International Marketing
An SME Perspective

Seán de Búrca
Richard Fletcher
Linden Brown

International Marketing

An SME Perspective

FT Prentice Hall
FINANCIAL TIMES

An imprint of **Pearson Education**
Harlow, England • London • New York • Boston • San Francisco • Toronto
Sydney • Tokyo • Singapore • Hong Kong • Seoul • Taipei • New Delhi
Cape Town • Madrid • Mexico City • Amsterdam • Munich • Paris • Milan

Pearson Education Limited

Edinburgh Gate

Harlow

Essex CM20 2JE

England

and Associated Companies throughout the world

Visit us on the World Wide Web at:

www.pearsoned.co.uk

First published 2004

© Pearson Education Limited 2004

This edition of International Marketing, Second Edition is published by arrangement with Pearson Education Australia Pty. Limited.

The rights of Seán de Búrca, Richard Fletcher and Linden Brown to be identified as authors of this work have been asserted by them in accordance with the Copyright, Designs and Patents Act 1988.

ISBN 0 273 67323 8

British Library Cataloguing-in-Publication Data

A catalogue record for this book is available from the British Library

Library of Congress Cataloging-in-Publication Data

A catalog record for this book is available from the Library of Congress

10 9 8 7 6 5 4 3 2 1
08 07 06 05 04

Typeset in 10/12pt Times by 35
Printed and bound by Ashford Colour Press, Gosport, Hants.

The publisher's policy is to use paper manufactured from sustainable forests.

To Evelyn and Darach

To my wife, Wendy Fletcher, and Jeff, Chris and Anne and the little people   RF

To Marie-Noelle – loving wife, fellow international traveller and life adventurer   LB

Brief contents

Part C International Marketing Strategy   461

Part D Contemporary Challenges in International Marketing   637

Contents

Part B The International Marketing Mix   223

7 International market selection and entry   224

Preface

International marketing by definition is the study of everyday marketing activities throughout the world. Traditionally, the focus of many international marketing texts is concentrated upon the needs of the multinational and global company. The treatment of the problems faced by small and medium-sized firms in undertaking international marketing is cursory. Yet it is small and medium-sized companies that make up the vast bulk of firms involved in international business. This is because across international markets there are only a limited number of global firms compared with the multitude of indigenous small and medium-sized firms.

A global or multinational approach to international marketing is not an operating strategy for indigenous small and medium-sized enterprises (SMEs) and is only partially appropriate to the local subsidiaries of global firms. For the majority of SMEs, globalisation is only a reality as far as potential competitors in both the domestic and the international markets are concerned. For these reasons, this book is written primarily from the perspective of small to medium firms rather than from the perspective of the global or multinational firm.

Of course we would have no effective understanding of the driving and restraining forces that underlie the international marketing imperative if we were to ignore multinational/global firms and the many branches or subsidiaries of such firms. Therefore, globalisation and its manifestations are covered in the book, but the focus is firmly on the role of the multinational/global firm as an international competitor and the role in international activities of managers of their local subsidiary or branch operations. However, such coverage is intended to sensitise firms to future trends and the underlying forces which may impact on their future international competitiveness.

Unlike most international marketing books, this text focuses on world coverage of international marketing activities, rather than a regional approach. This reflects the wide experiences of the authors and enables international marketing activities to be considered from both a western and Asia-Pacific perspective.

Four issues in international marketing are likely to increase in importance in the next few years – *environmentalism*, *ethics*, *multilateral trade relations* and the *impact of technology*. Environmental issues are frequently referred to throughout the book and, at the end of each chapter there is an ethical issue for discussion relating to the topic of the chapter. The evolution of multilateral trade relations will have a major impact on international marketing strategy and is discussed in Chapter 18. All chapters contain an 'Internet Infusion' illustrating how the topic of that chapter is impacted upon by the use of the Internet in international marketing. In addition, Internet exercises in the form of 'Web Workouts' are included in every chapter. While the impact of electronic commerce issues are integrated and addressed throughout the book, Chapter 19 is dedicated to exploring the potential benefits of the Internet as a new marketplace and outlines the challenges to established international marketers in migrating their business from 'place' to 'space' marketing. At the end of each chapter there is not only a list of references and suggested readings, but also a list of websites for organisations that are referred to in the chapter and for sources of additional and updated information on key issues.

Key features

- *Rigorous theory matched with a practice-oriented approach.* The book is rigorous in its coverage of international marketing theory and concepts but is equally concerned with presenting the material in a practical way with an extensive use of actual business examples from Europe, Asia-Pacific and the Americas. It takes a practical approach to understanding the international marketplace and organises material according to the decisions marketing managers face.

- *Special emphasis on the impact technology has on the international marketing landscape.* The impact of electronic commerce is central to the future of international marketing. All chapters contain an 'Internet Infusion' illustrating how the topic of that chapter is impacted upon by the use of the Internet in international marketing. In addition, Internet exercises in the form of 'Web Workouts' are included in every chapter. While the impact of electronic commerce issues are integrated and addressed throughout the book, Chapter 19 is dedicated to exploring the potential benefits of the Internet as a new marketplace and outlines the challenges to established international marketers in migrating their business from 'place' to 'space' marketing.

- *World coverage of international marketing activities rather than a regional approach.* Reflecting the wide experiences of the authors, international marketing activities are considered from both a western and Asia-Pacific perspective. The SME perspective forms the dominant thread and is integrated throughout the book. At the end of each chapter there is not only a list of references and suggested readings, but also a list of websites for organisations that are referred to in the chapter and for sources of additional and updated information on key issues.

- *Practical international marketing planning and strategy development approach.* Planning and strategy development for international marketing follows a series of steps and processes which are practised by most successful international firms. Most textbooks outline these steps well but fail to focus on the real life implementation issues. By focusing on a real-life example Chapter 13 outlines the marketing plan of a firm from situation analysis to implementation, addressing all the alternatives in the process.

- *Relationships and the network perspective to international marketing.* Comprehensive coverage of the network perspective to international marketing and the central role of relationships is provided.

- *Case studies and 'International Highlights'.* The cases represent the problems and issues confronting managers in international markets and involve firms from countries throughout the world. In addition, at least two 'International Highlights' are included in most chapters, providing a forum for classroom and tutorial discussion.

- *Contemporary challenges in international marketing.* Four key issues in international marketing are likely to increase in importance in the next few years – environmentalism, ethics, electronic commerce and multilateral trade relations. Environmental issues are frequently referred to throughout the book and at the end of each chapter there is an ethical issue for discussion relating to the topic of the chapter. The impact of international trade relations post-EU enlargement and 11 September 2001 will have an enormous influence on the international marketing activities of firms. Chapter 18 focuses on the role of international trade relations in international marketing and how multilateral trade relations have evolved and their likely directions in the years ahead. The impact of technology on international marketing strategy and practice is integrated throughout the text and a specific analysis is addressed in Chapter 19.

Book structure

The book is divided into four parts and a number of case studies have been selected to accompany each part.

Part A contains chapters on the various environmental variables that impact on international marketing. These include economic and financial variables, social and cultural, political and legal, and (unlike most texts) information and technology variables.

Part B commences with chapters on researching international markets, and selecting and entering international markets. These are followed by chapters on ways in which each of the marketing mix variables need to be modified when doing business in international markets. Included in this section are chapters on modifying products and services for international markets, promoting and advertising, pricing for profit and effective international distribution. The chapter on services marketing is written in response to the increasing demand for current information on services marketing as it relates to international marketing.

Part C is devoted to strategic considerations in international marketing with particular focus on devising marketing strategies for international markets. Chapters cover the planning process for international marketing, the gaining of competitive advantage, creating competitive international marketing strategies, issues involved in globalisation, and the formation of relationships, networks and strategic alliances. The chapter on networks, relationships and strategic alliances has increased coverage of the impact of networks and relationships on international marketing.

Part D covers contemporary challenges in international marketing, detailed discussion of which is rarely found in international marketing texts. Chapters are devoted to the impact of international trade relations on the international marketing activities of firms, and the role of electronic commerce in international marketing.

The structure of the book has been designed so that, through the selection of different parts or chapters, it can be used as a tertiary text at different levels. While of interest to the practitioner, this book is primarily designed for use in an MBA course or on a capstone undergraduate course. Moreover, the structure of the chapters – the introductory paragraphs, the international marketing highlights, the anecdotes, the case studies and web workouts – help to bring the real world of international marketing from a western and Asia-Pacific perspective directly into the classroom. At the end of each chapter there are a number of discussion questions which can be used either for self-testing or for examination purposes.

Supplementary materials

A wide range of supplementary learning and teaching aids accompanies this text. To access these, visit www.booksites.net/deburca.

Lecturer resources

- Instructor's manual – includes chapter overview, chapter outline and suggested teaching strategies.
- PowerPoint transparencies – for each chapter, a series of PowerPoint transparencies has been developed to follow the structure of the text.

Acknowledgements

No book is solely the work of its authors. Many people provided support, assistance valuable comments and suggestions. We are indebted to the following colleagues:

Dr Teresa Brannick	University College Dublin
Dr Brian Fynes	University College Dublin
Dean Mary Lambkin	University College Dublin
Dean Philip Bourke	University College Dublin
Professor Frank Bradley	University College Dublin
Professor Peter Turnbull	University of Birmingham
Professor Peter Naude	University of Bath
Professor James Ward	National University of Ireland, Galway
Professor Ken Miller	University of Technology, Sydney
Professor Nigel Barrett	University of Technology, Sydney

Special thanks go to academics and international marketing practitioners throughout Ireland, Australia and New Zealand who contributed their time and expertise in provid ing the case studies and marketing highlights which are a feature of this text. They are:

Evelyn Roche	University College Dublin
Carlos Sousa	University College Dublin
Angela Kennedy	University College Dublin
Peter McNamara	University College Dublin

Rosalind Beere   University College Dublin
Garrett Murray   University College Dublin
Carolin Grampp   University College Dublin
Cathal Brugha   University College Dublin
Tom Byrnes   University College Dublin
Gavin Lonergan   University College Dublin
Larry O'Connell   University College Dublin
Paul Brown   University College Dublin
Brian Fynes   University College Dublin
Thomas Downes   University College Dublin
Max Hayes   University College Dublin
John Fahy   University of Limerick
Thomas O'Toole   Waterford Institute of Technology
Declan Cahill   Waterford Institute of Technology
Chris Mulhall   Waterford Institute of Technology
Richard Burke   Waterford Institute of Technology
John Brennan   Waterford Institute of Technology
Eugene Crehan   Waterford Institute of Technology
Ann Torres   National University of Ireland, Galway
Mike Moroney   National University of Ireland, Galway
Will Geoghegan   National University of Ireland, Galway
Paul Ryan   National University of Ireland, Galway
Khaled M. Shaker   Maastricht School of Management
Vicente A. López   University of Santiago de Compostela (USC)
Jan Charbonneau   Central Queensland University
James Duan   Business Director, Ogilvy Interactive Worldwide
Nick Grigoriou   RMIT, Melbourne
Kimble Montagu   Monash University, Caulfield
Katherine Rodionoff   University of Technology, Sydney
Richard Fletcher   University of Western Sydney
Catherine Welch   University of New South Wales

We also owe a great debt to the people at Pearson Education who helped develop this book. It is their guidance, support and skill at managing the authors that has resulted in the finished product in which these acknowledgments appear.

Publisher's acknowledgements

We are grateful to the following for permission to reproduce copyright material:

Table 2.2 from *World Development Indicators 2002*, CD-ROM (Multiple user version) and Table 10.1 *World Bank Development Indicators 2000*, copyright 2002, 2000 by World Bank, reproduced with permission of World Bank in the format Textbook via Copyright Clearance Center; Table 2.5 from *Information Technology Outlook*, OECD © 2002, Table 5.1 from *ICT Database*, August, OECD © 2002, Table 9.1 from *World Trade in 2001 – Overview*, OECD © 2001; Table 6.1 and Figure 6.3 from Chapter 7 in I. Doole and P. Lowe (eds), *International Marketing Strategy: Contemporary*

Readings, London, Thomson Business Press (Lassere, P. 1997); Table 6.2 reprinted with permission from *Marketing News*, published by the American Marketing Association, E.H. Demby, 1990, Vol. 8, p. 24 (Demby, E.H. 1990), Figure 6.4 reprinted with permission from *Marketing Expansion in a Shrinking World, Proceedings of the American Marketing Association Business Conference*, published by the American Marketing Association, B. Gelb (ed.), 1978, pp. 86–90 (Corder, C.K. 1978), Figure 9.8 reprinted with permission from *Journal of International Marketing*, published by the American Marketing Association, P.G. Patterson and M. Cicic, 1995, Vol. 3, pp. 57–83 (Patterson, P.G. and Cicic, M., 1995), Figure 9.1 reprinted with permission from *Journal of International Marketing*, published by the American Marketing Association, P. Berthon *et al.*, 1999, Vol. 7, pp. 84–105 (Berthon, P., *et al.* 1999); Table 10.6 reprinted from *Industrial Marketing Management*, Vol. 24, Honeycutt, E.D. and Ford, J.B. (1995) 'Guidelines for Managing an International Sales Force' p. 138, with permission of Elsevier Science; Table 11.5 reprinted from *International Business Review*, Vol. 6, K.S. Craven, 'Examining the role of transfer pricing as a strategy for multinational firms', pp. 127–145, copyright 1997, with permission from Elsevier; Table 11.6 and Figure 2.2 from *Global Marketing Management: A European Perspective*, pp. 414 and 278, respectively, Harlow, Pearson (Keegan, W.J. and Schlegelmilch, B.B. 2001), Figures 3.2, 7.6 and 11.6 from *Global Marketing – A Market-responsive Approach*, pp. 161, 37, 37 and 458, respectively, Harlow, Pearson (Hollensen, S. 2001), reproduced with permission of the publisher; Table 19.2 from 'Making business sense of the internet', *Harvard Business Review*, March-April, pp. 128–133, published by Harvard Business School Press (Ghosh, S. 1998); Figure 1.1 from *Global Marketing Management* by Keegan, Warren, J., © 1995, reprinted by permission of Pearson Education, Inc., Upper Saddle River, NJ; Figures 1.2 and 1.3 and Tables 2.3 and 3.1 from *Principles of Global Marketing*, Keegan, W.J. and Green, M.C. (2000), Figures 6.1 and 7.3 from *Global Marketing Management: A Strategic Perspective* (2nd edn), Toyne, B. and Walters, P.G., Allyn & Bacon, Reprinted by permission of Pearson Education, Inc., Upper Saddle River, NJ; Figures 1.5, 8.2, 8.3 and 8.4 from *Global eCommerce – the Market, Challenges and Opportunities*, Bowne Global Solutions, January 2000, p. 4. All rights reserved; Figures 3.1 and 3.3 from *Culture, Consequences, Comparing Values, Behaviours, Institutions, and Organizations* (2nd edn), Hofstede, G. (2000), Sage Publications, Thousand Oaks, CA. © copyright Geert Hofstede. Reproduced with permission; Figures 5.1 and 5.3 from 'Metamorphosis in marketspace – paths to new industries in the emerging electronic marketing environment', Irish *Marketing Review*, Vol. 9, p. 56, Mercury Publications (Pattinson, H.M. and Brown, L.R. 1996); Figure 5.4 from *ITU World Telecommunications Indicators* database, reproduced with kind permission of ITU; Figure 5.6 on page 25 'The landscape of the technology adoption life cycle' from *Inside the Tornado* by Geoffrey A. Moore, copyright © 1995 by Geoffrey A. Moore Consulting, Inc., reprinted by permission of HarperCollins Publishers Inc; Figures 11.3 and 12.6 from *Export Marketing: A Practical Guide to Opening and Expanding Markets Overseas*, 2nd ed. By Noonan, C., reprinted by permission of Butterworth-Heinemann (Noonan, C. 1999); Figure 11.7 adapted with the permission of The Free Press, a Division of Simon & Schuster Adult Publishing Group, from *Power Pricing: How Managing Price Transforms the Bottom Line* by Robert J. Dolan and Hermann Simon, copyright © 1996 by Robert J. Dolan and Hermann Simon, all rights reserved, Figure 14.10 adapted with the permission of The Free Press, a Division of Simon & Schuster Adult Publishing Group, from *Competitive Strategy: Techniques for Analyzing Industries and Competitors* by Michael E. Porter,

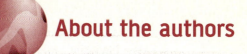

Dr Seán de Búrca joined the Department of Marketing, University College Dublin, having completed a Bachelor of Commerce Degree and Master of Business Studies Degree in Marketing. He received his PhD from the National University of Ireland, Galway. Prior to becoming an academic he worked on a number of engineering projects in Ireland, the UK and Australia, following his engineering studies. He joined FÁS (National Training and Development Authority), and held responsibility for the management, design and development of Business and Enterprise Development programmes and gained extensive management development experience assisting a wide variety of industrial, commercial and government clients. He currently lectures in international marketing, business-to-business marketing, marketing management and communications in the Department of Marketing, Smurfit Graduate School of Business, University College Dublin and was Director of the Executive MBA programme for four years. He has lectured in marketing at a number of universities and institutions, in France, Italy, Holland, Cyprus, Egypt, India, Australia, Singapore, Hong Kong, Vietnam, Hungary and Romania, among others. His main research interest is focused on the management of business-to-business relationships and he has been published widely in this area in management journals, international conferences and as a contributor to numerous books. He is a council member of the Irish Academy of Management and a member of the Marketing Institute where he was chairman of the Business to Business Forum. He also sits on the Education Committee of the Irish Institute of Purchasing and Materials Management. He is a member of the European Marketing Academy (EMAC) and the Industrial Marketing and Purchasing Group (IMP).

Professor Richard Fletcher holds the Chair of Marketing and International Business at the University of Western Sydney. He has a Master of Arts in Research from the University of Sydney, a Master of Commerce in Marketing from the University of New South Wales, and a Doctorate in Philosophy from the University of Technology, Sydney. Since becoming an academic in 1989, he has lectured on international marketing subjects at both undergraduate and graduate levels and created five new international subjects.

Fletcher's research interests are countertrade, emerging markets, internationalisation, networking, ethical issues and cultural impact. His research has been published in such journals as *Industrial Marketing Management*, *International Business Review*, *Journal of Global Marketing*, *Australian Marketing Journal* and the

Journal of International Marketing and Exporting. He is a member of the European Marketing Academy (EMAC), the Australian and New Zealand Marketing Academy (ANZMAC), the Academy of International Business, the Industrial and Marketing and Purchasing Group (IMP) and the Australian Institute of Export.

Prior to joining the University of Western Sydney, Fletcher was Director of Undergraduate Programmes in the School of Marketing at the University of Technology, Sydney. He also served as an Australian Trade Commissioner with 25 years' experience representing Australia's commercial interests overseas – in New Delhi, Bombay, San Francisco, Jakarta, Tehran, Libya, Los Angeles and Bangkok. During that period, he organised major Australian trade promotions in seven overseas cities, managed several trade missions, led two trade missions to Vietnam in the late 1980s, and participated in bilateral trade negotiations with various countries of behalf of Australia on a number of occasions.

Professor Linden Brown is Adjunct Professor of Marketing and Director of the Market Strategy and Information Technology (MSAT) Group at the University of Technology, Sydney. Linden is one of Australia's leading consultants and academics. His first degree, in Accounting and Economics, was followed by a PhD in Marketing at the University of New South Wales. He has lectured in marketing at a number of universities, including INSEAD in France in 1999, the Sydney Graduate School of Management and Public Policy, Melbourne Graduate School of Management, Royal Melbourne Institute of Technology, the University of New South Wales, and Cranfield University Management School, England.

Linden has published five books, the most recent being *Marketing*, co-authored with Philip Kotler, Gary Armstrong and Stewart Adam, published in 1998. His most recent published articles and working papers are in the field of electronic marketing, e-commerce and strategic alliances related to his specialist field of marketing strategy.

As director of the MSAT Group at the University of Technology, Sydney, Linden's research focus is with lead users of electronic business, focusing on the hospitality, telecommunications and computer industries. As a business practitioner, Linden has successfully initiated and developed a number of businesses in the transport, printing and food marketing areas.

He also has extensive experience as a marketing consultant in a range of industries, including: computer products and services, telecommunications, finance, retailing, hotels, building products, steel and minerals, and the education industry.

Linden has designed and conducted executive development programmes in strategic marketing for many Australian and international corporations since the late 1980s. He is particularly experienced in the use of marketing simulations as a tool for individual and team learning. Since 1994 much of his work has been in China as well as other Asian countries such as Taiwan, Japan, Malaysia and the Philippines.

He is founder and chairman of Inter*Strat, which has provided strategic marketing services to multinational companies since its incorporation in 1988.

Part A

The International Marketing Environment

1

The rationale for international marketing

Learning objectives

After studying this chapter, you should be able to:

● assess the driving and restraining forces that underlie the international marketing imperative;

● recognise various approaches and classification systems in international marketing;

● identify the underlying concepts of international marketing;

● assess, from the firm's perspective, the application of the 'wheel of international marketing'; and

● recognise the importance of global trade and the role of marketing in it.

The turbulent landscape of international trade

There is little doubt that a revolution is under way. The dynamics of international trade have always presented managers with complex and exciting challenges. The events of the past decade have certainly lived up to the notion of a revolution. The impact of technology has ensured that international companies everywhere have been faced with the thorny question of how to respond. Many companies have demonstrated a willingness and ability to meet these challenges and some have become masters of innovation. The roll-out of broadband technology will encourage more companies like Dell, Amazon, Google, Yahoo!, eBay and Ryanair to lead the way with new business models. Dell has gained industry dominance by building its sales and manufacturing around the Internet. Amazon, Google and Ryanair have created the standard in their markets and eBay has thrived when so many dot-coms have struggled and has become the leading US used-car dealer.

Recent political events will, however, necessitate a reshaped economy. Post 9/11, tighter scrutiny of cross-border transactions could impede the flow of goods, ideas and capital. Increased risks could reduce investor and corporate willingness to put money into high-risk innovations. The diplomatic tensions in the post-war stakes for business may make free-trade initiatives less likely and anti-war sentiment may strengthen public opposition to globalisation and capitalism.

Even though the dynamics of international trade increases in complexity, Forrester Research has estimated that successful cross-border transactions require participation by an average of 27 parties. Meanwhile, regional programmes such as the European Union (EU) and North American Free Trade Area (NAFTA) reduce the cost of trade but require detailed documentation to qualify shipments, putting extra burden on the process of international trade. At the same time, while the World Trade Organisation is trying to free up world trade, countries are increasingly entering into bilateral agreements with each other to keep other countries out of their markets.

Introduction

 While many US texts in international marketing focus on the activities of the transnational firm and the merits of a global as opposed to a local approach to international marketing, such approaches are not always relevant to small and medium-scale firms, apart from alerting them to the nature of the international competitive environment in which they are likely to operate. This is because across international markets there are only a limited number of global firms compared with the multitude of indigenous small and medium-scale firms. Table 1.1 shows the revenues for the world's top 10 firms.

The majority of exporters can be classified for the most part as:

● indigenous small and medium-scale exporters (SMEs)
● local subsidiaries of transnational firms.

A global or transnational approach to international marketing is not an operating strategy for the first category of firms above and is only partially appropriate to the second category. As far as the first group is concerned, globalisation is only a reality as far as potential competitors in both the domestic and the international markets are concerned. With the second category, executives in these subsidiaries are preoccupied with balancing the demands of the transnational corporation with the requirements of the local market and the regulations that circumscribe activities in that market. For these reasons, this book is written primarily from the perspective of firms in the above categories rather than from the perspective of the global or transnational firm. Although globalisation and its manifestations are covered in the book, such coverage is intended to sensitise firms to future trends and the underlying forces, which may impact on their future international competitiveness.

Table 1.1 The 2002 Global 10 largest corporations

Company	Revenues (US$ million)
Wal-Mart Stores	219,812
Exxon	191,581
General Motors	177,260
BP	174,218
Ford Motor	162,412
Enron	138,718
Daimler Chrysler	136,897
Royal/Dutch/Shell Group	125,913
General Electric	125,913
Toyota Motor	120,814

Source: www.fortune.com/fortune/global500

1.1 International highlight

How to stay ahead of globalisation – Intel, AMD, Gucci and Levis

When you are at the top the only way is down. For many companies staying at the top means fighting many challenges. Even companies as large as Intel face huge problems. To stay ahead it needs to develop new products and markets because its sales of microprocessors, which account for most of its revenues, have levelled off as the PC industry has matured. While Intel has little room for growth with over 80% market share, it cannot be complacent because its main rival Advanced Micro Devices (AMD) poses a real threat. AMD microprocessors have gained market share over the past five years by price-cutting. Its new product, Hammer, hopes to challenge Intel's Pentium chips head on. Hammer is a 64-bit chip and is intended for use in the desktop machine and low-end servers.

Intel, with its huge research and development budget, has not, however, stood idly by. Its new chip, Itanium, is suitable for use in powerful servers, mainframes and supercomputers. While sales volumes in these markets are low, margins are high.

Other companies have faced different kinds of challenges. Gucci, an Italian clothes label whose image was being destroyed by loose licensing and over-exposure in discount stores, saved itself by ending third-party suppliers, controlling its distribution channels better and opening its own stores.

Levis in its battle with retailers decided to seek help from the courts. The European Court of Justice decided that Tesco, a British supermarket chain, should not be allowed to import jeans made by America's Levi Strauss from outside the European Union and sell them at cut-rate price without first getting permission from the jeans maker.

The international marketing imperative

What is international marketing?

All of us live in an international marketplace. As you read this book, you may be sitting in a chair purchased from IKEA and imported from Scandinavia, and on your desk you may have a PC with a US brand but manufactured in Korea. The software may by designed in Bangalore, India, and the video recorder for screening the recommended international marketing film is a National Panasonic made in Malaysia. What a contrast to 150 years ago when students sitting at their desks would be surrounded by items all of which came from their country and in most cases from within a 120 km radius.

International marketing is the process of planning and undertaking transactions across national boundaries that involve exchange. Its forms range from exporting to licensing to joint ventures to wholly owned acquisitions to management contracts. Because the transaction takes place across national boundaries, the international marketer is subject to a different set of macroenvironmental factors and constraints deriving from different political systems, legal frameworks, cultural norms and economic circumstances.

Given these difficulties and differences, why undertake international marketing? The answer lies in the forces that both drive and restrain involvement in international markets.

Driving forces

The first of these forces is that of market needs. These needs transcend national boundaries and exist in many countries. International marketing is about catering to these needs. However, often in international marketing, these needs are created by promotion. The advertising campaign may focus on a global appeal but is adapted to the specific requirements of each culture. The marketing of diamonds by De Beers is an example of this. It promotes diamonds to announce an engagement in Japan where a diamond ring is not a traditional custom. In so doing, it is capitalising on the fact that the emotions that surround the engagement are universal and these can be harnessed to a new want – that of celebrating an engagement with a diamond ring.

A second driving force is that of technology. It is a universal, uniform and consistent factor that crosses national boundaries as everyone aspires to the latest technology. Of itself, technology knows no cultural boundaries – only in its application does culture come into play. When this happens, the modification is not in the technology, but rather in its application. If a company knows how to manage technology in one country, it has experience that is relevant to the rest of the world.

Cost is another driving force. Economies of scale deriving from supplying more than the domestic market can drive down research, engineering, design, creative and production costs. The cost pressure is becoming more and more intense when increasingly new products involve major investment and extended periods for development. The pharmaceutical industry is an example. It typically costs between US$40 and US$85 million to develop a new product from scratch in this industry and the average development period is about eight years. Rarely can these development costs be recovered from one national market alone, which is why such products are usually launched on a worldwide basis.

Communication has been revolutionised by the changes in information technology. As a result, knowledge of new innovations becomes disseminated throughout the world more rapidly than was previously the case and, as a result, everyone wants the latest product. The information revolution has also spawned media that overlap national borders and the global media have emerged. Customers in one country are increasingly exposed to messages about products that do not originate in that country.

Restraining forces

The first of these restraining forces is to do with differences between national markets. The differences usually are sufficiently pronounced to require adaptation of at least some elements of the marketing mix to suit local conditions. They may be a function of economic development, political system, legal requirements and cultural norms.

In addition, most countries implement some form of control over entry and access to their market. Such controls are to protect national values, local vested interests and domestic companies. This is achieved by both tariff and non-tariff barriers. With the progressive reduction of the former as a result of the activities of the World Trade Organisation, non-tariff barriers are becoming increasingly important as a control mechanism. Controls also apply to investment, acquisition by foreign interests, franchising and licensing.

Rationale

In the immediate post-war period, the ratio of world trade to total trade was much less than 10%. By the late 1980s this ratio had doubled, and at the end of the century hovered around 35%. World trade in manufactured goods now represents more than 35% of total output with more than 50% of this being intracompany transfers. Overall, the expansion of world trade over the past 50 years has been above 7% per annum, far outpacing world economic growth during that period. As a result of the continued expansion of world trade, there is an inescapable network of global linkages that bind countries, institutions and individuals closer together. A currency crisis in Thailand impacts on its Asian neighbours and on its trading partners in north Asia before adversely affecting countries in the developed world. In a similar way, acts of war such as the invasion by Iraq of Kuwait, and acts of terrorism such as the destruction of the World Trade Centre in New York can affect oil prices, stock markets, trade and travel throughout the world. Underlying the growth of the international economy since the Second World War is a number of factors. The most important of these are:

Change in management orientation   Perlmutter (1969) developed a typology whereby firms could be classified according to the orientation of their management, as follows:

- An *ethnocentric orientation* is underpinned by the belief that the home country is superior and that the approach used in the home country should be applied to every other country. This leads to the view that the products of the home country can be sold anywhere without adaptation, that foreign operations are secondary or subordinate to domestic ones, and, from a manufacturing perspective, foreign markets are mostly viewed as an opportunity to dispose of surplus domestic production.

- A *polycentric orientation* is the opposite of ethnocentrism and reflects the approach that each country is different and that no country is necessarily inferior to another. Therefore the home country approach is viewed as largely irrelevant and, to be successful, products must be specifically tailored to the differences in each foreign country. This leads to the view that each international subsidiary should develop its own unique business and marketing approaches.

- *Regiocentric orientation* views the region as the market and integrated strategies are developed for the region that take into account both the similarities and differences between the home market and the region. The world outside the region may be viewed from either an ethnocentric or polycentric standpoint.

- *Geocentric orientation* involves a world marketing strategy based on recognition that countries have both similarities and differences. The entire world is viewed as a market and a strategy is developed accordingly. It represents a synthesis of the ethnocentric and polycentric approaches and seeks to operate a global approach that is able to respond to local needs and wants.

Management of an increasing number of companies began with an ethnocentric orientation, then moved to a polycentric orientation and has now adopted a regiocentric or geocentric orientation in response to changing circumstances in the international marketplace.

International monetary framework The rapid growth in trade and investment has created a need for greater liquidity to facilitate the trading of goods and services between nations. Until 1969 exchange rates were fixed but, since that time, they have been allowed to fluctuate. International liquidity has been augmented by the International Monetary Fund (IMF) enabling its members to use special drawing rights (SDRs) in settling transactions involving reserves. This has overcome the limits on expanding liquidity imposed by earlier reliance on gold and foreign exchange.

The world trading system Following the Second World War nations did not want to return to the discriminatory trading practices of the 1920s and 1930s. The General Agreement on Tariffs and Trade (GATT) was born and the operations of this body did result in a lowering of the tariff barriers for industrial products. In 1994, following the conclusion of the Uruguay Round of the GATT negotiations, the World Trade Organisation replaced the GATT. It is in the process of addressing other issues which stand in the way of a more liberal world trade system, such as non-tariff barriers, barriers to trade in agricultural products, freeing up services trade, and issues related to investment.

Recent decades have been characterised by the emergence of an increasing number of regional trade groupings such as the European Union, ASEAN Free Trade Area and the North American Free Trade Area. These trade blocs are posing a threat to those outside the bloc and nations are rushing to join blocs lest they be commercially disadvantaged as a result. Regional trade groupings (RTGs) vary in terms of the degree of national sovereignty surrendered – from the European Union at one extreme to the looser arrangement of the Asia Pacific Economic Cooperation (APEC) at the other. Although a number of these RTGs were formed because of the perceived shortcomings of GATT, the extent to which such RTGs can coexist with the World Trade Organisation has yet to be determined.

Since 1945 the world has remained free of global conflicts and this has assisted the growth of the international economy. The passing of the cold war has further accelerated this process, as conflicts now are more likely to be local rather than global.

Communications and transport The time taken to transport goods as well as the cost of the goods have fallen considerably over recent decades. This has been due to the use of containerisation, larger vessels, improved waterside efficiency, electronic data interchange (EDI) and rationalisation of shipping services. The jet aeroplane has made face-to-face meetings in international business easier and cheaper whereas the ability to transmit data electronically has improved the ease and reduced the cost of staying in touch with international customers and representatives and facilitated the management of diverse operations around the globe.

Technology Never before has it been so easy to gather, analyse and disseminate information thanks to technologies such as the World Wide Web. Products can be produced more quickly and obtained less expensively from sources around the world. Advances in technology allow firms to operate in 'market space' rather than 'marketplace' by keeping the content while changing the context of the transaction. A newspaper, for example, can be distributed globally online, rather than delivered house to house, enabling unprecedented expansion in the ability to reach new customer groups. The burgeoning level of global investment means that an increasing number of people are working for companies owned by non-national interests. This global interdependence is not stable but continually changing as firms realign their international involvement. The recent pace of technology innovation grows faster each year, spurred by the increasing speed of transmission of ideas across national boundaries.

Approaches to international marketing

There are a number of different approaches to international marketing. These are based on increasing forms of involvement or commitment. They reflect the fact that since the Second World War, the international trading environment has become more complex and the interdependencies between firms in different countries much greater. The first of these approaches classifies firms in terms of management approach to international involvement.

From domestic to transnational

In this approach, firms are considered in terms of their orientation. The firm can operate as a domestic entity and in the past could be quite successful operating within the domestic market. Export marketing is the first stage in the firm exploring opportunities outside the home country. By leveraging its experience in the domestic market, the firm exports its products to international markets. This may involve a separate strategy to produce specifically for an international market or it may be the result of an attempt to dispose of surplus production or utilise excess production capacity. International marketing extends international involvement further, and usually includes a greater commitment of resources to the international market. For example, instead of relying on an international intermediary, the firm may establish its own direct representation in the foreign country. A further stage of involvement is operating on a multinational basis. This stage involves creating programmes specifically for each international market that take into account the differences and unique circumstances of each country. Finally, global or transnational marketing focuses upon leveraging the global assets of the firm by taking what is unique and different in each country in which it operates and combining the unique features to create the most globally competitive offering. The transnational firm does not have a centre from which decisions are dictated to operations elsewhere, but rather the various operations operate relatively autonomously. They are connected to each other in the interests of dissemination of information and global rationalisation.

From indirect exporting to foreign direct investment

In this approach, firms are classified according to the nature of their involvement in export-led or outward-driven international activities. This is based on the fact that initially firms may export not on a direct basis, but rather through an export intermediary (either an export merchant who takes title to the goods, or an export agent who receives a commission). From the perspective of the local firm, the sale is akin to a domestic one as little extra effort is involved because the goods are destined for the international market. The next stage is that the firm exports directly, but appoints an agent to represent its interests in the international market. This is the most common form of international involvement for small and medium-sized exporters. In this case, the agent receives a commission for arranging the distribution and sale of the products. Should the firm feel a loss of control over the marketing of its products in the international market because this is left to the agent, it can take the further step of establishing its own sales office in the market. This office is used to manage the distribution network necessary to get the goods to the final customer. It may be that tariff or non-tariff barriers either prohibit or make direct selling of the product uneconomic.

More advanced forms of international involvement result from such problems or from a desire to match competitive behaviour in the foreign market. These can take the form of transferring technology, for example when an arrangement is entered into for the product to be manufactured under licence in the foreign country. In this case, the licensee may pay the firm an up-front lump sum and a royalty based on the volume or value of goods produced using the firm's technology. In a similar vein, the firm may franchise its marketing and operating skills in the other country in return for a royalty payment and a contractual requirement on the part of the franchisee to purchase certain inputs.

A more common reaction in the face of import restrictions is for the firm to manufacture the product in an international market. This foreign direct investment can be via a joint venture with a local party in which management control and ownership is divided between the two parties, or via a wholly owned direct foreign investment. Wholly owned operations or direct foreign investments can be built from scratch or be acquired by buying out other firms in the international market. These latter options may not always be available because of restrictions on foreign ownership imposed by the foreign government.

From an export focus to a holistic focus

The approaches previously discussed are based on the assumption that the domain of international marketing is restricted to outward-driven international activities. This view does not match the reality of international business as the international involvement of firms can also be driven by inward activities such as importing. The stages of outward international involvement can be paralleled when international involvement is inward driven. Initially the firm imports through an agent based in the foreign market. Following this it imports directly. Then it may establish a buying office in the foreign market. The next stage of international involvement may require manufacturing the foreign product under licence or becoming the franchisee for an international operation. The final stage could be foreign direct investment in the supplying country to produce goods for sale in the international market so as to retain a competitive edge.

The reality of international business today is that outward and inward international activities do not operate in isolation from each other but are frequently linked. This linkage is manifested in two ways. In the first, an outward activity can lead to an inward activity and vice versa. This happens for example when the local licensee of a US firm is given the rights to license manufacture of the product in another market, or when the local franchisor gives the rights to its franchisee to extend the franchise to another market. The second type of linkage derives from more complicated forms of international involvement in which inward-driven international activities are directly dependent on outward-driven activities and vice versa. Strategic alliances, programmes of cooperative manufacture and countertrade are examples of growing international business practices in which inward and outward international activities are linked to each other. The international marketer needs to take this linkage into account and adopt a holistic rather than an outward-driven approach to international marketing.

Concepts underlying international marketing

There are a number of concepts that provide a rationale for involvement in international activities. These may have an economic rationale, such as comparative advantage or internalisation of activities; a marketing rationale, such as extending the life of the product; or an information rationale, based on extending the networks of relationships in which the firm is involved.

Comparative advantage

The theory of comparative advantage argues that a country can gain from international trade even if it has a disadvantage in production of all goods, or even if it is better than other countries at the production of all goods. The theory is based on the notion that a country should focus on what it does best rather than trying to produce everything. The following two-country/two-product model illustrates the concept. The two countries are the US and Spain, both of which produce apples and oranges. There is no money involved and there is no difference in the Spanish and the US product. Figure 1.1 illustrates that with any production mix between (A) and (E), total production is less at these production mixes than when there is concentration of production on the product in which each country has the greatest competitive advantage. For the US it is oranges, whereas for Spain it is apples. To calculate this comparative advantage, it is necessary to establish the production ratios for the two products. From a Spanish perspective, this is 0.80 (80/100) for apples and 0.33 (20/60) for oranges. Comparing what each country can produce under conditions of total specialisation, Spain has a comparative advantage in oranges whereas the US has a comparative advantage in apples.

Product life cycle extension

A well-known paradigm in marketing is that of the product life cycle. This states that products proceed through stages in their life from their inception to their abandonment. These stages are usually labelled 'introduction', 'growth', 'maturity' and 'decline'.

| Figure 1.1 | Comparative advantage – an example |

Source: Adapted from Keegan, Warren J., © 1995, p. 12. Reprinted by permission of Pearson Education, Inc., Upper Saddle River, NJ.

1. Production possibilities of United States and Spain (1,000 production units)

Before specialisation and trade (000 bushels)

	United States		Spain	
	Apples	*Oranges*	*Apples*	*Oranges*
Use of production units or production possibilities				
A 1,000 in apples, 0 in oranges	100	0	80	0
B 750 in apples, 500 in oranges	75	15	60	5
C 500 in apples, 500 in oranges	50	30	40*	10*
D 250 in apples, 750 in oranges	25*	45*	20	15
E 0 in apples, 1,000 in oranges	0	60	0	20

*Production in isolation.

2. Production and consumption after total specialisation and trade

	United States			Spain		
	Produces	*Trades: Imports (+) exports(–)*	*Consumes*	*Produces*	*Trades: Imports (+) exports (–)*	*Consumes*
Apples (000 bushels)	0	+30	30	80	–30	50
Oranges (000 bushels)	60	–12	48	0	+12	12

Trading price 30/12 = 2.5 apples = 1 orange
12/30 = 4 oranges = 1 apple

This paradigm is specific to a market. Given the differences between international markets, especially as far as levels of economic development are concerned, it is often the case that a product that has reached maturity in one country market may be at an introductory or growth stage in another. As a result, the life of a product in one market can be extended, by exporting it to an international market where the 'decline' stage has not yet been reached.

A related concept is that of the product trade cycle which incorporates the life cycle of markets. This concept proposes that the relationship between product and market proceeds through four stages. Initially the product is exported to the international market; then production commences in that international market; that market in turn exports to nearby markets; finally, because of rising production costs, it is no longer worthwhile producing it in the domestic market and the firm in the international market begins supplying the original domestic market. From a macro perspective, high-income, mass-producing countries such as the United States were initially exporters of many basic manufactures such as textiles and clothing but ultimately became importers. A second tier of developing countries initially imported the product before becoming exporters. A third tier of less developed countries initially imported, then began manufacture and finally exhibited the same trend from importing to exporting. The shift to low-cost production sources is only inevitable if the product remains the same. Continual product innovation can halt this process because it results in a different product with a different life cycle.

> *The evolution of the VCR illustrates the product trade cycle model. In the mid-1970s Japanese companies such as Sony and JVC produced VCRs for the Japanese market and for export. International customers were buying Japanese made goods even if they carried local brand names such as RCA. When the product category entered the growth phase, South Korean companies such as Goldstar and Samsung entered the international market in competition with Japan with a cheaper product due to their lower labour and other costs. When the product reached the mature phase, Japanese producers shifted production to low-cost producers in other countries such as Malaysia, Indonesia and Thailand.*
>
> *Source*: Adapted from Keegan and Green (2000), p. 408.

Figure 1.2 illustrates how countries at different stages of development move from importing to manufacturing to exporting then to importing. It also shows that whether the product is new, mature or has become a standardised product, impacts on the product trade cycle.

Underlying the above model is the assumption that the product originates in the advanced country, then trickles down to developing countries and then to less developed countries (as illustrated in Figure 1.3). This concept, however, may not reflect that behaviour of all firms, especially those that wish to introduce the product into all markets simultaneously as is the case with many 'born global' companies. This 'shower' approach recognises that we live in a global village where market opportunities may emerge simultaneously on a regional or global basis.

Internalisation

As firms consider their involvement in international activities, they are faced with either committing large resources so as to achieve the same degree of control over what happens to their product as they achieve in the domestic market, or committing fewer resources by relinquishing some control to others such as agents. The exercise of control involves the firm in internalising activities in the international market. This usually requires them to replicate their domestic operation in the international market in terms of activity, management and control. By internalising international activities within the firm, a number of problems frequently encountered in international marketing can be avoided. These include search and negotiating costs, protection of the firm's reputation, costs of contracts being broken, buyer uncertainty as to quality and maintenance of quality. Other problems that may be reduced by internalisation are:

- the management of the relationship with the foreign government;
- control over purchases and conditions of sale;

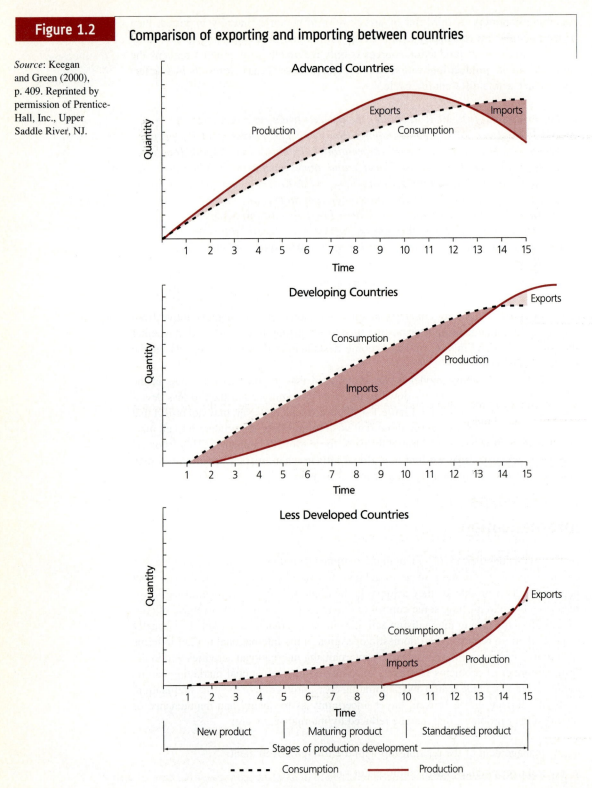

Source: Keegan and Green (2000), p. 409. Reprinted by permission of Prentice-Hall, Inc., Upper Saddle River, NJ.

Figure 1.2

Comparison of exporting and importing between countries

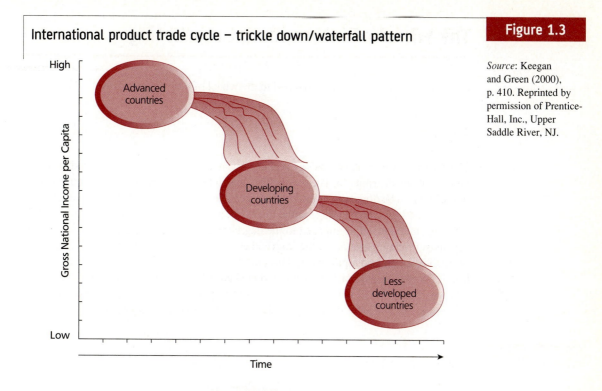

International product trade cycle – trickle down/waterfall pattern

Figure 1.3

Source: Keegan and Green (2000), p. 410. Reprinted by permission of Prentice-Hall, Inc., Upper Saddle River, NJ.

- consistency in the volume and content of promotional activities in the international market; and finally
- integration of activities in the foreign country market with activities in third country markets as well as in the home country.

Relationships and networks

The growing involvement of international business has led to the realisation that the tangible elements and the financial attractiveness of an offering in international markets may not be the main determinants of the purchasing decision. International marketing is perceived as more risky than domestic marketing. If the reasons for this are analysed, perceived risk is due to the parties to the transaction being unfamiliar with each other. The establishment of relationships becomes important in reducing this perceived risk. In the domestic environment, firms operate as members of an established network of relationships and the competitive position of the firm is as dependent on the contributions of other partners in the network as it is on the firm's own activities. Effective international marketing is often a matter of linking the domestic network of which the firm is a part, to an international network in such a way that network members derive advantage from their relationship with members of the other network. When searching for international agents to represent them or joint venture partners in international markets, the firm needs to study the network with which the other party is involved. The reasons for doing this include ensuring the compatibility of aspirations and effectiveness of reach, otherwise the new relationship is unlikely to deliver the anticipated benefits.

The wheel of international marketing

International marketing can be likened to the wheel of a bicycle as shown in Figure 1.4.

The hub

The hub of the wheel in this analogy is akin to the marketing mix variables – product, price, promotion and distribution. These variables, which lie at the core of any marketing operation whether it be domestic or international, can be controlled by the firm. Products vary in terms of usage patterns, stage in the life cycle, and the extent to which they are capable of being standardised as opposed to the degree to which they are sensitive to customer demands. Pricing varies according to whether it is determined by the marketplace or can be established on a cost-plus basis. This may be contingent on whether the strategy of the firm is short-term gain or long-term market share. Promotion can vary according to the relative importance of advertising, personal selling, trade promotion or public relations in the promotion mix for the product. Finally, distribution varies according to the willing-

| Figure 1.4 | International marketing task |

Source: Adapted from Cateora (1996), p. 8.

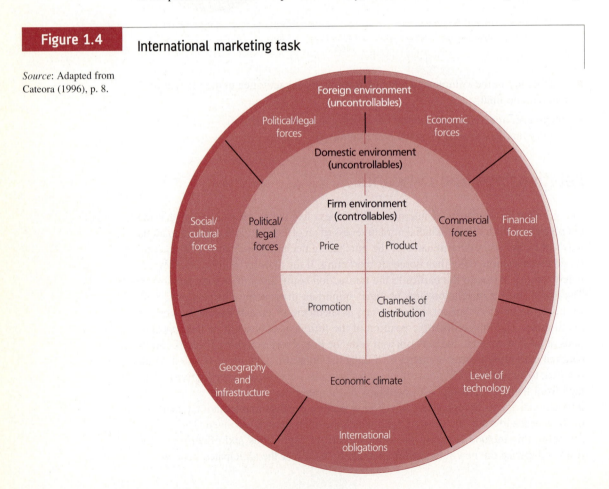

ness to accept risk as opposed to a desire to have control over the product from factory to final consumer. In international marketing, these variables will need modifying to take account of uncontrollable variables in both the domestic and international markets.

The spokes

The spokes of the wheel connect the hub to the rim and impact on the relationship between the hub and the rim. The spokes in this analogy are akin to regulations on exporting that are usually imposed by governments – for commercial, economic, political and legal reasons. These regulations can be commercially motivated and driven by a desire to protect the interests of domestic industry.

Regulations may also be driven by a desire to protect the country's image in the international marketplace. These are exemplified by export inspection requirements. Although usually on agricultural products, they can apply to manufactures. Lack of such requirements can have major repercussions on international trade as the UK recently experienced in its trade relations with the EU because of 'mad cow' and foot-and-mouth disease in its livestock.

Regulations may be imposed for economic reasons, such as balance of payments problems. Developing countries often ban their firms from accepting countertrade for products which are readily saleable in international markets for free foreign exchange.

Regulations are also imposed for security reasons particularly when a country does not want its defence technology to end up in the hands of nations it perceives as a threat to them. Allied to this are regulations imposed for political reasons such as embargoes on trading with a specific country due to either United Nations' sanctions (as with Iraq) or national prohibitions such as the ban on US companies trading with Vietnam until 1996 (Trading with the Enemy Act). Finally, restrictions may be due to legal agreements entered into between nations to control the degree to which each will compete with the other in each country's domestic market.

The rim

The rim cushions the impact of the bicycle on the road and, in this analogy, is akin to cushioning the impact of domestic marketing approaches on the international marketplace. The rim can be summed up in one word – 'sensitivity'. The main areas requiring sensitivity are the economic, financial, legal, political, social, cultural, infrastructure, technology and the country's international agreements and obligations. All the marketing mix variables at the hub of the wheel need to be substantially modified to take the above environmental factors into account if international business is to be successful. The extent of the modification will vary according to the nature of the product and the psychic distance between the home and international market.

The importance of world trade

The increasing importance of global linkages is reflected in the growing importance of international trade. As the recent Asian currency crisis illustrates, it is more and more difficult to isolate domestic economic activity from international market events.

Decisions that were once considered in the domestic domain are now being modified by influences from abroad and tailored to take into account global market forces.

> *Coca-Cola has responded to the Asian currency crisis by moving to increase its involvement in the region. It has moved to increase its equity in operations in Thailand, South Korea and Vietnam and has boosted marketing budgets in South-East Asia by 25–50% for some of its brands. It believes that a crisis is the best time to advertise because media is cheaper and competition sparser.*
>
> Source: Adapted from the *Far Eastern Economic Review*, 21 May 1998.

A reflection of the above is the change over recent decades in the pattern of diplomacy between nations. Whereas historically the main thrust of diplomacy has been on political relationships between countries, now commercial relationships are given equal importance. This trend is likely to continue due to absence of global conflicts and the cessation of the cold war. Achieving access for products, overcoming impediments to business and solving trade disputes account for an increasing percentage of the efforts of foreign diplomatic missions. The composition of international trade itself has been changing. In general, trade in primary commodities has declined while that of manufactures has risen. International trade in services has risen fastest of all.

Internet infusion

Adoption of the Internet has been faster than the adoption of any other technology in history. Electronic commerce has the potential to alter economic activity and the social environment. In the aftermath of the dot-com crash, many start-up companies that sold and/or purchased exclusively online have disappeared, and the popular perception of the growth in electronic commerce transactions has been less spectacular than predicted. Nevertheless, the volume of electronic transactions is growing and the Internet is increasingly used as a transaction channel, particularly for purchases. Networked business-to-business transactions will be US$2.4 trillion by the end of the decade, says Forrester Research Inc., but consumer e-commerce is slightly down on prediction. Despite recession, terrorism and war, the expected outcome for 2003 is projected to be US$95 billion. (See Figure 1.5.)

The adoption has been fastest in countries with high gross domestic product (GDP) and in countries where English is the first language or a widely spoken second language. The World Wide Web is an alternative to 'real world' environments, not a simulation of one. Success requires trust between vendor and customer and security issues still hamper the operation of electronic business.

The explosion of electronic business does call into question a number of fundamental principles in international marketing. These include:

● barriers to internationalisation by small and medium exporters (SMEs) – with the web, size is not a barrier to the same extent as it has traditionally been;

● incremental internationalisation – with the web, firms do not have to internationalise by moving from elementary modes of international behaviour to more advanced modes of international behaviour to the same extent;

Global Internet growth trends

Source: Plumley, D.J. (2000), p. 4.

Figure 1.5

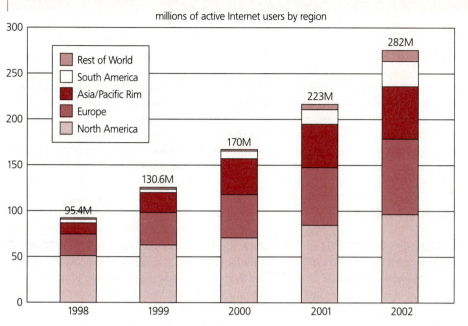

millions of active Internet users by region

Legend:
- Rest of World
- South America
- Asia/Pacific Rim
- Europe
- North America

95.4M (1998), 130.6M (1999), 170M (2000), 223M (2001), 282M (2002)

- need for international intermediaries – with the web, it is easier to locate international customers and deal directly with them rather than deal through international agents and distributors; and

- country screening – with the web, firms do not have to approach international business by moving from countries they are familiar with to more unfamiliar countries. This is because information is more readily available on the Internet and the medium is more interactive.

The Internet's low-cost communication ability allows firms with limited capital to become global marketers at an early stage of their development because the Internet connection can significantly enhance communication with international customers, suppliers, agents and distributors. Peterson, Balasubramanian and Bronnenberg (1997) argue that, as a marketing channel, the Internet has the following characteristics:

- an ability to inexpensively store vast amounts of information at different virtual locations;

- a powerful and inexpensive means of searching, organising and disseminating such information;

- interactivity and the ability to provide information on demand;

- the ability to provide perceptual experiences superior to the printed catalogue;

- facility to serve as a physical distribution medium for certain goods such as software; and

- relatively low entry and establishment costs for sellers.

Summary

This chapter introduces students to the reasons for undertaking international marketing and describes the dynamics of the international business environment in which the international marketer must operate. It examines various theories underlying the rationale for undertaking international business activities. In addition, the chapter explores various approaches that can be undertaken from an international marketing perspective to capitalise on the opportunities that exist in the international marketplace.

Ethics issues

Increasingly, social issues are influencing success in international marketing. Many of these social issues involve ethical considerations, which relate to all aspects of international marketing. Because of this, rather than have a separate chapter on ethical issues, at the end of each chapter there is an ethical issue for the student to consider that relates to the subject matter of the chapter. Following an ethical scenario in each case, a question is posed requiring the student to consider his or her position on the issue. This is designed to sensitise the student to the importance of ethical considerations in international marketing.

Web workout

Question 1 Go to the World Trade Organisation website (http://www.wto.org) and research sections on the latest news and key trade topics or resources. What opportunities do you see for international marketers in these areas? You may also join the world trade online forum (http://www.wto.org).

Question 2 (a) Visit the World Bank website (http://www.worldbank.org) and/or its research website (http://econ.worldbank.org) and evaluate the latest developments in global trade?
(b) What is the current focus of the World Trade Organisation (http://www.wto.org)? Does this help marketers to assess new market opportunities?

Question 3 Using Internet search engines such as Yahoo! or Google, research key trading networks within Europe and Asia-Pacific. Can you distinguish international marketing trading hubs?

Websites

Business Week www.businessweekeurope.com
CIA World Fact Book www.cia.gov/cia/publications/factbook/
Institute of Export http://www.export.co.uk

International Business Forum http://www.ibf.com/

International Monetary Fund http://www.imf.org/

JVC http://www.jvc.com/

News Corporation http://www.newscorp.com

Nike http://www.nike.com

OECD http://www.oecd.org

RCA http://www.rca.com

Sony http://www.sony.com

The Economist http://www.theeconomist.com.au

UNCTAD http://www.unctad.org

World Bank http://worldbank.org

Discussion questions

1 Discuss the extent to which a global approach to international marketing is appropriate.

2 Do the driving forces always outweigh the restraining forces in ensuring the attractiveness of international marketing to the firm?

3 Why is it necessary to adopt a holistic approach to international marketing?

4 Discuss the theory of comparative advantage and its limitations as an explanation for international trade.

5 Compare the product life cycle with the product trade cycle as explanations for involvement in international marketing.

6 In what ways do uncontrollable factors in the domestic environment impact on the application of the marketing mix variables in international markets?

References

Cateora, P.R. (1996) *International Marketing*, 7th edn, Irwin, Boston.

Keegan, W.J. (1995) *Global Marketing Management*, 5th edn, Prentice Hall International Inc., Englewood Cliffs, NJ.

Keegan, W.J. and Green, M.C. (2000) *Principles of Global Marketing*, Prentice Hall International Inc., Englewood Cliffs, NJ.

Perlmutter, H.V. (1995) in Bartlett, C.A. and Ghoshal, S. (eds) *Transnational Management*, Irwin, Chicago.

Peterson, R.A., Balasubramanian, S. and Bronnenberg, B.J. (1997) 'Exploring the Implications of the Internet for International Marketing', *Journal of the Academy of Marketing Science*, Vol. 25 No. 4, pp. 329–46.

Plumley, D.J. (2000) *Global eCommerce – the Market, Challenges and Opportunities*, Bowne Global Solutions, January, p. 4.

Rugman, A.M. (1999) 'Multicultural Enterprises and the End of Global Strategy', *Proceedings of the ANZIBA 1999 Annual Conference*, 30 September–2 October, Centre for International Business, University of New South Wales.

2

Appreciating the international economic and financial environment

Learning objectives

After studying this chapter, you should be able to:

- identify ways of segmenting the global economic environment and appreciate the ways in which countries differ from each other in terms of economic variables;

- evaluate international markets so as to predict likely outcomes of involvement;

- analyse the role of international bodies in regulating the international business environment;

- appreciate how the international financial system operates;

- recognise how foreign exchange variations impact on the successful undertaking of international business; and

- identify the role of aid in international business opportunities.

End trade barriers to cut poverty

Roughly one-fifth of the world's population lives on less that one dollar a day. The United Nation's millennium summit of 2000 pledged to halve the percentage of people living in these conditions by 2015. Probably no single change would make a greater contribution to fulfilling that pledge than fully opening the markets of the prosperous countries to the goods produced by poor ones. At present, farmers in poor countries not only have to compete against subsidised food exports, they also face high import barriers. In addition, the more value developing countries add to their products by processing them, the higher the tariffs they face. In Japan and the EU for instance, fully processed food products face tariffs twice as high as those on products in the first stage of processing. In effect, the already industrialised countries, while preaching the virtues of free and fair trade, practise protectionist policies that actively discourage poor countries from developing their own industries. Even in these conditions, developing countries' annual export earnings are more than US$1,500 billion. The minimum net gain if barriers were removed would be more than US$100 million a year – more than twice the amount of annual aid flows. Over time, as producers adjusted to the new export opportunities, the gain could be much greater. In addition, these opportunities would attract an increased flow of foreign direct investment to the developing countries which currently is only US$200 billion a year. In fact, the 49 least developed countries – home to more than 10% of the world's population – are missing out almost entirely on global trade and investment. Between them, they receive only US$12 billion in annual aid flows, only US$25 billion in export earnings and a paltry US$5 billion in foreign direct investment.

Source: Kofi Annan, Secretary-General of the United Nations, *The Irish Times*, 9 March 2001, p. 6.

Economic environment

Until the events of the Asian currency crisis of 1997 and more recently of 11 September 2001, it could be said that the global economy was growing strongly and was continuing on a path commenced at the beginning of the decade. Since 1990, developing economies had grown at about twice the rate of the industrialised economies (according to the IMF), Latin America was largely free of debt, and the end of the cold war had brought the economies of Russia and eastern Europe into the market-driven environment of mainstream international business. Also, China's casting off the shackles of a closed economy was hailed as an event of major importance. The pace of globalisation had increased rapidly, facilitated by the revolution in communications. Transnational companies employ approximately 10% of non-agricultural workers worldwide and nearly 20% in developed countries.

A major feature of the global marketing environment is the diversity of economic environments. The characteristics of each need to be appreciated if international marketing efforts are to be successful. There is available a substantial body of data which provides economic profiles on a country-by-country basis. This data is published by country sources, regional or economic grouping sources (European Union, OECD) and world sources. Included in the latter is the United Nations whose statistical yearbooks and monthly statistical reports provide data on items such as gross national product, gross domestic product, consumption, investment, government expenditure, production figures, imports, exports and demographic data. The United Nations statistical yearbook contains information on agriculture, mining, manufacturing, energy output and consumption, internal and external trade, transportation, wages and prices, health, housing, education and communication. To facilitate comparison all data is provided in US dollars. However, the way data is collected results in data from many developing countries being incomplete. Therefore some of this data should be treated as indicative because it may be understated. Table 2.1 is an example of the type of comparative data available.

The global economic scene

Recent trends

Keegan and Green (2000) comment that the most profound change in the world economy in the last 50 years is the emergence of global markets and global competitors who have steadily replaced local competitors. This change in the last two decades has been accompanied by a reduction in tariffs and to a lesser extent in non-tariff barriers. This means that the extent to which local firms are subject to import competition has increased. They attribute this to four factors:

1 Capital movements rather than trade are now the driving force in the world economy. Whereas world trade is running at US$5.5 trillion a year, the London Eurodollar Market turns over US$400 billion each working day.

Table 2.1 Demographic factors of selected countries

Demographic factors	Japan	China	Australia	Britain	US	Germany	France	Russia
Population (million)	127	1,272	19	60	286	82	59	145
Average population % growth rate (2000–2005)	0.1	0.7	1	0.2	0.9	0.0	0.4	0.4
Literacy rate %	91.2	80	99.5	100	94	95	90	85
GDP/pa US$	25,170	3,550	23,850	22,220	28,515	23,510	23,020	4,355
GDP growth %	2.6	9.6	3.2	3.4	0.3	2.8	2.2	5
Inflation %	1.9	2.7	0.3	3.5	2.3	2.1	1	14.6
Exports (billion)	411	145	60.2	251	633	512	274	88.7
People/per tel.	1.5	22	1.5	1.9	1.3	1.8	1.5	5.9
GNI/pc (US$)	33,090	655	20,170	20,860	28,480	25,860	24,040	2,965

Source: Various international sources, February 2003.

2 Production is no longer directly linked to employment. Although employment in manufacturing has declined, production continues to grow.

3 The world economy has more impact on economic outcomes within a country than the nation state.

4 The contest between capitalism and socialism is over, with the economies of socialist countries becoming increasingly market oriented.

These four factors have rendered former classifications of countries according to their economic system, less relevant than was formerly the case.

Economic systems

Since the Second World War, countries have been classified according to their economic system – as market, command or mixed systems.

Market allocation system   This system relies on the consumer to allocate resources. It is consumer choice that decides what is produced and by whom. It is the purchase decisions and purchase intentions on which producers in turn base their plans.

Command allocation   In this system, resources are allocated by government planners who determine in advance the number and specifications of each item to be produced. Under the command system, consumers are free to spend their money on whatever is available. However, the decision as to what will be available is determined by the state's planners.

Mixed system   In reality, there are no pure market allocation or command allocation systems as all market systems have a command sector (such as government regulation and involvement in production of some items) and all command systems have a market sector (for example when the country's government-owned airlines seek business in international markets). Because government is involved in all economic systems, classifications such as the above are a matter of degree. There is an overall trend throughout the world for governments to be less involved in economic participation. This is apparent in the move in both developed and developing countries towards the privatisation of government enterprises. Although there is a strong trend for command economies to move towards a market allocation system, this will be a slow process. Consider the remarks of Czinkota (1991, p. 27):

> ... all the announced intentions for change do not automatically result in change itself. For example, abolition of a centrally-planned economy does not create a market economy. Laws permitting the emergence of private sector entrepreneurs do not create entrepreneurship. The reduction of price controls does not automatically make goods available for purchase. It must be understood that there are deeply ingrained systemic differences in interests and values in command economies such as Vietnam. Highly prized and fully accepted fundamentals of the market economy such as reliance on competition, the agreement with profit motivation, and the willingness to live with risk on a corporate and personal level are not yet accepted or ingrained in former command economies.

Economic structure

As an alternative to classifying countries according to their economic system, it is possible to classify them according to their economic structure. This classification reflects the relative dominance in the economy of the country of the following:

Agriculture   Agriculture includes crop growing, hunting, fishing, grazing and forestry. Generally countries dependent on agriculture are among the economically poorer ones. The importance of agriculture to the wealth of nations has steadily declined in all countries.

Industrial   This group comprises mining, manufacturing, construction, electricity, communications infrastructure and gas. Industrial activity by low-income countries is more at the level of simply transformed manufactures, such as steel drums and extruded plastic products. The activity of middle-income and industrialised countries is more in the direction of elaborately transformed manufactures, such as computer-driven machine tools and telecommunications equipment. Within this classification, a distinction may be drawn between countries dependent on 'smokestack' (i.e. mature) industries and those dependent on high-tech industries.

Services   This involves all other forms of economic activity. It accounts for an increasing percentage of employment in all countries and is the fastest growing area of economic activity in all except low-income countries.

There are some problems with classifying countries in terms of economic structure. This is because within an economic sector, operations vary widely between countries. For instance, farming under the Common Agricultural Policy in the EU has little in common with subsistence rice farming in the Philippines. The same is true of labour-intensive operations in the textile industry of low-income countries compared with capital intensive high-tech manufacturing of telecommunications equipment in the US. An alternative classification is that based on stages of market development.

Table 2.2 Stages of market development

Income group by per capita GNI	2001 GNI (US$ million)	2001 GNI per capita (US$)	% of world GNI	2001 population (million)
High-income countries	25,104	26,710	81	959
Upper-middle-income countries	2,310	4,460	7	504
Lower-middle-income countries	2,733	1,240	8	2,163
Low-income countries	1,083	430	4	2,511

Source: Adapted from World Development Indicators database, World Bank, August 2002.

Stages of market development

This involves grouping countries according to GNI per capita. Table 2.2 shows four groupings of countries on this basis.

The stage of market development and the economic structure of countries act as an important reference point for the timing of investment by foreign corporations. Companies need to consider possible discontinuities in economic growth in terms of contingency plans for unexpected 'hiccoughs'. International Highlight 2.1 illustrates the implications of a dramatic change in economic conditions.

2.1 International highlight

Stages of market development: China versus India

China's superior performance in the past 20 years over India is largely due to its investment on and the constant improvement of its manufacturing sector, according to Richard McGregor of the *Financial Times*. Citing a report by McKinsey, McGregor claims that China has created a far more efficient and productive model for a developing economy. The transformation is driven not only by investment but also by rapid growth in labour productivity, an emphasis on exports, strong domestic demand fed by low prices and a stress on quality.

When compared with India, lower prices are not due just to cheaper wages (similar for both countries) but also to lower taxes and cost of capital. China can also manage its distribution more effectively by getting its exports to the US less than a month after leaving the factory compared with India's six to twelve months. As a result, China's GDP per capita has grown three times faster than India's. The report does concede that many Chinese firms are state owned and often fail to pay back their loans, but more than 70% of China's industrial output comes from private firms.

A multinational company like Nike produces 40% of its footwear in China, while Galanz has taken 30% of the global market for microwave ovens. In summary, the reason for their success comes down to lower taxes, import duties and raw materials costs as against India's higher indirect taxes.

Source: Richard McGregor, *Financial Times*, 8 November 2002.

Low-income countries　Often referred to as the 'third world' countries, they are characterised by dependence on agriculture with very basic, if any, manufacturing activity. They tend to have high birth rates, heavy reliance on foreign aid, low literacy, and are often characterised by political unrest. Examples of such countries abound in Africa and Central America, such as Ethiopia, Sudan and Nicaragua.

Lower-middle-income countries　These countries are at an early stage of industrialisation. Their industrial output supplies their growing domestic markets with basic items such as processed foods, batteries, tyres, textiles and building materials. They are also competitive producers for export of mature products that are standardised in nature and labour intensive, such as clothing. Examples are to be found in Vietnam and the Philippines in South-East Asia.

Upper-middle-income countries　These are industrialising countries that in Asia are referred to as 'tigers', such as Singapore, Taiwan and Korea. The percentage of population engaged in agriculture is small as people move to the cities and work in industrial or service sectors. Both wage rates and literacy are on the rise in these countries and they are formidable competitors with the high-income countries. Their economic growth tends to be export led.

High-income countries　Apart from several oil-rich nations, countries in this category reflect sustained economic growth. Sometimes referred to as post-industrial countries, this group is heavily dependent on services for income generation, is involved in information processing, places a premium on knowledge as a critical resource, and has an orientation towards the future. In these countries, new product development is a potent force for innovation and creativity. Countries in this category include the US, Japan and Sweden.

Knowledge as to how countries are categorised in economic terms is important for the international marketer. This is because it indicates the type and level of demand for various products in that country, the likely level of infrastructure that exists within the country, and the degree to which marketing is needed or allowed in that country. Apart from knowing what classification the country falls into, it is also necessary for the international marketer to appreciate how that country conducts its international trade.

International trade

International economic environment

Historically many countries have been dominated by a desire to protect domestic industry from foreign competition. Although in recent years tariff barriers (import duties on products entering the country) have fallen in most countries, they have in many cases been replaced by non-tariff barriers. Typical non-tariff barriers include import licensing (controls over the volume of imports), tariff quotas (limits on the quantity which may be imported at a specific tariff after which a higher tariff applies), quarantine restrictions (although intended to provide protection from diseases, these are often used as a protectionist measure) and standards (these often act as a barrier to entry due to their complexities and costs of conformity).

Electrical items manufactured outside the US cannot be sold there without Underwriters Laboratories Approval. This involves shipping a number of units to the US for testing which takes a considerable period of time and is very costly. As a result, few non-American electrical items are sold in the US.

There have been many attempts to regulate the international economic environment in the interests of freeing up trade between countries. The most noteworthy activity in this regard was the formation of the General Agreement on Tariffs and Trade (GATT) in 1948. This body is now known as the World Trade Organisation.

The World Trade Organisation (WTO)   Formed in 1995, the WTO involves 142 countries (as at 4 April 2003). It was an outcome of the GATT Uruguay Round of negotiations. The GATT established guidelines for the conduct of international trade and provided a forum for the negotiation of multilateral reductions in tariffs and non-tariff barriers. The members of its successor body, the WTO, account for in excess of 80% of world trade. Its central tenet is that the treatment accorded by one member to another must be accorded to all members and that there shall be no discrimination in treatment. Every member is to treat every other member as a 'most favoured nation' (MFN). Associated with this is the 'no new preference rule' whereby one country shall not accord a new preferential arrangement to any other country. Members are required to consult with each other concerning trade problems and the agreement provides a framework for negotiation. Rules also prohibit the placing of quantitative restrictions on goods entering one's country except for balance of payments reasons. This exception is often abused. A mechanism was also provided for resolving trade disputes. In 1974 there was a significant departure from this when a scheme was devised for assisting the less developed countries with a 'generalised scheme on preferences' (GSP). Developed countries were authorised to give products from such countries a margin of preference through a lower import duty, so that they could more effectively compete in developed country markets and improve their economic wellbeing.

Despite being raised in successive rounds of discussions in GATT, agricultural producing nations felt they were disadvantaged because the GATT failed to address their complaints. These complaints centred on claims that they were unfairly treated by the agricultural protectionism of industrial nations. This protectionism was exemplified in the Common Agricultural Policy of the EU and the Grain Enhancement Program of the US. In addition, while GATT had regulated trade in manufactures, it had not addressed investment or the fastest growing trade sector of services, nor associated problems such as intellectual property rights. At the conclusion of the GATT round of talks in Uruguay, GATT was replaced by the World Trade Organisation (WTO). The WTO is endeavouring to address the shortcomings of GATT through a broadening of its coverage of international trade to include agriculture, investment (Trade Related Investment Measures) and intellectual property (Trade Related Aspects of Intellectual Property Rights). Its effectiveness in these new areas is yet to be determined.

Many countries have supported multilateral forums, such as GATT and now the WTO, as vehicles for raising trade problems. This is because, for smaller countries with limited clout, the WTO offers a better chance of overcoming a barrier than does bilateral negotiations with a specific country. In bilateral negotiations it is necessary to give a concession in return, which is not the case in multilateral negotiations.

The second form of regulation of the international economic environment is in many respects a reaction to the perceived failure of the multilateral system to address the concerns of individual countries. Many nations felt that their concerns could be more effectively addressed by economic integration between like-minded countries.

Economic integration.   Since the end of the Second World War there has been a move towards economic integration. Nations are doing on a macro level what firms are doing on a micro level – banding together to improve their competitive position. Integration can take a variety of forms. These can be categorised as:

- *Preferential trading arrangements*: Participants reduce most restraints to trade between themselves but retain barriers to trade with countries which are not party to the arrangement.
- *Free trade areas*: This is a more formal version of the above and is the loosest form of economic integration. It involves the removal of all restraints to trade between members, although occasionally exceptions are made for certain products. The US–Canada agreement of 1989 and the European Free Trade Area of 1960 are examples. A more recent example is the successor of the US–Canada Agreement, i.e. the North American Free Trade Area (NAFTA) of 1994 that involved the addition of Mexico.
- *Customs unions*: As in a free trade area, the members dismantle the barriers to trade in goods and services among themselves. In addition, a common trade policy is established with respect to non-members. Usually this is a common external tariff whereby all imports are subject to the same tariff on products entering any member country. A well-known example is the one between Belgium, the Netherlands and Luxembourg of 1921.
- *Economic unions*: This involves freeing the movement of goods, services, capital and people so that not only the product but also the factors of production can move freely across borders. Under an economic union, members endeavour to harmonise monetary policies, taxation and government spending. Ideally this could lead to a common currency and fixed exchange rates. Various forms are compared in Table 2.3.

The stumbling block with economic unions is the surrendering of national sovereignty, as has been evident in recent moves in the European Union towards a common monetary unit (the euro), and major partners such as the UK are still resisting this change:

Twelve of the 15 members of the European Union have, as from 1 July 2002 adopted a common currency and exchange rates will be locked to a single continental currency – the Euro. These countries are Austria, Belgium, Finland, France, Germany, Greece, Ireland, Italy, Luxembourg, Netherlands, Portugal and Spain. Monetary policy of these countries was taken over as from 1 January 1999 by a newly created European Central Bank.

Source: Adapted from *European Union News*, Vol. 19, No. 4, 2001.

Table 2.3 Forms of regional economic integration

Stage of integration	Elimination of tariffs and quotas among members	Common tariff and quota system	Elimination of restrictions on factor movements	Harmonisation and unification of economic and social policies and institutions
Free trade area	Yes	No	No	No
Customs union	Yes	Yes	No	No
Common market	Yes	Yes	Yes	No
Economic union	Yes	Yes	Yes	Yes

Source: Keegan and Green (2000), p. 90. Reprinted by permission of Pearson Education, Inc., Upper Saddle River, NJ.

Within the Asian region, there is the ASEAN Free Trade Area which has expanded from the original six ASEAN members (Singapore, Malaysia, Thailand, Indonesia, the Philippines and Brunei) to include Vietnam, Laos, Cambodia and Myanmar. In addition, there is a looser grouping initiated by Australia in 1989 of APEC (Asia-Pacific Economic Cooperation). Originally this was to be a consultative body along the lines of the OECD (Organisation for Economic Cooperation and Development). It is now moving more towards becoming a free trade area. It includes the ASEAN nations, Australia, New Zealand, Canada, USA, Japan, South Korea, Chile and Mexico, and is viewed as a possible counterbalance to the EU and NAFTA.

Economic integration poses challenges for the international marketer. In the first place the exporting firm is now faced with supplying a larger market as goods going to one country can easily move to another within the economic grouping. This is facilitated by harmonisation of standards within that grouping. Forms of economic integration have implications for the appointment of representatives. For instance, does the firm appoint agents and distributors in each country or appoint an agent in one and distributors in each of the others? Regional trade groupings impact on foreign direct investment. The manufacturing operation established in one country is able to supply not only the market where the goods are manufactured but also markets in member countries as there are no tariff or non-tariff impediments to entry. On the other hand, economic groupings also increase competition, as domestic competitors are firms that can be based anywhere in the economic grouping, not just in the country where manufacture takes place.

In the early 1990s during the GATT Uruguay Round, many countries lost faith in the ability of the multilateral body to solve world trade problems and reverted to bilateral or regional trade arrangements. This trend was reversed in the second half of the decade with the euphoria surrounding the creation of the WTO. However, following the failure of the WTO meeting in Seattle in December 1999 to address world trade problems in a meaningful way, countries are again turning to bilateral arrangements and regional trade agreements. A more complete discussion of international trade relations issues is in Chapter 18.

Trade patterns

Trade patterns are usually measured in terms of a country's balance of payments, which is a record of transactions between residents of one country and those of all other countries. It represents the difference between receipts from foreign countries on the one hand and payments to them on the other. As the name implies, the overall total of these transactions must be in balance. Within the balance of payments account, any given category such as merchandise trade, services, and capital movements can either be positive or negative. The balance of payments is divided into:

- *Current account*: the record of merchandise and services traded as well as gifts and aid transactions between countries; and
- *Capital account*: direct investment, portfolio investment, short- and long-term capital flows.

A surplus or deficit in the current account will be compensated for by an entry in the capital account so that balance is achieved. The *balance of trade* is the relationship between merchandise imports and exports. It may be that within the current account, an unfavourable balance of trade is compensated for by a favourable trading position in services.

Consumption patterns   Both income and population impact on consumption patterns. Availability and statistics on such patterns vary widely between countries due to differences in sophistication and recency of data collection. Engel's law states that as income rises above a certain minimum, expenditure on food as a percentage of total income decreases. United Nations surveys have proved this by contrasting developed with developing countries. The share of income spent on necessities provides an indication as to how much consumers are likely to spend on other purchases. The nature of this other spending can be significant. In countries where the tendency is to rent accommodation rather than owning a home, disposable income levels are likely to be greater. Countries where the level of savings is high, such as Japan, will also exhibit different consumption patterns.

Another issue is the percentage of potential buyers or households already owning a product. In general, product saturation levels increase as per capita national income increases. For example, in countries where average income is high, the market for whitegoods is more likely to be saturated and is mostly a replacement market. In countries where income is low, regardless of need the majority of people cannot afford whitegoods. Consumption patterns are important for the international marketer because they influence the nature of demand in the international market.

Merchandise trade   Since the end of the Second World War, merchandise trade has grown at a faster rate than world production and it is the high-income countries that are responsible for more than 80% of imports and exports of merchandise. Of these countries, North America, Japan and western Europe account for approximately two-thirds of world imports and exports.

Services trade   This is the fastest growth sector in international trade. Statistics, however, are not as accurate for services as for merchandise trade. Evasion in payment for services can be a problem, as illustrated by the increasing international focus on enforcing international copyright and patent laws. The growth in services trade is one explanation for the increasing disparity in world trade between the developed and the developing nations. This is due to services involving intellectual capital. This is impacted upon by education levels and research expenditure that tends to be higher in developed nations.

Trading environment   The trading environment governs what firms can and cannot do when they go international. Trading environments are regulated by government. Most governments wish to control the international flow of trade into and out of their countries. In this they are motivated by:

- *financial issues* such as generating revenue from import duties and sale of import licences;
- *security issues* such as the sale of ingredients for chemical weapons manufacture to Iraq, or developing local industries so that the country can be self-supporting in times of conflict;
- *safety issues* such as importing defective aircraft parts from sources not approved by the original equipment manufacturer (OEM);
- *health issues* such as avoiding the entry of non-AIDS-tested plasma, anthrax etc.; and most commonly
- *protectionist issues* designed to safeguard domestic industry from import competition.

Barriers to the free flow of trade can be divided into tariff and non-tariff barriers. Tariff barriers usually operate as a tax on imports to make them less attractive to buyers. They can be imposed for either revenue or protectionist reasons. Tariffs can be either by value (ad valorem) or by volume (specific) or a combination of both. The way the tariff is applied influences its impact.

There are occasional cases where tariffs are imposed on exports. This can be for revenue reasons. Tariffs on exports can also be imposed when pressure is applied by another country seeking to protect its producers from an excess of import competition as happened in the case of Brazilian frozen orange juice concentrate entering the US market. Whereas with tariffs there is no limit as to the volume that can be imported provided the duty is paid, with quotas, the volume is controlled. The resulting restrictions on supply can force up prices, and profit margins may also increase, due to restrictions on supply. This happened with Japanese cars in the US market in the 1980s. The semiconductor industry in the US is another example of how quotas have been used to restrict local demand by forcing up prices. Quotas may be mandated by the government or voluntarily agreed to under threat of mandated quotas, as was the case above with the Japanese automobiles entering the US market.

Recent years have seen a general lowering of tariff barriers throughout the world. This has been the case not only in developed countries but also in a number of developing countries in the Asia-Pacific region. Non-tariff barriers include all other means of limiting trade between countries. Apart from those discussed earlier, they may also include government procurement restraints. An example is the 'buy national' policy of many governments. Limitations on trade between countries can also apply to exports as well as imports. Examples include the previous national embargo on trading with

South Africa, United Nations' sanctions against Iraq, and the US Trading with the Enemy Act which until 1994 prevented US firms doing business with Vietnam.

The growth of foreign direct investment (FDI) by 18% in 2000 was faster than that of other economic indicators such as world production, capital formation and trade. This global expansion of investment is driven by more than 60,000 transnational corporations with over 800,000 international affiliates. Developed countries remain the prime recipients of FDI, accounting for more than 75% of global inflows and most of this investment takes the form of mergers and acquisitions. In 2000, inflows into developed countries increased by 21% to just above US$1 trillion. By contrast, inflows of FDI into developing countries declined for the second year in a row (19%) and only amounted to US$240 billion (United Nations World Investment Report, *Promoting Linkages* (2001), p. 1).

Measuring markets

There are a number of different ways of assessing the size of economies in different countries. They include income, population, quality of life, infrastructure, debt and resources. These can affect the attractiveness of a market from an export or investment viewpoint in different ways.

Income

Countries are often classified according to levels of income and measured by gross national product or gross national income (GNI) per head. Although classifications of countries into groupings on this basis are somewhat arbitrary, the following guide, based on the World Bank's *World Development Report 2000/2001* figures, may be useful to marketers in appraising international markets (see also Table 2.2):

- low-income countries (also known as least developing of the developing countries or 'third world'), less than US$755 per head;
- lower-middle-income countries (also known as developing countries), US$756 to US$2,995 per head;
- upper-middle-income countries (also known as industrialising countries), US$2,996 to US$9,265 per head; and
- high-income countries (also known as advanced or post-industrial countries), more than US$9,266 per head.

The extent to which income varies between countries impacts on the ability of the country to fund future development. The degree to which average levels of personal income vary between countries also impacts on the ability of people to buy consumer goods. Income is a most important indicator of potential for a vast range of industrial and consumer goods. Income is usually measured and compared across countries in terms of GNI per capita and this is treated as a measure of purchasing power. However, it is only an approximate indicator because usage rates vary between countries and this may impact on affordability. In addition, variations between currencies can distort real income and standard-of-living figures. As a consequence, a consistent measure of real value needs to be applied to reflect the relative differences in the volumes of goods

Table 2.4 Purchasing power parities, gross domestic product per capita, 2001 at current prices (US$)

OECD member countries	Based on current exchange rates	Based on current purchasing power parities
Luxembourg	43,400	48,500
Norway	37,200	36,500
United States	35,200	35,200
Switzerland	34,000	29,900
Japan	32,600	26,400
Denmark	29,700	29,200
Iceland	27,100	29,300
Ireland	26,600	30,000
Sweden	24,600	26,000
United Kingdom	24,300	26,300

Source: Adapted from National Accounts of OECD countries.

produced and purchased. The use of 'purchasing power parities' achieves this objective by showing how many units of currency are needed to buy in country A what one unit of currency will buy in country B. Purchasing power parities for a number of countries are outlined in Table 2.4.

Population

People make a market. For basic and essential products, the more people there are the larger the size of the market. The significance of population size reduces with the sophistication of the product or service offered, as a person's hierarchy of needs becomes more important in determining what is purchased. The size of individual country markets varies from the largest – such as China and India each with in excess of 1 billion people – downwards. In predicting future trends in international markets, it is also useful to take into account population growth rates. Generally speaking, there tends to be a negative correlation between stage of development and population growth rates, with the less developed countries having higher growth rates than developed countries. There are exceptions to this, such as in China where the government-imposed one child policy has substantially lowered the population growth. Distribution of the population is significant. This distribution can be in terms of both age and location.

- *Age*: People at different stages of life have different needs. Increases and decreases in the percentage of the population in specific age groups is related to demand for particular products and services. In the developing world, the distribution towards younger people creates a different demand pattern from that in the developed world where the population distribution is towards older people whose needs and willingness to adopt new ideas and products differ.

- *Location*: In some countries the population is relatively evenly dispersed, as in
  many developing countries, but in other countries such as Australia it tends to be
  concentrated in a limited number of urban areas. Australia is the world's largest
  urbanised nation with 86% of its population living in urban areas. In the more
  developed countries in Asia there is a strong trend towards urbanisation as
  people move from the country to cities in search of employment. The degree of
  urbanisation and the movement from country to city are measures of significance
  to marketers. This is because in many developing countries there are usually wide
  differences in standards of living between country and city. China is a case in
  point. In addition, urban dwellers in different countries are more likely to exhibit
  similar patterns of consumption in contrast to urban and rural dwellers within the
  same country. Because globalisation of tastes is more apparent in cities, products
  targeting urban consumers may require less modification than those targeting rural
  consumers whose tastes are more likely to be traditional. The location of the
  population also assists in identifying pockets of purchasing power as well as the
  cost of researching the market or targeting international market segments.

Within large markets, there are many submarkets that may be more appropriate for the
firm given its limited resources and ability to supply. It is important to carefully define
the specific market to be targeted. For example, frequently when businesspeople visit
the US market, they are overwhelmed by its size. They think that if they could obtain
1% of the US market, they would be very happy. Unfortunately they do not focus on
which 1% of the market they wish to target, nor do they devise specific strategies to
secure that specific 1%.

Physical quality of life

Economic advancement is usually accompanied by a price tag. This aspect is increasingly being taken into account as evidenced by the requirement for environmental
impact statements to accompany development proposals. While wealthy countries have
the luxury of being able to trade off development for quality of life, this luxury eludes
many less developed countries whose citizens have little option other than to trade
away quality of life today in order to improve the lives of their children tomorrow. The
Physical Quality of Life Index is a measure of the level of welfare in a country and
takes into account life expectancy, infant mortality and adult literacy rates. Together
these three factors constitute a social indicator that provides a measure over time as to
how individual countries are advancing in terms of the quality of life enjoyed by their
citizens. This issue is further explored in Chapter 16 in the context of the macro aspects
of globalisation.

Infrastructure

Infrastructure generally refers to facilities and services necessary for the functioning of
the economy and includes energy supplies, transport and communications, commercial
and financial services. The availability and nature of infrastructure is important when
marketing in other countries. It can also affect the capability of a country to export its
resources. Not only does infrastructure impact on physical distribution, it also impacts
on the ability to operate in specific areas and cost of doing so (availability of power and

Table 2.5 Number of Internet hosts per 1,000 inhabitants

Turkey	3.63
Mexico	4.66
Slovak Republic	7.66
Korea	11.07
Poland	14.23
Portugal	13.82
Greece	17.37
Czech Republic	16.77
Hungary	19.20
Spain	26.17
France	27.20
Italy	40.44
Ireland	34.60
Japan	48.19
Germany	50.33
EU	53.04
Belgium	51.77
United Kingdom	69.71
Austria	84.12
Switzerland	74.09
OECD	100.60
Australia	91.08
Denmark	98.53
New Zealand	106.17
Netherlands	118.81
Norway	130.27
Sweden	177.02
Canada	183.07
Iceland	179.74
Finland	183.28
United States	275.26

Source: Adapted from OECD (2002) *Information Technology Outlook*.

water). Infrastructure also impacts on the ability to communicate messages to potential customers (availability and quality of advertising agencies and market research operations) and ability to finance activities (communications, banking and financial networks). The Internet is an example of a rapidly expanding communications technology that relies for its effectiveness on infrastructure being available to the customer. Table 2.5 shows the number of Internet hosts per 1,000 people in various countries. When the number of hosts per thousand people is compared between countries, the US has the highest with 275, but in Europe, Finland rates highest with 183 hosts per 1,000 people. All countries are experiencing rapid growth in hosts.

Debt

Another indicator of economic difference between countries is their level of indebtedness. As illustrated by the recent Asian currency crisis, this impacts on their ability to borrow to finance development (especially physical infrastructure), their attractiveness as markets, the extent to which foreign exchange is freely available and the likelihood of being paid. In many developing countries, interest on debt consumes a major percentage of export receipts. It can lead to debt crisis, the Argentinian crisis in 2002, and countries engaging in barter or other forms of countertrade. Figure 2.1 shows both the amount of debt and the percentage of debt to GNI for a range of developing countries.

Resources

Resource endowment varies from country to country and traditionally was an indicator of relative prosperity as reflected in commodity exports. In some cases the wealth of a country is almost totally dependent on a single resource (e.g. Libyan dependence on oil). In other cases the resource leads to other resource-related activity (e.g. water leading to rice production in Thailand). In some instances, the resource is geography, as happens when a country like Singapore lies across a strategic trade route that leads to entrepôt activities. Climate can also influence how a firm's product offering is received. For example, snow skis have limited appeal in Indonesia. Another resource-related issue is the source and diversity of a nation's export income. The greater the spread, the better the cushion against an economic downturn in a particular activity. On the other hand, in order to influence prices in an area, the country needs to be a major world

Figure 2.1	**Nations in debt**

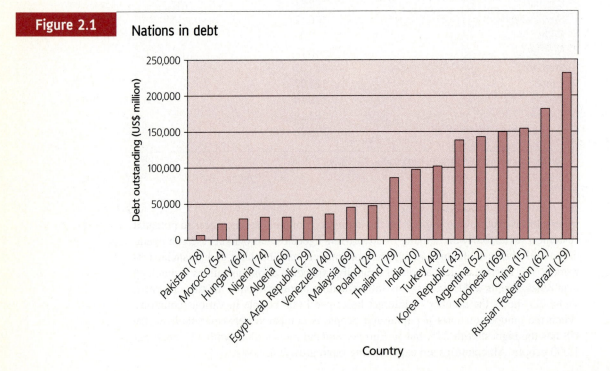

supplier in that field. Many less-developed economies are monocultures in which one industrial or resource sector dominates the economy, and often their opportunities are circumscribed by world prices for a product or activity over which they may have little influence.

Marketing implications

Although the most common relative measure of different markets is GNI, other measures which may impact on a market's attractiveness include the level of unemployment, consumer prices, level of productivity, trends in foreign trade, nature of balance of payments, exchange rate movement, the level of country indebtedness and foreign currency reserves. The international marketer needs to monitor the economic environment on both a global and individual country basis. This enables the targeting of specific markets, assessment of the best means of entering those markets, determination of the potential in those markets, evaluation of the best combination of marketing mix elements and estimation of future potential. The economic environment should be carefully considered when preparing plans and strategies for involvement in a country. This is because it impacts on the volume and nature of demand, the most appropriate form of market entry, the ability to compete in that market, the way products are to be delivered to customers in that market, and which segment of the market should receive most attention.

2.2 International highlight

Should we stay or should we go?

The political and economic climate in Zimbabwe is not considered to be rated as positive, according to international organisations such as the World Bank, the International Monetary Fund, the European community, many non-government organisations (NGOs) and many individual foreign governments.

The country is suffering a major foreign exchange crisis, fuel shortages, hyperinflation, record unemployment, falling exports, a withdrawal of investment and aid money, a decline in tourism numbers and a net contraction in the size of the economy. There have been government-sponsored forced seizures and violence on the commercial farms (which are responsible for much of the food production and export income),

and these activities have also spread to the manufacturing sector.

Allied with these events, the government has been accused of large-scale electoral corruption at the last national elections, widespread voter intimidation, and killings to ensure the return to government of the governing party. These matters are of considerable concern to international investors and international exporters to Zimbabwe, a number of which have a considerable stake in the economy.

Virginia Bonello, the international marketing manager of Farm Software, is particularly concerned since her company has been exporting its key product to Zimbabwe in recent years, targeting the commercial farming sector.

▶

The commercial farming sector in Zimbabwe appears to have a ready acceptance of new technology products and, until recently, had the financial resources (including the foreign exchange) to purchase such products. Farm Software offers software specifically tailored to owner-operated farms, allowing owners to plan their operational activities and to track expenditure and income on an annual basis. Specific packages exist for beef, dairy, crop farming and horticulture. After its establishment in 1993, Farm Software met with considerable success in Australia and New Zealand, before starting to export the full range of its software packages to South Africa (the first market in its international growth plans) in 1996.

The success of Farm Software products in this market led Virginia to commence exports to Zimbabwe in 1997, where sales of the beef and crop farmers' software packages were particularly strong in the first two years of operations. However, the political and economic climate changed in Zimbabwe shortly after this, with the government-sponsored farm seizures and violence having a major impact on commercial farm production. A number of farmers were brutally murdered, farm employees were severely intimidated, beef herds were slaughtered or stolen, and commercial crops were destroyed. Many farmers were forced to temporarily abandon their properties. This has led to a considerable decline in Farm Software sales in this market, as the commercial farming sector appears to be under considerable threat with the number of farms contracting, and the remaining operations being forced to scale down.

Commercial farmers in this market have been having difficulty accessing bank credit as a result of these problems, further reducing their ability to afford inputs such as farm software designed to improve the efficiency and productivity of their operations.

Furthermore, given the uncertain future of the commercial farming sector in Zimbabwe, the commitment of many farmers to improve their operations has been flagging, since the current government at any time may seize their properties.

Capital expenditure on infrastructure improvements in the commercial farming sector has almost ground to a halt, and farmers are having difficulty servicing their loans at high interest rates to the banks in Zimbabwe. Software packages are not being bought. As the international marketing manager for Farm Software, which is based in Sydney, Virginia Bonello has to prepare an export-marketing plan covering both the South African and the Zimbabwean markets for the next five-year period. Furthermore, Virginia has read reports in the international press that the political and economic meltdown in Zimbabwe may have flow-on effects into the neighbouring much larger South African market, where Farm Software sales have been strong since market entry in 1996. Already events in Zimbabwe have had an impact on the value of the South African currency, the rand, and foreign investment flowing into the latter country has been slowing, as investors judge the region as a whole, and fear flow-on effects.

This contrasts with the apparent stability of the Australian and New Zealand markets for Farm Software products, despite the presence of a greater number of competitors offering products similar to the various Farm Software packages. Virginia, in preparing the export-marketing plan is beginning to think that the domestic marketing manager (whole is responsible for both the Australian and New Zealand operations) has a much simpler market planning and management role. Unlike the domestic marketing manager, Virginia is under pressure to ensure that Farm Software's export marketing is a success, since the company's objective, almost right from its establishment in 1993, was to design and market products for a number of international markets.

Source: Al Marshall, School of Business & Informatics, Australian Catholic University.

Financial environment

The financial environment is the second major environmental influence discussed in this chapter. While the discussion of the economic environment primarily related to the economic situation within countries and regions, the following discussion of the financial environment primarily relates to the circumstances that affect relations and marketing opportunities between countries. Particular issues to be covered in this connection include foreign exchange, financial management and the international financial system.

Foreign exchange issues

The foreign exchange market is a market for currencies through which the currency of one country is exchanged for the currency of another country. Participants in the market include banks, governments, speculators, individuals and firms. The price of one currency in terms of another is the rate of exchange. As with many forms of financial trading, rates quoted can be either at the present time (known as the spot market rate) or at some time in the future such as 30, 60 or 90 days hence (known as the forward market rate). There is considerable gambling on rates, similar to the futures market for commodities or shares. This enables firms to hedge against a variation in the exchange rate and to negotiate a forward market rate that applies on the date on which receipt of payment is expected. In this situation, likely gains from a movement in the exchange rate are sacrificed to ensure protection from possible loss if the exchange rate moves the other way. Forward contracts for unstable currencies are very expensive and are not always available for lesser known or less frequently traded currencies.

Underlying the forecasting of exchange rates is the concept of purchasing power parity. This is based on the concept that a change in relationship between price levels in two different countries requires an adjustment in the exchange rate to offset the difference in price levels.

Dynamics

One of the problems which faces all people involved in international business is the risk that between the time a sale is agreed and the time that payment is received, the exchange rate may have changed. When this happens, the amount received in the currency quoted by the seller will be different from that which was expected when the contract was entered into. It could be that a major devaluation of the currency in the buying country occurred, as happened in Thailand in the last six months of 1997 and Argentina in 2002, or that there was a shift in the rate which, although small, had the effect of eroding the profit to be made on the transaction.

Forecasting

There are a number of factors that influence the forecasting of exchange rates in addition to the purchasing power parity of a country. The most important ones are economic and political.

Economic factors   The economic factors are as follows:

- Policy and performance can create a rate of growth higher than the world average. When this happens, the exchange value of a country's currency will increase.
- Real interest rates (nominal interest rate minus the rate of inflation) compared to the world average will also have an impact. If the rate is higher, it will attract capital from international markets and create a demand for the country's currency.
- Importance of the currency in the world's financial system. If a currency is desirable, like the US dollar, and included in baskets of currencies and held by individuals and institutions as a form of wealth in foreign countries, it is less susceptible to fluctuation. Also the spread between buying and selling rates for this currency is likely to be less.

Political factors   Political factors are important in the value attributed to a currency. Political factors include the philosophy of the party in power, the stability of govern-ments, the nature of the underpinning of power, sources of impending change and the nature of the government.

Managing foreign exchange risk

When a firm undertakes transactions in foreign currencies, the firm runs the risk of losses or gains from a change in the value of the currency involved. This exposure takes three forms:

1 *Transaction exposure.* The effect of outstanding contracts involving foreign countries on the likely receipts of the firm,
2 *Translation exposure.* The effect of translating results of international activities in the currency of the home country,
3 *Economic exposure.* The impact on the forward movement of the exchange rate arising from economic circumstances in the international market. Examples of exposure are impending tougher sanctions against Iraq and the impact on the tourism industry of foot-and-mouth disease in the UK.

Various strategies can be employed to reduce exposure to foreign exchange risk. These include modifying the risk. An example would be to borrow funds in the country with which the firm already has exposure so that the possible loss on foreign exchange is matched by profits when paying off that loan. Alternatively, risk modification can occur by shifting the risk by purchasing options and/or futures. Whereas options give the right to buy or sell currency at a specified price up until a specified date, futures are usually longer term and for larger values. They involve the right to buy an amount of a specified currency at some future time at a specified price.

Governments also intervene in free-floating foreign exchange markets. The motive for intervention is to support or depress the price of their own or other currencies, to dampen fluctuations in exchange rates or to manipulate the value of the currency for political or economic reasons. Sometimes governments attempt to discourage nationals from importing by making the currency more expensive in terms of that of major import sources.

Multiple exchange rates

When there is a difference between the official rate of exchange for a currency and what people think it is worth, a black market for the currency is likely to develop as existed in India for years prior to 1994. This situation can arise when the exchange rate is set by the government for political or balance of payments reasons and is not allowed to float according to demand or supply. When the situation gets out of hand, the government may give partial recognition to the problem by setting a different exchange rate for transactions by specific sectors such as a special rate for tourists visiting the country. On other occasions, the situation arises because the currency is pegged to a basket of other currencies and moves in step with them. If the relative weighting accorded to currencies in the basket does not reflect the relative market value of those currencies, then the float is skewed and the exchange rate does not reflect the market value of the currency.

In Vietnam in the late 1980s, there were three exchange rates for the dong. There was the official rate of 6.5 to US$1, a tourist rate of 12 to US$1, and an illegal black market rate of 300 to US$1.

Financial management

The discussion of financial management focuses on sources of funds and types of financial risk likely to be encountered in the international marketplace.

Sources of funds

In many cases it is necessary for firms to assist their customers abroad with financing. In countries where finance is a problem, it is often the case that the attractiveness of the financial terms will outweigh the price. The more attractive the finance (measured in terms of the rate of interest and/or the grace period and/or the length of the loan), the greater the chance of winning the business. Some of the more common sources of finance are banks, government and factoring.

Banks Banks provide trade financing depending on their commercial relationship with the exporter, the nature of the transaction, the perceived risk of the country of the borrower, and the availability of export insurance to reduce the risk. These institutions usually only finance first-rate credit risks. Often this means that banks do not insure transactions in promising or newly emerging markets. The increasing level of debt in the developing world and the lack of conformity by these countries to accepted 'western' financial practices, has increased the reluctance of the banking sector to finance transactions involving such countries.

Another factor may be the nature of the bank's international network. This may consist of a series of relationships with correspondent banks. A stage of increased international involvement is for the bank to establish representative offices in the more promising international markets from the perspective of either servicing its customers that seek international involvement or attracting new customers. The most resource-intensive form of bank involvement is acquiring equity in banks in other countries. This may increase the likelihood of the bank financing transactions in those countries.

Government When the risks are not commercially insurable or the government decides that it is in the national interest to fund a sale to a country that has a high credit risk, then it may extend the loan itself or underwrite a loan extended by a commercial institution. Official assistance can take the form either of a loan or a guarantee. In the latter case, governments often mix aid with credit to offer a blended loan. As Letovsky (1990) points out, this has resulted in an export credit war in which countries try to outdo each other in offering concessional loans so as to improve the chances of their firms winning international business. An example in the Irish context was the Export Insurance Relief funded by the government to assist cattle exporters to gain markets outside the EU.

Forfeiting and factoring With forfeiting, the importer provides the exporter with a promissory note at the time of shipment which the exporter then sells at a discount for cash. With factoring, the factoring house purchases the exporter's receivables at a discount giving the exporter cash. Where the exporter is still liable for buyer default, the discount is modest, but where the factoring house accepts liability, the discount tends to be large.

Figure 2.2 summarises different methods of payment and export financing in terms of whether they are short term or middle/long term.

Types of financial risk

There are a number of different sources of financial risk. Knowledge of these can assist in reducing or managing risk. International political, commercial and economic developments can quickly render the most careful financial judgements irrelevant. In addition, changes in the structure or ownership of the international party with whom the transaction is being undertaken can also have an unanticipated impact.

Figure 2.2	**Different methods of exporting financing**

Source: Keegan and Schlegelmilch (2001), p. 278.

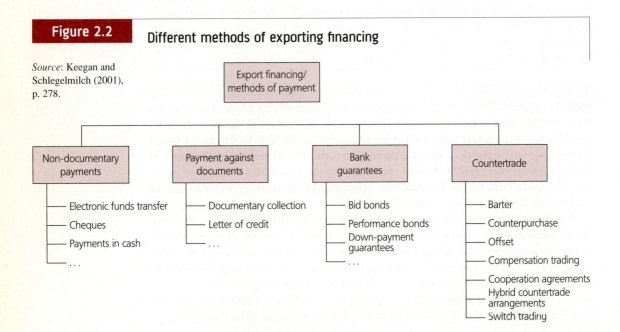

- *Commercial risk.* Commercial defaults usually result from changes to personnel in the firm, loss of a key customer by the buyer, the buyer encountering unexpected financial problems, or the buyer being threatened with a takeover bid. Slow payment by the buyer's other customers, such as government instrumentalities, or natural disasters, such as an earthquake, can also result in commercial default. While all these sources of change exist in the domestic market, lack of direct involvement in the international market as well as geographic and psychic distance, make the risks more difficult to anticipate when exporting to international markets.

- *Political risk.* This is beyond the control of either the seller or the international buyer. Often this is caused by the buyer wishing to pay, but the government of the host country delaying the approval to remit funds for balance of payments reasons. Other political risks include war, revolution, changes in official policy, cancellation of projects, change in the political party in power, and expropriation of firms in the host country.

- *Foreign exchange risk.* Fluctuating exchange rates impact on how much is actually received. As discussed previously, there are various mechanisms to minimise this form of risk, but as these impact on the cost of the transaction, the charges for minimising foreign exchange risk need to be factored into the price.

Coping with recession

Recession in the US and/or EU, the Asian currency crisis of a few years ago and the current Japanese economic recession, make it necessary for international marketers to have available plans to cope with recession. These can be short term and driven by the need to provide shareholders with continuous dividends, or long term, driven by the desire to cater for customer needs in the market encountering recession. Kotabe and Helsen (2000) propose eight strategies as follows:

- *Pull out.* Although a short-term, easy option, it does have long-term consequences, particularly in Asian countries where long-term, trustworthy relationships are an integral element of the business scene. Retail firms such as J.C. Penny and Wal-Mart who left Indonesia when its currency crisis occurred will find it very difficult to re-enter that market.

- *Emphasise a product's value.* Despite the recession, middle-class consumers will want to maintain their current lifestyle. In tough times, they will need reassurance that the products previously purchased without much thought, now represent value for money. This might be achieved by emphasising the quality of the product. This tactic was adopted by Procter and Gamble for its range of shampoos in Hong Kong.

- *Change the product mix.* The firm can shift the product mix offered in the market experiencing recession by pushing the relatively inexpensive elements of the range whilst de-emphasising the more expensive elements. Burberry, the UK men's clothing retailer, replaced its expensive jackets with its range of T-shirts in the windows of its Asian outlets during the region's currency crisis.

- *Repackage the goods.* So that loyal customers will keep buying the product in times of difficulty, the product can be offered in smaller packs at more affordable prices as was the case with Unilever's Magnum ice cream and its range of detergents.

- *Maintain stricter inventory.* This involves not only reducing unnecessary inventory but also improving product assortment by only offering what the customers in the market experiencing recession actually want. As a result, many companies do not restock slow-moving items.

- *Look outside the region for expansion opportunities.* Lower labour rates mean that plants in countries experiencing recession have a competitive cost advantage as sources of supply to other markets. Having one's plants in such markets focus on supplying international markets rather than the local market may be a strategy for coping with recession.

- *Increase advertising in the region.* A fall in exchange rates and a recession will mean that it is much cheaper to advertise in markets experiencing downturn. This, coupled with historical evidence that it is a mistake to cut advertising during a recession, suggests that advertising should be increased.

- *Increase local procurement.* Currency variations will make local sourcing cheaper than imported sourcing and this provides the opportunity for re-evaluating local sources of supply for inputs so as to improve competitiveness. Increasing local procurement offers greater protection against fluctuating exchange rates.

The international financial system

Background

Towards the end of the Second World War, the allied powers met to determine an international financial framework that would facilitate post-war reconstruction. This meeting resulted in the Bretton Woods Agreement that established:

- a world lending body – the International Bank for Reconstruction and Development (also known as the World Bank);
- a body to oversee the management of the international financial system and manage currency adjustments – the International Monetary Fund (IMF);
- a system whereby exchange rates were to be pegged to the US dollar. Nations agreed to maintain exchange rates to within ± 1% of the fixed rate. The US dollar was defined in terms of its gold value and convertibility into gold.

This system collapsed in 1971 due to mounting US balance of payments deficits. With reserves of US$11 billion in gold, but US$47 billion of currency held by foreign interests, there was no way the US could redeem dollars for gold if called upon to do so. The world moved to a foreign exchange market system. In effect this meant that currencies were free to fluctuate and foreign exchange rates were subject to demand and supply. The rates could be 'officially' influenced by governments intervening in the market by buying or selling their own currency if they wished to reduce or increase its value in terms of other currencies.

International Monetary Fund

The IMF has six objectives:

1 Promote international cooperation among members on international monetary issues.

2 Facilitate the balanced growth of international trade and contribute to high levels of real income, employment and production.

3 Promote exchange stability and orderly exchange arrangements and avoid competitive currency devaluation.

4 Foster a multilateral system of payments and transfers, and eliminate exchange restrictions.

5 Make financial resources available to members.

6 Seek a reduction of imbalances in payments.

Following the collapse in 1971 of the system established by the Bretton Woods Agreement, the IMF created a system of Special Drawing Rights (SDRs) to supplement both the dollar and gold as reserves. SDRs, often referred to as 'paper gold', represent an average base of value derived from the value of a group of the most important currencies. SDRs are allocated by the IMF to each member country on the basis of various factors, including share of gross world product and share of world trade. When members encounter balance of payments difficulties, they can exchange SDRs for currency held by other countries. The creation of SDRs has increased liquidity in the international business environment and some international contracts are written in SDRs to reduce exposure to foreign exchange rate fluctuations. SDRs play an important role by providing short-term financing to governments trying to clear current account deficits. Governments are able to do this because control over SDRs enables governments to operate as short-term lenders.

The IMF's lending capacity in recent years has led to a broadening of its role. Increasingly, the IMF operates as a financial consultant to governments of countries in financial difficulty. It organises a package of financial assistance measures for such countries but these are usually conditional on the country undertaking a package of financial remedies. The proposed remedies are often unpopular with politicians and people in the financially distressed country. Typical IMF demands are to cut government expenditure, establish realistic exchange rates, reduce growth in the money supply, curtail government subsidies and prepare an active programme to stimulate exports. These measures are based on 'western' economic rationalism and not on Asian relationship-oriented approaches to business. Because of this, there is often resentment towards the IMF and consequent claims that its conditions for assistance infringe national sovereignty. In response to criticism, the IMF has created a special fund (US$8.4 billion) to help the poorest of the less developed countries. This fund extends loans at concessional interest rates for up to 10 years.

The Thai currency was devalued in July 1997. The IMF became involved in structuring a rescue package and Thailand agreed to a number of measures, including approximately US$4 billion sale of state enterprises. However, two finance ministers resigned in succession after failing to get government support for tax increases sufficient to match IMF demands. When the Thai baht went *into 'free fall' in October 1997, the IMF became involved in restructuring the rescue package. Because of the size of the necessary package, the IMF sought assistance from other countries. The conditions imposed by the IMF, although accepted by Thailand, contributed to political instability resulting in a change in government in November 1997.*

The World Bank

The World Bank has approximately 150 members and had traditionally operated as a development bank channelling technical assistance and finance to developing countries. The primary focus of its lending programme until recently has been on project financing for economic and social infrastructure. Although some of its financing is provided by developed countries, most is raised on international capital markets. As a consequence, most of its loans are made at near-commercial rates. Its loans are usually repayable over 15 to 20 years with a grace period of 3 to 5 years. Each loan must be made to or guaranteed by the recipient country. Because poorer countries cannot afford to pay these high rates of interest, concessional finance is provided through the World Bank's subsidiary, the International Development Association. Another subsidiary provides funds for private sector investment projects – the International Finance Corporation.

In more recent years, the World Bank has been under pressure, particularly from the US, to move away from project financing towards activities which foster deregulation and more market-driven economic policies. On a number of occasions, the US has used its power of veto in the World Bank to impose on other countries its view of the world. This is regarded by many as being contrary to the spirit of a truly multilateral organisation.

From the time that the Socialist Republic of Vietnam was created in 1972 until US recognition in 1994, the World Bank was unable to fund development projects in that country despite the fact that a majority of the world's nations had long since recognised the regime. It was the US power of veto which enabled it to stop World Bank assistance to Vietnam and resulted in the strange situation whereby the United Nations Development Program funded feasibility studies in Vietnam against the day when the World Bank would be allowed to fund feasible projects.

International aid

The motives underlying aid vary. It is given for political, financial and altruistic reasons.

- *Political*: The purpose in this case is to increase the dependency of a regime in another country on the nation giving the aid or as a means of improving relationships between the donor and recipient nations.
- *Financial*: This is designed to assist firms to achieve increased business in international markets. It may be direct, as happens when aid is used to provide concessional interest rates on loans for commercial projects in international markets. It may be indirect, as happens when the aid is used to fund projects or supply products so as to demonstrate to the recipient country the quality of the donor country's products, services and improve its image as a source of supply.

- *Altruistic*: Most other countries still use their aid as a 'bait' for commercial purchases, but can vary according to whichever political party is in power.

Aid can be either a grant (gift) or a loan (usually at non-commercial interest rates and repayment periods). It can also come from different sources.

- *Multilateral aid* is extended by agencies such as the World Bank and the Asian Development Bank. These are bodies that extend concessional loans to their members, usually on concessional terms. Such aid is altruistic and tendering procedures involve a balance of decision making between the relevant agency in the recipient country and the experts in the bank responsible for development assistance to that country. These procedures are transparent and are designed to ensure that the bidder with the most appropriate offer and price is selected.

- *Bilateral aid* is that given by one country to another. It usually has strings attached and is motivated by political and economic considerations. Projects to be financed or products/services to be provided are usually worked out in advance in talks between the two countries and often in the context of political or trade talks. The only exception occurs when there is an unanticipated event, such as famine, earthquakes or floods, where one country seeks from another special help in times of need.

- *Non-government aid* is mostly extended by charitable bodies such as the Red Cross, Save the Children Fund or Freedom from Hunger campaign. Non-government aid can be offered on a country basis or on a global basis.

The flow of aid from the developed to the developing world has slackened somewhat as developed countries are finding it more difficult to balance their budgets. A UN resolution in the 1970s that each developed country should aim to give 1% of its GDP in aid was modified to 0.75% in the 1980s to reflect attainability and reality. The percentage of GNI given in aid by developed countries has fallen further in the 1990s with a decrease in availability of long-term, low interest loans offered on a bilateral basis.

A major problem with aid, whether it be motivated by altruistic or commercial considerations, is the involvement of the government of the recipient country. Leading UK economist Lord Peter Bauer has pointed out that often the governments of developing countries use aid to advance their political objectives or the individual objectives of the ministers responsible for the activity concerned, rather than to advance the welfare of the people. In countries where political divisions are on racial or religious grounds, aid can be used to advance the interests of one race or religion to the detriment of the other. This can backfire on the country giving the aid, cause negative publicity for firms involved in the execution of the project, and engender criticism of the donor country for violating global norms such as human rights and protection of the environment.

Marketing implications

The international financial system regulates financial transactions and provides opportunities for international business. Mechanisms exist for assessing and minimising the financial risks involved in international business. International bodies operate so as to facilitate the country's management of its international financial exposure and also to assist the less advantaged nations. They do this in case the financial problems of such nations cause recession or depression throughout the world. This is a reason why the IMF insisted that Indonesia in 1998 fully comply with its recommendations, rather than take the soft option of linking the rupiah to the US dollar. The international marketer needs to know the sources of funds when doing international business. If the funds are aid funds, payment may come from another country or from a multilateral agency. The international marketer also needs to monitor the financial situation in the economy of the foreign country. The financial state of the international economy provides an indication as to the likely stability of the exchange rate, the availability of funds, and the cost of funds. All these factors affect the attractiveness of the international market as well as the short- and long-term risks of involvement.

Internet infusion

The Internet has affected or has the potential to affect most aspects of modern life. It has led to digital 'haves' and 'have nots', especially as far as international trade is concerned. Issues that underlie this situation include:

- *Innovation versus control* – innovation takes place when it ruptures a stable structure. It prospers when demand is strong, when there is a stable investment climate and when infrastructure exists. However, innovation threatens the status quo and attracts the attention of regulators, including the taxman. The Internet is an example of a technology that has evolved at such a rapid rate that it is one step ahead of the regulators. The challenge for governments is to create regulation that is technology neutral and development supportive. Governments vary substantially in this respect.

- *Entrepreneurial versus social benefits* – although entrepreneurial activities associated with international e-business may be good for individual business interests, they need to be reconciled with macro issues which are the responsibility of governments, such as the right to privacy, social justice, security and public good.

- *'Bricks' versus 'clicks'* – the focus when implementing the Internet in international marketing should be on e-enabling traditional Internet business rather than on creating a parallel way of undertaking such business. This can be achieved despite the fact that 'clicks' requires a different focus as far as business development is concerned. This is because the products are often e-based, e-facilitated and digitally deliverable.

Source: Badrinath (2001), p. 5.

It is necessary to strike a balance as far as the above three aspects are concerned. This balance will depend on the state of e-readiness of the country with which it is proposed to do business electronically. E-facilitated trade should not be viewed as an alternative to traditional international trade because technology is a tool and it is up to the user to make the most effective use of this new tool called the Internet.

The Internet is rapidly developing as an international trading medium and its spread is likely to be in four waves. An appreciation of these waves is necessary in order to assess the appropriateness of trading with potential international trading partners via the Internet.

The first wave began in 1993 and basically involved North America and some Nordic countries. It evolved from an educational tool to a vehicle for corporate communications and transactions. The following are the characteristics of first-wave societies:

- advanced information societies;

- a marked clustering of information technology, telecommunications and content industries;

- very high levels of Internet usage;

- close cooperation on information technology issues between government, business and the general community to create national competitive strength based on information technology.

The second wave began in 1996 and involved northern Europe, North-East Asia, Israel, Singapore, Hong Kong, Australia and New Zealand. It is distinguished from the first wave only by the slower, large-scale commercial uptake of the Internet. The extent of these countries' development as information societies differs according to the type of information society these countries wish to create. Some countries, such as the UK and Germany, are virtually indistinguishable from first-wave countries whereas others lag behind in policy development and levels of online penetration. One factor could be the abundance of software in English and paucity in Japanese, Korean and some European languages. There are local factors at work impacting on Internet uptake, such as the attachment of large firms in North Asia to existing EDI networks and the impact of their existing systems, such as Minitel in France (a free service with text and e-mail capabilities delivered by France Telecom to 17 million households). Second-wave countries differ in their objectives for embracing e-business. Some see it as improving international commercial advantage and as a vehicle for accessing diverse new content and cultural enrichment. Others, while attracted by the international commercial advantages, wish to limit the social and political influence of the medium (e.g. Singapore, where a broadband intranet offering rich locally-oriented content operates at the highest speeds available in the world but where licensed ISPs regulate content provided from outside the system.)

The third wave began in 1998 and involved the use of the Internet by business and social elites in a number of the more developed of the developing countries in South and South-East Asia, Latin America, the Pacific Islands and the Middle East. Increasing local language content, improved telecommunications infrastructure, and greater foreign participation in both manufacturing and telecommunications is increasing the rate of Internet adoption. As this gathers momentum, the Internet will eventually cease to be a US-centric technology and become more of a global tool for trade with a majority of users living outside the US. This is evidenced in the slowing growth in Internet use in the developed world, the rapid growth in East Asia and Latin America where users are from narrow commercial and political elites interested in business rather than personal applications, and the rapid increase in Internet hosts in a small number of transition economies such as Brazil, the Czech Republic, Thailand and the United Arab

Emirates (DFAT, 1999, p. 100). The countries in this category have little in common, apart from a desire to improve competitiveness using advanced technology. Many of their governments are often downplaying social, moral and political aspects of the Internet in the interest of accessing online business benefits and reducing the gap between Internet 'haves' and their situation as Internet 'have-nots'. Their focus is on specific business benefits reflecting their economic circumstances and not on technology simply because it replaces labour. The transition to an information economy for most third-wave countries will be difficult because:

● there are major development problems, such as shortage of skills and capital and a large number of competing priorities;
● there are often serious deficiencies in telecommunications infrastructure which is capital intensive to remedy;
● Internet adoption problems encountered by countries in wave two will be intensified because business environments are geared to traditional forms of transaction and change is slow. Examples include the requirement in the Philippines that credit card transactions must be validated by a written signature and the combination in Russia of endemic credit card fraud and lack of any legal basis for online trade.

The fourth and final wave is unlikely to occur until at least 2002 and involves the least developed of the developing countries. This delay is due to:

● the lack of infrastructure to support significant Internet commerce; and
● governments shunning the Internet on political grounds.

Some of these countries however are interested in promoting online commodity trade because most of their exports are commodity related. Also, in countries where the Internet has been declared illegal, cross-border online trade is used to get around the restrictions. Due to the prevalence of poverty, the information society is an abstract issue for most of these countries that are more concerned with feeding the population and reducing disease by provision of clean water. In these countries, Internet security is a problem and necessary infrastructure often non-existent. Purchasing a computer is only affordable for a small elite because it costs between 10 and 15 times the average annual wage. Also, connecting to an ISP is astronomically expensive; in Bangladesh, 20 hours of access a month costs more than twice the average annual income (DFAT, 1999, p. 121). Some governments ban ISPs and the use of international phone lines to access them. Myanmar requires all faxes and modems not used in teaching or business to be registered with the government and, in Laos, the government screens Internet content available to subscribers, censors information exchanged, and approves each person, business and piece of equipment connected to the Internet.

Summary

From the perspective of the firm, the economic and financial condition of international markets influences the likelihood of undertaking profitable business with the countries involved. It influences selection of markets, the likely form of involvement in the selected market, and whether the involvement should be long term or short term in the first instance. Also of relevance is the degree to which the country is involved in the international financial system, how its performance is rated, and the degree to which it is economically stable and its currency subject to exchange rate volatility.

Ethics issue

The A to Z of the major corporate scandals over the past few years has shocked ordinary consumers everywhere. Below is a list of some of the casualties.

Arthur Andersen: The company's excellent reputation turned to notoriety when it was found guilty of complicity in the Enron scandal. In a classic conflict of interests, the firm was exposed as acting as both the firm's auditor and financial consultant.

AOL Time Warner: The world's largest media company admitted to inaccuracies in its accounts under new rules of disclosure by the Securities and Exchange Commission.

Elan: The Irish pharmaceutical company's share price dropped dramatically following an article in the *Wall Street Journal* which attacked its accounting practices.

Enron: Enron's story is one of massaged figures, hidden problems, bullied analysts, frightened employees and even suicide. The company investigation centres on 3,500 partnerships and other affiliates created by Enron to hide debt, inflate profits, push up share values and enrich top executives.

General Electric: Complicated bookkeeping worries GE investors in the wake of Enron. GE reported profits of US$2.1 billon in its pension fund in 1999 and 2000 despite the fact that the fund was losing money due to falling stock market prices.

Global Crossing: Filed for Chapter 11 bankruptcy and faces several major legal problems and is being investigated by the Securities and Exchange Commission, the FBI and the US Congress for alleged accounting irregularities.

IBM: Shareholders dumped IBM stocks in the wake of Enron fearing IBM's corporate structure was too 'complicated'. The company was criticised for using income from the sale of one of its businesses to offset expenses, instead of reporting it as revenue. Many critics said it made the company more efficient that it actually was.

Kmart: The huge US chain store filed for bankruptcy and has opened its own investigation after it was discovered to be overstating profits.

Merrill Lynch: The world's largest investment firm was charged with hyping up stocks to please companies with which it was doing business.

Tyco International: The US industrial conglomerate spent US$8 million on acquisitions in the last few years without revealing this to the public. Former Tyco chief executive and founder Denis Kozlowski was investigated for avoiding US$1 million in New York state tax after purchasing artwork valued at US$13 million with company funds.

WorldCom: Admitted that its auditor has misrepresented US$3.8 billion in expenses and defaulting US$4.5 billion in bank loans.

Xerox: Admitted to overstating its profits.

The problems revealed by these scandals were systemic, not the result of a few bad apples. Discuss. What is the underlying problem common in all the above cases? How can these issues be addressed in the future?

Web workout

Question 1 Visit the websites of three major local banks you are familiar with. Do they cater for international customers?

Question 2 Organisations such as E*Trade or Charles Schwab are considered to be the pioneers in online financial trade services. Visit their websites and establish whether these organisations are truly global companies?

Websites

www.eurnews.net

Dr Ed Yardeni's Economic Network http://yardeni.com

GATS – Fact and fiction
http://www.wto.org/english/tratop_e/serv_e/gats_factfiction_e.htm

IMF http://www.imf.org

IMF – Country Information http://www.imf.org/external/country/index.htm

TDC Trade – International Market Profiles http://www.tdctrade.com/mktprof/

Market potential indicators for emerging markets 2000
http://ciber.bus.msu.edu/publication/mktptind00.htm

Mondaq Business Briefing http://www.mondaq.com

TimeAsia http://www.time.com/time/asia

Tradecompass http://www.tradecompass.com/guest/index.asp

Tradeport – Country Library http://www.tradeport.org/ts/countries/index.html

Ernst & Young – Doing Business In series http://www.ey.com/GLOBAL/gcr.nsf/
EYPassport/Welcome-Doing_Business_In-EYPassport

www.bloomberg.com
www.reuters.com
www.marketwatch.com
www.ElectricNews.Net

Discussion questions

1 Discuss the trends likely to impact on the global economic scene in the first decade of the 21st century.

2 Classification of countries according to economic criteria is often a way of assessing their likely potential as markets. Discuss the merits of classification by economic system, economic structure or by stage of development.

3 There are a number of criteria which can be used to evaluate international markets. Which is most relevant for suppliers of:
   (i)   basic consumer goods;
   (ii) luxury consumer goods;
   (iii) industrial products;
   (iv) environmentally friendly products;
   (v)   infrastructure projects;
   (vi) mining equipment?

4 Discuss the role of the International Monetary Fund in enforcing financially responsible behaviour on the nations of the world. Is there a better alternative?

5 What are the most common forms of financial risk involved in doing business in international markets? What ways exist of minimising this financial risk for firms?

References

Annan, K. (2001) 'End Trade Barriers to Cut Poverty', *The Irish Times*, 9 March.

Badrinath, R. (2001) 'Playing @ the Digital Game', *International Trade Forum*, Issue 1, p. 4.

Craig, C.S., Douglas, S.P. and Flaherty, T.B. (2000) 'Information Access and Internationalisation – The Internet and Consumer Behaviour in International Markets', *Proceedings of the eCommerce and Global Business Forum*, May 17–19, Santa Cruz, CA, Anderson Consulting Institute for Strategic Change.

Czinkota, M. (1991) 'The EC'92 and Eastern Europe: Effects of Integration vs Disintegration', *Colombia Journal of World Business*, Spring, pp. 20–27.

Department of Foreign Affairs and Trade (DFAT) (1999) *Creating a Clearway on the New Silk Road: International Business and Policy Trends in Internet Commerce*, Commonwealth of Australia, Canberra.

Euromonitor (1996) *International Marketing Data and Statistics*, London, Table 2515.

European Union News (2001) Vol. 19, No. 4.

Financial Times (2002) 'Study Debunks Myths surrounding Manufacturing Miracle in China', 8 November.

Keegan, W.J. and Green, M.C. (2000) *Principles of Global Marketing*, Prentice Hall Inc., Englewood Cliffs, NJ, p. 54 and p. 90.

Keegan, W.J. and Schlegelmilch, B.B. (2001) *Global Marketing Management: A European Perspective*, Prentice Hall, Harlow, UK, p. 278.

Kotabe, M. and Helsen, K. (2000) *Global Marketing Management Update 2000*, John Wiley and Sons, New York.

Letovsky, R. (1990) 'The Export Finance Wars', *Columbia Journal for World Business*, Spring/Summer, pp. 25–34.

OECD (2001) *National Accounts of OECD Countries*.

OECD (2002) *Information Technology Outlook*.

United Nations (2001) *World Investment Report – 2001 Promoting Linkages*, United Nations, New York and Geneva.

World Bank (1997) *World Debt Tables, 1996*, Washington DC.

World Bank (2002) World Development Indicators database, August 2002.

3

Catering for the cultural environment of international business

Learning objectives

After studying this chapter, you should be able to:

- understand the impact of culture on international marketing;

- apply key cultural concepts when evaluating international marketing situations;

- evaluate the ways in which cultural differences impede international communication;

- undertake cross-cultural analysis;

- recognise the importance of social sensitivity, good corporate citizenship and appropriate ethical behaviours in international marketing; and

- recognise the need for cultural sensitivity when preparing for and conducting international negotiations.

Reinventing ice cream

Häagen-Dazs entered the European market with the objective of building the biggest ice cream brand in the world. Big multinational companies – Unilever, Mars and Nestlé, dominated the ice cream market in the 1990s. Häagen-Dazs managed to reinvent the ice cream market, positioning the product as a sensual and sophisticated adult treat – an indulgent experience to be enjoyed, but an affordable luxury. Traditionally ice cream was considered a seasonal product, mainly suitable for children. Häagen-Dazs managed to reposition it as a premium product, adult pleasure to be consumed year round, instead of a pleasure only during the summer months. They achieved this by targeting it at sophisticated and well-off adults, maybe married, maybe not, probably without children. They believed rightly that there was a 'European consumer', most likely to be the same all over Europe. The brand identity was built around the proposition of a genuine, sensual, adult treat. The brand name was Scandinavian, which gave it an association with nature, freshness and cleanliness. Brand values were communicated through a bold print campaign, through the ice cream parlours, through association with the arts and the association with the successful brand worldwide (Häagen-Dazs, from London, Paris, New York). These brand values were emotional values, highly relevant for adults, but not children, communicated in adult magazines and not on television. The packaging upgrade for Europe had pack sizes ideal for consumption by two persons – definitely not family. The price was high, relative to standard and economy ice cream, but also high relative to other premium ice creams (30 to 40 per cent higher in the UK) and there was a complete absence of price-related promotions. Their distribution consisted of posh ice cream parlours and food service accounts (restaurants, delicatessens and quality hotels), and branded freezers were installed in retail accounts. Their marketing strategy was highly consistent both internally and externally, which enabled them to overcome the cultural stereotypes we sometimes apply to products.

Introduction

 Knowledge of culture is essential for those engaged in international marketing. Whether buyers accept or reject a marketing offering will be determined to a large extent by the cultural influences impacting on their cognitive, affective and connotative behaviour. Often culturally determined preferences or reactions to a foreigner's approach will override what many managers think is rational economic decision making. To understand this behaviour and its impact on the decision-maker, the subtleties and dynamics of culture must be understood.

Definition

Defining culture has always been difficult. Fifty-one years ago Kroeber and Kluckholn found 164 definitions of culture. Some of the common characteristics of these definitions are that:

- culture is prescriptive in that it prescribes those forms of behaviour that are acceptable to people in a specific community;
- culture is learned, because people are not born with a culture but are born into a culture. The norms of the culture are acquired as people are raised in and exposed to the culture;
- culture is dynamic, because not only does it influence our behaviour but, in turn, our behaviour influences the culture reflecting its interactive nature; and
- culture is subjective, because people attribute meaning to issues on a subjective basis and these subjective meanings develop within the context of the culture.

From the above, there appear to be two broad dimensions of culture – first that it is learned, and second that it is shared. Therefore any definition needs to be broad enough to distinguish members of one group from those of another. Two such definitions are from Fletcher (2000): 'Culture is the total way of life in a society'; and Hofstede (2000): 'Culture is the collective programming of the mind'.

The impact of culture on international marketing

Culture is integral to the marketing concept which is based on satisfaction of wants and needs of potential buyers. Not only does culture condition these wants and needs, but it also impacts on the way messages concerning the ability of the product or service to satisfy the wants or needs, are received and interpreted. This is even more so in international marketing, where cultures differ markedly from one international market to another. Culture pervades all elements of the marketing mix – product, pricing, promotion and distribution – and the acceptability of each of these elements will be judged in the context of the culture that they are targeting.

Culturally related factors which impact on marketing

When considering culture in the context of international marketing, the following factors should be taken into account.

Knowledge

Knowledge of another culture can be either factual or interpretative. Factual knowledge conveys meaning about a culture, which appears straightforward. However, a fact may assume additional significance when interpreted within the context of a specific culture. For example, a firm wishing to do business in Indonesia and Malaysia would need to recognise that while business activities in both countries are largely controlled by the Chinese community, there are some differences. In Malaysia, this community makes up a larger percentage of the population and is subject to more government constraints because of the official policy to encourage the economic advancement of the Malay portion of the population. In Indonesia by contrast, the Chinese business community has very close links to government, and in its businesses there are usually powerful Indonesian political figures on the boards of directors of Chinese-owned firms. Issues of this kind may influence decisions like the appointment of an agent or the selection of joint venture partners.

Interpretative knowledge is based on feelings and intuition and is often influenced by past experiences. It can be erroneous if evaluated according to norms or behaviours in the home country. One way of acquiring such knowledge is to develop empathy for the host culture by associating with people from that country.

Sensitivity

Cultural sensitivity involves being aware of the nuances of the different culture, being empathetic with it and viewing it objectively rather than subjectively. It begins with an acceptance that other cultures in themselves are not right or wrong and one culture is not inferior to another but, rather, is different. Being culturally sensitive will reduce disharmony, alleviate aggravation, improve communication and pave the way for long-term international business relationships. Associated with cultural sensitivity is the need for the international marketing executive to evaluate the relevance of the cultural assumptions on which assessments are based, especially when those assumptions are embedded in the marketing executive's own culture.

Collectivism

Whereas in western societies decisions are generally made by individual consumers, this is often not the case in all cultures, especially in many Asian cultures. There, collectivism plays a greater role in decision making than individualism, because of the strength of family ties, strong affinity with the group to which the individual belongs, and sensitivity to the wishes of other members of the network. This behaviour stems from the broad definition of the family in Asian cultures, which is more extended than in western cultures. Often such behaviour is not reflective of the will of the individual, but rather of a consensus or compromise between the individual and members of the extended family.

Social conventions

These reflect the culture and have an influence on effective marketing practices in the foreign country. Many of these are related to eating – specifically the number of meals per day, time taken to eat the meal, the composition of each meal, the time at which the meal is eaten, the degree to which the meal is a social occasion as opposed to a functional occasion, and who prepares the meal and how it is served. These social conventions would be important background to a marketer of food. Culturally influenced social conventions apply to the marketing of most consumer goods and services but apply to a lesser extent to the marketing of industrial products. Such conventions also apply to occasions, which generate or restrict expenditure, such as weddings, New Year celebrations and Ramadan in the Islamic world.

Cognitive styles

The extent to which consumers are loyal to products varies between cultures. In the US and western countries, it is assumed that consumers are less loyal to products as evidenced by switching from one brand to another to test their benefits. In many Asian countries, consumers are more loyal and less inclined to switch brands on the basis of price or benefit comparison.

One of the issues in marketing is the degree of customer involvement in the purchase decision, with products being classified as high or low involvement. The nature of involvement in purchase decisions varies between cultural groups. In China (Yang, 1989) the overall level of consumer involvement is less than in the US and EU when the product is for private consumption, with the focus being more on the physical functions of the product than on the relationship between its price and quality. However, the opposite is the case when the product is purchased for its social symbolic value as it would be when it is intended as a gift. This is because the item is likely to be interpreted by the recipient as a measure of status, gratitude or approval.

The perception of risk is another culturally influenced cognitive variable. This is both in terms of extent and in terms of relative importance attributed to the various elements of risk – be they physical, financial or social. People in some cultures, such as in Africa, may be more susceptible to physical risk due to infrastructure or health inadequacies and seek reliability and protection when making a purchase. In western cultures, people may consider financial risk more important and are more likely to be concerned with cost in relation to value and affordability. People in Asian cultures, however, are more likely to feel most threatened by social risk and tend to be more concerned with whether the purchase might cause a loss of status in the eyes of their family or network.

Cultural universals

While there are clear differences, there are also universal tendencies in all cultures. These relate to the physical world, such as the desire to look beautiful or keep track of time; the social, such as the desire to cooperate, to be a member of a group, or to differentiate according to status; and the emotional, such as courtship, religious observance, or mourning.

Marketing can target these cultural universals although the way these universals are reflected in each culture will need to be taken into account because they are likely to differ. Cohen (1996) studied the cultural universals of right and left and explored how, throughout history, right has tended to be associated with good or superior and left with bad or inferior. This has its origins in the fact that because most people are right-handed, left-handedness acquires negative connotations. Although this right–left symbolism originates in physiology, it manifests itself through culture and is extremely deep-rooted. Cohen argues that by recognising the enduring nature of right–left symbolism and the way it is manifested in different cultures, marketers can avoid making blunders in their international promotional activities.

Elements of culture

In order to understand customers in the international market, it is necessary to be aware of their cultural heritage. Appreciating the intricacies of the culture is imperative in order to be effective in the foreign market. It should also be borne in mind that cultural differences are a matter of difference rather than exotica – culture exists in Dublin, Sydney, Moscow and Manchester just as it does amongst the Arctic Inuit and the Navajo Indians. To understand the significance for marketing of cultural differences in international markets, it is necessary to carefully study the elements of culture. These influences include the material, social, religious, aesthetics and language.

Material

Material culture consists of both technology and economics. The former relates to the techniques used to produce material goods. Certain skills related to an industrial society which are taken for granted in western society, such as an ability to read forms of measurement and gauges, do not widely exist in some other cultures which are agrarian based. In some cultures with a higher technology orientation, preventative maintenance is the norm, whereas in other societies, such as in Libya, cars are driven until they grind to a halt.

Economic culture relates to the level of demand: what kinds of products are sought; how these goods are produced; and how they get to the buyer. Included are associated infrastructure needs, such as availability of electricity to operate refrigerators and affordability in relation to purchasing power of local incomes, such as refrigerators being viewed as necessities rather than luxury items. Also included are the size and nature of average accommodation because this may influence the physical size of the refrigerator that will be sought. In Japan, for example, apartments are very small and communications links congested. This is likely to mean that in Japan the demand will be for small refrigerators that will fit into small apartments and can be delivered without being damaged.

Social institutions

These are the spine of the cultural process because they link the individual to the group. They include family, educational providers, political parties and social organisations. They are concerned with the way people relate to each other, how they achieve harmony in their relations with each other, how they govern themselves and how, in the process, they create norms for acceptable behaviour in the culture. These institutions generally provide rewards for conforming to rules. Roles performed and status within the society are influenced by the social institutions. Because of this and the impact of social institutions on values, behaviour and lifestyle, the nature of social institutions in the culture should be catered for when marketing to that culture.

Relations with the universe

Symbolic and sacred elements form the link between the material and the metaphysical world. Belief systems, such as those embodied in religion or superstition, impact on the value systems of a society in which legal, political and economic precepts are often based. Religion is one of the most sensitive elements of culture. It impacts on people's habits, the foods they eat, their perceptions of what is moral and immoral, the products they buy and the way they view life. Failure to fully appreciate religion's significance in a specific culture can easily cause the marketer to give offence. The following adaptation of an article that appeared in the *Wall Street Journal* is an example.

> *There are between 800 million and 1.2 billion in the world who embrace Islam, yet major international companies often unintentionally offend Muslims. A recent incident involved the French fashion house of Chanel that unwittingly desecrated the Koran by embroidering verses from the sacred book of Islam on several dresses shown in its summer collections. The designer said he took the design, which was aesthetically pleasing to him, from a book on India's Taj Mahal and that he was unaware of its meaning. To placate a Muslim group that felt the use of the verses desecrated the Koran, Chanel agreed to destroy the dresses with the offending designs along with negatives of the photos made of the garments. Chanel certainly had no intention of offending Muslims since some of their most important customers come from countries that subscribe to that religion.*
>
> Source: *Wall Street Journal*, 21 January 1994, p. 97.

The same religion may impact differently on business customs and practices in different countries. This is because there are other factors in the environment that modify the impact of religion. While Islam is the predominant religion in both Malaysia and Saudi Arabia, its impact on business is much less in the former than in the latter.

Superstition plays an important role in the belief systems of some cultures. To be dismissive of practices based on superstition because they are disregarded in the West is a certain way to give offence. Cutting the air with a knife to get protection from thunder and lightning (Thailand); sacrificing an animal to drive spirits away (Malaysia); and basing actions and decisions on predictions as to whether the day or time is auspicious (China) should be taken seriously by the foreign marketeer.

Aesthetics

Art, folklore, music, drama and dance all have a role in interpreting symbolic meanings in each culture. These aesthetic manifestations point up the uniqueness of a culture and need to be incorporated in marketing approaches to customers in that culture so as to enhance the appeal of and identification with the message. An appreciation of aesthetic values will improve the appeal of the product and its packaging as well as its promotional effectiveness.

Language

Language that members of a culture learn as they are raised, shapes their view of the world and their social behaviour. Languages differ in the way they convey meaning, the precision of the message, the degree to which things are implied as opposed to specified and the extent to which meaning is conveyed by verbal as opposed to non-verbal cues. Because of the influence of culture, simple translation from English into another language rarely conveys the meaning accurately. Culture determines the meaning attributable to words. When marketing in other countries, it is important to be aware of the meaning attributable to words in the language of that culture as well as to appreciate the role of idiomatic expressions in that language in conveying meaning. When translating from a foreign language into English, literal translation can yield hilarious results as the following collection of 'bloopers' shows, (Kelly, 2000).

- The lift is being fixed for the next day. During that time we regret that you will be unbearable (*Romania*).
- You are invited to take advantage of the chambermaid (*Japan*).
- Because of the impropriety of entertaining guests of the opposite sex in the bedroom, it is suggested that the lobby be used for this purpose (*Switzerland*).
- If this is your first visit to the USSR, you are welcome to it (*Russia*).
- Ladies are requested not to have children in the bar (*Norway*).
- The manager has personally passed all the water served here (*Mexico*).
- Drop your trousers here for the best results (*Thailand*).
- Ladies have fits upstairs (*Hong Kong*).
- We take your bags and send them in all directions (*Denmark*).
- Please do not feed the animals. If you have any suitable food, please give it to the guard on duty (*Hungary*).

Expressions of culture

Culture is expressed in a number of ways through symbols, heroes and rituals.

- *Symbols* are words, gestures, objects or pictures which carry a particular meaning recognisable only by those who are members of the culture. Jargon, dress, clothing and hairstyles and certain products fall into this category. Symbols are the most superficial element of culture because they are easily developed, often borrowed from other cultures, and quickly disappear.

| Figure 3.1 | The 'Onion Diagram': manifestations of culture at different levels of depth |

Source: Hofstede
(2000), p. 11.

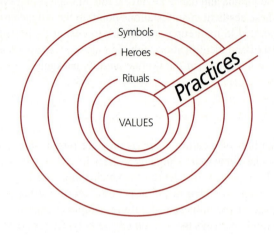

- *Heroes* are persons who, whether alive or dead, possess qualities which are highly prized in a particular culture and serve as models to emulate.
- *Rituals* are collective activities, which are an essential element of social activities within a culture. Ceremonies, ways of greeting and even sporting events are rituals for those involved.

Symbols, heroes and rituals are all practices. However, at the core of culture are *values* which may be considered as tendencies to prefer certain states of affairs over others. Usually, values embody contrasts such as evil versus good, ugly versus beautiful, and irrational versus rational. Values are usually the first things people learn, but this learning is implicit rather than conscious. Figure 3.1 illustrates this.

Culture as a collective fingerprint

Culture is a mark of identity not of superiority. Elements of culture will impact differently on different aspects of the marketing programme. Furthermore, although culture itself is dynamic in nature and constantly changing, it contains elements that are resistant to change. These must be understood so that the marketer will appreciate those aspects of the culture that might cause resistance to changes that the new product offering might generate. Culture is a total picture, although made up of different elements, and it cannot be separated into parts and be completely understood. It is not possible to select the best elements from each culture and arrive at an ideal combination. Usunier (1993) highlights our stereotypes in the following joke:

> *Heaven is where the cooks are French, the mechanics are German, the policemen are English, the lovers are Italian and it is all organised by the Swiss. Hell is where the policemen are German, the mechanics are French, the cooks are English, the lovers are Swiss, and it is all organised by the Italians.*
>
> *Source*: Usunier (1993).

3.1 International highlight

Creating favourable conditions – *feng shui*

Marketers in Asia have come to recognise that the supernatural attracts many Asians. Many folklores, taboos, superstitious and religious connotations by colours, numbers and symbols exist in Asia today. *Feng shui* is a particularly good example of this and is widely applied in Chinese culture, as well as in Japan and Vietnam.

Feng shui means 'wind and water'; it refers to the ancient art of geomancy – a calculated assessment of the most favourable conditions for any venture. A key focus of *feng shui* is its emphasis on the shape of mountains and the direction of water flows. It is believed that man's destiny could be enhanced if there is a correct alignment of the environment's *chi* (invisible energy) with the human *chi*. Thus *feng shui* involves the art of placing things, ranging from orientation of a building to the furnishing of the interiors, to influence the *chi* of a site. The philosophy maintains that excellent living conditions contribute to good health, which in turn leads to success and prosperity.

Some general guidelines for *feng shui* include where the front door of a business should face for a favourable orientation. For law firms, medical centres and shipping firms it should face north or east, while for accounting, finance, architectural and banking firms it should face northwest or southeast. North and southeast facing is appropriate for bars and retail stores. In addition to having *feng shui* the building must also face the water and be flanked by the mountains, but this should not block the view of the mountain spirits, which is why many Hong Kong offices have see-through lobbies to keep the spirits happy.

Sharp angles give off bad *feng shui*. The Gateway building in Singapore has two triangular towers, its sharp edges and jutting points giving off bad luck. The Gateway tries to compensate for this by being northeast–southeast facing; the building's sharp edges thus slice through oncoming winds to reduce their power.

Feng shui also incorporates numerology, which means addresses and opening dates must be chosen with care. The numbers 2, 5, 6, 8, 9 and 10 are deemed lucky, but not 4 which connotes death. The Bank of China is considered to have bad geomancy because of its sharp edges; the bank tried to compensate for this by opening its doors on 8 August 1988, as the number 8 connotes becoming rich.

Feng shui is big business in Asia. A company which consults an expert geomancer, and publicises it, signals to its customers and employees that it cares for their prosperity and wellbeing. Western firms in the Asian region have also come to adopt *feng shui* as they have adapted their business practices to the Asian culture.

Source: Adapted from Kotler, P., Ang, S.H., Leong, S.M. and Tan, C.T. (1996) *Marketing Management: An Asian Perspective*, pp. 724–725. Prentice Hall, Singapore.

An interesting concept was developed by Keillor et al. (1995, 1999) called the National Identity Scale (NATID). This scale identifies the importance placed by a nation or culture on its uniqueness and the specific elements that define that uniqueness. The scale measures national identity along four dimensions – national heritage, cultural homogeneity, belief system and consumer ethnocentrism.

Levels at which culture operates

Culture operates at various levels, each having an influence on negotiating or undertaking international business. To this point, the discussion has related to personal cultural differences. Culture also operates at the national, industrial and organisational levels. These levels are shown in Figure 3.2.

National

The national culture impacts on dealings with governments and is reflected in the values on which laws and institutions are based. National culture also influences the way the law is applied. This explains why in some cultures nepotism and cronyism can result in transgressors evading punishment and the tacit acceptance of some forms of bribery. One example of national culture is the insistence on the use of the national language as opposed to the most commonly spoken language among a group. The use of Malay in those Malaysian cities where the Chinese dominate is an example. Other examples include observance of hierarchical order as in Thailand; power being vested in certain elements in the community, such as in the Philippines where power resides among a handful of families; and religion dominating national life as happens with Islam in Saudi Arabia.

| Figure 3.2 | The different layers of culture |

Source: Hollensen (2001), p. 161.

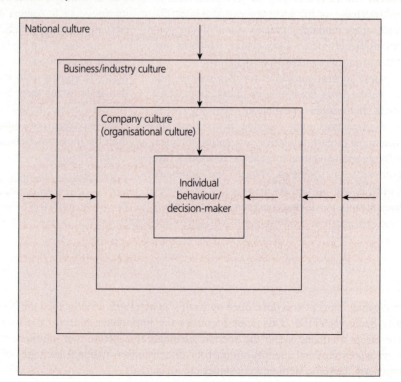

Starbucks has 1,300 stores outside the US and entered the German market with its first store in Berlin. However, it has run into some obstacles. The chain is named after Starbuck, the coffee-swilling first officer in Moby Dick. But in Germany, the name has other less happy associations: Starbuck was the nickname of Holger Meins, a member of the Red Army Faction (RAF) left-wing guerrilla group, which terrorised Germany in the 1970s. Rather than hot coffee on the high seas, Starbucks awakens memories of a bloody shoot-out in Frankfurt in 1972 and Meins' death after a prison hunger strike two years later. The chain could go the way of Wal-Mart, the US retailing giant which entered the German market with a roar only to be beaten to a bloody pulp by local supermarket chains Aldi and Lidl.

Finally, national culture influences the degree to which the practice in the society is to depend on law as opposed to trust, when business dealings are involved.

Industry

Culture impacts on negotiations with industry. Industry culture is reflected in the values and norms governing the activities performed by the industry in the other country. Manifestations of industry culture include credit policy, as exemplified in the issue of usury in Islamic nations, and attitude to the environment as seen in a number of Asian countries where concrete wins out over trees. It is also manifested in business relationships as indicated by the degree to which such relationships are confined to the transaction or extend beyond it and the importance of trust in the particular industry or profession. This can be seen in norms of negotiation – such as the norm to cement deals with a handshake, or the acceptance of kickbacks in an industry, as is the case in some countries where medical specialists give gifts to general practitioners who refer patients to them.

Organisational

Organisational culture impacts on negotiations with firms as opposed to individuals and is exemplified in the entering into of alliances or the arranging of takeovers. Organisational culture is reflected in the basic pattern of assumptions developed by the firm. These include its code of ethics and its attitude to employees. For example, in many Asian countries the employer is considered to be responsible for the welfare of the employee and his/her family, whereas in the US employees tend to be regarded as an expendable short-term resource. Another manifestation of organisation culture is reflected in the relationships between managers and staff. This is exemplified in the authoritarian relationship that operates in Japan compared with the egalitarian relationship that applies in the US, and in approaches to problem solving which is a group activity in many Asian cultures compared with an individual responsibility in the US. Decision-making style is also a manifestation of organisational culture. It varies markedly between Asian countries such as Japan where decision making tends to be by consensus of those likely to be involved in implementing the decision. In the US and EU, by contrast, decision making tends to be undertaken by senior managers and imposed on those below. Some manifestations of organisational culture are visible, such as the practice in Japan of starting the workday by singing the company song, and

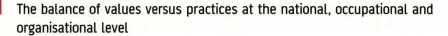

| Figure 3.3 | The balance of values versus practices at the national, occupational and organisational level |

Source: Hofstede (2000), p. 394.

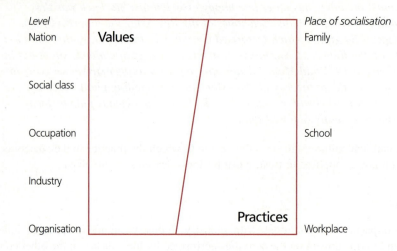

some are tacit, such as codes of company behaviour for personnel. In some transnational organisations, organisational culture can be very powerful and can reduce the impact of national, industry or personal cultures.

Hofstede (2000) found that at the national level, cultural differences reside more in values and less in practices and at the organisational level cultural differences reside more in practices and less in values. At the occupational level the balance is even, as shown in Figure 3.3.

Cultural concepts and cultural differences

In order to be able to understand how culture can impact on firms' international marketing activities, an understanding of key cultural concepts is necessary as well as how cultural differences manifest themselves in the international business environment.

Key cultural concepts

The following four concepts are important in understanding the impact of culture on international marketing.

Maslow's hierarchy of needs

A basic model for understanding the wants and needs of consumers, Maslow's model has been used by international marketers to appreciate how consumers in different countries behave in response to cultural stimuli. Maslow (1964) argues that

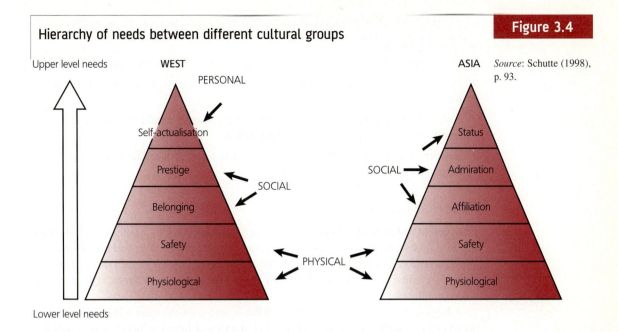

Figure 3.4

Hierarchy of needs between different cultural groups

Source: Schutte (1998), p. 93.

Upper level needs

WEST

PERSONAL

Self-actualisation

Prestige

Belonging

Safety

Physiological

ASIA

Status

SOCIAL

Admiration

Affiliation

Safety

Physiological

SOCIAL

PHYSICAL

Lower level needs

the needs of the individual form a hierarchy from physiological needs (hunger, thirst), to safety needs (security, protection), to social needs (sense of belonging, love), to esteem needs (self-esteem, recognition, status), to self-actualisation needs (self-development, realisation). Lower-order needs in the hierarchy such as hunger tend to be satisfied first and higher-order needs such as those related to self-esteem tend to be satisfied last.

Although culture can have an impact on needs at all levels, its impact tends to be greater where higher-order needs are involved – needs involving emotion and cognition. This aspect requires research in the specific international market as there may be cases where lower-order needs are not always satisfied first. Examples occur when people go without food in order to buy drugs or cigarettes, or forgo food in order to buy a refrigerator because owning a refrigerator increases social status and self-esteem in the local culture. In some societies, higher-order needs are encouraged at the expense of lower-order needs: Hinduism, for example, encourages self-realisation by focusing on acts which will improve one's position in the incarnations which follow rather than on one's present existence. Figure 3.4 shows Maslow's traditional hierarchy of needs based on research in western and Asian countries. The research indicates that both the specific needs and their rank order can vary between cultures.

Self-reference criterion

Often perception of the needs of the international market is blocked by our own cultural experience. The tendency is to evaluate the international situation in terms of our culture and this is also the basis used for evaluating and interpreting others in the negotiation situation. In short, the self-reference criterion (SRC) is the cultural baggage that the businessperson takes on when doing business in international markets. Many years ago, Lee (1966) developed a four-step systematic framework for reducing this myopic approach, which can be adapted to any business situation as follows:

1 Define the problem or goal in terms of your own cultural norms, habits and traits.
2 Define the problem or goal in terms of the cultural norms, habits or traits in the international market.
3 Isolate the SRC element in the problem and examine it carefully to see how it complicates the problem and its interpretation.
4 Redefine the problem without the SRC influence and proceed to solve the problem in the foreign market or negotiation.

Context and culture

Both verbal and non-verbal cues and messages are necessary to establish the full meaning of a communication. People in different cultures interpret verbal and non-verbal cues differently and this can be due to the influence of context in the culture. Cultures can be classified according to where they fall on a continuum between high- and low-context cultures.

A high-context culture is one where what is said conveys only a limited portion of the meaning which must also be interpreted in terms of how it is being said, where it is being said, and the body language of the speaker. In high-context cultures, much of the message will be implied in the context of the communication and is influenced by the background and basic values of the communicator. In a low-context culture, messages are mostly explicit and the words convey most of the meaning in the communication. The impact of non-verbal cues on intended meaning is far less and the status of the speaker is less important in interpretation of meaning. Figure 3.5 (adapted from Hall (1976)) illustrates where certain countries fall along a continuum from low- to high-context cultures.

Context impacts on most of the cultural variables in international marketing as shown in Table 3.1.

Psychic distance

Psychic distance, a perceptual concept, is a reflection of a range of environmental variables which differentiates one international market from another. The variables include linguistic, educational, political, developmental and cultural factors. Culture is the most important element of psychic distance because it is a product of many elements which are culturally influenced, such as belief systems, language barriers, differing attitudes to business, levels of education, material standards, infrastructure shortcomings and patterns of behaviour. Psychic distance is a measure of how far a country is perceived to be away from your own country in terms of a mental aggregation of the above factors. It is also a measure of how different the country is when compared to your country. Psychic distance acts to impede communication and understanding and can cause executives to prefer to deal with countries which are closer to their own in psychic distance terms. This may not always be desirable, as often opportunities are greater in countries which are distant rather than closer – lack of similarity can indicate greater potential for your products and services because the environments and hence the needs are more likely to be different.

Cultural context of various countries

Figure 3.5

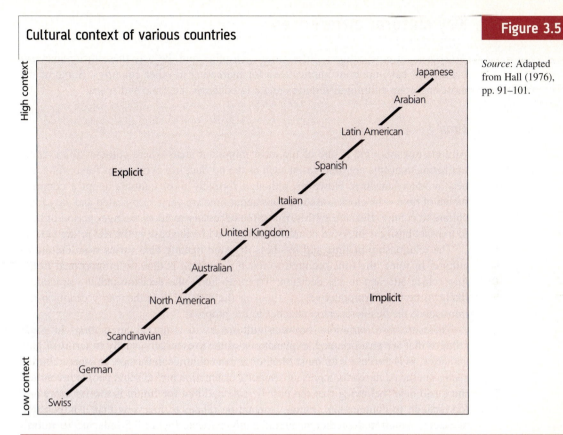

Source: Adapted from Hall (1976), pp. 91–101.

Table 3.1 Impact of context on cultural dimensions

Factors and dimensions	High context	Low context
Lawyers	Less important	Very important
A person's word	Is his or her bond	Is not to be relied upon; 'get it in writing'
Responsibility for organisational error	Taken by highest level	Pushed to lowest level
Space	People breathe on each other	People maintain a bubble of private space and resent intrusions
Time	Polychronic: everything in life must be dealt with in terms of its own time	Monochronic: time is money; linear; one thing at a time
Negotiations	Lengthy: a major purpose is to allow the parties to get to know each other	Proceed quickly
Competitive bidding	Infrequent	Common
Regional examples	Japan, Middle East	United States, northern Europe

Source: Keegan and Green (2000), p. 143.

Key cultural differences

Awareness of how cultures differ from each other and the way these differences are manifested has important implications for marketing in other countries. Some of the most important cultural differences relate to concepts, i.e. time and space.

Time

Attitude towards time is one of the most important areas where cultures differ. Most marketing concepts are time based such as the product life cycle, sales forecasting and new product launches. However, although formally most cultures adopt a common model of time – the clock – assumptions about time are very deep-seated and vary from culture to culture. Because of this, it is often necessary to allow a longer period of time to transact business in Asian countries than would be the case in the EU or the US.

The relationship of time and business decision making also varies from culture to culture. In some, the time required to reach a decision is directly proportional to the importance attached to the decision. To try to hurry the decision-making process is likely to be counterproductive, as it can in the eyes of the other party diminish the importance the businessperson attaches to the proposal.

There are also variations between cultures as to temporal orientation. In some cultures that are past oriented, explanations of the present are usually in terms of past activities, as is the case with most Mediterranean countries in Europe. In other cultures, such as in the Arab world, a present temporal orientation prevails and people favour the 'here and now' believing that the past is gone and that the future is too far away and too difficult to contemplate. Future orientation relates to the view that it is possible to master nature and predict or significantly influence what happens in the future. Whereas in the EU and US, it is normal to plan for the future, in some cultures, the future is considered too far away to consider and this manifests itself in a lack of willingness to plan forward and a resistance to establishing what are considered to be realistic lead times.

Temporal orientation is based on the 'western' assumption that time can have a past, present and future. To classify cultures according to whether they are past, present or future is to apply a notion of time that is not basic to many cultures. As an example, the Japanese are not time-based but rather have a view of time in which the future is viewed as a natural extension of the past.

> *In Japanese cultural time, the past flows continuously towards the present and also the present is firmly linked to the future. In philosophical terms, we might say that the past and the future exist simultaneously in the present.*
>
> Source: Hayashi (1988), p. 9.

Figure 3.6 reflects this, which the Japanese refer to as the Makimono time pattern.

Another dimension of time is the difference between monochronic and polychronic time. In the former, time is linear having a beginning and an end. It usually operates on the basis of doing one thing at a time and adhering to schedules. In polychronic time, time is cyclic and stresses the involvement of people who are likely to do several things at the same moment, change schedules and seldom view time as being wasted. In polychronic time the completion of a human transaction is more highly regarded than

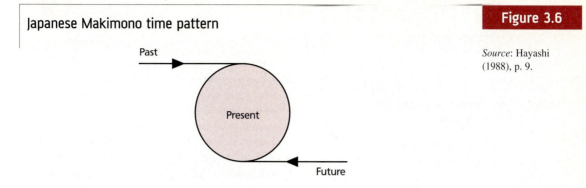

Japanese Makimono time pattern

Source: Hayashi (1988), p. 9.

Figure 3.6

keeping to a schedule. Examples of the differences in time and space can be seen in International Highlight 3.2.

Space

An important cultural manifestation relates to space. Space can be both physical and abstract. Physical space refers to a location such as a town or an office as well as personal proximity. In the western business environment, space often denotes status as reflected in the size of a person's office and its location. This is often not the case in other cultures.

Differences in attitudes to space can also be seen in matters of personal proximity. The size of these zones varies from culture to culture. Cultures differ as to who is allowed to enter each zone and what is considered an adequate sensory exchange within each zone.

Abstract space refers to a grouping of people based on common characteristics such as profession, education or religion. Abstract space gives rise to a number of issues. These include whether people are considered insiders or outsiders, the rights and obligations for group members, the extent to which outsiders can become insiders and how this might be achieved. This cultural concept is also reflected in language. For example, the word for foreigners in Japanese (*gai-jin*) means those from outside.

Language

This is another manifestation of cultural difference. The nature of discourse differs between cultures, with people in some cultures putting the justification first followed by the main point, and people in other countries putting the main point first and the justification afterwards. The degree of precision versus ambiguity with which language conveys meaning also varies and is linked to the issue raised earlier of high- versus low-context cultures. The frequent problem encountered by western businesspeople in Asia as to whether 'yes' means 'yes' or merely 'I hear what you are saying' (as in Japan), is an example. Some languages are tonal and this impacts on meaning. For example, there are five tones in Thai and the same word can have a number of different meanings depending on the tone used. The same is true of Mandarin where there are four different tonal levels. Script also differs and whereas many languages use a script involving individual letters which when joined together form a word, other languages such as Mandarin or Japanese are ideographic and based on symbols, each of which represents a concept rather than a letter.

3.2 International highlight

Differences in time and space

Time

When a businessperson travels abroad, it is within a time frame, and usually involves reference points fixed in time.

An UK business executive had planned a first visit to Indonesia. He intended to fly to Jakarta to arrive on Sunday evening, have a series of meetings on the Monday and leave for the United Kingdom on the Tuesday morning. Via fax, he had arranged five appointments on the Monday based on the number of outside appointments he could comfortably make in his headquarter city of London. His first appointment in Jakarta was at 9.30am on the Monday and although he was on time, he was kept waiting. When he was finally ushered in to see the Indonesian government official at 10.15am, his annoyance at the delay was reflected in his facial expression. As a consequence, the business discussion was strained because of this reflection of annoyance – heightened by the knowledge that not only would he be late for subsequent appointments but now he was unlikely to be able to keep the remaining four appointments before the close of business hours at 4pm. Unaware of the customs of the country, the UK businessman did not realise that the person he had been waiting to meet with considered that to tell his earlier visitor that his time was up, was far ruder than to keep his next visitor waiting 45 minutes.

Polychronic time in which several things are done at the same time and schedules change is a common experience in some cultures.

The tendency in some cultures to do several things at the same time can be rather disconcerting. Australia's senior diplomatic representative in Libya had frequent occasion to meet cabinet ministers (Heads of the Peoples' Bureaux) in their offices.

He was used to the 'western' notion that an appointment set aside a span of time exclusively for a 'one-on-one' discussion about matters of mutual interest. This practice did not operate in Libya, where inevitably on being ushered into the minister's office, he discovered there were a number of other people in the room and conversations were being conducted with a number of people simultaneously. Even on the occasion where the discussion just involved the minister and himself, it was likely to be interrupted by relatives or members of the minister's kin group, all of whom had immediate right of access without prior appointment and the right to command immediate attention to their problems.

Space

A US managing director with a large office in a corner position in a building with a good view over the city is inclined to judge the seniority of those executives he meets abroad by the size and location of their offices. When the executive visits Korea he finds things very different. He arrives for an appointment with a senior executive from one of the Chaebol (e.g. Lucky Goldstar, Hyundai, Samsung or Daewoo). He is confronted with a room of 50 people all labouring away at desks of the same size and is surprised when the receptionist goes to a person at a desk in the centre of the room to announce the visitor's arrival. This person escorts the visitor to an interview room, causing the American to wonder if he has been fobbed off with a junior clerk. The norm in Korea is for the executive to work in the midst of those he supervises rather than separate from them. To evaluate a person's importance in a foreign country in terms of one's own norms for office space and location can lead to serious misinterpretation of the status of the individual.

There are four ways of writing Japanese and each has a different image and effect. The four ways are **kanji** *which is a multi-stroke ideogram,* **hiragana** *or* **katakana** *which are simplified one- or two-stroke methods of representing the sounds of Japanese syllables, and* **romaji** *which is Roman letters used to spell out Japanised English. When used in advertising, for example,* **kanji** *gives a stiff, formal impression,* **hiragana** *imparts soft, delicate and often feminine mood, and* **katakana** *is used to express foreign words that have been Japanised in pronunciation and impart a crisp, direct feeling to the advertising copy.*

Different cultures vary also in the way meaning is conveyed, such as the way things are said, the pitch of voice, what is left unsaid and implied, gestures when speaking, and loquaciousness versus brevity. In some languages such as Indonesian, there are a number of words for 'you' that vary according to the status of the person speaking and the status of the person spoken to. Associated with this is the number of words to denote and the frequency of the use of honorifics indicating the degree to which hierarchy is the norm in the culture. It is also important that a businessperson visiting a different culture inquire as to the style and basics of the language. This is because it is likely that those contacted in the other culture, although able to speak English, will apply the thought patterns of their language when interpreting what is said.

Familiarity

Cultural differences are also reflected in familiarity and friendship patterns. These vary as far as the speed with which friendships are formed, superficiality, the obligation friendship imposes and motivation for the friendship. In many cultures, friendships are not based on business opportunism and are not formed quickly. In these cultures, once friendships are formed, they are much deeper, last longer and involve a real obligation to assist in times of need.

In different societies, the degree to which the individual is a private being varies, as does the way in which this privacy manifests itself. The easy assumption of familiarity involving back-slapping and the use of first names regardless of rank is considered in many parts of Asia to be an intrusion on a person's private world. Allied to this is the expression of emotion. Sensitivity to differences in this respect is important in business negotiation, especially when gauging the reaction to an offer or a statement. While a westerner might interpret a laugh or a smile as a sign of happiness, in other cultures it may indicate disappointment or annoyance.

Consumption patterns

These are reflected in different views of material possessions and dress. In many cultures, power is symbolised by material possessions and these are likely to be prominently displayed. Some years ago in India, when refrigerators were a status symbol in middle-class homes, refrigerators were likely to be given pride of place in the living room rather than located in the kitchen.

Another manifestation of differing cultural approaches towards material possessions is the habit in some cultures of bluntly demanding to know how much you earn and how much things cost.

Dress also can be an expression of cultural difference. Often what is considered formal and informal dress differs. In Indonesia, formal dress is a long-sleeved batik shirt rather than a suit, and in India the more formal alternative to a suit may be a Nehru jacket or even a homespun dhoti. In some hierarchical societies, such as Thailand, formal dress may be a uniform with indications of rank. Uniforms are worn not only by the military but also by officers in the public service. The tendency of westerners to dress informally in tropical countries is often not followed by the business community in that country. They, despite the climate, wear shirts and ties and expect foreign visitors to do the same. The foreign business visitor needs to dress for each occasion at the level of formality expected of that person as an outsider. Whether he adopts local or his own dress is an issue to be ascertained in advance lest the visitor be inappropriately dressed on the one hand or appear patronising on the other.

Differences in consumption patterns can impact on the product offered and the way it is promoted in the international market. The culture in which a person lives affects consumption patterns and also the meaning attached to certain products. When promoting the product to a new culture, it is easier to appeal initially to existing cultural requirements or expectations than to try to change them. Product promotion must be sensitive to the basic values of the country and the differences in the patterns of consumption. For example, promoting a 'do-it-yourself' timesaving device in a country with widespread unemployment may not only be pointless but could also lead to unfavourable criticism. The independence movement in India owed

Table 3.2 Corruption comparisons

Rank 1998	Rank 1997	Country	Grades 1998	Grades 1997	Change %
1	1	Singapore	1.43	1.03	36
2	2	Hong Kong	2.74	3.03	−10
3	3	Japan	5.0	4.60	9
4	5	Taiwan	5.20	5.96	−13
5	4	Malaysia	5.38	5.80	−7
6	10	China	6.97	8.06	−14
7	8	South Korea	7.12	7.71	−8
8	6	Philippines	7.17	6.50	10
9	11	India	7.40	8.20	−10
10	9	Vietnam	8.25	8.0	3
11	7	Thailand	8.29	7.49	11
12	12	Indonesia	8.95	8.67	3

Note: The Hong Kong-based Political and Economic Risk Consultancy (PERC) compiles an annual survey of corruption in Asia. The company ranked responses from 427 expatriates working in the region, who graded countries on a scale of zero to 10, with 10 being 'the most corruption imaginable'. PERC warns that respondents reported on their perception of the problem of corruption, not their actual experience.
Source: Political and Economic Risk Consultancy, Hong Kong, 1998.

much of its popular appeal to Gandhi's encouragement that people should spin their own cloth in the home instead of relying on imported machine-made fabric from Great Britain.

Business customs

An example of the many business customs and practices that are culturally influenced is that of bribery. The degree to which this is practised varies substantially from country to country as does the degree to which it is tacitly accepted. This applies to both the concept of bribery and the form the bribery takes. In some countries, minor bribery such as 'tea money' is accepted as an inescapable cost of doing business, whereas in others it is totally unacceptable. Table 3.2 provides a comparison between countries in Asia as to the alleged degree of corruption.

Figure 3.7 is a cross-cultural comparison grid using each of the key cultural variables. In the first column briefly detail the practice in your country. In the second column note the practice in the selected international market, and in the third column describe the appropriate course of action or behaviour modification that should be undertaken. This will heighten cultural sensitivity when approaching the international market.

Comparison grid

Figure 3.7

Variable	Attitude in your country	Attitude in international market under consideration	Modifcation required
Control over destiny			
Time			
Process vs task approach			
Status and relationships			
Technology orientation			
Space			
Language			
Business practices			

Culture and communication

Verbal communication

Although the differences in verbal communication between countries are immediately obvious to global marketers, some of the subtleties may not be. People interpret their world through language and the more important an item is in daily life, the more words are used to describe it, the more shades of meaning are attached to it.

Verbal communication differs from one culture to another. It differs not only in terms of language but also in terms of the relative importance of the variables involved – of who, what, how, where, when and why. A message is less likely to persuade when it does not reflect these variables in a manner appropriate to the culture of the recipient of the message. More specifically:

- *Who communicates the message and to whom* – cultures vary as to the degree to which people are free to communicate with each other. This may be due to hierarchy, status consciousness or through others acting as gatekeepers.

- *What message is communicated* – this is often determined by the function of the office held and the need to manage personal relationships. What is considered relevant varies by culture, with some interpreting relevance widely and others narrowly defining relevance as immediately applying to the situation.

- *How the message is communicated* – this involves choosing the channel (spoken or written) and the mode (face-to-face or phone). This will vary according to the channels available in a culture and factors such as speed, formality, legality and seniority.

- *Where the message is communicated* – cultures vary in terms of whether certain types of message must be conveyed in a formal setting (e.g. the manager's office) or an informal setting (whenever the occasion permits) and whether those messages conveyed in informal settings carry less weight than those communicated in more formal settings.

- *When the message is communicated* – some messages are communicated without warning, such as via telexes, and some at regular times such as at scheduled meetings. The acceptability of random versus scheduled conveying of messages varies between cultures.

- *Why the message is communicated* – although messages may be intended to inform or persuade, the relative weighting accorded to their motivation varies.

Non-verbal communication

It is not unusual when dealing in different cultures to receive contradictory signals and not to know what to believe or whom to trust. Care should be taken to spot non-verbal signals as these can supplement the verbal signals to yield a more accurate picture of reality. Morris (1977) developed a scale of non-verbal signals to be observed by the marketer. The most important of these are:

- *body stress signals* — perspiration, licking of lips, raising pitch of voice indicate stress;

- *lower body signals* – foot tapping, frequent crossing and uncrossing of knees can indicate impatience;

- *body posture signals* – body sagging or slumping can indicate boredom;

- *random gestures* – these can either confirm or contradict the verbal message – e.g. movements of the hands;

- *facial expressions* – are these consistent with other non-verbal signals and with verbal message?

Cultural adaptation and communication

Adaptation is an important concept in international marketing. This involves affirmative acceptance rather than just tolerance for a different culture. It does not mean that executives must forsake their own ways and totally conform to the other culture – rather that they are aware of local customs and are willing to accommodate those differences that cause misunderstanding. Cateora (1996) lists ten basic criteria for adaptation, namely: open tolerance; flexibility; humility; justice/fairness; adjustability to varying tempos; curiosity/interest; knowledge of the country; liking for others; ability to command respect; and ability to integrate oneself into the environment.

In order to apply these criteria of adaptation most effectively, it is important to understand business customs in terms of the following categories:

- *Imperatives.* These are customs that must be accommodated and conformed to if business relationships are to be successful. They vary from culture to culture and involve differing degrees of friendship, human relations and trust. Removal of one's shoes before entering the home of a Thai businessperson is an example of a cultural imperative.

- *Options.* Conforming to optional customs will enhance chances of a successful commercial outcome but is not mandatory. The Middle Eastern custom of male businessmen kissing each other on both cheeks is not expected of the western business executive. However, if he is sure of its appropriateness in context, this gesture by the foreign business executive indicates sensitivity to the culture, which is likely to be interpreted as a gesture of goodwill.

- *Exclusives.* These are customs in which an outsider may not participate. The foreigner is not welcome to participate and must be able to recognise them, because failure to do so is certain to give offence. Often these customs may be associated with religion, such as an unbeliever performing religious rituals belonging to a faith of which the person is not an adherent.

An ability on the part of the businessperson to perceive when they are dealing with a cultural imperative, a cultural option or a cultural exclusive, and the nuances associated with each in a particular culture, is likely to have a positive impact on cross-cultural communication.

Cross-cultural comparisons

Bilateral comparisons

Isackson (1980) found that countries regarded as being very similar in cultural background had significant differences in cultural attitudes and these impacted on business behaviour. For instance in the US, management was more crucial than technical superiority and personal time was viewed as less important and should be subordinated to work where necessary. He also found that in the US, negotiation should be undertaken by a powerful individual in the firm rather than by a committee, that loyalty was not highly important and authority should be questioned, and that maintenance of good relations should be subordinated to achieving profitable results.

An analysis of westerner–Japanese negotiations highlights culturally influenced differences in negotiation techniques as follows (Fletcher, 2000):

- When westerners negotiate outside their country, their members tend to pursue self-interest and operate as individuals first and as members of a team second. This enables the Japanese to quickly break down their bargaining position by finalising a negotiated price with one team member. This establishes the price point and reduces the negotiating position of the other members of the negotiating team.

- Westerners tend to reject authority and distance themselves from government. However, when they criticise their government, they may reduce their own credibility. This is because businesspeople in most Asian countries accept rather than reject authority and they use it in negotiation.

- In most Asian countries, formality is a state of mind and a reflection of the correct order of things. Hierarchy is inescapable and is respected. The individualistic approach in western society with its aggressive egalitarianism is viewed in many parts of Asia as an ill-disciplined affront to notions of order and formality.

- Whereas in the western approach the person takes over the function, in many parts of Asia the function takes over the person. In Japan the role of the leader of the delegation is known and the person appointed as leader conforms to the norms expected of the role. By contrast, the western businessperson uses their personality and abilities to be a more effective leader by modifying the leader's role to reflect personality and attributes.

Global comparisons

There are two researchers whose work deserves comment in this connection: Hofstede and Trompenaars.

Hofstede

The most comprehensive attempt to measure cultural differences on a global basis was by Hofstede (1980). He undertook a global survey of employees of IBM and came up with

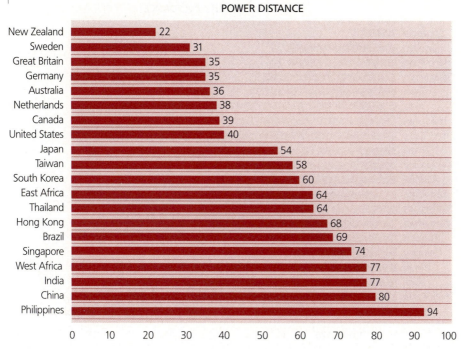

Hofstede's dimension of power distance and country differences

Figure 3.8

POWER DISTANCE

New Zealand	22
Sweden	31
Great Britain	35
Germany	35
Australia	36
Netherlands	38
Canada	39
United States	40
Japan	54
Taiwan	58
South Korea	60
East Africa	64
Thailand	64
Hong Kong	68
Brazil	69
Singapore	74
West Africa	77
India	77
China	80
Philippines	94

Source: Adapted from measures derived by Hofstede (1994).

four underlying dimensions of culture – power distance, uncertainty avoidance, individualism/collectivism and masculine/feminine. Subsequently, his work with Bond (1988) caused a fifth dimension to be added – long-term/short-term orientation. Figures 3.8–3.12 show where various countries lie in terms of each dimension.

● *Power distance.* This is the degree to which less powerful persons in a culture accept the existence of inequality and the unequal distribution of power as a normal situation. Although inequality exists in most cultures the degree to which it is accepted varies from one culture to another. In Figure 3.8 countries with a low power distance incline towards 0 and those with a high power distance incline towards 100. This figure places New Zealand as the lowest country in terms of power distance and Philippines as the highest. This reflects the egalitarian nature of New Zealand society compared with the Philippines society where inequality is accepted and where a handful of families control most of the wealth.

● *Uncertainty avoidance.* This is the extent to which people in a culture feel threatened by uncertain or unknown situations. They are nervous of situations that they consider unstructured, unclear or unpredictable. Cultures with strong uncertainty avoidance tend to be more active, aggressive, emotional and intolerant. Cultures with weak uncertainty avoidance tend to be more contemplative, less aggressive, unemotional and tolerant. Cultures with strong uncertainty avoidance tend towards 0 and those with weak uncertainty

Figure 3.9   Hofstede's dimension of uncertainty avoidance and country differences

Source: Adapted from
measures derived by
Hofstede (1994).

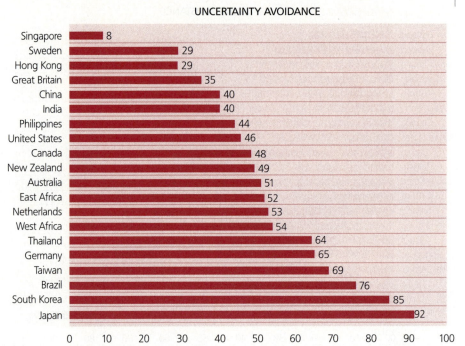

UNCERTAINTY AVOIDANCE

Singapore	8
Sweden	29
Hong Kong	29
Great Britain	35
China	40
India	40
Philippines	44
United States	46
Canada	48
New Zealand	49
Australia	51
East Africa	52
Netherlands	53
West Africa	54
Thailand	64
Germany	65
Taiwan	69
Brazil	76
South Korea	85
Japan	92

avoidance tend towards 100. Figure 3.9 shows a wide range of uncertainty avoidance from a very low rating for Singapore through to very high uncertainty avoidance for Japan.

● *Individualism/collectivism*. This reflects the extent to which people in a culture look after their own interests and those of their immediate family, and where ties are loose. The collectivist dimension reflects the extent to which people in a culture are members of a group and group needs should be subordinated to individual desires. Membership of the group confers status and plugs the individual into a network, but in exchange for this the group expects permanent loyalty of its members. In Figure 3.10 cultures with a high degree of collectivism tend towards 0, and those with a high degree of individualism tend towards 100. This figure shows that China is the most collectivist of societies and the United States the most individualist.

● *Masculine/feminine*. Cultures use the biological differences between the sexes to define different social roles for men and women. This is reflected in masculine cultures stressing material success and assertiveness and feminine cultures stressing quality of life and caring for the weak. In Figure 3.11 cultures with a high degree of focus on feminine values tend towards 0 and those with a high degree of focus on masculine values tend towards 100. In this figure, Sweden with its tradition of social welfare is shown to be the most feminine and Japan the most masculine of countries.

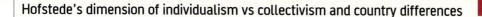

Hofstede's dimension of individualism vs collectivism and country differences

Source: Adapted from measures derived by Hofstede (1994).

Figure 3.10

INDIVIDUALISM VERSUS COLLECTIVISM

China	15
Taiwan	17
South Korea	18
Thailand	20
Singapore	20
West Africa	20
Hong Kong	25
East Africa	27
Philippines	32
Brazil	38
Japan	46
India	48
Germany	67
Sweden	71
New Zealand	79
Netherlands	80
Canada	80
Great Britain	89
Australia	90
United States	91

Hofstede's dimension of masculinity vs femininity and country differences

Figure 3.11

Source: Adapted from measures derived by Hofstede (1994).

MASCULINITY VERSUS FEMININITY

Sweden	5
Netherlands	14
Thailand	34
South Korea	39
East Africa	41
Taiwan	45
West Africa	46
Singapore	48
Brazil	49
Canada	52
China	55
India	56
Hong Kong	57
New Zealand	58
Australia	61
United States	62
Philippines	64
Germany	66
Great Britain	66
Japan	95

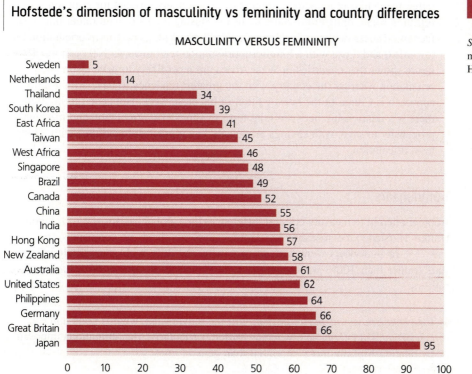

While Hofstede's work provides a useful insight into factors underlying differences between cultures and a global basis for comparison, there are some qualifications. The first relates to Hofstede's sample that consisted of IBM executives in each country. It is well known that IBM has a strong corporate culture and it is possible that this corporate culture could mask some of the differences between countries. The second relates to the fact that the actual survey was conducted in the late 1970s and since that time there have been changes within individual countries and a rise in the globalisation of world trade. The third qualification relates to the dimensions of national culture found by Hofstede. These are largely western dimensions and may not be appropriate measures of cultural differences in some Asian countries. In these cultures, a qualification such as collectivism does not necessarily exclude its opposite of individualism. Furthermore, the search for truth may be irrelevant in cultures whose members believe there is no such concept as a single truth. In such cultures in Asia, uncertainty avoidance may have only limited meaning. This raises the issue as to whether there are other dimensions that might have been overlooked because they are not important in western cultures. Hofstede recognised this latter shortcoming and in subsequent research with Bond from the Chinese University of Hong Kong, he arrived at a fifth dimension which was initially labelled Confucian Dynamism and subsequently long-term versus short-term orientation.

● *Long-term vs short-term orientation.* This is the extent to which cultures exhibit a pragmatic, future-oriented perspective as opposed to a historic short-term point of view. Cultures having a long-term orientation reflect the values of thrift, perseverance, concern for proper ways of doing things, building market share rather than chasing immediate returns to shareholders, respect for tradition, fulfilling social obligations and a focus on causing others to gain rather than lose face in business dealings. In Figure 3.12 cultures with a short-term orientation tend towards 0 and those with a long-term orientation tend towards 100 or more. This figure shows that countries in West Africa are most likely to have a short-term orientation whereas the country with the greatest tendency to have a long-term approach is China. In the latest edition of his basic work, Hofstede (2000) argues there is a relationship between long-term vs short-term orientation and marginal propensity to save, with savings propensity being greatest in cultures with a long-term orientation.

Trompenaars

Another attempt to measure cultural differences on a global basis was by Trompenaars. Unlike Hofstede, the research by Trompenaars involved 30 companies (not one), and 75% of interviews were with management and 25% with general administrative staff (rather than 100% with managers). Trompenaars arrived at five dimensions as follows:

● *Universalism versus particularism.* For the universalist, what is good and right can be applied everywhere whereas for the particularist, the obligations imposed by relationships are more important than general rules.

Hofstede's dimension of long term vs short-term orientation and country differences

Figure 3.12

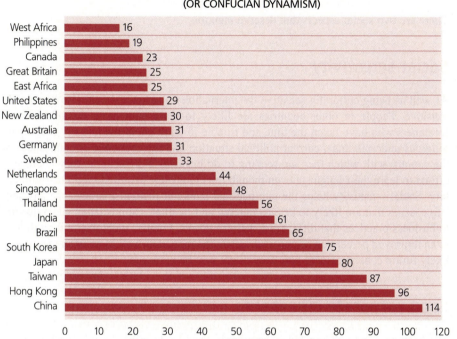

LONG-TERM VS SHORT-TERM ORIENTATION
(OR CONFUCIAN DYNAMISM)

Source: Adapted from measures derived by Hofstede and Bond (1988), and Hofstede (1994).

West Africa	16
Philippines	19
Canada	23
Great Britain	25
East Africa	25
United States	29
New Zealand	30
Australia	31
Germany	31
Sweden	33
Netherlands	44
Singapore	48
Thailand	56
India	61
Brazil	65
South Korea	75
Japan	80
Taiwan	87
Hong Kong	96
China	114

- *Individualism versus communitarianism.* Similar to the Hofstede dimension of individualism versus collectivism, this dimension is a matter of whether people consider themselves as individuals first or whether they set group obligations above individual desires.

- *Neutral versus affective.* In affective cultures, expression of emotion is viewed as natural whereas in neutral cultures, expression of emotion is repressed to give the impression of objectivity and 'being in control'.

- *Specific versus diffuse.* People in specific cultures get straight to the point whereas people in diffuse cultures discuss business only after relationships have been established. Should involvement in the contract or activity be confined to that contract or activity or should the 'whole' person be involved? In part this dimension approximates that of high context versus low context.

- *Achievement versus ascription.* In the achievement culture, status derives from one's own achievements, whereas in ascribing cultures status comes from age, sex, kinship, education, connections, etc.

Four of these five dimensions are different from those of Hofstede although, yet again, they measure western values.

Social aspects of the conduct of international marketing

There are two social aspects that deserve mention.

Social sensitivity

As well as being culturally sensitive the international marketer should also be socially sensitive. People in other countries are likely to react with more warmth towards foreigners who have taken the time and trouble to learn about the history, geography, religious underpinnings, current political situation and the economic circumstances of the country with which they are seeking to do business. Furthermore, they appreciate efforts to learn their language even though the knowledge acquired might be rudimentary. Social sensitivity helps the international marketer recognise in advance any sensitive issues that are likely to be encountered and facilitates appreciating and adjusting to business practices that differ from western norms. Finally, such sensitivity will lead to an improved perception of opportunities in the market as well as assist in identifying likely future constraints and how they might best be managed.

Good corporate citizenship

The term corporate citizenship is commonly used to describe the relationship of the firm with its various stakeholders. These are different in international marketing and include individuals, firms, groupings and governments in the foreign country.
According to Maigam (1997), corporate citizenship consists of:

- *Economic citizenship* – corporations should be productive and profitable while at the same time meeting consumer needs.
- *Legal citizenship* – corporations should fulfil their economic mission within a legal framework.
- *Ethical citizenship* – corporations should follow socially established moral standards.
- *Discretionary citizenship* – corporations should become actively involved in the betterment of the local communities in which they operate. Such activities are assumed voluntarily and do not produce a direct tangible benefit to the firm.

It is the discretionary element that can often make the difference in the award of contracts by governments in international markets. Firms that actively seek to employ locals in management, search out local sources of raw materials and other inputs, appoint locals of influence to the local directorship of the subsidiary or joint venture, and create opportunities for local shareholding are demonstrating good corporate citizenship. A proactive policy of good corporate citizenship will offset criticism of the firm as a 'foreigner' and head off nationalistic antagonism, especially in developing countries.

Ethical considerations

Ethics can be viewed as being culturally based assumptions of what is right and what is wrong. Views of correct ethical behaviour differ according to whether the person holds a:

- *relativist perspective* – what is ethical is determined by the host culture e.g. bribery is acceptable because it is customary in the host country; or a
- *utilitarian perspective* – what is ethical is that which delivers the greatest benefit to the greatest number of people, e.g. bribery is acceptable because it leads to contracts that create employment; or a
- *universalist perspective* – there is a universal set of acceptable ethical behaviours that should be applied to the conduct of business wherever it occurs, e.g. bribery is unacceptable under any circumstances regardless of circumstances or nature.

The problem with the relativist perspective is that consumers in the developing world are not as likely to be as well informed as their counterparts in developed countries; there is less regulation of the marketplace; and many of the developing countries do not have well-developed democratic institutions. The problem with the utilitarian perspective is that it is usually short term and can be detrimental in the longer term. The problem with the universalist perspective is that it assumes that one culture (western) has the right to define ethical behaviour for the whole world. This raises the issue of whether this perspective is appropriate in an environment of increasing globalisation and whether corporate codes of conduct, such as the Moral Authority of Transnational Corporate Codes, or ethical watchdogs such as Transparency International, really work. Are such bodies effective or are they another example of the 'West' imposing its values on the 'East'?

Ethical behaviours differ from country to country because of:

- *Popular attachments to governments* – if people respect the government they are less likely to break its laws in pursuit of individual gain. This is offered as an explanation as to why democracies in general are less corrupt than absolutist regimes.
- *Popular customs* – in many countries, gift giving is the norm in business and treated as an expression of friendship. While it may be argued that although the gift is trifling, the feeling is profound, it can easily degenerate into a situation where the more generous the gift, the more profound the feeling.
- *Level of economic development* – low levels of economic development intensify the role of government as a source of jobs and benefits. As economic development in such countries increases, government contracts become larger and the scope for incentives to secure the contract increases.
- *Relative size of the public sector* – as it grows, more aspects of life come under its control and with new rules, come new opportunities and incentives to break them.
- *Low income for public servants* – creates an unwritten convention that as the government cannot afford to pay its public servants properly, the cost of employing them should be shared between the government on the one hand

and those who benefit from the service provided on the other. An example of this is the payment of 'tea money' to the public servant to speed up the approval process or a facilitation payment to have a container cleared from the wharf in reasonable time.

- *Obscure political and legal environments* – poorly defined property rights, investment procedures and accounting standards all provide scope for questionable ethical practices. This tends to be exacerbated when the regime in power is unstable or does not exercise control over the whole country.
- *High level of government control and state ownership* – this enables politicians and bureaucrats to appropriate legal rights unto themselves and use their positions for personal enrichment or to raise funds for political election campaigns.

The international marketer needs to be aware of these differences and also of the laws regarding ethical behaviours that operate in both the home country and the host country. Where ethics are concerned the marketer is likely to be confronted by two sets of laws and two sets of behaviours when transacting international business.

Culture and international negotiation

Culture needs to be taken into account when preparing for international negotiations as well as when conducting international negotiations. In negotiation, there are usually two goals at stake:

- *Substance goals* – concerned with outcomes related to the content of issues involved; and
- *Relationship goals* – concerned with outcomes related to how well people involved in the negotiations can work with each other once the negotiations are concluded.

Many negotiations result in a sacrifice of relationships as the parties become preoccupied with substance goals and self-interest. However, effective negotiation takes place when both substance issues are resolved and working relationships are maintained or improved.

Background to negotiation

All aspects of business activity involve negotiation. It is involved when introducing a product/service to the market; when selling a product/service; when taking steps to ensure that the customer is satisfied; and when endeavouring to secure re-orders. In international business, negotiation is more complicated because the environment into which the product/service is being sold is different from the domestic market, especially in terms of the different cultural norms that apply. Cultural norms can critically affect the outcome of negotiations and many firms have lost significant international business because of cultural insensitivity on the part of those sent abroad to negotiate business on their behalf.

The environment of international negotiation

Underlying all international negotiations is the iceberg principle (Figure 3.13).

Just as the *Titanic* sank because the part of the iceberg above the surface of the ocean was small and the portion below the surface which it hit was very large, in international negotiations that which is obvious and on the surface is limited, and that which under-lies the motives and statements of the other party is substantial. Failure to appreciate what lies below the surface can either sink the negotiation or result in an unfavourable outcome. If unfavourable outcomes are to be avoided, then the underlying concerns, interests and needs of the other party should be researched, as should the impact of cultural differences.

Often cross-national comparisons are not soundly based in terms of the behavioural differences between nationalities and to assume that other countries can be compared with your cultural norms is erroneous. It should be remembered that people view negotiations through the 'eyes' of their own culture and carry this 'baggage' with them into international negotiations. The significance of culture to the conduct of the negotiation is not that it defines the outcome of the negotiation – rather that it influences the process of the negotiation and the underlying strategy of the bargaining. For example, is it the cultural norm to offer a 'take it or leave it' price or is it the norm to ask for more than you expect to receive and for the other party to offer less than they would expect you to accept, and for both parties to inch towards a mutually acceptable figure during the process of negotiation? Understanding the cultural background of the other party enables you to anticipate likely bargaining behaviour and respond with confidence.

The iceberg principle

Figure 3.13

Demand-offer

Sea level

Underlying concerns, interest and needs

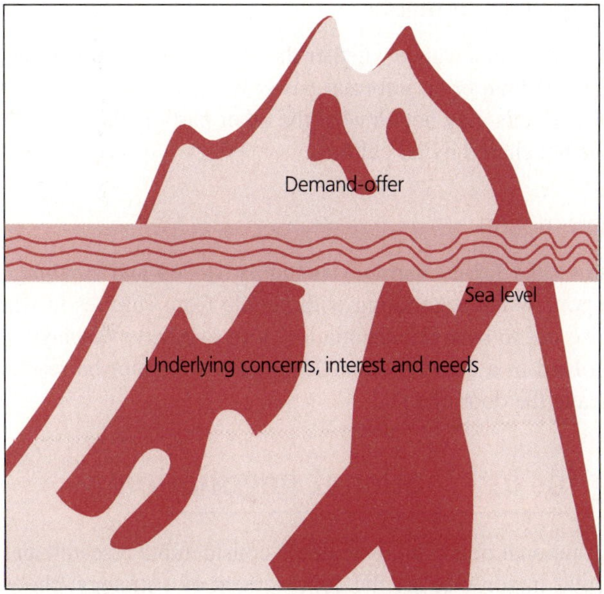

Culture and the conduct of negotiations

There are a number of culturally influenced factors that need to be kept in mind when negotiating with people from other countries.

Different approaches to thinking

Thought processes differ between cultures and this is manifested in the way the other party reaches agreement. An understanding as to how the other party thinks through problems will facilitate the planning of an appropriate negotiation strategy.

Self-esteem and 'face'

These are of differing degrees of importance to various cultures. In most Asian cultures causing a person to lose face is unforgivable. In these circumstances it is essential in negotiation that the other party is allowed to win some points so as to save face and maintain self-esteem. A linked issue is that of relationships. When relationships between an inferior and a superior are involved, it is important not to criticise or humiliate the superior in front of the subordinate. Relationships could involve membership of a particular caste, position in the social hierarchy, or links to power brokers or royalty. These linkages should be understood so as to avoid giving offence and understanding the value of the network to which the firm might be linked once the negotiation has reached an outcome.

Value systems

It is desirable to appreciate the aspects that are valued in the culture from which the other party comes. Heritage, history and traditions that are valued provide indicators as to which aspects of the proposal are most likely to appeal to the other side.

Appropriate degree of formality

It is useful to ascertain in advance whether the other party would prefer negotiations to be conducted on a formal or an informal basis. While a casual inquiry might elicit the response 'informal', this may not be what the other party really wants. The assumption of informality is not shared by all cultures.

Harmony and emotion

In many cultures (like Japan) harmony is highly valued and anything which disturbs it is frowned upon. When negotiating with people from cultures in which harmony is valued, it is wise not to sour the negotiation with excessive displays of emotionalism or become involved in a confrontation. If agreement cannot be reached, it is always advisable to 'leave the door open'.

Preparing for international negotiation

Success in international negotiations requires considerable research and advance planning. Of particular importance are the development of a strategy, choosing the correct negotiating team and researching the context in which the negotiations will take place.

Strategy

Developing a strategy which is culturally sensitive is a prerequisite for successful negotiation. A decision should be reached in advance in general terms as to whether your team should go out of its way to meet the expectations of the other side, or whether it should make no accommodation whatsoever, or whether it should aim for a compromise between the two extremes. In general, when planning negotiation strategy, executives should try to be themselves, avoid compromising personal integrity, be willing to modify behaviour to make others feel comfortable and show respect while being firm but friendly. The approach to negotiation should be to the degree appropriate to the culture, reflect respect for age, respect for tradition, respect for government and/or authority, an understanding of inequality and the reasons for it, respect for education, and recognition of local titles and symbols of rank.

Composition of the negotiating team

The following aspects, many of which can have cultural implications, should be borne in mind:

- *Numbers.* The number of people in the team should be matched to the number in the other negotiating team, although this can be expensive when discussions are held outside your country.
- *Status.* There should be a matching of the members of each team in terms of status. This facilitates harmony and an ability to enter into commitments without reference 'back home'. It also conveys the impression that your side is treating the negotiations as important.
- *Interpreter.* With the permission of the other side, an interpreter should be included as a member of your team. This enables the team to acquire a more accurate understanding of the views and sensitivities of the other side, and misunderstandings due to translation mistakes or imprecision of meaning are less likely to occur.
- *Tasks.* These should be defined in advance for each member of the negotiating team so that each member knows their role and members do not get in each other's way or inadvertently contradict each other, either in public or in private. Examples of possible roles are leader, negotiator, strategist, recorder, technical expert, sales expert, production expert or financial adviser.
- *Deployment.* Use the junior members of the team to argue over unpleasant details and test how far the other party will concede, while keeping the more senior persons to smooth over ruffled feathers, to resolve minor disputes and sign the final agreement.

Researching the context of negotiations

In undertaking this research it is necessary not only to seek information which confirms currently held ideas as to the appropriate negotiation approach, but also to seek out information which might contradict these assumptions.

- *The other negotiating team.* There is a need to research the likely composition of the negotiation team of the other party and the background of their team members so as to establish biases or likely areas of common experience or interest. It is also advisable to ascertain the planned location of discussions and whether there will be adequate and secure communications facilities available in case, during negotiations, it is necessary to refer an issue to head office. It is useful to ascertain the need for your team to provide either interpreters capable of translating what is being said as it is being said and/or translators to translate written documents and records of discussion. Although the other side might offer to provide interpreters/translators at their expense, there is always the doubt as to whether they will provide your team with a full and correct message if paid by the other party. Often the nuance of what is said or the accumulated context of the conversation is more important than the actual words and it is essential that the total sensitivity be communicated. Researching in advance the degree of autonomy the members of the other negotiating team have to make decisions is also useful. Another issue is, who is to be the decision-maker regarding the topic under discussion and whether that decision-maker is likely to be a member of the team. If any important decision-makers are not team members, it is useful to find out how they may be contacted and to extend hospitality to them if this is culturally acceptable. Finally it is desirable to establish what is likely to happen to the other party if negotiations are unsuccessful. Knowing how badly they want a successful outcome can strengthen your negotiating hand.

- *The competition.* It is also advisable to research which competitors are likely to be in the market. This research should include their strengths and weaknesses, whether they have done business in the market before, how their performance was judged, and whether they were they viewed as being culturally sensitive in their approach. Included in this appraisal should be an analysis of the influence exerted by the competitor's government, the connections and influence these competitors are able to bring to bear, and the competitor's connections in the market. The availability or otherwise of attractive competitors impacts on the strength of your negotiating position.

- *The firm's objective organisation.* It should be clearly established at the outset how badly the firm wants this international business. Whether the contract is to be viewed as a 'one-off' event or the start of a long-term relationship with that market, or as a vehicle to obtain a foothold in that market also needs to be decided. In this connection, it is necessary to determine the minimum acceptable package that can be agreed to in relation to each of the above strategies.

- *Alternative approaches.* It is useful to work out in advance a contingency plan if the original basis for negotiation proves unworkable. Such a plan could include an alternative approach that yields competitive advantage in a different way (e.g. offer a price in relation to usage so that, to the customer, the purchase becomes a variable as opposed to a fixed cost). Another alternative is to study all the elements of the offer so as to determine which elements are the most attractive to the other side; then as a fall-back position offer the most unique of these elements.

Stages in international negotiation

An understanding of the various stages through which international negotiations proceed will assist in deciding which strategies to pursue at each stage. The strategy most useful at the beginning of negotiations may be inappropriate as negotiations proceed. There are five major stages in most international negotiations.

Pre-negotiation stage

At this stage, it is necessary to work out the composition of the negotiation team and to formulate objectives and strategies. It is also necessary to conduct a preliminary analysis of the context of the negotiations, attempt an initial definition of likely problem areas, assess the position likely to be adopted by the other side and develop a desired agenda. Failure to prepare properly is likely to result in lack of commitment to a specific position and a willingness to grant concessions unnecessarily or too early in the negotiation. This stage also involves establishing rapport with members of the other team and the length of this stage is likely to be influenced by whether the other party comes from a low- or from a high-context culture.

Opening stage

During the second stage, the negotiating teams begin 'to get down to business' as opposed to conversation designed to build trust. The appropriate level of formality needs to be considered as does the exchange of business cards and any associated formalities (as in Japan). At this stage it is desirable to check that both sides have common understandings as to the topic of the negotiations, what has been previously agreed to, and how the relationship has developed to date. This exchange of information relating to the topics to be discussed is likely to take longer when the other party comes from a culture characterised by decision making by consensus. This is because more information will be required and many more people in the organisation represented by the other team will need to be provided with information.

Bargaining stage

This third stage is one in which the previously developed negotiation strategy needs to be applied. This is the stage where it is necessary to decide whether a broad agreement is negotiated first (such as intent to enter into a joint venture) or whether each aspect is negotiated individually for incorporation in a final agreement (such as human resource issues, financial issues, and technology exchange issues). Another aspect for consideration at this stage is the speed with which negotiations should be conducted. North Americans, in keeping with their 'time is money' approach, value a speedy approach, whereas in many Asian countries, the time devoted to negotiations is a reflection of the importance attached to the subject matter. To rush the negotiation in these circumstances is to send a signal to the other party that the issue is regarded as being of limited importance. In some cultures, negotiations are characterised by frequent restating of the position and in some circumstances this may be a deliberate ploy to give the party time to think. The bargaining stage is likely to be shorter in cases where the earlier stages have been protracted. At this stage, tactics are also important, as is knowledge as to what the other party considers acceptable behaviour. In some cultures, aggressive tactics are likely to be met with silence, changing the subject or by withdrawal from negotiations.

Concession and agreement stage

Complications at this stage often arise from contrasting styles of negotiation. Issues, such as volatility versus patience and trying to hurry resolution versus indifference to the time it takes to reach agreement, can be very important in reaching a mutually satisfactory outcome. The norm of the other party in agreeing to concessions is also important: are concessions made progressively throughout the negotiations or only during the latter stages of the bargaining? The issue of the nature of contracts is applicable at this stage. In high-context cultures formal contracts are disliked, whereas in low-context cultures they are sought because they provide the negotiators with feelings of security. A final factor at this stage is how each party views the negotiation in terms of the total relationship and whether both parties view it in the same way. Is the negotiation regarded as a single event or as part of an ongoing long-term relationship?

Post-negotiation stage

The final stage is where cognitive dissonance can set in and the parties question whether they made the right decisions and whether they are satisfied with the negotiated arrangement. In the interests of good relations and future business, it is good tactics after the deal has been concluded to give the other party an extra concession that they did not expect to receive. At the post-negotiation stage, another tactic common in some cultures, such as in India, is the practice of 'nibbling' – making further demands after the terms of the deal have been finalised. One way of handling this is to ask that the additional request be put in writing so that it can receive formal consideration when the agreement next comes up for review.

The atmosphere of international negotiations

Atmosphere is very important in the conduct of negotiations in all countries but this is especially the case with high-context cultures. The atmosphere that prevails during the course of negotiations can have a positive or negative impact on the outcome. It is likely to be affected by a number of factors, as follows.

Degree of mutual orientation

This will be a matter of whether both sides have the same view of the purpose of the negotiation and wish to achieve a mutually beneficial outcome. This mutuality of orientation is likely to be greater if both parties seek a 'win–win' outcome and view the exchange between them as improving the possibility of attaining their specific goals as opposed to maximising their own advantage by exploiting the other party.

Feelings towards the other party

The atmosphere of negotiations will be conducive to a successful outcome if both parties trust each other, if there is a genuine willingness to cooperate, if there is a strong commitment to the relationship, and if each side makes a genuine attempt to understand the other's motives and circumstances.

Openness versus secrecy

This factor will also impact on atmosphere and is often a reflection of differences in cultural values. The matrix in Figure 3.14 compares a range of different countries according to their tendency to be cautious in assessments on the one hand and a tendency to be open as opposed to secretive on the other. This ranges from Anglo-Saxon countries being transparent and optimistic at one end of the spectrum to the less developed Latin countries being secretive and conservative on the other.

Willingness to make cultural adjustments

This is often a matter of the position of the party in the negotiation and whether one party has a greater need to achieve a result than the other. In general, the greatest degree of cultural adjustment in the negotiation situation should be made by the seller rather than the buyer, by the party to the transaction with the least power, and by the party which wants a successful outcome the most.

Cultural differences in disclosure and assessment characteristics

Figure 3.14

Source: Adapted from Radeburgh and Gray (1993), p. 76.

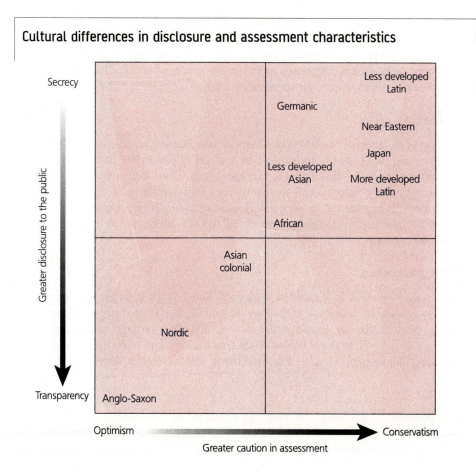

Internet infusion

Culture impacts on the way information is used, the credibility attached to information and the degree of trust exhibited in the Internet as a medium for information. The Internet is predominantly culturally geared to the American cultural norms of anti-government, individualism, populism and egalitarianism. This means that some people in other countries will consider that American culture is embedded in the Internet and this will lead to resistance to Internet use in cultures that are different from the US.

Global reach

One of the characteristics of the Internet is its global reach. This means that to be effective, e-marketers must address the diversity of the consumers' cultures. This is because nations and subcultures within nations differ from each other on various cultural dimensions. Those that appear to apply to Internet adoption and usage are as follows.

Time

The Internet is regarded as a medium that saves time because of its interactivity, ability to consummate a sale, and the speed of its information exchanges. This means that it will be valued in cultures where 'time is money' and punctuality is prized. In cultures that adopt a more relaxed approach to time and where time is subordinated to creating or maintaining relationships, the speed of the Internet is not likely to be valued as much.

Materialism

Because of its association with 'Americanness', the Internet is regarded in many countries as being associated with materialism and the dollar, rather than quality of life or improvement in the welfare of the average citizen. This association is reinforced by the perception that transnational companies are endeavouring to become global firms. The Internet is regarded as being a vehicle for achieving these aspirations. The adoption of the Internet in societies that are critical of materialism may be delayed because of this association.

Technical orientation

Technical orientation is a dimension along which countries differ. The Internet is strongly associated with new technology. Countries that are not strong in new technology creation may be countries that are not innovators or early adopters as far as diffusion of innovation is concerned. Such countries are less likely to invest funds in embracing the Internet because of its association with new technology.

Language

In its structure, content and form, language manifests the culture of those who speak it. This is reflected in word order, grammatical structure, number of words used to indicate shades of meaning, in discourse analysis (where the emphasis in the sentence comes), and specificity versus vagueness of meaning. As the Internet is specific rather than contextual and associated with the American direct style of communication rather than with oblique styles of communication, its adoption in some countries may be delayed because its directness could lead to giving offence.

Business customs and practices

Cultures vary in terms of acceptable business customs and practices. In some cultures these are specific and transparent while in others they are opaque providing room to manoeuvre, to repay favours and to provide a commercial return in circumstances where regulations eliminate the incentive. Because of the transparency of the Internet and the traceability of Internet transactions, people in cultures where business customs and practices are opaque and negotiable may be more reluctant to adopt the technology than people in cultures where business activities are more transparent. This is particularly the case where bribery is common or a significant percentage of international trade flows through unofficial channels.

Cultural concepts and the Internet

There are a number of underlying cultural concepts that impact on the influence of culture on international marketing.

High versus low context

It would seem that low-context countries are more likely to adopt the Internet than high-context countries. This may be because the Internet is not contextual and Internet messages convey all the intended meaning. This has led Fock (2000) to propose that communication behaviour of Internet visitors from high-context cultures will be different from that of visitors from low-context cultures and that perceptions of web messages by web visitors from high-context cultures will also be different from the perceptions of messages by visitors from low-context cultures.

Psychic distance

A comparison of these distances with rates of Internet adoption provides some indication that psychic distance is linked to a higher rate of Internet adoption. Research into the psychic distance of various countries from the US supports the above. Park (2000) concludes that the more psychic distance there is between American culture and the host culture, the less they (host cultures) are encouraged to use the Internet, or, at the very least, information dissemination on which the Internet is based can slow down significantly in the host country.

Ethnocentrism

Perlmutter (1995) developed a typology whereby firms could be classified according to the orientation of their management as still ethnocentric, polycentric, regiocentric or geocentric. Some researchers have found that ethnocentrism is related to a reluctance to adopt the Internet. Wheeler (1998) found that Islamic societies in the developing world reject technology associated with the western world as imperialistic, morally corrupt and harmful to local identity. She found that Kuwaiti companies use the

Internet not for business deals but rather to reinforce local identity or spread Islamic conservatism.

Culture and global comparisons of Internet adoption

Of Hofstede's dimensions, while logically it would seem that high uncertainty avoidance would be correlated with Internet adoption, there is no evidence for this and Park (2000) found the opposite. Similarly there would appear to be a logical connection between low power distance and Internet adoption as the Internet provides a facility for people to access information regardless of status. While Hofstede's classification of countries supports this proposed relationship, Park's research does not. There appears, however, to be a correlation between individualism and adoption of the Internet. Collectivist cultures put considerable pressure on members to conform to one another and this pressure for conformity and uniformity in collective cultures is not conducive to adoption of the Internet where diversity and different viewpoints are encouraged. This forgoing would suggest that individualistic cultures are more likely to use the Internet than collectivist cultures. Hofstede's classification of countries on this dimension tends to support the above suggestion. In addition, Park (2000) found that individualistic cultures are more prone to adopt the Internet than collectivist cultures. This he attributes to the autonomy, freedom and optimal flexibility that the Internet provides. Finally, it could be argued that the Internet is more compatible with feminine cultures where interdependence, interrelationships with other people and caring for other people are valued. This suggests that feminine cultures are more likely to adopt the Internet than are masculine cultures. Hofstede's classification of countries on this dimension provides some support for this proposition although there are some exceptions, such as Sweden, the Philippines and Japan. Park (2000) found strong support for the argument that feminine cultures were more likely to use the Internet than were masculine cultures. This he attributes to the fact that people in feminine cultures enjoy the anonymity that the Internet provides to avoid gender or ethnic identity.

One answer to the problems and differences associated with culture is to design ethnic portals if the ethnic market is large enough. The reach of such portals will not necessarily be confined to a country but will reach the ethnic group wherever they may be. Given the increasingly mobile nature of the global workforce, especially professionals, this could be an advantage – e.g. United Airlines could promote round trips to Kuala Lumpur for Malaysians worldwide using a Malaysian portal (Park, 2000, p. 2).

In designing ethnic portals for markets which are worthwhile in terms of numbers or purchasing power, it is necessary to take the host country's culturally influenced preferences into account. Procter and Gamble has designed country-specific localised websites of a different style and content, targeting the ethnic audience for each of its major markets, e.g. Brazil – (www.pantene.com.br); China (www.pg.com.cn); Germany (www.procterundgamble.de).

Summary

Cultural sensitivity is a critical aspect of doing international business and is particularly important in the conduct of international negotiations. There are a number of culturally related factors which impact on international marketing as well as various characteristics of culture itself which manifest themselves in different ways from market to market. Cultural sensitivity requires an understanding of the way that cultural differences impact on communication, awareness of the elements of culture which are likely to have the greatest impact, and a knowledge of the way culture operates at different levels – national, industry, organisation and personal.

There are a number of key cultural concepts that assist in classifying cultures in broad terms and these are reflected in the way culture manifests itself in an international business setting. Included in these are time, space, language, familiarity and consumption patterns. The way in which culture is communicated can be both verbal and non-verbal, and operating in a different culture will require some degree of adaptation. Cross-cultural comparisons, be they on a global or bilateral basis, highlight patterns of cultural difference and their implications for management. The work of Hofstede and Trompenaars in this respect needs to be considered in depth for the insights it can bring to an appreciation of the implications of cultural differences for international marketing. Social sensitivity, good corporate citizenship and appropriate ethical behaviour also play a role in successful international involvement. Cultural signposts abound in both planning for and undertaking international negotiations and apply differently at each stage of the negotiation process. Successful negotiation from a cultural perspective requires careful research, development of a strategy and management of the conduct of negotiations. Finally, the impact of culture on the atmosphere of negotiations is important, as are the different negotiating styles adopted by people from different cultural backgrounds.

Ethics issue

Your company, which makes small pumps, has been barred from entering the market in a large Asian country because of the collusive efforts of the local pump manufacturers. Your firm could expect to increase profits by US$3 million from sales in that market if the ban on your supplying the market were lifted. Last week a businessman from that Asian country contacted your management and stated he could smooth the way for the company to sell in his country for an inducement of US$300,000.

You are the international marketing manager for the company and have visited the country on a number of occasions and have some familiarity with the cultural norms and business practices that prevail there. Your board has sought your advice as to whether the inducement should be paid, the legality of doing so, and, if payment is recommended, how this might be handled.

Web workout

Question 1 Imagine you are about to embark on round-the-world travel. In order to work out the best deal and itineraries you may want to visit websites of one Asian, one European and one South American airline. As a customer, try to research the required information for your trip. Do these websites cater for non-English speaking customers?

Question 2 It is said that swimwear design cannot be differentiated or be country specific. Visit websites of major swimwear manufacturers such as Speedo, Spank, Adidas, Sea Folly, Arena or Zoggs. Do they cater for cultural differences or do they offer same deal to their global clients? What should they do?

Websites

Globaledge – Culture
http://globaledge.msu.edu/ibrd/busresmain.asp?ResourceCategoryID=17

Getting through customs http://www.getcustoms.com

Web of Culture http://webofculture.com/

Travelang http://www.travlang.com/

Cultural Perspectives Reports
http://www.ibrc.bschool.ukans.edu/about/publications/publications.htm

Discussion questions

1 Why, when doing business in other countries, is it important to analyse the impact of culture at the national, the industry and the firm levels as well as at the personal level?

2 Discuss how you would compensate for the self-reference criterion when marketing in Vietnam.

3 Illustrate the difference between high-context cultures and low-context cultures by comparing China with Germany.

4 Why is time so important as a cultural variable when doing international business? How would you take this variable into account during your first visit to Myanmar? What are the likely consequences if you don't?

5 Describe the ways in which cultural differences can act to impede communication between businesspeople of different nationality.

6 What are the shortcomings of Hofstede's criteria for assessing cultural differences on a global basis? Do you consider that his fifth factor adequately caters for the underlying differences between Asian and western cultural values?

7 Why is it necessary to prepare comprehensively for international negotiations? Prepare a list of issues you would research before leaving home.

References

Cateora, P.R. (1996) *International Marketing*, 9th edn, Irwin, Chicago, p. 114.

Cohen, J. (1996) 'The Search for Universal Symbols: The Case of Right and Left', *Global Perspectives in Consumer Research*, Haworth Press Inc., New York.

Fletcher, R. (2000) 'Cross-Cultural versus Cross-National Comparisons of Ethical Values and Behavior', *Advances in International Marketing*, Supplement 1, pp. 95–113.

Fock, H. (2000) 'Cultural Influences on Marketing Communication on the World Wide Web', Proceedings of the Multicultural Marketing Conference, 17–20 September, Hong Kong Academy of Marketing Science.

Hall, E.T. (1976) *Beyond Culture*, Anchor Press/Doubleday, New York.

Hayashi, S. (1988) *Culture and Management in Japan*, University of Tokyo Press, Tokyo, p. 9.

Hofstede, G. (1994) 'The Business of International Business is Culture', *International Business Review*, Vol. 3, No. 1, pp. 1–14.

Hofstede, G. (2000) *Cultures Consequences, Comparing Values, Behaviours, Institutions, and Organizations Across Nations*, 2nd edn, Sage Publications, Thousand Oaks, CA.

Hofstede, G. and Bond, M.H. (1988) 'The Confucius Connection: from Cultural Roots to Economic Growth', *Organizational Dynamics*, Vol. 16, No. 4, pp. 4–21.

Hollensen, S. (2001) *Global Marketing – A Market-Responsive Approach*, Prentice Hall, London.

Isackson, J. (1980) 'Differences in Cultural and Business Patterns between Australia and the United States', unpublished paper, San Francisco Institute for Management Development.

Keegan, W.J. and Green, M.S. (2000) *Global Marketing*, 2nd edn, Prentice Hall, Englewood Cliffs, NJ.

Keillor, B.D. and Hult, G.T.M. (1999) 'A Five Country Study of National Identity: Implications for International Marketing Research and Practice', *International Marketing Review*, Vol. 16, pp. 65–82.

Keillor, B.D., Hult, G.T.M., Erffmeyer, R.G. and Babakus, E. (1995) 'NATID: The Development and Application of a National Identity Measure for Use in International Marketing', *Journal of International Marketing*, Vol. 4, pp. 57–73.

Kelly, M. (1990) *The Milwaukee Journal*, 25 November, p. H5.

Kroeber, A.L. and Kluckholn, C. (1952) 'Culture: A Critical Review of Concepts and Definitions', Anthropological Paper, No. 4, Peabody Museum, Cambridge, MA.

Lee, J.A. (1966) 'Cultural Analysis in Overseas Operations', *Harvard Business Review*, March/April, pp. 106–114.

Maslow, A.H. (1964) 'A Theory of Human Motivation', in Levitt, H.J. and Pondy, L.R. (eds) *Readings in Managerial Psychology*, University of Chicago Press, Chicago, pp. 6–24.

Mead, R. (1990) *Cross-Cultural Management Communication*, John Wiley & Sons, Chichester, p. 151.

Morris, D. (1978) *Man Watching*, Triad/Granada, St Albans.

Park, H. (2000) 'A Cross-Cultural Analysis of Internet Connectivity', *Journal of Current Research in Global Business*, Fall, pp. 97–107.

Radeburgh, L.H. and Gray, S.J. (1993) *International Accounting and Multinational Enterprises*, 3rd edn, John Wiley & Sons Inc., p. 76.

Schutte, H. and Ciarlante, H. (1998) *Consumer Behaviour in Asia*, Macmillan Press, London, p. 93.

Trompenaars, F. and Hampden-Turner, C. (1997) *Riding the Waves of Culture: Understanding Cultural Diversity in Business*, 2nd edn, Nicholas Brealey Publishing, London.

Usunier, J-C. (1993) *International Marketing*, Prentice Hall, New York, p. 44.

Wall Street Journal (1994) 'Designer Apologises to Muslims', 21 January, p. A-7.

4

Avoiding the pitfalls of the international political and legal environment

Learning objectives

After reading this chapter, you should be able to:

- identify those aspects of the political-legal environment that affect a firm's international marketing;

- determine how the international political-legal environment impacts on each element of the marketing mix;

- outline which options are available to minimise political-legal risk;

- appreciate the way legal systems differ and the impact of these differences on the drawing up of contracts and the resolving of disputes; and

- identify the ways in which the impact of national laws might be minimised in the international environment.

The success of capitalism

The success of capitalism depends heavily on the political and legal landscape of the country. America's economic success and wealth is firmly based on what is considered market-based capitalism. This model of wealth creation is consistently cited as the superior way forward to generate the economics of growth needed for survival and growth in today's world.

The failure of Enron has caused many to reflect on the changes necessary to realign the system to function more in shareholders' interests. The most radical change suggested is to take responsibility for audits away from private accounting firms altogether and give it to the government. Another suggestion is mandatory rotation every four to five years to prevent individual auditors becoming too committed to their clients. The issues of accounting standards in some countries are too lax. These recent scandals have shown that all is not well with the governance of many big international companies. Companies need stronger non-executive directors, genuinely independent remuneration committees, more powerful internal auditors and a separation of the jobs of chairman and chief executive.

The success of market-based capitalism is much more likely in countries with a legal system based on English common law and with an independent judiciary. It does not seem to do as well in countries with a legal system based on European civil law. Common law is more flexible and quicker to change, provides greater investor protection and is less likely to accept state intervention.

Introduction

The political and legal risks faced in international markets are considerable. These risks are a major factor in deciding whether or not to enter a market and, if so, what form the entry should take so as to minimise risk. Although the international marketer may be plagued by government 'red tape', the investor is faced with a host of government laws and regulations which all increase the risk of doing business in the foreign country. In addition to the politics and laws of both the home and host countries, the international marketer must consider the global political and legal environment. This issue is explored further in Chapter 18. Political issues usually lead to laws and regulations, as a consequence of which political and legal issues in the international marketplace are often intertwined.

The national political environment is affected by a number of variables that form the context of all political activity. These include ideology, the economic system and the strength of nationalism. It is in the interests of international firms to continually monitor their activities in a market in relation to these variables because they contain the underlying forces that influence the degree of political risk. The major actor in the political arena in most countries is the national government.

The role of government in international marketing

Different types of national government

Knowledge of the various forms of government is useful in making an appraisal of the political environment for the firm. Forms of government are democracy, monarchy and dictatorship, as distinct from capitalism, communism and socialism which are economic systems characterised by varying degrees of market orientation (see Chapter 2). One can classify government as either open (e.g. parliamentary governments), or closed (e.g. absolutist regimes such as dictatorships).

Parliamentary governments

This form of government consults with citizens at intervals to ascertain their wishes and preferences. Policies are intended to reflect the desires of the majority and opportunity is provided for the population to take an active role in the formulation of these policies. Most industrialised nations can be classified as parliamentary democracies. Such forms of government can include monarchies provided they are constitutional such as in Great Britain or Thailand. The number of political parties in such governments may vary and some governments are made up of coalitions of parties rather than one party.

Absolutist governments

These dictate government policy without considering citizens' needs or opinions. Often these governments are to be found in newly independent countries undergoing some form of political transition. Absolute monarchs are comparatively rare, although dictatorships are not. Dictatorships need not involve one person but can involve a group such as the military in Myanmar.

Other governments

Most governments fall between these two extremes. Some monarchies and dictatorships have parliamentary elections (Saudi Arabia and South Korea); others hold elections but the results are suspect because of government involvement in voting fraud (the Philippines under Marcos and Nicaragua under Somoza); and others hold elections but ignore the results (Myanmar).

Thailand is a constitutional monarchy and elections mostly result in governments formed by a coalition of parties. In most ministries responsible for awarding government contracts such as communications, the usual practice is to have a minister and two deputy ministers. Each has responsibility for a specific area and each represents a different party in the coalition government. When bidding on a project involving the ministry, it is important for the businessperson to ascertain which minister has responsibility for the project. It is likely that this responsibility will be used to repay favours owed or indirectly to generate funds for the party.

Role of government in the economy

Government involvement in the economy presents commercial opportunities for firms where government undertakings are the purchasers. They can also provide targets for lobbying activity when governments are regulating access to the market. Further, governments can be solicited by the firm when government is facilitating foreign involvement in the market via investment incentives, free trade zones and the like.

Participator

An extreme form of involvement is the state trading company (STC) which is a common feature of the commercial environment in former communist countries. In almost all countries there are commercial activities undertaken by government, especially in areas related to transport, infrastructure, defence, health, education and public welfare. In some of these government will be the sole customer, for example water and sewerage, and in others it will be an important customer, for example airlines. Government ownership may preclude foreigners selling a competing product (e.g. the Thai Tobacco Monopoly), or owning an operation making a competing product. There is, however, a trend for governments to reduce their involvement in commercial undertakings, including those instrumentalities that deliver public services, via privatisation. Often this reduced involvement is driven by a need to sell off public sector enterprises in order to balance the budget or because of rising costs of public sector activities.

Soon after its emergency call to the International Monetary Fund in late July 1997, Thailand's government announced it would raise 100 million baht [€2.2 million], by privatising a host of enterprises including the Telephone Organisation of Thailand.

Source: *Business Review Weekly*, 6 October 1997, p. 26.

It is important for the businessperson to establish the degree of government participation in the area of interest in the international market. This is because selling to government is quite different from selling to the private sector. In addition, the pace of privatisation in the country should be considered because the government-controlled activity of today may be the privatised activity tomorrow.

Public servants in most countries, by comparison with employees in the private sector, have security of employment, are not financially accountable for their actions and tend to be remunerated (and promoted) on the basis of responsibility exercised rather than efficiency or savings achieved. These issues should be borne in mind when selling to public servants because they impact on what these individuals will consider to be appealing about the offer.

In dealing with government officials in international markets it is important to discover their real needs. Apart from macro interests, such as promoting economic development, expanding the tax base and providing national security, public servants are also likely to be concerned with how the deal will affect their ministry, the political party in power, their political patron and their own power and status.

Facilitator

Government can also operate as a facilitator to international business. Governments often attract new foreign investment and technology by providing a range of concessions such as tax holidays, duty-free import privileges, subsidised rent for factory sites, concessional loans or grants and discounted power and utility charges.

Regulator

Government regulatory activities are often tied in with government planning activities. It is not only former centrally planned economies that had five-year plans. Such plans exist in many developing countries and are the basis for economic development activities and funding, including aid. In many Asian countries, powerful government planning bodies exist such as Bappenas in Indonesia and the National Economic and Social Development Board in Thailand. International executives should be aware of and study these five-year plans because they indicate not only present priorities but the direction of likely future economic, welfare, industrial and infrastructure development. From these national plans come decisions as to how these priorities will be funded. Funding from within the country is usually by taxation. Some of the means of raising taxes impact on foreign firms, e.g. import duties, licensing fees and tax liabilities for foreign firms operating in the country. Governments also regulate in terms of setting mandatory standards and by imposing conditions for the repatriation of profits, dividends and royalties, as well as imposing rules covering foreign exchange and by setting exchange rates.

There are several other areas where the government acts as a regulator, which impact on firms doing business in international markets.

- Governments impose a variety of taxes on business in the domestic market. Many of these are hidden in the prices firms pay for their inputs. They all have the effect of raising costs of products and hence they impact on the competitive position of the product unless government refunds these taxes when the goods are exported. Payroll tax, road and haulage taxes, inspection fees, duty on imported components are just a few of these taxes.

- Governments impose embargoes on dealing with certain other countries. Sometimes these are applied by most countries and approved by the United Nations, such as the embargo on Iraq that commenced in 1990. In other cases these are imposed by one country alone such as the US embargo on dealing with Cuba. Embargoes distort the free flow of trade in goods, services and ideas for political rather than for economic reasons. When embargoes are imposed, they hurt not only the receiving country but often the firms doing business with that country. Embargoes imposed by governments, especially if directed by one country against another rather than unilaterally, do not usually succeed. This is because evasion is possible using devices such as countertrade or dealing through intermediaries based in countries that do not subscribe to the embargo.

    When President Clinton lifted the US embargo on Vietnam on 4 February 1994, it was estimated that the move would create about US$3.6 billion of business for US firms. Other countries such as France and Japan were likely to be disadvantaged by the US move. This is because they had for a number of years supplied Vietnam with goods that Vietnam might otherwise have sourced from the US and established joint ventures in Vietnam whose international partners might otherwise have been US companies.

- Boycotts are another form of restriction on trade and have come into prominence with conflicts in the Middle East. Arab nations have developed a blacklist of companies that trade with Israel. The US in turn has created a series of measures to prevent US firms complying with the Arab boycott. Boycotts can put firms in a difficult position if they are already trading with Israel on the one hand or substantially owned by US interests on the other. This issue can become very complex.

- Governments impose export control measures that are designed to deny or delay the acquisition of strategically important goods by current or potential enemies. In some cases, exports are controlled by legislation, as with the US Trading with the Enemy Act or the Munitions Control Act.

- Governments impose controls on imports. Often such controls are imposed for balance of payments reasons. Imports may also be banned in order to foster the development of domestic industries. Not only does this affect the exporter but, if the firm is manufacturing in the foreign country imposing the controls, the efficiency of that operation is threatened. This is because the import controls deny the firm access to the cheapest or best quality sources of inputs. A final reason for import controls is that certain goods are considered dangerous or environmentally unsuitable (such as toxic waste), regarded as a health threat (such as tobacco

4.1 International highlight

One country, two systems: getting business started in China

State-run businesses and private enterprise run side by side in China. Behind this, China is still a state-controlled economy supervised by powerful ministries in Beijing. The first step for any firm going to China is to find out which government agencies are in charge of its industry. Foreign investment projects need government approval – local, provincial and central. Without support from the right government authorities, even very attractive projects fail. This experience is not unusual for joint ventures in China. The political hurdles take time, endurance, patience and persistence for any business to make progress in this huge potential market.

products), or viewed as being unacceptable on religious grounds. Alcoholic drinks in many Middle East countries, such as Libya and Saudi Arabia, are forbidden because of religious beliefs.

● Joint ventures come under particular scrutiny in countries such as China. Since the first joint ventures in the early 1980s in China, the political process has played a decisive role in their success. Political appointees to the boards of companies such as Hewlett-Packard, one of the very early foreign companies in China, have acted as an important link to the political process. While this relaxed somewhat in the late 1990s, international business executives need to be aware of these factors and the complex web of politics and government networks before embarking on investment activities. International Highlight 4.1 gives further credence to the need for a long-term view when it comes to China.

Political approaches in international marketing

As the marketing concept evolved in the US, it tends to be practised most rigorously in countries that are close in ideological terms to that country. Although marketing has no ideology of its own, the way marketing functions are performed varies according to the ideological environment. Marketing managers are a product of their own countries and the underlying ideologies in them. Therefore marketing can operate effectively in countries that are ideologically different. This is apparent in the former centrally planned economies that are rapidly adopting a market orientation.

One approach that impacts on marketing is that of nationalism. A basic and pervasive force, nationalism is present to a degree in all countries. For many internationalising firms, nationalism can be a source of problems. Where nationalism is high, foreign firms tend to be regarded with suspicion and their products are discriminated against. In such circumstances, foreign firms are targeted for rigorous scrutiny and control and at worst the assets of the foreign firm can be expropriated.

Often nationalist pressure builds up when people consider a foreign government is interfering in the affairs of their own country. The US has often caused such manifestations of nationalism when it has applied pressure on other countries to liberalise their import regime for products, especially in the agricultural sector. Examples include pressure on Japan to liberalise rice imports and on the European Union to reduce grain and dairy subsidies.

Political stability and risk

This is a key concern for the international marketer. Political stability does not mean an absence of change as all markets are continually changing. Rather, political stability means that change should be gradual and non-violent. From a marketing perspective, the change should be such that it has a minimum adverse effect on business activities in the country. In this connection, it is necessary to be cautious of labels applied to political change. To assess political stability in a target international market, the firm should be aware of indicators of political instability. These indicators include:

- the degree of social unrest that is caused by underlying conditions, such as economic hardship, internal dissension, and racial, religious and ideological differences;
- the frequency of changes in the regime because these can mean changes in the attitude towards business if the new body in power has a different socioeconomic approach or a different degree of nationalism;
- the extent to which the country is divided culturally and/or ethnically as political borders often contain separate national groups (as in the former Yugoslavia);
- religious division, such as that witnessed in India and Lebanon; and
- linguistic diversity such as Tamil and Singhalese in Sri Lanka.

Following the attack of 11 September 2001 on the World Trade Centre, the risk status of many countries has been reassessed. This is not because risks have diminished, but because risks elsewhere have become greater, with an increase of 30% in the number of countries now categorised as 'high risk' or 'extremely high risk'.

Sources of political instability

Political sovereignty

Political sovereignty is to do with a nation's desire to exert control over foreign-owned enterprises operating within its boundaries. The rules evolve and are predictable. Many less developed countries impose restrictions on foreign business in order to protect their political independence from foreign economic domination and also the position of local firms in the domestic market. A common form of protection is an increase in taxes payable by foreign corporations. Political sovereignty is mostly encountered in dealings with developing nations.

Political conflict

Political conflict can be categorised as turmoil, internal war and conspiracy. Turmoil is generally an unanticipated upheaval on a major scale against a regime such as the overthrow of the Shah of Iran. Internal war is organised violence on a large scale against a government such as that which continues in Sudan and Afghanistan. Conspiracy is an instant planned act of violence against those in power, such as the assassination of Egypt's President Sadat. Political change does not always lead to a less favourable business climate in the long term although the climate may be adversely affected during the period of conflict. This is especially the case if the new government is more favourably disposed towards foreign enterprise than the previous one. This happened when Suharto replaced Soekarno as president in Indonesia. In addition, political conflict does not always lead to political risk. Therefore businesspeople should analyse each occurrence of political conflict and assess whether it is likely to have an impact on their current or proposed business activities in the selected country. This appraisal may cause the firm to change its mode of involvement in the market, for example from a greenfields investment to licensing, rather than totally withdrawing from that market. Political conflict can have direct effects on the foreign firm, such as damage to property, strikes and/or kidnapping of expatriate executives. It can also have indirect effects, such as shortage of inputs, removal of staff to serve in the military and new controls on the firm's operations.

Political intervention

Political intervention is when decisions by government(s) in the host country force the foreign firm to change its strategies, policies or operations. Usually this involves governments intervening in the operation of the firm to further their own interests. In many countries, power is exerted by a number of vested interests, many of which see foreign investment as a tempting target. The situation is particularly evident in cases where the foreign plant is located in a regional area where the local government has a degree of autonomy and imposes its own regulations on the firm in addition to those imposed by the central government. Sometimes such intervention can take the form of dictating membership of the board of the joint venture. It can involve making purchases from specified sources mandatory, charging special local taxes and insisting on the right to vet employees so that jobs in the firm can be used to pay off political debts or relationship obligations. Intervention can be more extreme and involve either expropriation or domestication.

- *Expropriation* is the official seizure of a foreigner's property on the excuse that the property seized is to be used in the public interest. This is recognised in international law as a right of a sovereign state provided the foreign party is given adequate compensation. Within expropriation, there are several distinct forms. Nationalisation refers to the transfer of a total industry to public control, regardless of nationality of ownership. Confiscation is expropriation without compensation. In recent times the incidence of expropriation has reduced because, with the reduction in aid, less developed countries need to attract technology to create an industrial base for survival, and expropriation discourages foreign investment (which is the chief source of technology transfer).
- *Domestication* is a process by which controls and restrictions placed on the international firms gradually reduce the influence of the foreign firm in the operation of the company. These conditions may have been spelled out as part of the original

approval or may have since been instituted by government fiat. Domestication is less radical than expropriation because it allows the foreign party to continue to operate in the country. It takes several forms. It can include gradual transfer of ownership to nationals and promotion of a large number of employees of the country to high levels of management as well as ensuring more decision making power vested in national employees. It also may include products being manufactured locally as opposed to being imported or assembled, and the introduction of specific export regulations which restrict the export activities of the foreign partner.

Nature of political risk

Political risk varies considerably from country to country. Countries that have a track record of stability and consistency are perceived to be lower in political risk than those that do not. Taking the previous discussion into account, there are four main types of political risk:

- *general instability risk*, which is risk due to internal threats such as revolution, or external threats to the government such as invasion;
- *ownership risk*, which is risk to property and the lives of the expatriate employees;
- *operating risk*, which is interference in the ongoing operations of the international company;
- *transfer risk*, which occurs when the firm is prevented from moving funds between countries or back home, e.g. repatriation of profits, capital and dividends.

According to Hadjikhani and Hakansson (1996):

Sometimes political risk can arise from the actions of a fellow national company. As an example, when Bofors of Sweden was accused of unethical involvement with Prime Minister Rajiv Gandhi and his Congress Party, other Swedish firms operating in India were affected to differing degrees.

Assessment

Because political risk is so pervasive, especially in developing countries, its assessment is increasingly important. Political risk assessment is necessary to identify the countries of today which may become the Irans or Iraqs of tomorrow, so that firms can protect themselves by minimising their exposure; it may reveal countries which are currently politically unstable; it can identify those countries which were considered a bad risk in the past but which are now less risky; finally it can help identify those countries that, although politically risky at present, are not so risky as to be excluded from consideration. These countries have a potential for risk that needs to be taken into account when planning entry strategy and involvement.

Jain (1996) offers a number of methods for determining political risk:

1 *The grand tour.* An executive team visits the country in which investment is being considered following the conduct of market research. A first-hand appraisal involving meetings with government officials and local business will yield information as to the likely level of political risk. This can be misleading however, because those contacted usually represent the establishment and not the sources of future political risk.

2 *The old hand.* This method employs an expert on the country as a consultant. Usually such people are educators, former diplomats or trade commissioners, local political figures or business identities. Not only will the capability and experience of the consultant be a determinant of the accuracy of the resulting report, but if the person is not a national, the quality will be affected by how recent is the consultant's experience of the country. If, on the other hand, the consultant is a national, the quality of the report may be influenced by the breadth of the consultant's network of local contacts.

3 *The Delphi technique.* This technique involves asking a group of experts on the country to share their opinions independently. Opinions are scored on various aspects of potential political risk. The experts are then shown the resulting score and given the opportunity to modify their opinion on each aspect. This process may be repeated several times and a decision made on the basis of the final round.

There are a number of political risk assessment indices published by bodies such as the Economist Intelligence Unit, which are updated at regular intervals. Frost and Sullivan (1985), using a worldwide panel of experts, compiles 18-month forecasts of regime stability, restrictions on international business activity, and controls on trade and economic policy for 85 countries. These forecasts develop general measures of risk not related to the specific situation of the firm.

A number of frameworks have also been developed to assist firms to make their own assessment of political risk. Douglas and Craig (1983) have a framework consisting of four dimensions of political risk – domestic stability such as riots and assassinations; foreign conflict including military action and diplomatic expulsions; economic climate such as inflation level; external debt; GNP and its distribution; and finally, political climate.

Any appraisal of a firm's exposure to political risk in a foreign country should at least cover three factors – product, external and company:

1 *Product-related factors.* These include an assessment of whether the product is a likely topic of political debate in terms of a number of questions:
   (a) What is the impact of adequate supply on the country's security or welfare?
   (b) Is the product a critical input for other industries?
   (c) Is the product socially or politically sensitive, as with food and drugs?
   (d) Does the product have national defence significance as with uranium?

2 *External factors.* These include the following considerations:
   (a) the state of relations between your government and the government of the other country;
   (b) the size of the international firm, because the larger it is the more threatening it may appear to be;
   (c) the extent to which the firm has visibility as a foreign business – the larger its visibility the greater its vulnerability.

3 *Company factors.* These factors include:
   (a) the general reputation of the firm as a good corporate citizen;
   (b) the extent of past contributions by the firm to the welfare and development of the host country;
   (c) the extent to which operations in the country have been localised.

There are a number of published political risk guides that assess various countries in terms of risk factors such as frustration of contracts, unfair calling of performance bonds and confiscation of foreign assets. The rate to cover the risk is given for each of these factors and in the case of contract frustration, information is often provided as to the waiting period before the contract is deemed to have been frustrated.

A preliminary indication of assessed political risk attributed to a country can be obtained from the LIBOR (London Interbank Offered Rate). This is the interest rate charged for loans between banks. Borrowers from a country with a high risk of default must expect to pay a high premium. The premium is a reasonable indication of risk since it reflects a lender's assessment of a country in terms of its debt level and payment history.

Managing the international political environment

A company involved in dealing with internationalisation can take a number of measures to minimise potential political problems.

Company behaviour

The firm can adopt a deliberate policy of political neutrality and convey the impression that its interests in the country are solely economic. Companies should also be conscious as to which political labels are acceptable and which are not because use of the wrong label can denote political sympathy for a particular group.

Companies should ensure that they combine investment projects with civic projects. If the firm has its manufacturing operation in a town, it should examine ways of becoming a major benefactor in that town by supporting education, health and community projects that will benefit its local workforce. Contributions to local infrastructure development are likely to benefit not only the community but also the company.

If the policies of the country could cause offence in either the domestic market or in other markets with which the company is involved, it may be necessary for the firm to wholly or partially disengage itself from a country. This is especially the case if that country is the target of sanctions as was the case with South Africa during the apartheid regime.

Another risk minimisation activity includes lobbying by the firm to influence political decisions. In the public arena publicity to focus on the benefits the firm's operation is bringing to the country can be a useful risk minimisation strategy. Finally, just as embassies monitor what the political opposition in a country is doing, so foreign firms should also be aware of the likely impact on their operations of the policies espoused by those who might form alternative governments. Such monitoring is likely to reduce surprises from political upheavals in the country.

Above all, firms should display political sensitivity in their dealings involving foreign countries. This applies both to the use of country names (see International Highlight 4.2) and to names used for geographical features.

4.2 International highlight

China punishes firm over its use of the term 'Taiwan'

China has threatened to punish Japan's Matsushita Communications Industrial Co. for making mobile phones that refer to Taiwan as a country. Its Panasonic brand of mobile phones includes the Republic of China in an electronic list of country codes. The Republic of China is the Taiwan government's designation for the island, a name Beijing rejects because it regards Taiwan as its own territory, although the two have been divided for more than five decades following civil war. A spokesman for China's Ministry of Information Industry said that Matsushita may have to cease assembly of mobile phones at its Chinese joint venture. The impending ban is likely to cover all five models of mobile phones the firm makes in China. Matsushita's Beijing operation, which has the capacity to make two million mobile phones a year, accounts for a fraction of the company's global output. However, getting on China's bad side helped drive down the price of Matsushita's shares on the Tokyo stock exchange by 7.9%.

Source: Adapted from *Wall Street Journal* (2001), Europe, 7–8 September, p. 7.

Both Iran and Iraq lay claim to the gulf of water that separates them. While the Iranians refer to it as the Persian Gulf (the name used by the United Nations), the Iraqis refer to it as the Arabian Gulf. In dealing with either country, using an inappropriate term on official documents, such as export labels or contracts, can cause serious difficulties for the business involved as well as for the firm's local partners or representatives.

In a similar fashion, it is unwise to categorise people who are located adjacent to each other in the same way. Despite geographical proximity and some cultural similarity, Arabs and Persians are completely separate peoples and resent being misidentified or grouped together. Arabs are of Semitic background and are originally from the Arabian peninsula and the Levant. Their language belongs to the same family as Aramaic and Hebrew. Persians are ethnically Caucasian and their language, Farsi, is of Indo-European origin.

Source: Adapted from DFAT (2000), p. 53.

Home government actions

Actions by the government or its representatives towards a foreign country can both enhance and retard the position of the firm in that country. Giving aid to countries, providing financial rescue packages, or according diplomatic recognition are examples of government actions that can enhance commercial prospects and reduce the likelihood of political problems for companies attempting to internationalise.

Criticising the leaders of countries can cause problems for firms. Problems can also be caused by the failure of government to control criticism in the media of actions by other countries. This difficulty is compounded when the media involved is owned by the government. Such nations find it hard to believe that this criticism does not reflect the views of the government.

Contribution to the host country

Firms that set out to be good corporate citizens of the host country are more likely to evade the consequences of political upheaval and minimise potential political risk. Good corporate citizens stimulate the local economy by linking their commercial activities to the host nation's economic interests and planned developments – buying local products whenever possible, forming alliances or joint ventures with local firms, establishing training programmes for local employees and demonstrably upgrading technology levels. Using the operation to generate exports, recruiting locals to occupy senior management positions and converting the firm from a private to a public company by listing on the local stock exchange, are additional ways of minimising political risk.

Localisation of operations

The greater the local ownership of an operation, the less likely it will be subject to political risk. Pressure to indigenise operations can come not only from political upheaval but also from established government changing its foreign investment policy, as happened in India in 1973. When a country for political reasons demands that foreign firms reduce their ownership and surrender equity to local interests, the firm has to decide on the degree of its disengagement. In their article 'Foreign Ownership: When Hosts Change the Rules', Encarnation and Vachani (1985) offer four alternative courses of action for the company:

- leave the country altogether (like IBM in India);
- totally indigenise your operations so it becomes a local company (like Colgate-Palmolive in India);
- negotiate an arrangement under the new law (like Ciba-Geigy in India);
- take pre-emptive action in advance of announced changes. Phased indigenisation is one such action and may enable the firm to benefit from a range of investment incentives. Another is to generate sizeable exports to step up the host government's dependency on the operation.

Globalisation

Firms that set up international operations may have operations in other countries and aspire to rationalise their operations globally. This may cause political problems because there can be a divergence between their maximising returns to their shareholders on the one hand and being a good corporate citizen of the countries in which they are operating on the other. Often these conflicts in interest cause problems in the company's relationship with the government of the host country. One frequent example of this is in the area of taxation. In order to minimise taxation liability on a global basis, firms structure international operations so that via transfer pricing the majority of profits are brought to account in the lowest tax regime countries in which the firm operates. This results in the host country not receiving the full tax revenue on the real profits earned as a result of activities undertaken within its boundaries.

Other problems arise when the firm wishes to reduce costs by standardising its product, pricing, promotion and distribution strategies on a global basis. This can create political problems, e.g. when the standardisation contravenes regulations in the host country. The issue has become more complicated with the global spread of communication through global or regional media and the Internet, because now national governments are less able to control messages received within their national borders.

Political risk insurance

In addition to actions to reduce risk and to avoid risk, firms can shift risk by insuring against it. The premiums for political risk will vary according to: (a) the country concerned; and (b) whether the company insures all its international transactions as opposed to only the risky ones. A range of politically induced risks can be insured against, including currency inconvertibility, expropriation of assets, and loss/damage due to war, revolution or insurrection.

Marketing implications – political

The international marketer should carefully examine the political climate in the international market before making a commitment to that country because the political situation may not be compatible with profitable business. Political sovereignty, desire by the government to assert its authority, and internal or external political conflict all threaten profitable business. The history of intervention by the governments of the country in foreign business activities should be studied, as should the form of such intervention. An analysis of political risk should be undertaken which covers the form of government, its stability, competence in economic management, frequency of changes in policy towards foreign investment and the nature of the relationship between the government and its people. An indication of general country risk should be obtained from a risk monitoring agency and then risk assessment techniques applied to cater for the individual circumstances of the firm in the specific international market.

Internet infusion

While the Internet empowers customers, it enables sellers to have unfettered access to information related to customers' preferences and buying profiles. This raises the issue of the right to privacy of citizens of a country and the ability of government to control its citizens and control what happens economically within its borders. The approach to protection of privacy versus commercialisation of data about people varies from country to country. Whereas, in general, Americans see privacy as a commodity and the issue one of control over property rights, Europeans tend to view privacy as an inalienable human right that should not be traded in the marketplace.

The Internet can threaten national sovereignty and political stability by providing a vehicle for minority groups within a national boundary to advance the cause of self-determination. With the advent of the Internet, the national government no longer has control over the media or the content of messages disseminated within its borders. Related to this is the issue of free speech. Whereas in the marketplace, governments have the power to regulate forms of speech, the content of which is regarded as reprehensible or offensive to national wellbeing, the new information infrastructure diminishes this control because censorship of the Internet has not proved possible to date. The Internet also makes it more difficult for governments to regulate national commerce in the interests of the economic wellbeing and safety of its citizens. How can governments license service providers such as doctors and lawyers who practise globally over the Internet?

Governments also collect taxes and duties and control capital flows into and out of their geographical jurisdiction. The Internet has increased the level of interference of external parties in these areas and facilitated evasion of the economic rents governments levy on external entities and transnational corporations in the national interest. Governments face a problem in regulating and levying taxes on Internet transactions because these might adversely impact on national competitiveness due to the effects on knowledge diffusion, investment flows and cost/price structures of industries compared to other nations. Whereas in the international marketplace, issues are addressed by public choice, with a focus on how firms in host countries might raise protectionist barriers against foreign firms, in marketspace, local firms will seek from government regulations that will give them advantages over other countries in attracting Internet companies. The emphasis shifts from protecting what you have to attracting what you have not.

The legal environment

International trade involves two or more countries and usually two or more legal systems. Hence the legal complexities are greater with international trade than they are with domestic trade. The international business executive does not need to be aware of the detail of the law as it applies in each international market. Rather the executive needs to be sensitive to the broad principles of law as it applies to doing business abroad and the way the law varies in implementation between different countries. Such sensitivity will alert the executive to legal pitfalls and to when to seek legal advice if entering into transactions or if faced with specific issues.

It is important to appreciate that there is no single uniform commercial law which governs international business transactions. Although the lack of such law and the need for it has been commented upon in international forums, nothing of importance has resulted. As a consequence, marketers have to operate under different legal systems whenever they internationalise. The legal environment for international business consists primarily of the laws and courts of the many nations in the world. These national systems vary in philosophy and practice, and each nation maintains a court system that is independent of those in every other nation. The differences between legal systems and the laws in various countries impact on the practice of international marketing in many ways.

4.3 International highlight

Gastronomic winds of change

The advocate-general in the European Court of Justice (2002) dealt a blow to Italian producers in their legal battle to show Parma ham sliced in Britain is no longer Parma ham. Mr Siegbert Alber found that the Asda supermarket chain could continue to market Parma ham sliced and packaged in Britain despite objections from the consortium of ham producers in the Italian city of Parma. The consortium had argued that slicing outside the area compromised the traditional production methods guaranteed by the Parma ham label. Mr Alber also rejected a similar argument that Italy's Grana Padano cheese could no longer be marketed under the label if grated outside the Po Valley. Findings by the advocate-general are not binding on the Court of Justice, but their opinions are adopted in most countries.

The case refers to EU laws that protect specialist foodstuffs by stating that only the goods produced in a particular region using defined methods can be marketed under traditional names. Hundreds of products, from Germany's Dortmunder beer to Greece's Kalamata olives, are covered by the rules. Parma ham producers launched court action in 1997 against Hygrade Foods, which buys smoked ham from Parma but slices and packages it in Britain. After a legal process that reached the House of Lords, the case was passed on to the European Court. French courts did the same to a complaint filed by two French companies that import Italian cheese. Mr Aber said a 1996 EU rule should be changed to make clear the slicing and grating did not have to take place in the region of production.

Differing legal systems and jurisdictions

In the global economy, there are a variety of legal systems. The two most common are common law and civil law. Therefore the international marketer must be aware of both the legal system which operates in the international market and the specific laws impinging on business activities and marketing practice.

Legal systems

Common law

This operates in the United Kingdom, Canada, the US and many of the former colonies and dominions of the United Kingdom. It is based on tradition, past practices, legal precedent and interpretation via court decision. The interpretation of what the law means on a specific subject is influenced by previous decisions of the courts as well by usage and custom. If there is no precedent, common law requires the court to make a decision that in effect creates a new law. Under common law, commercial disputes are subject to laws that apply to all matters, regardless of whether civil or commercial. This is because under common law, there is no specific recognition of commercial problems as such.

Code law

Code law derives from Roman law and is found in most countries where common law is not used. It is based on an all-inclusive system of written rules (codes) of law. The legal system is generally divided into three separate codes – civil, commercial and criminal. Because of its 'catch-all' provisions, code law is considered to be complete and caters for most contingencies. As an example, the commercial code governing contracts is made inclusive via a clause to the effect that 'a person performing a contract shall do so in conformity with good faith as determined by custom and good morals'. Under code law, the commercial code is given precedence over other codes when matters of business are involved. With code law, the courts adopt precedents to fit the case thereby allowing marketers a better idea of the judgement likely to be rendered.

Islamic law

Islamic law is based on the Koran and is applied by Islamic countries in varying degrees. It encompasses religious duties and obligations and also the secular aspect of law, especially relating to human acts. It defines a complete system of social and economic behaviour with the overriding objective of social justice. It is often applied in conjunction with code or common law.

Other legal codes

Included in this group are tribal or indigenous laws. Rarely are these laws applied by themselves but are usually applied in conjunction with the prevailing common or civil code of law.

The reality is that the legal system in most countries is a blend of different legal systems. Even in common law countries there are examples of code law such as the Uniform Commercial Code in the US. In Sri Lanka, the legal system is a blend of indigenous and common law. The following is a comparison of the two most common systems:

- *Industrial property rights*: under common law, ownership is established by use, whereas under code law, ownership is determined by registration.

- *Performance of contract*: under common law, impossibility of performance does not excuse compliance with contract provisions unless caused by 'an act of God'. Under code law, impossibility of performance is an acceptable excuse whether due to the elements, natural causes or unfavourable human acts.

- *Interpretation of contract*: operating under common law, the contract is a binding obligation; under code law, the contract is a piece of paper that operates as a memorandum of an understanding reached between buyer and seller.

International law

International law grows out of the agreement of two or more nations and implies a desire to lessen differences in the way countries treat legal problems. Generally, international law minimises the range of differences between national laws, e.g. international patent agreements. Traditionally, international law has only been concerned with relations between nations with a principal focus on political and military issues. However, the coverage in recent years has become much broader and now can include international trade and investment, taxation, labour relations, intellectual property and the environment. Whereas only nations used to be recognised as subjects for international law, today international organisations and their agencies are also covered. International law is reflected in the determinations of multilateral bodies such as the World Trade Organisation and the United Nations. Probably the most important attempt to promote harmonisation of international trade law was the establishment of the United Nations Commission on International Trade Law (UNICITRAL). It has produced a set of rules governing arbitration (1976); a convention on the carriage of goods by sea (1987); a convention on contracts for the international sale of goods (1980); and a model law on international commercial arbitration (1985). Increasingly, the determinations of regional bodies such as ASEAN have led to the creation of laws applied on a regional basis. Within the European Union, for example, one of the essential requirements for integration has been the harmonisation of laws of member states affecting international business. Once such harmonisation is achieved, then one common law is applied to the member states.

With both multilateral and regional bodies, after agreement is reached on issues that are to be binding upon their members, it is up to individual national governments to legislate the issue into their domestic law. For this reason, even when agreement is reached on matters to be covered by international law, implementation will vary widely between signatories. As a consequence, there is no such thing as international law for business activities, only the application of domestic law to international disputes. The need for a larger body of international law is likely to grow due to increasing problems in the area of protection of intellectual property and the information revolution rendering international boundaries of decreasing relevance.

Legal jurisdiction

A common legal problem in international business is determining which country's laws apply in the event of a dispute. This is decided according to whether the country is nominated in the jurisdictional clause in the contract, where the contract was entered into, or where the provisions of the contract are to be carried out. As the last two can differ, it is important to have a specific jurisdictional clause included in the contract so as to avoid the problem of determining jurisdiction after a dispute has arisen.

Where a jurisdiction is nominated, the law of that jurisdiction is likely to apply regardless of where the suit is filed. Where no jurisdiction is nominated, then the suit is likely to be heard in either the country where the contract was entered into or the country where the provisions of the contract are to be carried out. This can become the subject of dispute.

Jurisdiction can be further complicated when different sets of laws are alleged to apply, for example where:

- the practice of international law conflicts with national law as with the law of Japan;
- one nation endeavours to impose its laws on another, e.g. when the US attempts to enforce its anti-trust legislation extraterritorially;
- businesspeople operating in a foreign country are required to conform to the laws of their country of citizenship. For example there have been many US attempts to enforce the Foreign Corrupt Practices Act in matters of bribery.

Due to the above, when operating internationally, a businessperson can at the one time be subject to two or more sets of law, depending on the number of countries involved. The United States argues that where foreign transactions have a substantial effect on US commerce, they are subject to US law regardless of where they take place. Even within a foreign country, the businessperson may be subject to federal, state and municipal laws and regulations. The degree to which these overlap is often a function of development of law within the country and the extent to which it can be enforced. For instance, in some developing countries the central government has only token control over some regional areas within the national boundaries.

Law and the international marketing mix

The law as it applies to commercial activities varies between countries even when the countries operate under the same legal system. This situation complicates the creation of a common marketing plan for implementation in several countries at the same time. The laws governing each element of the marketing mix vary between countries.

Product

Both the physical and chemical aspects of a product are affected by laws seeking to protect consumers. Such laws may prescribe standards for purity, safety and performance. It is an offence to use lead-based paint on children's toys in some countries. Where countries have laws covering the same issue, the standards to which the product must conform can vary. Because nations differ in rigorousness or even the existence of standards, it is often necessary for a country to impose quarantine controls or ban products from certain countries of origin. There can also be instances where the regulations and laws applying to imports have been imposed more to protect the domestic industry than the health and safety of its citizens.

Laws also apply to packaging and may specify the type of outer packaging material and the nature of the container. Labelling regulations differ markedly between countries and even within a country. Labelling requirements may decree that the ingredients be specified, the packing or expiry date be shown, the volume of the contents be in metric or imperial measure; and the name and address of the manufacturer/and or importer be shown. Even the size of type for each piece of information is often prescribed.

Price

The free market system does not operate in many countries and national health laws and government price controls can have a significant impact on the prices that may be charged in the international market. Generally, price controls are motivated by a desire to protect consumers' interests or control inflation. Other laws relating to pricing may be motivated by a desire to ensure price competition in the market. These laws cover areas such as retail price maintenance, action to discriminate against competitors, limitations of licensing and franchising agreements, and collusive action in setting prices, whether directly or indirectly via mechanisms such as discriminatory rebates. In some countries, the prices of essential commodities are controlled, as are some non-essential items.

In Libya the price of television sets (all of which are imported) was subsidised by the government, as television was the main vehicle for the regime to convey its views to the people. A large percentage of viewing time was devoted to the activities of the government and Islamic matters.

Other laws that impact on pricing include those relating to dumping (selling goods below current domestic value in the country of origin) and transfer pricing (under-valuing the price of product exported from a foreign operation to another division of the firm so as to avoid/minimise tax payable in the country of manufacture). Also in this category are laws that relate to the size of the profit margin included in the price. Price is also affected by taxes such as sales tax, value added tax, import tax and port tax.

Distribution

There are laws in most countries covering physical distribution of products. These relate to shipping and to rights of carriage by air and sea. Regulation of airline services operates in the international airline industry and various liabilities for loss and damage to cargo by air or sea apply. Channel activities are also subject to different laws from country to country and the techniques permitted in one country are often prohibited in another, e.g. door-to-door selling is not permitted in France. In many former centrally planned economies, a foreign firm must use the state-owned national import/export company for the product category. This is especially relevant for firms doing business in South-East Asia where regulations in some countries, such as Indonesia, prescribe that the agency firm must be local rather than European or Chinese. Finally, many countries have regulations regarding the conditions under which a foreign firm might terminate a local agency arrangement.

Promotion

Promotion is a highly regulated element of the marketing mix in many countries. Most nations try to protect their members against deceptive, misleading or fraudulent marketing practices. Societies also try to regulate advertising in terms of propriety and taste. For example, nudity in advertising is relatively common in many countries, whereas it is illegal in Saudi Arabia and India. Some of the more frequent areas of regulation are:

- *Trade descriptions.* Legislation in this area seeks to bar statements which are deceptive or quotations from testimonials which are not wholly factual.
- *Prohibitions on advertising certain products.* Typical products are contraceptives, tobacco products, alcohol and drugs. In some countries, the prohibition is total; in others, qualifying statements are mandatory (e.g. the message on cigarette packets that cigarette smoking kills).
- *Prohibitions on using certain words and expressions.* Some words or expressions that might be misinterpreted by the consumer are prohibited.
- *Content and style of advertisement.* The degree of permissible advertising puffery and the use of comparatives and superlatives in describing products and offers varies between countries.
- *Other promotional elements.* These are subject to different laws in various countries and include the use of premiums (cash off or cash-back offers), contests, vending machines and catalogue sales.

Extraterritorial application of law

Marketing mix variables can be affected by extraterritorial application of law. This occurs when one country endeavours to apply its national law outside its boundaries. This can mean that international operations or subsidiaries are subject to the law of the home country as well as that of the host country. This can upset the host country that views this as a violation of its sovereignty. Examples occur when subsidiaries are prevented from trading with a country because of an embargo imposed by the home government, when the provisions of the home government's anti-corruption legislation is enforced on the subsidiary, or when the home country's anti-trust legislation is applied to the international operation. The US becomes involved in many international trade disputes because of its insistence on extraterritorial application of its laws.

The impact of law on international operations

Three additional areas in which the firm faces problems due to the application of different laws between countries are in relation to the environment, human resources and intellectual property. All these issues influence the operating of an office or a manufacturing concern in the foreign country, although legal issues relating to intellectual property can also affect firms merely exporting to the foreign market.

Environment

Environmental consciousness is an increasing focus of attention, both within countries and in multilateral forums. Therefore, not only are there laws in individual countries relating to environmental issues, but there is an increasing prospect of a body of international law on this subject. Accelerating this process is the growing consciousness that environmental problems cross national boundaries, as evidenced by the floods in Europe in 2002 and the forest fires in Indonesia and Malaysia in 1997 that caused substantial health problems in neighbouring countries such as Thailand and the Philippines. Global conferences on the environment are now almost an annual event and some countries are facing an ethical dilemma. Do countries accept internationally agreed targets for aspects such as greenhouse gas emissions knowing that there is no possibility of their reaching these targets, or do they, like the US and Australia in 2002, refuse to agree to the targets and incur strident criticism from the international community?

Environmental laws relate to packaging and include material used, recycling and extent to which packaging is wasteful of resources. Visual pollution such as advertising billboards is also a problem. Environmental laws also govern noise pollution and the requirement to indicate the level of energy consumption. In Germany, green marketing legislation is increasingly requiring the manufacturer to accept legal responsibility for the collection and recycling of packaging materials associated with the product. The European Union has now issued a global packaging directive to its members (which is less stringent than the German requirement).

Human resources

When operating in the international market, the firm will be involved in employing locals. This will mean conforming to the labour laws of the international country and accepting employment conditions different from those that operate in the domestic market. In addition, the firm will be involved in abiding by local laws regarding the employment of expatriate staff, the conditions under which they can enter the country and the length of time they can remain. Also, the firm will have to conform to laws and expectations for training locals to replace expatriate managers as required by the country's investment legislation. A final issue results from the fact that in many foreign countries, such as Saudi Arabia, there is a dearth of unskilled local labour. This then requires the employment of guest workers who are usually covered by employment laws that are different from those applying to nationals of the country.

> *Lack of sensitivity to this issue can be very costly as Mitsubishi found out when its US subsidiary was forced to pay €33 million in compensation to 289 female employees because its Japanese managers took no action to stop sexual harassment on the shop floor of its US plant. Mitsubishi tolerated practices at its US plant which were acceptable in Japan but were not acceptable in the US. In addition, the company was reluctant to interfere with supervisor–employee relations in another country. After vehemently protesting the charges, the company then adopted a more conciliatory tone, admitting to problems involving sexual harassment that required correction.*

Intellectual property protection

The ability to create and manage knowledge assets is a source of competitive advantage for firms in industrialised nations. The protection of such knowledge assets in the form of intellectual property through either withholding it from the public domain or securing the rights to its use is a very important issue in international marketing. The international protection of patents, copyright, trademarks, design, trade secrets and plant variety rights is inadequate and has recently attracted increased attention because of piracy of computer software. Often the costs of registration in a country may out-weigh the benefits, especially if this is a preventative measure designed to forestall future competition. Even if registration is proceeded with on this basis, a careful check of the local legislation and its interpretation is required lest prior use outweighs prior registration.

The fact of filing for protection requires that the party filing demonstrates the uniqueness of the intellectual property. This can mean that in order to justify protection, the item's unique properties must be revealed. This can lead to creating the competition that the seeking of protection was intended to avoid. For example, the firm may find that its logo or brand name has already been registered in the foreign country, in which case it is likely to have to buy back the rights of use from the holder in that market. Registration in one country often does not give protection in another unless both countries are parties to the same international convention on intellectual property, e.g. the Paris Convention, the Madrid Arrangement or the Inter-American Convention. The expense of filing for protection in a number of countries has belatedly caused the US to consider signing the Madrid Protocol of 1995. This involves a single enforcement and registration agency called the World Intellectual Property Organisation (WIPO). A US company could file one application with the US Patent and Trademark Office and obtain a single registration valid through WIPO in all participating nations. As at January 2001 the enabling legislation still had not been passed because of an earlier piece of legislation relating to Cuban trademarks, with which it was in conflict.

The Uruguay Round of the GATT addressed intellectual property for the first time in its closing stages (1992–94) and the resulting World Trade Organisation embodies a code covering intellectual property – Trade in Intellectual Property (TRIPS) – which contains comprehensive new rules to protect intellectual property and to govern disputes. Despite this, firms still face a threat as far as intellectual property is concerned when they venture abroad to countries with a weak institutional system for protection of intellectual property.

This can be illustrated in the case of China. China is one such country whose culture does not contain a strong tradition embodying the need to protect intellectual property rights. Historically, imitation of literary or artistic works from the past was a scholarly and respectable activity. However, this cultural inclination to revere the past and promote its reproduction is at odds with the enforcement of property rights of the work being imitated. In addition, during the communist era, the underlying concept of returning all wealth to the people militated against preserving an individual's ownership rights in intellectual property. As a result, foreign firms are reluctant to license sensitive technology in China except to firms in which they have direct ownership.

The Chinese government has somewhat belatedly recognised that this issue is a stumbling block to attracting foreign direct investment and has taken some measures to strengthen enforcement of intellectual property laws. However, in so doing, there is a further problem in that there are fundamental differences between Chinese and western interpretations of both the definition and purpose of licensing technology. In the first instance, regulations in China are based on technology transfer rather than technology licensing. The Chinese are uncomfortable with the notion of a licence as a temporary right to use a technology, and they view it as an instalment sale with the licensee gaining full rights to the technology at the end of the term of the licence. As far as purpose is concerned, the Chinese partner wants the technology to boost its profitability in the short term whereas the foreign party sees the licensing of the technology as a way of gaining access to China's market. The above illustrates that an understanding of the reasons underlying prevailing practice towards the protection of intellectual property is essential when deciding on the entry strategy to be adopted in foreign countries, especially in Asia.

Protection of intellectual property is often not as straightforward as it might seem, especially when ethical issues are involved.

4.4 International highlight

Drug giants told to reveal secrets

For a number of years, developing countries have been complaining about the high prices being charged in their domain by multinational pharmaceutical manufacturers for life-saving drugs. Whenever 'copycat' drugs appear in these markets, the drug companies lobby their domestic governments to pressure the developing countries to remove the 'copycat' pharmaceuticals from the market under threat of sanctions or withdrawal of preferences. This poses an ethical dilemma. On the one hand the government is being asked to protect intellectual property but on the other hand to condemn to a life of misery and eventual death those people (often in the millions) who cannot afford the branded item but only the 'copycat' item. This issue has recently flared up in South Africa with respect to AIDS drugs. Given the spread of AIDS in the African continent, the government of South Africa legislated to allow it to import cheap versions of medicines. Thirty-nine drug companies have challenged this law in Pretoria and the court has demanded that the multinational pharmaceutical firms reveal closely guarded details of their business practices including their pricing policies. In addition, international public pressure has resulted in parent governments of some of these multinationals (US, Germany as well as the EU and the WTO) backing South Africa's right to introduce the law and calling on the industry to drop the case.

Source: Adapted from the *Guardian*, 7 March 2001, p. 2 and *The Economist*, 10 March 2001, p. 75.

Reducing the impact

There are a number of ways in which the firm can reduce the impact of international laws on its international activities.

Transfer pricing

Transfer pricing involves the firm setting the prices at which it transfers products, technologies or services to its affiliates in other countries. If the price is set artificially high, then the profit earned in the foreign country is reduced, as is the amount of tax payable. As a result, greater profits are earned by the parent company. This is especially the case when affairs are arranged so that, via use of transfer pricing, most profits accrue in those countries where the rate of taxation is least. In recent years, there has been increasing attention paid by governments to this practice as they are missing out recouping tax revenue due to them from operations conducted within their jurisdiction. Increasingly, firms are being asked to prove that the transaction is truly 'arm's length'. Transnational companies will need to give greater attention to non-arm's-length transactions to ensure that efforts to achieve profit maximisation on a global basis do not expose the firm to charges of tax evasion.

International countertrade

Countertrade involves the linking of an import and an export transaction in a conditional way. Because goods supplied are either fully or partly paid for with other goods or services rather than with cash, one of the negotiating issues in such transactions is what value to place on the goods bought and the goods sold. The undervaluing or overvaluing of goods can influence the profit attributable to the transaction. As a result, countertrade can be used to avoid taxes, to evade anti-dumping legislation and to evade agreements on international prices.

Dumping

Dumping involves selling products in an international market below cost or below domestic prices. Dumping is prohibited by the World Trade Organisation via its Anti Dumping Code. Difficulties arise because although it is prohibited in international marketing, it is a common practice in domestic marketing. Dumping in domestic marketing is reflected in the 'loss leader' technique that is aimed at seizing market share, injuring competitors and increasing the degree of control of the market. During recent years, there have been an increasing number of complaints and government investigations into dumping. Government export incentive schemes can give rise to dumping charges. It has been alleged that the incentives are factored into the prices charged in the international markets enabling products to be sold below current domestic value in the country of origin.

Contracts and dispute resolution

When faced with a dispute in international business that cannot be settled by informal negotiation between the parties, there are three possible avenues for settlement. These are conciliation, arbitration or litigation.

Conciliation

This is the best approach if at all possible because it is least likely to close the door on future business. Sometimes it may be necessary to seek the intervention of a third party to convey to each side the views of the other side and clear up misunderstandings that might have arisen. In countries such as China, where business is largely based on trust and relationships, conciliation is preferred. Often, in Asia, this takes the form of the third party shuttling back and forth between the disputants trying to negotiate a solution. This 'shuttle' conciliation does save face for both parties in the dispute.

Arbitration

Many international contracts contain a clause requiring both parties to submit to arbitration before embarking on litigation. When arbitration is formal, the disputing parties usually present their cases to a panel of respected persons who will referee, determine the merits of the case and make a judgement that both sides agree to honour. Coddington (1994) summarises the advantages of arbitration as follows:

- Arbitration conventions such as the New York Convention to which almost 90 countries are signatories increases the ability of parties to enforce judgements.
- Arbitration hearings are usually in private and sensitive matters remain confidential to the parties concerned.
- Arbitration is likely to be quicker than litigation.
- The parties can choose the 'judges' who will sit on the arbitration panel.
- Unlike a court judgement, an arbitration judgement is unlikely to be appealed and more likely to be treated as final.

A number of formal arbitration organisations exist, such as the International Chamber of Commerce. In the case of this body, each party selects from an approved list one person to argue their case and the Chamber appoints a third member, who is usually a distinguished legal figure, to arbitrate. Success of arbitration often depends on the willingness of both parties to accept the arbitrator's rulings because not all countries have the necessary statutes to enforce arbitration determinations.

Litigation

This should only be used as a last resort. It is an approach whose victories are often spurious and it involves large costs, delays and aggravation that generally exceeds the benefit obtained. On occasion, the threat of litigation is sufficient to bring about a settlement. Other disadvantages of litigation are that:

- it usually closes the door on future business;
- it can create a poor image and damage public relations;
- there is the risk of unfair treatment at the hands of a foreign court;
- there may be difficulty in collecting the judgement;
- there is considerable opportunity cost – time and funds tied up in bringing legal action.

Marketing implications – legal

Whilst the international marketer is not expected to be a legal expert, it is necessary that there be an awareness of those areas where international law might impinge on international marketing activities. It is also necessary for the international marketer to be aware of differences in legal practices between the domestic market and the international market in which it proposes to do business.

In many countries, there is a difference between what the law says and what people actually do. This needs to be understood, as do the underlying reasons for this situation. Not only do legal systems differ from international market to international market, but the interpretation of laws also differs between countries following the same legal system. In some countries, the law is absolute and once it has been broken is modified via its interpretation, and in other countries, the law has some flexibility but once broken, its interpretation is rigid. To successfully transact business in international markets, the international marketer needs to be sensitive to the legal differences between domestic and the international markets.

Internet infusion

Global computer-based communications cut across territorial boundaries undermining the feasibility of applying laws based on geographic borders. New boundaries have arisen based on screens and passwords that separate the virtual world from the real world. This new boundary defines a distinct cyberspace that some would argue needs its own laws and legal institutions. These will have to cater for new phenomena that have no clear parallel in the real world and, in the process, define legal personhood, property rights, resolve disputes and establish a convention as to value in the international virtual marketplace. Furthermore, because of the speed and borderless nature of the Internet, this new law will have to cater for multiple jurisdictions, often simultaneously. It must accommodate persons who exist in cyberspace only in the form of an e-mail address. Internet business will increasingly be scrutinised by authorities in different countries and, with the growth in international e-business, the volume of international disputes is likely to escalate.

Recent examples include copyright infringement (e.g. Playboy, Sega), trademark infringement, buyer and seller being located in different legal jurisdictions (e.g. who is liable for taxes? Where has value been added?), intellectual property (e.g. website design, site ownership), violation of privacy, breach of regulations on promotion (e.g. whose regulations govern Internet sweepstakes?), and cyber squatting (who owns the site's domain name?). Solving the above issues is complicated because the laws that govern the Internet are still ill-defined and, in many cases, non-existent. Internet development moves faster than traditional lawmakers are used to. It is debatable whether the laws that apply in the international domain to bricks-and-mortar businesses will work for online commerce because many of the former were enacted at a time of slow-moving trains, not high-speed computers. E-business adds a new level of complexity to international business law and raises issues as to what constitutes a contract in cyberspace, international tax harmonisation and enforcement for online transactions and disparagement, defamation and consumer protection for online customers. Finally, there is a view in many developed countries that because the Internet is new, it is too early for government to become involved in regulating it lest, in the process, its growth becomes stifled. The consequence is that the firm using the Internet in international business may face multiple and contradictory national laws applying to the same transaction.

Summary

Figure 4.1 provides a summary of the way in which the international political and legal environment impacts on firms doing business in international markets.

Factors in the international and political environment affecting international business activities

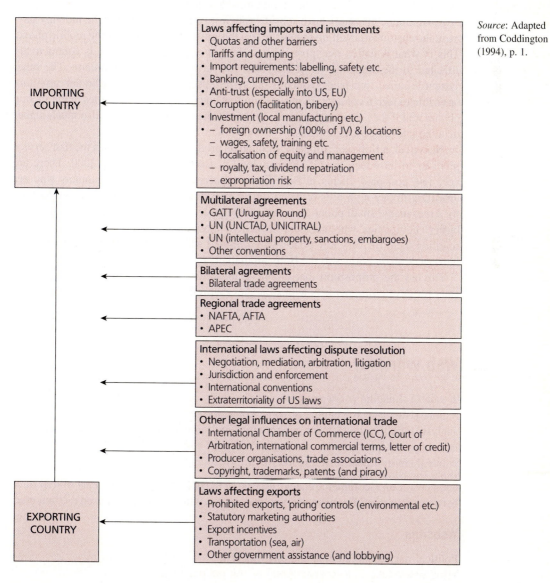

IMPORTING COUNTRY

Laws affecting imports and investments
- Quotas and other barriers
- Tariffs and dumping
- Import requirements: labelling, safety etc.
- Banking, currency, loans etc.
- Anti-trust (especially into US, EU)
- Corruption (facilitation, bribery)
- Investment (local manufacturing etc.)
- – foreign ownership (100% of JV) & locations
  - wages, safety, training etc.
  - localisation of equity and management
  - royalty, tax, dividend repatriation
  - expropriation risk

Multilateral agreements
- GATT (Uruguay Round)
- UN (UNCTAD, UNICITRAL)
- UN (intellectual property, sanctions, embargoes)
- Other conventions

Bilateral agreements
- Bilateral trade agreements

Regional trade agreements
- NAFTA, AFTA
- APEC

International laws affecting dispute resolution
- Negotiation, mediation, arbitration, litigation
- Jurisdiction and enforcement
- International conventions
- Extraterritoriality of US laws

Other legal influences on international trade
- International Chamber of Commerce (ICC), Court of Arbitration, international commercial terms, letter of credit)
- Producer organisations, trade associations
- Copyright, trademarks, patents (and piracy)

Laws affecting exports
- Prohibited exports, 'pricing' controls (environmental etc.)
- Statutory marketing authorities
- Export incentives
- Transportation (sea, air)
- Other government assistance (and lobbying)

EXPORTING COUNTRY

Internet infusion

Mobile services in Bolivia, NuevaTel PCS de Bolivia SA Mobile services is a booming industry and leading companies such as Nokia, Ericsson and Motorola are leading the way in developing the market. Although mobile technology development is very important for first world users, developing countries do not require the same level of sophisticated technology. Their communication needs are based on the simple need call and receive call.

Mobile services divide into mobile phone manufacturers, service providers and users. Service providers (mobile operators) are not interested in selling phones; they sell minutes of airtime but they depend on people having mobile phones, and users in turn need to get a mobile phone at a reasonable price.

Most mobile operators have subsidy policies; generally the higher the monthly payment the customer is willing to pay the less this customer will pay for the mobile phone. This is what is called the 'post-paid' system in which the customer is contractually attached to the company for at least one year at a given rate per minute. The other system is called 'pre-paid', which is the system used by customers who are unwilling or unable to sign a contract. In this system few companies grant subsidies to the mobile phones and if they do it is at a minimum level. The rate per minute is also much higher than the rates in post-paid plans.

NuevaTel, a Bolivian company, through its product VIVA GSM was the first service provider to introduce the GSM technology in Bolivia in November 2000. There are very few post-paid clients in Bolivia, most users being pre-paid customers who are unwilling to pay high bills or pay a lot for a mobile phone. These people are looking for a reasonable small phone for a reasonable price. They have started to look at 'refurbisher' companies who take old-fashioned phones and alter them inside and out, reselling them for very low prices with a limited warranty. NuevaTel has successfully introduced these phones to the Bolivian market.

Discuss the proposition that mobile manufacturers have a moral responsibility to cater for developing markets with strategies that reflect their needs.

Web workout

Question 1 Imagine you wanted to market security equipment in Brazil in the São Paulo region. Using a search engine of your choice, locate two websites that provide country analysis outlining investment opportunities and, in particular, the political climate for investment. Report on your findings. Will it be easy to market your product? Is the political environment fostering long-term investment?

Question 2 Can e-commerce change aspects of the political system that may restrict trade between countries? For example, you may research the impact of taxes on e-commerce.

Websites

Political risk, economic risk and financial risk
http://www.duke.edu/~charvey/Country_risk/pol/polindex.htm

International Trade Law Library http://www.intl-trade.com/library.html

Islamic & Middle Eastern law http://www.soas.ac.uk/Centres/IslamicLaw/Materials.html

Legal Information Institute http://www.law.cornell.edu/

eMarket Services http://www.emarketservices.com/

Auerbach's International Legal Checklists
http://www.tradenz.govt.nz/CWS/page_Article/0,1300,4411,00.html

Discussion questions

1 How can firms maximise the opportunities offered when foreign governments act as facilitators of involvement?

2 How can firms minimise the inconvenience to their international operations when foreign governments act as regulators of international commercial involvement within their borders?

3 What are the key differences between various forms of political instability?

4 What steps can you take to reduce political risk in the countries in which your firm is currently involved?

5 Discuss the circumstances in which international law can clash with national law as far as commercial matters are concerned. Will globalisation ever create a situation where international law will take precedence over national law?

6 Comment on circumstances in which national law can frustrate global marketing strategy and the potential savings that can result from globalisation.

7 Under what circumstances would it be worthwhile to file for protection of intellectual property in the international market?

8 When is it preferable to arbitrate as opposed to conciliate on the one hand and litigate on the other?

References

Coddington, I. (1994) 'Supplementary Notes on the Political and Legal Environment', University of Technology, Sydney.

Department of Foreign Affairs and Trade (DFAT), East Asia Analytical Unit (2000) *Accessing Middle-East Growth: Business Opportunities in the Arabian Peninsular and Iran*, Commonwealth of Australia, Canberra, p. 53.

Douglas, S.P. and Craig, C.S. (1983) *International Marketing Research*, Prentice Hall, Englewood Cliffs, NJ.

Encarnation, D.J. and Vachani, S. (1985) 'Foreign Ownership: When Hosts Change the Rules', *Harvard Business Review*, September–October, pp. 152–160.

Hadjikhani, A. and Hakansson, H. (1996) 'Political actions in business networks a Swedish case', *International Journal of Research in Marketing*, Vol. 13, pp. 431–447.

Jain, S.C. (1996) *International Marketing Management*, 5th edn, South Western College Publishing, Cincinnati, Ohio.

McGaughey, S.L., Liesch, P.W. and Poulson, D. (2000) 'An unconventional approach to intellectual property protection: the case of an Australian firm transferring shipbuilding technologies to China', *Journal of World Business*, Vol. 35, No. 1, pp. 1–20.

UNCTAD (1999) *Legal Aspects of International Trade*, United Nations, New York and Geneva.

5

The information technology environment

Learning objectives:

After reading this chapter, you should be able to:

- identify the key elements and drivers underlying the information technology revolution;

- identify the role of the Internet and its positioning within the new information infrastructure;

- determine how firms are capitalising on the information and technology environment to expand internationally;

- evaluate the significance of the international diffusion of innovation process and the role of lead users; and

- recognise the implications of the information and technology environment for changing industry structures.

What is happening in cyberspace?

Although the World Wide Web is the most popular medium to tap into information available on the Internet (the physical networks of wires and computers) it is not the most efficient or effective way of exchanging information. The killer application that has made the Net so talked about and used medium is e-mail. However, companies are now moving past this medium on its 11th anniversary. The web has been the catalyst to make the Internet a global phenomenon but it is a depository of relatively static web pages. A myriad of new non-web technologies will enable people to communicate and transact. The new concepts, such as wireless Net, peer-to-peer (P-2-P) communication, instant messaging or machine-to-machine communication, are proliferating.

Wireless Net. Wireless Net is expected to exceed more than 300 million users by 2003. Visionary companies such as DoCoMo and Nokia are investing in this area to find commercial opportunities. It seems that everyone in the world wants to use the Internet – especially while it's on the move. But the inconvenience of setting up a computer and finding a provider discourages people from connecting. Access is, however, much easier in Japan, where NTT DoCoMo, the country's leading mobile communications operator, provides Internet service automatically. Using their cellular phones, users simply connect to any laptop or PDA, dial a number and launch their browser. There are no additional manual setting procedures. This convenient service is called 'mopera' and is a part of many offerings that DoCoMo provides to achieve its vision for 2010 of providing a 'brighter future through convenient mobile communications'. DoCoMo is now using its wireless network profitably and is able to generate revenues for its partners. It is using micro-payment systems where participating content providers generate revenues per customer view for services such as horoscopes, stock quotes, birthday greetings or bill payments.

The peer-to-peer. The peer-to-peer concept was made famous by Napster, the Internet start-up. Its legal battles with major music record labels have popularised this music-sharing service. However, the P-2-P concept will have more far-reaching applications for businesses and their customers. This concept enables PCs to communicate with one another directly via the Net. To generate fees, companies will be able to charge for the software that lets people exchange data or better collaborate on projects.

Instant messaging. E-mail is the most popular non-web use of the Net. However, a new wave of instant messaging or chatting will take personal and business-to-consumer communication to the next level. Instant messaging is currently being developed for applications such as interactive TV. Companies such as Yahoo! and America Online are using these services on interactive TV and mobile phones.

Machine-to-machine. Computers and appliances are communicating with less and less human help. Smart fridges, TV sets or motor cars are making our lives even easier. For example, the e-Bay auction website enables a proxy bidding feature where users select bidding parameters such as maximum price and the auction automatically bids for the item. The next possibilities are for smart fridges that update their contents, or stationery cabinets that automatically place orders for replacement stationery.

International marketers have now more than ever the possibility of reaching international markets with their product or service. How will you transform your offer and delivery method?

Introduction

Technology is now the most dramatic force transforming the international environment. From biotechnology to computer technology we have seen a vast array of technological innovations in just the last ten years. New technologies impact or replace older ones. The motor car has hurt the railways, television has challenged the movies, and communications such as video-conferencing have affected the airline industry. In each case a level of substitution has occurred. More recently, as the quality of video-conferencing and other e-mail-style communications has improved while its costs have reduced, businesspeople have reassessed their need to travel. This decision has caused a consequent reduction in business travel for various purposes. New technologies create new markets and opportunities, but also pose a threat to those old technologies and industries that might be tied to them.

Scientists today are working on new products and services in communications, robotics, miniature electronics, solar energy applications, biological cloning, voice-activated and controlled computers and dispensing machines, and a myriad of other applications. Companies in the health industry such as Roche, telecommunications companies such as Ericsson, and software providers such as Microsoft, spend billions of dollars each year on research and development.

Many governments are assisting firms to set up 'science parks' to undertake research and development. Some industries, such as graphic design, are being revolutionised by information technology.

The paradigm shift caused by the information age and the convergence of industries using digital technologies has enabled international marketing to penetrate worldwide markets faster. Of the many technologies that will impact on international marketers in the new millennium in the fields of conservation, health, transportation and manufacturing and service, the pervading technology will be to do with information.

Many writers and commentators now believe that the new information infrastructure currently emerging will, more than any previous infrastructure, go well beyond transporting goods and services to *creating, developing, moving and delivering* them – thus transforming all parts of society.

This chapter looks first at how different technology infrastructure developments have transformed the business environment, with emphasis on the current revolution based on information and communication.

Infrastructure development and economic history – 'techno-economic paradigms'

Economic history dating from the Industrial Revolution in the late 18th century to the present day is typically classified through economic business cycles. Freeman and Perez (1988) directly challenged Keynes' and Samuelson's analyses of economic history as a set of business cycles as inadequate in their ability to explain and predict major structural crises and adjustment within the international economy.

Drawing from predominantly a Schumpeterian economic perspective, Freeman and Perez identified five longer-term Kondratiev cycles based on the application and diffusion of key technologies and resources throughout advancing nations within the international economy. These cycles are designated as 'techno-economic paradigms' and are classified as follows (Freeman and Perez 1988):

1st   – Early Mechanisation (1770s to 1840s)

2nd   – Steam Power and Railway (1830s to 1890s)

3rd   – Electrical and Heavy Engineering (1880s to 1940s)

4th   – Fordist Mass Production (1930s to 1990s)

5th   – Information and Communication (1980s to 2040s?)

Figure 5.1 outlines the five techno-economic paradigms with their associated key technology resources and infrastructure developments. Each techno-economic paradigm has a cycle of between 60 and 70 years with 10 years in an emergent phase in a previous paradigm and 10 years in a declining phase in a subsequent paradigm. To date, this pattern has pointed to a period of about 40 to 50 years when the paradigm is dominant. The transition periods are typically times when major structural crises and adjustments have occurred throughout the international economy.

Freeman and Perez (1988) contend that the diffusion of the key technologies and resources associated with each of these techno-economic paradigms radically transformed international markets at the macro country and industry levels and the micro business and individual level with all-encompassing outcomes including:

- emergence of new industries based on the key technologies and resources;
- effective solutions to the limitations of previous techno-economic paradigms;
- new infrastructure at both the national and international level;
- countries gaining technological and economic leadership positions from the application of key technologies and resources associated with the new paradigm;
- significant changes in spatial distribution and distance between associated production factors (including land, labour and capital sources) and market locations (marketplaces and customers);
- shifts in population density and urbanisation;
- radical changes in organisational forms associated with firms in new industries;

| Figure 5.1 | Techno-economic paradigms and key resources |

Source: Pattinson and
Brown (1996), p. 56.

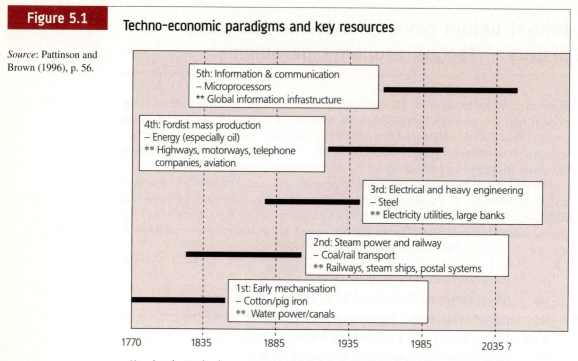

– Key abundant technology resource ** Major infrastructure developments

- new approaches to national and international regulation;
- new training and education systems;
- new services linked to the techno-economic paradigm;
- new innovative entrepreneurs.
- new political economists and philosophers.

Information and communication: the fifth techno-economic paradigm

The current fifth techno-economic paradigm is driven by the microprocessor and, to date, new infrastructure development can be divided into two phases. In the first phase a number of 'carrier branches' based on the microprocessor have emerged and evolved into new or redefined industries. These branches include:

- computer systems
- computer operating systems and software
- telecommunications equipment and optical fibres
- satellites
- consumer and professional electronics

- robotics, flexible manufacturing systems
- electronic networks
- information content providers
- information technology services.

In the second phase, all the 'carrier branch' industries are converging into a new information-based infrastructure that will be capable of providing most forms of data – namely, data, text, sound and image – through the requisite functions of generation, processing, storage and transmission.

The information revolution and the Internet

Access points to the new infrastructure include telephone networks, computer bulletin boards, commercial online services, satellite and broadcast television, cable networks, cellular networks, established corporate proprietary and open networks. The Internet is emerging as the fulcrum for the information infrastructure as it connects increasingly diverse networks. Figure 5.2 illustrates the Internet as a link between the different information technology, telecommunications and media networks and the new information infrastructure from an Internet positioning perspective.

The Internet's growth in the past ten years has been astonishing. Up until the early 1990s, the Internet was a research-oriented electronic mail network connecting technical, academic, defence and relevant corporate groups. The Net has transformed rapidly into the most powerful global network on the planet linking people and organisations from all walks of life.

Accessing the new information infrastructure: 'The planets of cyberspace' | **Figure 5.2**

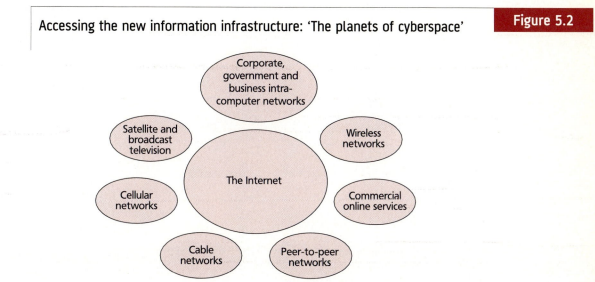

Two catalysts that have transformed the Internet into a system of universal usage are the development of the World Wide Web (web) and the Netscape Navigator browser. The web is a system of organising information on the Internet, where computer servers are identified as 'websites' and users can easily jump from one website to another using hypertext links. The architecture for the web was developed at the CERN Laboratories in Geneva, Switzerland, in 1991 and is continually evolving under the direction of the W3 Organisation based at CERN.

The Netscape Navigator browser software was the first to provide a low-cost, user-friendly interface (point and click) to the web for personal computer users via a modem. The Netscape Navigator browser was released in December 1994. By July 1995 over 6 million people were using the Netscape browser, being two-thirds of the total number of web users at that time – 9 million people (Fortune, 1995). The Netscape Navigator browser could be regarded as a 'killer application' whose impact may be as revolutionary as Gutenberg's printing press. Microsoft's Internet Explorer browser has been responsible for the huge growth in access by 2001. Today, Microsoft Internet Explorer is powering two out of every three Internet browsing occasions.

About 407 million computer users worldwide had access to the web in 2001. Forward estimates for the numbers of Internet users by 2005 vary from 500 million to 1 billion with about 80% accessing the Internet via the web (or 'descendants' of these technologies). It is conceivable that up to half of the world's population could have access to the Internet by 2015.

Commercial usage of the Internet either directly through the web or from intracompany networks through gateways or 'firewalls' to the web is also growing exponentially.

Table 5.1 highlights the percentage of household and businesses with Internet access.

Table 5.1 Households and businesses with Internet access

	% of households	% of business
Denmark	59.0	93.0
United States	51.0	85.0
Canada	49.0	71.0
Sweden	48.0	91.0
Netherlands	41.0	79.0
United Kingdom	40.0	65.0
Finland	40.0	91.0
New Zealand	37.0	84.0
Japan	35.0	92.0
Australia	33.0	86.0
Austria	19.0	84.0
Italy	19.0	72.0
Portugal	18.0	72.0

Source: Adapted from OECD, ICT database, August 2002.

User access to the World Wide Web

A key battleground to watch is the provision of access to the Internet. In the past the computing power and telecommunications associated with the Internet was under-written by academic, research and defence institutions. Today, a myriad of Internet service providers (ISPs) offer access to corporations and private citizens. The ISPs usually have their own leased lines connecting them to the Internet. A new breed of service provider referred to as application service providers (ASP) has emerged to offer a wider range of customised services to consumers to enable them to access and use the Internet much more effectively.

Figure 5.3 provides a schematic flow of user access to the web.

The impact and the importance in embracing the new economy can be seen in Table 5.2 as represented by research conducted by Forrester Research in 2001. It shows the growth and international dispersion of electronic commerce. Expected world sales through electronic commerce of US$6,790 billion in 2004 would represent about 8.6% of total sales, reflected as 12.8% of sales in the US, 8% in Asia-Pacific and 6% in western Europe.

Accessing the new information infrastructure entry to the web   **Figure 5.3**

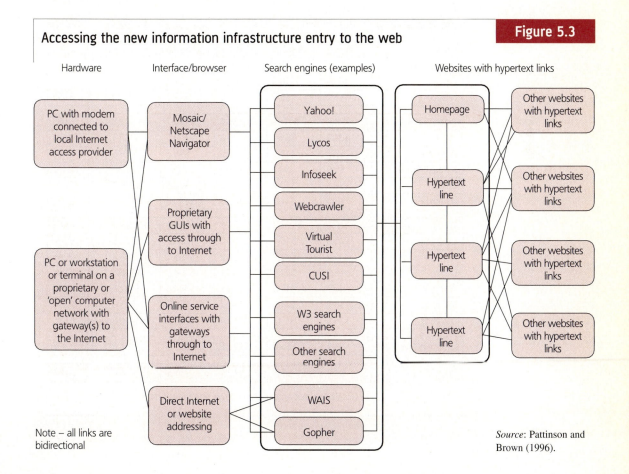

Note – all links are bidirectional

Source: Pattinson and Brown (1996).

Table 5.2 Expected growth of e-commerce by region

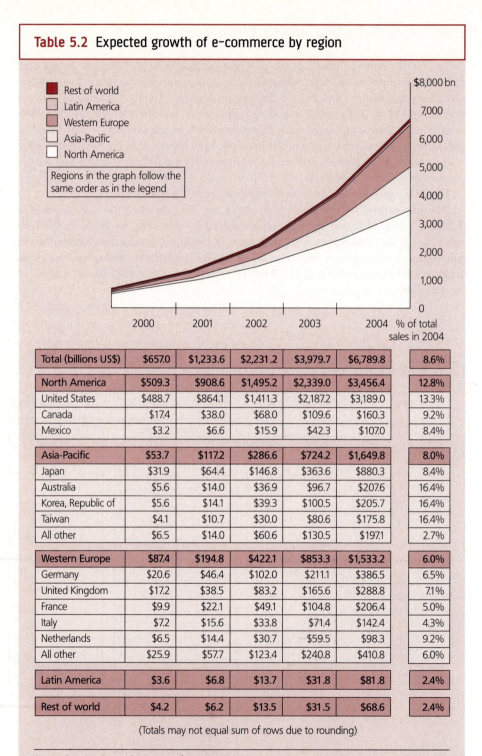

	2000	2001	2002	2003	2004	% of total sales in 2004
Total (billions US$)	$657.0	$1,233.6	$2,231.2	$3,979.7	$6,789.8	8.6%
North America	$509.3	$908.6	$1,495.2	$2,339.0	$3,456.4	12.8%
United States	$488.7	$864.1	$1,411.3	$2,187.2	$3,189.0	13.3%
Canada	$17.4	$38.0	$68.0	$109.6	$160.3	9.2%
Mexico	$3.2	$6.6	$15.9	$42.3	$107.0	8.4%
Asia-Pacific	$53.7	$117.2	$286.6	$724.2	$1,649.8	8.0%
Japan	$31.9	$64.4	$146.8	$363.6	$880.3	8.4%
Australia	$5.6	$14.0	$36.9	$96.7	$207.6	16.4%
Korea, Republic of	$5.6	$14.1	$39.3	$100.5	$205.7	16.4%
Taiwan	$4.1	$10.7	$30.0	$80.6	$175.8	16.4%
All other	$6.5	$14.0	$60.6	$130.5	$197.1	2.7%
Western Europe	$87.4	$194.8	$422.1	$853.3	$1,533.2	6.0%
Germany	$20.6	$46.4	$102.0	$211.1	$386.5	6.5%
United Kingdom	$17.2	$38.5	$83.2	$165.6	$288.8	7.1%
France	$9.9	$22.1	$49.1	$104.8	$206.4	5.0%
Italy	$7.2	$15.6	$33.8	$71.4	$142.4	4.3%
Netherlands	$6.5	$14.4	$30.7	$59.5	$98.3	9.2%
All other	$25.9	$57.7	$123.4	$240.8	$410.8	6.0%
Latin America	$3.6	$6.8	$13.7	$31.8	$81.8	2.4%
Rest of world	$4.2	$6.2	$13.5	$31.5	$68.6	2.4%

(Totals may not equal sum of rows due to rounding)

Source: Forrester Research Inc, www.forrester.com

Legend for graph:
- Rest of world
- Latin America
- Western Europe
- Asia-Pacific
- North America

Regions in the graph follow the same order as in the legend

Further analysis of Forrester's statistical forecasts within a global perspective indicate that by 2004 the US will account for 40% of Internet users and 50% of global e-commerce – almost double that expected in western Europe. Though the Asian crisis has modified earlier forecasts, e-commerce is expected to grow more than 30-fold in the Asia-Pacific region by 2004.

North America represents a majority of this trade, but its dominance will fade, because some Asia-Pacific and west European countries hit hypergrowth over the next two years.

The implications of globally linked networks or international markets are described in International Highlight 5.1.

5.1 International highlight

Electronic networks and electronic commerce

Impact of global information technology

In 2004 it is projected that over 709 million people will have access to the Internet (cyberatlas.com) using a myriad of services such as e-mail, web browsers, media players, on-board computers, and PDAs (personal digital assistants) in the process of interacting with one another for the purpose of conducting commerce. The number of networks that support this interaction is constantly growing and the predictions indicate that the size of such networks doubles every year (currently there are about 150,000 interconnected networks). Organisations such as Microsoft, Lucent, Cisco and IBM are investing heavily in new network technologies.

Technology over the past 20 years has been getting much faster and cheaper. This represents possibilities for new products and services that organisations can develop. The emergence of new services, such as video and multimedia players, depends on storage capabilities. In order to make these services fast and accessible the storage capacities are growing. Soon our storage devices will not be calculated in gigabytes but in yadabytes. In order to do so, the storage devices will need to embrace further miniaturisation and new ways of data storage using holograms.

The global network

Businesses embracing the concept of the globally networked business enable dissemination of the corporate information infrastructure to all key constituencies, leveraging the network for competitive advantage. The globally networked business is an open and collaborative environment that eliminates the traditional barriers to business relationships and between geographies, allowing diverse constituents to access information, resources and services in the most efficient and advantageous manner.

Organisations are embracing three key areas of the networked enterprise:

1. E-learning

E-learning is changing the way people around the world provide and receive education, information and training. By eliminating the barriers of time and distance, e-learning provides accountability, accessibility and opportunity to people and organisations around the world.

2. Internet commerce

Internet commerce, a key component of the globally networked business model, provides a company's customers and its partners with end-to-end solutions to conduct sales transactions.

▶

The myriad of Internet commerce applications accessed through such networks helps users place and manage orders for the company's products and services. The software applications streamline processes and deliver enhanced productivity, improved service, worldwide around-the-clock availability and faster access to a wider range of useful information.

3. Customer support

The globally networked business model opens the corporate information infrastructure, enabling the creation of innovative support offerings. Support applications provide customers with all the information they need to be successful. Removing the traditional barriers and re-engineering the information dissemination process allows new standards in business relationships to emerge, ensuring mutual benefits.

The challenges and possibilities for international or global marketing

Currently 80% of websites are in English but only 20% of the world population speaks English. This limits effectiveness and efficiency for non-English-speaking customers or potential customers. The recent developments in network speed and uniform infrastructure are enabling us to bridge this gap. Now users can go to the World Wide Web and view any page in their native language. Thanks to the interconnected networks this is being done in real time. The web page is being intercepted on the server and immediately translated and displayed in the viewer's native language.

Car manufacturers are also exploring these possibilities in car design. Soon they will be able to design their cars by interacting with the cars' users in real time via satellites where they will monitor engine performance and driving patterns to build more reliable and responsive cars.

The level of knowledge and usage patterns are gaining momentum despite the spectacular dot-com failures of 2000 and 2001, which could be attributed to very limited research on the extent of business activity on the web. Currently researchers such as Forrester.com, Gartner Group and those from academic institutions are presenting their findings about the shopping and trading services in the US, Europe and Australasia. This research indicates that the majority of users of these services browse for information but do not necessarily complete their transactions in the same electronic service channel, as there have been significant concerns about the security of financial transactions (Poulsen, 2001).

During the mid-1990s most companies connected to the web were experimenting in the environment by putting up homepages to gauge activity and interest in the new environment before deciding to invest further in electronic transaction and ordering systems. Hundreds of thousands of companies now have web homepages with some information about themselves and their products with references to toll-free numbers, contact numbers or e-mail addresses.

Between 1998 and 2001 many more companies were going further than the basic service by allowing customers to place orders or bookings directly through their web pages, although they still allowed the customer to complete the financial side of the transaction either by toll-free telephone call or by mail. Increasingly these companies are also offering special deals exclusively to web customers, such as Cathay Pacific USA's Cyber Traveller offers or Coca-Cola's special discount coupons to be redeemed in physical outlets.

Nevertheless, with the increasing robustness of the web environment in late 2001, significantly increasing numbers of companies have begun to fully utilise it as a genuine information dissemination environment. A large number of companies are now standardising their internal information architectures and transforming these into the web environment, hence the emergence of powerful information dissemination systems using web architecture. Examples of successful web-based systems include:

- EnronOnline now offers over 1,500 different products (from spot electricity and gas to complex derivative instruments and even hedges against the weather). Online trades now make up nearly two-thirds of the company's trading business.

- One of the most technologically advanced companies is General Electric. This old-economy icon now buys and sells more through its private online marketplaces – an estimated US$20 billion in 2001 alone – than is traded in all the independent B2B marketplaces put together.

- Merrill Lynch began researching its own customers. It soon discovered that even the most loyal customers had 'sandbox' accounts which they used to play with at rival online firms, and that those accounts were growing. As a result, Merrill Lynch now offers a full range of online services to its clients.

Electronic commerce is growing at a rapid rate in global industries. Financial services companies like Deutsche Morgan Grenfell are rapidly moving to online transactions. Media corporations have set up online news and information services which are becoming even more interactive and are embracing a wide variety of electronic networks, such as phone, wireless and the Internet, to attract and retain their customers.

This exploding growth of electronic networks and commerce has implications for the adoption and diffusion of innovations and presents both opportunities and challenges for international marketers.

Global markets and the new information infrastructure – the power of many, the power of three, or the power of lateral thinking?

Hamel and Prahalad (1994, pp. 39–40) assert that globalisation, deregulation and information technology are blurring boundaries in an increasing range of industries. Industry borders have been blurring between commercial banking, brokerage and investment banking, between computer hardware and software vendors, and between publishers, broadcasters, telecoms and film studios. In all these cases, industry structure has become very complex and almost indeterminate.

Internet infusion

The future of networks: collaboration powered by your friendly desktop

The proliferation of PCs onto our desktops went through a number of adoption phases. Each of these phases required a piece of software that would lead potential users to subscribe to the new idea. We have had word processing overtaking the typewriter, Excel spreadsheets overtaking calculators, and the Microsoft Windows operating system enabling desktop publishing. E-mail has exponentially grown as Internet communication.

But what about the peer-to-peer (P-2-P) network; will it be another killer application?

Typically, if you want to find a file or any information on the web, you would go to a search engine like Google or Yahoo!. You would then type in your search criteria and click on the 'search' button. Your computer then sends this information off to Google servers where there is a huge database of web pages. The server then sends these search results back to your computer, listing which web pages on the Internet have the data you have requested.

The P-2-P network process is different. Here you enter your search criteria and your computer asks ten other computers if they have it. Each of these in turn asks ten other computers if they have it. This process repeats itself until some computer indicates that it has it. You can then download this information directly. There are no servers between the user and the network.

The most prominent pioneers of this concept were Napster and Gnutella in providing free exchange of the music over the Internet network. The only problem was that the music companies were excluded from this new market which impacted on their traditional profit.

For companies with a large number of computers this new killer application may be 'just what the doctor ordered'. By using already idling PCs, P-2-P connections can tap into cheap and under-utilised computing power.

By linking users directly, P-2-P can create easier collaboration allowing a rapid formation of workgroups or team projects that will sidestep traditional barriers such as firewalls and ever-restricting intranets. P-2-P can also make this information proliferate through an entire enterprise by opening up the desktop PC of individual employees and allowing staff members to search each other's information more freely.

To date, the working proof of this concept has emerged primarily from non-profit organisations. For example, P-2-P networking is being used by Berkeley university in the US where over 3 million volunteers have downloaded a small P-2-P program and are now using joint computing power to analyse telescope data in the quest for finding extraterrestrial life (http://setiathome.ssl.berkeley.edu/). The P-2-P network has given the researchers the computing power of over three IBM US$100 million ASCI White supercomputers for free.

But the big online players such as Microsoft, Sun and Intel all have vested interests and issues with this concept. As a result they are also working on P-2-P projects. For example, Intel and Microsoft are working on a project called Hailstorm where the technology will be able to exchange a user's personal information to purchase an airline ticket and to pay for it via a personal credit card.

Will P-2-P running across different computer platforms and different languages become another tower of Babel and crumble, or will it become a new killer application for inter-networked countries, companies, conglomerates, consumers or consortia?

International marketers need to understand how these new technology applications can create international market potential.

Some observers believe that the global spread of the new information infrastructure will have dramatic structural impacts on many industries. At one end of the spectrum, Ohmae (1995) argues that boundaries (or markets) based on geopolitical criteria will decline in significance as most of the units based on this criteria cannot effectively manage the four Is – Investment, Industry, Information technology and Individual consumers – because these are all now globally oriented. Many companies and industries already exhibit this globalisation due to investment requirements for research and development and convergence and reshaping of industries. Industry convergence and the need for global alliances are occurring with media, publishing, entertainment and communication. Industries like pharmaceuticals, finance, telecommunications and airlines are becoming increasingly global as country standards become international and deregulation occurs. Also, a growing proportion of business customers and consumers are buying from global sources, particularly as electronic commerce and Internet access explode. However, smaller geoeconomic regions, such as Silicon Valley, southern China, the Kansai region or Penang, may be more effective at developing stronger economic couplings within a global economic environment.

Naisbitt's 'Global Paradox' (Naisbitt, 1994) points towards strongly integrated global economic and information systems but with many small 'units' driving the economy. These 'units' include much smaller geoeconomic states, small to medium-sized enterprises and units formed across borders based on common interests. The smaller units will emphasise their differences within the global economy. The possible impact of the Internet on small to medium-sized enterprises (SMEs) is considered further in the International Highlight 5.2.

At the other end of the spectrum, Sheth (2002) has proposed 'The Rule of Three', where three firms, one from each 'Triad' group, will dominate in many global industries. The Triad refers to the three economic regions of Europe (particularly the European Union), North America and Japan – regarded as the powerhouses of the world economy. Following Sheth's analysis, the three Triads as integrated units will exercise increasing market power over the next ten years.

Whether global markets evolve to many small corporations, or three large dominant ones, by 2005 most firms operating within the Triad markets will have to compete in a global market or face strong business pressures from global competitors – all with significant grounding in the new information infrastructure. However, future global industry analysis based on a *unidimensional* spectrum with many or few firms may prove to be myopic, because the new information infrastructure will be a driving force for the convergence from quite diverse backgrounds. Examples of industries where the breakdown of boundaries is occurring are the pharmaceutical industry and the cosmetics industry, hotels and hospitals, banking and insurance, media companies and telecommunications companies – and this is only the start of many different possible combinations.

5.2 International highlight

Global opportunities for SMEs through the Internet

Consider this scenario for SMEs!

The World Wide Web will reduce the competitive advantages of scale economies making it easier for small companies to compete internationally. Advertising costs, formerly a barrier to international marketing, will almost disappear as the web makes it possible to reach a global audience at low cost.

The importance of traditional intermediaries will be reduced as the Internet connects producers directly with end users. Price differentials between customers and between countries will be narrowed as consumers become more price-aware. The web will act as an efficient low-cost medium for conducting worldwide market research – gaining customer feedback, tracking customer behaviour and establishing virtual communities. In summary, the Internet will provide SMEs with low-cost access to global markets by reducing the barriers to internationalisation commonly experienced by small companies (Hamill, 1997).

But is it a gamble?

Most of us have heard of or played gaming machines whether in pubs, clubs or casinos. The chances are that you have played on Aristocrat machines. Aristocrat has been an Australian publicly listed company since 1996. The reason for 'going public' was to enable this SME to grow internationally.

Aristocrat has its machines installed in many of the glamorous casinos and clubs in America and Europe. Its website quotes it as the second biggest provider of gaming machines in the world. However, between 1996 and 1999 the game has changed significantly with the entry of new competitors. Those players are staking their claims on Internet gaming.

These virtual companies use the Internet to provide gaming services to their clients instantaneously and more cheaply than Aristocrat can do with its higher fixed costs structure. Furthermore

these online companies are directly competing with Aristocrat's objectives to grow internationally. As the Internet has no borders, the online gaming casinos are finding themselves winning customers from the countries that are usually hard to break into via traditional marketing means. This is especially evident in places such as China or India that have a large gambling population and rigorous government policies.

Research shows that the average gambler is continually seeking excitement and challenge and is looking for new ways of winning. Aristocrat has realised that Internet casinos have the potential to limit its business in physical places and also have the advantage of introducing new products instantaneously. It takes only a few minutes to upload a new piece of software (game) on the Internet site and make it visible to all of its players. In contrast, for Aristocrat's physical machines it takes between one and two years to introduce a new machine into the large clubs, and up to four years to do it in the smaller clubs. As a result Aristocrat is actively pursuing Internet opportunities and is developing online versions of its games. Aristocrat is using the Internet to source new business and form strategic alliances. It is continuing to follow its existing networks of casinos and is working in joint ventures to deliver online gaming to its traditional bricks-and-mortar clients. Its objective is also to win markets that it is not currently serving. Aristocrat is teaming up with some Internet companies (pure plays) to jointly develop lucrative Asian markets and bypass rigid regulatory frameworks that exist in the physical marketplace.

As banks, telecoms and computer firms increase the security, speed and infrastructure for electronic commerce, we can expect to see the most entrepreneurial SMEs rapidly take up international market opportunities accessible via the Internet.

Sources: Hamill (1997), pp. 300–323; Poon and Swatman (1997).

As firms become more information-based and service-oriented, they may run head-long into firms from other industries that have taken control of the basic transaction or information systems required to drive future growth within the former firm's industry.

Alternatively, firms that are augmenting their physical products toward information-based service offerings may find themselves forming strategic alliances with firms that may be in completely different industries – and even then the resultant virtual organisation may be in a new industry.

The challenge for strategic thinking posed by globalisation is not just the *unidimensional* convergence within an industry but the requirement to focus on *multidimensional* industry convergence. This requires lateral thinking to determine not only the sources of convergence but the new or redefining industries that will emerge as a result.

Industry transformation in a global economy connected to a powerful information infrastructure in 2005 will flow through to business transformation in organisational 'physicality', structure and orientation. (This is discussed in Chapter 19.)

The new information infrastructure in 2005

In 2002 the new information infrastructure exhibited many glaring constraints and limitations including:

- inefficient website search directories and processes inhibiting ease of access and use;
- slow access time and downloading of images, particularly in video and audio form. This was mainly due to the small amount of broadband-capable optical fibre laid and satellite access available;
- large amounts of out-of-date information on websites after the '2000–2001 tech wreck';
- perceived lack of security for transferring and processing financial transactions within the environment;
- uncertainty in many countries with regard to policies for investment, ownership, technology selection and rolling out for general public access to the new information infrastructure;
- major corporate rivalry in the development of technology and standards within the new infrastructure;
- concerns about how best to connect to and implement the new infrastructure within firms;
- resistance to implementation on cultural grounds.

By 2005, many of the technological constraints associated with the new infrastructure will have been overcome and high quality broadband access via optical fibre, microwave systems or satellites should be available to almost all businesses and over half of the population of the countries of the European Union, US and Canada, Japan, Hong Kong, Singapore, Taiwan, South Korea, Australia and New Zealand. Significant business numbers and population segments will have similar services in eastern Europe, Mexico, Brazil, Argentina, Chile, Uruguay, Venezuela, India, Indonesia, Thailand, Malaysia and South Africa.

Implications for international marketing

There are many implications for marketers in this new and increasingly global information-rich environment. Business customers and consumers have much quicker and more widespread access to business intelligence, company products and services, prices, new innovative concepts and potentially higher levels of service. The power of information is shifting from producers to consumers. Governments are having less influence than global corporations. Customers are expecting and demanding more. They are much more knowledgeable.

Firms can use information and communication technologies to access and service markets which previously were considered too remote or too expensive to address. They need to become lead users of these technologies to create added value for their international customers and consolidate relationships already established.

5.3 International highlight

The big gamble

'It requires no great leap of the imagination to believe that the convergence of mobile communications and the Internet will produce something big . . . but it may take longer than you think.'

Mobile communications and the Internet were the two major demand drivers for telecommunication services in the last decade of the twentieth century. Combine the two – mobile Internet – and you have one of the major demand drivers of the first decade of the twenty-first century. That's the theory, at least.

As Figure 5.4 shows, the two industries have exhibited remarkably similar growth patterns since the start of the 1990s, but with a lag of about two years. So, it requires no great leap of the imagination to believe that the convergence of mobile communications and the Internet will produce something big, perhaps even the mythical 'sum that is bigger than its parts'. In this view, the convergence of mobile communications and the Internet would produce innovations, new applications and new services that would not otherwise be possible. For instance, the service of knowing the location of a particular mobile user, combined with the service of targeted advertising, should theoretically make it possible for local businesses to attract users that are passing by, within a certain radius. Similarly, multimedia messaging services will open up visual, more exciting person-to-person communications. Thus, the mobile Internet could give birth to a whole new family of services.

Exploiting the new opportunities offered by the mobile Internet will require high levels of capital investment, possibly higher than ever before in the telecommunications industry. Investors want to see proof that a market for mobile Internet services exists. But operators can't provide that proof until they build the networks. Because of this 'chicken and egg' conundrum, the mobile Internet is potentially the biggest gamble the telecommunications industry has ever taken on. The lesson so far is that the pioneers get burnt fingers: to date, more than US$100 billion has been invested in acquiring 3G licences, even before network construction and service roll-out costs are taken into account. The timing of 3G investment could hardly be worse, with venture capitalists running scared of anything that has the word 'telecom' or 'Internet' in it. Consolidation is on their menu, not expansion.

Mobile and Internet – identical twins, born two years apart

Source: ITU World Telecommunication Indicators Database. Reproduced with the kind permission of ITU.

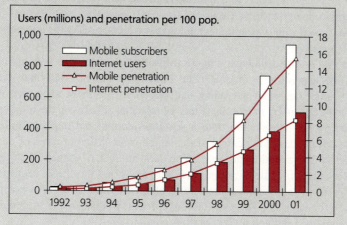

Mobile subscribers and Internet users (millions)

Penetration rates (per hundred inhabitants), worldwide

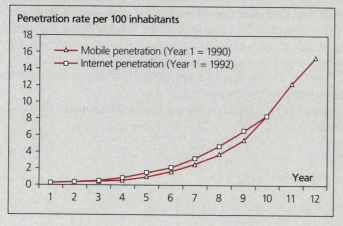

As previous waves of technological convergence have shown, we should not necessarily expect to see the commercial fruit of the mobile Internet for some ten or fifteen years yet. It will not happen straightaway, but that does not mean it will never happen. It is worth remembering that the 'hype' generated by a particular technological development often falls flat before market development begins to take off. Consequently, the popular view is that a particular development has 'failed', whereas the more accurate explanation is that market development has not yet got going properly. Those who forget their history are condemned to repeat it. So it is with some caution – and long-term vision – that the pioneers of this new wave of convergence must prepare their business plans.

Source: International Telecommunications Union (ITU) (2002) 'Internet Reports 2002: Internet for a Mobile Generation'. www.itu.int/osg/spu/. Reproduced with the kind permission of ITU.

Figure 5.4

International diffusion of innovation

The diffusion and adoption of technologies and products in international markets are key elements of the technological environment analysis. Diffusion refers to the movement of new products to and in international markets so that they are available to customers in those markets. However, the resistance of vested interests, having sunk investment monies into existing technologies, reduce or delay the competitive threat of the new technology.

Time lags in diffusion have a major impact on the costs and viability of a business. The diffusion process is characterised both by production lag-time, which elapses between initial output of a product and the commencement of its production in the foreign market; and by market lag-time, which elapses between the initial marketing of a product and its introduction into a specific international market. With market lag, there are differences in the extent of the lag between different types of products.

Typically the adoption process involves a number of stages, such as awareness, interest, evaluation, trial and adoption. Figure 5.5 shows the classic sequence of adopter categories from innovators, representing about the first 2.5% of a potential market, through to the laggards. This is based on a process of diffusion of a product, service or idea throughout a defined market or community.

The propensity of customers to adopt new products varies considerably from international market to international market and, according to Sheth and Sethi (1976), is a matter of differences in cultural lifestyle, strategic opinion leadership, economic environment and communication. In addition, the classification of consumers into innovators, early adopters, late adopters and laggards will also be affected by the following variables. The late adopters in one market might fall into the early-adopter category in some other country for certain products or services.

For a product to be more easily adopted in the international market, it should offer the following:

Figure 5.5

Adoption categories and curve

Source: Klopfenstein (2002).

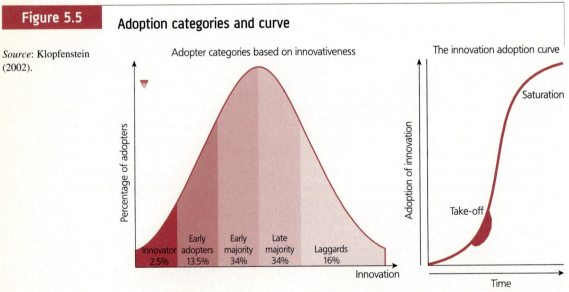

A relative advantage over existing alternatives in the market. If it does not,
it will have to offer a substantial price advantage in order to induce trial. The
advantage offered is situation-specific – products emphasising cleanliness and
sanitation are less likely to be perceived as offering the same advantage in India
where cleanliness has a lower priority because of circumstances, than in Germany.

Compatibility with local customs and habits. A freezer would be considered less
relevant in a country where shopping was a daily activity and fresh food was
the norm.

Ability to be divided and tried in small amounts. Divisibility is necessary so that
the potential international customer can determine its suitability without a major
outlay. Where the physical size or expense of the basic unit of the product is
great, other means of inducing trial should be applied, such as 'trial and money
back if not satisfied'.

Be observable in public. This is likely to induce trial and subsequent adoption.

Be as simple as possible. The more obvious the qualities of the product,
the greater the likelihood of its adoption in international markets.

A modification of life cycle theory has been proposed as the technology adoption
cycle for discontinuous innovations based on new technologies. The 'landscape' of this
cycle is shown in Figure 5.6.

It divides into six zones, which are described as:

1 *The early market* – a time of great excitement when customers are technology
   enthusiasts and visionaries looking to be first to get on board with the new paradigm.

2 *The chasm* – a time of great despair, when the early market's interest wanes but
   the mainstream market is still not comfortable with the immaturity of the solutions
   available.

The technology adoption life cycle

Figure 5.6

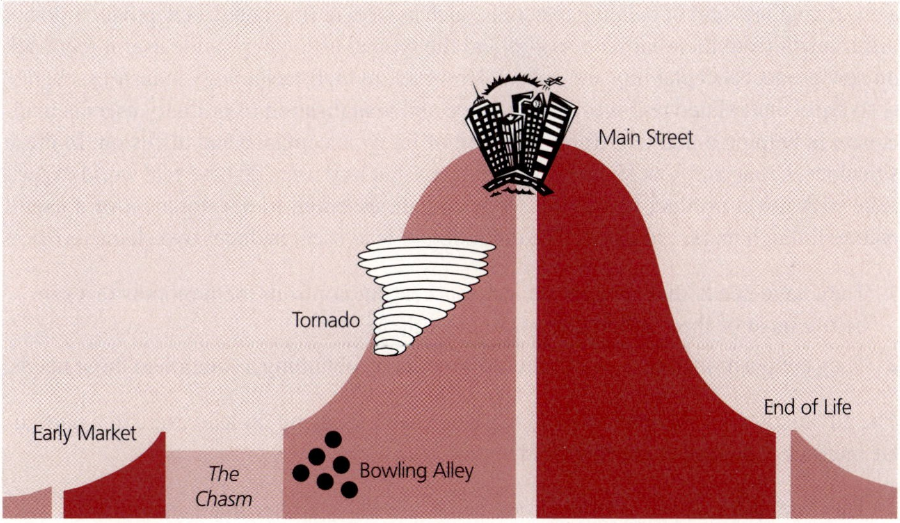

Source: Moore (1995)
p. 25.

Main Street

Tornado

End of Life

Early Market

The
Chasm

Bowling Alley

3 *The bowling alley* – a period of niche-based adoption in advance of the general marketplace, driven by compelling customer needs and the willingness of vendors to craft niche-specific whole products.

4 *The tornado* – a period of mass-market adoption, when the general marketplace switches over to the new infrastructure paradigm.

5 *Main street* – a period of aftermarket development, when the base infrastructure has been deployed and the goal now is to flesh out its potential.

6 *End of life* – which can come all too soon in high-tech products because of the semiconductor engine driving price/performance to unheard of levels, enabling wholly new paradigms to come to market and supplant the leaders who themselves had only just arrived.

Experience with high-technology products highlights the discontinuities occurring at different stages of the life cycle – particularly 'the chasm', when acceptance does not take place, and 'the bowling alley' which involves niche-specific solutions that need to be progressively broadened to appeal to a wider marketplace. Successful broadening of the conditions for general-purpose solutions encourages the pragmatist to adopt the product or service resulting in 'the tornado' of rapid market growth.

This is a major challenge in developing international markets and a firm can gain insight into a particular industry and market if it can identify lead users.

Lead users

It is frequently assumed that technological and product innovations are developed by technology or product manufacturers. Urban and Von Hippel (1988) show that for industrial markets the innovation process is distributed across users, manufacturers and suppliers. In some areas, such as scientific instruments, they have shown that users of innovations were the prime innovators. These users were also the primary instigators of diffusion of their innovations.

This has relevance to international marketing when related to the task of researching and evaluating needs for new products by analysing prospective users. In the relatively slow-changing world of building materials, such as steel or fibreboard, new products do not differ much from their earlier versions and the typical user can provide useful feedback on new product acceptability and appeal. However, in high-technology industries, change is so rapid that related real-world experience and visualisation of ordinary users is inadequate in helping a marketer form a picture of likely acceptance and diffusion. In these situations, Urban and Von Hippel (1988) suggest that lead users do have real world experience with novel product or service needs and are essential to development of a useful picture through market research. The definition of lead users includes two characteristics:

1 They have needs that are general in a market, but confront them months or years before most of the marketplace encounters them.

2 They are positioned to gain substantial benefits by obtaining a solution to those needs.

The advantages for the international marketer from focusing on lead users in a particular international market are threefold:

1 They are users whose present strong needs are likely to become general in a market in the future.

5.4 International highlight

Bluetooth versus Wi-Fi – the new connectivity technology

Named after the benevolent Danish king Harald Bluetooth, the much anticipated arrival of this new connectivity technology is hard to resist. With radio-based systems or wireless proving it can hold its own against fixed-wire connections, Bluetooth provides a simple method of inter-connecting a wide range of equipment, and it is this forthcoming convergence that is providing a catalyst for e-commerce in practically every corner of the world.

Personal computer and mobile phone users have waited almost a decade to benefit from some form of wire-free connection method (infra-red) because it has many problems that cannot be easily overcome. When there was a need to connect devices, the user specifically had to establish a connection, and ensure that the devices has an uninterrupted line-of-sight between them. Break the invisible beam, and the connection would be lost.

Bluetooth – being a radio-based system – offered considerable advantages, and by using low-power radio it allows a wide range of devices to 'talk' to each other without the user specifically having to bring the devices together and establish a connection. It enables laptop computers to surf the Internet via a nearby mobile phone; it allows commuters to download travel information into their phones; and it allows handheld devices to talk to nearby printers, without the need for cables.

Bluetooth is not getting all the attention; another wireless standard, called Wi-Fi, is arousing great excitement in the marketplace and many argue it will relegate Bluetooth to a minor role in cable replacement technology. However, it may not be fair to compare the two technologies as Bluetooth is designed for low-powered, short-range communication between devices, whereas Wi-Fi is a full-blown wireless Internet protocol for portable computers. There are many possible applications for Bluetooth: as a wireless payment mechanism in shops, as a replacement for key-cards to open doors, as an electronic travel pass. Using Wi-Fi to do these things would be far more complicated and expensive.

2 They can serve as a need-forecasting benchmark for market research.

3 They can provide new product concepts and design data to manufacturers because of their own attempts to satisfy their need.

As Herstatt and Von Hippel (1992) found in a lead user study of 'low-tech' industrial products, joint development of new product concepts by a manufacturer with lead users can reduce the costs of development and enhance success.

The challenge of today's high-technology environment for many marketers is to identify lead users in their targeted international markets as an input in the adoption and diffusion processes.

In the electronic world described earlier in this chapter, Hagel and Armstrong (1997) propose the concept of the virtual community – a group of consumers that have a common interest and similar needs. In this online interconnected community, they contend that power shifts from suppliers to consumers as the virtual community identifies its own needs and actively seeks solutions from a wide-ranging array of potential vendors. The lead user concept as applied to virtual communities is likely to play an important role in adoption and diffusion of new innovations. This application will be covered in some detail in Chapter 19.

Summary

The information and technology revolution in the new century is transforming the international business environment. Access to information and to the purchase of services and certain products via Internet or intranet systems provides the opportunity for businesses to instantly reach and be reached by international customers and prospects connected to these systems. This provides potential market penetration and speed of a totally different dimension from traditional marketplace activities.

The adoption and diffusion processes of new products, services and technologies need to be viewed in the light of this revolution. The identification of lead users in international markets is a particular challenge and opportunity for the firm. An understanding of how relevant industry structures are changing, globally and in country and regional markets, is an important aspect in reviewing the information and technology environment.

Ethics issue

The explosive growth of communications technology has resulted in a vast amount of information, public and private, being transmitted in cyberspace. Some of the lead users are global financial institutions and government agencies which hold personal and private information about their clients. As the value of information increases, particularly that associated with constantly updated detailed consumer profiles, the trading of such information is likely to become a substantial global industry.

How should financial institutions and governments respond? What ethical issues are involved?

Web workout

Question 1 How can firms use the Internet to create, develop, move and deliver services internationally?

Question 2 Surf the Internet and find two examples of small firms using their websites to generate international sales. Describe how they are doing it.

Discussion questions

1 What are the technology drivers of the fifth techno-economic paradigm – information and communication?

2 Look at the websites of Dell, Nike and Virgin and evaluate them in terms of potential for attracting international business.

3 How do lead users play a part in the adoption and diffusion of a new technology, product or service? Give an example.

4 How have international companies used virtual communities to generate growth? (This may be thought of as an extension of the 'user group' concept into the electronic environment.)

5 What are the likely impacts of technological change, globalisation and information technology on industry structures – globally and in local country markets?

References

Fortune (1995), 'The Rise of Netscape', 10 July, p. 105.

Freeman, C. and Perez, C. (1988) 'Structural Crises of Adjustment, Business Cycles and Investment Behaviour', in Dosi, G., Freeman, C., Nelson, R., Silverberg, G. and Soete, L. (eds) *Technical Change and Economic Theory*, Pinter, London, Summary of Section on Keynes (pp. 41–45) and Samuelson (p. 45).

Hagel, J. and Armstrong, A.G. (1997) *Net.gain: Expanding Markets through Virtual Communities*, Harvard Business School Press, Boston.

Hamel, G. and Prahalad, C.K. (1994) *Competing for the Future*, Harvard Business School Press, Boston, pp. 39–40.

Hamill, J. (1997) 'The Internet and International Marketing', *International Marketing Review*, Vol. 14, No. 5, pp. 300–323.

Herstatt, C. and Von Hippel, E. (1992) 'From Experience: Developing New Product Concepts Via the Lead User Method: A Case Study in a "Low Tech" Field', *Journal of Product Innovation Management*, Vol. 9, pp. 200–212.

Klopfenstein, B. (2002) 'Diffusion of Innovations on the Web', www.bgsu.edu/departments/com/diffusion.html (accessed 18 February 2002).

Moore, G.A. (1995) *Inside the Tornado: Marketing Strategies from Silicon Valley's Cutting Edge*, Harper Business, New York, p. 25.

Naisbitt, J. (1994) *The Global Paradox*, Allen & Unwin, Sydney, pp. 49–50.

OECD (2002) ICT database (accessed August 2002).

Ohmae, K. (1995) *The End of the Nation State*, Harper Collins, London, p. 80.

Pattinson, H.M. and Brown, L.R. (1996) 'Chameleons in Marketspace – Industry Transformation in the New Electronic Marketing Environment', *Journal of Marketing Practice*; *Applied Marketing Sciences*, Vol. 2, No. 1, pp. 7–21, Copyright MCB University Press.

Pattinson, H.M. and Brown, L.R. (1996) 'Metamorphosis in Marketspace – Paths to New Industries in the Emerging Electronic Marketing Environment', *Irish Marketing Review*, Vol. 9, pp. 55–68.

Poon, S. and Swatman, P. (1997) 'Small Business Use of the Internet: Findings from Australian Case Studies' *International Marketing Review*, Vol. 14, No. 5, pp. 385–402.

Poulsen, K. (2001) 'Cyber Terror in the Air', *Business Week*, 2 July.

Sheth, J.N. and Sethi, S.P. (1976) 'A Review of Cross-Cultural Buyer Behaviour', paper presented at the Symposium on Consumer and Industrial Buyer Behaviour, University of South Carolina, March.

Sheth, J. and Sisodia, R. (2002) *The Rule of Three: Surviving and Thriving in Competitive Markets*, Free Press, New York.

Time (1995) 'You Can Touch Cyberspace', Special Issue, Spring 1995, adapted in part from pp. 43–48.

Urban, G.L. and Von Hippel, E. (1988) 'Lead User Analysis for the Development of New Industrial Products', *Management Science*, Vol. 34, No. 5, May.

6

Researching international markets

Learning objectives

After studying this chapter, you should be able to:

- appreciate the role of market research in international marketing;

- discuss the research process as it applies to international marketing;

- identify sources of secondary data and secondary data issues in international marketing;

- recognise the differences between domestic and international market research;

- describe the techniques of conducting primary research in international markets; and

- appreciate the role and limitations of government agencies in providing information and export assistance.

Common international research mistakes

Information about international markets and the conditions that operate in them is essential if firms are to develop effective strategies to enter and develop business in those markets. This information is critical if mistakes are to be avoided and market research is necessary to obtain such information. Mistakes commonly occur because:

The need for research was ignored. Anxious to be the first into the market some firms often ship large quantities of product before doing market research. The results are often that they are left with these products as consumers fail to respond. Market research would have avoided this mistake.

Market research inadequate. Kentucky Fried Chicken entered the Brazilian market with the aim of eventually opening 100 stores. Sales from the initial store in São Paulo were disappointing. In deciding to enter the market, KFC had not researched all sources of competition. Street corner vendors sold low-priced charcoal grilled chicken virtually everywhere and this chicken was more appealing to local tastes than the KFC offering.

Market research was misdirected. An international soft drinks company conducted research in Indonesia to establish market potential. For cost reasons, it confined its research to urban areas, yet used the results to predict how the entire Indonesian population would react to the product. Based on the research, the results of which were encouraging, the company established large bottling and distribution facilities throughout Indonesia. Unfortunately there were major differences between urban and rural Indonesia. Sales proved to be disappointing as the product was purchased primarily by urban middle class Indonesians, tourists and visitors.

Failure to appreciate cultural differences. Coffee and its preparation are important in the life of the typical French household. Chase and Sanborn found considerable resistance when it attempted to enter the French market with its instant coffee. French consumers rejected the concept of instant coffee as it did not provide the ritual of coffee preparation that they viewed as inseparable from coffee. Prior marketing research would have alerted Chase and Sanborn to how deeply ingrained in the French culture was the ceremonial aspect of coffee preparation.

Source: Adapted from Douglas and Craig (1995), pp. 52–53.

Introduction

A study of blunders in international marketing leads to the conclusion that most could have been avoided if the manager had known more about the international market. Information is the key element in developing successful international marketing strategies, and necessary information ranges from general data for assessing market opportunities to specific information for making decisions about product, promotion, distribution and price. Major mistakes occur in international marketing because the firm and its managers do not adequately understand the international business environment. Unfortunately, many firms either do not believe that international market research is worthwhile or they consider that, given the potential for business, such research is not warranted in cost or manpower terms. Considering the international marketplace is more complex than the domestic market and that information is critical for informed decision making, the need to conduct market research in foreign countries is at least as great, if not greater, than is the case in the domestic market. Keegan and Green (2000) offer a series of anecdotes to illustrate the costs of failure to undertake market research in advance of entering international markets. Their anecdotes attribute international market failures to not appreciating local market tastes, not understanding why the preference for a local product was entrenched, projecting research based on large cities as representative of the total population in countries that were predominantly rural, not appreciating local preference for products in a particular form and not recognising that the same product might be served on different occasions in different countries.

International research decisions

The types of marketing studies required for doing international business relate to the market and the marketing mix variables of product, promotion, price and distribution:

- whether to enter, leave or expand activities in the international market;
- whether to add, delete or modify products in the international market;
- how to determine the appropriateness of promotional activities such as copy design, media selection and sales compensation in the international market;
- how to assess the relationship between price and demand and resultant profitability of operating in the international market; and
- how to ascertain distribution channels in and the logistics of getting products to consumers in the international market.

For each of the above, more specific research tasks can be established. Using the variable of 'market' as an example, the marketing decisions to be taken and the intelligence that needs to be gathered would be as follows.

Go international or concentrate on the domestic market? Assess the global market demand and the firm's likely share in view of local and international competition and compare these to opportunities in the domestic market.

Which markets to enter? Rank world markets according to potential, local competition and political situation.

How to enter target markets? Ascertain the size of the market, international trade barriers, transport costs to and within the chosen market, strength of local competition, government regulations impacting on imports and investment, and political stability.

How to market in selected market? Gather intelligence on buyer behaviour, competitive practices, distribution channels, promotional media, pricing practices and government regulations.

International market research

While the above points could in most instances apply equally to domestic as to international market research, they are being applied in a different environment. Because the international environment is so different from that with which the firm is already familiar, international market research is more complex than domestic market research. The four major differences relate to the different parameters involved, the new environments in which research will be undertaken, the increased number of factors involved, and the broader definition of competition.

When doing research in other countries, the firm must cope with parameters not found when carrying out research in the domestic market. Some of these are import duties, fluctuating foreign currencies, and logistics such as port facilities. Information must be obtained on these as they impact on business decisions. In addition, the way a firm may be required to operate in another country, such as via a joint venture or a licensing arrangement, may require extra information for business decisions. International market research will need to include this information.

When going international, the firm is exposed to a different environment in which many of the assumptions that guided its decision making in the domestic market are unlikely to apply. These assumptions will need changing to take into account the culture, the politics, the economics, the stability, the language and the social structure of the other country. Additional areas where information will need to be obtained include the legal regulations and enforcement effectiveness as well as the level of technology in the society. Managers are a product of having operated in their domestic business environment and assumptions made on this basis will need to be re-evaluated. Information gathered in international market research must include issues that reflect the differences in the international environment. Such information is essential if the manager is to begin to appreciate the different structures, the type of regulation and the different patterns of operating which govern business activities in the other country. Not only are the factors to be taken into account when operating internationally, different, but they are also more numerous. This is particularly the case when entering or operating in more than one international market. Apart from the number of factors that need to be researched, the interaction between them requires study and this adds to the complexity of international market research.

Finally, when operating in another country, the firm exposes itself to a broader range of competition: (a) the competition is likely to be from local firms which receive some form of government protection or preference and from other suppliers of imported products; and (b) it is likely to come from substitute products or other products with a similar end use application. As an example, devices that are labour saving in one market face competition from cheap manual labour in another. For this reason, international research should determine the breadth and nature of competition in the international market.

Stages

Figure 6.1 shows a number of stages to be undertaken when preparing a market research plan for international markets. In the first place, it is necessary to define the problem to be researched. Some familiarity with both the international market and the underlying strategy of the firm's involvement is necessary because if the problem is not properly defined, the data gathered may not be useful. The next stage is to develop the research plan and this will involve selecting a research design that will minimise the problems of collecting and comparing between countries to ensure reliability. The collection of data is then undertaken. This may be on the basis of secondary sources, primary data gathering or a combination involving gathering secondary data first and then undertaking primary research to verify or add to it. Intertwined with this stage is the next stage of interpreting the data. Interpretation involves an awareness of the biases

Figure 6.1	The research process and international issues

Source: Adapted from Toyne and Walters (1993), p. 366. Reprinted by permission of Pearson Education, Inc., Upper Saddle River, NJ.

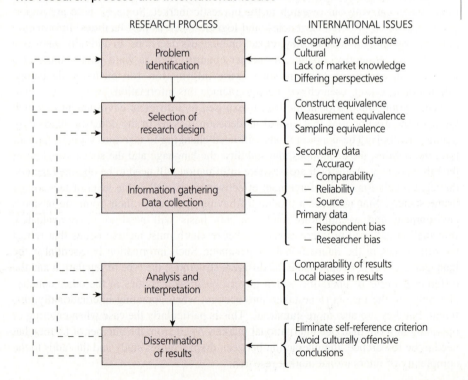

that can creep in, such as respondent bias and researcher bias, as well as taking comparability of data. The final stage is to summarise the findings and prepare the research report. This involves ensuring that the findings are communicated to all those people in the company taking and influencing decisions on matters covered by the report.

Issues

There are a number of general issues that need to be kept in mind when engaging in international market research. These relate to selection of markets and comparability of results.

If market research is being used to decide which international market to enter, then the research should consider the issue of degree of stability of the market. This is because there may need to be a trade-off between stable markets with low returns and less stable markets with higher rates of return. Such research will need to include the source of the instability and whether the political instability impacts on the stability of the commercial environment, the stability of the economy and the currency. The issue of psychic distance (see Chapter 3) also impacts on the selection of markets and the research needs to cover language impact and cultural differences so as to ascertain whether the perceived psychic distance is a real barrier. Research should also ascertain what the legal restraints are in the foreign country on carrying out research and what is the cost of research in relation to the apparent size of the market.

Although much of the following is discussed in more detail later in the chapter, comparability of results can be affected by the nature of the language in which the data is collected. Languages vary in their degree of precision with which meaning is conveyed. Answers to a questionnaire couched in a precise language, such as German, may give a different result from answers to a questionnaire couched in a language which tends to be imprecise in meaning, such as Thai. The use to which products are put is another variable impacting on comparability as is the method by which they are sold. As an example, bananas are sold by number in Germany whereas in the UK they are sold by weight. To ensure comparability, it is important that the same segment be researched in each market and that allowance be made for any differences in socioeconomic conditions. Socioeconomic conditions impacting on comparability include affordability, social class, educational levels and family composition issues. If the data source is secondary, then another issue is the reliability of statistics available in the international market. Finally, comparability can be affected by the difference in the marketing environment between countries, as figures from research in socialist countries may reflect different conditions from figures from research in a marketing-oriented country.

International research process

The international research process involves defining the problem, developing a research plan, collecting data, interpreting data and summarising the findings in a research report. Before undertaking international market research, it is useful to ask the following questions:

- What information is needed and what will happen to the information when obtained?
- From where can the information be obtained?
- Why is the information needed?
- When is the information required?
- What is the information worth in monetary terms?
- What is the likely cost of not getting the information?

The answers to these questions will influence the approach to be adopted in the research process.

Problem formulation

At the problem formulation stage it needs to be established who the decision-makers are, the objectives of the research, possible courses of action to obtain the information and the consequences of each alternative course of action. In international marketing, those who design the research and those whose decision making is the subject of the research are geographically separated. Because of this, it is often difficult for the researcher to arrive at a well-defined understanding of the research problem. This leads to two areas of difficulty in formulating the research problem to be investigated. The first relates to the cultural norms and values of the party commissioning the research. Known as the self-reference criterion (see Chapter 3), this refers to people's tendency to view the international situation in terms of their own background. To avoid mistakes due to the self-reference criterion, it is necessary to isolate the influence of the self-reference criterion and view the research problem from the perspective of the foreign parties involved.

The second problem area is lack of familiarity with the foreign environment to be investigated. Lack of familiarity can lead to false assumptions and poorly defined research problems. This can be overcome by some preliminary research into the general conditions in the international market. For many markets, there exist omnibus surveys conducted by market research agencies. These are conducted at regular intervals, contain a large number of consumer-related questions and are administered to a very large sample of consumers. Subscription to such surveys, where available, can assist in avoiding some mistakes at the problem formulation stage.

Research design

This refers to the framework for studying the issue to be researched. Its purpose is to ensure that the study is relevant to the problem and that it employs effective procedures. Researchers need to be familiar with problems that are unique to conducting research within and across countries and cultural groups. Three issues that are critical when designing this research are construct equivalence, measurement equivalence and sample equivalence.

Construct equivalence

Basic concepts such as beauty, youth, sex appeal, wealth, etc. are often used in market research questionnaires where the motivation for buying products is related to self-image or social values. Although these are seemingly universal concepts, their meaning can vary from country to country. Construct equivalence is concerned with whether both researcher and the subjects of the research view a particular phenomenon or concept in the same way. Problems arise due to social, cultural, economic or political differences; perspectives may be neither identical nor equivalent.

This difference in perspectives can impact on *functional equivalence*. It relates to the function served by an action as a result of which, differing interpretations might be placed on an activity in cross-cultural research. As an example, in Asia shopping is often undertaken by servants, in some European countries it is considered a social activity, whereas in other markets it tends to be regarded as a chore.

The difference in perspectives may also impact on *conceptual equivalence*. This refers to the concepts used by the researcher to identify an activity. Difficulties arise because many concepts are culture bound and are not equivalent when applied across national boundaries. This impacts on the selection of terms to use in the research instrument or the words used to grade or measure the responses. As an example, what is considered reliable in one country may not be considered reliable in another because the experience of the consumer with the product category may have been different. Reliable might mean something quite different to a car owner in Germany where sales of Mercedes and BMW are high compared with a car owner in India used to, say, the locally produced Hindustan Ambassador of 1950s design.

Difference in perspectives impact on *definitional equivalence*. Definitional equivalence relates to the categories used by the researcher to group data. Examples include the different meanings given by persons from different cultures to classes of products, roles performed by families and inclusions in occupational categories. For example, in Europe, businesspersons are accorded relatively high status, but in other countries where status is based on education or caste, this may not be the case. Sometimes businesspersons come from a despised minority group, as is the case with the Chinese in Indonesia.

Difference in perspectives impacts on *temporal equivalence*. In international marketing, temporal equivalence cannot be assured by simultaneous measurement because seasonal, religious, cultural, political and economic factors can intervene. For example, gift-giving seasons do not coincide between countries and they are often influenced by religion, i.e. Hanuka in Israel, Ramadan in Iran, and Christmas in Europe. In addition, reverse seasons between the northern and southern hemispheres affect research in areas such as fashion clothing.

Finally, difference in perspectives can be impacted on by *market structure equivalence*. When countries are not equivalent, there will be differences in the level of awareness of products and the availability of products. Aspects of market structure causing these differences are the nature of distribution channels in the foreign country, the advertising coverage in the market, the availability of product substitutes and the intensity of competition. There is a world of difference between the market structure in Vietnam and that in the UK.

Measurement equivalence

This deals with the methods used by the researcher to collect and categorise information. A method of measurement that works well in one culture may fail in another, and special care is needed if the reliability and validity of measurements taken in different countries are to be assured, so that the results can be compared. A distinction is necessary between two kinds of measuring instruments, etic and emic.

The *etic approach* to research uses general cultural variables such as individualism vs collectivism and cultures are compared in terms of these variables. Therefore, etic instruments are those that are culturally universal and when translated can be used in other cultures. Each measurement in the instrument, however, will need to be tested in advance of use to ensure that it does not contain any cultural biases. Etic instruments are very difficult to create and are not often used.

The *emic approach* to research takes the idiosyncratic traits of each culture to explore actual business behaviour in a culture. Therefore, emic instruments are tests constructed to study a phenomenon in one culture only. When the emic approach is used, country-specific instruments have to be created for each country involved in the research in order to ensure comparability of results. When developing emic instruments to measure the same phenomenon between different cultures, it is necessary to ensure gradation, translation and scale equivalence.

Gradation equivalence refers to equivalence in the units of measurement used in the research instrument. While it is normal to ensure equivalence in monetary and physical measurements such as volume, it is also necessary to aim for equivalence in items such as product grades, procedures, safety standards, quality and similar issues that vary from country to country. Perceptual cues also vary from country to country as is illustrated in the following:

> *The colour green has positive associations in Muslim countries due to it being the colour of Islam. As an example, in Libya Gaddafi's treatise on global reform is known as the 'Green Book', and the focal point for popular rallies in support of Gaddafi in Tripoli is called 'Green Square'. By contrast, in some Asian countries, green is associated with disease because of its connection with dense, green, humid jungles.*

Translation equivalence applies to both verbal and non-verbal language. Context, whether high context where much is implied or low context where most of the meaning is stated, will impact on translation equivalence because expectations will differ. For example, in high-context cultures, more meaning may be conveyed in non-verbal ways such as by gestures. Languages differ in how precisely they convey meaning and the number of words used to indicate shades of meaning. Differences also occur in the degree to which meaning is asserted as, for example, when 'yes' means 'definite agreement' or merely that the person is listening, and 'no' means 'definitely not' as opposed to 'I will need to think further about it'. Usunier (1996) points out that translation equivalence may be further divided into lexical equivalence, idiomatic equivalence, grammatical equivalence and experiential equivalence. To this might be added character equivalence.

● *Lexical equivalence* refers to whether the translations in dictionaries exactly match. If the English dictionary gives the word for 'hot' in French as 'chaud', does the French dictionary give the English word for 'chaud' as 'hot'?

● *Idiomatic equivalence* relates to a linguistic usage that is natural to a native speaker. In this case the equivalence is not in the words but in a different phrase to convey the intended meaning.

● *Grammatical equivalence* deals with the ordering of words and the construction of sentences. Whereas English proceeds in an active way, with the subject followed by the verb and then the circumstances, many other languages such as Japanese start by explaining the circumstances before dealing with the subject or the action. This can result in sentences much longer than those in English.

- *Experiential equivalence* is about what the word means to a reader/listener in terms of their experience. Translated terms should refer to real items and real experiences, which are familiar to the cultures involved in both languages. As an example, languages used by those living in hot countries are likely to have a number of words for degrees of heat and few words for degrees of cold whereas the reverse applies to those living in very cold countries.

- *Character equivalence* arises because different languages are written in different scripts. In most European languages, meaning is conveyed by letters making words and words forming a sentence. In many Asian languages such as Chinese or Japanese, meaning is conveyed by ideographs which are word pictures, each one of which has meaning which needs to be translated as a phrase. Translation can be complicated because these ideographs can be highly contextual.

The difficulties that can arise from translation equivalence were highlighted at the 1994 UN World Conference on Population Development in Cairo.

> *At this Conference, the Americans raised the concept of 'reproductive health'. This was translated into German as the equivalent of 'health of propagation' into Arabic as 'spouses take a break from each other after childbirth'. The equivalent in Russian became 'the whole family goes on holiday' and in Mandarin as 'a holiday at the farm'.*
>
> Source: Adapted from Bohnet (1994) as cited in Usunier (1996).

To overcome the problems of translation equivalence, there are a number of techniques that can be employed. The most commonly used is back translation which involves having the questions translated from English into the target country's language by one translator. The translated questions in the other language are then translated back into English by another translator. A second technique is parallel blind translation which involves a number of translators translating the questions from English into the other language independently of each other. The translations are then compared and discrepancies resolved. Another technique is the random probe approach whereby several probe questions are included in both the English and translated versions to ensure that the respondents understand the questions in the same way.

Scale equivalence

When developing an instrument for collecting data it is important to ensure not only that the same scale is used in each questionnaire but also that the meanings that respondents attach to each point in the scale are the same. Many questionnaires employ a version of a Likert scale. In countries such as the UK, these have 5 or 7 points, whereas in other countries such as Germany, there may be 10 points. This is important when comparing secondary data and other research between countries. Another problem area is differences between countries in the weight attached to respondent scores. The relative importance placed on scale values can vary as can the interpretation of values given. In countries where people tend to be definite, there is more likely to be a

| Figure 6.2 | Extracts from a questionnaire used in a study of Aboriginal health |

Source: Spark (1999).

Does eating SUGAR cause diabetes? (Tick one circle or dot)

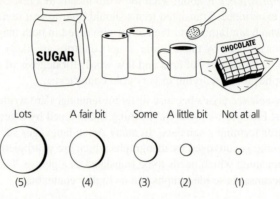

Lots	A fair bit	Some	A little bit	Not at all
(5)	(4)	(3)	(2)	(1)

How WELL are most people in your community? (Tick one circle or dot)

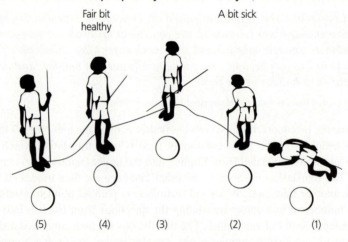

Fair bit healthy   A bit sick

| (5) | (4) | (3) | (2) | (1) |

spread of responses around the mid point of the scale compared with countries where people are more equivocal.

The problem is even more complicated when conducting research in developing countries or in developed countries among underprivileged groups. This can be overcome by using pictorial scales such as that employed in a survey of Aboriginal health (see Figure 6.2). Devices used included different sized circles and climbing a hill.

Research by Sood (1989) involved translating nine scale terms into Arabic, Chinese, Farsi, French, German, Korean and Spanish and asking respondents to place values on the translated items. The average values of the translated terms were then compared with the average value of the English terms to see whether there was a measurement equivalency problem. He found significant differences in the way measurement terms were interpreted between countries and concluded that intuitively developed rating scales, even with careful translations, resulted in poor comparability in research results.

Sampling equivalence

Because of social, cultural, economic and political differences, there are unique problems in international marketing which are not found in domestic marketing. The first relates to identifying and making operational, equivalent population samples to test in two or more countries. While it is possible to define a population for research by using externally imposed criteria (e.g. location, income, age or education), comparison and equivalence will be affected by internally generated criteria (e.g. personality and psychological characteristics). External definitions of population, such as income classification, ignore the fact that the same income group may have different lifestyles in different countries. Furthermore, internal definitions could result in inclusion of people in one country with a high interest in the product and inclusion in another country of people with a low interest. As Toyne and Walters (1993, p. 374) state, 'it cannot be assumed that either externally imposed or internally generated population definitions are comparable'.

The second problem area in sampling equivalence concerns the scope and representative nature of the sample. It is necessary to select comparable samples from each population in the research. Often this is expensive and time consuming and some markets may not warrant the expense of obtaining truly representative samples. Here it may be necessary to sacrifice representativeness of the samples in order to enhance the comparability of selected variables in the survey instrument.

Research in developing countries

The lack of sampling resources and the obstacles encountered when sampling a poor, mobile and illiterate population prevented the sampling of large segments of the Egyptian population. This forced researchers to abandon more precise sampling techniques in favour of a more realistically obtained convenience sample consisting of 500 consumers living in Cairo in the summer of 1990. The test instrument was hand delivered due to the lack of a reliable postal service. The sample, with a response rate of 67% was skewed in favour of educated and professional consumers. Although the above did not result in a proportionate representative sample, it was acceptable to the researchers in the circumstances. This was because poorer people are more reluctant both to form and express opinions, tend to be negative towards market research, and are more inclined to be biased towards issues which are socially sensitive. Due to the hardship they face because of economic circumstances, the cost of reaching poorer areas and respondents with low education is prohibitively expensive and such respondents have a general mistrust of strangers which obstructs the conduct of market research (Al-Khatib et al., 1995).

Data collection

There are two ways of gathering data for undertaking research into international markets. One method involves collecting from the international market, data specifically related to the purpose of the study. This is referred to as primary data. The other method is to check on what has already been gathered for other purposes and what information

6.1 International highlight

Market research booming in Russia

With official statistics hopelessly outdated or incomplete, Russian marketers are turning to the private sector for market information. Official statistics don't count the rapid growth of small companies in the service sector that are hiding from the tax authorities. These are listed however in the figures for new company registrations which exceed 300,000. However, a private research agency, Mobile, estimates that only 8,000 of the above companies actually advertise

their activities or do business. The difference between the two figures reflects the legal fiction that managers use to hide from taxation. Mobile analyses real commercial activities in the absence of reliable official statistics, by devising ways of tracking sales, surveying dealers and checking claims against how much they advertise, the prices they publish and the amount of electricity they consume. For example, media advertising provides a vast database of offers to sell which are then checked against price lists, sample surveys of sales figures and media circulation figures. It is believed that in Russia there is a mathematical relationship between advertising volume, turnover and profitability. By tracking advertising in the media every 36 hours, Mobile claims it can reliably pinpoint changes in buying and selling patterns in Russia. Despite smuggling and other unofficial commercial activities, using indirect measures and surrogate indicators enables private sector research firms to provide reasonably accurate secondary data on the market.

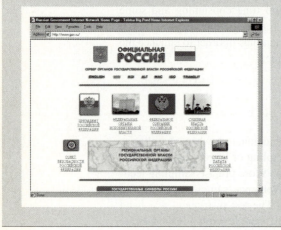

Source: *BRW*, 9 June 1997.

is already available. This is secondary data. Usually secondary data is obtained before the collection of primary data is undertaken as secondary data might obviate the need for primary data or reduce the number of areas for which primary data needs to be gathered. For this reason we discuss secondary data first.

Secondary data

Sources

Often referred to as preliminary desk research, much of the secondary data on international markets can be gathered at home. This can involve a study of export statistics in the home market, a study of export statistics of other countries with whom you are likely to be competing in the target market, and finally a study of the export statistics in the target market itself. The home market study is likely to indicate whether exports are taking place already, where the exports are going, the volume and value of these exports and whether there is a seasonal pattern. The study of other countries may reveal comparative export prices, competitive export quantities, the magnitude of import trade to the markets in which you have an interest, and any seasonal trends. The study of the target market is likely to show the key sources of supply, the volume by source of supply and values on a cost, insurance and freight basis (CIF) by source of supply, enabling you to assess your level of competitiveness (Noonon, 2000, pp. 37–39).

There are six major sources of secondary data related to doing international business:

- *International agencies.* The United Nations, EU, the World Bank, the International Monetary Fund and the Asian Development Bank gather a wide variety of economic and social information on different countries. This information is publicly available. It suffers from the drawback of being supplied by each member country, which may use different criteria for collecting and classifying the information, and from being dated, because it takes time to collect and analyse information from all around the world.

- *Home government.* The Department of Foreign Affairs and Trade and trade promotion bodies are the main government agencies which supply information on international markets. Other government departments can supply information in the areas of their specialisation on international markets – such departments being those responsible for primary industry, energy, defence, education and transport.

- *Consulting firms.* Many consulting firms, including accounting firms, specialise in services for international firms. Some firms such as PriceWaterhouseCoopers will conduct original research for a fee and issue newsletters on specific markets, produce information about various countries in material such as 'Guide to the Market in . . .', and may continuously track, analyse and forecast economic and business conditions in a number of countries.

- *Government representatives.* Trade commissioners can, in the area for which they are responsible, provide updates on market conditions, and a general background on the market. They can undertake more detailed research on the market for the firm's product/service for a fee. Information can also be obtained from embassy and consular officials as well as the international representatives of other government departments. In some international markets, state governments have representatives who will assist firms from their state with information on market conditions.

- *Databases.* Electronic databases provide international marketing information and updates on international trade statistics. Online databases, such as the Internet, link computer users worldwide and allow firms to find out about international developments in their field of interest. The interactive nature of the medium enables firms to discuss the information provided so as to check and improve its relevance to their needs.

- *Other commercial interests.* Other organisations which provide information to firms on international conditions and opportunities include the chambers of commerce and industry associations. Banks through their network of representative offices can also provide their clients with international market information, as can legal firms. Information will be of different degrees of importance as shown in Figure 6.3 which illustrates the results of a survey conducted in countries in the Asia-Pacific region.

Figure 6.3	Sources of information in Asia-Pacific

Source: Lasserre
(1997).

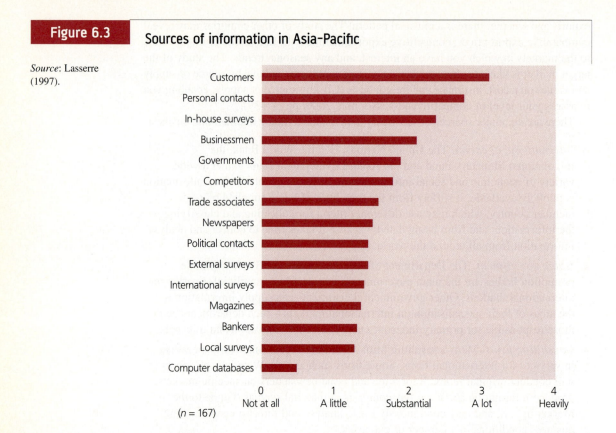

(*n* = 167)

As shown in Table 6.1, in different countries various sources of secondary data have different degrees of importance. This needs to be kept in mind when gathering data.

Problems with secondary data

Unfortunately much of the secondary data available in western markets is not available in many developing countries. In some countries, data gathering is only of recent origin. Although the situation is improving through the efforts of the United Nations and other multilateral bodies, there are still problems in cross-country comparison of secondary data. These problems relate to availability, age, accuracy, reliability and comparability.

- *Availability of data.* Detailed data on numbers of manufacturers, wholesalers and retailers is not available in many developing countries because there are no government agencies which collect such data on a regular basis. In these circumstances, it is necessary to commission private agencies to supply secondary data as in the Russian example mentioned in International Highlight 6.1.

- *Age of data.* The desired data might be available but, because it was collected some years previously, it is outdated. Many countries collect data at different frequency levels and difficulties arise comparing such international data; for example, data collected every four years in one country might only be collected every ten years in another country.

Table 6.1 The most used sources of information, by country, by rank of importance

---

Japan	Singapore	Taiwan
Customers	Government	Customers
Government	Political contacts	In-house surveys
In-house surveys	In-house surveys	Competitors
Personal contacts	Customers	Government
Local surveys	Business contacts	Personal contacts

Korea	Hong Kong	China
Customers	Customers	Customers
In-house surveys	Personal contacts	Political contacts
Personal contacts	In-house surveys	Newspapers
Business contacts	Trade associations	Personal contacts
Political contacts	Magazines	Magazines
	Business contacts	

Indonesia	Philippines	Malaysia
Customers	Personal contacts	Customers
Competitors	Customers	Personal contacts
Personal contacts	Local and international surveys	In-house surveys
Business contacts	Business contacts	Competitors
		Trade associations
		Local surveys

Thailand	Vietnam
Personal contacts	Trade associations
Customers	Personal contacts
Business contacts	
Competitors	

Note: Only sources which, on average, are used substantially, a lot or heavily are reported.
Source: Lasserre (1997).

- *Accuracy of data.* Problems arise in this connection because the definition used for certain indicators varies across countries, and the quality of the information becomes compromised by the mechanisms that were used to collect it. Whereas in developed countries, data collection mechanisms are sophisticated, in developing countries this is not the case due to lack of resources and skills.

- *Reliability of data.* Official statistics in some countries are not accurate: the data might have been selectively collected for statistical purposes; may be overly optimistic to reflect national pride; or may be incomplete because it does not reflect a sizeable 'black' economy.

- *Comparability of data.* As mentioned, the factors above make it difficult to compare data between countries. Another factor contributing to comparability problems with secondary data is the manner in which the data is collected. In some developing countries, especially where literacy is a problem, data can be estimated rather than accurately gathered and very frequently data is reported in categories which are too broad to be compared with classifications which apply in developed countries.

To check whether the secondary data can be relied upon, it is useful to ascertain, for each data source, who collected the data and whether there was any party that might benefit from the data being misrepresented. Other issues to inquire about include the purpose of having the data collected, how the data was collected, and whether the data is consistent with other related factors. As an example of consistency checking, data on the sale of infant formula could be compared with number of women of childbearing age and with birth rates. In general, the availability and accuracy of secondary data increases as the level of economic development improves. When confronted by contradictory information, one possibility is triangulation – the obtaining of information on the same item from at least three different sources to check if there are any reasons for the contradiction. In the case of wine, such triangulation might reveal that the import figures for Singapore were by value and those for Thailand were by volume, or that one country categorised all sparkling wine as champagne, while another categorised as champagne only that sparkling wine which originated in the Champagne region of France.

Primary data

Primary research is undertaken to fill specific needs for information. Although the research may be done by an agency rather than the firm because it is being carried out for a specific purpose, it is different from secondary research which cannot supply the answers to specific questions. Different environments, attitudes and market conditions add to the complexity of conducting primary market research in other countries. Furthermore, collecting primary research is expensive in terms of both money and time and therefore care is necessary in designing the research to ensure that it is conducted economically and that the effort is justified in terms of the costs involved.

Sources

The firm can obtain primary research by visiting the international market and checking at first hand the impressions formed as a result of the secondary research undertaken at home or commissioned from the international market. Participation in trade missions can be a useful way of gathering primary data. Another way is to visit the international market at the time of a major trade display of products in the firm's area of expertise. The show itself provides a useful venue for gathering information on competitive offerings, the state of development of the market, and likely reaction to the product to be offered. The most common source of primary research for the firm is for it to commission a firm in the international market to undertake specific research on its behalf. Such research is usually intended to obtain answers to questions that are directly related to the firms' decision making with respect to that market.

Issues

A wide range of issues need to be considered when conducting or evaluating primary market research. These include the ability of the respondent to communicate opinion, their willingness to respond, sampling where field surveys are to be undertaken, the ability of the respondent to understand the question or issue, bias on the part of the respondent, non-response bias and interaction bias between the researcher and the respondent.

- *Ability to communicate opinion.* The respondent's ability to express attitudes about an item or concept depends on their ability to recognise the usefulness or value of the item or concept. Opinions and attitudes are difficult to form if the respondent is unfamiliar with the concept or the item is not widely used in the community. The more complex the concept, the more difficult it is to design research to elicit useful opinions about it.

- *Willingness to respond.* Culture may influence this in two ways. In the first place, culture can influence who in the household expresses opinions to outsiders. In Muslim countries, this is generally the male in the household and a male interviewer is not allowed to interview a female. In the second place, there may be a reluctance to tell interviewers what the respondent actually thinks or to reveal the actual situation. This may be due to secrecy reasons such as covering up tax evasion or fear of the state.

- *Sampling.* As was evident from the example in International Highlight 6.1, sampling in field surveys can be a major issue in undertaking primary research in many countries. The types of problem encountered in drawing up a random sample can include no officially recognised census, lack of other listings that can serve as a sampling frame, inaccurate or out-of-date telephone directories and no accurate maps of population centres from which cluster samples can be taken.

- *Language and comprehension.* Differences in idiom and difficulty in arriving at an exact translation create problems in obtaining the specific information sought and in interpreting respondents' answers. This is because equivalent concepts rarely exist in all languages. Literacy can also be a problem in developing countries where literacy rates are low and written questionnaires are largely irrelevant. Within a country, there can be a number of different languages and dialects (as is the case in India where different languages are spoken in each of the four southernmost states). This can impact on the conduct of primary research.

- *Respondent bias.* This can include social biases, such as telling the interviewer what it is believed the interviewer wants to hear; social desirability biases as exemplified by giving answers which are believed to reflect desirable social status or educational levels; and topic biases which result from some topics being taboo in some cultures (as with sex in India).

- *Non-response bias.* Often this is a matter of reluctance to answer personal questions or questions on particular topics. It can also be a matter of members of some cultures being more reluctant than members of other cultures to respond to market research questions. As a consequence, non-response rates vary substantially between countries.

● *Interaction bias.* Many primary research studies require interaction between researcher and respondent. This can be influenced by the location where the interaction occurs and whether there are others present when the interaction occurs. In the first instance, the formality of the location may influence the formality of the response because responses to interviews conducted in a home may be more relaxed and forthcoming than responses to interviews conducted in an office or in a rented interview room. In the second instance, when others are present the interviewee may be more inclined to provide a socially acceptable response rather than a response reflecting what is actually felt. Another source of bias is difference in social status between interviewer and interviewee which can inhibit expression of frank opinion.

The problems of conducting international primary research are compounded when emerging markets are involved.

> *With the last census conducted in 1988, with infrastructure in disrepair, with long held traditions of secrecy, obtaining a representative sample for the purposes of conducting national research in Russia is a nightmare. The absence of telephones in many parts of the country precludes telephone polls and requires data be gathered using personal interviews which are both time consuming and expensive. According to Vsevolod Vilchek, director of sociological research for Russia's public television channel, obtaining a representative nationwide sample of 3,000 people to poll is an impossibility and attempts to do so fail by a wide margin of error. On average, he stated, 15% of people approached to participate in a poll refused to participate, and many people do not know how to answer questions. If difficult questions are posed, you cannot count on people telling you what they actually think. A question about attitude to privatisation is likely to yield a positive response of 20%, a negative response of 30% and a don't know type response of 50%. This is due to people not understanding what the word 'privatisation' means.*
>
> *In the case of China, there are problems in defining the sample frame, of proportionately very small sample sizes, difficulty in framing questions so that the meaning is appropriate and accurate when translated, very low response rates, and over-simplification of responses, especially when Likert scales are employed.*
>
> Source: Adapted from David Hoffman (2001) and Newman et al. (2001).

Techniques

Cultural and individual preferences vary substantially among nations. These are important for determining the most appropriate research technique to use. Executives usually prefer to collect large amounts of data through surveys so that the data can be manipulated statistically. Executives in other countries such as Japan prefer to gather research through visits to dealers and other channel members and match this with hard secondary data, such as statistics on sales, imports and inventory levels. Techniques for gathering primary research can vary according to whether the data is to be collected in a real world or controlled environment. Surveys are an example of the former, whereas focus groups are an example of the latter.

Also influencing the selection of the technique for gathering primary data will be the extent to which the data to be gathered is subjective or objective and the degree to which it is to be structured or unstructured. Subjective, unstructured data is more likely to be collected by qualitative research whereas objective, structured data is more likely to be collected by quantitative research.

Qualitative research techniques

Qualitative techniques include interviews, focus groups, observation and Delphi studies.

Interviews   These constitute the primary form of research for executives visiting the international market. If the interviews are with knowledgeable or influential persons, they can be a major source of information because opinions expressed are a result of that person analysing a variety of other opinions and sources of information. However, because of the risk of bias, the objective of the interview should be to gather in-depth information as opposed to a wide variety of materials.

Focus groups   These are a popular form of exploratory research in international marketing. Focus groups consist of small groups of potential customers, usually between 8 and 12 people, facilitated by a professional moderator. A free-ranging discussion takes place around a series of predetermined topics. In an international setting the moderator needs to be familiar with local language and patterns of social interaction, e.g. people from some cultures such as Japan are more reluctant to offer criticism than are people from cultures such as Hong Kong. In countries where non-verbal language is important, the moderator needs to be skilled at interpreting the degree to which body language adds to meaning.

Observation   In international marketing, observation can shed light on issues not previously understood or practices not previously encountered. Observation is useful when researching how consumers in different countries actually behave and for this reason it can be obtrusive or unobtrusive. Problems can arise with unobtrusive observation when people discover that their behaviour has been observed and become resentful.

Delphi studies   These are a technique for aggregating the views of a number of experts who cannot come together physically. These experts are people who are very knowledgeable about a particular issue as opposed to the general interviewee who only has limited knowledge. Participants are asked to identify major issues relating to the topic, rank their statements according to importance, and give a rationale for their ranking. The aggregated responses are then returned to all participants who are asked to indicate their agreement or disagreement with the aggregate ranking. Repetition of this process occurs until a degree of consensus has been achieved. Using mail, e-mail or fax, it can obtain the opinions of informed individuals at a reasonable cost, despite their being separated by large distances.

6.2 International highlight

Toyota makes design changes for the US female market

Toyota sent a group of its engineers and designers to southern California to observe how women get into, out of and operate their vehicles. They found that women having long fingernails encountered difficulty in opening doors and operating knobs on the dashboard.

Based on their observations, the Toyota engineers and designers redesigned some aspects of both the exterior and the interior of Toyota automobiles intended for sale in the US.

Source: Adapted from Czinkota and Kotabe (1994).

Quantitative research techniques

The commonest instrument for the gathering of primary data in international marketing is the questionnaire. Preparation of questionnaires for administration in international markets requires care with both wording and sequencing of questions so as to ensure that results from one country can be compared with results from another. (The elements to be considered in this connection were discussed earlier in this chapter.) When difficulties arise in ensuring that concepts will be rated the same across different countries, it may be necessary to use pictures rather than words, as in Figure 6.4.

In selecting the sample from which to collect the data, a sampling plan should be drawn up which addresses issues such as: What is the target population? How many people should be surveyed? And how should the prospective respondents be chosen from the target population? Usually, a larger sample will be required from heterogeneous countries such as India than will be required from more homogeneous countries such as Thailand.

When preparing the sampling plan, it is necessary to decide how prospective respondents are to be contacted. Data collection methods can vary from mail to telephone to personal interviews, e.g. shopping intercepts. The use of these methods varies from country to country as illustrated in Table 6.2 and the custom of the country regarding method of data collection needs to be taken into account.

Questionnaire design should take account of format, content and wording so as to achieve both cultural sensitivity and a low non-response rate.

- *Question format.* Questions can be structured or unstructured. The latter, being open-ended questions, capture a greater amount of in-depth information but increases the potential for interviewer bias. Another issue to be taken into account is that some societies prefer indirect questions and others have no problem with direct questions. Sensitivity to this issue is important to reduce the non-response factor. A typical example relates to age. Should the question be phrased: 'How old are you?' or, 'In what year were you born?'

- *Question content.* Content impacts on willingness to respond. Information available to respondents may vary because of different education levels and access to different communication infrastructure. Questions should also be adapted to societal restraints such as tax evasion and the black economy. Where these

The funny faces scale

Source: Corder (1978), pp. 86–90.

Figure 6.4

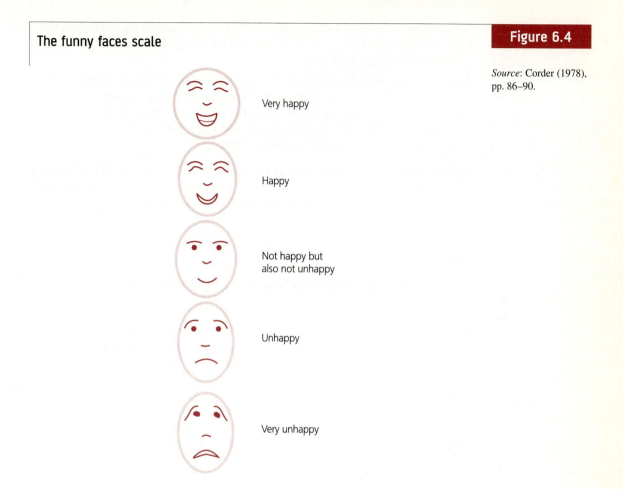

Very happy

Happy

Not happy but
also not unhappy

Unhappy

Very unhappy

Table 6.2 Comparison of European data collection methods

	France	Netherlands	Sweden	Switzerland	UK
Mail	4	33	23	8	9
Telephone	15	18	44	21	16
Central location/streets	52	37	–	–	–
Home/work	–	–	8	44	54
Groups	13	–	5	6	11
Depth interviews	12	12	2	8	–
Secondary	4	–	4	8	–

Source: Demby, E.H. (1990) 'ESOMAR Urges Changes in Reporting Demographics, Issues Worldwide Report', *Marketing News*, 8 January, p. 24. Reprinted by permission of the American Marketing Association.

constraints apply questions must be asked indirectly lest the respondent feels that a truthful answer will end up in the office of the tax commissioner or lead to a charge of black market activity.

● *Question wording*. The potential for misunderstanding spoken or written words should be reduced by careful attention to the impact of language and culture on the design of questions. Words used should be simple rather than complex, unambiguous rather than ambiguous and, where culturally acceptable, the questions should be couched in specific terms.

Using a poorly designed data gathering instrument in international marketing will yield poor results. For this reason, any instrument should always be pre-tested, preferably with a sample drawn from the population it is intended to survey.

Interpretation

In research the same situation can be interpreted in different ways, as the following story indicates:

> *There's a story told about difficult markets along the following lines:*
>   *Two shoe company salesmen get the nod to open the first international sales territories. Joe goes to Zimara and Bob to Didyuri Doo. After one week, Joe sends a cable back to headquarters that reads 'Coming home tomorrow. No possibilities in Zimara. The natives don't wear shoes.' Bob isn't heard from in the first week, nor in the second. Because Didyuri Doo was so remote, people at HQ began to worry. In the third week a cable arrived which said 'Fantastic sales opportunity!! Natives are all barefoot. Everyone here needs shoes!!'*
>
> Source: Adapted from Zhan (2000).

The final step in the research process involves interpreting the data, following which a report is prepared. There are many issues that must be taken into consideration at this stage ranging from cultural interpretations to different concepts of the product in various countries. As an example, in Australia, beer is considered to be an alcoholic beverage, whereas in southern Europe, it is regarded as a soft drink. This relates to comparability of data collected in different cultural contexts. Affecting comparability is how reliable the data is likely to be. This can be a matter of accessibility on the one hand and quality on the other. Accessibility of information varies from one country to another. Factors impacting on accessibility can be the stage of development of the country, its market research infrastructure, extent of freedom and dissemination of information, and the degree to which the political regime is democratic or authoritarian. Comparability is also influenced by variation in the quality of information available as this also varies between countries. It can vary in terms of reliability, detail and whether it is short- or long-term.

Interpretation of research results in international marketing requires a degree of scepticism because the data has been collected under varying circumstances that can result in errors in both collection and analysis. Substantial biases in answers to questions on attitude for example can arise because of cultural differences. If researchers wish to compare answers given to the same question by respondents from two culturally distinct environments, they may need either to standardise or normalise the data before interpreting it (see Craig and Douglas, 2000, Chapters 7–9). Standardisation involves taking the questionnaire scale and setting the mean answer for each respondent at zero. Differences from that mean are then expressed in terms of standard deviations. Normalisation occurs when differences are expressed in terms of deviation from the country's or cultural group's mean. Interpretation of data gathered on an international basis also involves a high degree of cultural sensitivity because of selective perception due to cultural biases. This can be minimised by ensuring that at least one of those interpreting the data from a particular country is either from that country or is well acquainted with business customs and practices in that country.

Interpretation of statistics also requires consideration of purchasing power parity (PPP). This refers to a method of comparing the size of economies using international price comparisons to reflect the domestic purchasing power of the local currency (Table 6.3). This is more accurate than the traditional method of comparing countries' gross national income (GNI) via converting to US$ by applying the official exchange rate to the local currency. This traditional approach does not reflect the fact that prices of services and other non-traded goods tend to be much lower in developing countries. As a consequence, PPP measures of developing economies are frequently higher than estimates based on exchange rate calculations.

In preparing the final report, it is important to comment on the reliability as well as on any limitations relating to the facts as presented. The report should:

- identify the sources of the data because different sources of data justify differing degrees of confidence;
- where appropriate, identify by name and title those interviewed as this enables the recipient of the report to assess the value of the information it contains;
- simplify statistical computations so as to facilitate understanding by the recipient; also the way the data was obtained should be fully explained; and
- spell out alternative courses of action resulting from the research so that management is able to make an informed decision.

Finally, international marketing research is not just confined to establishing a market for a product or service. It may be specifically directed to understanding the international market and how it operates, so that a specific segment of that market can be targeted. This is illustrated in a case about China.

Ogilvy Brand Consult, a recently established marketing advisory firm, has researched China's middle class through a study of brand buying behaviour. They established four key segments within the marketplace. These were 'seekers' or those considered to be leading social change, 'adapters' or those who follow the seekers but wish the pace of change to slow somewhat, 'tolerators' who struggle physically and emotionally with the new system, and 'resisters' the most traditional members of the middle class, who tend to adopt new opinions and behaviours slowly.

Source: Adapted from Song and Wong (1998).

Table 6.3 GNI measures for selected countries, per capita 2001, Atlas method and PPP: the top ten and bottom ten countries based on capita income

	Population (thousands)	GNI per capita		PPP measures	
		US$ 2001	Rank	US$	Rank
Low-income countries		430		2,040	
Ethiopia	65,816	100	205	710	200
Burundi	6,938	100	205	590	203
Sierra Leone	5,141	140	203	480	207
Guinea-Bissau	1,226	160	200	710	200
Tajikistan	6,224	170	197	182	1150
Niger	11,192	170	198	770	198
Malawi	10,526	170	197	620	203
Eritrea	4,204	190	196	700	189
Chad	7,917	200	194	960	190
Mozambique	18,071	210	191	100	187
High-income countries		26,710		27,680	
Singapore	4,103	24,740	10	24,910	20
Sweden,	8,893	25,400	9	24,670	21
Hong Kong, China	6,874	25,920	8	26,050	14
Iceland	284	28,880	7	29,830	5
Denmark	5,350	31,090	6	27,950	7
US	283,962	34,870	5	34,870	2
Norway	4,519	35,530	4	30,440	4
Japan	127,100	35,990	3	27,430	10
Switzerland	7,209	39,070	2	31,320	3
Luxembourg	444	41,770	1	1	1

Source: Adapted from World Development Indicators database, World Bank, August 2002.

Other issues

Some final issues in international market research for consideration include new techniques for market research that have recently been developed in advanced countries, managing the international research process and undertaking test market activities.

New international research techniques

Recent years have seen an increasing use of various forms of scanner data as a vehicle for international market research and comparison between markets in developed countries. Most non-durable consumer goods are sold with a barcode to facilitate scanning at the point of sale.

Scanner data is collected more frequently, is more accurate, enables shifts in sales volume and market shares to be spotted quickly, and can be used as the basis for an automatic order to replenish system. In countries such as Japan where scanner data has met with some resistance, consumer panels are used. Two approaches are used. One is to issue members of the panel with an ID card to use when checking out at the cash register so that purchasing information is entered every time the panel member shops. The other method is to provide the panel member with a scanner and the member scans all purchases made on returning home after shopping.

Another advanced form of data gathering for market research purposes is to use people meters to track TV programmes as they are watched and then correlate viewing behaviour with purchase transactions. Referred to as single source data, this approach allows companies to gauge the effectiveness of their advertising.

The use of these technologies in cross-country comparisons in consumer research is at present confined to the more developed countries – even then comparability is patchy due to the reluctance by retailers to release their scanner data for competitive reasons, and uneven use of these new technologies.

Managing international research

This involves two aspects: the selection of a research agency, and coordination of global research activities.

Selecting a market research agency

There are three choices. The first is to select a research agency based in the geographical area. In all developed countries and in many developing countries, such agencies exist. The need to use a local agency depends on the level of physical distance.

The second option is to select a research firm that specialises in the industry of which the firm is a member. These firms are more likely to understand research issues peculiar to the industry and may have undertaken multi-country research studies for the industry or have undertaken individual studies for the industry in other countries.

The third option is to hire a firm that is either a multinational agency operating in many countries or has alliances with agencies in other countries. Such agencies rely on branches and/or associates in all developed countries and in many developing countries, but the client deals with only one office located in the domestic market. Examples of firms with extensive networks of international offices are SRG International of New York and AC Nielsen of Chicago. By using them for surveys, interviews and analyses, clients avoid the hassle of managing research projects from a distance, not to mention the headaches over cultural differences and translation into the other language.

Coordination and management of market research

International marketing research may need to be carried out both at headquarters and in the host country. Marketing research at headquarters is useful for short-term planning and strategy formulation, whereas marketing research in host countries is necessary for tactics to achieve goals, short-term market planning and day-to-day activities. Marketing information is important at all levels of the organisation and it is important that a balance be achieved between centralising functions at headquarters in the interests of achieving economies and devolving responsibility to the regional or national levels so that the research has a 'local look and feel'.

As can be seen from Table 6.4, costs of various forms of market research vary widely from country to country and this is illustrated by benchmarking other countries in relation to western Europe or the United States. For example, using western Europe as a cost benchmark (i.e. 100), usage and attitude studies for various countries ranged from a high of 234 in the USA to a low of 13 in India.

Given this variation in cost, the issue arises as to the desirability of coordinating cross-country market research. Coordination facilitates cross-country comparison of results and also provides the benefits of timeliness, cost savings, centralisation of communication and quality control. The degree of coordination depends on the conflicting demands of users of the market research. Headquarters tend to favour standardised data collection, sampling procedures and survey instruments, whereas local users tend to favour country-customised research that takes into account the peculiarities of their local environment. The ideal approach should embody both the etic and emic approaches referred to earlier in the chapter. If coordination is attempted, then all user groups should be involved and multi-country research should make some provision for particular circumstances of specific countries. It can do this by adding some country-specific items to the standardised questionnaires.

Test marketing

Should a 'go–no go' decision to launch into an international market be made on the basis of market research or should the firm do what is commonly done in the domestic market and conduct a field experiment otherwise known as a test market? An international test market operation is advisable if the decision to proceed would involve new capital investment in production facilities in the domestic market. In such a case, using existing excess capacity, the firm could supply an international test market location with product so as to assess sales potential, reception to planned promotional strategy, degree of price elasticity and to analyse ways of achieving cost-effective distribution.

The international test market selected should be a microcosm of the larger market that would be targeted if the test market in successful. This means that it should reflect the same characteristics of demographics, lifestyles, economics and culturally influenced behaviours. It should also reflect the same commercial impediments, incentives and media availability as the larger market.

In developed countries, locating a test market city is possible because test marketing is a well-established practice. In developing countries, especially where there is a wide gulf in socioeconomic conditions between rural and urban areas as in Thailand, test market locations may not be available. One possibility is to launch in one location and, if results are promising, then progressively roll out the launch to other locations. This can be within a country: for example, you could use San Diego as a test market, then roll out the launch to the rest of California; if this is satisfactory, extend the launch nationwide. This can be done on a country-by-country basis within a geographic region. Using ASEAN as an example, the initial test market could be Singapore, followed by

Table 6.4 Cross-country comparison for market research studies

Usage and attitude survey		
Western Europe	100	
North America	220	
USA		234
Canada		202
Japan	181	
Australia	136	
Central/South America	100	
Brazil		114
Argentina		105
Mexico		92
Colombia/Chile/Venezuela		67
South Africa	102	
Middle East	96	
Saudi Arabia		106
UAE		84
Pacific Rim	87	
Hong Kong		140
Indonesia		63
Taiwan/S Korea		92
Eastern Europe	61	
Hungary		48
Czechoslovakia		65
Poland		62
Russia		81
North Africa	50	
Egypt		49
Turkey	45	
India	13	

Telephone tracking study	
USA	100
Canada	106
Japan	103
USA	100
Australia	80
Taiwan	78
Brazil	59
Hong Kong	48
South Africa	47
Argentina	34
Hungary	27
Turkey	26

In-home product test		
Western Europe	100	
North America	318	
USA		283
Canada		362
Japan	297	

Central/South America	190	
Brazil		225
Mexico		150
South Africa	188	
Australia	157	
Middle East	151	
Saudi Arabia		165
UAE		129
Pacific Rim	144	
Hong Kong		152
Indonesia		73
Taiwan/S Korea		187
Eastern Europe	119	
Hungary		94
Czechoslovakia		111
Poland		127
Russia		155
North Africa	100	
Egypt		102
Turkey	77	
India	25	

Four group discussions		
Western Europe	100	
Japan	194	
North America	129	
USA		135
Canada		115
Pacific Rim	90	
Hong Kong		92
Indonesia		53
Taiwan/S Korea		133
Central/South America	82	
Brazil		107
Argentina		53
Colombia/Chile/Venezuela		51
Mexico		83
Australia	74	
Middle East	70	
Saudi Arabia		72
UAE		69
South Africa	51	
Eastern Europe	50	
Hungary		51
Czechoslovakia		53
Poland		48
Russia		45
North Africa	33	
Egypt		45
Turkey	51	
India	17	

Source: ESOMAR.

Malaysia, then Thailand, the Philippines and Indonesia. The weakness of this approach is that these markets differ from each other and the Singapore results may not be an accurate predictor of acceptance of the product in Thailand.

Many firms skip the test market stage when marketing internationally because they consider that, having announced their intention to introduce their product into a market, if they do not do so in all areas, their competitors may launch nationally and pre-empt them. Test market operations are costly and the results may be misleading if the conditions in the test market cannot be replicated in the wider market should the product eventually go to a national or a regional launch.

Government export assistance

For many firms, the government is a vital element in their researching the potential of and entering international markets. The government can assist with export promotion which Seringhaus (1986, p. 55) defines as 'all public policy measures that actually or potentially exporting activity either from a firm, industry or national perspective'. Government assistance is provided to improve the firm's international competitive position and in the process enhance a nation's competitiveness. From the firm's perspective, export promotion measures create a pro-exporting attitude, deal with specific export problems and assist in making exporting a positive experience for the firm (Diamantopoulos et al., 1993). The level and type of assistance a government can provide is restricted by the World Trade Organisation with the result that for the most part government assistance is restricted to 'back-up' services. Assistance differs between countries depending on national trade policy and the prevailing view towards government intervention in the business sector. Some countries have a pure government export promotion organisation (e.g. Australia, New Zealand and export boards in most EU countries), whereas others have privately funded bodies (e.g. Austria). Government export promotion programmes provide both indirect and direct assistance as illustrated in Figure 6.5.

Indirect measures, while not specifically designed for export, can generate export benefits via enhancing future competitiveness. They include assistance to firms to improve their productivity, research and development incentives, support to firms to create and employ innovative technology, assistance with manpower planning, incentives for undertaking activities in specific regions or industry sectors and fiscal measures such as tax and investment incentives.

Direct measures are intended to enhance the firm's export competitiveness. They include the activities of government departments that supply standardised and customised market information and give advice on exporting in general and export marketing in particular; programmes that provide assistance to firms extending from awareness to market entry; and programmes that cover a firm's financial risks through insurance and financial arrangements.

The focus of all programmes is on exporting and as such does not reflect the reality of current international business which involves varied forms of international involvement including licensing, franchising and strategic alliances. Given that inward and outward international activities are often interdependent, governments in future may need to adopt a less restrictive approach towards assistance for encouragement of international involvement.

Government assistance programmes

Figure 6.5

Source:
Diamantopoulos et al.
(1993), p. 6.

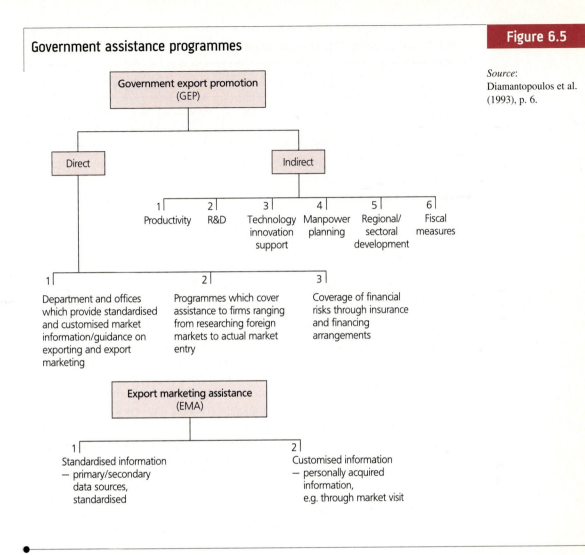

Government export promotion (GEP)

Direct   Indirect

1 Productivity 2 R&D 3 Technology innovation support 4 Manpower planning 5 Regional/ sectoral development 6 Fiscal measures

1 Department and offices which provide standardised and customised market information/guidance on exporting and export marketing

2 Programmes which cover assistance to firms ranging from researching foreign markets to actual market entry

3 Coverage of financial risks through insurance and financing arrangements

Export marketing assistance (EMA)

1 Standardised information — primary/secondary data sources, standardised

2 Customised information — personally acquired information, e.g. through market visit

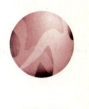

Internet infusion

The Internet is a significant tool for international market research. It extends both the depth and the breadth of the search process because, in addition to company sites, consumers can also access product category sites, retailer sites and consumer dominated sites (e.g. bulletin boards and chat rooms). With the Internet, the initiative in the search process shifts to the consumer, resulting in topic-focused rather than sequential, process-oriented search. Also, the search process is influenced by the fact that the information provided is timelier and it is cheaper than acquiring it via conventional sources.

The information environment on the Internet differs from that in the marketplace in that due to the majority of sites being located in western countries, Internet sites in general reflect the conventions and symbols of western culture. As a result there may be difficulty in the interpretation and retention of information where communication crosses cultural and linguistic boundaries. Specific areas of concern are:

Table 6.5 Internet penetration by language

	Languages spoken		Internet sites	
Mandarin	1,025	35%	9.9	6.6%
English	497	17%	129.0	85%
Hindi	476	16%	–	0%
Spanish	409	14%	9.6	6.4%
Russian	279	9%	1.4	1%
Arabic	235	8%	0.95	<1%
	2,921		150.85	

Source: Craig, Douglas and Flaherty (2000), p. 31.

- *Language.* There is predominance in the use of English on the Internet (57% of users are English speakers). This implies that non-English speakers have access to a much more limited range of information, although there are signs that a global Internet vocabulary is starting to emerge. Using other languages is impeded by their having a number of spoken dialects (e.g. Mandarin is the written form of Chinese but there are many spoken forms) and meaning conveyed in the spoken form in some languages varies by tonality.

- *Information misinterpretation.* Because there are no filters on accessing Internet information, there is greater scope for misinterpretation and miscommunication of messages on the Internet, especially by non-native English-speaking or non-western consumers.

- *Information credibility.* As 'word of mouse' replaces 'word of mouth', it is much more difficult to assess the objectivity or biases of the presenter of the information.

- *Product cues.* On the Internet, consumers are faced with a truncated set of cues and an absence of olfactory and sensory cues. This leads to a greater reliance on objective cues such as price and product description. The latter can be termed 'digital' cues because they can be conveyed on the Internet, whereas the former can be considered as 'non-digital' cues.

Market research often has as its major focus the understanding of consumer behaviour. In traditional marketplace models, cultural factors are viewed as key factors in explaining geographic variations in behaviour. However, these factors play a much lesser role in 'virtual' markets. There, a cyber culture dominates and local culture acts as a contingency variable that mediates behaviour. Compounding the situation is that access to information can be acquired in one geographic sphere that is totally separate from the geographic sphere in which the resulting transaction will occur. Some related international issues for market research:

- Diffusion of innovation – geographic proximity will no longer be as important as the Internet provides not only a vehicle to rapidly communicate the latest developments but also a conduit to deliver them.

- Complexity of evaluations – consumers now have to evaluate stimuli and make choices based on heterogeneous and often unfamiliar cues (e.g. Does the hotel stars rating system mean the same in all countries?).

- Country of origin effect – the role of national culture in the formation of values and behavioural norms is likely to decline in importance. This will occur as consumers via the Internet become exposed to stimuli from other countries. As they become more global in outlook, country of origin becomes less salient as a cue.

- Opinion leaders – models focusing on the role of personal influence are no longer likely to apply to the same extent. With the proliferation of chat rooms, bulletin boards, etc., the role of such influence becomes more diffuse and depersonalised.

With the Internet, the degree of consumer involvement in the purchase process becomes less and the distinction between high and low involvement goods also becomes less meaningful. Another factor is that the consumer who uses the Internet is different from the consumer who does not (in terms of demographics and innovation adoption). This has implications for international market segmentation.

Summary

Although undertaking international market research is fraught with more difficulties than domestic research and available information on which to base decisions is far less perfect, international market research is necessary to ascertain whether a market for the product does exist and, if so, how that market should be approached. It is a useful vehicle for learning in advance what changes need to be made to the product, what pricing strategy should be adopted, how best use can be made of the available media and which channels of distribution are likely to prove most effective. When carrying out international market research, considerable care is necessary to ensure that at each stage of the research process differences between the domestic and the international market are recognised and compensated for. If this does not happen, in all probability the research results will be irrelevant because there will be no basis for comparison. These differences must be taken into account not only when collecting secondary and primary data, but also when analysing and interpreting the data. Despite the fact that international market research is complex and at times frustrating, it does reduce uncertainty and provide a better basis for informed decision making as far as commitment of resources to international activities is concerned. In the process, firms should take maximum advantage of government assistance programmes, especially as far as provision of information is concerned and facilitation with conduction of primary research.

Ethics issue

You are the export manager of a major German pump producer that has been exporting small quantities of pumps to Indonesia for years. Sales have not grown with the market. For the last year you have been endeavouring to persuade your managing director that a manufacturing operation in Indonesia would give the firm a major share of what has been both an expanding market and a source of cheaper pumps as a hedge against competition in the German market from Taiwanese imports. In order to strengthen your argument, and without the knowledge of your managing director, you commissioned primary research on current and future prospects in Indonesia for your firm's pumps. Today two reports arrive on your desk. One was from the Jakarta office of PriceWaterhouseCoopers advising that in the short term there would be a severe downturn in the Indonesian market for pumps because of the flow-on effect of the currency crisis. In the longer term and within five years the market would recover and expand. The other report was from your Indonesian agent advising that representatives of the only other firm in the world with your advanced technology, US-based 'Pumps R Us', had recently been in Jakarta talking with the Indonesian Investment Promotion Authority (BKPM), about incentives for establishing a manufacturing operation in Bandung to supply the Asia-Pacific region.

Given the conservative approach of your managing director, if you were the export manager, would you show the Indonesian agent's report to him?

Web workout

Question 1 Visit the website of a well-known car rental company, a PC manufacturer and seller, or an airline. Browse through the website to find out whether it has a country-specific website. Are there any survey, quizzes, specific offers or FAQs (frequently asked questions) that are different in each country website?

Question 2 Using search engines such as Yahoo!, Hotbot or Google, research information about a country or a market of your choice. Are there any research agencies that you are most impressed with? Is there any valuable country or market analysis freely available?

Websites

Comparative country data http://www.pangaea.net/data/compara1.htm

globalEDGE™
Serves as a gateway to specialised knowledge on countries, cross-border business transactions, cross-cultural management and as a global business knowledge portal; it provides a wealth of information, insights, and learning resources on global business activities. http://globaledge.msu.edu

International Market Research http://www.stat-usa.gov/

Tradeport – Market Research http://www.tradeport.org/ts/planning/

Market Research http://www.knowthis.com/research/marketingresearch.htm

Brint – Business Researchers' Interests http://www.brint.com/interest.html

Web Resources for International Trade http://www.fita.org/webindex/index.html

Global Business Web http://www.gbw.net/content/index.htm

AC Nielsen http://www.acnielsen.com/

Kentucky Fried Chicken http://www.kfc.com.au

Mercedes http://www.mercedes.com

Toyota http://www.toyota.com.au

World Trade Organisation http://www.wto.org

Trade New Zealand http://www.tradenz.govt.nz/CWS/page_Index/

The Literati Club Website http://www.emeraldinsight.com/literaticlub

Discussion questions

1 What are the factors that cause international market research to differ from market research in the domestic?
2 Outline the stages in an international market research plan.
3 Why is the issue of equivalence a major problem in cross-cultural market research? Do the suggested techniques overcome all the problems of translation equivalence?

4 Which sources of secondary data are more important for industrial than for consumer goods?

5 Discuss the problem of cross-comparison of secondary data between countries.

6 What are the main areas of bias in primary research in international markets and how would you compensate for these?

7 Under what circumstances is qualitative research preferable to quantitative research in the international environment?

8 Discuss the issues involved in deciding which type of market research agency you would employ to undertake international market research for your company.

9 What criteria would you apply in selecting an international test market location?

References

Al-Khatib, J.A., Dobie, K. and Vitell, S.J. (1995) 'Consumer Ethics in Developing Countries: An Empirical Investigation' in Delener, N. (ed.) *Ethical Issues in International Marketing*, International Business Press, New York.

Bohnet, M. (1994) 'Was Wurde in Kairo wirlick beschlossen?' *BMZ*, Bonn, October.

Corder, C.K. (1978) 'Problems and Pitfalls in Conducting Market Research in Africa', in Gelb, B. (ed.) *Marketing Expansion in a Shrinking World*, AMA, Proceedings of American Marketing Association Business Conference, Chicago.

Craig, C.S., Douglas, S.P. and Flaherty, T.B. (2000), 'Information Access and Internationalisation – The Internet and Consumer Behaviour in International Markets', *Proceedings of the eCommerce and Global Business Forum*, 17–19 May, Santa Cruz, CA. Anderson Consulting Institute for Strategic Change.

Czinkota, M.R. and Kotabe, M. (1994) 'Product Development the Japanese Way' in Czinkota, M. and Ronkainen, I. (eds) *International Marketing Strategy*, Dryden Press, Fort Worth, pp. 285–291.

Demby, E.H. (1990) 'ESOMAR Urges Changes in Reporting Demographics, Issues Worldwide Report', *Marketing News*, 8 January, p. 24.

Diamantopoulos, A., Schegelmilch, B.B. and Katy Tse, K.Y. (1993), 'Understanding the Role of Export Marketing Assistance: Empirical Evidence and Research Needs', *European Journal of Marketing*, Vol. 27, No. 4, pp. 5–18.

Douglas, S.P. and Craig, C.S. (1995) *Global Marketing Strategy*, McGraw-Hill, New York.

Hoffman, D. (1996) 'Russian Voters' Poll Position: Fear, Uncertainty', *The Washington Post*, 23 May, p. A31.

Keegan, W.J. and Green, M.C. (2000) *Principles of Global Marketing*, Prentice Hall, Englewood Cliffs, NJ.

Lassere, P. (1997) in Doole, I. and Lowe, P. (eds) *International Marketing Strategy: Contemporary Readings*, Thompson Business Press, London, Chapter 7.

Newman, P., Minghua, J. and Ibrahim, N. (2001) 'The Meaning of the Brand to the Young Educated Biejing Consumer: a Comparison Between Local and Foreign Fashion Goods', *Proceedings of the Conference of the Academy of Marketing*, July, University of Cardiff.

Noonon, C. (2000), *Export Marketing: A Practical Guide to Opening and Expanding Markets Overseas*, Butterworth-Heinemann, Oxford.

OECD (2001) National accounts of OECD countries.

Seringhaus, F.H.R. (1986) 'The Impact of Government Export Marketing Assistance', *International Marketing Review*, Vol. 3, No. 2, pp. 55–66.

Song, T. and Wong, L. (1998) 'Getting the Word Out', *China Business Review*, Vol. 25, No. 5.

Sood, J. (1989) 'Equivalent Measurement in International Market Research: Is It Really a Problem?' *Journal of International Consumer Marketing*, Vol. 2, No. 2, pp. 25–41.

Spark, R. (1999) 'Developing Health Promotion Methods in Remote Aboriginal Communities', PhD Thesis, Curtin University of Technology, Perth.

Toyne, B. and Walters, P.G. (1993) *Global Marketing Management: A Strategic Perspective*, 2nd edn, Allyn and Bacon, Boston.

Usunier, J-C. (1996) *Marketing Across Cultures*, 2nd edn, Prentice-Hall, London.

World Bank Development Report (1995) World Bank, Washington DC.

World Development Indicators database, World Bank, August 2002.

Zhan, S.E. (2000), 'Penetrating Difficult Markets', *World Trade*, January, pp. 84–86.

Case study 1

Inditex-Zara (1974–2002): from local to global

Vicente A. López, **University of Santiago de Compostela (USC)**

Introduction

A growing number of clothing companies, such as C&A, Benetton, Stefanel, Marks & Spencer, Cortefiel, The Gap, Max Mara, Adolfo Domínguez and Calvin Klein, have expanded their geographical boundaries and become truly international in character. At the same time this has the effect of pressuring local domestic firms into defending their markets by gaining international experience. The forces of globalisation are evident.

The clothing industry

Even though the clothing, fashion and textile industry is undoubtedly dominated by SMEs, little by little larger firms are generating a growing percentage of the industry's income. However, the concentration of this sector varies depending on the countries considered, as we can see in Table 1.

A myriad of forces are coming together which are triggering the globalisation of industries. A detailed analysis shows that among the most significant past and present trends in the clothing industry are the following:

- Most of the industry groups have been immersed in a process of restructuring their activities.

- The main growth strategies pursued are diversification of products (for example into accessories) and diversification of markets.

- There has been a significant increase in the industry's concentration level, for example Cortaulds (UK) was taken over by Sara Lee (US); Inditex (Spain) acquired Massimo Dutti (Spain) and Stradivarius (Spain).

- Growth by acquisition is the main approach taken by companies to increase their number of well-known brands and distribution networks. In some cases the brand acquired is a key player in another sector and only needs restyling to be adapted to the clothing market.

- Based on the 1998 sales of the top twelve global corporations (Table 2), four US firms have attained a 61.3% market share against a 38.7% market share generated by eight European companies.

Table 1 Industry concentration

Country	Clothing industry		Textile industry	
	Top 3 firms	Top 5 firms	Top 3 firms	Top 5 firms
UK	22%	33%	43%	52%
France	28%	35%	21%	28%
Germany	35%	46%	14%	20%
Italy	20%	25%	9%	12%
US	na	na	23%	31%

Source: Adapted from Euratex (Bulletin 2000/1).

Table 2 Clothing industry (1998): market share of the twelve big firms

Company	Country	Market share (%)
Sara Lee	US	18.7
Levi Strauss Associates	US	15.08
VF Corporation	US	13.95
Calvin Klein	US	13.57
Holding di Partecipazioni	Italy	8.85
Adidas Konzern Clothing	Germany	6.15
Benetton Clothing	Italy	5.56
LVMH Clothing	France	5.12
Triumph International	Germany	3.87
Zara International	Spain	3.82
Marzotto Abbigliamento	Italy	2.71
Max Mara Fashion	Italy	2.6

Source: Adapted from Stengg (2001).

The historical origins of the Inditex Corporation

The origins of the company date back to 1963, the year in which Amancio Ortega Gaona, the founder (currently the chairman of the board of directors), commenced business activity as a maker and seller of ladies' lingerie in A Coruna, a Galician city in the northwest of Spain. In May 1975, the first Zara store was opened in A Coruna. This first outlet consisted of 350 square metres and acted as the benchmark for the future development of the Group. All further stores had a similar store design, with similar window dressing, merchandising and product mix based on a balanced price–quality relationship with a clear fashion vision.

In the Spanish market, Zara's retail chain and Cortefiel (another domestic firm) were the catalyst for the growth of a new and attractive market segment demanding designer-styled clothes with a medium quality and at a reasonable price. The concept at the time (late 1970s and early 1980s) was not new because companies like The Gap, The Limited (US), C&A (Germany) and Next (UK) had very similar fashion concepts.

The Group and its chains

The Inditex Group was formed in 1985 as the head of the corporate group and currently is composed of approximately one hundred companies dealing with activities related to textile and clothing design, production and distribution. Zara, Pull & Bear, Massimo Dutti, Bershka, Stradivarius, Oysho and Kiddy's Class are the fashion retail chains of the Corporation, selling more than 90 million garments yearly. All garments are fully designed by the Group. Sales generated by their own stores accounted for 88% of its 2001 revenues, franchises accounted for 6%, other textile sales accounted for 5% and other services 1%. Inditex put out an initial public offering in 2001 on the Spanish Stock Market. Inditex's products are not available via catalogues or through its web page. A description of some of the group's companies is outlined below.

Zara

Zara is the benchmark store of the Inditex chain and was the first outlet opened in A Coruna in 1975. To date there are 527 outlets covering approximately 30 countries, accounting for 74.2% of Inditex's revenues. Each year approximately 10,000 different models are designed which enables the stores to renew their collections twice a week with fresh designs.

Pull & Bear

Pull & Bear was launched in 1991 to service a growing new generation of urban, active and informal young people aged from 14 to 28 anxious to buy a modern image at competitive prices. A wide range of clothes, accessories and cosmetics are sold in these outlets. The design of these outlets has to cater for additional services with added value for this type of costumer, for example they offer music, video images, video-games, the Internet, magazines and a coffee area. There are currently 293 outlets in 15 countries generating 6.6% of the Group's income.

Massimo Dutti

Inditex acquired a 65% share of the Massimo Dutti Group in 1991. To date there are 247 outlets operating in 17 countries. These outlets focus on high quality brands at a medium price for independent, modern urban consumers. The range also includes tailored suits, shirts, informal leisurewear, footwear and accessories. Sales account for 7.4% of the Group's revenues. In 1995 Inditex took 100% control of Massimo Dutti.

Bershka

Bershka was founded in 1998 to address the needs of the younger female generation between the ages of 13 and 23. There are 193 outlets operating in nine countries with revenues totalling 6.6% of Inditex's turnover.

Stradivarius

Stradivarius was bought by Inditex in 1999 because of its positioning and high growth potential. It targets young women between the ages of 15 and 25 with a taste for the latest styles in international fashion. They currently have 148 outlets operating in seven countries generating 3.3% of the revenues of the Group.

Oysho

Oysho was launched in 2001 to meet the needs of a growing number of customers demanding the latest lingerie fashion products at attractive prices. The product mix includes sleepwear, clothing for sports, hosiery, swimwear, home wear, accessories and cosmetics. The stores are located in high streets and in shopping centres. The location strategy is similar to Zara. The selling area is greater than the average of the sector. There are currently 75 outlets operating in 11 countries representing 0.5% Inditex's turnover.

Kiddys Class

Kiddy's Class was created to market clothing products for children to compete directly with Gap Kids or Benetton O12. It currently has 51 outlets accounting for 1.4% of Inditex's turnover.

Internationalisation of Inditex

The first country targeted for international expansion was Portugal in 1989. Inditex gained considerable knowledge and experience from this expansion particularly in how to select, penetrate and consolidate new countries. France was the next port of call mainly because it represents a reference for a fashion corporation. They decided on the French market even though it was known as a difficult one to enter. They were conscious of the fact that Marks & Spencer had great difficulty in entering the market. Indeed, Zara's openings moved at a slow rate in the beginning mainly due to difficulty in finding state-of-the-art locations.

It was not until 1991 that Zara decided to open its first store in the United States (Lexington Avenue, New York). Even though they made losses they decided to remain in the

US market to build international brand aware-ness and to generate market intelligence by inter-acting with competitors like The Gap, Banana Republic and The Limited.

A joint venture with a local company was used to enter the Mexican market in 1993.

By January 2003, Inditex was represented in more than 30 countries with 1,586 stores.

Marketing mix strategy

The product strategy is based on 'one product for one global market' with some adaptations to suit local climates. Inditex continually focus on market needs in designing their products. They learn from the market through two mechanisms: firstly, by getting information daily from every store all over the world and secondly, from the reports of the international team responsible for capturing the fashion trends in universities, coffee shops, discotheques, pubs, restaurants and competitor stores. They use a target pricing approach eased on market needs assessment instead of using a production focus in establish-ing price (Figure 1).

Their communications strategy does not follow the traditional intensive advertising approach adopted by many companies in the fashion industry (for example Benetton's campaign). Instead they rely on the stores them-selves, with state-of-the-art locations, as the key builder of the company's image.

With respect to their manufacturing process, approximately 50% is carried out directly in the Corporation's factories. Local subcontractors and other manufacturing locations account for the remainder. However, up to 80% of all the products sold are manufactured in Europe. Inditex is a good example of a vertical retailer versus highly vertically disintegrated firms like Benetton or Mango. They embrace market-based design coupled with lean production with just-in-time processes and an informal structure that enables them to create and disseminate knowl-edge faster. These elements can be interpreted as a critical resource in terms of a quick response to market demands. For example, Inditex only needs three weeks to design, produce and dis-tribute a new product to a store compared with an industry average of nine months.

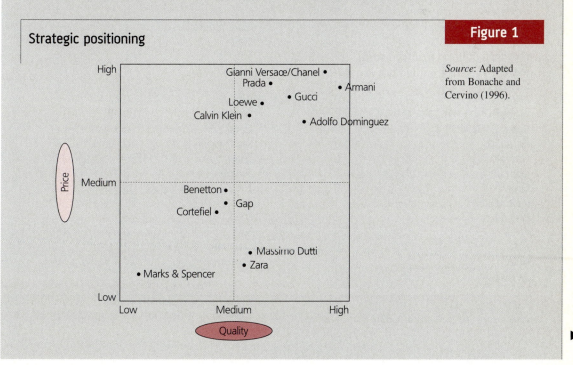

Strategic positioning

Figure 1

Source: Adapted from Bonache and Cervino (1996).

Appendix

Table 3 Number of stores and selling space*

Chain	Number of outlets		Selling space (sq m)	
	Own	Franchises	Total	Average size
Zara	476	31	488,400	910
Pull & Bear	220	29	38,500	144
Massimo Dutti	135	88	43,000	182
Bersha	146	5	49,800	337
Stradivarius	86	34	33,800	270
Oysho	34	0	5,900	na

*At 31 January 2002.

Table 4 International sales by chain (2001)

	%
Zara	60.8
Pull & Bear	31.3
Massimo Dutti	38.8
Bershka	32.3
Stradivarius	20.5
Oysho	33.3
Total	54

Source: 2001 Annual Report.

Table 5 Stores by country*

Country	Number of outlets		Country	Number of outlets	
	Own	Franchises		Own	Franchises
Andorra	0	2	Kuwait	0	4
Argentina	8	0	Lebanon	0	4
Austria	3	0	Luxembourg	1	1
Bahrain	0	2	Malta	0	2
Belgium	16	12	Mexico	41	14
Brazil	7	0	Netherlands	4	2
Canada	4	0	Norway	0	1
Chile	3	0	Poland	0	2
Cyprus	0	9	Portugal	109	31
Czech Republic	1	0	Qatar	0	2
Denmark	2	0	Saudi Arabia	0	14
France	68	0	Spain	730	39
Germany	17	0	Sweden	0	3
Greece	29	0	Turkey	5	0
Iceland	0	1	UK	11	0
Ireland	0	2	US	8	0
Israel	0	24	UAE	0	15
Italy	3	0	Uruguay	2	0
Japan	5	0	Venezuela	20	0
Jordan	0	1			

*At 31 January 2002.
Source: 2000 and 2001 Annual Reports.

Table 6 Stores by chain and country*

Country	Zara	Pull & Bear	M. Dutti	Bershka	Stradivarius	Oysho
Andorra	1		1			
Argentina	8					
Austria	3					
Bahrain	1		1			
Belgium	14	1	12			1
Brazil	7					
Canada	4					
Chile	3					
Cyprus	2	2	1	2	2	
Czech Republic	1					
Denmark	2					
France	67				1	
Germany	15		1			1
Greece	20	6		2		1
Iceland	1					
Ireland		2				
Israel	9	15				
Italy						3
Japan	5					
Jordan			1			
Kuwait	2	1			1	
Lebanon	2		2			
Luxembourg	1		1			
Malta		2				
Mexico	27		14	14		
Netherlands	3		2			1
Norway			1			
Poland	2					
Portugal	38	35	30	19	11	7
Qatar	1				1	
Saudi Arabia	6	3	3		2	
Spain	225	175	144	105	100	20
Sweden			3			
Turkey	5					
UK	11					
US	8					
UAE	4	3	3	3	2	
Uruguay	2					
Venezuela	7	4	3	6		

*At 31 January 2002.
Source: 2000 and 2001 Annual Reports.

Discussion questions

1 Identify the key elements and drivers that contribute to the competitive advantage of Inditex.

2 Visit the web pages of Inditex's competitors, for example Sara Lee (www.saralee.com/) and Benetton (www.benetton.com/), identify and describe the segments in which Inditex, Sara Lee and Benetton compete. How has Inditex positioned itself against its competitors?

3 How has Inditex internationalised?

4 Identify the cultural differences and challenges facing Inditex in the different country markets. How has Inditex addressed these issues?

5 Critically evaluate Inditex's international marketing strategy.

References

Bonache, J. and Cervino, J. (1996) 'Caso Zara: el tejido internacional', in *Multinacionales Españolas I. Algunos Casos Relevante*, Pirámide, Madrid.

Cervino, J. and Cruz, I. (1998): 'Caso Adolfo Domínguez: el pragmatismo gallego en la moda internacional', in *Marketing Internacional. Casos y ejercicios Prácticos*, Pirámide, Madrid.

Euratex Bulletin (2000/1).

Inditex annual reports (1999, 2000 and 2001).

Stengg, W. (2001) 'The textile and clothing industry in the EU. A survey', *Enterprise Papers*, No. 2.

WWW: Inditex, Sara Lee, Benetton, Mango, Cortefiel, Adolfo Domínguez, Gap, Massimo Dutti, Limited and Next.

Case study 2

Jurys Doyle Hotel Group plc

Mike Moroney, National University of Ireland, Galway

Introduction

Jurys Doyle is Ireland's largest hotel group with an established international presence. The Group underwent major development and expansion from the late 1980s, including acquiring Doyle Hotels in 1999. By 2002, Jurys Doyle managed 30 properties, with a stock market value of €500 million, a tenfold increase since 1989. Notwithstanding its achievements and committed future growth plans, 2002 was a watershed for the Group. Most senior managers had retired in the previous two years, while the new millennium presented a tougher environment for the hotel industry. The right strategy, properly executed, would be critical to continuing success.

Industry background

The state of the hotel industry depends on economic growth, which gives rise to increased business travel and corporate demand for conferences and meeting rooms. In addition, greater affluence results in increased use of hotel accommodation and facilities. After strong recovery in the late 1980s from previous fiscal mismanagement and stagnation, the Irish economy stalled in the early 1990s, due to a currency crisis and global recession. From the mid-1990s, a robust international backdrop and the double-digit growth of the 'Celtic Tiger' economy were favourable to the hotel industry, particularly the upmarket segment. However, the new millennium heralded a coordinated global downturn, with immediate and direct impact on the hotel sector.

As one of the world's largest industries, tourism is also a major determinant of the success of the hotel sector. Hotels cater for a sizeable minority of tourists, and for a higher proportion of tourist expenditure on accommodation, food, beverages and entertainment. Globally, tourism experienced healthy growth in the 1990s, with increases in numbers and receipts of around 5% annually. However, post the millennium, tourism suffered from the soft economy and from a series of exogenous shocks, including major terrorist incidents, the international spread of new infectious diseases and the second Iraq war. In 2001, global tourist activity declined by 1%.

In Ireland, the annual number of tourists exceeds the population by two-thirds (reflecting, in part, the country's large emigrant diaspora). From 1988 to 2000, foreign tourists grew by 7% p.a. and spending rose by 10.2% p.a. Ireland's strong growth reflected increased marketing (a relaxed, safe, scenic, unpolluted environment), development of new and improved products (interpretive centres, hiking trails, championship golf courses), greater and cheaper transport access, and upgrading of tourism infrastructure, with the aid of €1.1 billion in European Union (EU) led structural funding from 1988. Dublin was the major beneficiary, accounting for 35% of foreign spending in 2001 (up from 30% in the mid-1990s) due to the increasing popularity of city breaks, economic expansion and the city's role as the primary access point to the island. In 2001, foreign visitors fell by 4%, as foot-and-mouth disease in the UK compounded global factors. While there was a small recovery in 2002, tourism numbers remained below 2000 levels, in part reflecting high consumer prices (12% above the EU average), poor summer weather, development pressure on the environment, erosion of traditional Irish hospitality and the strength of the euro.

In terms of markets, Britain consistently accounts for half (and latterly more) of total tourists to Ireland, but for only two-fifths of spending. By contrast, North American visitors have the highest spend per head, are predominantly holidaymakers and 28% stay in hotels (compared with only 8% of Europeans, 16% from Britain and 14% of total tourists in 2001). But the North American market is also the most volatile. Although Europeans visit in large numbers, many are 'back-packers', staying in hostels and spending relatively little. In aggregate, domestic trips exceed the number of foreign visitors. However, average spend is only one-third the foreign level, 40% of trips are 'visiting friends/relatives' and seasonality is pronounced. Domestic trips declined from 1993 as increasing affluence led to more Irish holidaying abroad. Nevertheless, a 25% increase from 2000 to 2002 counterbalanced soft overseas markets.

The hotel sector in Ireland

There were 863 hotels in Ireland in 2002, 44% of the accommodation room base. In terms of luxury, facilities and price, hotels are graded from 5-star (6% of the total) down through 4-star (14%), 3-star (47%), 2-star (10%), 1-star (3%) and other (20%). Dublin has a higher proportion of 5-star (11%) and 4-star (19%) rooms, almost half the national total in these grades. By 2002, there were 42,235 hotel rooms in Ireland, double the 1988 level. The largest rises were in 3-star and 'other' hotels. Growth was strongest in Dublin, whose share of rooms rose from 22% in 1996 to 29% by 2001. (46% of visitors to Dublin in 2001 stayed in hotels.) Other trends include higher marketing spending, greater competition,

---

Table 1 Tourism and hotel industry trends

Year ended April	Actual performance					Est.	% Change	
	1988	1993	1996	2000	2001	2002	93–00	88–02
Tourism								
Foreign tourists (000)	3,007	3,814	5,289	6,737	6,448	6,600	+77	+119
Great Britain	1,465	1,783	2,590	3,494	3,416	3,700	+38	+153
Mainland Europe	398	945	1,177	1,451	1,344	1,400	+54	+252
North America	401	422	729	1,058	907	800	+151	+100
Other (inc. N. Ireland)	743	664	793	734	781	700	+19	−6
Domestic trips (000)	N/A	7,833	6,170	6,556	7,488	8,250	−16	N/A
Total spending (€m) (exc. carrier receipts)	1,227	2,009	2,696	3,947	4,416	4,700	+96	+283
Hotels								
Number of hotels	680	679	713	844	849	863	+24	+27
Occupancy (%)	55	58	62	68	66	N/A	+10 pt	+13 pt
Total rooms (000)	21.0	23.2	26.4	38.1	39.8	42.2	+64	+101
Dublin rooms (000)	4.2	5.0	5.8	11.1	11.7	N/A	+122	+179
Hotel bednights (000)	5.01	7.06	9.20	14.80	15.00	N/A	+110	+199
Foreign	2.53	3.75	5.07	8.10	7.30	N/A	+116	+189
Domestic	2.48	3.31	4.13	6.70	7.70	N/A	+102	+210

Sources: Irish Tourist Board, Central Statistics Offce, Horwath Bastow Charleton Hotel Survey.

more investment in business, conference and leisure facilities, increased emphasis on quality of service, a general upgrading of bedrooms and the 'ground floor' (bar, restaurant, lobby), and the emergence of a quality budget segment.

Reflecting the economic and tourist boom, the number of guest bednights trebled between 1988 and 2001. (Hotel usage by foreign visitors rose from 30% in 1996 to 36% in 2000; in addition, one-quarter of Irish holidaymakers consistently stay in hotels.) As a result, occupancy levels increased sharply, from 55% to 68%, while average pre-tax profit per room almost doubled between 1996 and 2000, from €5,250 to €9,895. In general, room rates, occupancy and profitability were substantially greater in high grade hotels and in Dublin. The difficulties experienced by the industry post the millennium were reflected in performance, and occupancy and pre-tax profit per room fell in 2001 (to 66% and €9,067, respectively). The decline, which continued into 2002, would have been greater but for the buoyant domestic market.

Jurys Doyle Hotel Group

Jurys opened its first boarding house in Dublin in 1881. In 1970, the flagship Jurys hotel moved from Dublin city centre to a large site in the exclusive Ballsbridge area. By 1989, Jurys Hotel Group operated three upmarket hotels in Dublin, Cork and Limerick. New management comprising Walter Beatty (Chairman) and Peter Malone (Managing Director) expanded the Group through the 1990s. Hotels were bought or built in Ireland and the UK and the 'budget plus' Jurys Inns concept was developed. In 1999, Jurys acquired the family-owned Doyle Hotels for €245 million, to attain 'sufficient critical mass and scale . . . internationally'. Doyle comprised 11 high grade hotels, well located if architecturally functional, with over 2,000 rooms in Dublin, London and Washington. Jurys quickly integrated the Doyle operations to optimise occupancy and yield, streamline capabilities and achieve purchasing economies and synergies. By 2002, Jurys Doyle Group managed thirty 3-star, 4-star and 5-star hotels and inns in 12 cities in Ireland, the UK and US, with over 6,000 rooms and 4,000 employees.

Group strategy is to develop a balanced (year-round) portfolio of properties in major city centres. All properties are in either city centre or urban locations with upside regenerative potential. The Group manages two distinct types of properties, with both types in five cities (six by end 2004). Jurys Doyle Hotels are 'cosmopolitan, down-to-earth hotels offering genuine Irish hospitality in prime city centre locations'. The Group

Table 2 Jurys Doyle properties and rooms at end 2002

	Hotels	Inns	Total	Hotels	Inns	Total
Ireland	9	5	14	1,915	1,045	2,960
of which Dublin	*7*	*2*	*9*	*1,631*	*425*	*2,056*
United Kingdom	6	6	12	1,047	1,559	2,606
of which London	*3*	*2*	*5*	*597*	*469*	*1,066*
US *(all Washington)*	2	1	3	447	75	522
Group Total	17	12	29	3,409	2,679	6,088
Total by end 2004	18	18	36	3,634	4,287	7,921

Sources: Jurys Doyle Hotel Group, industry and media commentaries.

distinguishes its three 5-star flagship Dublin hotels with their high-profile, stand-alone identities. In general, Jurys Doyle Hotels are 4-star, luxurious and comfortable with a wide range of facilities. The Jurys Doyle brand is actively promoted and marketed, with corporate and event-related business comprising 75% of total custom.

Jurys Inns are 3-star, 'simple, no fuss yet welcoming accommodation in the city centre'. The Inns were established in the early 1990s based on high levels of customer service (albeit of limited range) and operational efficiency. The Jurys Inn brand is separately marketed and has a distinct value-for-money identity (based on a fixed, per room rate) that attracts a more tourist-based clientele. The Inns have spearheaded the Group's expansion (particularly in the UK) and will account for 55% of total Group rooms by the end of 2004, by which time two-thirds of Inn capacity will be UK based. The Inns concept has proved tremendously successful. Unusually high occupancy rates of 90% are consistently attained. In addition, the Inns achieve gross margins of between 40% and 50%, compared with around 30% for the Group's 4-star and 5-star hotels.

Jurys Doyle Hotel Group provides a consistent quality service and experience based on professionalism and friendliness. The Group has invested substantially in facilities and people. By 2002, the annual refurbishment expenditure on

Table 3 Jurys Doyle Hotel Group finances and operations

Year ended April	Actual performance						% Change p.a.	
	1989	1993	1996	2000	2001	2002	93–00	89–02
Financial (€m)								
Revenue	24.1	33.4	62.6	219.0	252.2	266.4	+31	+20
Operating Proft	3.1	5.0	13.2	60.8	74.9	73.4	+43	+28
Earnings Per Share (¢)	8.6	7.6	23.5	68.3	72.4	66.0	+37	+17
Operating								
No. of Hotels/Inns	3	7	11	30	31	29	+3 p.a.	+2 p.a.
No. of Rooms	683	1,155	1,867	5,889	6,128	6,088	+26	+18
No. of Employees	701	894	1,354	3,610	4,011	4,017	+22	+14
Ratios (€000)								
Revenue/Room	35.3	28.9	33.5	37.2	41.2	43.8	+4	+2
Op. Proft/Room	5.1	4.4	7.1	10.3	12.2	12.1	+13	+7
Revenue/Employee	34.4	37.3	46.3	60.7	62.9	66.3	+7	+5
Op. Proft/Employee	4.4	5.6	9.8	16.8	18.7	18.3	+17	+12
Gross Margin (%)	N/A	20.1	26.3	32.6	36.4	35.7	+13 pt	N/A
Operating Margin (%)	12.7	15.1	21.1	27.8	29.7	27.6	+13 pt	+15 pt
Net Assets/Share (€)	1.16	2.44	2.34	7.41	7.40	10.77	+17	+19
Gearing (%)	34	23	29	68	81	53	+45 pt	+20 pt

Sources: Jurys Doyle Hotel Group, industry and media commentaries.

its properties was over €14 million. Technologically, the Group has been a leader in online booking and wireless Internet access in rooms. Marketing data warehousing and the use of property management and SAP enterprise planning and reporting systems have enhanced internal management. Building on Exceptional Customer Care Programmes launched in 1994, the Group has put in place numerous human resource initiatives, such as management development, leadership and accountancy programmes; specialised staff training and mentoring; an employee handbook; student placement; and work–life balance measures. In an environment of employee shortages and in an industry characterised by casual and contract labour, benefits for the Group have included employee retention, reduced absenteeism and greater flexibility and productivity.

The new millennium heralded significant change for Jurys Doyle Hotel Group. A new Chairman (Richard Hooper), Chief Executive (Pat McCann) and Finance Director (Paul McQuillan) took up office within a two-year period. (Like his predecessor, Pat McCann rose through the ranks.) The new management team faced challenging market conditions compounded by economy-wide cost pressures. The Group responded with cost controls and measures to maximise revenues, including cross-selling between properties, a guest loyalty programme and the development of dedicated meeting rooms and new eating formats. In addition, three non-core Irish 3-star hotel properties (totalling 280 rooms) were disposed of for profit. At the same time, the Group entered commitments to expand its bedroom stock by 30% by the end of 2004. Notwithstanding these efforts, the Group issued

Table 4 Profile of Gresham Hotel Group

OPERATIONS	City	Leisure	Total	FINANCES/RATIOS	€m
Number of Hotels	6	4	10	Year End December	2002
Dublin	1	1	2	Revenue	55.3
Rest of Ireland	1	3	4	Operating Profit	4.6
London	1		1	Earnings Per Share (c)	0.27
Europe	3		3		
				Revenue/Room	39.8
Number of Rooms	843	548	1,391	Operating Profit/Room	3.3
Dublin	288	103	391		
Rest of Ireland	113	445	558	Revenue/Employee	70.7
London	188		188	Operating Profit/Employee	5.9
Europe	254		254		
				Operating Margin (%)	8.3
No. of Employees			778	Net Assets/Share (€)	1.73

Note: Apart from the 4-star Gresham Hotel in Dublin city centre (288 rooms) and the 4-star Carat Hotel (90 rooms) in Amsterdam, all Group hotels are 3-star.
Gresham Hotel Group reported for 11 months in 2002. Numbers presented have been annualised.
Sources: Gresham Hotel Group, industry and media commentaries.

▶

a profit warning at its annual general meeting in spring 2003 due to the continuing downturn in its key markets.

Gresham Hotel Group

Formerly Ryan Hotels, Gresham Hotel Group operates 10 hotels in nine locations in Ireland, Belgium, Netherlands, Germany and the UK. Founded in 1947, the Group engaged in several activities but, by 1980, was entirely a hotel operator. The Group has a chequered history. In 1983, it was forced to sell a well-located London property and a decade later it sold one hotel in Dublin and two in West of Ireland resorts.

The Group's properties are in either suburban or edge-of-town locations and Gresham has a mid-market concentration with significant tourist trade. In the 1990s, the Group redefined its strategy, involving a twofold focus on year-round, quality city hotels and on value-for-money leisure hotels. In 1999, the Group assumed a new brand name and rebranded several hotels. Since the millennium, performance has been severely hit. An Israeli hotel chain, Red Sea, acquired 28% of the equity and control of the Board, while bids have been received for individual properties. The stock market value of the Group at end 2002 was around €60 million, a 60% discount to net asset value.

Discussion questions

1 Outline the major opportunities and threats facing Jurys Doyle Hotel Group in 2002.

2 Describe Jurys Doyle's strategies for its two business and discuss whether they are consistent.

3 Describe the core competences on which Jurys Doyle's strategies are based.

4 As part of its future strategic direction, evaluate whether Jurys Doyle Hotel Group should acquire Gresham Hotel Group.

Case study 3

The battle for the skies: Do low fare airline passengers expect low service quality?

Gavin Lonergan MBS, **UCD Business Schools**

The airline industry has been one of the most heavily regulated industries in the past. Criticism was frequent as this highly regulatory system resulted in high-cost airlines and high fares (Barrett, 1993). However, the trend in recent years has been to significantly liberalise economic controls over pricing, service levels and market entry in the airline industry. The first major step of official EU liberalisation came in 1987 and was followed by two more packages, in 1990 and 1992. The three packages combined effectively liberalised air transport within the EU. The past two decades have seen enormous changes in the way economic regulation in the airline industry is viewed. The long-standing tradition in many countries for their major airlines to be publicly owned is also changing as privatisation takes place and commercial carriers are allowed to compete in traditionally protected markets.

With full deregulation, any qualified airline could fly anywhere within the European Union without the need for government approval. With this liberalisation came the first widespread competition for national flag carriers, then still mostly state-owned. Almost 80 new entrant airlines emerged across the European Union in the deregulation euphoria of the mid-1990s. However, if the US experience is replicated in Europe, the vast majority will not survive, as only two airlines established during US deregulation in the 1970s are still flying today. In fact, there are signs that this experience is being replicated in Europe illustrated by the fact that 17 of the 56 airlines founded since 1995 went bankrupt within their first year of existence.

Europe's two leading low-fare carriers are Ryanair and EasyJet/Go. They are not only expanding their route networks but are also setting up bases in continental Europe where low-fare airlines are few and far between. Both use the pricing advantage afforded to them by low and flexible cost structures to win market share from full-service carriers and to stimulate new demand at price points that were previously unexploited.

These low-fare airlines are modelled on Southwest Airlines, a Texas-based carrier that was the first to exploit the deregulation of America's skies in 1978. Labour is cheaper than in traditional airlines and cabin crews undertake non-core duties such as cleaning, speeding up turnaround times to 20 minutes and allowing aircraft to be used for 15 hours a day, twice as much as in a conventional airline. The Southwest way can substantially reduce costs compared to those of a mainstream airline. Table 1 outlines the operating costs for conventional, full-service airlines versus low-cost airlines. As can be seen, the cost per seat kilometre for a low-fare airline is as low as one third that of a full-service airline.

Low-fare airlines are aggressively competing with the more established traditional airlines such as British Airways, Air France, KLM. These low-cost airlines are steadily eroding the profit margins and market share of their more established rivals. It can easily be seen from Table 1 how no-frills airlines such as Ryanair and EasyJet can charge such low prices for their fares. However, what effect do these low fares have on consumer expectations of service quality? Understanding customer expectations of service quality is a prerequisite to meeting and exceeding those expectations (Parasuraman et al., 1991). In today's competitive marketplace, this is vital for success. Without knowing and understanding customer expectations, how does

►

Table 1 Operating costs, conventional vs low-cost airlines

	Cost per seat-km in 2002 (US cents)
Conventional	
Aer Lingus	15.07
SAS	13.86
Air France	12.85
British Airways	11.98
Alitalia	10.05
Low-cost airlines	
Ryanair	5.04
EasyJet	6.04

Source: Doganis, R. (2001) *The Airline Business in the 21st Century*, Routledge, London.

one attempt to meet or exceed them? Numerous assumptions are made on the role of price in the formation of service quality expectations. Many of these assumptions stem from the consumer behaviour literature where the focus of research has been on tangible products. However, research into services pricing in general is scarce and in relation to price–quality relationships, it is virtually non-existent.

There is a consensus that providing a quality service is a prerequisite for survival in today's marketplace. There is also a consensus that perceived service quality involves a comparison by consumers between expected service quality and experienced service quality. Pricing poses a serious challenge for the airline industry that requires active participation from marketers who understand the needs and behaviours of customers and from operations managers who recognise the importance of matching the demand for the service to the capacity available to meet that demand (Lovelock, 2001). Zeithaml

and Bitner (2000) outline three key ways in which service pricing is different for consumers:

- customer knowledge of service prices;
- the role of non-monetary costs; and
- price as an indicator of service quality.

Pricing of services such as airline travel is difficult and complicated due to the intangibility factor inherent in services and the related problem of perishability. The consumer behaviour literature indicates that consumers often fall back on heuristics or mental rules-of-thumb especially when limited problem solving occurs or in the absence of product information. When product information is incomplete, opinions are often formed on the basis of covariation or perceived associations among events that may not actually influence one another. For example, a consumer may form an expectation of quality based on price, brand name, country of origin, etc. According to Clow et al. (1997), price is a cue often used by customers in forming service quality expectations and in evaluating the quality of the service relative to how much they paid.

Research undertaken by Lonergan (2002) into the effect of price on service quality expectations of airline customers unveiled some interesting insights. Passengers from a low-fare airline and a full-service airline were interviewed and in the case of the low-fare passengers, almost half expected 'poor' or 'very poor' service quality. This compares with 8% of passengers from the full-service airline who expected similar levels of service quality.

This was followed up with a question on how those expectations were formed. It emerged that price was the key indicator for both sets of passengers, albeit more pronounced for low-fare airline passengers. Full-service passengers were then asked the level of quality they would expect if travelling with a low-fare airline and low-fare airline passengers were asked the same question in reverse. Again, the findings were interesting. Full-service passengers expected significantly worse service quality if they were flying with a low-fare airline while the opposite held for low-fare passengers. The key reason for these opinions was the pricing levels of each airline.

These findings pose some important questions for both types of airline. Price was clearly shown to be the most important indicator of service quality for airline passengers. The data for both sets of passengers illustrated that price is the major cue used to form quality expectations. In total, 60% of passengers use price as the key indicator when forming quality expectations. This equates to 68% of low fare passengers and 52% of premium or full-service airline passengers. The more an airline passenger pays, the less of an impact price has on quality expectations. However, although price has less of an impact as the price increases, it is still the most important indicator of quality for all passengers. Apart from price, previous experience of the airline also plays an important role in the formation of service quality expectations. Word-of-mouth and overall corporate image have limited importance while corporate advertising has minimal importance.

It is important that low-fare airlines such as Ryanair understand that the service quality expectations of their passengers, because of the low price charged, are likely to be below average. This gives the low-fare airlines some leeway in terms of the level of service quality they provide. Passengers will be less disappointed when they do not get free refreshments or there is a lack of in-flight entertainment. Also, passengers are likely to be more forgiving when mistakes occur or things go wrong. If service quality expectations are low, it is easier for the airline to meet and exceed them. However, as quality expectations are dynamic, and it has been shown that previous experience also plays an important role, exceeding quality expectations will raise those expectations for any subsequent journeys.

Although service quality expectations are primarily based on price, this does not mean that very low quality is acceptable in return for a very low price. Customers have a minimum service quality expectation and failure to meet this minimum level will cause substantial dissatisfaction regardless of how cheap the flight was. The minimum quality expectation is based on the outcome of the flight (technical quality) rather than on the process elements (functional quality) (Grönroos 1984). In other words, if low-fare airlines get the basics right, customers are likely to have their expectations met and become satisfied customers.

Overall, low-fare airlines are in a very strong position because they can develop customer loyalty simply by getting the basics right. The pressure is firmly with the traditional airlines who must rise to the challenge laid down by these new low-cost competitors.

References

Barrett, S. (1993) in Banister, D. and Berechman, J. (eds), *Transport in a Unified Europe: Policies and Challenges*, Elsevier Science.

Clow, K., Kurtz, D., Ozment, J. and Soo Ong, B. (1997) 'The Antecedents of Consumer Expectations of Services: An Empirical Study Across Four Industries', *Journal of Services Marketing*, Vol. 11, No. 4, pp. 230–248.

Grönroos, C. (1984) 'A Service Quality Model and Its Marketing Implications', *European Journal of Marketing*, Vol. 18, No. 4, pp. 36–44.

Lonergan, G. (2002) 'The Role of Price on the Formation of Service Quality Expectations', MBS thesis, Michael Smurfit Graduate School of Business, University College Dublin.

Lovelock, C.H. (2001) *Services Marketing: People, Technology, Strategy*, 4th edn, Prentice-Hall International.

Parasuraman, A., Berry, L. and Zeithaml, V. (1991) 'Understanding Customer Expectations of Service', *Sloan Management Review*, Spring, pp. 39–48.

Zeithaml, V.A. and Bitner, M.J. (2000) *Services Marketing: Integrating Customer Focus Across the Firm*, 2nd edn, McGraw-Hill.

►

Discussion questions

1 As head of marketing with a full-service premium airline, explore the branding and communications issues that may need to be addressed following a decision by the CEO to follow a low-fare business model.

2 Although airlines such as Ryanair and EasyJet follow a no-frills, low-fare business model, there are wide differences in the price paid by passengers on the same flight. Discuss the challenges facing a low-fare airline from a marketing communications perspective as a result.

Case study 4

Marketing activities using B2B online technology in the pharmaceutical industry: the case of CiraNet in Egypt

Khaled M. Shaker, MBA, Maastricht School of Management, The Netherlands

Introduction

CiraNet is a result of a merge between Citibank, Egypt and Raya Group. Its main focus is on creating a well-designed B2B marketing network through the Internet within the pharmaceutical industry in Egypt.

Pharmaceutical industry overview

The Egyptian pharmaceutical industry is considered one of the oldest strategic industries in the country. It was founded in 1939 with the establishment of the Misr Company for Pharmaceutical Industries. The industry developed slowly between the 1960s and 1980s, following nationalisation schemes which brought the industry under full government control. With the launching of reform programmes in 1991, pharmaceutical companies gained greater autonomy and an increasing number of private sector companies entered the market. At present there are 30 pharmaceutical manufacturing companies of which 8 are public and 22 are privately owned.

The Egyptian pharmaceutical market was valued between at approximately €75 million in 2002 with over 9% of products locally produced. Egypt is the largest producer and consumer of pharmaceuticals in the Middle East Arab market. The Middle East region also absorbs most of Egypt's pharmaceutical exports, which represents approximately 6% of total production. The US plays an active role in the industry through foreign direct investment and pharmaceutical imports.

The Egyptian drug industry is mainly drug formulation rather than research based. Local manufacturers import their ingredients either from their licensors or from numerous suppliers worldwide. Pharmaceutical raw material or final products are imported from France, Switzerland, Belgium, Germany, the UK and the US. The public sector's share of the market is 29%, while the private sector's share is 71%. The government is putting special emphasis on upgrading its health care. This will have an enormous impact on the pharmaceutical industry, which is striving to obtain technology transfer and branch into new products.

CiraNet background

In today's global economy, more and more companies are turning to the Internet as a primary channel to conduct their businesses by means of e-commerce technology.

CiraNet, the leader in B2B e-commerce in Egypt, was formed at the end of August 2000 as a joint venture between Raya Holding and Citibank. Raya Holding's expertise in the implementation of information technology and telecommunications projects, together with Citibank's competence as a leader in electronic financial services and e-commerce worldwide, laid a solid foundation for CiraNet's operations.

CiraNet unveiled a pioneering initiative through the launch of CiraNet Pharma, the first digital marketplace for the pharmaceutical industry in Egypt. The pharmaceutical industry was designated as CiraNet's proving ground for several reasons according to Sameh Montasser, Managing Director of CiraNet:

We chose the pharma industry because of its size, and the fact that it is a true marketplace, in the sense that it is not monopolistic – there are many buyers and sellers.

▶

The industry was already one of the most automated and sophisticated in Egypt, thanks to the large number of multinationals operating high-tech factories and distribution centers.

CiraNet Pharma is the first online business-to-business trade exchange targeted at all players in the pharmaceutical industry. CiraNet Pharma fosters and facilitates trading relationships between pharmaceutical manufacturers, distributors and pharmacies. The exchange is a neutral website that buyers can log on to and place orders with multiple manufacturers and distributors in one place. For both buyers and sellers the exchange provides centralised order placement, billing, payment and customer service.

CiraNet Pharma is not just a trading hub; it offers its services as a portal for the pharmaceutical community. This portal contains news, directories, event listings, Q&A and chat rooms tailored to the pharmaceutical industry. CiraNet Pharma aims to be Egypt's Internet marketplace for purchasing and selling various products including drugs, cosmetics and medical supplies.

The development of CiraNet Pharma is based on CiraNet's extensive research and knowledge of the pharmaceutical industry. Such research demonstrated the significant growth witnessed by the pharmaceutical market and its huge potential to positively respond to the system and become fully automated.

CiraNet Pharma offers compelling benefits to all its trading partners. Working with CiraNet Pharma, trading partners can increase their sales and exposure, control their inventories and cash flows. A supplier working with CiraNet Pharma puts his product details online where all information related to product descriptions including packaging and prices are presented according to international standards. Details are updated regularly. This results in major reductions in costs, particularly those related to designing, printing and catalogue distribution. Costs are also reduced because of the speed of executing orders and transactions. In addition, as the collection cycle is shortened, suppliers enjoy better control over their cash flows. Also with the variety of payment methods, receivables are no longer a headache.

CiraNet Pharma offers buyers the possibility of processing orders online. All transactions can be accessible 24 hours a day. A buyer can browse catalogues and place orders easily, review order status, invoices and pay online. Buyers have instant access to information concerning new product releases, promotions and marketing programmes. Working with CiraNet Pharma, buyers can increase profitability and reduce purchasing and inventory costs.

Our main objective at CiraNet is to offer value added services through the establishing of an online marketplace that allows all producers, distributors and buyers to have secure business deals. Different parties interested in a certain deal can search for the terms of the deal online.

Source: Sameh Montasser, Managing Director of CiraNet.

Through its call centre, CiraNet provides its customers with the required support and allows them to promote and sell their products over the phone. Another promising field for CiraNet is in the development of applications and systems for the CiraNet Pharma site by its sister company Mega. After thorough market scanning, Raya and Citibank had decided to hand the project to Mega because of its capability to develop the systems for CiraNet Pharma in a record time to international standards and at a much lower cost.

In phase 1, CiraNet Pharma is expected to focus its activities on the Egyptian market. Future plans include expanding CiraNet Pharma's B2B offerings to the entire Middle East and Africa regions. The ambitions of CiraNet do not stop at these borders. Rather it plans to continue to penetrate the largest industries in Egypt to become the leader in e-commerce in the Middle East.

CiraNet used the Infomediary model to develop the B2B online exchange in the pharmaceutical industry. The model represents an innovation made possible by Internet/Web-based

technology. The concept of Infomediary enables a company to sell information about a market and creates a platform on which buyers and sellers can do business in a marketplace. It is literally a virtual market and typically earns commissions or transaction fees for its service. The basic premise is that in the virtual market space, the information regarding the product is as valuable as the product itself.

CiraNet's strategy and activities

In order to achieve its goals in a very short time CiraNet used different strategies to enter the pharmaceutical market.

Market scope strategy

Market scope strategy is concerned with market coverage. CiraNet deliberately decided to concentrate on the B2B Egyptian market in the pharmaceutical industry.

> *It was very encouraging to us to enter this industry, because it has very special characteristics and is a strategic industry in Egypt. We deliberately targeted this well educated segment in Egypt because we believe these doctors and pharmacies' owners will respond quickly to our new concept of selling and buying on the Internet and using our call centres to place orders.*

(Mr Khaled Shash, Manager)

Market entry strategy

Basically there were three market entry positions the company considered: (a) to be first in the market, (b) to be among the early entrants, or (c) to be a laggard. CiraNet decided they wanted to be the first to enter the market.

They thought that if their business model was successful it would completely change the nature of their transactions to one where high speed and efficiency in executing orders and delivery would be the order of the day. Transactions would take much less time starting with the placing of the order through CiraNet's site on the Internet or through the phone, and then going through the process in which CiraNet contacts the supplier either online or by phone, ending with the final order being delivered on time by the supplier to the pharmacies.

Initial marketing contacts

At first CiraNet approached their customers directly, by conducting seminars and making presentations to their customers in Egypt's biggest hotels. They also invited companies that provided pharmacies with various operational equipment for managing their own internal processes.

Marketing promotions

CiraNet offered each of their pharmacy customers who owned a PC a free fax modem, and if the pharmacy had no PC they leased them one with the proviso that the cost of the lease would decrease the greater the amount of transactions with CiraNet.

Training courses

CiraNet provided training sessions for its customers on the usage of the Internet in order to execute orders online. There were also training courses for the different applications of Microsoft Office. The call centre organised and supported all the issues related to training. If one of the service users had difficulty using any of the applications the call centre was there to give them assistance.

Discussion questions

1 Outline the main issues faced by CiraNet in developing their business model for the pharmaceutical industry.

2 Perform a SWOT analysis on CiraNet and evaluate their competitive advantage, if any.

Case study 5

The cat that conquered the world: Hello Kitty and the spread of Nippon culture

Jan Charbonneau, Lecturer, School of Marketing and Tourism, Central Queensland University

We recognize and accept that we have failed to meet everyone's expectations. We sincerely apologize and ask for your forgiveness for any inconvenience and disappointment this may have caused. We wish to extend our sincere apologies and thanks to the Singapore Police Force, Ministry of the Environment, Singapore Civil Defence Force, and everyone who has been inconvenienced during this promotion.

Stephens (2000), reporting on a full-page statement by McDonald's Singapore appearing in Singapore newspapers, January 2000

'During this promotion'? They can't possibly mean a marketing promotion, can they? The police, government and civil defence forces needed for a marketing promotion? The answer is yes – a marketing promotion, needing the forces of law and order. McDonald's in Singapore underestimated the appeal of a white kitten with bow and no mouth and her mouthless boyfriend and the chaos caused when consumers felt they might miss out. The kitten in question is, of course, 'Hello Kitty' and her boyfriend, 'Dear Daniel'. And the promotion – buy a burger meal and get a 22 cm high Hello Kitty or Dear Daniel for S$2.60, a major savings compared with the regular retail price.

When McDonald's began the promotion on New Year's Day 2000, it had 2.4 million dolls on hand (in 12 different sets), which according to their estimates was sufficient quantity for a six-week promotion. What McDonald's failed to add into their calculations was first, the broad-based appeal of Hello Kitty, and secondly, the Singaporean phenomenon known as *kiasu*, roughly translated as 'the fear of missing out'. *Kiasu* led thousands of Singaporeans to wait in line all night to be the first through the doors to get the increasingly scarce dolls. Queue jumping led to the arrest of six people and the injury of a policeman. One man was charged with disorderly behaviour over protests after McDonald's opened a different door from the one he had been waiting at for 12 hours. At its height, this McKitty McFrenzy generated almost 300,000 daily visits to McDonald's. And they were not all prepubescent girls. Grandparents lined for hours to get the toys for their grandchildren (or so they claimed!). Fathers fought for the toy for their children (again, so they claimed!). And over 20s wanted Hello Kitty and Dear Daniel for traditional Valentine's Day love gifts.

McDonald's acknowledged that it was caught unawares and had seriously underestimated demand. To quell the negative publicity (which reached world media) they resorted to selling vouchers for Hello Kitty and Dear Daniel dolls dressed in Chinese wedding outfits, redeemable when stocks arrived in July 2000. Embarrassed by garbage bins overflowing with discarded burger meals in the early weeks of the promotion, McDonald's introduced a system where the

cost of the meal could be donated to charity. By mid-February 2000, S$37,000 had been donated to charity compared to estimated takings of S$11.7 million for McDonald's. All for a little white kitten!

When Sanrio of Japan created Hello Kitty in 1974 – yes, she's in her late 20s! – little did its founder, Shintaro Tsunji, know that he was creating a multibillion dollar empire that would not just take hold in Japan but would lead the charge of Nippon culture not only throughout Asia but the rest of the world. Hello Kitty and her boyfriend Dear Daniel have been joined by Tuxedo Sam, the penguin, and My Melody, the rabbit, among others and adorn a range of products and services that is exceptional even in today's merchandising culture. The characters adorn standard merchandise, such as clothing, stationery, housewares, video games and automatic bank teller, credit and phone cards. Hello Kitty cafes serving kitty-shaped waffles and Kitty Colada drinks continue to be extremely popular in Hong Kong and throughout Asia, as is the Hello Kitty Megastore in Causeway Bay, selling mega volumes of Hello Kitty merchandise. Hong Kong television even has a Hello Kitty sponsored weather report – read by newsreader Wincy Miaow! In the late 1990s, Sanrio opened Puroland theme park in Tokyo for Hello Kitty affectionados, creating a powerful rival for Disneyland Tokyo, especially among visitors from Taiwan and China. The turn of the century saw Sanrio launching a Hello Kitty hotel to cater for the 'Kittyra', as Hello Kitty fans are known in Japan.

If you are initially thinking that Hello Kitty appeals only to young girls and perhaps some young boys, consider the following items of Hello Kitty merchandise for sale throughout Asia: Hello Kitty watches adorned with Austrian Swarovski crystals; Hello Kitty notebook computers complete with Hello Kitty mouse and reasonably powerful computing capabilities; companion Hello Kitty fax machines; powder blue Hello Kitty Yamaha motorcycles; Hello Kitty jeeps by Daihatsu (sorry, no whiskers on the bonnet); Hello Kitty body-fat monitors; Hello Kitty toilet paper; and believe it or not, Hello Kitty condoms! While the characters appeal primarily to prepubescent girls in North America (although pop sensations Christina Aguilera and model Tyra Banks are fans and American stores carry T-shirts and tank tops in women's sizes), Hello Kitty's appeal throughout Asia is much broader as witnessed by the merchandise for sale. That said, Sanrio's corporate-owned Kitty Boutiques generated sales of US$1.2 billion in the United States in 2000, indicating either an extremely lucrative prepubescent market or a broader appeal than believed. Sanrio, listed on the Tokyo Stock Exchange, has a Hello Kitty line that covers an estimated 15,000 products, with 100 new items released every month. Sanrio also licenses approximately 500 companies to make Sanrio-approved items. As can be imagined, Hello Kitty is also a hot kitten in the black market, with a booming trade in knock-off merchandise. A visit to any Asian street market will reveal stall after stall of Hello Kitty products, a large number likely not Sanrio-approved.

Sanrio makes sure that store shelves always have new merchandise, stopping production after a few months and keeping products on the shelves for only a limited time. This strategy has increased the collectible value of the merchandise. Remember the S$2.60 McDonald's Hello Kitty doll? In early 2001, a six pair set was offered for sale on the Internet for S$470. Hello Kitty has kept up with technology. For example, www.dreamkitty.com, a Canadian online boutique, provides an ever-changing array of Hello Kitty merchandise. A quick search of the Internet using the search terms 'Hello Kitty' will reveal an amazing array of retail sites and chat rooms devoted to Kitty and Daniel.

To understand the Hello Kitty phenomenon in Japan, you have to understand *kawaii* ('hou Q' in Hong Kong). Literally, 'kawaii' means cute but figuratively means things that are desired to fulfil

▶

one's life. Kawaii culture originated with 15- to 18-year-old girls in Japan who became the holy grail for advertisers and marketers in the fashion, publishing and cute-little-gadgets industry. As one industry observer stated, 'it's not how much they spend . . . it's that they all buy the same things'. If an item is hot, such as pocket pagers (called pocket bells in Japan) or mobile phones, market penetration can reach 100% in a matter of weeks.

The core values of *kawaii*, however, have spread far beyond its original members, and extended beyond Japan throughout Asia. Hello Kitty has given birth to a mega publishing, media and merchandising industry, including Sailor Moon, Pokemon, Digimon, Dragonball Z and the Power Puff Girls aimed at kids – essentially those below the age of 18. Hello Kitty has also led the charge of Nippon culture throughout Asia. Consumers in Hong Kong, South Korea, Taiwan, Singapore, Malaysia and other Asian cultures view 'Made in Japan' as 'way cool', embracing all things Japanese. Asian consumers, especially young adults – a prime target for marketers – find they can relate more to the ideals, concepts and imagery expressed in Japanese music, movies, media, clothing and merchandise than they can to American or European popular culture. While American pop culture still dominates, with Hollywood films generating the biggest box-office draws, Asians are increasingly turning away from the 'Baywatch'-inspired beach/body images and family values expressed in music such as US rap lyrics. And increasingly, they are turning to all things Japanese.

Four out of five comic books sold in South Korea are Japanese; Japanese pop music acts sell out in Taiwan and Singapore, and while most Taiwanese consumers cannot read Japanese, owning karaoke videos with lyrics in Japanese is considered a status symbol. According to HMV's commercial director for Greater China and South-East Asia, 'Asians like to have stars they can identify with, instead of always looking to the West . . . Japanese stars modify western music to make it more suitable for Asian listeners'. J-pop is taking over more floor space in music shops and on commercial broadcasters such as Star TV's music channel. Japanese soap operas, operating on larger production budgets than their Asian counterparts, have a loyal Asian following that rivals those of their American counterparts. Nippon culture provides an Asian dimension to popular culture not understood by western artists and designers – or marketers. Japanese animated films draw heavily from Chinese myths and traditions, with characters using their life energy (*ki* in Japanese, *qi* in Chinese) and group allegiances to prevail. Compare the American icon Superman, who singlehandedly fights evil, with his Japanese counterpart Ultraman, who enlists the support of his extended family to fight evil and even performs Buddhist funeral services for his victims. Asian fashion designers realise that the western aesthetic of the tall curvaceous blonde does not match the dark hair, skin and slimmer bodies of Asian consumers, and design accordingly. Japanese fashion and entertainment has created an image of quality among Asian consumers, with great attention to detail. Japanese marketers have capitalised on the Asian preference for group activities and the role of the extended family, something most western marketers have difficulty understanding. Japan's focus on innovation and short product development cycles match the lucrative youth market's short attention spans and mania for the newest, brightest and most bizarre. This fixation with all things Japanese suggests an emerging Asian identity, replacing past adulation of all things western. Asian consumers are increasingly becoming more comfortable with Japan's values and lifestyle with its focus on family ties, respect for elders and the emotion of personal relationships. According to one Sony talent scout, 'a decade ago, we Asians had no modern image of ourselves. We had no cultural identity to match' (*Newsweek International*, 1999).

Despite memories of wartime brutality and long-standing restrictions on Japanese imports, Japanese culture has succeeded in penetrating Asian markets, representing a profound generational change. While Asia's youth may have been raised at their elders' knees on stories of Japanese occupation and wartime atrocities, it has not restricted their desire for all things Japanese, leading to the more benign invasion of Japanese pop culture, spearheaded by Hello Kitty. In Taiwan, those who follow Japanese trends even have a name: *harizu* or 'Japan-crazy tribe'. Trade on the black market of restricted products flourishes, with sales increasing even further when restrictions are lifted. Even South Korea is allowing some Japanese items to be legally imported – for example, award-winning films and records – and has removed restrictions on J-pop live performances. Japanese culture cafes and teahouses are quickly replacing American fast food restaurants as preferred meeting places for South Korea's younger generation. The joint staging of the 2002 soccer World Cup by South Korea and Japan may have opened the doors even further to Nippon culture. Approximately 1.5 million Asians are studying Japanese, up 29% from 1995–1999, all the better to understand the latest trends. One Thai scholar believes that Thailand can learn from Japan, what he considers the most civilised country in Asia, while a Hong Kong scholar believes that Hong Kong consumers admire the richness of Japanese culture, epitomised by the tea ceremony, compared with the money focus of Hong Kong culture. A South Korean academic, commenting that Japanese culture now ranks second in terms of global market share behind the United States, believes that 'Culture is like water. It flows from stronger nations to weaker ones. People tend to idolise countries that are wealthier, freer and more advanced, and in Asia, that country is Japan' (*New York Times*, 1999). Geographic and cultural closeness, the expansion of Asian media and television broadcasting coupled with aggressive marketing and packaging have also fuelled the invasion of Nippon culture.

While not to the same extent as in Asia, Nippon culture has spread to the western world, with Hello Kitty remaining the poster girl for all things Japanese. In 1959, French philosopher Alexander Kojeve wrote that 'The interaction of the West and Japan will result not in a vulgarisation of Japan but rather in a Japanisation of the West' (*Marketing*, 2000). He would likely look at American basketball players sporting Japanese calligraphy tattoos, the popularity of brands such as Sony (from televisions to stereos to Playstation 2), the popularity of 'Tokyo chic' fashion, the translation of obscure Japanese anime and television into English, called 'fansubbing', and the never-ending array of innovative and downright bizarre products emanating from Japan as support for his beliefs. The Internet has facilitated an almost constant cultural exchange bridging geographic and time boundaries between Japan and the rest of the world. Consider, for example, that the demand for Pokemon was well established through Internet chat rooms long before Nintendo America began their promotional campaigns. And this is likely to continue as long as innovation remains the 'Viagra of Japan'. And its likely Hello Kitty will still be around to welcome her grandchildren as new ambassadors of Nippon culture, to Asia and the world!

Discussion questions

1 Explain the appeal of characters like Hello Kitty to younger consumers in both Asia and the western economies, taking note of cultural and group influences.

2 Explain why characters like Hello Kitty appeal to a broader audience in Asia. Do you think that Hello Kitty will be able to generate the same level of broad appeal in western countries?

3 What factors have lead to the spread of Nippon culture throughout Asia? Do you see the spread continuing? If so, why; if not, why not?

►

4 One scholar remarked that 'Young people can mistakenly regard Japanese culture as their own' ('Cute Power', *Newsweek International*, 1999). Discuss this from the perspective of market segmentation and the impact on individual Asian cultures?

5 Many believe that much of the spread of Nippon culture has been fuelled by massive marketing campaigns. What responsibility do marketers have towards consumers in terms of both the acknowledgment and preservation of individual cultures?

References

AsiaWeek (2001) 'Your Money: Trends: Hello Kitty', 9 March.
Entertainment Weekly (2001) 'Hello, again', 4 May.
Marketing (2000) 'Turning Japanese', 21 September.
New York Times (1999) 'Japan Beckons, and East Asia's Youth Fall in Love', 5 December.
Newsweek International (1999) 'Cute Power! Asia is in love with Japan's pop culture', 8 November.
Stephens, J. (2000) 'In a McKitty Frenzy', *AsiaWeek*, 10 February.
Time International (1999) 'She's a Material Girl', 3 May.

Case study 6

HP-Compaq: a new beginning

Seán de Búrca and Evelyn Roche, **UCD Business Schools**

Introduction

In May 2002 two rival giants in the computer industry, HP and Compaq, merged. Months of vicious politics preceded the merger. HP board member Walter Hewlett, supported by David Packard, both sons of the co-founders, opposed the merger vehemently. In their view the merger would increase HP's exposure to the troubled commodity PC market instead of building on its strengths in the highly profitable printing and imaging business.

Many workers in the company opposed the merger, 15,000 jobs were at stake and corporate cultures of HP and Compaq did not seem compatible. The decision by HP's AGM in favour of the merger was a victory for Carly Fiorina, HP's CEO since July 1999. After an 18-month struggle, the companies merged to create an US$87 billion global technology leader.

Background

In 1939 Bill Hewlett and Dave Packard, two Stanford electrical engineers, founded their company Hewlett-Packard (HP) in a car garage. The company started in the post-Second World War era producing electrical instruments and consumer electronic products including oscilloscopes, signal generators and electronic calculators. After a string of failures, Hewlett-Packard's first successful product, an audio oscillator, turned out to be better than anything else on the market and earned a US patent. Disney Studios ordered eight units to help produce the animated film *Fantasia*. During the 1940s HP products continued gaining high esteem among engineers and scientists. The company went public in 1957. In the 1960s HP continued its steady growth in the test-and-measurement market and branched out into related fields like medical electronics and analytical instrumentation. In 1966 HP developed its first computer. The 1970s were marked by significant growth in earnings and employment, with HP passing the US$1 billion mark in sales in 1976. That year HP introduced the world's first pocket-sized scientific calculator, the HP-35C, which rendered slide rulers obsolete.

In the 1980s HP became a major player in the computer industry with a full range of computers, from desktop machines to portables to powerful minicomputers. During this period HP made its entry into the printer market with the launch of inkjet printers and laser printers that connect to personal computers. At the end of the decade the company had ballooned into a multinational company with 104 divisions, 123,000 employees worldwide and 19,000 products with sales of over US$47 billion.

In the beginning of the 1990s the company failed to meet Wall Street's expectation of high revenue growth rates. The company attributed the slow growth to the weak Asian markets and price competition in hardware. Analysts, however, questioned whether HP had a viable long-term strategy, particularly with regard to the opportunities offered by the Internet.

The merger

In July 1999, Carly Fiorina took over the management of HP. Under her leadership HP intend to focus on three key areas:

- intelligent, connected access devices;
- infrastructure solutions; and
- applications that can be delivered over networks as web services.

▶

In order to accelerate the implementation of this strategy Fiorina and Compaq Computer Corporation chief executive officer Michael Capellas jointly announced the merger of both companies in 2001.

HP's position in the PC market

Protagonists of the merger with Compaq, led by HP chief executive Carly Fiorina, argued that the merger would improve economies of scale of its PC business. Those opposed to the merger were concerned that it would increase HP's vulnerability to the shrinking PC market. In 2001 there was a worldwide decline in PC shipments of –5.2%. The decrease was mainly the result of falling demand among home users (–11.7% in shipments).

The global recession compounded by September 11, Enron and WorldCom scandals affected consumer confidence. In addition, World Cup soccer fever made consumers focus more on games and TV than PCs. A number of structural developments are affecting the PC industry specifically. Firstly, PCs are not becoming obsolete as fast as they used to. From a consumer perspective, software applications are constrained by the speed of Internet connections and not by the capacity of the PC. Secondly, consumer attention is shifting to devices such as handheld computers, personal organisers and Internet-capable mobile phones. As a result of fierce competition the profit margins on PCs have become very small.

In this shrinking market HP/Compaq are losing ground to Dell, which has managed to increase its share of worldwide vendor shipment. It is difficult for HP to compete with Dell's build-to-order model and HP's dependence on retail makes it more vulnerable to market fluctuations. While HP/Compaq's capital is tied up in inventories prone to obsolescence, Dell holds only four days of finished goods at hand. HP/Compaq have to reduce the inventory overhang by selling at discount prices.

The marketing strategy of the merged company faces some serious challenges. Some argue that in order to compete with Dell the company should adopt the Dell direct sales model. This is easier said than done. Initial restructuring efforts in this direction showed only slow progress. Nevertheless HP is venturing into the Dell direct selling approach. This may cause tension with the retailers. It is still questionable whether direct selling and retail selling are compatible options for one company. Dell's attempts in the past to enter the retail market were not successful. Trying to do both, direct selling and retail selling, might mean failing completely.

At the same time HP/Compaq are trying to preserve the shelf space and thus the 60% retail market share of the two brands combined. For that reason the company have announced that it will continue selling both HP and Compaq computers to a segmented market. Compaq PCs will target consumers that want to set up a home office and connect wirelessly to the Internet while the HP PCs will be positioned as home entertainment devices and as digital imaging machines for photography enthusiasts. HP can sell more add-ons such as printers and digital cameras which have higher profit margins.

In response to the sluggish PC market HP's Personal Systems Group are focusing on a broader portfolio of products than PCs. While PCs will constitute the largest product, emphasis will gradually shift to other products to include mobile devices moving from laptop to handset. HP believes that widening the portfolio in this direction offers tremendous opportunities.

HP's position in the printer market

Printers are HP's strength with almost 50% of the world's market. HP has captured over 75% market share in the black-and-white laser printer market and in the colour inkjet printer segment HP has 46% market share. However, HP's position in imaging and printing is not without its challenges. A serious weakness according to some critics is that HP's profitability in printing and imaging is largely the result of overpriced printing cartridges. 'Selling expensive ink' is not a very sustainable strategy, according to the critics.

Competition is not sitting on the fence. Dell Computers decided to move into the lucrative printer market. In an agreement with Lexmark, they are producing Dell printers and setting up a head-on battle with HP for supremacy in the printer market. The agreement with Lexmark, the number two printer manufacturer, is for the company to develop and produce Dell inkjet and laser printers along with peripherals. The printers went on sale to customers using Dell's direct sales model in the first half of 2003.

With Dell joining the printer market, the market is expected to become more competitive. On the other hand it will be interesting to see whether the direct sales model works for printers. Dell's success in the PC industry is to a large extent based on the elimination of large inventories of end products. This can only be achieved when customers are prepared to wait for a week or two before their made-to-order PC will be delivered. It remains to be seen whether they will be equally patient buying a printer.

HP's position in the server market

IBM is the leader in enterprise systems – supplying servers, storage and software to companies. Servers are a major loss maker for HP.

The divisions of HP and Compaq combined lost US$233 million in the second quarter ending 30 April 2002, compared with US$1 million profit a year earlier. The main competitors in the high-end server market are Sun, IBM and HP. Middle and small companies' demand is growing as the performance of low-end products gets better and better. The focus is shifting to low-end products, a market which has become very competitive.

After the merger HP divided its server products into two: the UNIX server based on HP products and the Intel-based server based on Compaq products. HP gave up the production of HP's servers of PA-RISC, Alpha and Tandam, and turned to Intel-based products – the Itanium processor family (IPF). However, their applications are still limited which hampers the growth of this market. While Sun and IBM remain formidable competitors in the high-end server market, Dell, focusing on the Wintel operating platform, is a looming threat for HP in the low-end server market. However, its made-to-order model may not work very well in this market.

Discussion questions

1 Discuss the competitive position facing HP/Compaq and outline a strategy for the future.

2 Should HP-Compaq continue with their co-branding strategy approach?

Part B

The International Marketing Mix

7

International market
selection and entry

Learning objectives

After studying this chapter, you should be able to:

- identify the different problems faced in selecting an international market as between firms inexperienced and experienced in international business;

- assess a country's attractiveness in terms of the potential, membership of trading blocs, competitive intensity and entry barriers;

- create a portfolio of the most attractive international markets to enter given the circumstances of the firm and the potential offered by the market;

- recognise the different available modes for entering the international market and the advantages and disadvantages of each; and

- adopt a holistic view of the way the internationalisation of the firm impacts on selection of entry mode in terms of inward-driven, outward-driven or linked forms.

Small exporters lead the way

Better communication, speedier travel and lower tariff barriers have made foreign markets more accessible to small companies. From America to Germany small exporters are leading the way abroad. Exporters tend to fall into one of three categories. Some start life as exporters and include many high-technology firms. Others become exporters over time by gaining experience and consolidating their home market before looking to the international markets. These firms are often motivated to look to the international market because of a downturn in the domestic market. Finally, many firms are encouraged to export by government agencies often before they are ready. Governments do this for balance of payments reasons.

Czinkota and Ronkainen (1998) argue that small and medium-sized companies typically pass through five stages: firstly they start with ignorance about foreign markets; then they become aware of exports but do nothing; next they send staff to conferences; in the fourth stage they pick up a few trial contacts and begin to export. Only at the fifth stage, with export sales accounting for around a sixth of the total, do they acquire an export mentality.

Introduction

Whether the firm is experienced or new to international business, two of the most critical questions involved in the decision to go international and which impact on the resulting profitability of international involvement are:

- Which of the vast range of international markets should the firm enter?
- What mode of entry should the involvement in the selected market take?

As far as market selection is concerned, this is complicated by changes in the international business environment. These changes, involving the formation of regional trade groupings, the creation of strategic alliances between firms, and the exponential spread of information technology, are resulting in a breaking down of barriers between countries and the need to view the world as a global entity rather than as a series of national markets. As a consequence, choosing the most appropriate international market to enter has become more difficult. As markets can now stretch across national boundaries, geographic segmentation may no longer be an appropriate basis for market selection. While this may be true for large or transnational firms, most firms are small to medium-sized and when they venture international are still likely to do so on a country-by-country basis. For such firms it is useful to have a systematic procedure for selecting individual markets to enter.

Decisions as to the form of market entry (such as exporting, joint ventures or franchising) logically follow the decision as to the most appropriate market to enter. However, market selection and entry are linked because the attractiveness of markets is influenced by the strategic thrust of the corporation, competitive action in those markets and government regulation relating to the permissible forms of foreign entry. For example, a ban on the imports into the market may mean that a joint venture is the only viable entry mode. This may make the market unattractive to a firm without the resources to establish a joint venture or to a firm whose international strategy is focused around export rather than foreign direct investment. Deciding on the most appropriate form of market entry involves understanding each of the various modes available and the conditions under which one mode might be more suitable than another.

Alternative approaches to market selection

Selecting an international market can impact on the other activities of the firm. This is because the outcome may influence the profitability of the firm in its domestic as well as in its other international markets. Not only will this impact be on overall profits but it might also impact in other areas such as its global reputation. This is illustrated in situations like the impact on Union Carbide following the Bhopal calamity; the security of a firm's intellectual property (in countries where intellectual piracy is common); and the physical risk to its personnel (in countries like Cambodia).

Underpinning the selection of markets to enter should be a strategic orientation that treats market entry selection as part of the firm's overall strategy, linked both to its resource base and a distinctive competence on the one hand and its position in relation to competitors on the other.

In isolating the markets that offer the greatest potential, it is necessary to take the situation of the firm and the circumstances of the international market(s) into account. In doing so, the characteristics of the individual markets, as well as the extent to which one international market is integrated with another, needs to be considered. Where there is an integrated group of international markets, entering one may facilitate subsequent or simultaneous entry into others.

In addition to balancing the firm's strategic orientation with the characteristics of the international market(s), market entry decisions should also take into account:

- the structure of the global industry of which the firm is a part – consideration of the structure of the industry recognises that in whatever it does, the firm is part of a network and the strengths deriving from this network can affect the decision as to which market to enter; and

- the strategy of current or potential global competitors – the inclusion of competitor strategy recognises that markets are dynamic and the fact of entering an international market is likely in many instances to provoke a competitive reaction, either from firms in that market or from firms in other countries.

Selection of international markets involves comparison. This can be difficult because the quality of data varies from country to country. Although the expansion of global databases and international online services has helped comparison, difficulties remain because of differences between countries in both recency and rigour of data collection. These limitations make a structured approach to international market selection desirable.

There are various approaches to market selection and these have different implications for small and medium-sized as opposed to large-sized firms. The first approach focuses on whether to enter international markets on an incremental basis (this entails moving from one to another only after establishing a presence in the first); or whether to enter a number of international markets simultaneously and, on the basis of experiences decide on which markets to concentrate. The advantages of incremental entry are that it enables the firm to gain experience at a measured pace, requires the commitment of fewer resources and involves less risk in terms of exposure. However, this approach involves greater competitive risk as competitors may leapfrog into other markets. For instance, after seeing how successfully a firm is doing in Thailand, competitors may move immediately into Malaysia, Indonesia and the Philippines which were potential target markets for the firm following its establishing a presence in Thailand. The incremental approach, however, may preclude achieving economies of scale and result in a haphazard approach to entering international markets. The simultaneous entry approach does enable the firm to acquire international experience rapidly, facilitates achieving economies of scale in international activities and is likely to prevent pre-emption by competitors in other markets. Offsetting these advantages is the fact that it is a resource-intensive strategy and one that entails higher operating risk.

The second approach to international market entry focuses on whether a concentrated as opposed to a diversified approach should be adopted. If a firm decides to concentrate its resources in a limited number of markets, it is likely to have a more focused effort, encounter reduced operating risks and costs, and benefit from economies of scale in exploiting information and acquiring experience. On the other hand, it will have all its 'eggs in one basket' and if something happens to the selected markets (such as the events in the former centrally planned economies 1989–91, or the Asian currency crisis of 1998), the firm is in an exposed position. In addition, this approach leaves the firm largely ignorant about potential in the rest of the world. A diversified strategy spreads both risk exposure and broadens knowledge of potential in a variety of markets, as well as offering greater strategic flexibility. It can, however, result in the firm spreading itself too thinly, may affect its ability to be competitive as economies of scale prove elusive, and may require greater management resources at the firm's headquarters.

Screening for market selection

Analysing the attractiveness of individual markets

The purpose of screening is to enable the firm to arrive at a portfolio of attractive international markets. The following approach, based on two grids developed by the Australian Trade Commission (AUSTRADE) in 1990, compares the attractiveness of the international market with the competitiveness of the firm in order to decide the merit of entering the specific international market.

The first grid, which relates to the international market, involves rating the characteristics of the market, the competitive conditions, the financial and economic conditions, and the legislative and sociopolitical conditions for the category of products/services to be offered by the firm. Figure 7.1 shows specific criteria.

The second grid, which relates to the local firm, involves rating management characteristics, marketing characteristics, technology attributes and production related competencies in terms of potential competitiveness in the international market. Figure 7.2 shows the specific assessment criteria.

As a result of the ratings of individual characteristics on both export market attractiveness and firm's competitiveness, an overall assessment of both aspects is arrived at from which the suitability of entering the international market can be determined. Countries that rated high for the firm on both export market attractiveness and competitiveness would constitute a portfolio of attractive markets for the firm to consider entering.

A screening approach

The 'grid' approach, which involves an analysis of each country, is time-consuming and may be beyond the management resources of many small and medium-sized firms. An alternative approach might involve commencing the selection procedure by

Export market attractiveness

Figure 7.1

Country/Market: ....
Product Category: ....
Size of imports (A$ Equivalent) ....

ASSESSMENT CRITERIA	[1] #	RATING [2]					COMMENTS [3]
		--	-	0	+	++	
MARKET CHARACTERISTICS							
• Growth of imports							
• Predictability of imports							
• Degree of market segmentation							
• Degree of customer concentration							
• Sensitivity to quality/performance							
• Availability of close substitutes							
• Sensitivity to imports							
COMPETITIVE CONDITIONS							
• Concentration of domestic industry							
• Concentration of exporters							
• Complexity of distribution system							
• Threat from domestic or foreign new entrants							
FINANCIAL AND ECONOMIC CONDITIONS							
• Industry pricing practices							
• Industry payment terms							
• Currency parity							
• Import tariffs and charges							
• Need for concessional financing							
• Foreign exchange conditions							
• Cost of doing business							
• Barriers to entry not elsewhere identified							
LEGISLATIVE AND SOCIOPOLITICAL CONDITIONS							
• Political stability							
• Trade legislation							
• Consumer or environmental legislation							
• Registration and licensing legislation							
• Cultural affinity							
• Foreign investment legislation							
• Labour legislation and practices							
• Intellectual property protection							

Critical Hurdles   Overall Assessment

[1] # the most important issues in determining the attractiveness
     of the market
[2] Rate the assessment criteria from -- (very negative) to ++ (very
     positive)
[3] The comment, based on knowledge of market conditions, should
     substantiate the rating given to the assessment criteria in each case

Source: Australian
Trade Commission
(1990).

Figure 7.2	Evaluation of firms' competitiveness

Country/Market: ....
Product Category: ....
Australla's Share of Imports ....

ASSESSMENT CRITERIA	[1] #	RATING [2]					COMMENTS [3]
		--	-	0	+	++	
MANAGEMENT RELATED							
• Adequacy of management resources deployed							
• Span of international contacts/alliances							
• Effectiveness of institutional support							
MARKET RELATED							
• Sophistication of market intelligence							
• Effectiveness of distribution network							
• Appropriateness of pricing approaches							
• Advertising/promotion capability							
TECHNOLOGY RELATED							
• Product design/development capabilities							
• Adequacy of technological investment							
• Customer service/support capabilities							
• Breadth of product line							
PRODUCTION RELATED							
• Cost competitiveness of operation							
• Adequacy of scale of operation							
• Consistency of quality control							
• Effectiveness of logistics capabilities							
• Control of key inputs supply							
• Packaging and labelling							

\# Critical Hurdles   Overall Assessment

[1]   # the most important issues in determining the attractiveness
      of the market
[2]   Rate the assessment criteria from -- (very negative) to ++ (very
      positive)
[3]   The comment, based on knowledge of market conditions, should
      substantiate the rating given to the assessment criteria in each case

Source: Australian
Trade Commission
(1990).

considering all markets in the world and then screening markets in relation to a succession of criteria. Unsuitable markets are progressively eliminated from consideration. The result is likely to be a small group or cluster of markets that offer the greatest potential. As the selection procedure moves from stage to stage, a greater degree of analysis is likely to be required. As a consequence, most effort is put into studying those markets that are likely to offer the most promise in relation to the characteristics of the firm and the opportunities of the market.

The approach to progressive screening described below and shown in Figure 7.3 is a modified version of that developed by Toyne and Walters (1993). It is made up of five stages.

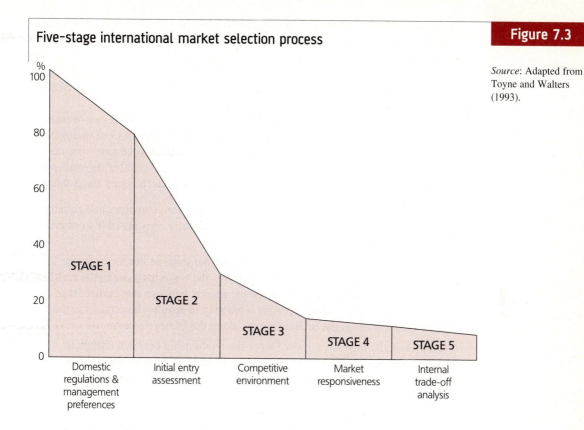

Figure 7.3

Five-stage international market selection process

Source: Adapted from Toyne and Walters (1993).

Stage 1

Stage 1 involves answering the following questions relating to domestic considerations.

Question 1. Which international markets are of no interest to the firm regardless of their apparent potential? This issue, while often irrational, impacts on market selection. It is often due to the prejudice or preference of the senior executives. For example, an unhappy holiday experience in India may result in a refusal by the CEO to contemplate exporting to that country.

Question 2. Which remaining international markets should be excluded because of regulations initiated by or involving support of the government? These regulations may be political, such as an embargo on trading with Iraq, defence-related (export of defence equipment only allowed to friendly countries), or have economic/protectionist motives.

At the conclusion of this portion of the analysis, it is likely that around 20% of world markets can be excluded from further consideration.

Stage 2

Stage 2 involves answering the following questions relating to macroenvironmental factors in international markets and an initial assessment of general prospects. The second step, described as 'initial entry assessment', screens out economically unattractive markets.

Question 3. Which remaining international markets have the least attractive political and social environments? This question can be assessed by considering the political and economic environment, the domestic economic conditions and the external economic relations of the country. At this stage of the analysis, economic considerations could also be included, such as the ease with which profits can be repatriated, freedom to convert local currency and the volatility of the exchange rate.

Question 4. Which remaining international markets are least attractive because of their nature and potential size? There are a number of simple ways for estimating likely demand sufficient for a screening activity. These not only involve assessing current demand but also likely future demand as well as untapped or unfilled demand which may exist in a particular market. Some of the more common techniques are as follows:

- *Demand pattern analysis.* By analysing local production, inventory and patterns of international trade for a product in an foreign country, it is possible to estimate consumption trends and market opportunities.

- *International product life cycle.* By comparing the stage of the life cycle for the product in the international market compared to the stage in the domestic and by reflecting on what happened in the domestic market between that earlier stage and the present one, it is possible to predict what may happen to the product in the international market as the product moves along the life cycle curve.

- *Income elasticity measurements.* This is the relationship between change in demand for a product divided by the change in income. This measure can be used for predicting change in likely quantity demanded for a particular product category.

- *Proxy and multiple factor indices.* When information about the product in the international market is unavailable, it is possible to estimate likely demand using demand patterns for another product or service that is correlated with demand for the firm's own product/service. For example, electrification of villages will be associated with demand for refrigerators. A multiple factor index involves two or more proxy variables believed to correlate with demand for the product.

This second stage of the analysis may indicate that demand for the product/service does not exist in a further 50% of world markets.

Stage 3

By Stage 3, only about 30% of world markets remain. In this stage and the next, the more expensive and time-consuming elements of evaluation are applied to the remaining limited number of countries offering potential. During this phase, it is important to answer the following questions relating to the likely competitive environment in the international market.

Question 5. Which remaining international markets have substantial entry barriers to protect domestic industry or conform to trade relations arrangements with other countries? These barriers may relate to entry, exit and the marketplace. Entry barriers can be both tariff and non-tariff (e.g. quotas, quarantine or standards). Such barriers also include aspects that impinge on the form of international market entry, such as regulations relating to local content and ownership. Exit barriers may relate to repatriation of profits, dividends and capital, taxation issues and technology transfer.

Marketplace barriers can include access to skilled personnel, availability of warehouse space, transportation, allocation of critical inputs such as power and water, and control over prices.

These barriers may take different forms all of which would serve to rule out markets from further consideration. This is reflected in the composition of the markets in Japan and China. In the former, the main barrier is the complex and multi-layered distribution system which underpins a major sector of business activity and generates significant employment. In China, by contrast, the tariff and non-tariff barriers are a continuing legacy of the previous regime, designed to create a climate for the development of indigenous industry. Although in both countries the barriers are being lowered, they still continue to operate as a substantial impediment to firms wishing to enter these markets.

Question 6. Which remaining international markets should be avoided because competitors (both domestic and foreign) are already well entrenched in them? This will require some knowledge as to whether the competitors are local or foreign, and how they will react to entry into their markets. With each competitor or potential competitor, knowledge as to relative strengths and weaknesses in relation to your firm's operation helps establish whether a market should be excluded because of potential competitive reaction. There are a number of competitive strategies which might influence selection of markets. These include entering a market so as to pre-empt the entry of others, entering a market in which there are already competitors and confronting them, and entering a market where large competitors do not exist. The latter strategy might be designed to both build up share of market and gain experience for attacking more competitive markets in other countries at a later stage.

This third stage of the analysis is likely to screen out a further 15% of countries.

Stage 4

Stage 4 involves answering the following questions relating to the degree to which markets are unlikely to respond to, or prohibit, certain market activities.

Question 7. Which remaining international markets are not large enough to justify the marketing effort that will be necessary to gain a satisfactory market share? This requires an assessment as to what share of the total market in the country the firm can reasonably expect to obtain, given domestic and other foreign competition and affordability of the product. In cases where this demand is not sufficient to justify risk or costs of entry, the market should be excluded from further consideration.

Question 8. Which remaining international markets are unlikely to respond to those marketing activities which are considered necessary to effectively establish the product/service in the marketplace? It will need to be determined whether the market allows or prevents the firm achieving its objectives. These may be couched in terms of product (e.g. achievement of brand identity and product line extension), and in terms of pricing (e.g. such as the ability to achieve acceptable levels of return on investment and match changes in competitors' pricing). The market will also need to be assessed in terms of whether the firm will be able to achieve its objectives in promotion (e.g. securing media coverage, optimising sales force effectiveness and attaining advertising objectives), plus its objectives in distribution (e.g. achievement of coverage, building up appropriate inventory levels and the ability to modify the channel when this becomes necessary).

Question 9. Which remaining international markets prohibit the form of presence that your firm considers optimal and can afford when entering a new international market? The answers to previous questions and the firm's preferred way of operating internationally may indicate as to what form of market presence would be most appropriate for each market. It is necessary to establish whether the desired form is permissible (because some may not be allowed), and whether those forms which are allowed are likely to be profitable. If the company always operates internationally via licensing its technology and the government limits the size of allowable licensing fee, then the attractiveness of the market may be questionable. Before the reforms of the Indian economy in 1993, the Indian government restricted royalty payments to 3% maximum, taxable at 50% yielding 1.5% net. Most international firms found this figure unattractive.

Question 10. Which remaining international markets are unattractive because of costs and problems of reaching them? Answering this question involves ensuring that reasonable logistics links exist both between the domestic and international market and within the international market. The impact of the cost of logistics on the ability to both compete and satisfy demand also need to be considered. Also relevant in selecting a market is whether these links are reliable and timely – that delivery can be relied upon; that the time taken for goods to reach the destination does not adversely impact on the ability to compete; and that the goods arrive in an acceptable condition.

Completion of this fourth stage of the analysis is likely to exclude another 10% of countries.

Stage 5

The fifth stage involves eliminating markets because of internal trade-offs. At this point, it is likely that around 5% of markets remain for consideration. It may be useful to create a weighting system that reflects the goals of the firm and perceived importance to the firm of circumstances in the international market. This weighting could then be applied to answers to the final two questions. Appraising the remaining countries in relation to these final questions is likely to result in only a few markets being contemplated for entry. This step involves answers to the following questions:

Question 11. Which remaining international markets are no longer attractive because of the extent to which resources need to be committed and changes made to existing company resources? Some of the remaining markets may require more resources than others. Trade-offs are likely – first, between markets which require more resources and those which require less in terms of anticipated pay-off; second, between resource requirements of specific international markets and using those same resources to expand activities in the domestic market.

Question 12. Do any of the markets still under consideration fail to meet the company's objectives or match its competitive advantages? This last question recognises that market attractiveness does not exist independently of a firm's competitive strategy. The process by which the remaining markets have been arrived at should mean that the answer is 'no'. However, it is useful to pose a check question of this type at the conclusion of the screening process.

With the several remaining markets having promise, no final decision should be made until these markets have been visited by a responsible executive to see whether the impressions of potential are justified. It is only then that they should be ranked in order of attractiveness.

Market selection in the new millennium

In the new millennium, it is increasingly likely that for both the novice international firm and the experienced one, international market selection will be increasingly influenced by strategic objectives, such as establishing a competitive position, transferring risk and rating market investment against profitability. While international market selection will still require a 'fit' between the requirements of the prospective markets and the firm's competences, these markets may not parallel geographic boundaries and may be a result of cultural similarities. There may be a need for change in the traditional patterns of international market selection to cater for a world 'that values choice, speed, information, collaboration, market convergence, business cost reduction and increased consumer value' (Walton and Ashill, 2001). Their research also suggests that, in the future, international market selection will be increasingly influenced by the desire to select the right partner and the need to transfer risk to other markets in order to even out one's risk exposure between countries. It will also be influenced by the desire to capitalise on the potential of e-commerce in international markets and the need to gain insider status in emerging regional trading blocs.

The literature on market selection is intended to provide a path for the novice exporter to follow. Experienced exporters may be driven by different considerations when selecting subsequent markets to enter. Two recent studies illustrate this: Brewer (2001) found that experienced firms seek out new country markets on the basis of expected commercial returns; Clark and Pugh (2001) found that UK-based multinationals, in selecting further markets to enter, were more likely to be influenced by the affluence of the market than by its size, and by the extent of geographical separation rather than by its cultural distance.

Internet infusion

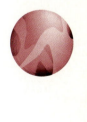

Whereas market selection prior to the introduction of the Internet was based on country, with the advent of the Internet this may no longer be the case. This is because with e-business marketing, the Internet has created a cyber marketplace structured around Internet access and commonality of interests and consumption needs. The Internet is rapidly changing the significance of national boundaries in defining market areas. No longer do businesses have to be structured around political boundaries. The attractiveness of markets will more likely now be rated in terms of ease of Internet access, influenced by both infrastructure (PCs and telephone access) and language. Consumers without Internet access will be restricted to information from traditional sources and have a more limited range of product offerings. As Internet access is unlikely to be available in the least developed of the developing countries (LLDCs), this factor will make them less attractive as markets for those firms using the Internet as a marketing vehicle. On the other hand, consumers with Internet access in geographically isolated or distant markets can become linked into the global market structure. This will be of particular benefit to them. Market selection will also be influenced because the Internet establishes direct channels of communication between exporters and importers and reduces the need for intermediaries, such as international agents. In some cases, however, reintermediation occurs and traditional intermediaries are replaced by cyber intermediaries (e.g. search engines) that perform matching functions.

Modes of entering international markets

Having identified promising international markets, the next issue is the mode of entry that is most appropriate for the market(s) selected. Although this is treated as a separate decision to market selection, it is often directly related because of a preference by the firm for a specific mode of entry. Modes of entry can be divided into those that aim to sell the product and those that aim to transfer know-how to the host country. Further discussion of various modes of entry as they relate to effective internatonal distribution can be found in Chapter 12.

Export-based entry

These forms for entry are driven by a desire to sell either a product/service or technology internally with the minimum commitment of resources.

Indirect exporting

Indirect exporting refers to the use of agencies in the home country to get the product into the foreign market. Indirect export can be subdivided into export agents who receive a commission for exporting goods produced by firms, and export merchants who buy the goods from the manufacturer and subsequently export them. In addition, firms can export using specific agencies established to market international products in their category. This is often referred to as cooperative exporting. Cooperative exporting has long been a feature of the export of agricultural products and takes the form not only of cooperative associations but also of statutory corporations set up by governments which involve government, trading and grower representatives. To varying degrees these bodies set conditions and influence or control the export of the product category. Another form of indirect exporting is that of piggybacking, whereby an inexperienced exporter uses the facilities of an experienced exporter to enter and market products into an international market. This can be initiated by government, e.g. when a government trade promotion agency initiates a 'foster firm' scheme for inexperienced exporters. It can also be encouraged by the private sector, e.g. when an industry group encourages those members which are successful in international business to seek opportunities internationally for newer and smaller members.

7.1 International highlight

Starbucks enters China

Starbucks has followed in the path of McDonald's and Kentucky Fried Chicken (KFC) in its successful entry of the Chinese market. Given that the Chinese are devoted tea drinkers the success of Starbucks is outstanding. They opened their first outlet at the China World Trade Centre in Beijing in 1999. American companies often come under pressure in China for political reasons. In recent years McDonald's and KFC have suffered a downturn due to international events – for example when the Chinese Embassy was bombed in Belgrade. Given this cultural and political landscape, companies have taken at times surprising decisions in the Chinese market. Starbucks opened an outlet in a souvenir shop in Beijing's Forbidden City; as a result, many critical articles appeared in the local media. However, the outlet is still selling coffee and Starbucks has no plans to close it.

Direct exporting

In this case, the firm itself contacts the international buyers and either sells direct to the end user or arranges for firms in the target market to act as agents and/or distributors for its products. The firm establishes its own export sales organisation which becomes responsible for all marketing activities in respect of international sales. This group identifies potential markets and segments and is involved in export documentation – shipment, and planning both strategy and marketing activities in the international market. While direct export entails a greater commitment of resources, it enables the firm to exercise more control over the conditions under which its products are sold. For many small and medium-sized firms, direct exporting is the dominant form of foreign market involvement. Another variant that is becoming increasingly important, especially with the advent of the Internet, is direct marketing. This is proving to be a very useful entry mode for small firms and firms initially entering a new international market.

Establishing a sales office in the international market

Whereas direct exporting involves appointing a non-employee in the international market to represent your firm and set up a network of distributors, establishing a sales office in the international market represents a further commitment of resources beyond what is entailed in the usual form of direct exporting. Establishing a sales office in the international market also enables a greater measure of control over what happens to the product in that market. The office controls not only the selling of the product or service but also its promotional programme. This refinement enables the firm to set up and control its own distribution channels.

Licensing

Licensing enables a firm to earn foreign income from its technical innovations, its brand, its corporate image or its other proprietary assets without engaging in either manufacturing or marketing internationally. It usually involves an 'up-front' payment for the transfer of know-how and a royalty linked to volume produced and sold in the international market. Although there is a minimal commitment of resources involved, this form of market entry provides limited return especially in cases where the licensee does not fully develop the potential that the market has to offer. A further disadvantage is that licensing agreements are usually for a fixed term during the course of which the firm is prevented from entering the market directly. In addition, there is a risk that licensing might lead to 'cloning a competitor' should a licensee export to other markets in competition with the licensor or continue to manufacture the product after expiration of the licensing period. However, with an increasing number of countries accepting the new World Trade Organisation regime on intellectual property protection, this risk has diminished. A final problem occurs when the licensee produces substandard products under the company's brand and the firm's global image suffers as a result.

Franchising

Whereas international licensing usually applies to products, in the services industry the variant of international franchising is becoming increasingly common, especially in the global expansion of hotel and fast-food chains. The franchisor gives the franchisee the right to undertake business in a specified manner under the franchisor's name in return for a royalty payment that usually takes the form of a fee or a percentage of sales. Many of the advantages and disadvantages that apply to licensing apply to franchising. In particular, one of the problems of international expansion in both the retail and hospitality sectors is the cost of purchasing or renting sites and this responsibility is usually that of the franchisee. Franchising is also important where contact with customers and the well-managed operation of the business are critical to success. The franchisor can lay down guidelines for this interface to ensure a uniform projection and include in the franchising agreement penalties or threat of abrogation of contract for non-compliance. Successful franchising involves the establishment of performance standards and mechanisms for monitoring and control. Because of this, franchising can often be more resource-intensive than licensing.

Manufacturing-based entry

Often referred to as direct foreign investment (DFI), this can take a number of forms, varying from limited equity involvement to total ownership of the international operation.

Joint venture

The most common form of manufacturing-based entry into international markets is that of the joint venture, especially entering Asia. This is because the governments of many Asian countries have foreign investment laws that mandate some local equity in any investment in their country. Joint ventures are a means of the firm limiting its equity exposure in an international market and can provide a vehicle for entering markets where the economic systems and marketing environments are so different from the home ones that it is necessary to have a local partner in order to be successful.

Where the object of the joint venture is the building of a major infrastructure project, a number of foreign firms might be involved in a consortium together with local interests from either or both the public and the private sectors. When the manufacture of products is involved, the more common form of joint venture is that between an international firm and a local firm. The international firm brings to the joint venture technology and production expertise while the local partner provides access to the distribution network as well as familiarity with the local marketing environment.

As a mode of entry, joint ventures reduce the capital and other resource commitment required, involve a spreading of risk, and result in access to contacts and expertise in penetration of the local market. The main disadvantages are the risk of conflict between the international firm and its joint venture partner, problems of communication and management when different cultures are involved, and the fact that the international firm has only partial control. Because of this, joint ventures are likely to have a limited lifespan unless the partners can develop an agreed corporate mission and agree on a common strategy and mode of governance.

Acquisition

This involves entering the international market by acquiring an existing company. It is an entry technique often employed by multinational firms that are cash rich; however, it is often beyond the resources of small and medium-sized firms. Acquiring an existing operation enables rapid entry into the international market in that it usually provides an established distribution channel and existing customer base. It is a desirable strategy in cases where the industry is highly competitive or where there are substantial entry barriers for a new entrant. Such a move requires considerable research lest the equipment is outdated, the assets of the company are overvalued, labour laws inhibit change and increased productivity, or the intellectual assets of the firm cannot be protected. Many larger corporations like Electrolux have adopted this approach.

7.2 International highlight

Aventis – Bridging the gap between France and Germany

The successful merger between Hoechst, a German drugs and chemical group, and Rhône-Poulenc, a French rival, has been hailed as a great success for the new company Aventis. The results for the last two years have outstripped their rivals'. The merger of the two big European companies of roughly equal size was difficult and in the end was one of compromise. The head office was put in Strasbourg, on the border but in France, while the top jobs and plant cutbacks were shared between the two nations. Aventis has not only managed its merger well, it has three major drugs and its market share in North America has grown to 40%.

Greenfield operation

This occurs where a firm decides to build its own manufacturing plant in the foreign country using its own funds. This is an attractive entry option if there are no suitable firms to acquire or the firm needs to establish its own operation because of technology or logistics considerations. It enables firms to utilise the latest production technologies while at the same time selecting the most attractive locations in terms of labour costs, local taxes, land prices and transportation. Firms wishing to rationalise their operations on a global basis are more likely to find this the most attractive entry option despite the costs in terms of capital and management.

Relationship-based entry

These forms of entry are more reliant on the creation of relationships than those discussed previously. They occur where a considerable degree of cooperation is necessary in order to achieve success. This is because the level of resource commitment by the international firm is usually modest and both parties to the transaction have a mutual stake in the outcome.

Contract manufacturing

In this case, the firm contracts the production to a local manufacturer but retains control over the marketing of the product. It is a strategy suitable in circumstances where the international market does not justify establishing a manufacturing operation and where there are high barriers to imports. It requires little investment and is a relatively quick way of entering the international market. Because brand name and company reputation are involved, it does require the exercise of quality control by the international firm so that the contract manufacturer meets the firm's quality and delivery standards. Contract manufacture can also include cooperative manufacture. This is becoming an increasingly common feature of global business. It entails either various parts being produced in differing countries like the Airbus aircraft, or different functions being carried out in differing countries. For example, Fujitsu and NEC now conduct R&D in one country, component manufacture in another, assembly in a third and servicing in a fourth.

Strategic alliances

Although this term is sometimes used in a broader context as a market entry strategy, strategic alliances refer to collaborations between firms in various countries to exchange or share some value-creating activities. The firms involved might be competitors in the one market and see collaboration as being necessary in order to enter and compete in another international market. Alternatively, the alliance may be between a group of firms whose activities complement each other. These strategic alliances can involve joint R&D, shared manufacturing (as is common in the automotive industry), the use of common distribution channels or any other activities in the value chain. In distribution alliances, the members both agree to use an existing distribution network. The Star Alliance between United Airlines, SAS, Air Canada, Lufthansa, Air New

Zealand, Austrian Airlines, Varig, ANA, Singapore Airlines and Thai International is an example of such an alliance as this involves pooling of route information, common access to frequent flyer programmes and sharing of passenger traffic on certain routes using code share flights. Strategic alliances are discussed in greater detail in Chapter 17.

Countertrade

Countertrade involves the linking of an import and an export transaction in a conditional manner. It includes barter, counterpurchase, buy-back, offsets and debt exchange, all of which can result in a firm entering the international market. In countertrade there is a mutually dependent relationship between buyer and seller.

Evaluation of entry modes

In viewing these modes of market entry, it is important to recognise that they involve a trade-off between degree of control on the one hand and commitment of resources on the other. This trade-off exists between forms of exporting. For instance, with indirect exporting, commitment of resources is minimal and the degree of control non-existent, whereas with direct exporting, more resources are required but there is more control over what happens to the product/service and how it is represented. A similar trade-off applies to contractual forms when comparing licensing the manufacture of a product on the one hand with entering into a joint venture on the other. Even within the category of wholly owned subsidiaries, buying out an established operation involves less commitment of management resources but less control. This is because employees are inherited who do things a different way. In a greenfield operation building an operation from scratch will absorb considerable management time but will be totally controlled by the firm from the start. The latter will operate according to the way the firm usually does business. In addition, it can be argued that moving from one group of modes to another, such as from export to contractual to wholly owned subsidiaries, also involves the same trade-off between resources and control.

Theories of market entry

Considerable research has been undertaken into the factors that cause firms to manufacture in a foreign country rather than export to it. Two theoretical approaches are summarised below. (Full details can be found in the references at the end of this chapter.)

Dunning's eclectic paradigm

Dunning (see Brouthers et al., 1996) argues that entry modes are influenced by OLI (**O**wnership, **L**ocation, **I**nternalisation). The paradigm has its origin in the concept that different countries have different factor endowments that could be mobile or immobile

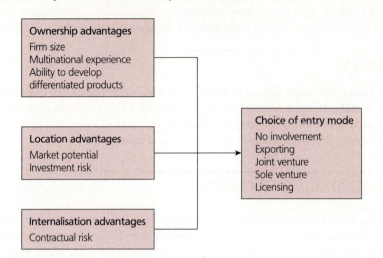

Figure 7.4   A schematic representation of entry choice factors

across national boundaries. The more uneven the geographic distribution of factor endowments, the greater the likelihood of production taking place in the foreign country. The second concept underlying the paradigm is that of market failure which arises because different countries have distinct political and economic institutions. Market failures can be structural (barriers to entry, government intervention) or transactional (economies of scale, risk, etc). This theory is relevant to explaining not only the location of economic activities across national boundaries, but also the division of that activity between multinational and uninational firms. The OLI paradigm describes the degree to which the firm has advantages due to its:

- *Ownership.* Is it sufficient to offset the costs of operating in a foreign environment? In order for a firm of one nationality to compete with those of another by producing in the latter's own country, they must possess advantages specific to the nature and/or nationality of their ownership. These advantages can take the form of asset advantages and transaction advantages.

- *Location.* Is it more advantageous for the firm to exploit its assets through manufacture internationally than via export from its home market? Location advantages are benefits that arise from a company performing certain operations in a specific location driven by lower labour costs, tax incentives, proximity to state of the art research etc.

- *Internalisation.* Is it more profitable to capitalise on its unique assets by foreign direct investment than selling the rights to their use via licensing arrangements? In other words, is it more beneficial for a company to make direct use of its competitive advantage in a foreign country rather than to sell it or lease it to someone else?

The appropriateness of this OLI paradigm is likely to vary according to the selected form of market entry. Pinto et al. (2001) found that as far as the financial services sector was concerned, the OLI advantages were greatest when the firm used acquisition as its market entry mode and least effective when it set up a wholly owned subsidiary.

Williamson's transaction cost approach

In the article by Anderson and Gatignon (1986), Williamson's 'transaction cost approach' is used to argue that the foreign entry mode selected should be that which maximises long-run efficiency measured in terms of the risk-adjusted rate of return on investment. It is suggested that control is the most important determinant of risk and return and that high-control entry modes (e.g. wholly owned subsidiaries) increase return on the one hand and risk on the other. By contrast, low-control modes (e.g. licensing) involve less commitment of resources but also have lower returns. The authors postulate that the extent to which the chosen entry mode should provide control is a function of:

- transaction-specific assets including specialised physical or human investments such as proprietary processes or products at an early stage of the product life cycle;
- external uncertainty reflecting unpredictability in the chosen international market due to economic and political factors;
- internal uncertainty related to difficulties in exercising control over the agent in the international market due to lack of experience, culture and linguistic knowledge and familiarity with business customs and practices;
- free-riding potential, which refers to the agent's ability to exploit the relationship for personal advantage such as by degrading the brand name or by taking on the line to neutralise its competitive impact.

On the above basis, high control modes of entering foreign markets should be chosen when the firm possesses transaction-specific assets, when external uncertainty is high, when it is difficult to control the agent's performance, and when there is considerable opportunity for agents to take advantage of the relationship.

Information for market entry and expansion

The information necessary to enable decisions to be made as to the nature of involvement in a specific international market can be categorised according to whether it relates to factors internal or external to the firm.

Factors internal to the firm

The characteristics of management and the characteristics of the firm can impact on decisions made about both the form of market entry and the form of expansion.

Management characteristics

One of the often-overlooked resources that firms can use to improve their prospects for successful entry of international markets is the previous international exposure of its executives. Research has shown (Barrett, 1986; Fletcher, 1996) that country of birth, years spent abroad, and frequency of international business trips have a positive impact on the executive's willingness to engage in international activities. Other relevant characteristics of managers influencing international expansion decisions are planning orientation, knowledge of different cultures and business practices, experience with international transactions, adoption of a strategic approach to international business, espousal of a marketing orientation, and willingness to take a long-term view of international involvement.

These characteristics influence the management objectives of the firm. They often influence the trade-off between resources committed and control of international activities discussed earlier in this chapter.

Firm's characteristics

Research by Fletcher (1996) has found that international involvement is affected by:

- the problems of competing in the domestic market (especially with competitors who enjoy economies of scale due to international activities);
- the willingness to commit resources to international activities;
- the nature of the domestic market for the firm's products and excess capacity within the firm;
- the ability of the firm to make the necessary resources available for market entry and expansion;
- the extent to which products are high-tech; and
- the size of the firm.

Factors external to the firm

Factors external to the firm can impact on the form of market entry which is most appropriate for the firm. They can act as either incentives or impediments to international involvement. They include the international nature and attractiveness of the product category, receipt of unsolicited export orders, reversal of seasons between local and international market, the overall potential of the selected international market, government regulations and trade barriers (including embargoes and less obvious barriers, such as deliberate administrative delays, local content requirements) and assistance offered by the government and other external bodies, in both the domestic and international markets.

Nature and attractiveness of the product category

The physical characteristics of the product, such as its weight, value, perishability and composition, will influence where to locate its production. When the product incorporates such assets as a high level of technology or a well-known brand name, management may be reluctant to participate in international operations where it loses control over the production process. For this reason, the nature of the product category can be a very important determinant of entry mode especially when deciding between licensing/franchising on the one hand and foreign direct manufacturing on the other.

The potential of the international market

The greater the potential of the international market, the more likely it is that the firm will be willing to commit resources to market entry and development. Potential can be a matter of the size of the market, maturity for the product category involved, and the growth rate in the market. As previously discussed, the more advanced stages of entry involve a greater commitment of resources; therefore the greater the potential, the more likely the firm will engage in a more advanced stage of activity in that market. Potential, however, can be negatively impacted by political and environmental risk. If these factors are high in the international market, participation in that market is likely to involve a lesser commitment of resources. Another factor impacting on the form of entry is accessibility to the market. If the market is difficult or expensive to access this may result in some form of manufacturing in that market rather than exporting to it.

Another external factor to consider is marketing infrastructure. A number of questions are relevant:

- Is the general attitude in the market towards marketing positive or negative?
- Do the marketing intermediaries exist that your company is used to, such as advertising agencies, market research agencies or media buying groups?
- Do the media exist on which the company's domestic marketing is based? If so, are they available to the firm and viable for the marketing of its product in the selected market?

The answers to these questions may influence whether the firm engages in a mode of entry where it is responsible for marketing or whether it engages in a mode of entry where responsibility for marketing is left to a local party.

Government regulations and trade barriers

There are situations where government regulations prevent imports into a market, restrict manufacture of a product category to local firms, or only permit manufacture in less attractive geographical locations in that market. The Thai government, for example, will only provide investment incentives for foreign firms prepared to locate manufacturing facilities outside Bangkok. The attractiveness of these incentives varies according to the extent to which the facility is located in areas accorded high priority in terms of Thailand's industrialisation and economic development plans. A similar situation prevails in China. Hence the form of entry may be prescribed by the host government. Trade barriers such as tariff and non-tariff barriers like import quotas, quarantine barriers, mandatory local standards, may also influence the form of entry.

An indirect trade barrier of increasing importance is environmentalism. The trade-off between the need for foreign exchange and industrial development on the one hand and the degree to which environmental regulations are enforced on the other varies from country to country. Criticism of international firms engaging in environmentally damaging activities, even when allowed by the host country, is likely to increase and could impact on decisions to become involved in a particular market. This issue has recently been highlighted in the growing debate concerning the Three Gorges Project in China. Environmental considerations can therefore impact on the cost of various forms of market entry and on decisions between contractual forms of entry and wholly owned subsidiaries. Even with a contractual form of entry, if something goes wrong it is likely that the foreign firm will be both criticised and pursued in the courts for compensation, rather than the local partner. (Union Carbide and the Bhopal calamity in India is a case in point.)

Allied to government regulation is involvement of a target country in a regional trade grouping. This is a factor of increasing relevance in today's international business environment. The individual country's market may not be large enough to justify an entry mode other than export. However, membership of a regional trade grouping aiming towards a common external fiscal boundary and free trade/industrial rationalisation among its members, may make contractual or wholly owned subsidiary modes much more attractive. This is because insider status in one country enables access to all the others, e.g. the Industrial Development Agency in Ireland has managed to attract to Ireland some of the largest multinationals in the world on the basis of their access to the EU.

Assistance from government and other bodies

The nature of assistance available from one's own government may influence choice of entry mode. In general, government assistance is focused mostly on export and to a lesser extent on establishing joint ventures. It is unlikely to be available for relationship-based entry forms. Incentives offered by host governments also have an influence on entry mode. If a foreign country has an attractive package of investment incentives, the firm may elect to establish a joint venture in the international market rather than export to it.

Approaches to internationalisation

An examination of what has been written about selecting an international market and the best way of entering an international market indicates that most studies have focused on the novice exporter. However, even the novice will learn by experience and become more adventurous by first entering difficult but potentially more rewarding markets and, secondly, attempting new entry modes involving greater commitment and control. The larger firm, already knowledgeable about international activities, will also learn by experience and increase its degree of internationalisation. An understanding of the process by which firms increase their international involvement is necessary.

Internationalisation has usually been depicted as an incremental process of limited commitment in the face of uncertainty. However, according to Rosenzweig and Shaner (2000), a number of major changes in recent years – ranging from deregulation of industry, to newly emerging markets, to the revolution in information technology –

have changed the pattern of internationalisation. As a result, firms face lower barriers to international growth and more firms which are smaller and limited in resources can expand internationally. This has meant a surge in international activities requiring firms to internationalise more rapidly than in the past. The various approaches to internationalisation are as follows.

Stages approaches

The earliest group of theories to explain this process were the so-called 'stages approaches' – firms started with the mode of entry which required the least commitment of resources and with experience gradually increased their commitment of resources to international activities. Typical of these approaches were those of Bilkey and Tesar (1977), based on the theory of diffusion of innovation; Cavusgil (1980), based on progressive reduction of uncertainty; and Reid (1991), who argued that firms moved from awareness (of export potential) to intention (to begin doing something about exporting) to trial (attempt exporting) to evaluation (of the results of initial exporting) to acceptance (of exporting as a good thing). These theories, summarised in Fletcher (2001), were somewhat static although logical.

Learning approaches

A second group of theories applied learning theory and recognised that internationalisation is a dynamic process. They focused more on an evolutionary, sequential build-up of foreign commitments over time and recognised the role that psychic distance can play in the process. For instance, firms commence their international involvement in nearby markets that are most similar to the home market and as they learn more about the export process, become willing to try markets which are more distant in terms of cultural background, political system and economic circumstance. Typical of this group of theories of internationalisation was that of Johanson and Weidersheim-Paul (see summary in Fletcher, 2001), who argued that from a position of no export activity, firms first exported via an intermediary and then on a direct basis. This often involved establishing a sales subsidiary in the international market. This stage could be followed by some form of production in the international market.

Both the above theories are incremental and imply that firms repeat the process in all markets rather than apply their experience in one market when entering another using an entry mode requiring a greater commitment of resources.

Contingency approaches

A third group of theories of internationalisation are based on contingency theory, whereby the firm evaluates and responds to an opportunity as it occurs, regardless of whether the market is close in psychic distance terms or whether an advanced mode of entry is required. Exponents of this approach (Okoroafo, 1990), argue that factors internal to the firm as well as external situations or opportunities will cause firms to leapfrog stages and select one that is the most appropriate for the international market.

Network approaches

The fourth group of approaches is based on the network paradigm that emphasises the role of linkages and relationships in the internationalisation process. The approach here is that firms become involved in international activities by establishing linkages with networks in other countries. The network of the exporting firm in the home market, including those firms which provide inputs and facilitate the activities of the firm, becomes linked to the network of the buying firm in the international country, including those firms which distribute, facilitate, service and on-sell the product. Using this approach, Johanson and Mattsson (1988) describe modes of entry in terms of the position established in international networks as:

- *international extension* – entering a international network that is new to the firm;
- *international penetration* – consolidating and building upon an already established position in an international network;
- *international integration* – coordinating the positions already occupied in networks in different countries.

These authors believe that the degree of internationalisation of the firm in terms of the nature of its product network should be compared to the degree of internationalisation of the market in terms of the national network for the product in the selected country. They arrive at four categories of firm.

- *Early starter* – firms in this category often begin exporting to nearby markets using agents so as to take advantage of positions in the market occupied by firms in the network in that country.
- *Lonely international* – because this firm has considerable international experience and because the international market is not highly internationalised, this firm is likely to experience little difficulty in entering the network in that country.
- *Late starter* – this firm may be 'pulled' into becoming involved in the foreign country by members of its network at home such as customers or suppliers. Being 'pulled' it may become involved in a more advanced stage of internationalisation and/or in markets perceived to be more psychically distant.
- *International among others* – firms in this category can easily use their position in the international network in one country as a way of entering networks in other countries. For example, they may use production capacity in one to supply another.

The network approach caters for the current dynamic situation in international marketing whereby internationalisation not only involves outward-driven activities but also inward-driven activities as well as activities in which import and export transactions are linked and mutually dependent. As such, because of its focus on the need for buyers (importers) and sellers (exporters) to build up knowledge about each other, it is the only approach with a capacity to cater for more advanced forms of international market entry, such as strategic alliances, cooperative manufacture and countertrade.

A holistic view of internationalisation

Fletcher (2001) looked at market entry modes in a broader way in an endeavour to consider what actually happens to firms when entering international markets as opposed to theories built around what firms should do. His research is based on a definition of internationalisation developed by Welch and Luostarinen (1988) – it is 'the process of increasing involvement in international operations'.

The research endeavours to accommodate recent trends in the international business environment such as the information superhighway, rising fixed costs, shorter product life cycles and converging consumer tastes. These trends have resulted in more complex forms of international behaviour which are imposing an increasing requirement for global cooperation in order for firms to be globally competitive.

A broader approach to market entry is necessary. This is illustrated in Figure 7.5.

Firms can enter markets via both inward and outward activities. As with outward activities, inward activities can occur as a series of stages involving increasing commitment of resources. Alternatively, they may be the result of experience, with each activity being incremental to the previous one and influenced by the learning that has taken place. Further, they may be the result of contingencies in either the firm or the international market or be the result of relationships arising out of connections into the international network. Figure 7.5 shows the modes of inward driven entry in markets.

Figure 7.5 also shows that in addition to outward and inward modes of entry, there is a third category of linked forms of entry into international markets. In the case of countertrade, the linkage of outward and inward forms is conditional. It is often either a condition of doing business directly mandated by a government or the direct result of a set of conditions created by government, such as the non-availability of foreign exchange. Given that countertrade is estimated to account for between 15 and 20% of world trade, this form of international market entry should not be ignored. Also strategic alliances are becoming increasingly popular due to a desire to achieve economies of scale, reduce R&D costs and overcome protectionism. These alliances are intended to improve international competitiveness by serving customers in a global environment, bringing products to market more quickly, introducing products into several countries simultaneously, lowering costs by focusing on core competences and reducing promotion costs by marketing under one brand. Such alliances are built upon

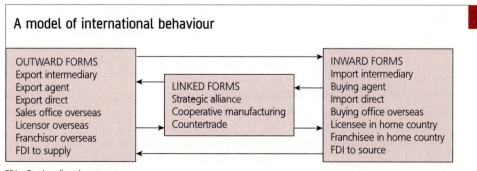

A model of international behaviour

Figure 7.5

OUTWARD FORMS
Export intermediary
Export agent
Export direct
Sales office overseas
Licensor overseas
Franchisor overseas
FDI to supply

LINKED FORMS
Strategic alliance
Cooperative manufacturing
Countertrade

INWARD FORMS
Import intermediary
Buying agent
Import direct
Buying office overseas
Licensee in home country
Franchisee in home country
FDI to source

FDI = Foreign direct investment

Figure 7.6	Inward/outward internationalisation

Source: Hollensen
(2001), p. 37.

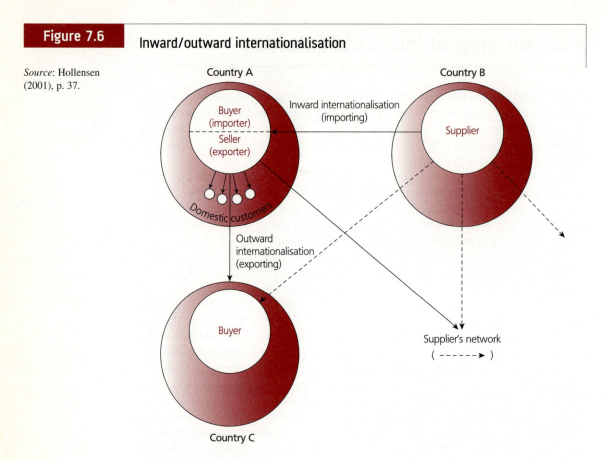

entering international markets, cooperating with a party in that market and gaining competitive strength by becoming involved with that firm's network.

Another reality of international marketing is that outward or export-led involvement can often lead to inward or import-led involvement and vice versa. This happens for example when the licensee in the international market is given the rights to license manufacture of the product in another country, or when the joint venture partner is allowed to set up manufacturing operations in another market. This interconnectedness between inward and outward forms of internationalisation is illustrated in Figure 7.6.

Finally, Welch and Benito (1996) propose that, on occasion, international entry can also be associated with exit from an international market – either exiting from one form of involvement in order to undertake another or exiting from one market in order to strengthen an established position in another. They refer to this as de-internationalisation. It can occur when political or economic conditions in a country change and the firm exits but re-enters when conditions improve as is the case with the history of IBM's involvement in India. This is analogous to what happens in the home market when firms rationalise, downsize and refocus on core competences, all in the interest of greater market share or profitability. In view of the above, there is need for a broader definition of internationalisation than those previously discussed. One such definition is by Calof and Beamish (1995), viz: 'Internationalisation is the process of adapting firms' operations to international environments.'

Internet infusion

When marketing using the Internet, the availability of the necessary infrastructure in a country will influence the form of market entry. Infrastructure availability may not be the same in all countries and the existing infrastructure prior to the introduction of the Internet will influence how the Internet develops in that country (e.g. Europe's advanced digital phone infrastructure will result in greater use of mobile phones for accessing the Internet). E-business firms can only internationalise by dealing with countries that are Internet enabled and use the Internet. A country with a large percentage of the population using the Internet is more attractive as a market for e-business firms to enter. Global technology parity involves availability of both computers and accessible telecom services in a country. E-business firms cannot implement an internationalisation strategy in countries where this parity in technology is absent. The higher the level of technology parity a country exhibits, the faster the e-business firm is able to move into it.

Another factor impacting on form of entry when the Internet is involved is the extent to which there is legal protection of intellectual property rights in a given country. The lack of such protection is detrimental to e-business firms since the core competences of such firms are centred on know-how and the development of patent and software technology. The better the legal protection, the more rapidly the e-business firm will move into a country. As with the internationalisation of traditional firms, cultural distance is significant for determining the speed of internationalisation of e-business firms. For example, language and using it properly may delay e-business firms in preparing their websites and portals.

Research by Zhao and Du (2000) found that:

- E-business firms were much more likely to enter markets that were culturally distant than were traditional firms.
- E-business firms began international activities much sooner after establishment (2.71 years) than traditional firms (21 years).
- E-business firms entered a larger number of foreign markets a year (3.62) than did traditional firms (1.60).
- The internationalisation of e-business firms was neither incremental nor sequential but rather a function of acquired knowledge.
- High degrees of technological parity and legal protection of intellectual property rights were necessary preconditions for the internationalisation of e-business firms.

Because of the Internet characteristics of interactivity and speedy access to information, a knowledge of international markets is acquired more quickly in marketspace than in the marketplace and, as a result, Internet-driven internationalisation is more likely to follow a contingency process of responding to opportunities as they occur. The relevance of the incremental approach to internationalisation is called into question by the explosion of international business activity on the World Wide Web, particularly as technology now exists to provide small and medium-sized enterprises with a low-cost gateway to international markets.

Summary

Selecting international markets is one of the most difficult decisions to be undertaken by the international marketing executive. This is because selecting the wrong market can not only be costly in profit terms but can also result in management disenchantment with any future involvement in international operations. The difference between the novice and the experienced firm is a matter of accumulated international experience; both need to adopt a systematic approach to market selection which takes the circumstances of the firm and the circumstances of the market into account. The form of market entry is another issue which merits careful consideration because some modes, while requiring greater commitment of resources, also allow a greater degree of control and have the potential for greater profitability. In selecting the mode and form of involvement, current business issues such as the information revolution, the linking of networks, the operations of the transnational firm and regional trade groupings need to be taken into account. A more holistic view of market entry should be adopted catering for inward, outward and linked forms of international behaviour.

Ethics issue

Your company has a large amount of capital tied up in manufacturing plant for milling grains. Your main market has recently introduced environmental protection legislation to come into force 12 months hence, which will make this equipment unusable because it gives off more dust than the new legislation allows. Although this machinery will be written off, the company wishes to dispose of it as profitably as possible. You have been advised that potentially profitable opportunities exist to establish joint venture milling operations in Vietnam and Laos. Research also indicates that there is no environmental protection legislation in these countries or restriction on the supply of secondhand milling equipment provided a joint venture is being established.

You are the international marketing manager for the company and the board has called for recommendations for disposing of the firm's current milling machinery with minimum loss. Would you recommend entering into a joint venture in either Vietnam or Laos?

Web workout

Question 1 Choose a product you are familiar with and then select a country that you believe that this product should be marketed to. Using the Internet, research the number and the size of competitors operating in this market? Should you still try to market your product in your previously selected market? Why? Why not?

What would be your next choice of country based on the research you have just conducted?

Question 2 Select a product/service different from that chosen in Question 1 and from your knowledge pick what you believe is the most unattractive market for your chosen product/service. Why do you think this market is unattractive? Next using the Internet, research this country, focusing on competitors, and other socioeconomic dimensions. Has your opinion as to the attractiveness or unattractiveness of this market changed?

Websites

Trade Development homepage www.ita.doc.gov/td/td_home/tdhome.html

Capturing the flag www.exporter.com

Country background note (US Department of State) www.state.gov/r/pa/bgn

New Zealand government web pages www.govt.nz

Foreign Trade online www.foreign-trade.com/articles.htm

Discussion questions

1 Discuss the pros and cons of:
   (a) simultaneous versus incremental entry into international markets;
   (b) concentrated versus diversified market entry strategies.

2 (a) Take a product you are familiar with which has not previously been sold internationally and, applying a progressive selection procedure, arrive at the three most promising markets for the product.
   (b) Take a product you are familiar with which is already being sold in several international markets and, applying a progressive selection procedure, arrive at the three most promising markets that could be considered when expanding international business for the product.
   (c) What different factors would you consider in the case of a product never exported compared with the one already exported to several countries?

3 What factors would you consider if you were a French manufacturer of catamarans in choosing between Mexico, Indonesia and Japan as the next country to enter?

4 What would be the advantages and disadvantages of licensing the manufacture of your product internationally as opposed to manufacture under a joint venture arrangement?

5 What aspects of the international market might cause you to settle on an entry mode which gives you less control over how your product is marketed but requires less investment of resources?

6 It is often argued that theories of international marketing should be based on a process approach (i.e. what actually happens) rather than on a structured approach (using a predetermined model to explain or predict what should happen). Which of the approaches to internationalisation most closely follows the process approach and why?

7 (a) In what circumstances would you enter an international market via an inward form of international involvement?
   (b) When should you contemplate a linked form of market entry and how do you ensure that the relationship is beneficial to both parties?

References

Anderson, E. and Gatignon, H. (1986) 'Modes of Foreign Entry: A Transaction Cost Analysis and Propositions', *Journal of International Business Studies*, Vol. 17, No. 3, pp. 1–26.

Australian Trade Commission (1990) *AUSTRADE User Guide*, Sydney.

Barrett, N.J. (1986) 'A Study of the Internationalisation of Australian manufacturing Firms', PhD Thesis, University of New South Wales.

Bilkey, W.J. and Tesar, G. (1977) 'The Export Behaviour of Smaller-sized Wisconsin Manufacturing Firms', *Journal of International Business Studies*, Spring/Summer, pp. 93–98.

Brewer, P. (2001) 'International Market Selection: Developing a Model from Australian Case Studies', *International Business Review*, Vol. 10, pp. 155–174.

Brouthers, K.D., Brouthers, L.E. and Werner, S. (1996) 'Dunning's Eclectic Theory and the Smaller Firm: the Impact of Ownership and Locational Advantages on the Choice of Entry-modes in the Computer Software Industry', *International Business Review*, Vol. 5, No. 4, pp. 377–394.

Calof, J.C. and Beamish, P.W. (1995) 'Adapting to International Markets: Explaining Internationalization', *International Business Review*, Vol. 4, No. 2, pp. 115–131.

Cavusgil, S.T. (1980) 'On the Internationalisation Process of Firms', *European Research*, Vol. 8, No. 6, pp. 273–281.

Clark, T. and Pugh, D.S. (2001) 'Foreign Country Priorities in the Internationalisation Process: a Measured and an Exploratory Test of British Firms', *International Business Review*, Vol. 10, pp. 285–303.

Czinkota, M.R. and Ronkainen, I.A. (1998) *International Marketing*, 5th edn, Dryden Press, Orlando, p. 249.

Fletcher, R. (1996) 'Countertrade and the Internationalisation of the Australian Firm', PhD Thesis, University of Technology, Sydney.

Fletcher, R. (2001) 'A Holistic View of Internationalisation', *International Business Review*, Vol. 10, pp. 25–49.

Hollensen, S. (2001) *Global Marketing – A Market-Response Approach*, Prentice Hall, Harlow, UK.

Johanson, J. and Mattsson, L.-G. (1988) 'Internationalisation in Industrial Systems – a Network Approach', Reprint Series, no. 1, Department of Business Administration, University of Uppsala, in Hood, N. and Vahlne, J.-E. (eds) *Strategies in Global Competition*, Croom Helm, New York.

Johanson, J. and Wiedersheim-Paul, F. (1975) 'The Internationalisation of the Firm: Four Swedish Cases', *Journal of Management Studies*, Vol. 12, No. 3, pp. 305–322.

Okoroafo, S. (1990) 'An Assessment of Critical Entry Factors Affecting Modes of Entry Substitution Patterns in Foreign Product Markets', *Journal of Global Marketing*, Vol. 3, No. 3, pp. 87–104.

Pinto, J.C., Shaw, V. and Fahrhangmehr, M. (2001) 'Foreign Market Entry Modes in the Financial Services Sector: An Empirical Testing of Dunning's Eclectic Model', *Proceedings of the European Marketing Academy Conference*, Bergen, 8–11 May, Norges Handelshoyskole.

Reid, S.D. (1981) 'The Decision-maker and Export Entry and Expansion', *Journal of International Business Studies*, Vol. 12, No. 2, pp. 101–112.

Rosenzweig, P.M. and Shaner, J.L. (2000) 'Internationalisation Reconsidered: New Imperatives for Successful Growth', *Proceedings of the Annual Meeting of the Academy of International Business*, Phoenix, AZ, 17–20 November, Thunderbird University.

Toyne, B. and Walters, P.G. (1993) *Global Marketing Management*, 2nd edn, Allyn and Bacon, Boston, Chapter 9.

Walton, G. and Ashill, N. (2001) 'International Market Selection: Challenging the Status Quo', *Proceedings of the Conference of the Academy of Marketing*, Cardiff, 1–4 July, University of Cardiff.

Welch, L.S. and Benito, G.R.G. (1996) 'De-internationalisation', Working Paper 5/96, Department of Marketing, University of Western Sydney, Nepean.

Welch, L.S. and Luostarinen, R.K. (1988) 'Internationalisation: Evolution of a Concept', *Journal of General Management*, Vol. 14, No. 2, pp. 34–55.

Young, S., Hamill, J., Wheeler, C and Davies, J.R. (1989) *International Market Entry and Development*, Harvester Wheatsheaf, Hemel Hempstead, UK, Chapter 1.

Zhao, J.H. and Du, J. (2000) 'Electronic Commerce and International Business: A New Test of Internationalisation Theory', *Proceedings of the e-Commerce and Global Business Forum*, Santa Cruz, CA, 17–19 May, Andersen Consulting Institute for Strategic Change.

8

Modifying products for international markets

Learning objectives

After reading this chapter, you should be able to:

- determine how products spread to international markets and what influences their adoption by consumers in other countries;

- develop specific strategies for marketing international products;

- know when to tailor products to suit the needs of customers in international markets;

- recognise how the international marketing of industrial products differs from that of consumer goods; and

- develop an awareness of the complexities of branding and packaging products in the international marketplace.

McDonald's rise in France

While McDonald's worldwide losses are growing, the situation in the French subsidiary is the opposite. Every week a new McDonald's opens in France. However, the modus operandi is somewhat different. In the US, McDonald's have tried to speed up the service by streamlining the menus. In contrast, France has focused on making McDonald's a destination restaurant. They have upgraded their interiors and have added extras such as music videos that entice customers to stay longer. They have not streamlined their menus but instead have added items such as hot ham and cheese sandwiches. French customers spend twice as much as their US counterparts. In addition the French subsidiary has addressed the ongoing criticisms concerning their shopfront designs, by adapting their designs to fit in with the local architecture. This updated styling has come at a cost as it is estimated to increase the cost of outfitting by as much as 20%. However, it has made a big difference in the French market as sales have soared. Whether McDonald's could achieve similar results in the US market is questionable as customers there have traditionally gone for quick service and cheap food.

Introduction

 Because a product is successful in the domestic market, there is no guarantee that it will be successful when exported to other countries. In the international market, as in the domestic market, a marketer must always establish local needs and then take them into account. While some products have universal appeal and require little change before being offered internationally, other products have narrower appeal and must be modified before being offered to buyers in other countries. In general, it is easier and cheaper to modify a product than to try to change a consumer's preference. Often this most basic of marketing concepts is ignored in international marketing.

This is even more often the case when the firm becomes involved in international operations rather than simply exporting to foreign countries. When the firm ventures abroad, it is faced with a need to reappraise its domestic marketing strategies so as to take into account the differing circumstances of the international markets and the changes such international involvement will make to the total strategic approach of the firm. International involvement will require a redefinition of the business, a leveraging of the existing capabilities of the firm and a reappraisal of the firm in relation to its competitors – not only domestic, but also foreign. Such a reappraisal will involve adopting a different approach to segmenting the market and a different strategy when positioning the product or service.

The product

What is a product?

A product is a collection of attributes – physical, service or symbolic – which yield satisfaction to the buyer or end user. Products can be further defined in relation to the different marketplaces in which they are found:

- local products have potential in only one market;
- international products have potential to be extended from the domestic market to a number of international markets;
- multinational products are products offered to many international markets but which are adapted to suit the needs of each market; and
- global products are designed to meet the needs of market segments that are the same the world over.

A product is often considered in a narrow sense as something tangible that can be described in terms of its shape, dimensions, colour and form. This misconception applies in international marketing and many people have the idea that it is only physical products that can be exported. The reality is that intangible products (often called services) can be exported. One of the largest earners of export income in many countries is tourism, a very intangible product. In many instances the actual offering to the international market consists of both a tangible and an intangible product, the totality of which is useful or satisfying to the buyer.

Kotler (2000) believes that this utility or satisfaction can be best appreciated by categorising the elements of a product into the core benefit, the basic product, the expected product, the augmented product and the potential product, all of which may need changing when venturing abroad. The *core benefit* consists of the fundamental benefit or service that the customer is really buying. The *basic product* is the item actually purchased and its functional features. The *expected product* is the attributes and conditions that the buyer expects to receive when purchasing the item and may also include the styling, the packaging, the quality, the brand name and the trademark. The *augmented product* consists of items that exceed customer expectation and may also involve repair and maintenance, installation, instruction book, delivery, warranty, spare parts and credit facilities. Finally, there is the *potential product*, which embraces the possible augmentations and transformations that the product might undergo in the future (e.g. the possibility to add more memory to a computer).

Each of these elements may need modification when the product is offered to buyers in other countries. Such modification may be required for:

- competitive reasons, e.g. when someone else has registered the brand name;
- for legal reasons, e.g. when the manufacturer is required to show weights and volume in imperial measure;
- for linguistic reasons, e.g. when dealing with a bilingual market, such as Canada, where instructions must be in both French and English;
- for fiscal reasons so as to qualify for a lower rate of duty due to the changed product being eligible for a different tariff classification;
- for cultural reasons, e.g. when the colour of packaging needs to be changed because it denotes the colour of death;
- for economic reasons, e.g. when consumers in the international market cannot afford the product in its current form; and
- political reasons, such as government regulation on the way firearms are described and sold.

International product strategies

Product diffusion and adoption in international markets

Diffusion refers to the movement of new products to and within international markets so that they are available to customers in those markets. Typically the adoption process involves a number of stages – awareness, interest, evaluation, trial and adoption. The propensity of consumers to adopt new products varies considerably from international market to international market (see Chapter 5).

Although there is no shortage of new ideas, few are successful in commercial terms. According to Ambler and Styles (2000), of the 20,000 new products that appeared on US supermarket shelves in 1994, only 10% were on sale two years later. They argue that the majority of innovations are incremental and, for the most part, marketers develop what already exists by appreciating customer needs, seeing what is available, and filling the gap between.

While the international marketer may be in the fortunate position of seeing which products survive being launched locally before deciding which ones should be launched in other countries, this is becoming increasingly impractical as product life cycles shorten, the cost of bringing new products to market escalates and global competition intensifies. Increasingly, international marketers need to be involved at the birth if not at the conception of new products. Their presence enables a reduced possibility of failure by ensuring that issues are addressed, such as how the innovation compares with those coming from other countries (as international innovations could be future competitors in the domestic market), and what problems were encountered when these innovations were launched in other countries. According to Ambler and Styles (2000), the international manager can adopt three strategies for cross-fertilising innovation:

- *Passive* – encourage various national units in the organisation to learn from each other. The international manager cross-fertilises the ideas but contributes nothing of his/her own.
- *Pacemaking* – the international manager creates a portfolio of the best innovations available throughout the organisation and uses incentives such as research funding to persuade other divisions of the company to adopt them.
- *Participative* – in cases where the global market demands a global product, the international manager becomes actively involved in forming/leading an international task force to come up with the desired global innovation.

In order to do business in international markets, it is necessary to make changes in both business attitude and strategic posture. It may be necessary to redefine the business in which the firm is engaged, leverage the core competences or expertise of the firm so as to achieve economies of scope, and redefine the competitive approach that the firm will adopt when doing business in an international market.

Redefining the business

Businesses tend to be defined in terms of the benefits they provide to the customer, the segments of the market they occupy, the technology they employ, the nature of the value chain in which they are involved, the stage in the life cycle of the product they market, and the form of their involvement in the market. Each of these factors can change when the firm ventures abroad and, as a result, there is likely to be a need to redefine the business when going international.

Customer benefits

Consumers around the world have many different needs and will perceive products as satisfying these needs to differing degrees. While some of these needs are basic and universal, such as the desire to improve living standards, people's ability to satisfy these needs is not universal. The economic, political and social structure of a country affects the ability of consumers to satisfy their needs and the methods they use to do so. As a consequence, the same product will offer different benefits to customers in different countries.

Customer benefits will also vary according to whether the product is regarded in the international market as a low involvement or high involvement purchase. What might be a low involvement purchase in one country can be a high involvement purchase in another, especially where there are differences in standards of living between the two countries.

The degree of difference between brands can also vary between countries depending on the benefits the item is perceived to confer and the availability of choice between brands in the specific international market.

Customer segments

Entering or expanding activities in an international market may result in the firm targeting different segments from those targeted in the home market. Unilever, a transnational company, markets the same brand of products in different markets and often the product serves different segments in one market as opposed to another. For instance, Domestos is a remover of bathroom plaque in Australia, whereas in Germany it is a general purpose cleaner. For Unilever, the definition of its Domestos business would be different in Australia from what it is in Germany. As a consequence, while the manufacturer might initially think that it is offering the same standard product in different countries, consumers may impose a differentiation of their own on the product and the uses to which it is put. Frequently this is due to the availability of other products in the same category in the international market.

Technology

The technologies that are used in the domestic market may be either too sophisticated or too unsophisticated for various international markets. The appropriateness of different technologies will be a matter of levels of education, availability of infrastructure, the R&D environment, the cultural attitude towards innovation and the relative cost of various factors of production. As an example, in a country where labour is very cheap, the attractiveness of labour-saving technology is not as significant as in countries where labour is expensive. Also, in countries where the average skill levels of labour are low, the ability to sell products whose application requires skill is likely to be somewhat restricted.

Another issue is the social cost associated with the importation of high technology products and projects. Will the costs of associated social dislocation such as unemployment and resettlement be greater than the benefits resulting from the technology? Even if they are less, will there be an unacceptable political cost? The Three Gorges Project in China is a case in point, because while the economics of this power generation project look good, the social costs are huge and have aroused worldwide criticism. This issue of appropriateness can impact on how the business is defined in a particular international market.

Value chain

Production is defined as value-creating activity. Added value is achieved by converting inputs of lesser worth into outputs of greater worth. There are going to be many elements in the chain that are perceived by the customer to offer value over which the firm has little direct control as indicated in Figure 8.1.

Elements of the value chain may lie at the input end (e.g. raw materials, delivery, infrastructure support such as power, water and gas), and also the output end (e.g. warehousing, performance of intermediaries, servicing and warranty performance, and transport facilities and infrastructure). The degree to which the firm can participate in the value chain in a foreign country in the same manner as it does in the domestic market will be impacted upon by the existence and relative efficiency/cost of elements of the value chain in that country. If the opportunities for participating in the value chain in the foreign market are restricted, then the firm has to decide whether to become directly involved in elements of the value chain in that country, which back home in the domestic market it leaves to other suppliers. An alternative is to supply elements of the value chain from affiliates or subsidiaries in other countries, as happens when transnational companies undertake a global rationalisation of activities. The degree to which it is possible to replicate the domestic situation in the international market as far as the value chain is concerned will impact on how the business is defined with respect to that particular market.

| Figure 8.1 | **The value chain** |

Source:
Porter (1990).

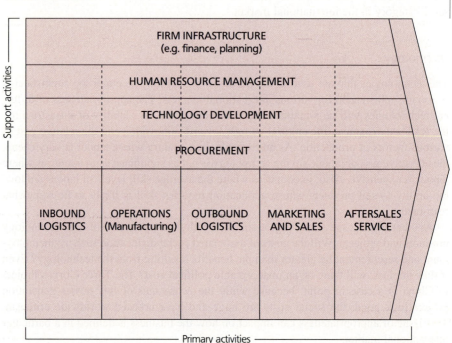

Product life cycle

This aspect impacts on how the business is defined in the international market. The theory of product life cycle argues that, like people, products have a life and move through stages from introduction to growth to maturity to saturation and, finally, to decline.

The international product life cycle (briefly commented on in Chapter 1) describes this process as related to the spread of products across national boundaries. Products which are at a decline stage in the domestic market may have their overall life extended if they can be marketed in a country where the product is not known or where, if it is known, it has not yet reached the decline stage. Conversely, a firm with a product at the growth stage, and believing it is ripe for export, needs to avoid international markets where that same product class is at a decline stage.

Bicycles are an example of a product that is at different stages of the product life cycle in different countries. Whereas in industrialised countries, bicycles are at a decline stage of the market, in the late 1980s they were at a growth stage in Vietnam and are now at a mature stage following the recent and rapid introduction of motor scooters. In the late 1950s and early 1960s British motor car producers launched two models which did not prove popular in the UK market and rapidly reached the decline stage. These were the Morris Isis and the Hillman Hunter. The life cycle of both models was extended in terms of contributing to company profitability by their manufacture being licensed to foreign countries without a domestic automobile industry. Manufacture of the Morris Isis was licensed in India as the Hindustan Ambassador and manufacture of the Hillman Hunter was licensed in Iran as the Peykan.

Onkavist and Shaw (1983) developed a five-stage description of the international product life cycle:

1 *Local innovation.* The firm in developed countries has developed an innovation because consumers are relatively affluent and have relatively unlimited wants.

2 *International innovation.* With the domestic market saturated, firms look to international markets to expand sales and profits. Initially the products tend to go to markets where the psychic distance is least.

3 *Maturity.* Growing demand in advanced nations provides the stimulus for firms to start local production of the imported product. As export markets, these countries tend to be replaced by other markets further down the development scale.

4 *Worldwide imitation.* The innovating nation runs out of new export markets as the product is produced in many countries. Economies of scale suffer and costs in the domestic market rise as export markets dry up.

5 *Reversal.* Other countries with the technology and cheaper labour costs are more efficient producers than the innovating country and these countries commence supplying the innovating country which ceases production. The last imitators now are able to undersell manufacturers in the original market.

There are many examples of the international product life cycle. The textile, clothing and footwear industries illustrate the involvement of the low-income developing countries and the automotive industry the involvement of the middle-income developing countries. (This issue was explored in Chapter 1.)

Leveraging capabilities

When considering the direction in which the firm should proceed in the international market, there is a need to understand the extent to which the new capabilities acquired as a result of exposure to one international market can be leveraged so as to provide the firm with competitive advantage in another. The new skills and assets resulting from exposure to one international market can be leveraged in respect of further operations either in that market or in another international market. Initially, when entering an international market, the firm's core competences centre on production capabilities but, as the market develops, attention shifts to taking the competences and leveraging them internationally both across products and across product lines within a single country. Leveraging takes three forms: shared physical assets; shared external relationships; and shared information and expertise.

Shared physical assets

Apart from the case of branching into new product lines in a country because of excess capacity, the firm may share its physical assets by undertaking work for another firm in the form of contract manufacture, contract packaging or partial (or component) manufacture. It may also perform functions for an affiliate in another country so that the sharing of physical assets takes place across national borders. In most cases this sharing of physical assets is based on the firm using those physical resources in which it has a competitive advantage.

Shared external relationships

The very fact of commencing operations or even exporting to another country leads to the firm becoming involved with established networks in that country. These networks are an important asset of the firm and form part of its competitive advantage in that market. In such circumstances, the phrase 'one thing leads to another' applies and these relationships in the international market can be used to the advantage of the firm. The network applies to all elements of the value chain in the international market. There are differences between countries as to the extent to which business is conducted on a competitive as opposed to a cooperative basis. Although in reality, even in marketing-oriented countries, there is a great deal of collaboration between enterprises, there are strong indications that collaboration is increasing globally. This is indicated by the fact that the share of the international market held by countries where cooperation is a strong feature of business life, e.g. Japan, Korea, Taiwan, China and the countries of ASEAN, is expanding.

Shared information and expertise

There is a powerful incentive for the sharing of information and leveraging expertise – the costs of developing and bringing a product to market are escalating. An example of this is in the pharmaceutical industry where the costs of developing, trialling and obtaining approval for a new drug can run into several million dollars. The need to achieve large market size becomes more and more important in order to amortise these costs, so relationships of this kind are becoming increasingly necessary in order to be able to compete. By leveraging information and expertise through these relationships, reciprocal benefits are likely to flow. This in turn may improve the firm's competitive position in the domestic market as the international involvement may yield economies of scale because costs of development can be defrayed over a larger base. The sharing of information and expertise applies not only to R&D and production activities but also to sources of supply and marketing functions. There are many cases where international involvement as an exporter has led to the firm becoming the importer of products that fit well into its existing distribution network in the home market.

Understanding product market structure

The structure of the market for a product varies from one country to another and often from market to market within a foreign country. This is particularly so where there are different ethnic groups in the one country, as is the case with Malaysia, which has significant populations of Malay, Chinese and Indian ethnic origin. This structure is defined by market boundaries, differentiation, branding and the size of the market. The prevalence of different ethnic groups is increasing due to increased mobility brought on by choice, economic hardship and expansion of the EU.

Identifying the product market boundaries

The boundaries of a market are likely to differ from country to country in terms of the product's use, the functions it performs, what the product category includes, and the activities of competitors. As Craig et al. (2000) point out, this is the case with soft drinks. In Australia, beer is viewed as an alcoholic beverage whereas in other markets it is treated as a soft drink. In the US, the soft drink market only includes sodas (fizzy drinks) whereas in South-East Asia it includes fresh fruit juices, and in other countries, such as Europe, cordials and fruit concentrates.

Product differentiation and branding

The form in which the product is currently available in the international market is important, e.g. whether soft drink is sold in bottles or cans. Also to be considered is whether the product to be offered should be differentiated from competitors' offerings by changing the form in which it is presented or the benefits claimed for it, such as varying the size of the pack or the claimed end-use application. In addition, the nature of the other products with which the use of the product is associated can vary and impact on the need to differentiate the offering. In countries such as India where washing of clothes is done by hand, bar soap is used, whereas in western countries, where washing is usually by machine, synthetic detergents are most commonly employed.

The significance attributed to branding in a market can also influence its structure. In markets emerging from a subsistence level or markets which are changing from a command to a market economy, branding is less important than it would be in a highly market-oriented environment. The significance of brands differs between segments within an international market. This is evidenced by Japanese yuppies' preference for imported designer-label clothing. The significance of branding in market-oriented economies will also vary according to positioning of the product in that market.

Dimensions of the product market

The above issues point to a need to place some dimension on the market for the product or service in the foreign country. In some countries, where the product is at a mature stage of the product life cycle, the potential is likely to be low and the market mainly a replacement one. In markets where the stage of the life cycle is one of growth, the potential is much larger, especially if these countries have large populations and high rates of economic growth. Other factors include age distribution of the population, and the degree to which the market is concentrated in major cities or dispersed throughout the country. Also relevant is the extent to which the market is fragmented and in the hands of many small firms or concentrated in the hands of several major conglomerates.

Tailoring products to suit international markets

In some cases, it may be possible to take a product made in the domestic market and modify it to enhance its appeal in selected international markets. In other cases, it will be necessary to create a product from scratch for the target international market. In other situations it may be necessary to design a product to appeal to global markets from the outset.

8.1 International highlight

DVD success story

Despite initial sluggish sales, the DVD is now considered to be the most successful format launch in consumer electronics history. Even if you still use Windows 98, a brick-sized mobile phone and the cassette deck of your hi-fi on a regular basis, chances are you will be familiar with the various types of 'special features' added to your DVD movie releases. You may have noticed DVDs steadily taking over more and more of the shelf space set aside for VHS cassettes at your local rental store. The market for DVD has primarily been driven by Hollywood films and box sets of cult American television programmes. Most people in the consumer electronics industry believe that, despite its breakthrough success, DVD will only fully replace VHS as the standard format for home video when it is both recordable and affordable. Meanwhile, as most manufacturers are working to integrate or converge entertainment and information functions onto one device, the first DVD players with the ability to connect to the web have already been showcased. But the ability to record and to download DVDs from the web could hurt the catalogue sales of DVD videos and albums and the rentals market, increasing demand for sophisticated anti-piracy technology to protect copyright held by studios and record companies.

Modifying products for international markets

The extent to which modification of a product is required will vary according to whether it is a consumer good or an industrial product. Even within these groupings, the need for modification will vary according to the environmental sensitivity of the item being offered. In some instances, product modifications are voluntary in order to enhance appeal to customers; in other instances, they are compulsory in order to conform to product standards or government legislation.

Product standards and regulations

Product standards in different countries determine whether the product needs to be adapted to conform to the local standard in that country or not. Standards can be either technical or mandated by government. Technical standards are enforced by the market in that consumers will not or cannot buy the product unless it conforms to the accepted standards. Often standards issued by government are a device for keeping out foreign products. Some countries such as Japan may demand that, despite tests having been completed in the country of origin, tests must also be carried out in their country, often at considerable expense. This exclusion can also be achieved by requiring the international firm to comply with cumbersome certification requirements. Onerous and costly testing and certification requirements are illustrated in the case of electrical goods entering the US which are required to undergo Underwriter's Laboratory testing. This time-consuming and costly process has served to exclude many imported electrical products and whitegoods from the US market.

Most countries have a national standards body such as the National Standards Association that sets standards, often in the interests of protecting the consumer. Sometimes these bodies are in the public sector and sometimes in the private sector, e.g. the Underwriters Laboratories in the United States. There is also a trend to set international standards such as the international quality management standard ISO 9000. Standards are most common in pharmaceuticals, automobiles, electrical appliances and foods. In some instances regulations may prevent a product from entering an international market and in others the regulations may operate as a disguised non-tariff barrier.

Measurement and calibration

Another reason to modify international products for sale is to ensure that they conform to weights and measures legislation in the foreign country. Not only do some countries use imperial rather than metric measures, but the norm or legal requirement is that the weight or measure must be stated on the pack in a specific manner, such as in millilitres rather than centilitres or by volume rather than by weight. With products there can be requirements relating to statement of capacity, voltage or speed. Increasingly, with products intended for sale in several markets, it is necessary to show measurement or calibration in multiple ways in conformity with varying requirements in each market. This may require a significant modification to the product or its packaging as happens with multi-voltage electrical appliances.

Trademarks

Trademarks, and other forms of protection for intellectual property such as patents and copyright, may necessitate modification of the product together with its branding and packaging. The brand might already be registered in a foreign country. It may be that the brand, due to intellectual piracy, has acquired a poor reputation in the target international market, which means that a different brand name should be used when introducing the product. It sometimes happens that another party in the foreign country has a patent on the process used in the domestic market that prevents the firm selling or at least manufacturing the product in the target country without further modification. Abuses of trademarks and patents are particularly prevalent in developing countries.

Climate and usage

Products need to be modified in order to be able to operate effectively under different environmental or climatic conditions – changes will be necessary in the interests of both utility and marketability. Climatic conditions need to be borne in mind, particularly when packaging a product for shipment to ensure that the goods arrive in good condition.

Another factor is that of usage patterns. These often reflect affordability, as with the sale of cigarettes in single sticks in parts of Asia. Usage patterns also reflect the environment as exemplified by the demand for small, quiet air-conditioning units in Tokyo. Here, people live in very small flats in close proximity to each other in a very humid climate. Usage patterns also reflect social customs, e.g. in parts of Europe people shop daily because shopping is a social event.

Language and symbolism

This issue impacts particularly on the packaging and labelling of products because different symbols are interpreted differently from country to country and they can affect the way the product is perceived. The same applies to the use of brand names because the use of a global brand name can give a negative connotation to a product if the brand has a different meaning in another language. This is discussed in more detail later in this chapter.

Other issues relating to the need to modify the product are the acceptability of colours used on the product and its packaging, the need for visual as opposed to written instructions, and in the case of products destined for a number of markets, the use of several languages on the packaging, labelling and instructions for use.

Style, design and taste

The above factors may necessitate modification to the international product in order to improve its marketability. This will affect the size of packaging in relation to the size of the product and the quality and nature of the packaging. For example, the Japanese tend to judge the quality of the product by the elaborate nature of its packaging, whereas the environmentally conscious Germans are critical of unnecessary packaging and highly conscious of environmental issues associated with disposing of packaging materials. Colour preferences and religious/social acceptability of specific colours vary from country to country and need to be taken into account in the formulation of the product as well as its packaging. Taste is another variable which is particularly important with foods and beverages. Although modifying products involves extra costs, the costs can be more than offset by enhancing the appeal of the product to a wider market in the target foreign country. It often necessary to change the formulation of the product and its design features. Sometimes design changes may be a matter of local taste but, in other situations, the changes are virtually mandated because government-imposed tariff or non-tariff barriers require the use of local inputs if the barriers are not to be prohibitive. A further aspect is that features associated with a product in one country may be different or not be required for the product in another. An example is motor vehicles that must be sold with air-conditioners in countries such as Saudi Arabia and with heaters in others such as Sweden. Even within the one geographic area, the features required of a product may vary due to affordability. For this reason, a fully optioned vehicle is likely to be more marketable in the United Arab Emirates than on the other side of the Gulf in Iran.

Technology issues and performance standards

With high-technology products, performance standards are likely to differ from one country to another. This is often because the degree of technical infrastructure varies between countries. In a country plagued with power blackouts or brownouts, technology which is sensitive to consistent voltage in the power supply may be of dubious value unless it can be supplied with its own generator which significantly increases its cost. In addition, products developed in technologically advanced countries often exceed the performance standards needed in less developed countries where labour is a more significant factor of production than capital. In these countries, customers prefer products which are simpler but which will last longer under local conditions, especially as the purchase is likely to account for a greater percentage of average annual income.

Warranty and servicing issues

Customers buying products are buying utility, function and performance as well as image and status. This utility, function and performance involves warranty provision. In many cases, products are sold with a package of service attributes. These can take the form of linked servicing programmes such as free service for one year, or warranty programmes like 30,000 km or three years with a motor vehicle. Expectations regarding these as well as the cost of providing them will also vary from country to country on the basis of use conditions, government regulation, cost of providing the warranty service, and the availability of competent persons to provide that service in the foreign country. During the oil price hikes of the late 1970s and early 1980s, there was a healthy appetite for luxury motor vehicles in oil-rich countries such as Libya. However, because local repair and servicing facilities were primitive, it was not uncommon to see relatively new vehicles abandoned by the side of the road because they had been driven without major servicing until they stopped. In circumstances of this kind, having a standardised servicing and warranty policy worldwide does not work. Another related challenge and dilemma is whether to conform to the local expectation knowing that this may impact on the firm's international reputation or whether to provide the same service package/warranty provision as in the domestic market when this may make the firm less competitive in the international market.

The next aspect of tailoring a product for international markets involves the decision as to how to develop a product specifically for the new market.

Developing a product for the international market

In cases where it is not possible either to export an existing product in an unaltered form to an international market or to modify it to ensure its appeal in an international market, it may be necessary to develop a product specifically for that market. Robinson (1961), when considering the implications for developing products specifically for less developed countries, listed a number of factors and their implications for product design:

- Level of technical skills may necessitate product simplification.
- Level of labour costs will impact on automisation or manualisation of the product.
- Level of literacy will impact on visualisation of instructions and simplification of the product.
- Level of income will impact on the degree to which quality is built in and price charged.
- Level of interest rates will impact on inventory holding decisions,
- Level of maintenance will impact on changes in tolerances and nature of guarantee offered.
- Climate will impact on operating conditions and packaging to protect product.
- Isolation will create the need for a simplified and reliable product due to difficulties and expense of repairs.
- Different standards will require recalibration and resizing of the product.

As an alternative to designing a new product for an international market from scratch, it may be possible to take existing technology and apply it to the needs of the international market. Applied research, as opposed to fundamental research, has been a strong point with the Japanese and has made a significant contribution to their success in international business.

Czinkota and Kotabe (1990) describe this process as incrementalism, as opposed to the giant leap. The incremental approach of the Japanese emphasises continued technological improvement aimed at making an already successful product even better for the customer. It also enables the pace of new product introductions to be accelerated.

The stages to be followed in developing a new product for an international market are:

- *Generating ideas.* The ideas to be generated should tap new or existing markets, complement existing product lines or improve existing products in the international market. Sources of such ideas should come not only from domestic sources such as consumers, employees, competitors, etc., but also from sources in both the target international market and other countries.

- *Screening ideas.* As not all ideas generated from the search process may be suitable for the selected international market, some sorting out will be necessary. A list of acceptable ideas should be developed based on compatibility with the firm's distinctive competence, ability of the firm to convert the idea into a product offering, the export potential of the idea and the fit of the idea with the firm's competitive position in the industry of which it is a part.

- *Business evaluation.* Although new product ideas might be acceptable to the firm, they may not represent the best use of funds and should be subject to a cost–benefit analysis. This analysis with respect to the selected country would consider current and potential demand, likely competitor response and potential for expansion into other markets.

- *Product development.* This is the next stage for those ideas which still indicate promise following the cost–benefit analysis. Details of the product are worked out and tangible and intangible benefits are specified. Considerations influencing the

8.2 International highlight

From the Internet to the mobile

According to Fergus Cassidy of the *Irish Times*, the single greatest achievement of the Internet has been to come up with an alternative broadcast model. First it started with sending text via computers over the telephone lines. That was followed by images and then sound and video.

It took generations before television created the infrastructure that supports its ubiquitous presence in society today. Yet it took only a decade for some computer code and copper wires to create an alternative. While it can compete with the range and quality of the moving images and sound of broadcasting, its uniqueness is its two-way, one-to-one and one-to-many facility. Not just voice, but sound and image.

Building it was unique – an experiment in public/private partnership on a massive scale. The public telephone utilities were handed over to the private sector sometimes for a song. As computer networks were connected around the world, oceans of information flooded across the wires.

Now the mobile phone's time has come. Starting with voice, then texting and now images, cellular technology has also built an alternative broadcast system. Put voice and images together, add some transmission speed and decent screen and you have got television. Mobiles have brought text messages out from behind the inaccessible complexity (for many) of computers and software. Mobile phones are the Internet the way it was envisaged by the media and entertainment companies. The mobile networks were built to their liking. Not an alternative method of broadcasting but an alternative to the Internet, with one big difference, the mobile is only for one-to-one communication, not one-to-many.

The mobile is private enterprise's Internet, a private network, devoid of any public service or universal access dimension: pay-per-view brought into the communications arena with gusto.

development of the product include its core benefits, where it is to be positioned in the international market, and the role of the other marketing mix variables in enhancing the product's appeal.

- *Test marketing.* This involves selecting a small section of the international market to test consumer reaction to the product. The town or area selected should be a microcosm of the wider market so that the results of the test can be assumed to predict the average reaction of those to be targeted in the wider market. On the basis of results from the test market, decisions can be made as to whether to launch the product in the wider market and if so whether any modifications to the product are necessary before the launch.

- *Product introduction.* This is the final stage of product development. Further modification might still be required depending the reaction to the product. This may depend on whether reaction in the wider international market proves to be the same as in the test market, or whether the conditions under which the product is used or consumed in the target international market impact on the acceptability of the product or the nature of the reaction of competitors.

An alternative to exporting a tailored product is to offer the same international product as manufactured in the domestic market. This involves the issue of the relative merits of standardisation as opposed to adaptation.

Creating a global product

An alternative to the usual approach of taking a domestic product and offering it in a standard or an adapted form is to design a international product which can be offered internationally as well as in the home markets virtually simultaneously.

The phrase 'born global' is increasingly being used to describe firms that commence operations with a focus on the global market rather than simply on the domestic market. Often these firms offer products or services that are suitable for small, niche markets and the size of that niche in the domestic market is insufficient to ensure the viability of the concept underlying the product. In these circumstances, the design of the product and its proposed marketing must ensure its appeal to potential buyers in a wide variety of countries. Products that are not culturally sensitive are likely to be able to be offered with little modification on a global basis. However, products that are culturally sensitive may need to be designed so that a base product is offered which is capable of modification in the international market to enhance its acceptability.

Designing global products is very much a concern of transnational companies. No longer is the focus on the Italian subsidiary designing products for the Italian market, the German subsidiary for the German market, and the Malaysian subsidiary designing products for the Malaysian market, but rather on a global product to which each subsidiary contributes according to the relative advantage each has to offer. The Italian subsidiary in this example might contribute the design, the German subsidiary the R&D and the Malaysian subsidiary the labour-intensive elements of the manufacture. Another advantage of this new approach is that experience and technology can be more rapidly transferred between subsidiaries as the desire of each subsidiary 'to protect its own turf' is lessened.

8.3 International highlight

Wining over the Europeans

Since the beginning of the 1990s, Australian wines have been selling in Europe in huge volumes. In the UK, for example, sales of Australian wines in 2000/2001 were valued at A$683 million (equivalent to 164 million litres). While in part this is due to European winemakers, such as Veuve Cliquot and Moët et Chandon, establishing operations or buying equity in Australian vineyards, it has also been due to Australian winemakers modifying the product, packaging and labelling to suit European requirements. Whereas others just made wines first and tried to sell them, the Australians worked out what the European consumer wanted and at what price and then came up with a suitable offering, according to British wine master Jasper Morris. Critical in this process was Australia's agreeing to European Community demands. These were that Australian winemakers cease using the names of European winemaking regions (e.g. Champagne, Burgundy, Moselle and Chablis) on their products and conform to European regulations as to the percentage of a variety that can be in a blend before the wine can be called by its varietal name. This marketing challenge has resulted in an upsurge in the use of Australian regional names of winegrowing areas and Europeans are now asking for Coonawarra Pinot Noir and Hunter Valley Semillon.

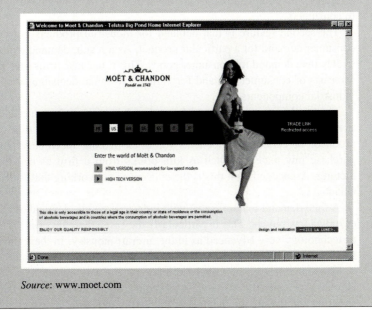

Source: www.moet.com

To date, the discussion in this chapter, when referring to product, has generally treated it as synonymous with consumer goods. Industrial products are widely marketed between countries and have features additional to those mentioned above. These must be taken into account if international marketing efforts are to be successful.

Marketing industrial products internationally

Industrial products

Firms marketing industrial products internationally face similar problems to those encountered when marketing consumer goods abroad. However, these firms also face a number of problems unique to industrial products, which in part derive from the different nature of industrial marketing.

Unique features of industrial marketing

Demand for industrial products is characterised by four features. The first of these is that industrial products are usually purchased for reuse in creating other products. It may well be that the product is also a consumer good in some applications, e.g. a computer. However, the intent behind the purchase is important. When the product is purchased to create another product, it is an industrial product. With many products, different marketing campaigns are needed to sell them to industrial buyers as opposed to consumers.

The second feature is that demand for industrial products is usually derived from consumer demand for a particular product. As a result, demand tends to fluctuate more widely than demand for consumer goods. This is because firms such as Volkswagen use forecasts of consumer demand for vehicles to make decisions as to their purchase of industrial components.

The third feature of demand for industrial products is that it is often reciprocal – two companies may buy and sell to each other at the same time. As an example, a producer of ceramic components for brick-making machinery may be expected to purchase raw materials such as kiln bricks from a firm owned by the brick manufacturer. Associated with this is the concept of networking that is discussed in detail in Chapter 17.

A final demand feature is that with industrial goods, demand often rests in the hands of only a few buyers. This is particularly the case where investment in a process is high or technology very advanced as in the aircraft industry. In these circumstances, industrial marketers experience a high volume of demand per customer.

The above features are likely to influence the way industrial products are marketed abroad, especially the way industrial buying decisions are made, the industrial buying situation and the unique features of marketing industrial products abroad.

Industrial buying decisions

Whereas in consumer marketing, the decision to purchase is usually made by the individual or the immediate family, in industrial marketing the decision is either made by a much wider group or influenced by a wide range of people in the organisation.

In some cases, companies have purchasing committees. Bonoma (1982) categorised those who make or influence decisions relating to the purchase of industrial products as follows:

- *initiator* – the person who makes the initial request for the product such as the line manager on the factory floor;
- *decider* – the individual or group that formally decides what product to buy;
- *influencer* – those within the organisation who influence buying decisions. They can be located in a variety of different sections, from sales to accounts to R&D to production;
- *gatekeeper* – the person who controls access to those who make or influence purchasing decisions. For an executive, this may be a secretary, and for a person on the factory floor or in the laboratory, it may be a supervisor;
- *user* – the person who uses the product; and
- *purchaser* – the person who agrees to the purchase and negotiates the terms of sale. Often this is the purchasing department.

In international marketing, the problem is how to reach those parties when they are located abroad. Because of this difficulty, it is important that the network of agents and distributors established in the target international market have contacts at all levels and lobby the firm's interests at all levels.

Industrial buying situation

Buying decision making is likely to be influenced by the nature of the purchase. In general, the less routine and the larger the purchase, the more people are likely to be involved in making and influencing the decision. There are three categories of buying situation, all of which influence decision making for industrial products in the international market:

- *Extensive problem solving.* This usually applies when the buying situation is unique or unusual such as with a one-time purchase of an expensive piece of capital equipment. In this situation, there is unlikely to be any initial preference for a supplier.
- *Limited problem solving.* This usually involves industrial products of considerable importance to the buyer on technical or financial grounds. The buyer usually has had some experience with purchasing these products previously and there tend to be supplier preferences. With these products, partially structured purchasing procedures are likely to be in place.
- *Routinised purchasing behaviour.* This applies when products are purchased on an ongoing basis. Supplier preferences are well established and purchasing procedures are likely to be well structured. Raw material inputs and standardised products such as stationery purchases typify products in this category.

Features of the international market for industrial products

There are a number of unique features of international markets for industrial products. The most important are summarised as follows:

- *Different characteristics of buyers.* While it can be argued in general that cultural and other local differences are likely to be more important with consumer than with industrial products, in Asian countries cultural norms can be important in industrial procurement. This is especially the case with those countries where relationships are considered to be equally if not more important than price, functionality or quality.

- *International market potential.* The level of economic development and industrialisation in other countries can be critical factors in the demand for industrial products. The existence of an abundance of cheap labour will influence demand for products such as capital plant.

- *Targeting decision makers.* This is complicated in other countries because it is often difficult to pinpoint who is involved in the decision-making process. In Asian countries, many buyers are family-owned companies which compounds the problem.

- *Government control.* Foreign governments exercise control over supply from abroad for security, protectionist, political or revenue reasons. The nature of the regime in the foreign country also determines the extent to which the government is a major purchaser of industrial products. In some countries, there are very close relationships between business and government, as in Japan, and this can impact on the ability of the firm to supply products in competition with local sources.

- *Service support.* The need for service support varies greatly for different types of industrial goods. For this reason, selling industrial products requiring high levels of support will create problems in countries such as Libya, where the available level of such support is basic.

- *Direct contact between buyer and seller.* In cases where the domestic supplier does not operate in the foreign country there will be a need for an intermediary between buyer and seller. This will reduce the likelihood of direct contact between buyer and seller with the result that there will be a reduction in the degree of control that the firm is able to exercise over the marketing of its industrial products abroad.

- *Terms of sale.* Because costs of industrial products tend to be higher than with consumer goods and the contracts may cover a longer period of time, the critical factors in the terms of sale in international markets may extend beyond price and include credit terms and countertrade proposals.

Branding and packaging for international markets

Branding and packaging are two important additional issues related to the international marketing of products that need to be taken into account when modifying products for international markets.

Branding

Brand names are a critical element in making an impact on the customer. Should there be one international brand or different brands for each market? If the company uses its own brands, it may want to use multiple brands in the same international market to target different customer segments as it does in the domestic market. However, if the brand name does not travel well or create positive images in the mind of the international customer, modification of the brand name will be necessary. A major issue is whether to promote local country specific brands or establish global and regional brands with appeal across countries. Onkavist and Shaw (1989) have produced a list of advantages and disadvantages of alternative branding strategies for the international marketplace (see Table 8.1).

In countries where the language is ideographic (word pictures), English brand names will require change, e.g. in China the translation gives an international brand not just a Chinese name but also a distinctive local image. A good brand name in Chinese should have desirable connotations, desirable sound and tonal associations, and attractive calligraphy. Chinese native speakers tend to encode verbal information in a 'visual mental code' according to Fan (2001), whereas English native speakers rely more on a 'phonological code' and judge a brand name based on whether the name sounds appealing. Often there can be a paradox between the global brand and the image that the translated version creates.

> *When Ansett Airlines of Australia commenced its service to Hong Kong several years ago, it was surprised to discover that the Chinese strongly disliked the name Ansett. Enquiry revealed that the word Ansett, when translated, meant 'to die peacefully' which was not regarded as a confidence-building name for an airline!*

Obviously there is a need to use ideographs for the brand name that create a favourable image for the product. As Fan (2001) points out, this situation also provides an opportunity to treat the renaming as a value-adding process and create a unique global-local image that enhances the original brand equity.

Building global brands

Building a global brand involves using a standardised product. Its success depends on a growing convergence of consumer tastes and the coordination of global promotion.

Table 8.1 A perspective on branding

Advantages	Disadvantages
No brand	
Lower production cost	Severe price competition
Lower marketing cost	Lack of market identity
Lower legal cost	
Flexible quality and quantity control	
Branding	
Better identifcation and awareness	Higher production cost
Better chance for product differentiation	Higher marketing cost
Possible brand loyalty	Higher legal cost
Possible premium pricing	
Private brand	
Better margins for dealers	Severe price competition
Possibility of larger market share	Lack of market identity
No promotional problems	
Manufacturer's brand	
Better price due to more price inelasticity	Difficulty for small manufacturers
Retention of brand loyalty	with unknown brand offering
Better bargaining power	Brand promotion required
Better control of distribution	
Multiple brands (in one market)	
Market segmented for varying needs	Higher marketing cost
Competitive spirit created	Higher inventory cost
Negative connotation of existing brand avoided	Loss of economies of scale
More retail shelf space gained	
Existing brand's image not damaged	
Single brand (in one market)	
Marketing effciency	Market homogeneity assumed
More focused marketing permitted	Existing brand's image when
Brand confusion eliminated	trading up/down
Advantage for product with good reputation (halo effect)	Limited shelf space
Local brands	
Meaningful names	Higher marketing cost
Local identifcation	Higher inventory cost
Avoidance of taxation on international brand	Loss of economies of scale
Quick market penetration by acquiring local brand	Diffused image
Variations of quantity and quality across markets allowed	

Table 8.1 (*continued*)

Advantages	Disadvantages
Worldwide brand	
Maximum marketing effciency	Market homogeneity assumed
Reduction of advertising costs	Problems with black and grey markets
Elimination of brand confusion	Possibility of negative connotation
Advantage for culture-free product	Quality and quantity consistency
Advantage for prestigious product	required
Easy identifcation/recognition for	Opposition and resentment in less
international travellers	developed countries
Uniformed worldwide image	Legal complications

Source: Onkavist and Shaw (1989) Table 1, p. 24.

One of the advantages of global branding is economies of scale in advertising – a uniform image appeals to globe-trotting consumers. Global brands are also important in accessing the best distribution channels and intermediaries in other countries. In developing global brands it is necessary to decide what brand image to project. Research by Roth (1995) found that in countries where the degree of separation between high and low power distance individuals is great (as in China), brand images should stress social and sensory needs.

Modification of brand names

Czinkota and Ronkainen (1998, p. 321) refer to the work of NameLab of California who offer the following suggestions in connection with checking the appropriateness of a brand name in an international market:

- *Translation* – translate the brand name directly into the foreign language. While this is achievable with languages using the same script as English, problems arise with languages which use ideographic script such as Japanese or Mandarin.

- *Transliteration* – testing the brand to see if it denotes the same meaning in another country as it does in the domestic. Whereas in English, Coca-Cola has no meaning in itself, in China it means 'tasty and happy'.

- *Transparency* – avoids brand name problems of transliteration, translation and prior registration of trademarks by developing an essentially meaningless brand name. Omo is an example.

- *Transculture* – because the product category has a foreign image which is associated with desirable attributes, the brand name used is a foreign word associated with the country having a positive image for the product category.

Brand name strategies

For the firm operating in a number of markets or on a global basis, the following options are available:

- *Use the same brand name worldwide.* This is appropriate when the company markets one product and has wide international distribution for it. This approach works when there is no conflict between the brand name and the culture of different countries. 'Pepsi' is an example of this. The use of a single brand name worldwide both creates customer identification and results in savings in promotion costs.

- *Modify the brand name in each market.* This is appropriate when the marketing strategy is to identify with the local market. While the same brand name is used, add-on words create local identification, e.g. coffee called 'Nescafé' and shampoo called 'Sunsilk'.

- *Different names in different markets.* This is necessary when the brand name cannot be translated into the local language or when the firm wishes to create a local identity. Often local brands are adopted as a result of acquisition. These may have a strong local loyalty due to promotion by the previous owners.

- *Company name as a brand name.* Many firms use standard trademarks for all their products and allow the use of local brand names in different countries. These trademarks which can take the form of letters, symbols and logos, act as a form of corporate identification. Because the trademark is identified with both the product and the company, it often conveys a stronger corporate message to the consumer than the brand by itself. When successfully undertaken, this approach can create an umbrella that lends strength to the individual brands and creates the impression of strong corporate identity, e.g. the 3M company.

Packaging and labelling

The main function of packaging is to ensure that the product gets to its intended recipient in a serviceable shape and pleasing form.

Protection. Protecting the product is particularly important in international marketing as the product usually travels longer distances, is handled and transferred more frequently, and its transit involves changes in both climate and temperature to a greater extent than in the domestic market. The degree to which packaging will need to be different for exported products will depend on transit time, mode of transport and transportation conditions. Another problem impacting on packaging requirements is the higher incidence of pilfering in a number of international markets. Although containerisation has reduced this, pilfering can still occur at the stage when the container is opened for inspection on arrival at the international port. Clear handling instructions in both English and the languages used at the transit points as well at the final destination will facilitate safe handling. The use of universal symbols, such as a glass to denote 'fragile', is becoming increasingly common.

Promotion. Packaging can also act as a vehicle for promoting the product or the company's image in international markets. The same cultural sensitivities that are taken into account with labelling should also be observed when designing the outer package. The size and the shape of the package can be important for those markets where the goods are displayed in or sold from the outer container and where the package in an empty or after-use form still has value. There should be consistency between the colours, messages and logos used on both the product and the outer packaging so as to maximise the packaging's promotional value.

Convenience. This applies to both intermediaries in the international distribution channel as well as to the final consumer. For the intermediary, convenience is a matter of ease of handling, ease in opening to facilitate bulk-breaking, conformity to shelf layouts, efficient pricing and retail labelling, as well as protection of the product. From the consumer's point of view, the package should be one that is easy to carry or shift, is aesthetically pleasing and, where appropriate, has use or assembly instructions which are clearly illustrated or written in the consumer's language. The packaging should be in a form that is compatible with storage facilities in the user's household. For example, in countries where refrigerators are not the norm or are very small, a six pack is not a convenient way of packaging beverages.

Another aspect of packaging in international marketing concerns environmentalism. There is increasing concern as to the environmental implications of disposing of packaging materials. This is particularly the case in the more developed countries where the volume of packaging generated has increased in line with the greater focus on elaborate packaging as a form of marketing. The European Union, led by Germany, wants to reduce the amount of packaging material that is generated and increase the recycling of the essential packaging that remains. It requires that 60% of all packaging material must be recyclable and this figure is to rise to 90% by 2003. These regulations impact on international firms marketing their products to countries in the European Union.

There are a number of areas where governments impose regulations on packaging. Regulations mostly relate to labelling and marking and are designed to both inform and protect consumers. These vary from country to country as indicated by 'warnings' on cigarette packets. The languages used on packages are often prescribed by governments, as is the form in which volume or weight of contents should be indicated. Government regulations also specify that a list of ingredients is shown on the pack, and the manner in which this must be shown also varies between countries.

The use of multiple languages in the labelling of products in international marketing is a primary consideration in providing information to consumers. Regulations in many countries require that detailed product composition and nutritional data be provided, as well as a warning of any hazards that might ensue from the use of the product. Firms may wish to provide instructions for correct assembly or use which have implications for how the message is communicated on the label. In these cases, simply translating the text from English into the other language is unlikely to be sufficient. In some countries, such as Canada, information on the label is required to be in all official languages used in a country or a region. Often this can result in crowded or impractical labels, with the result that manufacturers are increasingly using icons, diagrams and cartoons to instruct consumers in the use of their products.

Internet infusion

According to Craig et al. (2000), there will be three categories of products in the Internet environment – physical products, transaction-related products and virtual products.

Physical products – with physical products (e.g. cosmetics), information search can be conducted online and in many countries, but completion of the transaction either requires the consumer to go to a physical location to purchase the product or requires the product to be delivered to the consumer in a given location. In this case, the final stage of the transaction relies on traditional market infrastructure and the merchant relies on physical infrastructure to deliver the goods (e.g. Amazon.com's warehouses in each major geographic region).

Transaction-related products – with transaction-related products (services such as rental cars, air tickets), information search is conducted online but actual consumption is tied to a given time and location. Although delivery of a physical product is not involved, an organisational infrastructure is needed to ensure delivery at the time and location requested (e.g. at the airport check-in desk).

Virtual products – with virtual products (such as music, software, news broadcasts) there is no physical location and consumption is anywhere in the world. There are no physical or geographic constraints to search, transaction or consumption. Table 8.2 provides a typology for each of these categories of product.

The value chain will differ when the Internet is involved. The physical value chain treats information as a supporting element of the value-adding process, not as the source of value itself. The physical value chain differs from the virtual value chain because of the enhanced role of information in the latter. The latter consists of a realm where products and services exist as digital information and are delivered through information-based channels. Here the value-adding steps are virtual in that they are

Table 8.2 Internet product typology

Key dimensions	Product type		
	Physical products	Transaction-related products	Virtual products
Ease of reaching a global segment	Difficult	Moderate	Easy
Degree of product standardisation	Varies	Moderate	Customised
Role of information	Complement	Enhancement	Equivalent
Role of infrastructure	Infrastructure constrained	Conforms to infrastructure	Unconstrained by infrastructure

Source: Craig et al. (2000), p. 30.

performed through and with information. Often the physical and virtual value chains exist side by side. An example is with airlines, which now sell tickets in both the marketplace and marketspace. In many cases, the virtual value chain has its origins in the physical value chain as happens with 'just in time' (JIT) and 'total quality management' (TQM) that have had the effect of increasing the dependency of client companies on their suppliers. There are five steps in the virtual value chain – gathering, organising selecting, synthesising and distributing information. These value-adding steps allow companies to identify customers' desires more effectively and fulfil them more efficiently. This, for example, happens when a car manufacturer shifts its R&D from the physical to the virtual value chain. Then it can engage customers in the firm's new product development, wherever they are located around the world. Whereas the physical value chain is linear (a sequence of activities with defined inputs and outputs), the virtual value chain is non-linear (a matrix of potential inputs and outputs that can be accessed and distributed via a wide variety of channels).

Plumley (2000) has a series of figures illustrating the physical value chain, the e-business value chain and the international e-business value chain.

Figure 8.2 shows a physical value chain. At each step, the company has opportunity to add value to the previous input. Firms that execute the key linkages between steps in the chain will tend to enjoy a competitive advantage. Poor linkages or poor execution will remove significant value and hence reduce competitive advantage.

Figure 8.3 shows the basic e-commerce value chain. Here, the supply, manufacturing and inventory elements are integrated, rather than separate functions. An e-commerce platform is added and this is followed by a secure transaction support element. The e-commerce platform and transaction support elements in a single country site are complex, especially when integrated into inventory and supply chain logistics systems.

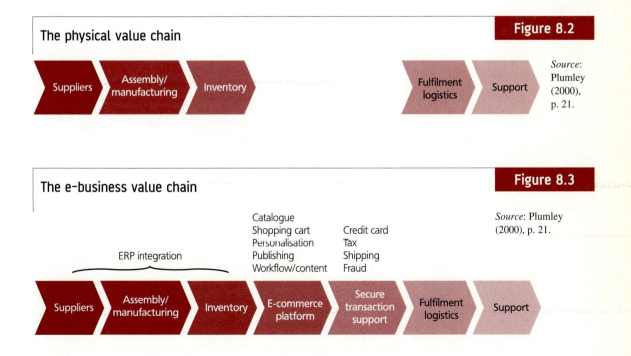

Figure 8.2

The physical value chain

Suppliers → Assembly/manufacturing → Inventory → Fulfilment logistics → Support

Source: Plumley (2000), p. 21.

Figure 8.3

The e-business value chain

ERP integration

Catalogue
Shopping cart
Personalisation
Publishing
Workflow/content

Credit card
Tax
Shipping
Fraud

Suppliers → Assembly/manufacturing → Inventory → E-commerce platform → Secure transaction support → Fulfilment logistics → Support

Source: Plumley (2000), p. 21.

Figure 8.4   The international e-business value chain

Source: Plumley
(2000), p. 22.

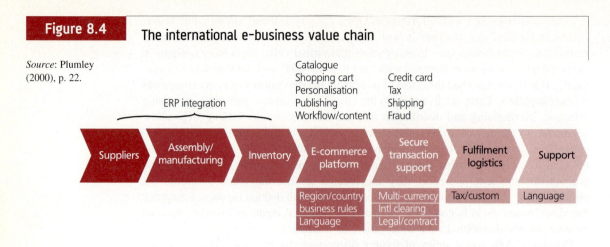

Figure 8.4 shows the international e-business value chain. This builds individual country business rules into the e-commerce platform, and currency clearing and legal requirements into the transaction support element. In this figure, single-country sourcing and inventory management are assumed for the sake of simplicity. However, even with this simplification, there are now additional layers of both features and processes involved in the most complex portions of the system, each with varying levels of dependency.

Summary

Developing a strategy to embrace international as well as domestic markets is one of the challenges faced by the firm when management decides to engage in international business. The strategic marketing approach of the firm is no longer focused only on the domestic market but also on the international markets. Tailoring products to suit international markets requires not only modifying existing products to improve their fit, but also developing new products from scratch to meet specific international require-ments. This may involve creating a global product. There are a number of unique issues relating to the marketing of industrial goods and services which need to be taken into account as do specific issues relating to branding and packaging.

Ethics issue

Jans Johanson is the director of product development for ANS, the Dutch manufacturer of automobile axles. The ANS company received a large contract from Malaysia six months ago to manufacture axles to be used in a new line of four-wheel drive vehicles to be introduced to the market by the Proton company. The contract is vital to Johanson's firm that has recently fallen on hard times due to import competition. Just prior to receiving this contract, half the employees, including Johanson, were scheduled for indefinite layoff. Final testing of the transaxle assemblies was completed. However, when Johanson began examining the test reports, he noted that the transaxles tended to fail when both were loaded at more than 20% over rated capacity and subjected to strong torsion forces as occur when a vehicle brakes hard for a curve down a mountain road. Although the specifications accompanying the order from Proton called for transaxles to carry 130% of rated capacity without failing, Johanson knows that the Malaysian firm has no means of testing the transaxles once they have arrived in Malaysia. Johanson showed the test results to the Managing Director who indicated that he was already aware of the problem. The Managing Director advised that given the low likelihood of occurrence and the fact that there was no time to redesign the assembly, he had decided to ignore the report as they would lose the contract if they did not deliver on time.

   If you were Johanson, would you show the results to the Malaysian automobile manufacturer?

Web workout

Question 1 Visit a website of your favourite snack food or consumer electronics (e.g. www.nestle.com or www.sony.com). You should search their global and their country-specific websites looking at products and brand names in their portfolio. Is the packag-ing of your favourite snack (or are the features of the consumer electronic item) the same in all the markets?

Question 2 Consider launching a dairy snack food in the German market. Using the Internet, research how and what kind of packaging is used by competing brands in the marketplace? In what ways would you adapt your product to suit your selected international market?

Websites

Selling your product abroad www.morebusiness.com/running-your-business/marketing/

Search engine for Asian Products http://www.asianproducts.com/

Discussion questions

1 Prepare a matrix. Along the horizontal axis show the following countries: Canada, Vietnam, Spain and Japan. On the vertical axis, list each of the six factors to be taken into account when redefining the business and considering international markets. In the cells indicate how these factors would differ for each of the four countries.

2 Modifying a product to facilitate its sale in international markets will involve extra costs. To what extent are these costs discretionary and how would you assess whether the costs are worthwhile?

3 For what kinds of products do you expect customer needs to be worldwide? Why?

4 In what ways does the product's packaging need changing when the product is being marketed in another country?

5 You have been asked to develop an international product for sale throughout the EU or ASEAN region. What are the criteria you would apply in the development process and what are the stages from conceptualisation to market introduction?

6 What factors decide whether a similar product can be marketed in different international markets and whether modifications are necessary?

7 How does the international marketing of industrial products differ from that of consumer goods?

References

Ambler, T., and Styles, C. (2000) *The Silk Road to International Marketing – Profit and Passion in Global Business*, Financial Times/Prentice Hall, London.

Beeby, M. (1998) *Australian Financial Review,* 14 May, p. 26.

Bonoma, T.V. (1982) 'Major Sales: Who Really Does the Buying?' *Harvard Business Review*, May–June.

Business Review Weekly (2000), 10 March, p. 60.

Butler, G. (1998) *Australian Financial Review*, 14 May, p. 34.

Craig, C.S., Douglas, S.P. and Flaherty, T.B. (2000) 'Information Access and Internationalisation – The Internet and Consumer Behaviour in International Markets', *Proceedings of the eCommerce and Global Business Forum*, Santa Cruz, CA, 17–19 May, Andersen Consulting Institute for Strategic Change.

Czinkota, M.R. and Kotabe, M. (1990) 'Product Development the Japanese Way', *The Journal of Business Strategy*, November–December.

Czinkota, M.R. and Ronkainen, I.A. (1998) *International Marketing*, 5th edn, Dryden Press, Orlando.

Fan, Y. (2001) 'The National Image of Global Brands', *Proceedings of the Academy of Marketing Conference*, Cardiff, 2–4 July, University of Cardiff.

Jacob, R. (1994) 'The Big Rise; Middle Classes Explode Around The Globe', *Fortune*, 30 May.

Kotler, P. (2000) *Marketing Management: The Millennium Edition*, Prentice Hall, Englewood Cliffs, NJ.

Onkavist, S. and Shaw, J.J. (1983) 'An Examination of the International Product Life Cycle and its Applications within Marketing', *Columbia Journal of World Business*, Fall.

Onkavist, S. and Shaw, J.J. (1989) 'The International Dimension of Branding', *International Marketing Review*, Vol. 6, No. 3, p. 24.

Plumley, D.J. (2000) *Global eCommerce: The Market, Challenges and Opportunities*, Bowne Global Solutions, January.

Porter, M. (1990) *The Competing Advantage of Nations*, Macmillan, London, p. 41.

Robinson, D. (1961) 'The Challenge of Underdeveloped National Markets', *Journal of Marketing*, October.

Roth, M.S. (1995) 'The Effects of Culture and Socio-economics on the Performance of Global Brand Image Strategies', *Journal of Marketing Research*, May, pp. 163–175.

9

Marketing services
internationally

Learning objectives

After studying this chapter, you should be able to:

- recognise ways in which the international marketing of services differs from the international marketing of goods;

- appreciate how the unique characteristics of services marketing require a different strategic approach when introducing services into an international market;

- develop market entry strategies for the international marketing of services; and

- assess ways in which the Internet can overcome some of the problems traditionally encountered in international services marketing.

Microsoft's European battle

The successful outcome of Microsoft Corporation's anti-trust actions in the US does not mean that its battle in the European arena will be easy. Microsoft's rivals, including Sun Microsystems, AOL Time Warner, Nokia and Oracle, have presented new complaints to the European competition commissioner, Mario Monti, that might push the balance against Microsoft. They argue Microsoft is using its Windows monopoly to establish dominance in other markets from instant messaging to digital moviemaking software. They want Monti to force Microsoft to tear out the applications, stripping Windows down to the bare essentials. From Microsoft's perspective this runs contrary to its long-term PC strategy objective. The Windows XP operating system is designed to provide users with a host of applications. Microsoft wants to have the freedom to innovate based on this operating system.

Monti's original anti-trust case is based on Microsoft adding its Media Player into the Windows 98 operating system. The new complaints are more serious for Microsoft as they give the perception that Microsoft is now more than ever using its Windows monopoly to establish dominance in other markets.

Introduction

The international services trade is increasingly important to the economies of most countries, especially industrialised countries. The marketing of services in an international context needs to be considered separately from goods. This is because opportunities for growth are better and the barriers to trade in services are different from those for goods. The commercial services trade is now around 20% of total world trade. The international services trade is growing at 16% per year compared with only 7% per year for goods. A detailed comparison of the share of goods and commercial services in the total trade of selected regions and economies is outlined in Table 9.1.

Table 9.1 Share of goods and commercial services in the total trade of selected regions and economies, 2001

	Exports			Imports		
	Value	Share (%)		Value	Share (%)	
	Total (US$bn)	Goods	Commercial services	Total (US$bn)	Goods	Commercial services
World	7,520	80.6	19.6	7,500	80.7	19.3
North America	1,291	76.8	23.2	1,603	85.7	14.3
Latin America	413	85.6	14.1	436	83.7	16.3
Western Europe	3,106	78.2	21.8	2,983	78.3	21.7
Africa	179	82.7	17.3	160	76.6	23.4
Asia	1,947	84.5	15.5	1,813	80.4	19.6
European Union (15)	2,830	78.4	21.6	2,744	78.0	22.0

Source: Adapted from OECD (2001) *World Trade in 2001 – Overview*.

The nature of services

Services are different from products and have a number of distinguishing characteristics that are critical in their marketing. Services can be anything that can be bought or sold but cannot be dropped on your foot! Services can be distinguished from products in that they can bring about a change in those who use them, as happens with education; can bring about changes to the goods to which they are applied, as with engine design; can be embedded in products, as with aftersales service on a car; or can exist on a stand-alone basis, as with a haircut.

Other features of services are that they can combine both tangible (e.g. aircraft and food and drink) and intangible elements (e.g. inflight service and transportation); they can be experiential (i.e. you do not know what you will get until it is delivered, e.g. an operation); they can be delivered in real time (e.g. filling a tooth); they can be delivered face to face (as with a university lecture); and often they need to be taken on trust (e.g. when you have your car serviced).

The marketing paradigm for services

The marketing characteristics of services are:

- *Intangibility*. The fact that services often cannot be touched or felt can be compensated for by stressing tangible cues associated with the service, by using 'word of mouth' to promote them, by creating a strong image for the company supplying the service, and finally by having a programme of post-purchase communication to lessen any feeling of cognitive dissonance.

- *Inseparability*. Because production and consumption of many services occur at the same time and the consumer becomes part of the service, selection and training of personnel becomes very important.

- *Heterogeneity*. Because of the high labour content in the provision of most services, output can vary in quality. This can be reduced by customising the service (as with ladies hairdressing) or by industrialising it (as with carpet cleaning).

- *Perishability*. Because services cannot be saved or stored, it is necessary to devise strategies to cope with fluctuating demand. These might take the form of having a flexible pool of part-time employees to call on at periods of peak demand as in the hotel industry or by implementing yield management strategies as with airlines.

Figure 9.1 shows the additional marketing mix variables that apply with services.

As with goods, the 'four Ps' can apply to services. The *product* could be the content of the degree; the *price* could be US$1,500 per subject; the *promotion* would be to advertise the MBA in the *Financial Times*; and the *place* would be delivery on campus or delivery in a downtown location or delivery via a residential programme. In addition, with services marketing, three additional 'Ps' apply. These are *personnel* as with the

---

7 Ps – services paradigm

Figure 9.1

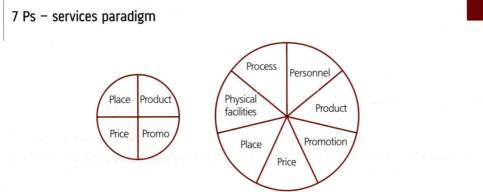

lecturer; *process* as with enrolment in the degree programme; and *physical* facilities as with quality of lecture halls and content of the library.

Lovelock et al. (2001) argue that rather than focusing on generic differences between services and goods, one should focus on the process by which services are delivered. They categorise services as:

- *People-processing services.* Customers become part of the production process that becomes simultaneous with consumption (e.g. passenger transportation, lodging and health care). Customers must either travel to the place in which the service is provided or the service provider must travel to the customer. In both cases, the service provider needs to maintain a local geographic presence.

- *Possession-processing services.* These involve doing something to physical products to improve their value to customers (e.g. transporting freight; repairing motor vehicles; servicing capital and plant). The service provision facility may be either in a fixed location or mobile. A local geographic facility is necessary when the service supplier needs to provide service to physical products in a location on a repeated basis. In some cases, electronic technology obviates this by enabling diagnosis of a problem from a distance, as with telemedicine.

- *Information-based services.* These involve collection, interpretation and transmission of data to create value (e.g. banking, consulting, accounting, education). Customer involvement in the production of these services is minimal and modern global telecommunication enables them to be delivered from a central hub to almost any location. Local presence requirements are limited to an automatic teller machine or a fax or a computer.

The content of services marketing and delivery

The services encounter involves not only traditional elements of marketing but also internal marketing within the organisation. Because of the high involvement of people in the supply of the service, there will need to be considerable emphasis within the company on training people to provide the service and the development of a service culture within the firm. This is likely to involve training people in the firm who provide service and also those who are in direct contact with customers. It will also involve a greater emphasis on relationship marketing than is necessary when simply dealing with goods, because services marketing emphasises retaining and managing relationships with customers on an ongoing basis especially when there is a 'face-to-face' element in the service provision. This is reflected in Figure 9.2.

The delivery of services typically involves backstage or invisible elements such as the kitchen in a restaurant, and front stage or visible elements such as the actual meal, the table setting and the waiter service. In general, the backstage elements are low in contact with the customer whereas the front stage elements are high in contact with the customer. Services will vary according to the extent to which they are low contact or high contact and this will affect the relative weight given in the firm to the operations system to provide the service, the system to deliver the service, and the system to market the service. Figures 9.3 and 9.4 illustrate the differences between low and high contact services.

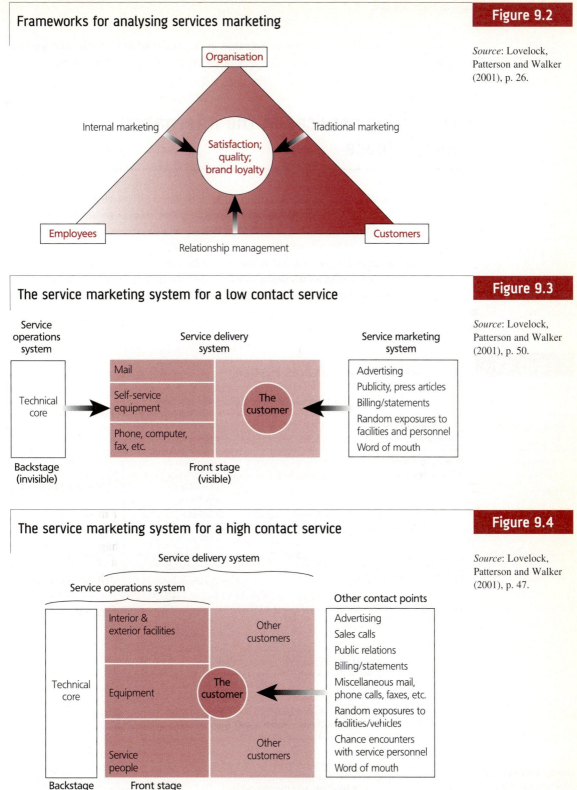

Frameworks for analysing services marketing

Figure 9.2

Source: Lovelock, Patterson and Walker (2001), p. 26.

Organisation

Internal marketing

Traditional marketing

Satisfaction; quality; brand loyalty

Employees

Customers

Relationship management

The service marketing system for a low contact service

Figure 9.3

Source: Lovelock, Patterson and Walker (2001), p. 50.

Service operations system

Service delivery system

Service marketing system

Technical core

Mail

Self-service equipment

Phone, computer, fax, etc.

The customer

Advertising
Publicity, press articles
Billing/statements
Random exposures to facilities and personnel
Word of mouth

Backstage (invisible)

Front stage (visible)

The service marketing system for a high contact service

Figure 9.4

Source: Lovelock, Patterson and Walker (2001), p. 47.

Service delivery system

Service operations system

Other contact points

Technical core

Interior & exterior facilities

Equipment

Service people

Other customers

The customer

Other customers

Advertising
Sales calls
Public relations
Billing/statements
Miscellaneous mail, phone calls, faxes, etc.
Random exposures to facilities/vehicles
Chance encounters with service personnel
Word of mouth

Backstage (invisible)

Front stage (visible)

In recent years, there has been an increase in the extent of low contact service due to both self-service and electronic delivery of an increasing range of services.

Marketing services in the international marketplace

The transformation of the services economy has stimulated the international marketing of services. Figure 9.5 shows the factors underlying this. Issues to be considered in relation to each of these factors are described below.

Internationalisation in general. There has been a hollowing-out effect caused by low-tech, labour-intensive operations being transferred to the less developed countries. This has resulted in a demand for the value-added intelligent services necessary to support

---

Figure 9.5 Transformation of the services economy

Factors responsible for transformation of the service economy

Internationalisation	Government regulation	Social changes	Business trends	Advances in technology
• 'Hollowing out' effect	• Deregulation/ privatisation	• Increased consumer expectations	• Relaxation of professional association standards	• Convergence of computers and telecommunications
• Increased services trade	• New trade agreements in services	• Increased affluence and leisure time	• Marketing emphasis by non-profit organisations	• Miniaturisation
• Global customers		• More women in the workforce	• Outsourcing of non-core services	• Digitalisation
			• Quality movement	• Enhanced software
			• Franchising	

Increased demand and competition

Facilitated by information technology

Growth and focus on services marketing and management

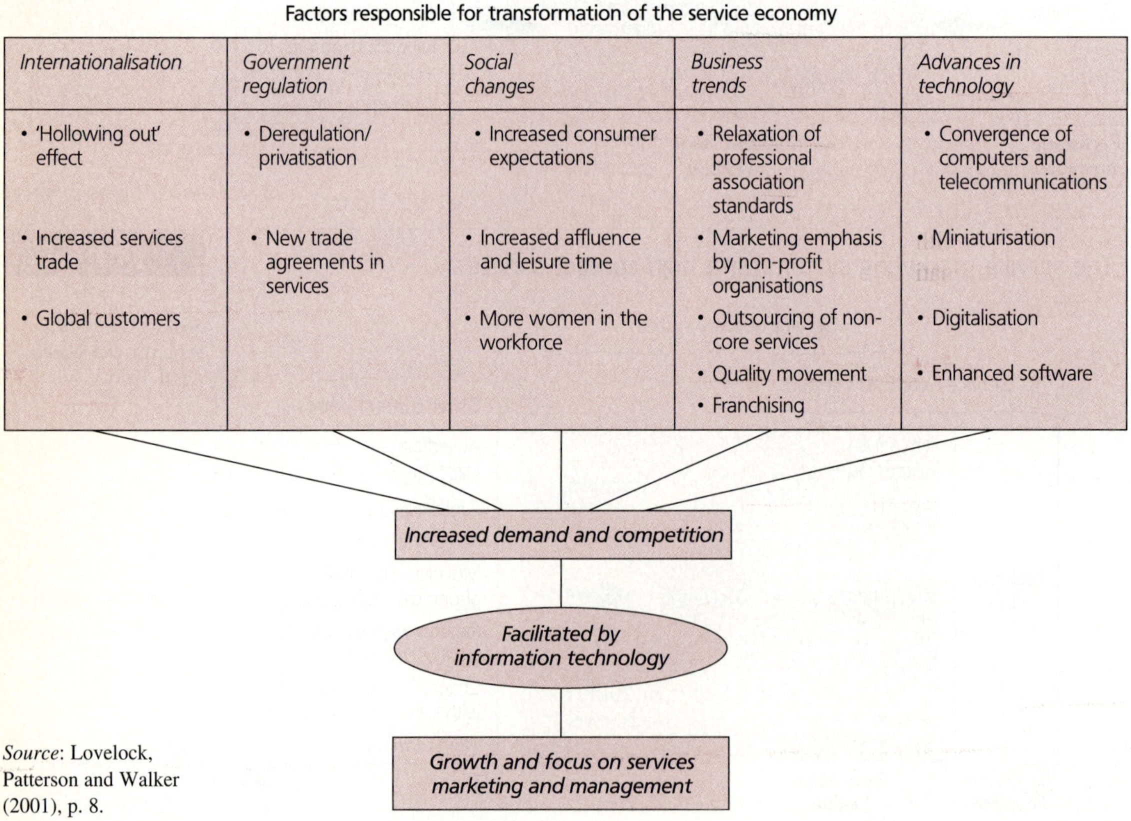

Source: Lovelock, Patterson and Walker (2001), p. 8.

a more high-tech manufacturing sector. Firms in this sector find there is a need to go international in order to survive; and when they do so, their service suppliers are forced to follow them abroad. This factor has partly been responsible for the growth of service trade internationally.

Government regulation has decreased. This is especially the case internationally in the service industry with banks, airlines and telecommunications. The World Trade Organisation has been working on freeing up trade in services and has introduced the Trade in Intellectual Property Agreement (TRIPS). Increasingly, government is privatising its business undertakings with utilities and by outsourcing the services it needs, as opposed to undertaking them 'in house'. Deregulation has often occurred in response to public pressure as with shopping hours. This has strengthened private sector provision of services and ability of the private sector to compete in service provision internationally.

Social changes. Rising expectations, greater affluence and more focus on leisure and quality of life have caused increased expenditure on services such as tourism. Furthermore, the increase in the percentage of women in the workforce has bought about a larger demand for labour replacement services such as purchasing food supplies via the Internet.

Business trends. A number of business trends have facilitated internationalisation of services. The spread of franchising is one such trend, as is the creation of international standards for services (e.g. ISO 9000) and moves towards international recognition of standards of professional practice (e.g. accountancy standards).

Advances in technology. These have lessened the constraints on provision of services traditionally imposed by national boundaries and caused international service providers to rationalise activities on a global basis. This is evident in the media, transportation and telecom sectors. Advances in technology have also created new international markets for services as with the Internet and facilitated existing services activities as with the tracking of international airfreight.

Drivers of internationalisation of service firms

These can be divided into firm-level drivers and industry-level drivers. Within each category are a number of specific drivers. Although these apply to the marketing of both goods and services, their application to services involves the following.

Firm-level drivers

- *Market seeking.* This usually involves small and medium-sized service exporters seeking new markets because of their apparent higher growth potential.
- *Client following.* This involves service firms following their clients into international markets to provide the same services as they do in the domestic market, for example in the banking and advertising industry.

- *Domestic market pressure.* This occurs when the domestic market becomes saturated and there is pressure from forces within the market for the service provider to go international.
- *Unsolicited orders.* These usually result from the service firm having an international reputation or a technology that is innovative which has application to an international project

Industry-level drivers

- *Common customer needs.* In general, standardisation is less likely with services that with goods. Within services, the potential for standardisation is greater the less the provider is involved in the delivery because this increases the extent to which customer needs are likely to have more features in common.
- *Scale economies.* These are driven by the opportunity to spread fixed costs. With services, such economies are more likely to come from standardised processes than from a physical concentration of activities.
- *Government drivers.* These can take the form of incentives from one's own government for exporting services, or barriers placed in the way of services exports by the government in the international market to protect local service industries.

9.1 International highlight

Advertising in China

Throughout the 1990s the advertising industry in China underwent a period of immense growth. The advertising spend showed double-digit growth each year since 1994 and this trend is forecast to continue until at least 2004. In 2001, advertising spend reached US$8.5 billion. Of this, newspapers, magazines and television dominated – accounting for $1,737 million, $68 million and $4,334 million respectively. The balance consisted of radio, outdoor, cinema and online. Online accounted for $12 million.

Given the size of the advertising market, as well as the geography and size of the country, reaching the consumer can be a difficult task. There are over 10,796 newspapers, 2,197 magazines, 1,211 radio stations and 747 television stations that will accept advertising. China's major cities absorb most of the advertising dollars, with Shanghai accounting for 17%, Beijing for 15% and Guandong for 11% of all advertising expenditure.

Despite the growth in advertising, there are still many obstacles to be overcome by the international advertiser. International advertising agencies continue to be highly regulated, given their potential to influence public opinion. Foreign advertising firms are limited to a 51% equity in joint ventures. The Ministry of Foreign Trade Economic Cooperation (MOFTEC) and the State Administration for Industry and Commerce (SAIC) are the key regulatory bodies for the advertising sector. However, there are other organisations such as the Ministry of Radio, Film and Television that also exercise control over the advertising industry.

Source: Adapted from a presentation at DCMA, Singapore and based on data by Forrester Research, 2000.

● *Competition drivers.* These often occur because the service provider finds it necessary to go international in order to protect its position in the domestic market, especially if costs can be lowered. If the service providers do not take this step, then there is an increased risk that firms in the international market may use that market as a base from which to internationalise their operations.

● *Information technology drivers.* The ability to centralise information hubs on a global basis is a motive because it strengthens the firm's competitive position. Rupert Murdoch's involvement in satellite TV in order to monopolise sports coverage is an example of this factor.

Issues in services exports

When firms engage in international trade in services, they face most of the same problems as they would with international trade in goods. There are, however, a number of additional problems that influence firms' international marketing strategies.

Delivery issues. Unlike goods, the export of services can also be inbound. This happens when the recipient of the service enters the provider's country to receive the service (e.g. tourism and education). In some cases, the international services export can be inbound (e.g. telemedicine) or outbound (e.g. surgeon flies to the international country to perform the operation).

Infrastructure requirements. Services exports are often dependent on the presence of an existing infrastructure in the international market. Taking tourism as an example, there is a need for the existence of airports and resorts in the country before tourists can be attracted to the market. With financial services and call centres, there is a requirement for telecommunications and informational facilities. Exports of technology require an education infrastructure that fosters creativity and innovation as well as the provision of an R&D infrastructure to create an entrepreneurial environment.

Direct contact needs. When the export of services involves simultaneous production, exchange and consumption, there is a need for much more face-to-face contact and for buyer and seller to be in the same location. The firm has to supply the service in person direct to the international market because it cannot be shipped there and, when direct contact is involved, each service transaction is unique. In these circumstances, controlling quality is likely to be a greater problem than with goods. Finally, because services cannot be inventoried, the opportunity to reduce variance in overall demand by diversification of production/supply from abroad is lessened.

Greater protectionism. Government often regards the service sector of its economy as having special cultural or strategic significance. It strives to protect this sector via the use of non-tariff barriers or by prohibiting investment in service sectors of the economy. Table 9.2 provides examples of barriers to the international marketing of services.

Table 9.2 Selected barriers to the international marketing of services

Type	Example	Impact
Tariff	Tax on imported advertising	Discriminates against international agencies
	Tax on computer services contracts	Prices international service providers higher than domestic providers which stand alone
	Higher fees for university students from outside the country	Decreases international student enrolment
Non-tariff National buying policies	US government buying training services only from US companies	Discriminates against international suppliers
Prohibited employment of foreigners	Priority to Canadian citizens	May prevent supplier from going to buyers
Distance	International business education	May raise cost of bringing supplier to buyer, buyer to supplier
Direct government competition	Indonesian monopoly on telecommunications	Must market services to government
Scarce factors of production	Lack of trained medical workers in Biafra	Limits production of services
Restriction on service buyers and sellers	North Korea limiting the number of tourists allowed to enter and exit the country	Limits the restricted industry

Source: Adapted from Dahringer, Lee D. (1991), 'Marketing Services Internationally: Barriers and Management Strategies', *Journal of Service Marketing*, 1991, Vol. 5, pp. 5–17.

Economies of location. Because services tend to be more jointly demanded, supplied and consumed than goods, there is advantage to be gained from concentrating some service activities in certain cities or in certain countries. The creation of 'technology parks' is an example of this. The concentration of global banking, insurance and financial services in specific centres such as Singapore, Tokyo and London reflects the above.

Quantifying international services trade. One of the problems with services exports is that they have not received the same focus of attention as goods exports do. Possibly this is because media and government tend to underplay export achievement in the services sector due to their embedded nature. Certainly this factor, together with their

Figure 9.6

Classification of services exports

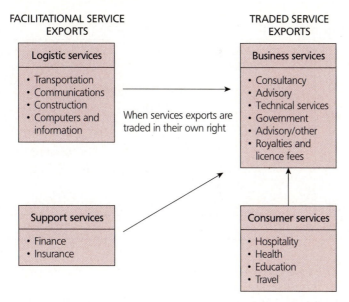

intangibility as well as their variability in location of delivery, have made it difficult to accurately measure the volume of services exports.

Categorisation of services exports

According to the L/E/K *Partnership Report* (1994), services exports can be categorised according to the function they perform – as either 'facilitational' or traded. Within the category of 'facilitational', services exports can be logistical or support. With the traded services category, exports can be either business services or consumer services. This is reflected in Figure 9.6.

Services exports can also be categorised according to different stages of development of the markets. Figure 9.7 contrasts the nature of the services export with the stage of development attained by a market.

- *Infrastructure-related services exports* – these are essential for a nation's industrialisation and the flow is usually from a provider in a middle-income country to a buyer is a low-income country.

- *Adaptive services exports* – these are services exports that facilitate trade (often computer aided), and because of the technology involved, the flow tends to be from high- or middle-income countries to countries with growing middle classes.

| Figure 9.7 | Framework for targeting export service markets |

Source:
L/E/K Partnership
(1994), Fig. 45.

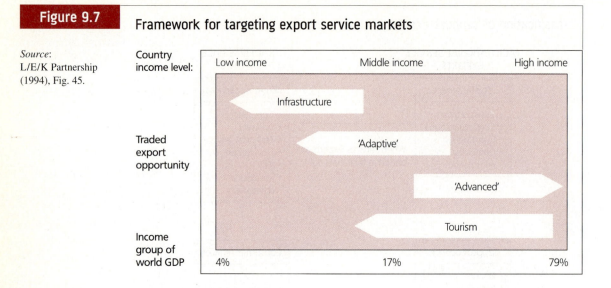

- *Advanced services exports* – these are generally high-tech or information-based exports and the flow is from middle-income to high-income countries or from one high-income country to another.

- *Tourism exports* – because of the importance of levels of disposable income for tourism, the flow tends to be from high-income to middle- and low-income countries.

Patterson and Cicic (1995) have developed an alternative framework for classifying firms involved in the export of services. Their typology focuses on the dimensions of 'face-to-face' contact on the one hand and 'intangibility of the service' on the other.

As shown in Figure 9.8, services offered in international markets can be:

- *Location-free professional services* – a permanent presence in the international market is not necessary to deliver these services. Firms exporting these services internationalise using direct representation such as sending their personnel to the international market.

- *Location-bound customised projects* – these are longer term and require considerable personal interaction between client and service provider as well as the need to establish a permanent presence in the international country. Firms in this category mostly internationalise by following major clients into the international market.

- *Standardised service packages* – generally these services are linked to the supply of goods, such as software and technological training, and as such tend to be standardised. Services in this category are mostly exported by small firms whose internationalisation involves direct representation, agency arrangements or franchising.

Portuguese Shoe Show (MOCAP)

Pornographic! This was the classification that the police authorities in Saudi Arabia used in order to classify the advertising and promotion content of MOCAP.

During recent years firms have increasingly committed themselves to global markets. The intensification of competition on a global scale has led to an increasing number of firms seeking opportunities in international markets to achieve their objectives, as well as to safeguard their market position and survival. The firms' expansion into new markets serves as the catalyst for significant growth opportunities. Achieving success in export markets is, however, not an easy task, due largely to the multiple, diverse and idiosyncratic nature of foreign environments. For firms to be globally competitive it is, therefore, crucial that they recognise these differences and adjust their practices according to the cultural specifics of a particular host country. It is amazing in this era of globalisation the ease with which we ignore cultural heterogeneity between countries. The following example is about the Portuguese footwear industry and demonstrates how cultural differences between the countries are often neglected.

The footwear sector of the Portuguese economy has registered its greatest growth in the last twenty years. During the first quarter of 2001, Portuguese footwear exports increased 16% reaching €765 million, representing a 6.4% increase in volume and 46 million pairs. As a result, the Portuguese footwear industry ranks second in Europe and ninth worldwide in exports. It exports approximately 90% of its production; Europe is still the main market despite the recent efforts to enter new markets. However, in spite of the large investments which have characterised the sector in the last decade (average annual investment of €100 million), resulting in some of the most advanced factories in technology worldwide, Portugal still faces problems with its own image. That is, clients do not perceive products 'made in Portugal' to be of high quality. In order to change this image, a campaign called 'Portugal Quality Shoes' was developed by APICCAPS (Portuguese Footwear, Components, Leather Goods Manufacturer's Association) in close cooperation with ICEP (Portuguese Investment, Trade and Tourism Office).

Among other initiatives APICCAPS and ICEP have organised Portuguese companies' participation in trade fairs in several countries, supported companies in the development of business relationships with non-traditional markets, and organised a Portuguese Shoe Show (MOCAP) held twice a year in Portugal.

At the last MOCAP show, Saudi Arabian officials characterised the promotion content for the Portuguese Shoe Show as pornographic. Now, how can an advertising campaign that features shoes be considered pornographic? This campaign was used in Europe to promote MOCAP and was considered to be very well developed. Nevertheless, the posters and the leaflets inviting local managers to visit the Portuguese Shoe Show did not get through Customs. The material was apprehended and destroyed for being considered of pornographic nature.

This example reflects that management theories and practices that reflect the values of the country in which they originate should be culturally translated before they are exported to other countries. The notion that there is one correct way in management must be rejected. Simply because a marketing strategy – in this case the images on the posters – is effective in one country does not guarantee its success in another. Differential cultural orientations will lead to differing beliefs and preferences, which subsequently will have an impact on the effectiveness of management strategies and policies. It is, therefore, crucial that managers recognise these differences and adjust their practices according to the cultural specifics of a particular host country.

Source: Carlos Santos, Research Fellow, Smurfit Graduate School of Business, University College Dublin.

Figure 9.8	A typology of service firms in international markets

Source: Patterson and Cicic (1995), pp. 57–83.

Degree of face-to-face contact

	Low	High
Low **Degree of tangibility** **Pure services**	**Cell 1** **Location-free professional services** Typical firms: executive recruitment, market research, environmental science consulting, transportation, finance and insurance, information technology, product design services. • Degree of customisation: low • Firm size: small (median size = 25 employees) • Foreign ownership = 14% of sample	**Cell 2** **Location-bound customised projects** Typical firms: project management, engineering consulting, management consulting, human resource development consulting, larger market research firms, legal services. • Degree of customisation: high • Firm size: largest in sample (median size = 160 employees) • Foreign ownership = 9% of sample
Services bundled with goods **High**	**Cell 3** **Standardised service packages** Typical firms: software development, installation/testing of new hardware/ equipment, development of distance education courses, compact disks. • Degree of customisation: low • Firm size: small (median size = 40 employees) • Foreign ownership = 13% of sample	**Cell 4** **Value-added customised services** Typical firms: on-site training, computer hardware consulting, facilities management, accommodation services, catering, software training and support. • Degree of customisation: high • Firm size: medium (median size = 55 employees) • Highest incidence of foreign ownership = 21% of sample

● *Value-added customised projects* – because of their nature these services require considerable interaction with the customer if delivery is to be successful. With these services, the service component adds considerable value to the physical goods element. Firms exporting these tend to internalise both by following their customers into international markets and by filling unsolicited orders.

Services and international market entry

Figure 9.9 shows that the range of entry options for services differs from that for goods. While each stage involves the same trade-off as between commitment of resources and desire for control, the role of the agent may not be as important and licensing is replaced by franchising.

As with the export of goods, protectionist pressures from international governments can force providers of services to change their entry strategy from one of export to one

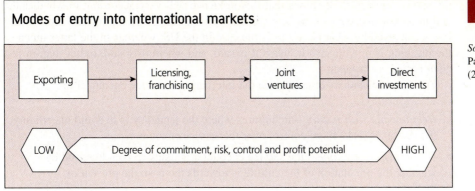

Figure 9.9

Modes of entry into international markets

Source: Lovelock, Patterson and Walker (2001), p. 377.

of greater involvement in the international market. For example in the education sector many universities that are involved in the provision of programmes internationally are under pressure to increase the local content.

Services exports and cultural sensitivity

As a general rule, services are more culturally sensitive than goods. This is because services are delivered in 'real time', the process of service delivery involves interaction, services are people-specific, services are delivered in a cultural setting and customers judge the process as well as the outcome. Table 9.3 illustrates cultural influences on

Table 9.3 Cultural influences on the service encounter

Cultural dimension	High context	Low context	Service encounter implication
Relationship with nature	Control over nature	Controlled by nature	Customer expectation of degree of control in service encounter
Relationship with time	Past (tradition)-oriented	Future (goal)-oriented	Customer expectation of provider flexibility in time spent at service encounter
Relationship with activity	Task (doing)-oriented	Experience (being)-oriented	Customer emphasis on process versus outcome of service
Relationship with others	Group-oriented	Individual-oriented	Customer expectation of significance of personal relationship in service encounter

the service encounter. It shows that this influence will vary according to whether the culture is low in context or high in context (see Chapter 3). In the former, most meaning is conveyed by what is said as is the case in the US, whereas in the latter much of the meaning is in who says it, when it is said, and where it is said, rather than in just what is said, as in Japan.

Specific implications of culture on the international service encounter are:

- *Relationship with nature* – in cultures where the tendency is to avoid uncertainty, the customer seeks more control over the service encounter.

- *Relationship with time* – the service encounter is likely to be influenced by whether the orientation of the culture is towards the past, the present or the future.

- *Relationship with activity* – context influences whether the customer for the service places emphasis on the process (as in high-context cultures) or on the outcome of the service delivery (as in low-context cultures).

- *Relationship with others* – in high-context cultures, front-line employees are more likely to respond to the wishes of the customer, whereas in low-context cultures they are more likely to implement management directives regardless of customer wishes (e.g. whereas airline check-in staff and gate agents in Asia tend to be polite and, where possible, flexible, in the US such staff are often inflexible and abrupt in manner, citing company regulations).

Services marketing and the issue of standardisation

The possibilities of standardisation of the offering across countries are fewer with services than with products. This is due to personal elements involved in their provision. However, some services are more amenable to standardisation than others. This has implications for marketing because of the search for economies of scale when transferring the offering from one country to another. Figure 9.10 illustrates this by comparing the source of the service with the type of service provider.

Examples of services falling in cell 1 would be the local restaurant; in cell 2 selling insurance via a local agent; in cell 3 offering a Visa credit card via a local bank; and in cell 4, TNT parcel express.

Figure 9.10	**Potential for standardisation of different services**

	Local service provider	Multinational service provider
Local service product	Local service provided locally for domestic market (1)	Local service provided by multinationals in various countries (2)
Transnational service product	Transnational service provided locally only (3)	Transnational service provided internationally (4)

Internet infusion

Marketing international services in marketspace As the Internet matures into a global medium for the trading of services, cross-border online trade will increase dramatically in both scale and diversity. This is most likely to occur in business-to-business trade in services because firms use the Internet to link international supply chains. Digitally delivered services have the potential to intensify international trade, particularly in financial and professional services. This is because the Internet gives firms more flexibility in locating their operations and it facilitates the internationalisation of small and medium-sized enterprises (SMEs).

As illustrated in Figure 9.11, the web is a developing marketing channel for services that not only transcends national boundaries but informs, investigates, interacts, distributes, elicits feedback and supports the services transaction.

Virtual services go international

Figure 9.11

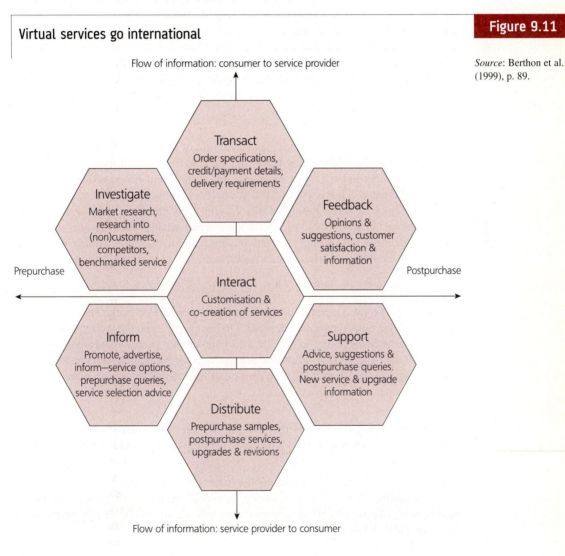

Source: Berthon et al. (1999), p. 89.

Flow of information: consumer to service provider

Transact
Order specifications, credit/payment details, delivery requirements

Investigate
Market research, research into (non)customers, competitors, benchmarked service

Feedback
Opinions & suggestions, customer satisfaction & information

Prepurchase

Interact
Customisation & co-creation of services

Postpurchase

Inform
Promote, advertise, inform—service options, prepurchase queries, service selection advice

Support
Advice, suggestions & postpurchase queries. New service & upgrade information

Distribute
Prepurchase samples, postpurchase services, upgrades & revisions

Flow of information: service provider to consumer

As pointed out earlier, difficulties in the international marketing of services are sometimes created by the fact that they are characterised by intangibility, simultaneity, heterogeneity and perishability. These difficulties can often be reduced by using the web as a vehicle for international services marketing.

Intangibility. The web can be used to provide tangible cues when marketing the intangible, i.e. something to compensate for the fact that customers cannot see the service they are receiving. This happens when airlines sell you an electronic ticket and you receive confirmation via electronic means. The web can also address the issue of intangibility by providing the customer with a sample in cyberspace as happens with the MP3 music site. Having a 'visitor's book' on your site also addresses this issue as it provides a record of who visited the site and when.

Simultaneity. Because of the simultaneous nature of production and consumption of the service, demands for a customised offering are frequent. The web is ideally suited for customisation because its capacity is based on information technology, data storage and data processing instead of reliance on employees at a physical location. The web facilitates the customer by innovating and offering suggestions to improve the service outcome. It also facilitates interactivity between customer and provider as exemplified by a customer being able to customise the content of a web page so that it allows people to interact with each other.

Heterogeneity. The web facilitates standardisation of customer treatment as when you receive the same form of greeting when logging onto a website. It removes some of the variable treatment in the service encounter due to different personalities encountered in the marketplace. This is evident for example when booking travel via the web as opposed to booking travel through a travel agent. Data gathering is facilitated by web usage. The conduct of focus groups via the Internet enables focus groups to be conducted with more customers, more attentively, and in real time. It also means that everyone in the firm, not just the interviewer, can listen to what the customer has to say about the service.

Perishability. To overcome this problem, international service marketers are using web sites to manage both supply and demand. On the supply side, the web gives the international marketer the ability to provide a 24-hour service to customers anywhere in the world. On the demand side, firms can use the web for promotion, pricing and service bundling to stimulate demand (e.g. to dispose of last-minute remaining seats on a flight or at a concert).

There are strategic implications for using the Internet in marketing services internationally. Lovelock et al. (2001) have come up with strategic implications as follows:

Customer service. The web enables SMEs to provide almost the same level of service when marketing services internationally as would be the case if they had used a salesperson. Given the cost differences, the web enables SME service providers to internationalise more easily.

Pirating the value chain. Participants in the value chain have the opportunity with the web to take over the role of other members in the chain and provide customers with better value as a consequence. This happens when the producer of the service uses the web to replace physical delivery and the use of international intermediaries. An example would be when publisher Pearson Education delivers content of publications to libraries in other countries.

Digital value chain creation. Innovation can be achieved and new services provided from afar. SMEs located anywhere can engage in online collaboration in R&D, service design and promotion with international alliance partners.

Creating a customer magnet. Firms that create a strong brand equity on the Internet will create confidence among their customers about returning to the site again.

Summary

The international marketing of services is different from that of products because of both the different nature of services and the way they are delivered to the customer. Although the categorisation of goods and services is arbitrary because many services are dependent on goods and vice versa, the general differentiating characteristics of services which impact on their being offered internationally are their perishability, their intangibility, their inseparability and their heterogeneity. Because services are more dependent on people, on availability of information and material infrastructure for delivery, their provision to international customers is often complicated, especially as they may be delivered in the supplying country as with tourism or in the foreign country as with consultancy. Because of their characteristics, the provision of international services is more culturally sensitive than with products and more subject to government regulation and non-tariff barriers. It is more difficult to standardise the service offering in international markets and most attempts to do so focus on the mode of service delivery rather than on the service itself.

Ethics issue

Biometrics are automated methods of recognising a person based on a physiological or behavioural characteristic. Among the features measured are: face, fingerprints, hand geometry, handwriting, iris, retina and voice. Governments, the military and private firms are introducing systems that record personal identities and can validate physical or logistical access to buildings or computer networks. There has also been increased pressure from governments for the introduction of secure national identity cards with embedded microchips that can store personal information. Many systems are based on biometrics. As the level of security breaches and fraud increase, more firms and governments are introducing biometrics for greater security. While many politicians acknowledge the sensitive nature of biometrics and public perceptions that it could be used to undermine privacy, they criticise films that depict biometrics being used as methods for social control.

What opportunities are open to applying biometrics to the delivery of public services? Is there a role for proactive public relations?

Web workout

Question 1 Institutions, such as banks, universities or colleges, are considered pure service organisations. Visit some of your well-known banks and universities and assess how these organisations can enter new markets using the Internet. What services can they provide?

Question 2 Using any Internet search tool identify the best-rated European universities for the provision of MBA programmes. How have these universities used the Internet to position themselves in the international education market?

Question 3 Appreciating the sensitivities between cultures, how can you introduce a new product using the Internet? You may want to visit some global companies in food and consumer electronics for ideas and examples.

Websites

Globaledge knowledge room
http://globaledge.msu.edu/KnowledgeRoom/KnowledgeRoom.asp

David Maister http://www.davidmaister.com/

'Additional Thoughts on International Services Marketing'
http://globaledge.msu.edu/KnowledgeRoom/featuredarticles/0007.pdf

Discussion questions

1 Discuss how the international marketing of services involves different marketing approaches from those required when marketing products in international markets.

2 Which of the ways of categorising services exports are the most appropriate in the Internet age?

3 Why are services exports more subject to cultural sensitivity issues than the exports of products?

4 What are the factors responsible for the increased attention now being focused on the international marketing of services?

5 Take a service provider with which you are familiar and outline various strategic options for entering the new EU post-Nice Treaty countries.

References

Berthon, P., Pitt, L., Katsikeas, C.S. and Berthon, J.B. (1999) 'Virtual Services Go International: International Services in the Marketspace', *Journal of International Marketing*, Vol. 7, No. 3, pp. 84–105.

Dahringer, L. D. (1991) 'Marketing Services Internationally: Barriers and Management Strategies', *Journal of Service Marketing*, 1991, Vol. 5, pp. 5–17.

L/E/K Partnership (1994) *Intelligent Exports and the Silent Revolution in Services*, Commonwealth of Australia.

Lovelock, C.H., Patterson, P.G. and Walker, R.H. (2001) *Services Marketing: An Asia-Pacific Perspective*, 2nd edn, Prentice Hall, Sydney.

OECD (2001) *World Trade in 2001 – Overview*.

Patterson, P.G. and Cicic, M. (1995) 'A Typology of Service Firms in International Markets: An Empirical Investigation', *Journal of International Marketing*, Vol. 3, No. 4, pp. 57–83.

10

Promotion in international marketing

Learning objectives

After studying this chapter, you should be able to:

- identify the stages which apply to the international communications process;

- evaluate the factors which cause international communication to differ from domestic communication;

- assess the extent to which modifications are necessary when using print media in international markets;

- recognise the advantages and disadvantages of visual and aural media for promoting in the international marketplace;

- prepare a plan for effective participation in international trade displays;

- maximise the advantages of participating in an international trade mission; and

- evaluate the impact on international promotion and advertising of issues such as 'country of origin' and 'standardisation versus differentiation'.

Advertising in the nude

Both Procter & Gamble (P&G) and Yves Saint Laurent (YSL) have recently launched controversial advertising campaigns featuring nude men. The French fashion house Dior was forced in 2002 to withdraw its nude Sophie Dahl advertisement in several markets following consumer complaints. Its competitor YSL has again opted for so-called 'porno chic' in a print campaign for its new M7 after-shave. The advertisement featuring a full frontal male nude will appear in European fashion glossies such as French *Vogue*. Not to be outdone, P&G's new black-and-white television advertisement for Lacoste Homme aftershave features a male model drinking a cup of tea and wandering around his stylish apartment in the nude.

Introduction

This chapter focuses on promotion in international marketing rather than on international promotion. It is primarily concerned with the management of promotion both in and across a number of nations. Promotion in international marketing plays the same role as it does in domestic marketing – that is communication with audiences to achieve desired outcomes. Any consideration of communications strategy in the international marketplace must take into account that there are four elements in the promotional mix. The first is advertising – a non-personal presentation through any medium that is paid for by a sponsor. The second is public relations – a non-personal form of communication based on conveying messages to publics or exchange partners designed to create a favourable image for the organisation. Personal selling involves direct communication between buyer and seller. The final element is sales promotion, which involves techniques to stimulate a short-term response. The relative importance of these techniques will vary from international market to international market, depending on government regulation, media availability, marketing acceptability and promotions infrastructure. As a consequence, the relative importance of elements within the promotion mix will vary when the firm promotes in international markets, as will the need to modify each element of the promotion mix prior to its implementation.

Communication theory

Promotion is a major form of communication in international business. Its essence is the transmission of a message from the seller or exporter to the buyer or importer. However, the firm will have many 'publics' with which to communicate besides the international customer. These 'publics', located in both the domestic and international markets, include the general public, the government, the media, the firm's suppliers, employees, stockholders and intermediaries, and other firms in the industry. The communication objective will vary from 'public' to 'public'. Whereas, for example, the objective with the media might be to obtain favourable coverage, the objective with the government may be to obtain fair or favourable treatment. Also the most appropriate promotional tool will vary according to the 'public', with public relations being used to influence government in contrast to using advertising to influence customers or intermediaries.

The communications process

Figure 10.1 shows the communications process. There are three major elements. These are the sender, the medium through which the message is conveyed, and the receiver of the message. This process of communication is influenced by both

The communication process

Figure 10.1

Source: Griffin (1994), p. 11.

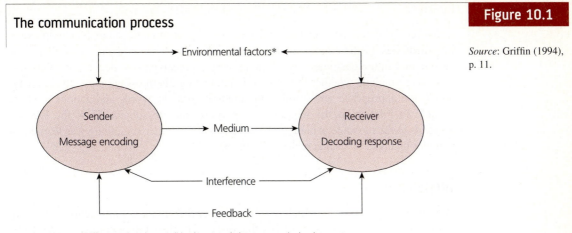

*Differences in culture, politics, laws/regulations, economic development, competition, education, infrastructure and technology

environmental factors and noise or interference in the transmission of and/or receiving of the message.

Sender

The sender of the message, although usually a person, can also be a brand or a company or a combination of all three. The message must be appropriate to the medium being used and in a form that the intended recipients can understand. As an example, an Australian TV commercial intended for use in the United States should not involve broad Australian accents because these will not be comprehensible to Americans.

Before being sent, the message is encoded so that it is suitable for the medium to be used and will appeal to its intended audience. Encoding ensures that the message will be interpreted correctly and, for this reason, literal translations on the one hand and plays on words on the other should be taken into account and eliminated.

Medium

The medium can take a wide variety of forms ranging from a letter to a phone directory to a billboard to a television commercial. Not only must the medium be appropriate for the environment in which it is to be used but it must also be appropriate for the product or service being promoted. Some media are more appropriate for some products than for others. As an example, expensive perfume is more likely to be promoted in glossy magazines than on billboards because of the image that accompanies the product and the expectations that have been created by the product. It is necessary first to check that the medium used in the domestic market is available in the foreign country. Then it should be determined whether it has a similar impact in terms of cost per potential customer reached, is technically able to convey the message without distortion and is similarly regarded in relation to the image of the product category. The medium selected must be suitable for conveying the attributes of the product. For example, television is most appropriate for demonstrating a product whereas direct mail is most appropriate for sampling a product.

Receiver

Those receiving the message can be from a wide spectrum and can include employees, intermediaries, media editors, those who can influence decision-makers as well as past, present and future customers. How the message is received will depend on many factors. These include whether the content is interesting, the message clear, the language translation appropriate and whether the pictures, sounds, words and actions used are suitable in relation to the message, its purpose and its subject. How the receiver responds to the message is likely to be a function of whether something was learned, or attitudes changed or further action stimulated.

Interference

Interference creates noise, which has the effect of disrupting communication. A major source of noise is competitive activity that often takes the form of confusion created by competitors' messages being transmitted at the same time. If faced with this problem, one solution is to seek a different medium for the message. Interference can also occur because of distortion due to poor quality reproduction or transmission of print, audio or visual material. Another source of interference is that of appropriateness of the medium. Apart from its suitability for the target audience, there is also the issue of editorial compatibility between product and medium as with contraceptives and a Roman Catholic-owned radio station. Also, this includes location of the advertisement and editorial content. For example, in a magazine, an advertisement on a feminine hygiene product should be adjacent to an article on beauty rather than to an article on cooking. A final source of interference relates to the degree to which receivers were receptive to the message. For example – were they distracted at the time the message was received? Were they preoccupied with other things? Would receiving the message at that time cause irritation? An example would be the screening of soap commercials during coverage of the opening ceremony of the Olympic Games.

Environmental factors

The effectiveness of promotion as a form of communication will be impacted upon by a number of factors. These include sensitivity to social norms, the degree to which local tastes and preferences are catered for, the extent to which religious mores and standards of behaviour are conformed to, the awareness of media alternatives and the constraints attaching to each in the international market.

Feedback

The feedback loop in Figure 10.1 enables an assessment as to whether the communications objectives are being achieved. Depending on the form of promotion employed, this feedback can be immediate, as with personal selling, or drawn out, as with assessing the effectiveness of advertising. Also, the feedback may be voluntary, as indicated by orders placed, or involuntary, as with research to assess the effect of print and visual advertising.

The factor in the application of the communications model with the most impact on international promotion is culture. This is because the message encoded in one culture may not work in another. In international promotion, it is necessary to establish a common frame of reference for both sender and receiver. Included in this is overstatement versus understatement as the norm, as well as harmony in expectations as to size, distance, punctuality and location. The message to be conveyed should also take account not only of culturally influenced differences in spoken or written language, but also differences in the silent language of the body and accompanying gestures.

Constraints in international marketing communication

The constraints on international marketing communication vary from international market to international market but the most important are:

- *Language differences.* The diversity of languages in world markets, even within the one country, provides a challenge because, when venturing abroad, the firm will need to communicate in a variety of languages other than English. Technological accuracy or perfect translation is not sufficient as use of the other language must be motivating – what Terpstra and Sarathy (2000) term 'language of the heart'.

- *Marketing acceptability.* This varies from country to country depending on politics, history (e.g. former centrally planned economy) and level of economic development (generally speaking, marketing is less acceptable in the poorest countries).

- *Media availability.* Media available in the domestic market may not be available in many countries or, if they exist, they are not allowed to be used for promotion other than by government. In addition, the volume of each medium available in each country varies. Even in developed countries this is the case, with a lesser volume available in rural as opposed to urban areas. Associated with this is the variation between countries in the number of viewers, listeners, or readers per TV set, radio set, or newspaper copy.

- *Intermediary availability.* The availability and effectiveness of advertising agencies, media buying groups and market research institutions also vary from country to country and this variation can be a constraint on international promotion, especially where it is intended to replicate the domestic approach in the international market.

- *Activities of competitors.* In some markets, the competitors are other international firms, local firms and in many a combination of both. This creates a different situation from market to market. Competitor activities may require either an increase or a reduction in promotion in a given market at any time.

- *Government controls.* The final constraint is that national governments regulate promotional activities within their borders in the interests of protecting their citizens, their firms and their culture. Such regulations can impact on the media, the message, the budget, media ownership and operations of promotional intermediaries.

Factors in international communication

International communication, whether it be verbal, visual, written or oral, will be influenced by a variety of contextual factors. These may be a mix of culture, language, education, economic development, media infrastructure or government regulation.

Culture

Culture affects what people like and dislike, how they interpret signals and symbols, as well as their attitudes towards and biases against particular products and services. These issues need to be taken into account when developing the message to be communicated and deciding on the medium to be used. As a consequence, symbols, brand names, celebrity endorsements, colours in promotional pieces and copy platforms used in the domestic market may be inappropriate in another country. The same is true of certain colours and numbers. Figure 10.2 provides detail as to colours and numbers that would be appropriate to use when promoting products in Chinese communities.

| **Figure 10.2** | **Perceptions of colours and numbers** |

Source: Jacobs et al. (1991).

COLOUR	PERCEPTION
Grey	Inexpensive
Blue	High-quality
Green	Pure Trustworthy Dependable Sincere
Red	Happy Love Adventurous
Yellow	Happy Pure Progressive
Purple	Expensive Love
Brown	Good-tasting
Black	Powerful Expensive High-quality Dependable Trustworthy

The Chinese consider the following numbers lucky and would prove advantageous if used with a product: 8, 11, 13, 15, 16, 17, 18, 25, 29, 31, 32 and 39.

Hall (1976) divided cultures into those that were high- and those that were low-context cultures and argued that cultures fell somewhere along a continuum between these two extremes. High-context cultures are those where the social context that surrounds the act is much more important than written or legal documentation. China is an example of a high-context culture. Low-context cultures are those where the social context is unimportant and it is the written word or legal agreement that counts, as in the UK or the United States. Knowing where a culture falls along this continuum provides a useful guide as to how to communicate effectively with people in different cultures.

In high-context cultures communications approaches should imply rather than directly state the obvious, whereas in low-context cultures the reverse applies. Dulek et al. (1991) categorise the application of context to international communication as described below.

Conversational principles. The first of the four conversational principles involves recognising that in high-context cultures people want to know considerable detail about the executive and the company represented. This means that advertising and promotion should feature the company, its credibility and its background to a great extent. The second relates to clarity in communication and the need to avoid assuming that elements of the message which are taken for granted in the domestic market will also be taken for granted in the other country. In international promotion, it is necessary to speak clearly, use a presenter without a strong accent, speak slowly, and avoid jargon or cliches or slang. The third principle is focused on identification with the international recipient. This can be achieved by including phrases or words from the language spoken by the recipient and by allusion to history or contemporary events in the receiver's country. The fourth requires attention to body language. When recipients of the message cannot understand the spoken word, they are likely to rely for meaning on the body language of the presenter or the tone of voice used when the communication is made. The body language in commercials needs to be consistent with the message being communicated.

Presentation principles. The first of these presentation principles involves respect for cultures that are more formal. The desire for structured, as opposed to more natural, presentations will impact on the format and content of the promotional communication. The second presentation principle involves respecting and appealing to the different way foreign audiences react to promotional messages. The third requires patience with cultures where messages are drawn out or subject to interruption – rather than fast paced or brief. In some cultures the length of the message is often viewed as an indication of the importance the promoter attaches to its subject.

Written word principles. It is important to vary the structure of the message according to the context of the culture. Only in low-context cultures should communication be organised so that the central point is directly and immediately stated. A second principle requires that the style of writing be adapted to the culture to which the readers belong. In high-context cultures this means that there should be more emphasis on politeness and decorum in the message. In cases where there is doubt about the ability of the recipient of the communication to understand the language in which it is conveyed, it is necessary to either provide a translation or communicate the message visually as well as verbally.

Trade names, brands and slogans may have to be changed as well as translated when used in other markets. A brand name or slogan that is effective in the domestic market may mean something offensive or ludicrous in another language.

Other cultural issues that can affect international communication are whether social hierarchies are respected or egalitarianism prevails. This will impact on the content of the message and possibly on the background used in the promotion or advertisement. The role of women in a culture also has an impact on the target of the communication and the content of the message.

Language

The ability to translate words from one language to another is no guarantee that the same message is being communicated. Often meaning is culturally influenced and a portion of meaning is often lost in translation. For this reason, it is preferable to translate the idea or concept into the other language rather than the words used in English. Furthermore, because English tends to be the language of international business, it is mostly American or English cultural norms that are communicated when English is translated into other languages. These cultural norms are often not those of the target international market. In promotion, the culturally sensitive elements of the other culture need to be taken into account to enhance the impact.

Languages also vary in the degree to which they convey meaning precisely. In markets where language tends to be imprecise, the communication needs to be longer than in markets where a more precise language is used. Another aspect of language is the acceptability of use of foreign words in communications regarding certain products, e.g. French words are commonly used when perfume is promoted internationally. Finally languages vary as to the extent to which words commit the speaker. As an example, does 'yes' mean 'yes' as in the UK, or 'maybe' as in Thailand, or 'I hear what you are saying' as in Japan?

Context is important, as this will influence the interpretation put on the message. For this reason, it is necessary to check the context in the international market where the target of the promotion is. The context consists of the people involved in the communication, when the communication is made, and where it is made. The way the message is projected will influence the way it is interpreted. This can be a matter of the tone of voice, the overlap of conversations in the communication, the speed of speaking, the degree of personal involvement in what is said and the emphasis on talking rather than listening. All the above vary from country to country and can impact on how the message is received. This is illustrated by the following story.

The slogan 'Put a Tiger in Your Tank', although often regarded as a perfect example of a standardised advertising campaign, is not as standardised as it might seem. It is not fully equivalent from one country to another. A study of the back translations of the advertisements shows that in Northern European countries, such as Holland and Germany, the power of the tiger is located in the tank; and in France the power of the tiger was located in the engine. In Asian countries, such as Thailand, the tiger may be regarded as a danger for the local population and its image is that of the jungle rather than of power.

Source: Adapted from Usunier (1996).

Education

Different media have different educational requirements. In markets where literacy is low, it may be necessary to communicate messages in visual or aural modes rather than in writing. In addition, the level of education in the international country will influence the content of the promotional or advertising message. In countries such as India where literacy rates are low, it may be necessary to use media that are visual or aural and if print media are used, then ensure that it is the visual elements which convey the message. Other media may need to be considered, such as billboards, mime, puppet shows, movies and posters. Those promoting social services, such as health and contraception in less developed countries, frequently have to devise innovative promotional vehicles for communicating with people with limited education and literacy.

Economic development

The level of economic development impacts on how many people in the international market can afford the product. It also influences who has a need for the product and the acceptable level of sophistication of the product to be offered to that market. This factor can also impact on which media the people can afford to patronise as well as which media are available. In some countries, the higher the per capita GNP, the higher the percentage of GNP accounted for by advertising expenditure. However, as a country's income rises, so does the incentive to engage in advertising and promotion. This has the side effect that, despite the greater need for advertising in such countries, the effectiveness of particular advertising messages is reduced because of the volume of persuasive messages.

Media infrastructure

Countries differ as to availability, reach, cost and effectiveness of media and this alters the optimal promotional mix from one country to another. Whereas in some countries the same media might not be available, even in countries where it is, it may not be available in the same form. To achieve national coverage in India would require 100 newspapers and involve overlap in coverage and scheduling problems. By contrast, national coverage in Japan could be achieved by advertising in three newspapers.

Another problem has to do with differing levels of demand from one country to another. Where media availability is limited in relation to demand, either because of controls on advertising volume or lack of media, the time lag for advanced bookings may restrict its use for promotional purposes. In South Africa, for example, TV advertising must be booked one year in advance. A further constraint may relate to the production of commercials. Some countries have local content requirements for commercials that specify that they must either be produced in the host country or employ a number of local actors.

The issue of reach is also important in comparing effectiveness between countries. In many countries, it is not only circulation or home viewing figures which count but also the number of readers per copy or the number of viewers per TV set which is important. In the villages in India, it is not uncommon for up to 20 people to watch the communal village TV set. The degree to which various media are used and acceptable for promotion and advertising varies from country to country. Table 10.1 illustrates the different usages of media for promotion in a range of mostly developed countries.

Table 10.1 Penetration of the information economy – selected countries

Countries	Daily newspapers	Radios	Television		Mobile phones	Personal computers	Internet hosts
			Sets	Cable subscribers			
			per 1,000 people				per 10,000 people
	1996	1996	1997	1997	1997	1997	1998
Argentina	123	677	289	156.3	56	39.2	15.92
Australia	297	1,385	638	38.1	264	362.2	400.17
Austria	296	740	496	132	144	210.7	163.45
Belgium	160	792	510	361.8	95	235.3	150.65
Canada	157	1,078	708	261.4	139	270.6	335.96
China (Hong Kong)	739	695	412	61.5	343	230.8	108.02
Denmark	309	1,146	568	238.6	273	360.2	358.85
Finland	455	1,385	534	170	417	310.7	996.13
France	218	943	606	27.7	99	174.4	73.33
Germany	311	946	570	210.5	99	255.5	140.58
Greece	153	477	466	–	89	44.8	37.98
Ireland	150	703	455	147.4	146	241.3	121.85
Italy	104	874	483	0	204	113.0	55.69
Mexico	97	324	251	15.2	18	37.3	8.75
Netherlands	177	963	541	371.8	110	280.3	327.85
Norway	588	920	579	160.2	381	360.8	705.28
Portugal	75	306	523	38.5	152	74.4	45.34
Russian Federation	105	344	390	78.4	3	32.0	8.88
Saudi Arabia	57	319	260	–	17	43.6	0.02
Spain	99	328	506	10.8	110	122.1	61.9
Sweden	446	907	531	218.1	358	350.3	429.86
Switzerland	330	969	536	346	147	394.9	289.32
Turkey	109	178	286	8.1	26	20.7	4.30
United Kingdom	332	1,445	641	40.2	151	242.4	0.01
United States	215	2,115	847	245.9	206	406.7	975.94

Source: http://www.worldbank.org/data/wdi/pdfs/tab5-11.pdf. *World Development Indicators 2000* by World Bank, Copyright 2002 by World Bank. Reproduced with permission of World Bank in the format Textbook via Copyright Clearance Center.

Government regulation

Governments in most countries regulate the use of media for promotion in the interests of protecting their citizens from undesirable influences. Such regulations relate to the product that can be promoted, the content of what is said, by whom it is said, how it is said, the time at which it is said and the medium used. The above impacts on advertising and promotion to differing degrees from one country to another. Restrictions on media access may take the form of bans on advertising on certain media. For example, until recently, advertising was not allowed on TV in Indonesia.

Regulations can also govern the ratio of advertising to editorial and can set a limit on the maximum number of minutes advertising allowed per hour on TV. In some countries, advertising is banned altogether (e.g. in Libya), because it is contrary to the prevailing political philosophy. Government regulation can also apply to the content of advertising or promotion. In some countries, content regulations are motivated by a concern to protect moral and religious values (e.g. in Thailand the showing of underwear on billboards is prohibited). In other instances the ban is driven by a desire not to expose children to undesirable influences. In this case the ban may apply to promoting certain products in publications read by children or on TV or radio in the hours before children go to bed. Regulations on promotion to children vary markedly from country to country and change frequently.

Government regulations can also apply to sales promotion and can influence which sales promotion tools are allowed in the interests of ensuring that consumers are protected and that competition is conducted fairly.

The above factors often mean that an innovative approach to international promotion and advertising will be necessary.

Content of international communication

Although words are a means of communication and not the communication itself, many of the blunders in international advertising and promotion are due to words being translated literally rather than meaning being translated. This is often the case when the language of the other country is written in a script based on symbols rather than letters, e.g. Japanese or Chinese.

The richness of language and ability to convey shades of meaning vary from country to country. Where the language lacks ability to convey shades of meaning, it may be necessary to alter the balance in the advertisement between copy and visuals in print media or between voice and visuals in TV, so that the visual elements convey the shades of meaning. This requires an understanding as to how consumers in the international market arrive at a decision to purchase and how the message to capitalise on this process must be modified in order to maximise the advertisement's appeal. Promotion must be undertaken to fit in with the decision process involved in purchasing.

The management of promotional communication

The management of international communication involves six steps. These are illustrated in Figure 10.3 and discussed below.

1 *Isolate the communication problem to be solved.* This may be a matter of increasing awareness, improving brand image, increasing sales, differentiating the product or service from that of the competition or increasing market share.

10.1 International highlight

There's no accounting for taste

Australian beer has been exported to the United States for several decades. For most of that time, the second most popular beer has been the Queensland brew XXXX. This is despite the hilarity that results from the verbalisation of the brand name being Fourex which is the name of a major selling brand of condoms. Even the adventurous Madison Avenue types baulked in the mid-1980s when it was proposed to replicate the highly successful Australian promotional program for XXXX in the US. This was because the campaign was built around the slogan 'I feel a XXXX coming on'.

Figure 10.3   The main steps in the management of promotional communication

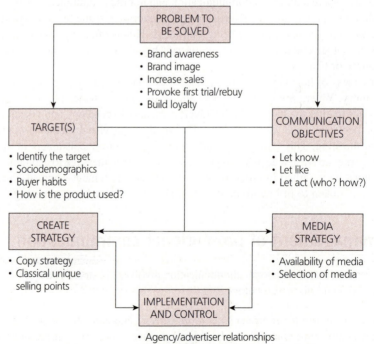

2 *Identify the target population.* Are there specific segments and what are their characteristics in terms of demographics, lifestyle and consumption habits?

3 *Define the communications objective.* Is the objective to convince buyers to like the product, or to stimulate repeat purchase, or to motivate people to act? Alternatively, the objective might be one of general education.

4 *Establish the creative strategy.* This may involve selecting particular themes for the promotion or stressing a unique selling proposition.

5 *Design a media plan.* This will specify which media to use, when to use them, and how to optimise the media mix to best reach the target audience. Critical to this will be whether the media are available in the international market and their degree of effectiveness.

6 *Implement and monitor the promotional campaign.* This can involve pre- and post-tests of a promotion's effectiveness as well as research into different aspects of the campaign.

Decision process

There are five stages in the decision process:

1 *Need recognition.* This involves the recipient being made aware that they have a need for the product or service. The communication should reinforce or draw attention to the basic need that the product/service fulfils.

2 *Information search.* This will vary with the nature of the product. With impulse purchases, the search is instantaneous; with frequent purchases the search is casual; and with high involvement purchases the information search is extensive. The message should provide information commensurate with the expected search needs for each of the above categories in the international market.

3 *Evaluation and comparison.* As part of this process, potential purchasers may seek information from independent assessors of quality and value. They may also try a number of products before making a final decision or they may base their decision on that of a referent, e.g. a well-known local figure who endorses the product. At this stage, the communications objective is to assess the importance in the international market of the comparison process and facilitate it in such a way that the product is not disadvantaged.

4 *Vendor and product purchase decision.* This aspect of the decision process involves deciding – the type of outlet to buy from such as supermarket versus pharmacy; incentives to purchase such as couponing, bundling, free gifts or discounts; unique packaging or point of sale material; product support such as warranties or extended periods of free maintenance; and the extent of information provided with the purchase as to its ingredients or contents.

5 *Post-purchase evaluation.* This element of the decision-making process involves convincing the customer after the purchase has been made that they have made the right decision. This will ensure that the customer becomes an unpaid advocate for the product with friends and acquaintances and may encourage repeat purchasing by the customer. Attention at this stage will reduce cognitive dissonance.

As the above five stages of the decision-making process vary between international markets, it is necessary to ascertain how each operates in the chosen market and formulate a message strategy.

Message strategy formulation

The advertising message is likely to differ depending on whether national or international appeals are to be used. If national appeals are employed, then the message will need to differ from that used in the domestic market for a number of reasons. These include:

- *Linguistic and cultural nuances.* These give rise to various subtleties which impact on how the message will be received and need to be taken into account to improve the effectiveness of the communication. An associated issue is that of language overlap. The message, while directed to one country market, may also be received in an adjacent market, as happens with radio and TV in Europe. To maximise this benefit, the message should also be crafted to appeal to customers in this adjacent market.
- *Different products.* Some product groups are more sensitive to cultural differences between markets than others and the extent of such sensitivity for the same product will vary between international markets. This degree of cultural sensitivity will need to be taken into account in deciding on the extent to which the advertising message should be localised.
- *Different users.* Some products will have different uses in different markets. Differences in the buyer's consumption pattern need to be taken into account because similar appeals are less feasible where the product does not meet the same needs or is not used in the same way.
- *Different media alternatives.* Not only does availability vary from market to market but also the relative importance of different media varies within each market. The suitability of different media for communicating different messages varies and if the media used in the domestic are not available in the international location, then a different message strategy may need to be devised.
- *Communication sophistication.* The expectations of both media and the messages they convey vary from country to country and especially between developed and developing countries. This must be taken into account when formulating messages. As local needs vary, the above needs to be evaluated in the light of these needs, otherwise the message may be irrelevant. For example, the Italian design house Diesel has broken all the rules in the luxury goods handbook but has succeeded. Its ads have mocked the glamorous images used to market haute couture by using obese models. It believes its use of humour and irony is fundamentally different from Benetton's effort to build brand recognition by using controversial social messages.
- *Business priorities.* Whereas in some countries business priorities are driven by the short-term goal of maximising returns to shareholders, in other countries, such as Japan, business priorities focus on achieving long-term growth in market share. Where the former priorities dominate, the communication strategy is likely to concentrate on stimulating instant purchase, whereas in countries where the latter predominate, the communication strategy is more likely to concentrate on image creation.

- *Status of marketing.* This varies throughout the world. In countries such as the US, where marketing is highly acceptable, the volume of promotional expenditure is likely to be high and sizeable promotion is expected to accompany market entry. In countries such as the former centrally planned economies, promotional expectations remain low despite moves towards a market economy.

The above points are exemplified in the situation several years ago when Procter & Gamble ran television advertisements in Japan. The advertisements compared its Pamper brand of babies' nappies to Brand X in a way which aimed to show that Brand X was inferior to the Procter & Gamble product. The advertisements were unsuccessful because hard-edged comparative advertising that is acceptable in the US is considered insulting in Japan.

Pull strategies in international promotion

Strategies that are targeted directly towards the international customer or end-user will need to be crafted correctly so as to appeal to that customer or end-user. Pull strategies involve advertising, publicity and public relations.

Advertising

This can include newspapers, magazines, trade publications, telephone directories, television, radio, cinema and outdoor and transit advertising. In general, advertising is the most high-profile of the various communications activities. Although it is the most powerful aid to positioning a product or service in a market, it is also the most expensive. It differs from other forms of promotion in that it is paid for; it involves non-personal presentation; and it uses media.

Between-country differences

Advertising differs from one country to another in terms of:

- *Usage.* Variations relate to the extent of advertising, the expectations of local buyers as to what advertising will achieve and the degree to which advertising is politically acceptable.
- *Form.* The relative weight given to press, radio, TV and other media will vary from country to country as will the availability of different media for promotional purposes.
- *Content.* What can be said or included, and what cannot be included, are a matter of both taste and government ruling (see earlier). It is often not appropriate to replicate local advertising approaches in other countries because of cultural differences and sensitivities.
- *Presentation.* This should conform to local expectations and, if in doubt, 'play it straight'. Humour in advertising or advertisements that are situation-specific rarely cross national boundaries. In the presentation of the message, go for either a

10.2 International Highlight

A tale of two cities

Source: Corbis.

In Tokyo, companies are not concerned about differentiating themselves from competitors, as is the case in the EU and US. This is because they feel that if the approach worked for others, then it should also work for them. The Japanese approach towards using celebrities also differs. Whereas in western cultures celebrities are used because their association lends strength to the claim for the product, in Japan they are used to lend dignity and elegance to the image of the product. In Tokyo, advertisements in general are oriented towards creating mood and nuance around the product rather than aggressively marketing it. In South-East Asia, advertisements, which virtually ask for the order, as many do in the US, are considered impolite because asking for the order is bad manners. The above example illustrates the need to tailor the advertisement to the preconceived notions existing in the international market.

A study of advertisements on buses in Bangkok is illuminating. The first thing noticed is that on most buses, the advertisements on the side of the bus adjacent to the footpath are different from the advertisements on the rear of the bus or on the side of the bus adjacent to the traffic. Further examination reveals that the advertisements on the side of the bus adjacent to the footpath are usually for low-unit price, high-volume consumer goods, whereas the advertisements on the other parts of the bus body are for higher-value luxurious items. Investigation reveals that this is deliberate because those who walk can only afford low-cost basic items while those who drive cars are the only ones in a position to purchase high-priced luxury products, many of which are imported.

neutral background or one that most readers, listeners or viewers can identify with regardless of their background.

McDonald's is making an effort to soothe local sensitivities. Ronald McDonald, the firm's Disneyesque mascot, was replaced in its French advertising by Asterix, a French comic-strip character who stands for Gallic individuality and symbolises local resistance to imperial forces.

Media usage by form varies widely between countries. And the usage of various media vehicles changes over time as is illustrated in the case of the US in Table 10.2.

Media selection

Of the media available in the international market, a selection will need to be made based on a number of criteria, each of which will vary in relevance to the international market. In the first place, it is important to be specific as to which is the target. It may be that the audience should be the total population or it may be special interest groups only. A second factor impacting on media selection is the nature of the product or

> ### Table 10.2 Percentage of advertising expenditure by medium in the US
>
> | Medium | 1959 | 1969 | 1979 | 1989 | 1999 |
> |---|---|---|---|---|---|
> | Newspaper | 47.9 | 44.2 | 42.7 | 41.3 | 37.16 |
> | Magazines | 19.9 | 19.9 | 14.2 | 12.1 | 8.3 |
> | Television | 20.7 | 20.7 | 31.2 | 34.3 | 40.1 |
> | Radio | 8.9 | 8.9 | 10.2 | 10.6 | 12.65 |
> | Outdoor | 2.6 | 2.6 | 1.7 | 1.4 | 1.32 |
>
> *Source*: www.adage.com/

service to be promoted. Different media will be more suitable for promoting some products rather than others: if the product needs to be demonstrated, TV would be a preferable medium to press or radio; if the product is at an early stage in its life cycle, then a medium which appeals to innovators and early adopters may be most appropriate. A third factor is the type of message to be conveyed: if it is a complex message, then print may be preferred to radio (because of the limitation of the voice medium) or TV (because of cost due to the need for lengthy explanation and demonstration). A fourth factor impacting on international media selection is the objective of the campaign: if the campaign is to inform rather than to persuade, then technical journals or specialist publications may be preferable to newspapers or mass-circulation magazines.

Print media

Print media consist of headlines, illustrations, body copy and signature/theme/ incentive to action. To ensure the advertisement's appeal, each of these components of the print advertisement may need to be modified when the advertisement is used internationally. In general, the major disadvantage of print media is that they are restricted to the visual senses, whereas some products may also need an audio effect (e.g. the throaty roar of a powerful car engine).

Newspapers   Although newspapers are the print medium with the greatest global spread, newspaper circulation characteristics vary considerably, which influences the cost-effectiveness of this medium. Newspaper editions can be morning or evening, or circulated less frequently than daily. In addition, newspapers can be standard or broadsheet and this has implications for advertising layout and positioning. Newspapers vary widely in terms of both number of copies sold per thousand population and the number of readers per copy. The scope of distribution varies and the fact that the newspaper is distributed nationally does not always indicate a larger circulation. For example in the US, the local newspaper, *Los Angeles Times*, has a much larger circulation than the national newspaper, *US News and World Report*.

The language used in the newspaper will influence its suitability as a promotional vehicle. It is necessary to inquire whether all newspapers are printed in the same language or if there is a bilingual press? In India, for example, the daily metropolitan newspapers containing economic and financial news are in English, while regional daily newspapers are printed in the language of the region. The physical characteristics

Figure 10.4	Differences in page layout for newspapers

Source: Griffin (1994).

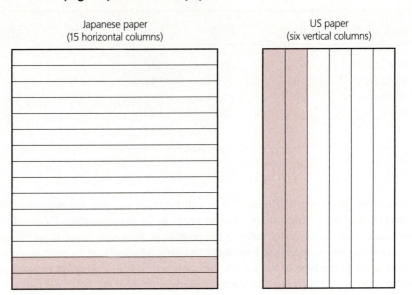

Japanese paper
(15 horizontal columns)

US paper
(six vertical columns)

of newspapers will impact on advertising. This is not only a matter of standard versus broadsheet but also of column width and column direction. Figure 10.4 shows the differences in typical page layout between US and Japanese newspapers. Finally, newspapers can carry a number of different forms of print advertisement – classified, display and supplements.

The advantage of newspapers from a promotional perspective is that newspapers can cope with detailed information and are flexible in terms of coverage. The immediacy of the news that they feature improves the currency of the advertising messages, there is scope for cooperative advertising with retailers if consumer goods are being promoted and there is flexibility as regards shape and size of advertisements. The disadvantages of newspapers are that more than one newspaper may be required to cover the target market, that much of the circulation is likely to be wasted and that the paper and print-ing ink used can reduce the quality of the reproduction. There are also limitations on the use of colour, the life of the message is very short and is usually only one day and the medium is not suitable for the conveying of emotion or for demonstration.

Magazines   Magazines are a selective way of reaching a more targeted audience as, in general, magazines are audience-specific rather than general in appeal. Their availability varies considerably from international market to international market and, in general, the less developed the country the fewer the number of magazines likely to be available. Due to the nature of the editorial content, magazines are likely to have a higher reader involvement than newspapers. Also magazines are likely to have a long life and a greater number of readers per copy. The placement of magazines in waiting rooms and office foyers extends both their life and readership. This medium uses better quality paper and colour reproduction than newpapers, enhancing the suitability of it for promotion of products requiring quality graphic representation. The image of the magazine lends prestige to the goods and services promoted therein. To a greater extent than newspapers, magazines can provide reader attention devices, such as samples and perfume strips.

The disadvantages include the fact that magazines appear usually monthly and rarely weekly. There are long lead times for placement of advertising, deadlines are less flexible and greater forward planning is necessary. Readership is not as immediate and separate language issues can be a problem. In developing countries, infrastructure shortcomings can make magazine circulation a problem and the auditing of circulation numbers in such countries is problematic. The production costs for full-colour advertisements is high, relative to circulation, and the purchase price can be a disincentive as far as the target audience is concerned.

There is a range of regional magazines such as the *Far East Economic Review* or global magazines with regional editions such as *Vogue* or *Time*. In-flight magazines of airlines are another category of publications which cross national borders. In evaluating such magazines, it is desirable to undertake research to make sure that they cater for the segment claimed and that this segment is one that is relevant to the international aspirations for the product.

Other print media   There is a plethora of trade publications available in the more developed countries and some of these find their way to the less developed countries. These are particularly useful if marketing industrial products internationally because they cater for a select audience, most of whom are either in a position to buy the product/service or influence the purchasing decision. One advantage of such media is their interest in new product development and a willingness to feature, along with the advertisement, an editorial piece on the product and its underlying technology.

Commercial sections of telephone directories are another print medium that is available in most countries. The 'Yellow Pages' are available for example in Vietnam in Ho Chi Minh City, Hanoi and in Danang. Often 'Yellow Pages' are the first reference point in the search process. A predominantly local medium, the challenge when using this form is how to get noticed. This can be a matter of the size of the advertisement, the illusion created of the firm's status in the industry, the ability to convey a message of reliability and a 'bait for action', such as 'phone us for the lowest prices'. A key feature of this medium is its wide usage.

Posters, billboards, signage and transit media   Although not print media, the above are forms of advertising which require careful research as to consumer response patterns in international countries if they are to be effective.

Transit advertising on a vehicle is exemplified in International Highlight 10.2. Transit advertising can also be inside the vehicle, such as a bus or a train. This form of advertising is important in countries where private transportation is expensive (Japan) or restricted (Singapore, where mass transit is the norm).

Posters, billboards and signage can also lead to additional publicity in other media e.g. when TV covers an event in the area. It is necessary to ascertain in advance whether there are any regulations in the international country governing what products can be promoted in this manner and what can be said about or claimed for the product, using this medium. Cigarette advertising in many countries is subject to restrictions where outdoor advertising is concerned. Other advantages of this form of advertising are that it can achieve a striking effect due to size, it can build audience coverage quickly and it can reach a broad or selective audience depending on placement. It has geographic and seasonal flexibility and it is not dependent on outlay by the recipient, as with papers, TV or radio. On a cost per viewing basis, it is relatively inexpensive. Its disadvantages are that the viewing span is brief when viewed from a moving vehicle and that because it is usually non-intrusive, it may blend into the background and not be noticed. There is the possibility of a high percentage of wasted viewers, and there is limited opportunity to deliver a written message. Because of its outdoor location there is likelihood of weather and climate damage and, if small quantities are required, the cost of design and artwork may be prohibitive.

Visual media

The main forms of visual media are television and cinema, although some might consider the Internet a visual medium.

Television   The key promotional factors with television are its ability to incorporate attention-getting devices, conveying the message with drama, suspense or humour, and the ability to make a claim and prove it. These advantages are facilitated by its having a continuous story line from introduction to close; using a mix of voices, sounds and music; and being able to capture the way the product appears and performs by showing 'in use' situations. Although regulations on television commercials vary from country to country, new forms such as satellite TV and some forms of cable TV may reduce the ability of nations to control what their citizens view when the signal is beamed in from outside its borders. Because different countries gained TV at different times, the quality of transmission can vary as does the audience reach. These factors need to be taken into account when evaluating the cost per reach of this medium in international markets.

Advantages include the ability to involve the additional sensory effects of sound and motion and an ability to show change and demonstrate outcomes. In addition, it delivers a captive audience because viewers must make a deliberate effort to avoid seeing the commercial. Furthermore, TV can deliver a national or a major regional audience and it can impart credibility to the advertiser's message because it tends to be regarded as a source of informed opinion.

The main disadvantage is one of cost and this excludes many advertisers. Cost is not just in the rate per minute but also in the expense of producing TV commercials. The audience receiving the message tends to be non-selective. Also the availability of advertising time in association with programmes that deliver large audiences is limited, costly and often subject to government regulation. The life of the message is short which means that this medium cannot be used by the customer as a vehicle for search and product selection. Finally, advertising intensity on this medium often causes noise due to conflicting claims by other advertisers of similar products.

Cinema   Overall its importance is diminishing but it is still important in some countries, especially those with lower incomes. It is a medium targeted at a local audience and therefore suitable for international test market activities. The audience characteristics need prior research as audiences differ from country to country. In India, for example, cinema audiences are predominantly male.

Audio media

Radio   This is the main form of audio media and it relies on the sense of sound. The mental picture created can be added to by use of sound forms other than voice.

10.3 International highlight

Advertising with local knowledge and understanding

Heineken has moved its US$10 million advertising account to McCann-Erickson in Ireland. This is the first time in five years that the beer account will be managed by an Irish advertising agency. The move back to a Dublin-based agency reverses a trend, which in recent years has seen the creative work for most major beer brands being done by UK or American agencies. Due to international brand alignment, the Heineken current campaign in the Irish and UK market has been very obviously a US-generated campaign by the Lowe group. Heineken is aware how alcohol advertising can cause adverse publicity. Indeed, the Irish Advertising Standards Authority recently banned three beer advertisements. Part of the problem was that the campaign for Coors, Guinness and Carlsberg were developed outside the market and so were somehow out of touch with the cultural reference points. This was one of the reasons Heineken was interested in a local agency that it believes will have local knowledge and understanding. McCann-Erickson is part of the McCann-Erickson WorldGroup.

Commercials are usually measured by the number of seconds, and the number of words that can be conveyed in a 30-second slot can vary according to the language used. In English, for example, it would be 65 words. When creating a radio message it is necessary to address a number of issues in relation to the international audience and market. These include adherence to strategy and ensuring that the script contains the essential elements of the message to be communicated. Also required is that the commercial be sufficiently simple for the listener to grasp the principal idea; that the commercial stimulates interest (rather than a yawn!) by having some attention-getting device at the start and that the language used is simple and the sentences short. Finally the commercial should be memorable and suitable for frequent repetition – a use of a jingle or a catchy tune can help achieve this outcome.

The advantages of radio are its relatively low cost and its ability to deliver messages at or away from home as with drive-time radio. Some stations have a highly selective audience and radio also has the advantage of short lead times for placing advertisements, low production costs, and a large number of local radio stations whose existence facilitates geographic segmentation. Disadvantages involve the limited effectiveness of this medium in delivering to a nationwide audience, a fatigue factor from listeners hearing the same message over and over again, and noise from a competing stations all airing a large number of commercials each hour.

Global media

There are an increasing number of media that transcend national boundaries. There are media that operate in a region rather than in a country, such as the footprint map of satellite TV (e.g. Rupert Murdoch's Sky Channel). In addition, there are media that are targeted at a global segment (e.g. prestige magazines like *National Geographic*), and new forms of media that are global in design (e.g. the Internet).

Global print media   Global print media consist of general newspapers, such as *US News and World Report* and the *International Herald Tribune*. It can also involve a newspaper that has a number of different country editions such as the *Wall Street Journal* (European and Asian editions plus special editions in 25 countries). The *China Daily* of the PRC is published by satellite simultaneously in China, the US and Europe. Magazines are more likely to be global because the news they contain is not so perishable. Some magazines emanate from one location and are distributed in many countries, such as *The Economist*, and others are produced in a number of languages in a number of different locations, such as *Time* that publishes 133 different editions, or *Reader's Digest* that publishes 41 editions. The internationalisation of magazines has increased with international consolidation among magazine publishers.

Global visual media   CNN is the leader and reaches consumers in over 100 countries and has a number of competitors. The biggest growth is in satellite television which is the most prominent form of global visual media and has already impacted on other media with local or regional coverage. Satellite messages can be received via rebroadcasting in traditional form on the cable network or per medium of a satellite dish. Beaming messages into other countries, as happens with Star TV in Hong Kong being able to access 4.8 million homes in mainland China, opens up new opportunities for international promotion.

Global audio media   International commercial radio is important, especially in western Europe where a number of commercial stations reach several nations (e.g. Radio Luxembourg). Such global media are useful for reaching non-literate populations. In addition, there are a number of national radio networks such as the BBC that currently do not accept advertising. Should this change with privatisation, then this will create another powerful medium for global or regional promotion.

Internet   The Internet removes many barriers to communication with customers by eliminating the obstacles created by geography, time zones and location and in the process creates a 'frictionless' business environment. The long-term growth of the Internet raises the opportunity for cross-border information flows and transactions. At present the Internet is mostly an English medium. In 1998 it was estimated that of the online population of 178 million users, 60% of the population used English, 28% other European languages and 12% Asian languages. By 2005, it is estimated that the majority of Internet traffic will be in languages other than English. This trend is likely to be the result of increased adoption in less developed countries.

Global media and national boundaries   Not only do global media spread information across national borders, but this development makes it increasingly difficult for national governments to prevent their citizens from receiving the messages which may come from environments with different social values and political systems. Most governments have regulations governing advertising but global media call into question the degree of enforceability of these regulations as well as issues of national sovereignty.

Language and mass media

There are three aspects of language and mass media that require comment. These are use of foreign words, impact on advertisement layout and translation problems.

Foreign words are often used in advertisements to enhance the image of the product. The foreign word can create an association with a country or a region and this can enhance awareness as well as identification. Foreign words are often embodied in logos which result in their reinforcing the image of the product being promoted. Sometimes foreign words are used in advertising because the local language is incapable of conveying precise meaning or because a technical term only exists in one language and most in the field are familiar with that term. Usually it is European words that are used as foreign words in advertisements.

Language affects the layout of advertisements because different languages, regardless of whether written in characters or script, require different amounts of space to convey the same message. Thai, for example, requires 35% to 50% more space than English. This means that in an advertisement the balance between visual and written elements may need to be reviewed when advertising in international markets or more space needs to be paid for per advertisement. Similarly with spoken advertising, the number of words required to convey the idea or concept may result in a longer radio or TV commercial.

It is important to translate the concept rather than the words when translating an advertisement from one language to another. Failure to do so results in mistakes such as 'full aeroplane' in English becoming 'pregnant aeroplane' in French or 'body by Fisher' becoming 'corpse by Fisher' in German. Any translation must be made culturally relevant in the target language and this may cause not only the original English text to change but also the tone of the advertisement to alter. It is desirable once the advertisement has been translated into the other language to arrange for a back translation from the other language into English, to ensure that the correct concept and message is being conveyed.

Publicity and public relations

These activities can be regarded as communication between an organisation and its 'publics' to achieve specific objectives based on mutual understanding. The publics of the firm are broader than the market it serves and include all those that are affected by the firm's operations – customers, general public, stockholders, government, media, suppliers, employees, activist groups, financial community and distributors (Terpstra and Sarathy, 2000, p. 505). In normal situations, publicity and public relations can be used to create or enhance a favourable image. In the international arena, it is a useful way of combating nationalistic criticism. In crisis situations, publicity and public relations not only facilitate a response to criticism but also provide the opportunity to explain proposed remedial action and to head off criticism harmful to the corporate image. In the international scene, however, publicity and public relations must be culturally sensitive and attuned to local customs and commercial practices. Apart from public relations activities, sponsorships and loyalty programmes are becoming increasingly important publicity activities in international marketing. Underlying the increasing importance of public relations is the view that marketing today must do more than manage the 4Ps – it must also try to manage the environment, especially political power and public opinion. This concept of mega-marketing is particularly important when doing business in countries where the firm is likely to lack a deep understanding of the culture and the politics.

News releases

In many countries, being 'foreign' may be newsworthy itself. Ways of securing news releases are to hold international press conferences to announce a new product, a different strategy or a significant linkage with a local interest. No matter how good the public relations consultant might be, it is always necessary to have a newsworthy message to convey, otherwise the 'take up' of the press release will be less than enthusiastic. Associated with this is support for good causes in the international country, which lessens the image of the firm being yet another foreign company 'trying to rip us off'. This support might take the form of a donation, an endowment, making a gift of physical property with the name of the firm carved/labelled on the gift, or a promotional campaign with a percentage of sales/earnings going to a nominated charity.

Sponsorships

These relate a company or a brand to an event in order to benefit from the exploitable commercial potential associated with that activity. The most talked-about recent events in this connection were the 2000 Sydney Olympic Games and the 2002 World Cup. Globally, sponsorships are big business with the value exceeding US$5 billion annually. Sporting activities attract most sponsorships with the arts coming second. Usually the sponsor contributes funds to defray a portion of the production costs of the event.

Sponsorships have grown as a promotional vehicle. This is because funding by public bodies has been cut back and funds have to be obtained from other sources. The globalisation of mass media increases the reach of the sponsor's message in relation to a specific event such as the global coverage Coca-Cola obtained as a result of its sponsorship of the Olympic Games in Atlanta. Changing lifestyles and technology have delivered larger audiences for sports and arts events. As traditional forms of promotion become more expensive and message clutter via these media increases, there is a desire for new, 'less spoilt' forms of promotion and extensive possibilities exist for the sporting or arts figure to endorse the sponsor's product.

Research by Thompson and Quester (2000) has found that sponsorship effectiveness is directly related to the degree to which sponsors are willing to leverage their investment with additional forms of promotional expenditure.

Public relations activities

The attraction of public relations is that the resulting messages come across as news and therefore have more credibility than advertising. Public relations consultants value the space occupied by the PR release in the print media or the number of minutes coverage on TV or radio as being worth around three times the value of advertising rates. Public relations do not lead to immediate sales but improve cumulative favourable awareness. In international marketing, PR is particularly useful if the product is not widely known or if there is a country of origin image problem. When used abroad, PR releases should not simply be newsworthy but should have an intriguing application, identify with the needs of the international market and be supported with good quality photographs, preferably showing 'in use' situations with which international readers/viewers can identify.

Public relations can also be used to correct misleading impressions or unfavourable images in the international country as the following example illustrates:

After the Asian crisis began in 1997, the Thai baht dropped dramatically in value. A government campaign was launched urging consumers to 'buy Thai, eat Thai'. Even the revered Thai king urged his subjects to 'buy Thai'. Research by Damask/BBDO Thailand showed that 80% of the respondents believed that buying 'foreign' products hurts Thailand. Thai TV news broadcasts on this issue frequently used McDonald's 'golden arches' as a backdrop. Instead of fighting this campaign in a direct way, McDonald's began to promote the idea that it contributes to Thailand's foreign exchange reserves rather than draining them. Dej Belsuk, CEO of McThai, the joint venture with 51% Thai ownership, noted that for every dollar of imports, McDonald's exports seven dollars worth of goods, not only to other Asian countries but also to Europe. Customers did not know that up to 90% of a typical meal served by McDonald's consisted of locally grown products. McDonald's used tray mats to convey such information as well as the TV and the press. After Dej Belsuk appeared on TV, there was a noticeable recovery in sales. The advertising of the next new product launch was built around traditional Thai images to reinforce local identification.

Source: Adapted from *Business Asia*, 29 June 1998, p. 3.

The use of public relations in Asian markets varies considerably, depending on how the market and the government view it as a promotional vehicle. In China, it has long been used to promote official policies to the population and was used extensively in the international domain by the government to support its successful bid to host the 2008 Olympic Games. By contrast, in Vietnam, many local businesses still view it as advertising and human relations, although this is slowly changing due to the PR activities of foreign firms operating in that country.

Loyalty programmes

These are sales promotions in which loyalty is acknowledged in the form of meaningful rewards to the customer – usually in the form of the marketer's own product. This reduces the cost of the programme as happens with frequent flyer schemes. When using such schemes in international marketing, it is necessary to ascertain whether the scheme is regarded favourably or suspiciously in the international country and whether the reward is perceived as offering the same value as it would be in the domestic market. For example, a free domestic flight or hotel night might be a most attractive reward in a poor nation but a lesser incentive in a rich nation.

Agencies

There are intermediaries available in international markets to assist with many forms of promotion, including advertising, media buying, exhibition organisation and public relations. The intermediary not only knows the local scene and what is culturally acceptable, but also knows how to work with what is available in the international market. When engaging an international intermediary, the firm is buying access to a network of contacts as well as the service the intermediary provides. Table 10.3 shows the world's leading advertising agencies in terms of both gross income and billings.

Advertising agencies can be local or international and many international agencies were domestic agencies that followed their international clients, such as Lintas of the

---

Table 10.3 World's top advertising agencies 2001

Rank/Company	Headquarters	Worldwide gross income 2001	% chg	Billings 2001
1 WPP Group	London	$8,165.0	2.5	$75,711.0
2 Interpublic Group of Cos.	New York	7,981.4	−1.9	66,689.1
3 Omnicom Group	New York	7,404.2	6.0	58,080.1
4 Publicis Groupe (includes Bcom3 Group)	Paris	4,769.9	2.0	52,892.2
5 Dentsu	Tokyo	2,795.5	−8.9	20,847.8
6 Havas Advertising	Levallois-Perret, France	2,733.1	−2.1	26,268.5
7 Grey Global Group	New York	1,863.6	1.7	12,105.7
8 Cordiant Communications Group	London	1,174.5	−7.0	13,388.0
9 Hakuhodo	Tokyo	874.3	−13.0	6,862.2
10 Asatsu-DK	Tokyo	394.6	−8.7	3,500.6

Notes: Figures are in US dollars in millions. Ranked by gross income in 2001 by all marketing-related activites.
Source: Ad Age Agency Report. Taken from Adageglobal.com (30 April 2002).

UK and Dentsu of Japan. In some cases these agencies operate autonomously in international markets, and in others, such as Dentsu, they form joint ventures with local agencies. International companies will need to decide whether all communications services in the international market should be provided by one full service agency or whether different services, such as creative or media buying, should be supplied by local specialist firms. Because the exporter is highly dependent on the agency in the international market, selection should be undertaken carefully. Whether to choose a local or the subsidiary of an international agency may be determined by what is available in the international market and the international strategy of the firm. Of particular relevance will be the extent and the quality of the coverage the agency provides, the other marketing services it can provide (e.g. market research, public relations etc.) and its size relative to the exporter. If the agency is large and the exporter's billings are modest, the service provided by the agency may be indifferent. If the reverse is the case, or the size of client and agency are in balance, then the agency is likely to try harder and devote more attention to the account.

Exhibition organisers offer similar advantages to locally based advertising agencies abroad and can facilitate not only participation in a trade show but also involvement in associated promotional activities. Media buying is a specialist activity and media buyers can plan advertising strategies in the international market. Using the strength of their local media contact networks and bulk buying shared among their clients, they can obtain media exposure at favourable rates. They are also useful in countries where media availability is restricted and in evaluating alternatives when the media used in the domestic market is not available. Public relations firms are important in promoting in markets where cultural sensitivity is an issue because they can assist in positioning the product or service in an acceptable way.

Evaluating advertising effectiveness

This is more difficult in many international markets than it is in the domestic market due to market size and the lack of market research vehicles for this purpose (e.g. the regular surveys of Nielsen), and the distance and communications gap between the market and the international marketer. As a consequence, international marketers will have to undertake their own research or devise surrogate indicators along the lines of those mentioned in Chapter 6.

Push strategies

Push strategies in the international marketplace primarily involve sales promotion and personal selling.

Sales promotion

Sales promotion plays a much more important role in international marketing than it does in domestic marketing. In part this is due to the focus in international marketing on introducing new products to the marketplace and getting them into local distribution channels. Whereas in the domestic market, sales promotion is often in the form of contests, coupons, sampling, premiums, money-off deals etc., in international marketing the most important form is the trade show. Where the former are used they must be attractive to the buyer in the international country, acceptable from a social and cultural perspective and conform to local regulations as to acceptable forms of promotion.

Trade shows

One of the oldest forms of trade promotion, trade shows, dates back to the medieval fairs. They are an affordable form of promotion for smaller firms venturing abroad for the first time and are a convenient way of testing reaction to the product. They are particularly important for international business-to-business marketing because trade promotion is more important than advertising where industrial products are concerned. Trade shows provide the opportunity for meeting potential purchasers without making an appointment and, because there are exhibitors of both local and imported competitive products, they provide an opportunity for gathering intelligence on the market. As complementary products are being promoted at trade shows, they are also a means of finding potential agents and distributors from among other exhibitors at the show, as well as from visitors. Trade shows provide the opportunity for potential buyers to see and demonstrate the product. They are important in creating credibility for an imported product from an unknown source of supply. They are also an economic medium for sales promotion. It is generally accepted that a visitor to a trade show costs the exhibitor less than making a sales call.

Figure 10.5 shows that trade shows can perform a selling function, a promotion function and a network-creating function. The selling function involves primarily

Figure 10.5	Three conceptions of trade fairs

Source: Adapted from
Rossen and Seringhaus
(1996), p. 1181.

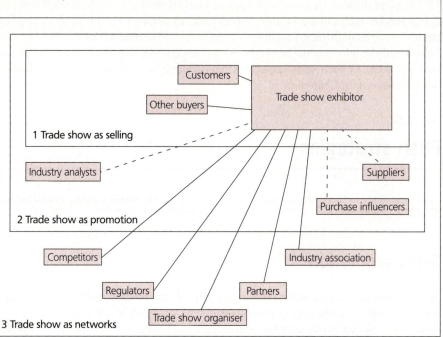

customers and other buyers, while the promotion function includes suppliers, influencers of the purchasing decision, and industry analysts. The network-creating function includes other stakeholders, such as competitors, regulators, show organisers, partners and industry associations.

Trade shows take a number of forms. They can be open to the public or for the trade only or a combination of trade-only days followed by one or two public days at the end. Shows open to the public are useful for consumer goods or products already available in the international country or in cases where the specific objective is to reinforce awareness. Trade-only shows in foreign markets are more suitable for industrial products, for firms seeking representation or for promoting items of large unit value.

Trade shows can also be classified according to whether they are general or specialised. The general trade show covers a wide variety of unrelated products and is usually mounted to create an awareness of the range of products a country wishes to promote in the international country. They are often mounted in countries where the trade show infrastructure, such as convention centres and exhibition halls, is sparse and specialised trade shows are non-existent. The emphasis is on a public rather than a trade audience, especially if the show is to mark a specific event of an 'Expo' type. Specialised trade shows concentrate on narrow product categories, such as mining equipment, and are usually only open to the trade. Although they are smaller than general trade displays, some can be quite large, such as the COMDEX computer show in the US where the number of exhibitors runs into thousands. Often the specialised show is the major event in the calendar of a specific industry and may attract a regional or global audience rather than just a national one. Often new product launches are timed to coincide with the industry's annual trade show.

The range of opportunities to display goods in the international country is extensive. These include:

- the firm hiring space in a hotel and setting up its own display and inviting potential buyers to view it;
- mounting a display in embassy premises and arranging for the Trade Commissioner to issue invitations; and
- the firm participating in an organised trade show on its own account.

Effective participation in international trade shows usually requires research in advance, active involvement in attracting an appropriate audience, contingency plans to overcome infrastructure problems, an understanding of visitors' motivations, and a realistic appraisal of results.

Research   This is necessary to establish what is the best trade show for the firm in the target country, in terms of the current stage of penetration of that market and objectives for that market. Research is also necessary to ensure that the audience profile matches objectives and to see whether a significant percentage of the audience attracted to the show is relevant in terms of participation objectives. In this connection it is useful to obtain an indication as to what percentage of the audience is local as opposed to regional or global. Research is also necessary to establish the full cost of participation as this is easy to underestimate. Such costs can include renting space, dressing the exhibit, connecting facilities, such as power and water, shipment and clearance of exhibits, putting up customs bonds, provision for emergency air freight if shipment is delayed, hire of furniture and equipment for the exhibit and hire of local people to assist and interpret. Costs should also take into account sending executives to man the exhibit, supplementary promotional activities in conjunction with participation to attract visitors to stop at the firm's exhibit including direct mail, advertising and PR activities, and a contingency of at least 10% of the total costs.

Attracting an audience   Although in many cases the trade show organisers promise an audience and have a publicity campaign to attract an audience, it is desirable for the firm to supplement this with its own campaign. Such a campaign should be aimed at ensuring that the visitors to the trade show are aware of the stand before their visit. Advertising in the trade show catalogue is useful, particularly if the catalogue is distributed in advance of the trade show. Publicising a competition in advance, entry to which requires a visit to the stand, is also useful. A technique employed by many trade exhibitors is to have a competition which would be drawn from business cards left in a large goldfish bowl at the stand. In advance of the show, the competition would be publicised in industry publications or via notices slipped under the doors of delegates' hotel rooms.

Another way of attracting an audience is to operate additional events timed to coincide with exhibiting at the trade show. These could take the form of a technical seminar or a cocktail party held at the hotel recommended for the accommodation of exhibitors by the trade show organisers.

Infrastructure issues   Unless the firm already has an agent in the country and the exhibits are supplied from the agent's stock, then the exhibit material has to be shipped from the home market. Goods should be shipped well in advance of the normal shipping time to allow for contingencies. The manager of the exhibit should arrive in the country at least three days before the show opens. This enables full recovery from jet lag (depending on the distance travelled) and allows time to take action to correct mistakes at the exhibit site and to oversee the dressing of the stand. It also provides the manager with the opportunity to telephone key contacts and invite them to visit the stand. A local person should be hired as a translator and a 'Mr (or Ms) Fixit'. It is important to become familiar with customs procedures for entry and disposal/reshipment of exhibit material. It is also necessary to develop a fallback plan to cater for contingencies. This could include knowing what type of generator to hire if power is not connected to the exhibit and having plenty of spares in the exhibit shipment in case of local problems, such as damage in transit or pilferage. It is also desirable to remain in the city several days after the display closes to oversee disposal/reshipment of display goods and to follow up with promising contacts made as a result of participating in the trade display. A final infrastructure problem relates to staffing the exhibit. It is essential that the exhibit be staffed at all times. Because manning trade displays is exhausting, local conditions can create health problems for visitors, it is therefore important to have sufficient people to man the stand to give reasonable breaks and to allow for any of the above contingencies.

Visitor motivations   Visitors attend trade shows for different reasons. Adopting a customer orientation to attracting the right prospects to the exhibit requires an understanding of their reasons. Research has shown that these reasons can be categorised as viewing new products or developments; strong interest in the field of activity covered by the display; seeing a particular product or meeting a specific company; attending a training session held in conjunction with the trade display; or obtaining technical information. Exhibition organisers are often able to provide this information based on questionnaires completed by visitors to the display in previous years. Table 10.4 shows the results of research in this connection.

Measuring outcomes   Outcomes should be measured against specific rather than 'rubbery' objectives. Specific measures could include: (1) the number of leads generated and the quality of sales from those leads; (2) the number of potential agents/distributors located and the likelihood of establishing a good distribution network as a result; (3) the number of visitors to the exhibit and the percentage who displayed active interest and accepted literature on the product; (4) the sales which were actually made at the display; and (5) a realistic appraisal of sales likely to directly result over the next 12 months.

Technical seminars

This form of international promotion is particularly useful when marketing an international product or service that embodies a technology new to that market. It involves hiring a venue with audio-visual or screening capability and mounting a seminar designed to attract people interested in the technology being promoted. The invitees can be those who make the purchasing decision, those who influence the decision, and those in regulatory authorities whose approval might be needed to market the new technology. Seminars are particularly appropriate for reaching 'influencers', as opposed to

	Totally unimportant (1)	Unimportant (2)	Medium (3)	Important (4)	Essential (5)	Average (6)
Table 10.4 What the visitor is looking for						
Buying exhibited products	43.3	24.2	17.2	9.6	5.7	2.10
Contracting potential suppliers	5	3.1	9.4	34.6	47.8	4.17
Seeking new ideas/carrying out market research	2.5	6.3	12.6	41.5	37.1	4.04
Finding out about competitors	8.8	11.3	21.4	33.3	25.2	3.55
Discovering new lines or new products	1.9	1.3	6.9	47.8	42.1	4.27
Discovering new applications of the product	24.1	15.2	17.1	25.9	17.7	2.98
Obtaining information about the operation of industrial machinery not easily transportable and investigating technical features by specialised staff	24.3	13.5	20.9	24.3	16.9	2.96
Meeting specialists		23.6	24.8	36.9	14.6	3.29
Comparing market prices	14.5	10.7	17.6	32.7	24.5	3.42

Source: Munvera and Ruiz (1993), p. 1032.

purchasers, and can facilitate their early involvement in development projects where new technology is relevant. A prestigious venue is necessary and the seminar must have education or information value. It is also very suitable for products which require demonstration or complex explanation. Technical seminars are valuable in cases where there is a degree of uncertainty about the technology if it has not been seen in the country before, or where it has not yet been accepted as a natural solution to a specific type of problem situation.

Personal selling

Although personal selling involves both salesforce activities and trade missions, it is the latter which is a promotional activity mostly found in international marketing.

Trade missions

Trade missions are like a series of blind dates as they are designed to introduce parties who for the most part are unknown to each other. The facilitation is via the mediation of a government or chamber of commerce that acts as a sponsor for the members of the trade mission. Trade missions can be inward or outward. Inward trade missions involve bringing the buyers to the home market. The members of the inward mission are then introduced to firms that wish to develop relations with them. Inward missions can also be organised by the government of the international country but paid for by the host government as part of their aid activities or under the framework of a bilateral agreement between the countries. Research by Wilkinson and Brouthers (2000) shows that trade missions are a highly effective vehicle for attracting foreign direct investment.

Outward trade missions, however, are the most common and involve exporters visiting the international market. These missions can be:

- *general* and designed to create an awareness of the country as a source of supply. Usually these missions do not include competing firms;
- *policy-related* such as creating an awareness of national capability in an area of activity involving government;
- *product-category* and confined to an industry or industry segment. This type of mission can often involve competing firms;
- *project-related* and consisting of a range of non-competing firms with the collective capability to undertake the project for which tenders are likely to be called.

Most trade missions are sponsored by government, which gives them credibility and improves the access in the international country for members of the mission. These missions are led by a senior political figure, as is often the case with general trade missions, or by a senior government official, as with policy-related or project-related missions, or by a leading industry figure as with product-category missions. The leadership is important because it influences the level and extent of access, the degree of publicity obtained, and the attendance at mission hospitality functions.

Trade missions can also be sponsored by industry associations or chambers of commerce and are confined to members of that association or chamber. The credibility tends to be less although this can be compensated for in part by having the commercial section of the embassy make VIP appointments for the mission leader and host mission social functions.

The advantages of a trade mission as a form of international trade promotion are that it facilitates the acquisition of information on the international market, enables access to decision-makers at a senior level and puts mission members in contact with planners and regulators. It also generates publicity for the member's products/services because the mission has news value and assists in relationship building, since the initial introduction was as a member of the trade mission. In addition, there is the benefit of sharing experiences with other mission members which leads to synergy (resulting in a deeper investigation of the market) and the production of a trade mission report, which assists future credibility in the market. Because the trade mission is mobile, it can cover more ground by visiting regional areas. It is better than many other forms of international trade promotion which are anchored in one place. There are also efficiencies in the amount of time spent in the international market due the organisation of appointments, transport and hospitality in advance of the mission's arrival. Disadvantages relate to the possible existence of competitors on the mission, the long planning time required, the fact that participation is generally by invitation only, and the fact that fewer contacts can be made than at trade shows.

Salesforce activities

Personal selling in international markets is different from personal selling in the domestic market because it involves crossing national borders and managing relationships with people from a different cultural background. Often the firm is unknown in the other country and there may be a country-of-origin problem with the product or service. These problems, which do not exist back home in the domestic market, can be overcome by a sensitive approach and a selling strategy that concentrates on relationship building. Selling internationally requires a prior understanding of the norms regarding introductions to new contacts, the getting-to-know-you phase of the relationship and expectations as to the conduct of the initial interview. Some strategies in selling in a new international market are noted below:

- Be prepared. Study the culture, the politics, the geography, the history, the industry structure, the role of the client in that industry and the background to the client's operation. This will create the impression that the salesperson has taken the trouble to learn about the client and the environment within which the client operates.

- Slow down the pace of negotiation if you're in Asia, or speed up the pace if you're in the US, depending on the norm in that country. Exercise patience because delays in reaching a decision may be due to time being spent on researching the accuracy of your firm's claim.

- It is important not to try to hurry a decision in countries where the time taken to arrive at a decision is proportional to the importance of the decision. In the eyes of the other party, to hurry a decision diminishes the importance the executive attaches to the negotiation.

- Be careful of body language and the way it is interpreted in the other country. It is important to be sure that body language is consistent with the meaning of the spoken words, and that any gestures/actions are not offensive in the local culture.

- Spend time on relationship building in cultures where this is valued before getting down to business. It is important to understand the role of entertainment in the target market, especially when to offer, how lavish is the expectation, the form it should take, and the preferred location.

The criteria for recruiting, selecting and managing the salesforce in another country will differ markedly from those in the domestic for a variety of social and cultural reasons as exemplified in the following:

- *Japan*: individual recognition of sales reps is still at odds with the nation's team approach to business.
- *Saudi Arabia*: finding qualified sales reps is difficult because of a labour shortage and the low prestige of selling.
- *India*: salesforce management is difficult in a market fragmented by language divisions and the caste system.

Source: Terpstra and Sarathy (2000), p. 485.

One of the issues that will need to be addressed is whether the selling should be undertaken in the international market by a member of your own sales team or by a national

Table 10.5 Contingency factors in selecting sales force nationality

Technology level	Management orientation					
	Ethnocentric		Polycentric		Regiocentric	
	Developed	Less developed	Developed	Less developed	Developed	Less developed
High	Expatriates	Expatriates	Expatriates	Host-country nationals	Expatriates	Third-country nationals
Low	Expatriates	Expatriates	Host-country nationals	Host-country nationals (agents)	Third-country nationals	Third-country nationals (agents)

Source: Reprinted from Honeycutt and Ford (1995), p. 139, with permission of Elsevier Science.

of the international country. Often this depends on the technical sophistication of the product or service involved, as illustrated in Table 10.5.

The advantages and disadvantages of using professional expatriates, as opposed to your own employees or as opposed to locals, are set out in Table 10.6.

Brochures

It is not sufficient for the salesperson to be knowledgeable about and culturally sensitive towards the international market. Such sensitivity must also be reflected in the material they distribute. Apart from local regulations with handout material, e.g. content, local expectations/norms as to size and quality; and cultural requirements, e.g. appropriate colours, care is needed with translation, graphics and with what is depicted in the brochure lest its impact is misleading, irrelevant or inappropriate.

Direct mail

At the consumer level in international marketing, direct mail is used to reach high-income groups and international travellers. At the commercial level, it is often used as a substitute for a repeat sales call and as a supplement to other forms of promotion such as inviting attendance at an exhibit at a trade display. It can also be used as a means of obtaining qualified sales leads for local agents in the international market.

Difficulties with operating international direct-mail campaigns often relate to differing postal regulations between countries, different envelope and paper sizes, variable quality of direct mail lists especially in terms of recency and targeting. Other problems can be due to the decision-making units in companies being different from country to country or there being different reactions in the country to direct mail solicitations. Whereas in some countries there is a tendency to treat commercial direct mail as junk (as in the US) or environmentally wasteful (as in Germany), in other countries it tends to be regarded more as a source of information (as in Indonesia).

Table 10.6 Advantages and disadvantages of different sales types

Category	Advantages	Disadvantages
Expatriates	Superior product knowledge Demonstrated commitment to high customer service standards Train for promotion Greater HQ control	Highest cost High turnover Cost of language and cross-cultural training
Host country	Economical Superior market knowledge Language skills Superior cultural knowledge Implement actions sooner	Need product training May be held in low esteem Language skills may not be important Diffcult to ensure loyalty
Third country	Cultural sensitivity Language skills Economical Allows regional sales coverage	Face identity problems Blocked promotions Income gaps Need product or company training Loyalty not assured

Source: Reprinted from Honeycutt and Ford (1995), p. 138, with permission of Elsevier Science.

Communication in emerging markets

It is apparent that there is a need to tailor the communications to the market being targeted. This is particularly important when promoting products in emerging markets where the mass of the world's population is located and where future markets for products and services are likely to be based. Research by Fletcher (2001) tested the applicability of the communications model (shown in Figure 10.1 at the beginning of the chapter), to both the urban middle class and the lower urban/rural groups in a typical Asian emerging market, viz. Vietnam.

As far as sender-oriented aspects of the model were concerned, research in Vietnam showed a greater focus on utilitarian appeals than aesthetic appeals; an even split between preference for information as opposed to persuasion, although information was definitely preferred to persuasion among the lower urban/rural group; and a definite need for the message content to be politically sensitive. Appeals to group benefit were preferred among the lower urban/rural group. There was a small preference for messages that appealed to cultural universals and a definite preference for messages that appealed to long-term loyalty rather than stimulating a short-term reaction. There was a preference that the presenter of the message should be a Vietnamese, especially among the lower urban/rural group. The findings revealed a modest preference for use of testimonials in advertising and that a high degree of power distance should be reflected in both the presenter and the message content. There was a definite preference for messages to be encoded in specific rather than in abstract terms and that messages should rely on verbal rather than on non-verbal stimuli.

Concerning medium-oriented aspects, it was found that there was widespread usage of radio among lower urban/rural but little usage among the urban middle class. The reverse was the case with TV. Internet usage was moderate/low among the urban middle class but virtually non-existent with the lower urban/rural group. The extent of government control over media was high and the availability of infrastructure (e.g. computers, coaxial cable and TV sets) was more of a problem among the lower urban/rural group for whom affordability was an even greater issue.

With respect to receiver-oriented aspects, the research showed that promotional messages tended to be received in a group situation, especially among the lower urban/rural sectors. The way people responded to messages was more likely to be influenced by a desire to conform than by individualistic behaviour. Message response was not highly dependent on literacy/education levels, although this was somewhat of a factor with the lower urban/rural group. Finally it appears that message response is more likely to be influenced by emotional appeals among the lower urban/rural group than is the case with the urban middle class.

Concerning the interference aspect of the model, whereas group or ethnic affiliation did not create interference to a major extent among the urban middle group, it did have a greater impact among the lower urban/rural group. On the other hand, local or regional loyalties tended to override the individual reaction to messages to a much greater extent. Although government controls over the media are high, the directives seem to have only limited impact on individual reaction to messages, although this impact is greater among the lower urban/rural group.

As far as feedback was concerned, in general it was found that there was little reluctance to express an opinion and that obtaining a reaction to promotion via market research was not all that difficult.

Issues

There are a number of issues unique to promotion and advertising in the international marketplace. Two of the most important are country of origin and the possibility of standardisation as opposed to differentiation in approach.

Country of origin

Country of origin provides the customer with a tangible cue for evaluation when other less obvious features are difficult to assess. Its importance is directly linked to product and brand knowledge and the greater the knowledge of the product or brand, the less the need to use country of origin for evaluation (Lampert and Jaffe, 1998). The country of origin can either add to the image or detract from the image of the product, depending on whether the image of the country in the specific product category is positive, negative or non-existent. With globalisation, country of origin is becoming a more complex issue.

Research by Mort and Duncan (2000) in Australia found that increasingly 'owned by' was just as important a country of origin cue as 'made in'. As the following indicates, 'made in' often does not mean what is implied. Volkswagens are now German engineered rather than German made; Ikea furniture is now Swedish designed rather than Swedish made; although 'Yoplait is French for yogurt', the product is made in Ireland and Australia not France, and the nuts in 'Queensland Fruit and Nuts' are from China rather than Queensland. Known as 'captions cues', the use of misleading, deceptive or ambiguous country-of-origin cues is a widespread practice in international marketing (Mueller et al., 2001).

The above examples indicate that with the increase in the number of global firms, although products are produced in a variety of locations, they are being promoted as associated with whichever country has the strongest country of origin image. Country-of-origin image can be embedded in the brand name as with Alitalia Airlines or *France-Soir* newspaper; and it can be indicated through a brand name which sounds like a word in a particular language, such as Lamborghini or Toyota; or in the manufacturer's name, such as Nippon Steel. Country of origin can also be included as part of the logo or package design – examples include the stylised kangaroo on the Qantas logo or implied by the uniforms worn by salesforce or delivery people, e.g. the red, white and blue uniforms of Domino's delivery people could indicate association with the US. Country image can also be conveyed by images, such as a bowler hat to indicate British, by use of personalities identified with a country, such as Paul Hogan for Australia, or by geographic association, e.g. the Rocky Mountains for Coors Beer.

One subject of current research is whether the country image comes first followed by beliefs and then attitudes or whether beliefs or attitudes come first and lead to an evaluation about products from that country. The first is termed the 'halo construct' and operates where consumers are unfamiliar with the product. The second is termed the 'summary construct' and operates where consumers know the product and form conclusions about the country of its origin based on their experience of products from that source.

Standardisation versus differentiation

Earlier discussion points to the need for international promotion and advertising to be tailored to the needs of each country. Yet there is a move towards globalisation which implies that promotion and advertising approaches should be standardised in the interests of economies of scale and because customers worldwide are being driven by the same needs. Also communications improvements are making customers in one country aware of what customers are demanding in another. Despite this, only about 10% of the *Fortune* 500 firms were committed to standardised global advertising. Although the trend is increasing, even transnational firms are not adopting this practice on a wide scale.

In deciding whether to try for a global approach in promotion and advertising, it is necessary to establish the extent to which the product/service on offer appeals to global customers. These are customers that read, watch or listen to global media, who travel widely, are reasonably homogenous in their tastes, and have universal needs. A standardised approach can reduce communication costs. Although creating a global advertisement is very expensive, as British Airways discovered with its 'Manhattan Landing' campaign, it can be amortised over a large number of markets, and it needs to be kept in mind that, of total advertising costs, media costs are far greater than production expenses.

Global campaigns enable greater control over the promotion activities of a subsidiary and improve the firm's ability to maintain a consistent brand image. In general, standardisation of campaigns is more likely to succeed with luxury goods because of the nature of the customers and their ability to afford the luxury item. Such campaigns will need to be print or poster campaigns, which are more dependent on graphics than text. Technical products are also more likely to be amenable to standardised campaigns because of the limited and more specialised nature of the target audience. Products targeted at the youth market may also be amenable to standardised campaigns. This is because there is an increasing youth culture stimulated by music, film and communication, and youth tend to be more homogenised because they have not yet internalised traditional cultural values to the same extent as their parents.

> *Coca-Cola's latest global advertising campaign, involving over US$300 million is the largest in the company's history and illustrative of things to come. Its creation involved marketing directors from 13 regions around the world creating ads for their own markets based on 11 story ideas, all with the tag line 'Life tastes good'. It includes 31 television executions tailored to consumer tastes and trends in different countries and a radio song that will run in 20 versions recorded by local artists worldwide. This approach will mean that ads will differ from country to country but will have a consistent message.*
>
> Source: Adapted from *USA Today*, 20 April 2001, p. 5b.

Many international firms adopt a variation of the doughnut approach to standardisation. This involves having a standard frame of reference for all advertisements (the ring of the doughnut containing brand name and uniform global message) and a core which relates content or application to the individual country market. The standardisation can be further extended by all advertisements using similar colours and similar layout. As the following commentary indicates, when a company with a principally domestic orientation becomes involved in international activities, a standardised promotional approach will be riddled with pitfalls unless it is careful to take national preferences and behaviours into account.

> *Many US carriers expect to generate a substantial portion of their revenues from foreign routes in the years ahead. To stay competitive in what has become a global business, carriers such as United, American and Delta are accelerating their expansion into international markets. The core concept remains the same regardless of the market: for example to provide quick simple meals for business executives who want to eat soon after takeoff and then sleep or work undisturbed for the rest of the flight. Some aspects of service have to be adjusted to national preferences. German passengers, for example, are very particular about the use of formal titles when they are addressed by attendants; Japanese customers dislike being touched. Some of these challenges will be met only after a learning experience as shown by the following examples from United's Asian expansion:*

- *the map that United inserted into its sales promotion brochure left out one of Japan's main islands;*
- *United's magazine ad campaign, 'We know the Orient' listed the names of Far Eastern countries below pictures of local coins. Unfortunately, they did not match;*
- *most Chinese business travellers were shocked during the inauguration of United's concierge service for first-class passengers from Hong Kong. To mark the occasion, each concierge proudly wore a white carnation – a well-known symbol of death in Asia.*
- *United's in-flight magazine cover showed Australian actor Paul Hogan (Crocodile Dundee) wandering through the outback. The caption read 'Paul Hogan camps it up'. Hogan's lawyer alerted the airline that 'camps it up' is Australian slang for flaunting one's homosexuality.*

Source: Adapted from Zeeman (1987).

Because of the large numbers of fiascos in international advertising due to cultural insensitivity and failure to undertake sensitivity research in advance, awards are given each year for the most notable fiasco. These are known as the Chevy Nova awards, in honour of GM's fiasco in trying to market this car in South and Central America where in Spanish, 'No va' means 'it doesn't go'. Some recent nominees for the award are:

- *Coors* – which put its slogan 'turn it loose' into Spanish where it was read as 'Suffer from diarrhoea';
- *Clairol* – which introduced its curling iron under the brand name 'Mist Stick' into Germany only to find out that 'mist' is slang for manure;
- *Frank Perdue's* – whose chicken slogan, 'It takes a strong man to make a chicken tender' was translated in Spanish as 'it takes an aroused man to make a chicken affectionate';
- *American Airlines* – who, when it wanted to advertise its new first-class leather seats in Mexico, translated its 'Fly in leather' campaign literally which came out as 'Fly naked' (*vuela en cuero*) in Spanish;

10.4 International highlight

Brand building on the Internet

Ask people what they believe to be the most famous e-brand and they will probably answer Amazon.com. Amazon.com has achieved brand awareness through massive advertising campaigns in traditional media as well as through a substantial level of word-of-mouth communication, or viral marketing as it has become known. The brand awareness has come at a cost as the company has only recently turned a profit. This is largely due to the huge marketing costs associated with building and maintaining a successful e-brand. In the Internet space, competitors are just a 'click away' and brand awareness can fade like morning mist if marketing efforts aren't maintained.

- The European vacuum cleaner manufacturer that told its US audience that 'nothing sucks' like it.

- A famous tonic water brand was translated for the Italian market as 'toilet water'.

- A well-known cola company's campaign, built around the premise that it brought a generation alive, translated into Chinese as 'brings your ancestors back from the grave'.

Internet infusion

A survey by *The Economist* in 1997 revealed that 75% of customers who shopped on the Internet went on to purchase goods through traditional channels. This suggests that the Internet plays a more important role as a worldwide advertising and promotional vehicle than it does as a selling tool. However, compared with other media, the spread of the Internet has been much faster. The Internet has the characteristics of both broadcast mass media and direct response advertising. It is more like newspapers than TV, but the medium and response convenience are closer to TV than newspapers from the perspective of impact on consumers.

Whereas in the traditional model of communications in the international market-place, there are clear-cut distinctions between the sender, the message and the recipient with control of the message being with the sender, in marketspace control of the message is shared between the sender and the receiver. This is because of the interactivity of the medium, the ability of the medium to carry back a message in reply, and the impact of information technology on time, space and communication.

The web represents a change away from a push strategy in international promotion where a producer focuses on convincing an agent or a distributor to stock products, towards a pull strategy in which the producer communicates direct with the customer. The web in comparison with other forms of advertising tends to be high on information, low on generating an emotional response and poor on reinforcing existing behaviour.

Web advertisements are often targeted to a user profile which in turn impacts on the way the message is received. Increasingly, the ads displayed on this international medium are specific to user interests and pop up as these interests are revealed when the user navigates the web. In order to provide value to the potential international customer and maintain interest, the website must be attractive and user friendly. This involves an appealing design, being available in the buyer's language (or one with which the buyer is likely to be familiar) and being aesthetic in terms of colour and background (taking into account the buyer's cultural norms). It should be easy to navigate, contain the information the buyer is likely to want and be easy to access. Having a website is not enough in itself to attract 'hits' from international buyers. It is necessary to promote the site by both traditional and electronic means. Some recommended techniques are to put the firm's URL on all correspondence, in traditional advertisements and highlight it as part of other marketplace promotion activities.

Summary

International promotion and advertising requires a different blend of activities from promotion and advertising in the domestic market. There are some promotional techniques which are much more important when promoting in international markets than in the domestic market such as trade shows and trade missions. All forms of advertising and promotion will require substantial modification to take into account the circumstances of specific international markets. Although there are unique issues when promoting in international markets, such as country of origin and the potential for standardisation, research in advance is essential if promotional activities in other countries are to be effective. In a nutshell, the elements of the promotion mix will need modifying as will the balance between various forms of promotional activity.

Ethics issue

You are in Ho Chi Minh City for a trade show where your exhibit is a feature attraction. The show is due to open in three days' time. An hour ago you received a fax from your European head office advising that due to a mistake at your firm's warehouse, there were a large number of items in the consignment not mentioned in the list of goods on the manifest previously submitted to the Vietnamese customs authorities. The customs clearance agent for the show responsible for handling all exhibit goods has advised that if the discrepancy is drawn to the attention of the Vietnamese authorities, they will impound your consignment for at least a week. This will mean it will not be available for the trade show. However, the customs agent has mentioned that through a contact, he could arrange that the consignment not be inspected but this would require a 'donation' of €3,000 to the Customs Officers Welfare Fund.

How would you respond if faced with this predicament?

Web workout

Question 1 Often the difficulty in promoting products/services in international markets stops companies from pursuing their global or international reach. Select a product or service you are familiar with. Next, using your favourite search engine, research a competitor's products/services for your chosen international market. How do they promote their products? Are they fully utilising the power of the Internet to effectively and efficiently market their products? What would you do?

Question 2 Select a product or service you think could benefit from international trade. Visit a major portal, such as Yahoo!, AOL or Netscape, and then analyse its promotional/advertising capabilities. How can these portals be used to effectively and efficiently promote your selected product or service?

Websites

AC Nielsen www.acnielsen.com

Expoguide (information about trade shows) http://expoguide.com

Discussion questions

1 How does each stage of the communications process require modification when promoting in international markets?

2 Rate in terms of importance, factors in international communications when promoting machine tools in India.

3 What are the factors impacting on the effectiveness of communicating messages to international markets?

4 How do newspapers differ from magazines as promotional print media for accessing international customers?

5 Will global media eventually replace national media? What are the factors that underlie the rise of global media?

6 Why are trade shows an ideal medium for the new exporter to introduce products into the international market?

7 How do technical seminars differ from trade shows? When would you use a technical seminar in preference to a trade show?

8 What are the key features of a trade mission which facilitate its use as a vehicle for researching opportunities in the international market?

9 What are the characteristics of an effective international salesperson as opposed to a domestic salesperson?

10 Under what circumstances is the doughnut principle preferable to complete differentiation when promoting in international markets?

References

Dulek, R.E., Fielden, J.S. and Hill, J.S. (1991) 'International Communication: An Executive Primer', *Business Horizons*, January/February, pp. 20–25.

Fletcher, R. (2001) 'The Complexities of Communicating to Customers in Emerging Markets – an Exploratory Study', *Proceedings of the Australia–New Zealand Marketing Academy Conference*, Auckland, 3–5 November, Massey University.

Fletcher, R. and Melwar, T.C. (2001) 'The Complexities of Communication to Customers in Emerging Markets', *Journal of Communications Management*, Vol. 6, No. 1, pp. 9–23.

Griffin, T. (1994) *International Marketing Communications*, Butterworth-Heinemann, Oxford, UK.

Honeycutt, E.D. and Ford, J.B. (1995) 'Guidelines for Managing an International Sales Force', *Industrial Marketing Management*, Vol. 24, March, pp. 138–9.

Jacobs, L., Keown, C., Worthley, R. and Ghymn, J. (1991) 'Cross-cultural Comparisons', *International Marketing Review*, Vol. 8, No. 3.

Meuller, R.D., Broderick, A.J. and Mack, R. (2001) 'Captious Cues: The Use of Misleading, Deceptive or Ambiguous Country of Origin Cues', *Proceedings of the Conference of the European Marketing Academy*, 8–11 May, Bergen, Norges Handelshoyskole.

Mort, G.S. and Duncan, M. (2000) 'The Country of Origin Effect: A Study of the "owned by" cue', *Proceedings of the Conference of the Australia–New Zealand Marketing Academy*, Gold Coast, 28 November–1 December, Griffith University.

Munvera, J. and Ruiz, S. (1993) 'Trade Fairs: Visitors' Viewpoint', *Proceedings of the 23rd Conference of the European Marketing Academy*, Barcelona, 25–28 May, p. 1032.

Rossen, J.R. and Seringhaus, F.H.R. (1996) 'Trade Fairs as International Marketing Venues: a Case Study', Paper presented at the 12th IMP Conference, University of Karlsruhe.

Terpstra, V. and Sarathy, R. (2000) *International Marketing*, 8th edn, Dryden Press, Fort Worth, Texas.

Thompson, B. and Quester, P. (2000) 'Evaluating Sponsorship Effectiveness: the Adelaide Festival of Arts', *Proceedings of the Conference of the Australia–New Zealand Marketing Academy*, Gold Coast, 28 November–1 December, Griffith University.

Usunier, J.-C. (1996) *Marketing Across Cultures*, 2nd edn, Prentice Hall, Europe.

Vardar, N. (1992) *Global Advertising: Rhyme or Reason*, Paul Chapman Publishing, London.

Wilkinson, T.J. and Brouthers, L.E. (2000) 'Trade Shows, Trade Missions and State Governments: Increasing FDI and High-Tech Exports', *Journal of International Business Studies*, Vol. 31, No. 4, pp. 725–734.

Zeeman J. (1987) 'Service – The Cutting Edge of Global Competition: What United is Learning in the Pacific', Presentation at Academy of International Business, Chicago, Illinois, 4 November.

11

International
pricing for profit

Learning objectives

After studying this chapter, you should be able to:

- assess the importance of the pricing decision in the international context;

- learn how to apply a range of alternative international pricing strategies;

- discuss factors that must be considered in setting prices;

- compare different approaches to setting international prices so as to ensure an optimal outcome;

- determine the constraints that apply to setting international prices; and

- appreciate the role of international pricing for the global firm and the rationale for transfer pricing.

Anti-dumping actions

India has consolidated its position as the World Trade Organisation's (WTO) most aggressive user of anti-dumping measures against imports. WTO rules allow member states to set aside free trade regulations and impose anti-dumping tariffs if detailed investigations show that dumping is taking place.

Analysts say that although not all investigations lead to tariffs, they usually have an immediate impact on imports because importers are obliged to post bonds against eventual duties.

India overtook the United States, traditionally the champion of anti-dumping actions, for the first time in the second half of 2002 when it instigated 51 investigations against Washington's 35. Anti-dumping actions can be challenged through the WTO's dispute settlement system and, if found unjustified, the country applying must withdraw them. Several anti-dumping actions by the US, as well as other WTO members, have been declared illegal by neutral WTO trade judges, and developing countries have often accused Washington of abusing them to keep out goods competing with domestic products.

Introduction

 The role of pricing in international marketing is analogous to the selection and purchasing of a fine expensive wine. In the same way as wine to be tasted is sipped rather than gulped, international price setting requires research to establish the most appropriate price to charge. Just as the making of fine wine is a compromise between the objectives of the winemaker and the wishes of the consumers, so the setting of prices in international markets is a compromise between the strategic objectives of the firm and the estimated demand at various price levels. In the same way as the winemaker does not totally control the price to be charged because of the requirement to add excise or sales taxes, prices charged for products sold in other countries are often regulated by governments. There are elements such as import duties which add to the price and the consumer's perception of value, but over which the domestic supplier has no control.

International pricing issues

A number of issues influencing the setting of prices in the international environment need to be considered in advance of a decision as to the most advantageous price. These include a variety of internal and external factors that are interrelated and together influence the pricing decision. First the role of price and the nature of the pricing decision are considered.

The role of price

Price is the only marketing variable that produces revenue. It is an integral part of the product when marketed in international markets as it is difficult to think of a product without considering its price. Price is important because it affects demand. Demand and price are usually inversely related. Price, however, is also related to other elements of the international marketing mix and does not exist in isolation from them. Price can be the subject of controversy, not because consumers object to paying for products or services, but because they wish to see a relationship between price and perceived value. Price must be set at equivalent or lower than perceived value for this reason.

Reference prices

The price that an international buyer pays for a product or sees being demanded for a product becomes the reference price against which other products are likely to be evaluated. Reference prices are not constant and are modified by market experience. In

international marketing, buyers establish a range of prices around the reference price and anything outside this range is unlikely to be acceptable unless it has unique or different features, in which case it becomes a different product. Within this range of prices, however, price in international marketing is often used as an indicator of quality until experience indicates otherwise. When price is perceived as being similar for alternative products, then product quality or value as communicated through the brand becomes the deciding factor in the decision to purchase. For example, regardless of relative merits, the Proton Saga, which sells for less than the Volkswagen in Malaysia, tends to be regarded as being of lesser quality because of both price and the international reputation of the Volkswagen brand.

Nature of the pricing decision

Pricing is the only variable in the international marketing mix which can be changed at short notice without cost implications. The form of market entry will depend on whether the price is decided by the firm or by an intermediary, such as an international agent. In cases where the firm sets the price, the decision will be a different one when the product is being introduced to an international market for the first time as opposed to when changing the price in an existing market. With a new product, flexibility to set prices will be increased the more innovative the product, the greater the capacity of consumers to afford the product, and the smaller the degree of competition in the market. With existing products, the ability to change prices will be increased as the firm acquires more knowledge about the international market and increases the share it already holds in that market. This ability will also be influenced by the extent to which the market is free or regulated.

The price element of the purchase

The price that is charged for a product is not only for the physical product but also for an associated bundle of other attributes that come with the purchase, any one of which can positively or negatively impact on the perceived value. This can be illustrated in the case of a motor vehicle. Here the price may include extra features such as air conditioning or power steering and a warranty that has a greater perceived value if it is 3 years/30,000 kilometres instead of 1 year/10,000 kilometres. It may also include servicing in the original price or extended servicing available at a concessional price; discount for repeat purchase; affiliation with credit card frequent flyer programmes as with Star World; or discount for bulk purchase as with fleet owner discounts. When pricing for international markets, it is useful to ascertain what bundling of benefits is included with the price so these can be matched if necessary or introduced if not usual in the market so as to gain a competitive edge.

Complexities of international pricing

International pricing is a more complex activity than domestic pricing because of the larger number of variables involved and the greater degree of uncertainty. For this

reason, international pricing requires more care and effort, and approaches that merely extend domestic pricing rarely succeed. The variables are both internal and external.

Internal

Internal variables are those which relate to the firm's overall strategy and practices. They include corporate goals, the degree to which the firm wishes to control prices charged to the international consumer, the firm's usual approach to costing and the extent to which the company is internationalised. For example, does it insist on the same FOB price for all international markets or does it charge different FOB prices to different markets to take account of varying circumstances? This may be a matter of whether the firm views export as an extension of its domestic sales effort or as a separate strategic activity.

External

External variables include actions by competitors both in the domestic market and in the international markets, the levels of demand both in the domestic and international markets, and legal constraints on price setting. They also include government regulations and imposts on exports by the domestic government and on imports by the international governments, as well as exchange rates and general economic conditions in the domestic and the international markets.

Nature of the product or industry

The nature of the product or industry impacts on price because a specialised or technically advanced product is likely to have fewer competitors than a 'me too' product. When the product has unique advantages, price will have a more static role in the international marketing mix. However, some industries face dramatic fluctuations in the price of raw materials or are more susceptible to predatory pricing practices by foreign competitors. This can impact on prices of the finished product offered. For example, a rise in the price of coal might cause a rise in the price of steel that in turn might result in a price rise in the cost of automobiles. Technically complex products in general have greater servicing requirements, longer production times and greater sales lead times than simple, non-technical products. A final product-related issue impacting on price is the level of service expected to be provided to support the product in the international market. Expectations as to service provision differ from country to country and constitute a cost that must either be factored into the price or charged for separately.

Location of production facilities

Companies with production or assembly facilities in other countries find it easier to respond to fluctuations in exchange rates and cost of inputs. This is because they are able to supply from a variety of sources rather than simply one source and can source from the plant in whichever country offers the greatest competitive advantage at a particular time.

Several years ago one of the authors was visiting the Philippines together with a group of students undertaking projects in international marketing research. He noticed in a major supermarket chain that the Kellogg's products came from five different countries. Inquiries to the chain's buying office revealed that the office varied its sourcing of Kellogg's lines according to whichever source had the most advantageous exchange rate to the peso at the time of the purchasing decision.

Location and environment of the foreign market

The location of the international market also impacts on the operational costs of exporting to that market. Such costs include undertaking market research, visits to that market by company executives, communicating with the market and promoting in that market.

One environmental factor is climate. Climatic conditions can add to price. Examples include climatic conditions in international markets requiring termite proofing or stronger packaging because the product in being transported over unpaved roads, or weatherproofing because of monsoon rains.

Economic factors can also influence the price that can be charged in international markets. These include the rate of inflation and fluctuations in the exchange rates. Also having an impact on price are political factors such as perceived risk of dealing with a particular country. The firm may wish to charge a higher price to compensate for such factors. Certainly its credit insurer, such as the Export Finance Insurance Corporation, will charge a higher premium to compensate for the greater risk of doing business in the international market. Such premiums become a cost that will need to be reflected in the price charged.

Chosen system of distribution

The channels of distribution often dictate export pricing. The nature of the distribution influences the degree of control the firm is able to exercise over the price charged to the final customer in the international market. The length of distribution channels varies from country to country. When the firm has a subsidiary in that market it is able to exercise more control over the final price than when the firm operates in the market through an independent agent or distributor. By reducing the number of intermediaries between the manufacturer and the final customer in the international market, the firm is able to reduce the international escalation in the price of its product. In international business, intermediaries are usually employed because the manufacturer does not have a physical presence in the international market. For this reason, the distribution channel in international marketing usually adds more to costs than in the domestic market because of the involvement of at least one additional intermediary. This disadvantage can be overcome if the firm is able to localise manufacture in the international market by techniques such as partial assembly or shipment in bulk and contract packing.

The costs and margins of a given channel vary from country to country as shown in Figure 11.1.

Figure 11.1	Cost variability of the same channel in different countries: medicines (US dollars)

Source: Terpstra and Sarathy (2000), p. 561.

Country	Manufacturer's price $	Wholesaler's markup $	Retailer's markup $	VAT $	Total $
Germany	100	25	92	24	241
Switzerland	100	21	99	none	220
France	100	12	56	34	202
United Kingdom	100	18	59	14	191
Italy	100	10	38	9	157

One of the problems encountered by international firms in competing in the Japanese market has been the extended and complex nature of the Japanese distribution system that involves several layers of distributors and subdistributors. Each of these adds to the price of the final product often making international products uncompetitive.

Government regulations

These can affect prices charged in international markets, and in domestic markets these regulations can involve export inspection costs (particularly with agricultural products) and the costs of conforming to standards imposed by the domestic government on export products. Other costs include the effect of local taxes when applied to products to be exported. These include payroll tax and excise rates and have the effect of reducing the host country's competitive advantage when doing international business. Import duties can also add to costs of exported products. Although there is provision for the refund of duties paid on components used in finished products that are subsequently exported, the bureaucratic procedures involved may not make the claiming back of duties worthwhile.

Competition in the international market

When setting prices for the international market, it is necessary to take competitors' prices into account. It is also necessary to take into account the price of substitute products which perform the same or a similar function. The OPEC price hike of the 1970s illustrates this. In this case it was substitute energy products such as coal tar sands and wind power, as well as the advent of competition from non-OPEC producers such as Britain and Norway, that created a ceiling on the price which OPEC countries were able to impose on the global market for oil. In setting international prices, it should be remembered that the entry by an international firm into a new foreign market is likely to provoke a competitive reaction that may manifest itself in price cutting. The likelihood of competitor reaction will be influenced by the firm's relationship to the international market. This is because the reaction will be different if the international firm is a leader in the market compared with its being a challenger or a follower. The anticipated extent of competitor reaction should be taken into account in setting prices.

Culture

Because price is a decisive element in the interaction between buyer and seller, culture plays a role in price setting and negotiation. In the first place, culture influences the bargaining over price. In some cultures, everything is negotiable and no one believes that the first price offered is anything but a negotiating ploy and a ceiling that can be negotiated downwards. In these cultures, the offer by the buyer is treated as a floor price that can be negotiated upwards. In other cultures, prices are not negotiable and the price sought is the result of careful consideration as to what is a fair price and, once put on the table, is inflexible. In markets where negotiation is the norm, the international firm should consider using a higher list price so as to leave room for negotiation.

In some cultures (e.g. many Islamic countries), interest is regarded as usury, yet buyers still want extended payment terms. In such cases, the international firm may need to load into the price the opportunity cost of funds 'tied up' rather than charge interest for delayed payment.

Another culturally influenced aspect of pricing is that price is viewed as a surrogate indicator of quality. The degree to which this occurs will vary between cultures as illustrated by Usunier (1993) who contrasts northern and southern Europeans. The former consider that goods should be expensive in order to limit their consumption based on the Lutheran value system, and prefer durable, lasting goods in line with a thrifty, austere view of life. In the case of southern Europeans, they are less concerned with a price/quality relationship and support implicit spending in order to satisfy immediate needs – allegedly more in line with the Roman Catholic philosophy.

A final cultural variable is the acceptability of loading the price to cater for various pay-offs in order to get the business. This is a form of disguised bribery that influences price setting. The degree to which this practice is the norm varies from country to country. Inquiries in this connection will enable the international firm to decide whether it wishes to do business on this basis.

The factors mentioned above are summarised in Figure 11.2.

International pricing strategy

Having considered the issues influencing the setting of international prices, it is necessary to set prices within the context of the overall strategic approach of the firm. Price is an essential element of the overall marketing mix, but only one factor in the buying decision. Because of this, there needs to be a high degree of consistency between the approach to product market pricing and other aspects of the marketing programme. Figure 11.3 highlights a number of additional factors that affect pricing decisions. Not only must the marketing strategies of the supplying firm be taken into account, but also the distributor's needs, the requirements of trade buyers, competitor activities and the market environment need to be considered.

In addition, it is necessary to factor into the price the terms of sale and the terms of payment that fit with the firm's overall approach to international business. The strategic approach to pricing differs between companies and between the differing cultures of countries. A comparison of the difference in strategic orientation taken to pricing by Japanese companies and their western counterparts is described in International Highlight 11.1.

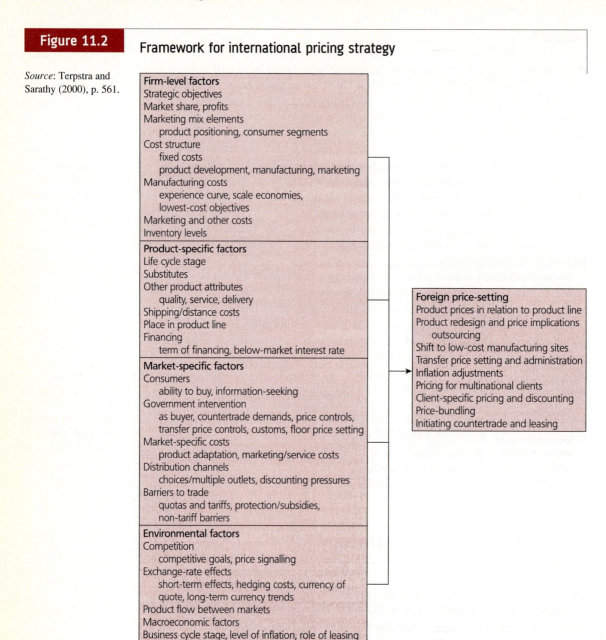

Source: Terpstra and Sarathy (2000), p. 561.

Figure 11.2 Framework for international pricing strategy

Firm-level factors
Strategic objectives
Market share, profits
Marketing mix elements
    product positioning, consumer segments
Cost structure
    fixed costs
    product development, manufacturing, marketing
Manufacturing costs
    experience curve, scale economies,
    lowest-cost objectives
Marketing and other costs
Inventory levels

Product-specific factors
Life cycle stage
Substitutes
Other product attributes
    quality, service, delivery
Shipping/distance costs
Place in product line
Financing
    term of financing, below-market interest rate

Market-specific factors
Consumers
    ability to buy, information-seeking
Government intervention
    as buyer, countertrade demands, price controls,
    transfer price controls, customs, floor price setting
Market-specific costs
    product adaptation, marketing/service costs
Distribution channels
    choices/multiple outlets, discounting pressures
Barriers to trade
    quotas and tariffs, protection/subsidies,
    non-tariff barriers

Environmental factors
Competition
    competitive goals, price signalling
Exchange-rate effects
    short-term effects, hedging costs, currency of
    quote, long-term currency trends
Product flow between markets
Macroeconomic factors
Business cycle stage, level of inflation, role of leasing

Foreign price-setting
Product prices in relation to product line
Product redesign and price implications
    outsourcing
Shift to low-cost manufacturing sites
Transfer price setting and administration
Inflation adjustments
Pricing for multinational clients
Client-specific pricing and discounting
Price-bundling
Initiating countertrade and leasing

Preliminary planning

There are a number of approaches to establishing the price to be charged in international markets. These relate to both the firm's corporate and marketing objectives and conditions in international markets. The corporate and marketing objectives could include earning an acceptable return on investment. They may also involve maintaining prestige and image as is the case with consumer goods such as brands of perfume sold

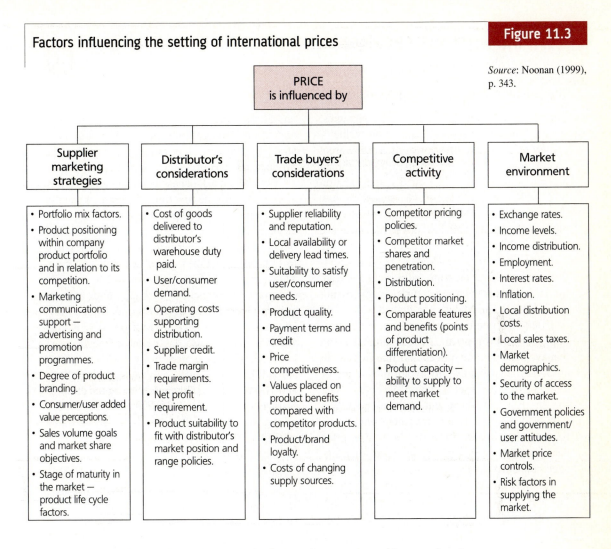

Figure 11.3

Factors influencing the setting of international prices

Source: Noonan (1999), p. 343.

PRICE is influenced by

Supplier marketing strategies	Distributor's considerations	Trade buyers' considerations	Competitive activity	Market environment
• Portfolio mix factors. • Product positioning within company product portfolio and in relation to its competition. • Marketing communications support – advertising and promotion programmes. • Degree of product branding. • Consumer/user added value perceptions. • Sales volume goals and market share objectives. • Stage of maturity in the market – product life cycle factors.	• Cost of goods delivered to distributor's warehouse duty paid. • User/consumer demand. • Operating costs supporting distribution. • Supplier credit. • Trade margin requirements. • Net profit requirement. • Product suitability to fit with distributor's market position and range policies.	• Supplier reliability and reputation. • Local availability or delivery lead times. • Suitability to satisfy user/consumer needs. • Product quality. • Payment terms and credit. • Price competitiveness. • Values placed on product benefits compared with competitor products. • Product/brand loyalty. • Costs of changing supply sources.	• Competitor pricing policies. • Competitor market shares and penetration. • Distribution. • Product positioning. • Comparable features and benefits (points of product differentiation). • Product capacity – ability to supply to meet market demand.	• Exchange rates. • Income levels. • Income distribution. • Employment. • Interest rates. • Inflation. • Local distribution costs. • Local sales taxes. • Market demographics. • Security of access to the market. • Government policies and government/user attitudes. • Market price controls. • Risk factors in supplying the market.

in many countries. It may also include a desire not to trigger a competitive reaction that could destabilise the international market or a desire to defend an existing position in a country where the firm already operates.

To achieve these objectives, it is necessary to decide upon the pricing strategy to be adopted. One strategy is price *skimming*. This strategy is appropriate when the intent is to achieve the highest possible return in the quickest period of time. It assumes that the product is unique and that there exist groups of customers prepared to pay a high price. It also assumes that competitive reaction will be sufficiently slow so that a return can be obtained before competitors force down the price. Another strategy is *market pricing*. This applies when there are similar products to those of the firm already available in the international market. Competitive prices determine the price to be charged and both production costs and marketing of the product must be adjusted to this price. This approach assumes a good knowledge of the competitive situation in the international market. It also assumes that the life cycle for the product in that market will be of sufficient duration to warrant entry by the firm into the new international market.

11.1 International highlight

The Japanese way: competing on value

International marketing by Japanese companies, such as Honda and Toyota, is based on 'value' – quality products at prices lower than their direct competitors. While most Japanese international marketers think of product quality and function first, 'value' is also seen to be created by low price. Starting with 'value packaging' which combines high quality and low price, the Japanese marketer then adds value through advertising and after-sales service backed by strong distribution channels. Over time additional service, image and status is provided through advertising and styling to sell 'value' at a higher price.

Often the international marketer in a firm does not control price. Accountants and top management monitor prices and margins as do corporate legal counsel to avoid allegations of dumping or price discrimination. To compensate for this lack of control international marketers will set list prices at an acceptable price positioning, then make frequent short-term price changes. This is particularly the case for packaged consumer goods.

Japanese marketers prefer to hold prices so that intermediaries maintain margins and they are against sudden price wars. Sony, Panasonic and Sharp prefer to compete on product features and brand image, not price. The Japanese strategy is to set a low price, then position the product in terms of features and image.

Thus, when a Japanese company enters a foreign market for the first time, the product usually enters with a very low price. In the past, this was at the lower end of the market. Today it is more likely to be at a higher price point – but relative to competition, lower prices are still common. This strategy differs from some US and EU countries who expect to exchange their success at home for a killing abroad. Firms from a variety of industries, such as McDonald's, Kodak and Ericsson, tend to flaunt their domestic market leadership as a reason for premium prices abroad. European auto companies, such as Saab and BMW, also use their foreign connection to extract consumer goodwill in the form of higher prices. So far, with less confidence in the status of their own country, the Japanese have largely avoided this strategy.

Source: Johansson, J.K. and Nonaka, I. (1996), *Relentless– The Japanese Way of Marketing*, Harper Business, USA, pp. 126–129.

A final strategy alternative is *penetration pricing*. Here, the product is offered at a low price, so as to rapidly build sales volume and market share. The downside is low returns per unit sold. For success, this strategy requires mass markets, price-sensitive customers and a situation whereby production and marketing costs fall as sales volumes rise.

As far as market conditions are concerned, answers should be obtained to the following questions:

- What international market segments should the firm concentrate on?
- Who are its major international competitors?
- What are the competitive strengths of the international competitors?
- Why and how do the international consumers buy?
- What are the major segments in international market for the product/service?

Terms of sale

One of the aspects in which international pricing differs from domestic pricing is in the terms of sale. Terms of sale have evolved with experience of the requirements of international trade over time. Recently these have been codified to yield uniformity by the International Chamber of Commerce and a series of International Commercial Terms (incoterms) have been arrived at. The most common are:

- *Ex-works* (EXW) – the price at the point of origin (the factory). All other charges are to the account of the buyer.
- *Free alongside ship* (FAS) at a specified port of export – this is the price of the goods delivered to and unloaded at the wharf of the port from which they will be exported. The buyer is responsible for the cost of loading, freight and insurance.
- *Free on board* (FOB) – the price of goods delivered and loaded onto an international vessel. The buyer is responsible for freight and insurance.
- *Cost and freight* (C & F) – the price of the goods delivered to a nominated international port where the goods will be disembarked. The buyer is responsible for insurance, customs clearance etc.
- *Cost, insurance and freight* (CIF) – the landed price at the port of destination including insurance. It is a more comprehensive basis for sale and can also include port charges, unloading, wharfage, storage, heavy lift, demurrage, documentation charges and certification charges.
- *Delivered duty paid* (DDP) or *delivered duty unpaid* (DDU) – the price delivered to the premises of the international customers and includes inland transportation.

The difference between DDU and DDP is whether the seller also pays the duty.

Increasingly, exporters are quoting more inclusive terms such as CIF or DDP as this makes it easier for the international buyer to compare the price of the goods on offer, with the price already being paid or quoted by other potential sources of supply. The international offer is more attractive if the seller assumes responsibility for the goods until they are delivered to the buyer and the buyer is not burdened with extra administration because the goods are being supplied from international markets rather than from local sources.

The point of delivery determines the point at which the risk shifts from seller to buyer as shown in Table 11.1 – the closer the point of delivery to the buyer's operation, the lower the risk for the buyer; the further the point of delivery from the buyer, the lower the risk for the seller.

Terms of payment

Terms of payment are extremely important because they impact on how payment is received. If payment is not received, or not received in a timely fashion, the entire international marketing effort is likely to be defeated. An integral part of any international marketing strategy is which method of payment is acceptable and what are the terms and costs of alternative payment methods. Decisions on this subject need to be related

Table 11.1 Shift of risk from seller to buyer

Terms of sale	EXW	FAS	FOB	C&F	CIF	DDP
Point of delivery						
Suppliers warehouse	X					
Export dock		X				
On board vessel			X	X	X	
Buyer's warehouse						X
Transit insurance met by	Buyer	Buyer	Buyer	Buyer	Seller	Seller

Source: Adapted from Onkavist and Shaw (1990), p. 696.

to the firm's reasons for going international, international market entry and growth strategies, and resources available for international marketing activities.

In more specific terms, the terms of payment relate to the degree of risk the exporter is willing to assume and the terms of sale that are most preferred. Often it is not the price alone that motivates purchase, but also the payment terms that go with it. The extent of credit allowed on the export transaction will not only impact on the profitability of the transaction but will also involve credit insurance premiums. If the exporter funds the credit this may require inclusion of either interest on borrowings in the price at the domestic end or the opportunity cost of interest forgone. In deciding whether it is necessary to offer credit, the exporter will need to take into account: the amount involved together with the likelihood of default; the terms offered by competitors; and the ability to finance the transaction or secure funds to be able to offer the finance. The basic methods of payment vary in attractiveness to both buyer and seller as illustrated in Figure 11.4.

Most attractive to the exporter is cash in advance because there is no risk and funds are immediately available. Most attractive to the importer is shipment on consignment which means that, although the seller retains ownership, any outlay of funds is deferred until the buyer receives the goods. However, rarely in international business are international buyers willing to deal on a 'cash in advance' basis or sellers willing to deal on a consignment basis. The next most attractive option for the international importer is selling to them on open account. This involves delivering the goods or services without a guarantee of payment and is generally only used in cases where the exporter has already had successful dealings with the importer from whom continuing constant business is expected in the future. Supporting open account transactions is usually an underlying sales contract or agreement. Documentary collection provides the exporter with additional security in that transfer of goods from seller to buyer only occurs if accompanied by documents transferring ownership (title) from seller to buyer. Included in such documents is usually a bill of exchange or draft. This is a written order addressed from the seller to the buyer requiring the buyer to pay immediately (sight draft), or at some time in the future (time draft), a specific sum of money in favour of the seller. The main disadvantage of this payment method is that it does not obligate the buyer to accept the goods, unless this is specified in an underlying sales contract.

Attractiveness of different methods of payment

Figure 11.4

Source: Chase Manhattan Bank (1984), p. 5.

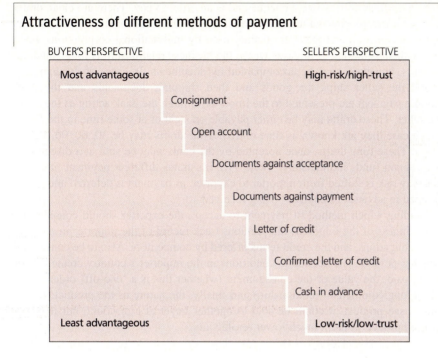

BUYER'S PERSPECTIVE   SELLER'S PERSPECTIVE

Most advantageous   High-risk/high-trust

- Consignment
- Open account
- Documents against acceptance
- Documents against payment
- Letter of credit
- Confirmed letter of credit
- Cash in advance

Least advantageous   Low-risk/low-trust

The commonest term of payment instrument is the *letter of credit*. It is issued by a bank (usually in the international country) at the request of the buyer, following the buyer depositing funds with the bank. The letter of credit contains a promise by the bank to pay the specified amount of money on presentation of a draft or written demand to receive payment by the seller or the seller's representative.

- *Irrevocable or revocable*. An irrevocable letter of credit cannot be changed or cancelled without the agreement of the beneficiary (the exporter). This guarantees payment. All letters of credit are irrevocable unless stated otherwise.

- *Confirmed or unconfirmed*. When the letter of credit is confirmed, another party (usually a bank) assumes any risk that the exporter will not receive the sum in the currency specified, including risk due to foreign exchange movements.

- *Revolving or non-revolving*. Non-revolving letters of credit are valid for one transaction only, whereas revolving letters of credit can involve a number of transactions, provided that the amount specified in the letter of credit is not exceeded at any point in time during its validity.

Letters of credit are widely used because they effectively substitute the credit of the bank for the credit of the buyer. From the exporter's point of view, the most attractive letters of credit are those which are both irrevocable and confirmed. The availability of letters of credit also can assist exporters secure preshipment financing. Letters of credit are specific concerning the goods to be shipped and will not be met if the consignment is in any way different from that specified in the letter of credit or attached documents. Letters of credit are promises to pay but not a means of payment. Actual payment is made by a *draft*. A draft is like a cheque and is an order to pay. There are clean drafts which are orders to pay without the need for any other accompanying documents (shipping documents) and these are mainly used by multinational corporations when dealing with subsidiaries or in cases where the business relationship is long standing. Most drafts, however, must be accompanied by documents. In cases of documentary collection the seller ships the goods and then shipping documents and the draft demanding payment are presented to the importer through the bank acting as the agent for the seller. These drafts may be either payable on sight or at some time in the future (in which case they are known as time drafts). Time drafts may be 30, 60, 90, 120 or 180 days. These time drafts, once accepted by the bank, may be sold at a discount in order to obtain funds immediately. Table 11.2 illustrates different payment methods, and the way risk is shifted from importer to exporter, as payment is deferred and goods are shipped in advance of payment being received.

In deciding which method of payment to accept, the exporter should consider the creditworthiness of the importer, the previous track record of the importer in meeting payment obligations, and the credit terms offered by competitors. Also to be considered are whether political and economic conditions in the importer's country create risk of not being paid, the value of the consignment (whether this is a 'one-off' order or the start of a long commercial relationship) and finally, the nature of the product. If it is a standardised product, it could be sold to another buyer at a discount, but if it is a customised product it has a much lower resale value.

Table 11.2 Attractiveness of payment methods to buyer versus seller

Method	Payment	Goods available to buyer	Risk to exporter	Risk to importer
Cash in advance	Before shipment	After payment	None	Relies on exporter to ship goods as ordered
Letter of credit	When goods shipped and documents comply with letter of credit	After payment	Little or none depending on letter of credit	Relies on exporter to ships goods described in documents
Sight draft, documents against payment	On presentation of draft to buyer	After payment	Buyer can refuse goods	Same as letter of credit unless he can inspect goods before payment
Time draft, documents against acceptance	On maturity of draft	Before payment	Relies on buyer to pay draft	Same as above
Open account	As agreed	Before payment	Relies completely on buyer to pay his account	None

International price setting

In establishing the price to be charged, it is first necessary to decide which principles of costing are to be applied. Following this, the exporter should estimate the minimum price that is acceptable to the firm and assess the maximum price that the market is prepared to pay. Finally, it is necessary to determine which price point between the minimum and maximum is likely to yield the greatest profit.

Full versus marginal cost pricing

An issue to determine in advance of calculating the price to be charged in the international market is the cost recovery strategy to be adopted. It needs to be decided whether full costs, which include both fixed costs and variable costs, should be recovered. The alternative is only to recover in the price charged internationally the variable costs associated with the specific international business transaction. These are known as marginal costs and are basically the costs of producing the extra units for the international order. It is assumed with marginal costing that the fixed costs have been amortised in the price charged in the domestic or other markets.

It may be argued that fixed costs have already been covered during activities in the domestic market and therefore the costs of production for the international market should be based on variable costs only. This argument has merit as long as the firm has excess capacity in its domestic operation. When this capacity is exhausted, then additional capacity must be installed, and to amortise this it is necessary to recover full costs (both fixed and variable) from the international market. On the assumption that excess capacity does exist, Table 11.3 details the circumstances when marginal costing is most appropriate and when full costing is likely to be achievable.

Traditionally, there are two approaches to setting international prices – cost-plus and marketplace pricing. Used separately they won't lead to the optimal price to be charged. The optimal price may result by combining the two approaches.

Cost-plus pricing

	$
Cost of production in the domestic market (depending on strategy and corporate policy, this can be wither full or marginal cost)	100.00
Costs of getting goods to the international customer (freight $10; insurance $5; delivery to wharf $2; agent's margin $15; additional costs of marketing in international market $5)	37.00
Less export incentives and subsidies (e.g. Export Market Development Grants Scheme – EMDG)	–10.00
Minimum acceptable profit	13.00
TOTAL	140.00

This is the fbor price below which the business is not worth having

Table 11.3 Assessment of the need for marginal costing

Factor	Strongly agree 2	Agree 1	Neutral 0	Disagree −1	Strongly disagree −2	Weight	Score
Low product differentiation							
Committed to exporting							
Strong fnancial resources							
High excess capacity							
Possible economies of scale							
Strong growth potential in the export market							
Follow-up sales potential good							
Price sensitivity high							
Competitive intensity high							
Can offer favourable terms of sale and fnancing							
Total						1.0	

If the total score for the weighted rating of the 10 factors is positive, then serious consideration should be given to some degree of marginal costing.

The cost-plus approach is simple to calculate, requires little if any market research and may be suitable if the product to be exported is of leading edge technology and has no competitors in the international market. However, this approach ignores most of the factors that should be considered when setting prices discussed earlier in this chapter.

Marketplace pricing

	$
The price of a competitive product in the international market (excluding duty)	250.00
Adjust for quality difference between competitive product and domestic product (assuming it is slightly better than the domestic item)	−5.00
As the domestic product is unknown in the international market it will need to be priced at a lower fgure to encourage switching	−25.00
Costs of getting product to the international customer (freight $10; insurance $5; delivery to wharf $2; agent's margin $15; additional costs of marketing international $5)	−37.00
Add subsidies and export incentives (EMDG)	10.00
Pro-rata costs of management time to develop international market	−3.00
TOTAL	180.00

This is the ceiling price which is the most that can be expected

The marketplace price requires research to establish what are the competitive prices in the international market, and includes more of the factors influencing price discussed earlier in this chapter. This approach is suitable for products already available in the selected international market and takes account of the competitive environment.

Optimal price setting

If there is no positive gap between the ceiling and the floor price, then the market cannot be pursued at a profit and should be abandoned unless favourable price and cost dynamics are expected in the future. If there is a positive gap, then the challenge is to decide which price should be charged in the range between the floor and the ceiling price. Basic laws of demand and supply indicate that the lower the price, the greater the quantity demanded and the greater the probability of a sale. However, the profit levels per item will vary at different price levels. The challenge is to set a price between the floor price and the ceiling price that yields the largest overall profit. One technique for establishing this price is decision analysis. In the case above, this price will be somewhere between the floor of $140 and the ceiling of $180. To work out the optimal combination of profit per unit and volume it is necessary to estimate the probability of sales at each price point.

Unit price ($)	Unit profit ($)	Profitability ($)	Expected profit per unit ($)
140	13	0.80	10.4
145	18	0.70	12.6
150	23	0.60	13.8
155	28	0.50	14.0
160	33	0.40	13.2
165	38	0.30	11.4
170	43	0.20	8.6
175	48	0.10	4.8
180	53	0.05	2.6

Based on the hypothetical example above, the price most likely to yield the optimum profit is $155 per unit.

Mismanagement of price setting

It was argued earlier in this chapter that price often sends a signal to buyers as to the quality that they might expect, especially if buyers are unfamiliar with the product. Mismanagement of price setting can send the wrong signal to the buyer. In addition, mismanagement of price setting can result in different prices being charged in different countries and unless there are substantive reasons for this difference, 'grey markets' can result. This is an issue touched upon later in the chapter and explored in depth in Chapter 12. Once customers in the target market learn of discrepancies between the price charged in their market and the price charged in other markets, they are likely to pressure the firm for price reductions or larger discounts. Finally, mismanagement of price setting creates an adverse impression of the firm as either a 'gouger' or an 'incompetent'.

The Japanese approach to price setting

The Japanese approach does not treat costs as a given. Rather the Japanese decide in advance what costs they must achieve in order to ensure a price that will deliver them dominance of the international market. This target cost is then used as a target for the designers, the engineers and for those who wish to be suppliers or subcontractors to the Japanese firm. Once initial profitable entry into an international market has been achieved, the pressure to lower the target costs continues so as to ensure that the market position is protected from competitors and expanded. Figure 11.5 illustrates the difference in approach between western and Japanese firms to the setting of prices. A more detailed comparison of Japanese and western approaches to pricing tactics is in International Highlight 11.2.

An illustration of the periodic cost reductions in Japanese international pricing strategies and their effect on pricing is shown in Figure 11.6.

| Figure 11.5 | Comparison between western and Japanese firms' price setting |

Source: Robert (1993).

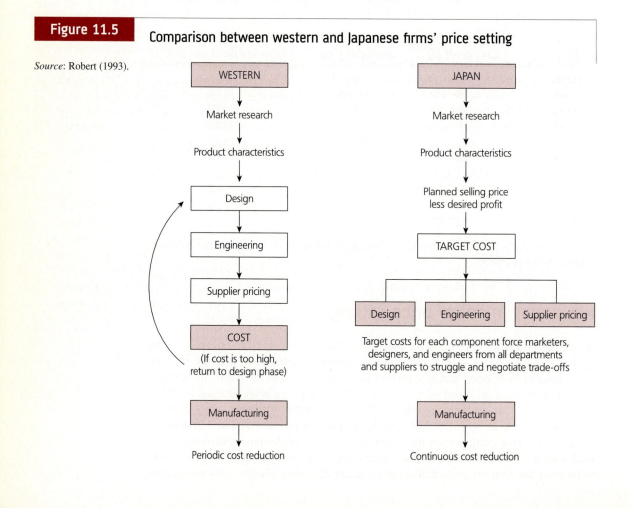

11.2 International highlight

The Japanese way: setting target prices by the cross-functional product team

Source: Corbis

As a Japanese company establishes its international image, you might expect the low-price entry tendency to change. But with a few exceptions, such as Sony, it is still unusual for a Japanese company to capitalise on its newly established brand name and charge a premium price. And they do not raise prices to higher levels because of large yen shifts. Their objectives are far too long-term for such a profit-oriented tactic. Japanese international prices are generally set and kept at very competitive levels.

Unlike western companies, Japanese companies do not set prices to provide a reasonable margin over costs in the long term; it is the other way around. Companies set prices so that the company can compete effectively in its markets – costs must come down to provide a profit at this price. While a western pricing approach treats production costs as given, Japan's unit production costs must accommodate a low enough price.

The company first analyses the intended market to identify a target price, then sets the target costs so as to achieve a reasonable profit margin at that price. If the team cannot meet this cost target, it uses value engineering to pinpoint areas where costs can be reduced.

In selecting the target price, competitive pricing is the typical approach in line with the positioning against competing brands. The actual target price chosen involves a trade-off between product quality and functionality. Adding features increases functionality and justifies a higher target price, as do higher-quality materials. The firm's feasible trade-off possibilities within the target price are termed the 'survival zone'. The choice of positioning in this zone involves a consensus between the product development team members drawn from many functional areas within the firm (including design, production engineering, manufacturing and marketing).

The derivation of the cost target first involves subtracting a target profit margin from the target price. At Nissan, for example, the target margin is determined by ten-year profitability projections for existing and planned product mixes, given forecasted sales levels. When entering foreign markets with an existing product, the company chooses the price level typically based on competition in the market. But in these cases, the costs involved tend to be marginal costs rather than the average costs involved in the targeting approach. Hence, the company generally has more leeway in lowering prices when entering international markets. As a result many Japanese products are less expensive in other Asian countries than in Japan.

Source: Summarised from Johansson and Nonaka (1996), pp. 126–129.

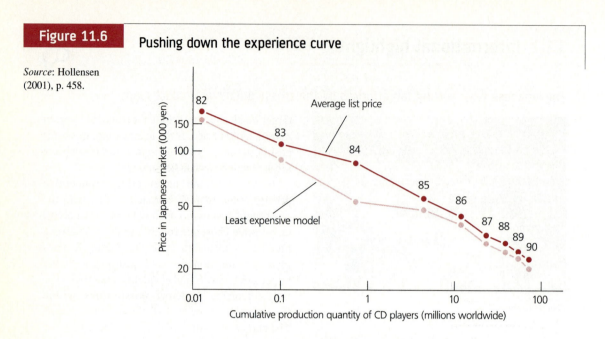

Figure 11.6

Pushing down the experience curve

Source: Hollensen
(2001), p. 458.

An alternative approach to price setting

Traditional approaches to price setting in international marketing tend to view the product as being a tangible item rather than a bundle of services or satisfactions. Given the increasingly augmented nature of products traded internationally and the fact that in many cases what is traded and has value is the service rather than the tangible product, an alternative approach to international pricing is to charge for the service rendered rather than the product. In the process, a fixed cost can be converted into a variable cost, adding to the appeal of the offer. An often cited example of this is the aircraft tyre manufacturer that, instead of putting a price on each tyre, offered a contractual arrangement whereby the airline was supplied with tyres as needed and charged on the basis of the number of aircraft take-offs and landings.

Another approach is to redesign the product so that it is price competitive in the international market. This may involve switching manufacturing locations to take advantage of lower labour costs, the redesign of the product so that its manufacturing costs are reduced, or the sourcing of cheaper materials and inputs.

Pricing and foreign currency fluctuations

Since the early 1970s, an increasing number of currencies have been allowed to float or have been linked to a basket of other currencies rather than to a single currency such as the US dollar (see Chapter 2). This volatility in foreign exchange rates has important implications for pricing.

The exporter can either maintain a stable price which will cause the foreign currency price to rise or fall; maintain a stable price in the foreign currency which will cause the price to fluctuate; or arrive at a combination of the two policies so as to protect returns

Table 11.4 Strategies for exporters to cope with currency fluctuations	
When the currency is weak	*When the currency is strong*
● Stress price benefts ● Expand product line and add features ● Shift manufacturing and sourcing to domestic market ● Exploit export opportunities in all markets	● Undertake non-price competition by improving quality, delivery and aftersales service ● Improve productivity and engage in cost reduction ● Shift sourcing and manufacturing offshore

to the exporter without pricing the product beyond the capacity of the international market to afford it. Table 11.4 explores options for the exporter to cope with currency fluctuations.

It is not always the case that variations in exchange rates will be passed on to the importer by the exporter in the form of higher or lower prices. Known as 'exchange rate pass-through' (Clarke et al., 1999), research has shown that the extent of such 'pass-through' will be influenced by:

● the size of the economy of the export market ('pass-through' is greater for small countries);

● the level of industry concentration in the target international market (the greater the concentration, the greater the 'pass-through');

● whether the exchange rate variation in the export market is an appreciation or a depreciation (greater likelihood of 'pass-through' for appreciations than for depreciations);

● the proportion of foreign exporters to domestic firms in the international market ('pass-through' greater as the number of export competitors in a market increases);

● the type and height of non-tariff barriers in the export market (import quotas discourage 'pass-through');

● country of origin of exporter – some countries use export pricing in a more strategic manner (e.g. Japan) than others do (e.g. European countries) – the more strategic the approach to pricing, the less the likelihood of 'pass-through'.

Currency inconvertibility

It may be that the country has restrictions on the convertibility of its currency or that due to balance of payments reasons or political change, currencies that were previously freely convertible are no longer so. This has cost and pricing implications as the artificial exchange rate may diverge significantly from the freely floating or the black market rate. This may result in having to deal on a countertrade basis and the additional cost of doing so will need to be factored into prices asked.

Responding to price changes in international markets

Accelerating technological advances, shorter product life cycles and more rapidly changing input costs increase the likelihood that either prices of competitive products will change or the ability to afford the product will vary after the product has been introduced into an international market. This will necessitate a review of the firm's pricing policy with respect to that market. Alternatives include:

- Maintain current price as a holding action until it can be established how deep will be the price change and how long it is likely to last. This is especially useful when price escalation is due to a movement in the exchange rate which could well drop back to its earlier level.
- Reduce the price if there is an immediate likelihood of losing customers because most competitors have already reduced their prices.
- Raise price and justify the increase by offering a demonstrable product improvement.
- Reduce the price and enhance the perceived value as a way of creating barriers to other firms contemplating entering the market.

Other ways of responding to price changes in international markets focus on reducing the cost of goods as supplied to that market. These include:

- Reduce the number of intermediaries in the distribution channel or the firm undertakes some intermediary functions itself. If the market is large enough, a sales office might be established in the market to replace the local agent.
- Eliminate costly features, reduce product quality or offer an 'economy' version of the product. The extent to which this is possible will depend on what features your competitors offer with their product in the international market.
- Ship and assemble from components in the international market for this purpose – a contract assembler might be employed (e.g. motor vehicle assembly in Thailand) or you might establish your own assembly operation. Establishing such an operation in a free trade zone can be very attractive because duty is not paid on the components until the assembled product leaves the free trade zone. As well, governments often provide incentives to set up in such zones such as tax holidays, concessional rents etc.
- Modify the product so that it is classified for tariff purposes in the other country as eligible for a lower rate of duty. This requires an expert to study various eligible tariff classifications and convince local authorities that the product is eligible for the lowest one.
- Reduce the basis of valuation for duty by switching from full cost to marginal cost, or by reimbursing distributors for service functions performed instead of including this cost in the price.
- Manufacture the product in the international country or in another country where costs are less. As duties are less if products are supplied from a fellow member of a regional trade grouping to the target country, it may be possible to source some components or accessories from such countries as a way of lowering costs.
- For markets where sales are declining, allow 'grey markets' to develop (see Chapter 12 for a full discussion of this topic).

Constraints on setting prices

The foregoing assumes that the firm is free to set any price it wishes to charge in the international market. Even in the domestic market, this is not always possible because there may be regulations controlling prices, or regulatory bodies that influence prices charged. There may be moral pressure as to what is an appropriate price which can happen when a firm's pricing activities receive unwelcome publicity on widely watched TV consumer programmes. Additional constraints operating in the international market are mostly due to governments wishing to protect domestic firms from foreign competition and from restrictive pricing practices by foreigners, which may drive domestic firms from the market.

Restrictive trade practices

Knowing what constitutes a restrictive trade practice in a country is important for making pricing decisions. What is acceptable as a pricing strategy in one country may be viewed as a restrictive trade practice in another. Restrictive trade practices take many forms, the most common of which are:

- horizontal price fixing, such as price fixing between competing firms;
- vertical price fixing, such as price fixing in the distribution chain as between suppliers, distributors and retailers to maintain retail prices;
- allocating or dividing up markets;
- export or import cartels;
- boycotts;
- monopolies or monopolising practices;
- mergers or consolidations;
- price discrimination.

Most of these restrictive trade practices are price related. Legislation against restrictive trade practices can include:

- complete prohibition (where the act is illegal and courts are not interested in motives or results such as with 'anti-trust' legislation);
- practices which have to be notified and subsequently investigated (need to establish whether public interest has been adversely affected or not or whether injury has occurred, as with mergers);
- practices which can continue without interference (unless it can be demonstrated that an abuse has occurred, as with price discrimination).

Restrictive trade practices are not only regulated by national laws, but may also be covered by multinational agreements such as the World Trade Organisation and regional agreements like the European Union.

Dumping

Dumping refers to the practice of selling products at a price lower than the current domestic value in the country of origin. It would be logical to expect that because of freight, insurance and the involvement of an extra party in the distribution channel, prices would be more expensive for the firm's product in an international country than in the country where it is made. Exceptions to this occur when taxes are imposed on domestic products by the government that do not apply when the goods are sold internationally. Examples of such taxes are import duty on components, sales taxes and payroll taxes. However, when the firm uses profits obtained in the market to subsidise entry into an international market, or engages in predatory pricing to quickly obtain market share in another country, it may be accused of dumping its products.

Governments, via export incentive schemes, facilitate dumping by firms and on several occasions certain countries (especially the US) have invoked the GATT Anti-Dumping Code against other countries.

Many countries apply an 'injury' test to evaluating dumping charges – the firm must prove that it has been actually injured by the dumped goods from another country.

Dumping can take several forms:

- *predatory dumping* which occurs when a foreign firm intentionally sells at a loss in another country in order to increase its share of market, usually at the expense of domestic producers;
- *sporadic dumping* which occurs when a firm solves excess inventory problems in the home market by selling at any price it can get in an international market. This avoids a competitive war in the domestic market;
- *unintentional dumping* which occurs when there are time lags between the dates of the transaction and the arrival of the goods in the international market. The firm's involvement in dumping in this case is usually because there has been a movement in the exchange rates in the intervening period, making the landed price to the international customer less that the cost of production in the domestic market.

When a firm feels that it is being injured by dumping from another country, it can complain to its government which may take action to impose a penalty to nullify the price advantage from the dumping action. The government can either impose an anti-dumping duty equivalent to the dumping margin, or in cases where the foreign government is subsidising exports as with an export incentive programme, impose a countervailing duty to offset the price advantage the imported product has received as a result of the subsidy. Sometimes the threat of potential anti-dumping action against a product from another country is used as a device to 'persuade' that country to voluntarily restrain the volume of its exports of the product to that market. The US has used this approach to restrict imports of motor vehicles and semiconductors from Japan.

Devaluation and revaluation

Devaluation and revaluation are other aspects of international marketing affecting price over which the exporter has little control. Until the last decade, one currency was pegged to another and currency movements were reasonably stable. Since that time most countries have moved to a floating exchange rate system whereby the currency is pegged to a basket of currencies reflecting the country's most important trading partners. This has resulted in much greater volatility in exchange rates. With this floating exchange rate system, devaluation and revaluation automatically take place when currencies fluctuate in relation to each other. Devaluation of the importing country's currency causes the costs of goods imported to be more expensive in the importing country. However, if the goods being imported contain components from another country, the relationship to final price of those imported components will have an impact. This depends on moves in the exchange rate between the importing country and the country from which the components are imported.

Revaluation of the importing country's currency on the other hand causes goods to be cheaper in the importing country. Because price impacts on demand in the international market, the firm will have to decide whether to vary its prices in response to a movement in the trading currencies. In some circumstances, the firm may wish to absorb some loss by not passing on the full cost of the devaluation in the importing country. In other cases, it may take a windfall profit by not passing on all the gain resulting from a revaluation of the currency of the importing country. As discussed earlier, the impact of this factor on price and profit can be reduced by taking out forward foreign exchange cover through the company's bank.

Administered pricing

The government of a country can dictate to a foreign supplier what prices can be charged in the market. It does this because it considers its main responsibility is to its citizens, not to the foreign supplier. It can dictate prices by establishing margins, establishing price floors and ceilings and making its approval necessary before price changes can be made. It can also dictate prices by competing in the market on its own account, by granting subsidies, and by taking over control of all purchasing or selling of the product. This happens in many socialist countries. Sometimes the government will import the product at world market prices and subsidise the price to the local consumer, in pursuit of political objectives (as happened with colour TV sets in Libya in the 1980s).

Government may either directly or indirectly control the price at which products can be sold in other ways. If it wants to discourage consumption, as with luxury items for example, it can mandate a very high price or load the products with duty and tax to ensure a high price. If the products are politically sensitive or necessities, it can dictate a low retail price. When selective price controls are implemented, usually foreign companies are more susceptible than local companies because they lack political influence with government that local firms are able to bring to bear. Subsidies imposed by governments on the price of products often make it difficult for firms to compete in an international market.

It is not only governments in foreign markets that interfere with the ability of the firm to charge a price of its own choosing. Competitors in the market can also interfere by banding together and colluding to fix prices, reducing price competition and foreign competition. Because no country favours or permits totally free competition, it is relatively easy for local industry to have their government turn a blind eye to restrictive practices when directed against foreign firms, especially if the domestic industry is likely be injured by the import competition. Industry groups also engage in price setting and disguise these activities under a variety of names (e.g. trade associations, communities of profit, informal inter-firm arrangements, licensing agreements and cartels).

Inflation

Once a price is set, it may need to be adjusted periodically because of inflation. While the exporter has no control over such inflation or its rate, sensitivity to inflation is necessary in order to protect the long-term profitability of involvement in the international country. In countries which experience very high inflation rates (e.g. some South American countries), consumers cannot commit themselves to purchases over a period and the pricing proposal will need to take this into account. At the wholesale level, this impacts on inventory holding and, at the promotion level, it stimulates use of instant media, such as the daily press and TV, rather than long-term promotional vehicles, such as catalogues and magazines. One answer for the exporter when dealing with a country with high inflation levels is to post prices in the currency of a less inflationary country such as the EU or the US.

Global pricing strategies

Just as with the other marketing mix variables, the transnational firm needs to consider the degree to which it will benefit from a global pricing strategy as opposed to operating a different pricing strategy for each individual market.

Global versus local pricing strategies

While some products and services are more amenable to a global pricing approach than others, such as those targeting affluent segments and those with a technical edge, for most products and services, affordability will vary from country to country and from segment to segment within each country. This will influence the extent to which a global as opposed to a differential pricing policy is realistic. The alternatives to consider are listed below.

Standard world prices

This ethnocentric strategy involves setting a standard price at corporate headquarters and applying it in all markets, after taking into account exchange rates and sales taxes imposed at the other end. The importer is responsible for paying freight and insurance. Such an approach ignores both the competitive environment and conditions in that market.

Market differentiated prices

This polycentric approach involves a different price for each market to reflect market conditions such as affordability and source and nature of competition, as well as the strategic objectives of the firm. Usually subsidiaries or intermediaries in the international country are allowed to charge whatever they feel 'the traffic will bear'. One of the dangers of this approach is that of grey markets in which others buy the product from markets where it is cheaper and make a windfall profit by reselling in a market where prices are higher.

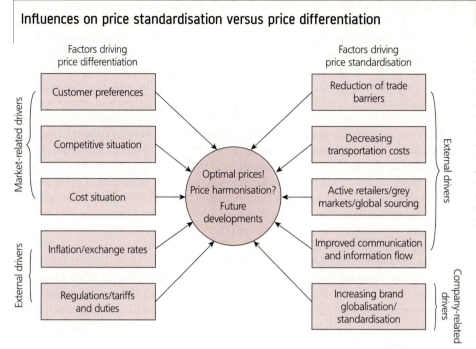

Figure 11.7

Influences on price standardisation versus price differentiation

Factors driving price differentiation

- Customer preferences
- Competitive situation
- Cost situation
- Inflation/exchange rates
- Regulations/tariffs and duties

Market-related drivers

External drivers

Optimal prices! Price harmonisation? Future developments

Factors driving price standardisation

- Reduction of trade barriers
- Decreasing transportation costs
- Active retailers/grey markets/global sourcing
- Improved communication and information flow
- Increasing brand globalisation/standardisation

External drivers

Company-related drivers

Source: Adapted with the permission of The Free Press, a division of Simon & Schuster Adult Publishing Group, from *Power Pricing: How Managing Price Transforms the Bottom Line* by Robert J. Dolan and Hermann Simon. Copyright © 1996 by the Free Press. All rights reserved.

Modified pricing policy

This geocentric approach balances the global strategic objectives of the firm with the recognition that market conditions in each international market will vary. Local costs plus a return on invested capital create the long-term price. This will be modified by short-term strategic considerations of the company, such as rapid market penetration or disposing of a domestic surplus or testing the market.

In developing pricing strategies for global markets, firms will need to consider how their actions will be interpreted by buyers in various countries. Research has shown that in countries with individualistic cultures, negative outcomes of a price increase are more likely to be blamed on others such as the retailer, whereas in collectivist cultures, negative outcomes of a price increase are more accepted by the individual and not as likely to be blamed on the retailer or other party (Maxwell, 2001).

Figure 11.7 summarises the factors that drive price differentiation and those that drive price standardisation in international marketing.

Transfer pricing

Transfer pricing does not happen with simple exporting but rather with international investment when a firm has divisions operating in different countries. Multinationals are able to exert a huge influence on the global economy. The 300 largest multinationals account for approximately 25% of the world's productive assets (*The Economist*, 22 May 1993). Multinationals derive their competitive advantage from utilising operations in a variety of countries to their advantage. Their normal operations involve the transfer of raw materials, goods and services between divisions both within and between countries. Since the entities are related, but operate separately, some method must be arrived at to value these intercompany transfers. The usual mechanism is transfer pricing which applies to goods sold within the corporate family from an operation in one country to an operation in another. It is a means of maximising the profit of the corporation as a whole rather than that of a branch or a division. It is achieved by arranging corporate affairs so that profits are brought to account as far as possible in the country with the lowest taxation regime. This is effected by reducing the prices of goods shipped from a subsidiary in a high-tax country to a subsidiary in a low tax country so little profit is earned in the high tax country. While this practice might be rationalised as tax avoidance and not tax evasion, it effectively denies the high-tax country a legitimate tax return on activities undertaken within its borders. This leads to the government of the high-tax country accusing the transnational of not being a good corporate citizen. It also leads to bad public relations resulting from critical press articles attacking, for example, the small tax contribution to the local economy by transnational companies as a whole. The Internal Revenue Service in the US alleges that foreign companies overcharge their American subsidiaries and in the process have avoided paying up to US$8 billion in taxes annually (Fraedrich and Bateman, 1996, p. 270).

There may be motives other than tax for transfer pricing. These include liquefying frozen assets. When restrictions on foreign currency transfers prevent a firm extracting its profits from a country with foreign exchange problems, transfer pricing enables such profits to be repatriated by underinvoicing goods to a subsidiary in another country. Yet again, such action is designed to circumvent the regulations of the host country. Transfer pricing may also be used to maintain or create a competitive position in another country. The transfer price can enable profits earned in one country to subsidise entry into another. In this case it has a result akin to dumping and, as such, may be contrary to regulations in the host country. Transfer pricing may also allow the firm to institute price reductions in response to slack demand or a decline in the wellbeing of the economy of the international country. A final transfer pricing objective includes the acquisition of goods or raw materials – in this case, the price set is such that the manager, forced by company policy to purchase from an international affiliate, pays no more than world market price despite the affiliate's product being more expensive. Table 11.5 (see Cravens, 1997) summarises the motivations for transfer pricing. It indicates that while tax avoidance is not the only motivation, it continues to be the most important.

There are five possible methods of transfer pricing between national divisions of a company and these vary in terms of their intent to evade host country regulations and taxes.

1 Sale at the local manufacturing cost.
2 Sale at local manufacturing cost plus a standard mark-up.
3 Sale at the cost of the most efficient producer in the company plus a standard mark-up.
4 Sale at negotiated prices based on those prevailing in the international market.
5 Arm's length sale using the same prices as quoted to independent customers.

Of these, arm's length pricing is most acceptable to tax authorities in the host country. With this 'Basic Arm's Length Standard' the tax authority compares the sale price with the selling price set by independent buyers and sellers in similar business environments. Although governments in many countries are targeting firms using transfer prices to evade taxes and regulations, eliminating the practice is proving difficult. Table 11.6 illustrates the principles of transfer pricing and shows how profits can be manipulated through transfer pricing.

Table 11.5 Motives for transfer pricing

Objectives	%
Taxation-related	
Manage tariffs	4
Comply with tax regulations	7
Manage the tax burden	40
	51
Internal management-oriented	
Equitable performance evaluation	7
Motivation	9
Promote goal congruence	5
	21
International or operational	
Cash transfer restrictions	2
Competitive positions	21
Reflect actual costs and income	5
	28

Source: Cravens (1997).

Table 11.6 Basic principles of transfer pricing

Country X (high tax)		Transfer price manipulation	
'Ex factory' costs	100		100
Tranfer price ('arm's length') to subsidiary in market Z	120	Artifcially low transfer price	105
Profit	20		5
Local tax (50%)	10		2.5
Net proft	10		2.5
Country Z (low tax)			
Buys from X	120		105
Duty (20%)	24		21
Cost warehouse	144		126
Sells at (marketable price)	160		160
Profit	16		34
Tax (5%)	0.8		1.7
Net proft	15.2		32.3
Corporate net proft			
(2 markets)	25.2		34.8
Government tax/duty	34.8		25.2

Source: Keegan and Schlegelmilch (2001), p. 414.

Internet infusion

There are a number of features of the Internet that can directly or indirectly impact on international pricing. The first of these is that the Internet lowers the cost of acquiring information and this can translate into lower prices in terms of the quality of competitive data obtained and the costs of obtaining general market information on the potential in selected international markets. In the second place, the Internet reduces transaction costs because of its interactivity and timeliness. This reduction in transaction costs improves efficiency which can also translate into lower prices. The third area where the Internet can impact on international pricing is its potential to link the exporter directly to the international buyer. This eliminates the agent or at least the distributor in business-to-business marketing and also the wholesaler and possibly the retailer in business-to-consumer marketing. Known as 'disintermediation', this has a major impact on pricing in international marketing where there is likely to be at least one more step in the distribution channel than is the case with domestic marketing. Each extra stage in the channel results in one more profit margin being added to the final price. A fourth area where the Internet impacts on pricing is its ability to provide the consumer with a customised offering. Generally, customers are prepared to pay more for a product or service that is specifically tailored to their needs, especially if they have had an input into the design of the offering which is possible due to the interconnectivity of the Internet.

With the Internet, geography becomes less relevant and competition increasingly comes from elsewhere in the world. In international marketing, the Internet exposes the firm to a greater degree of international competition, especially when buying is conducted via Internet auctions. As pointed out earlier in this chapter, governments in many countries influence prices charged within their domain so as to support domestic policies and protect national enterprises. With the Internet, government power over pricing is reduced, consumers become aware of different prices prevailing in other countries and will either pressure government to reduce the differential or use the Internet to evade existing government regulations. As an example, some governments ban the use of 'price off' coupons. When such coupons are offered over the Internet, government can do little to stop their nationals making purchases using such coupons. The purchase may be at a dumped price and government can do little to stop this, and applying countervailing duties is unlikely to be practical, especially on small-value consumer items. Finally, the goods entering the country as a result of an Internet purchase may be liable for duty so as to protect local producers or raise revenue. But will it make economic sense to collect the duty on a small-value item such as a book from Amazon.com?

The paperless world of the Internet has the ability to reduce shipping costs by as much as 30%. Furthermore, costs will fall further as online networks come on stream with the facility to handle both fulfilment and settlement of international trade transactions. Already TradeCard has formed an alliance with the Thomas Cook Group whereby once exporter and importer have decided to transact, TradeCard provides an electronic payment guarantee charging customers one-tenth of the average cost of a letter of credit. In the area of shipping, the Internet facilitates small shippers banding together under the aegis of a trade portal and achieving the same rates that apply to large shippers thus enabling small exporters to lower their delivered price and compete more effectively.

Summary

In this chapter, most of the factors influencing pricing for international markets have been discussed. Cavusgil (1988, 1996) summarises these in his decision framework for export pricing. He argues for a formal decision-making procedure that incorporates and weights the relevant variables. This framework, he suggests, will result in a more profitable pricing policy. The steps in this decision framework are:

- *Verify the potential of the market* – use both formal sources such as government, market research firms and industry bodies; as well as informal sources such as trade shows, trade journals and local intermediaries.
- *Estimate the target price range* – calculate both the floor and the ceiling price discussed earlier in the chapter.
- *Estimate sales potential* – estimate the size and concentration of customer segments, likely consumption patterns, competitive reaction and distributor expectations.
- *Analyse the barriers to import, distribution and transactions in the international market* – these barriers may include quotas, tariffs, taxes, anti-dumping measures, price maintenance, exchange rates, remittance of funds and relevant government regulations.
- *Review in relation to corporate goals and preference for pricing policy* – make a decision as to whether to insist on full-cost pricing or accept marginal-cost pricing (if full-cost is not attainable), and the ability to obtain normal profit margins.
- *Check consistency of proposed pricing approach with the current pricing approach* – if the firm already operates in the target market, the recommended pricing strategy should be compared to the strategy currently in place. It is also important to ensure that export pricing policies are consistent between international markets to reduce potential problems such as those with 'grey markets'.
- *Implementation* – decide on specific prices for both distributors and end-users, arriving at a recommended pricing strategy and deciding on specific pricing tactics.
- *Monitoring* – this should be a continuous activity, because the international market is likely to be more volatile than the domestic market due to daily movements in the exchange rates, an increased level of competition and government restrictions of pricing activities, especially by foreign firms.

Ethics issue

Your company has enjoyed a successful business exporting concrete pumping equipment from the US to Thailand over the last decade. Due to the Asian currency crisis, the rate of the Thai baht to the US dollar has moved from 18 to 28 = $1. This has forced the major customer, the Ministry of Public Works, to seek cheaper sources of supply. You have heard that a Malaysian firm is likely to be awarded the next tender as the movement of the Malaysian ringgit to the Thai baht has only been from 15 to 18 = M$1. Currently your product incurs an import duty of 50% due to its being classified as construction equipment. Your Thai agent advises that because of his political connections he could 'arrange' for your concrete pumping equipment to be classified on entry as pumps that incur a duty of 5%. This difference in duty would comfortably enable you to compete and retain the business but would require you to falsely describe your equipment on shipping invoices and bank documents.

If you were the US firm's export manager, would you recommend the above course of action to the managing director? List both the positive and negative side effects of reclassifying the product for duty purposes in this way.

Web workout

Question 1 Visit a website for a global computer company such as Dell (www.dell.com) and compare its pricing strategies in the markets it operates in. Do the prices seem different?

Question 2 Select a well-known product and what you believe is a global product. Using a search engine, research online 'auctions' and online 'shopping malls' that are selling your chosen product. Are the prices similar to or different from the prices that you would pay for this product locally?

Websites

AC Nielsen www.acnielsen.com

Expoguide (information about trade shows) http://expoguide.com

Discussion questions

1 In what ways is the role of pricing in the international market (a) similar to and (b) different from the role of pricing in the domestic market?

2 What influence do distribution strategies have on international price setting?

3 Outline an international pricing strategy that is a 'win–win' outcome for both importer and exporter.

4 Under what circumstances does marginal costing for export constitute dumping?

5 Develop a strategy for reducing potential constraints by a foreign government on the price you can charge in the international market.

6 Under what circumstances is transfer pricing likely to be acceptable to a government and when is it regarded as impugning their national sovereignty?

7 Discuss the circumstances when a global price is (a) the most appropriate course of action, and (b) an inappropriate course of action for a firm.

References

Cavusgil, S.T. (1988) 'Unravelling the Mystique of Export Pricing', *Business Horizons*, May–June, pp. 54–63.

Cavusgil, S.T. (1996) 'Pricing for Global Markets', *The Columbia Journal of World Business*, Winter, pp. 67–78.

Chase Manhattan Bank (1984) 'Dynamics of Trade Finance', New York, p. 5.

Clarke, T., Kotabe, M. and Rajaratnam, D. (1999) 'Exchange Rate Pass-Through and International Pricing Strategy: A Conceptual Framework and Research Propositions', *Journal of International Business Studies*, Vol. 30, No. 2, pp. 249–268.

Cravens, K.S. (1997) 'Examining the Role of Transfer Pricing as a Strategy for Multinational Firms', *International Business Review*, Vol. 6, No. 2, pp. 127–145.

Dolan, R.J. and Simon, H. (1997) *Power Pricing: How Managing Price Transforms the Bottom Line*, The Free Press, New York.

Fraedrich, J.P. and Bateman, C.R. (1996) 'Transfer Pricing by Multinational Marketers: Risky Business', *Business Horizons*, January–February, pp. 17–22.

Hollensen, S. (2001) *Global Marketing – A Market-responsive Approach*, Pearson Education Limited, London, p. 458.

Johansson, J.K. and Nonaka, I. (1996) 'Relentless – The Japanese Way of Marketing', *HarperBusiness*, US, pp. 126–129.

Keegan, W.J. and Schlegelmilch, B. (2001) *Global Marketing Management: A European Perspective*, Prentice Hall, Harlow, UK.

Maxwell, S. (2001) 'Biased Attributions of a Higher than Expected Price: A Cross Cultural Analysis', *Proceedings of the European Marketing Academy*, 8–11 May, Bergen, Norges Handelshoyskole.

Noonan, C. (1999) *Export Marketing; A Practical Guide to Opening and Expanding Markets Overseas*, 2nd edn, Butterworth-Heinemann, Oxford.

Onkavist, S. and Shaw, J.J. (1990) *International Marketing: Analysis and Strategy*, Maxwell Macmillan, New York, Chapter 16.

Robert, M. (1993) '*Strategy Pure and Simple: How Winning CEOs Outthink their Competition*', McGraw Hill Inc.

Simon, H. and Dolan, R. (1997) *Profit durch Power Pricing*, Campus, Frankfurt, p. 168.

Terpstra, V. and Sarathy, R. (2000) *International Marketing*, 8th edn, Dryden Press, Fort Worth, Texas.

Usunier, J. (1993) *International Marketing: A Cultural Approach*, Prentice Hall, UK, Chapter 10.

12

Effective international distribution

Learning objectives

After reading this chapter you should be able to:

- appreciate the role of distribution in the international marketing mix;

- compare alternative international channels of distribution;

- integrate the alternative distribution strategies available to the international marketer;

- discuss techniques for managing international distribution channels;

- perceive how differences in international wholesaling and retailing impact on other elements of the distribution channel;

- relate global issues of standardisation and grey markets to international distribution; and

- examine the impact of physical distribution in international marketing on international competitiveness.

The elusive agent

Source: Digital Vision.

When many firms begin doing business in international markets, they commence their involvement by appointing an agent or distributor. Usually this occurs on their first visit to the market during which they establish the agreed parameters of the arrangement. Frequently, following their return home, they mostly ignore the agent, expecting that business will automatically flow. Some months later they become disillusioned because orders have not eventuated and they blame the agent for their failure to penetrate the market. Usually as part of their international expansion, the international would draw up a business plan for the market and a marketing plan for the agent. They would regularly visit the agent to monitor activities and readjust the plan to the needs of the new market and the capabilities of the agent.

Introduction

A channel of distribution is an organised network of agencies that combine to link producers with users. Distribution is the physical flow of goods through channels. A channel is useful in that it makes a product or service available in a convenient location to the customer (*place*), makes the product or service available when the customer wants it (*time*), packages or reprocesses the product or service into a form that the customer can use (*form*), and advises the public about the product and its attributes (*information*).

Distribution channels in international marketing can be a basic source of competitive advantage on the one hand and a cause of problems on the other. This is because small exporters have difficulty in establishing effective channels to distribute their products in the international market and because the headquarters of transnational firms often fail to understand that channels differ from country to country. In addition, channels involve relationships, and skill at managing these relationships will determine the success of firms' international marketing efforts. They also often involve long-term legal commitments and obligations to another party in another country that can be difficult to terminate or change. It is important that the right distribution channels be established in the international market because when goods cross borders, title is transferred to persons in another country, control is more difficult to exercise and the competitive environment is fiercer. Distribution channels in international marketing can be of varying length as indicated in Figure 12.1.

There are a number of different forms by which products can be entered into international markets. These have already been discussed in Chapter 7 as far as their implications for market entry are concerned. These forms can be categorised as follows.

Indirect export – use of an export intermediary

Export intermediaries can be export merchants. These merchants, based in the home market, buy the goods from the firm and ship them to their international customers. The merchant takes title to the goods and the sale in this instance is like a domestic sale.

With the export agent, the agent sells goods in the international market on behalf of the domestic producer and receives a commission on the sale, although they do not take title to the goods. International firms also establish buying offices in international markets and these offices take title to the goods at the time of purchase and usually are responsible for shipment of the goods to their international headquarters or affiliates. In all cases where an export intermediary is involved, the producer has little influence over the final price or control of the marketing of the international products. The benefit is that the producer does not have to spend time developing the international market.

Another form of indirect export is 'piggybacking'. Here a manufacturer uses its established distribution network in the international country to sell another company's product range along with its own. Usually a non-competitive product, the additional item often fleshes out the product range that the established exporter is able to offer in the international market. In other cases, if the original product is seasonal and the new one sells in the reverse season, then the piggyback operation enables the firm to keep

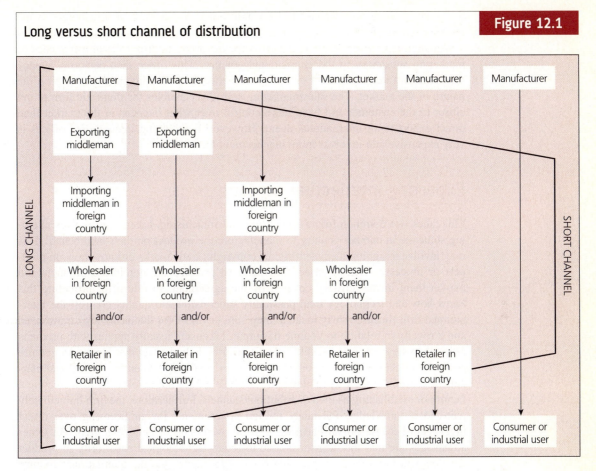

Figure 12.1

Long versus short channel of distribution

Source: Adapted from Keegan (1995), pp. 542, 545.

their sales and distribution operation in the international market busy throughout the year. An example would be a firm that sells both barbecues and oil heaters in a market.

Direct export

The commonest form of market entry for small to medium-sized firms is through the appointment of an agent or distributor. Unlike indirect exporting, the manufacturer undertakes the exporting rather than delegating the task to others. As such, the manufacturer is responsible for organising initial market contact, market research, physical distribution, export documentation and pricing. The advantages are not only direct contact with the international market, but also increased control, improved marketing information and acquisition of international marketing expertise. Often an agent is appointed who then appoints distributors according to the established practice in the international market. Agents represent the domestic company in a defined territory and receive a commission on sales made. They do not take title to the goods although they are responsible for promotion and may receive funds from the domestic firm to promote the product. They are responsible for establishing the network of distributors in the territory for which they are appointed.

An alternative form of direct export is for the domestic firm to establish a sales or marketing subsidiary in the international country. This office then performs agency functions and may sell direct or through a network of distributors depending on the nature of the market. The sales/marketing subsidiary enables the domestic firm to get closer to the customer and have more control over what happens in the market than direct export to an international agent. However, maintaining international offices is very expensive and involves more management time.

Exporting intellectual content

This takes two common forms – licensing and franchising. Licensing involves allowing someone in another country to manufacture the product on their own behalf. This may involve assigning the patent rights, copyright, trade marks or know-how on products or processes. The licensee undertakes to produce the nominated products and market them in the territory covered by the agreement. In return for providing this know-how and technology (and possibility supervision and quality control) the international firm (licensee) may make a lump sum payment for the technology transferred and a royalty in relation to volume of output. Licensing usually applies with products rather than services. Advantages to the licensor include the fact that it does not require an outlay of capital and therefore is a means for small firms to enter international markets. It is also a quick way to gain entry because it does not involve the firm erecting a factory or establishing its own distribution channels. Furthermore, the firm immediately gains local knowledge and many foreign governments favour licensing over direct investment because no surrendering of local ownership or control is involved. Other advantages are that the licensor is able to retain technological superiority in product development in its field, overcoming barriers to import into the international country and gaining additional revenue from a product at the tail end of its life cycle. Licensing agreements usually cover one or more of the following: a patent covering the product or process involved in its manufacture; manufacturing know-how not subject to patent protection; technical assistance; marketing assistance and the use of trade marks.

Franchising is somewhat similar and usually applies at the wholesale/retail level, and particularly with services. Hollensen (2001) describes it as a marketing-oriented method of selling a business service to usually small independent investors with working capital but little business experience. In international marketing, franchising involves allowing the party in the other country access to brand name, design, packaging, marketing systems, training, bulk buying advantages as well as production systems. In return, the franchiser receives payment for items provided and a royalty or share of profits for the marketing and systems support supplied. The rapid recent growth in international franchising has been largely due to the general decline in international trade in manufactures and its replacement by services. The 'business package' supplied by the franchisor is likely to include, where relevant, trade marks, copyright, patents, trade secrets, business know-how and geographical exclusivity. It may also include the right for the franchisee to appoint subfranchisees. Other elements of the package might include managerial assistance in setting up the operation, centrally coordinated advertising and store fit-out.

Both forms of distribution based on intellectual property run the risk of the franchiser being 'ripped off' unless it sets a minimum amount for royalty payments and establishes a system for monitoring turnover. Another risk is that the transfer of intellectual property can result in the franchiser 'cloning a future competitor'.

Manufacturing in international markets

This can take the form of assembly, contract manufacture, joint venture or acquisition. The extent of the firm's involvement in production and marketing varies with the approach it chooses. Assembly involves shipping the product to the international market either in 'knocked-down' form, as with motor vehicles, or as component parts. Frequent motives for this include duty rates on parts being much lower than on the finished product, transport costs on components or kits being lower than on built-up units, and assembly being a relatively unskilled task which can often be done more cheaply in the international market, especially if that market is in a developing country.

Assembly

Often such assembly takes place in a Foreign Trade Zone (FTZ). These have been established in over 50 countries by, or with the blessing of, government, with the aim of attracting industry to their shores and creating employment that would normally be driven away because of trade barriers. Usually, the government and/or zone administrators provide a range of incentives to encourage foreign firms to locate there. These incentives can include tax holidays, duty-free admission of goods and plant, subsidised rents, infrastructure and facilities (e.g. power and water). Specifically, such facilities enable the foreign firm to bring goods into the country without paying duties as long as it remains within the zone or bonded warehouse. Many allow processing, assembly, sorting and repacking within the zone. Other advantages include the economies of being able to ship in bulk to a country without paying customs duties until the goods are released into the distribution channel, and take advantage of the lower labour costs available in that market for relatively unskilled assembly. To a large extent, the advantages of operating in a Foreign Trade Zone will depend on the duty rates because the zones are designed to compensate for high tariff barriers. Where barriers are low, they are not as attractive as many of the other advantages such as bulk shipping, and low cost labour can be obtained outside these zones. The Bataan Export Processing Zone in the Philippines is an examples of such a zones.

Contract manufacture

Contract manufacture occurs when the international firm produces goods for the domestic firm, has no title or rights to the output and is paid for the manufacturing process. Marketing remains the responsibility of the domestic firm. The goods could be destined for the country in which they are manufactured, for third countries or, as is increasingly the case, for the domestic market. Contract manufacture is usually driven by the attraction of cheap labour costs and access to raw materials. It involves relatively little risk to the firm (apart from a potential for pirating of the technology) and no outlay of investment capital. Contract manufacturing is an attractive option if the firm's expertise is in marketing or branding rather than in manufacturing. This is often seen with textiles, clothing and footwear. It avoids problems due to unfamiliarity with the country, such as labour issues, while at the same time allows the firm to claim that the product is made locally.

Joint ventures

Joint ventures are the most common form of manufacturing in international markets by firms. Joint ventures are foreign operations in which the international company has sufficient equity to have a say in management but not enough to dominate the venture. The domestic firm, in conjunction with a partner in the international market, builds and operates a manufacturing facility. The contribution by the local firm can vary and may include equity, buildings, local contacts, market knowledge and access to raw materials. Often the percentage of equity that the local firm must have is dictated by the local government as a condition of the awarding of investment approval. In a number of developing countries, this must be at least 51%, which can cause problems when the contribution of the local firm is far less than that of the international company. In order to encourage development of new industries, export-generating industries or location of new industries in poorer parts of the country, international governments often grant new joint ventures investment incentives ranging from tax holidays to duty-free import of raw materials and components. Compared with other forms of manufacture discussed above, joint ventures potentially deliver greater returns from equity participation compared with royalties, greater control over production and marketing, better feedback from the market, and greater hands-on experience in international marketing.

Acquisition

A final form of manufacturing in international markets involves acquiring an existing operation or building a plant from scratch (greenfield operation). This option requires considerable investment, involves building up a base of contacts and requires considerable research as to conditions in the market. Another disadvantage is that it is more susceptible to expropriation than the joint venture because of its lack of local equity. It does have the advantage that the international firm retains total control of the operation from production to marketing to delivery to the final customer. The laws of many countries put conditions on greenfield investments and prohibit or restrict acquisition of existing businesses.

Strategic alliances

Strategic alliances are another way of being able to distribute products in international markets. They cover a variety of non-equity contractual relationships, frequently between competitors in different countries. Cross-border strategic alliances have become a popular vehicle for international expansion in cases where firms face internationalisation pressures. These are an increasing phenomenon in international marketing and are discussed in depth in Chapter 17.

Distribution strategies

Developing distribution strategies for getting goods to the international marketplace often involves dependence on intermediaries. Kim and Frazier (1997) have developed a typology for the necessary degree of commitment between supplier and intermediary under different situations. They contrast the circumstance of high versus low environmental uncertainty with both the extent to which intermediaries add value to the finished product in the hands of international customers (low value-added versus high value-added) and the degree to which the intermediary can replace the firm as a supplier. An adaptation of their typology is shown in Figure 12.2.

Cell 1 depicts 'market exchanges'. In this form of interaction between supplier and intermediary, both parties have a very low commitment to the relationship and can easily change partners.

Cell 2 depicts 'short-term relationships'. In this form of interaction, both parties have a 'low' rather than a 'very low' commitment to the relationship influenced by the higher perceived degree of environmental uncertainty and volatility in the distribution channel.

Cell 3 depicts 'supplier domination'. In this form of interaction, intermediaries have greater difficulty in replacing suppliers than suppliers have in replacing intermediaries. Because the environment is stable, this domination of the channel by the supplier is likely to continue beyond the short term.

Cell 4 depicts 'supplier leadership'. In this form of interaction, suppliers are dominant because of the low value added by intermediaries, but the uncertainty of the environment makes it difficult for suppliers to manage without the intermediary,

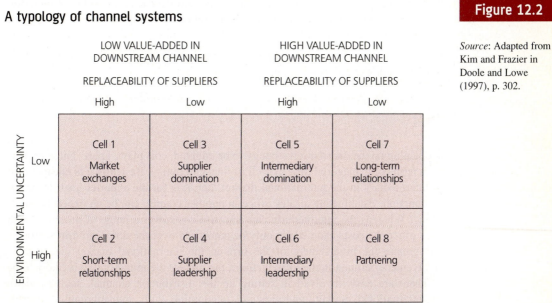

A typology of channel systems

Figure 12.2

Source: Adapted from Kim and Frazier in Doole and Lowe (1997), p. 302.

	LOW VALUE-ADDED IN DOWNSTREAM CHANNEL		HIGH VALUE-ADDED IN DOWNSTREAM CHANNEL	
	REPLACEABILITY OF SUPPLIERS		REPLACEABILITY OF SUPPLIERS	
	High	Low	High	Low
Low	Cell 1 — Market exchanges	Cell 3 — Supplier domination	Cell 5 — Intermediary domination	Cell 7 — Long-term relationships
High	Cell 2 — Short-term relationships	Cell 4 — Supplier leadership	Cell 6 — Intermediary leadership	Cell 8 — Partnering

ENVIRONMENTAL UNCERTAINTY

with the result that both parties have a medium degree of commitment to the overall relationship.

Cell 5 depicts 'intermediary domination'. In this form of interaction, the intermediary adds considerable value to the product and suppliers are not difficult to replace. In this situation, suppliers have a greater stake in investing resources in the relationship than do intermediaries.

Cell 6 depicts 'intermediary leadership'. In this form of interaction, intermediaries are in the dominant position because the value they add is high. However, because environmental uncertainty is high, intermediaries have a greater need to coordinate with suppliers.

Cell 7 depicts 'long-term relationships'. In this form of interaction, both parties are highly committed to each other because suppliers are difficult to replace and intermediaries add significant value. The combination of the right channel member and strong channel ties can yield a distinct competitive advantage.

Cell 8 depicts 'partnering'. In this form of interaction, the uncertain environment reaffirms the need for both parties to work closely with each other and creates a strong motivation to closely coordinate the channel relationship. It leads to a high level of joint activities between the parties.

The above typology can assist the firm in developing a strategy for deciding on the relationship that it needs to establish with a potential intermediary. It involves balancing a realistic perception of the relative strengths of both itself and the international intermediary with the degree of uncertainty in the international environment.

A consideration of the specific factors to be taken into account when planning the distribution system should take into account the following:

- a distribution system is the major link between a company and its customers;
- a distribution system takes considerable time and capital to build and is not changed easily;
- the way the distribution system is structured will have a strong influence on both the market segments that can be reached, and on the ability to execute certain marketing strategies; and
- the distribution system influences companies' ability to penetrate new international markets or expand existing ones.

Cost

In deciding on the distribution strategy to be adopted, cost plays a part. These costs can be in terms of managerial time as well as financial outlay. Basically it is cheaper to use an intermediary in the international market than it is for the exporter itself to perform the function. Establishing a sales office in another country can be an expensive undertaking. Whereas the intermediary can amortise costs over a range of products, with a sales office the costs can usually only be amortised over the domestic firm's products. The greater the involvement of the firm in the international market (see forms of involvement outlined in the introduction), the greater the initial outlay is likely to be.

There are costs involved in setting up the distribution channel, such as visiting the international market, interviewing, negotiating with and appointing members.

Maintaining the channel also involves expenses such as those that would be incurred by regular visits to the international market and providing promotional support for channel members. Finally, there are associated logistics costs, such as providing, funding and replenishing inventory. Costs vary according to the relative power of the supplier as opposed to the intermediary. The greater the power of the intermediary, the greater the likelihood that costs such as promotion and inventory carrying will be met by the domestic firm.

Another issue is that of cash flow to parties in the distribution channel. A decision needs to be made as to who extends credit to customers – is it the domestic supplier or is it the intermediary in the international market?

Control

The use of intermediaries will lead to a degree of loss of control over how the firm's products are marketed in the international market. The looser the relationship between the domestic firm and the intermediary (see the Kim and Frazier typology discussed earlier), the less control the supplier can exert. In addition, the longer the distribution channel, the less the likelihood that the supplier can have any say over the marketing mix variables of price and promotion in the international market. Therefore, the greater the importance of exercising control over the distribution channel, the greater the likelihood that the firm will become directly involved in distribution activities in international markets.

From a strategic point of view there is a trade-off between desire for control and the wish to minimise commitment of resources to the international market. Where control is important, the firm is more likely to establish its own salesforce in the international market as opposed to working through agents and distributors. Often firms new to a market commence operations using an intermediary because of the intermediary's specialised knowledge of the market. With experience of dealing in the market, the firm may replace the agent with its own local sales office so that it can directly monitor the network of distributors.

Commitment

Commitment impacts on distribution strategy. One indicator of commitment is the degree and manner in which it is intended to cover the selected international market. Alternatives are to distribute the product through the largest number of intermediaries catering for the largest number of market segments; to select only one market segment and choose a limited number of intermediaries for that segment; to select multiple segments but only one or several intermediaries for each chosen segment; or finally, select only one intermediary who will cater for all segments in the international market. One constraint on the above is that of the potential profit to the intermediary of representing the firm's product. It may be necessary for the intermediary to seek exclusive distribution for the whole market on the basis that without it the firm's line would not be worth handling. On the other hand, a single agent may be a better strategy when entering a new international market because:

- single representation eliminates confusion among local buyers;
- the larger volume represented by the sole agent may attract larger distributors;
- promotion of the product to the trade will be without contradictory claims because it is coordinated by only one agent;
- sales and promotional activities can be more effectively coordinated;
- logistics will be more economical;
- a sole agent is more likely to cover minor (and possibly currently unprofitable) segments of the international market because of its exclusivity for the whole market;
- the relationship between the principal and the international intermediary is likely to be better because of the larger stake each has in the success of the other.

Nature of the market

Distribution strategy will be affected by the economic health of the country. This is because the investment of resources will vary according to the distribution mode employed. Before the currency crisis in Brazil, Argentina and Indonesia, firms may have contemplated opening their own sales office in these markets; such firms now are more likely to rely on an international agent until they can see how the crisis and subsequent political upheavals will be resolved.

Another issue is whether the selected distribution channel is vulnerable to political change, such as being outlawed or nationalised. In some countries (e.g. Libya) intermediaries are not allowed, in others they must be government undertakings (as in China). In a number of countries, retailing is also controlled by the government. In some cases (e.g. Japan) this control is exercised to protect the small retailer who is considered part of the social fabric. Regulations on retailing can take the form of zoning the location of stores (especially supermarkets and large retail complexes), control over hours of opening and requirements governing health and safety. In non-socialist countries governments often engage directly in retailing (e.g. various State Government Liquor Control Board retail outlets in Canada) and in wholesaling (e.g. Thailand Tobacco Monopoly).

Customer characteristics in the international market influence distribution channels because they dictate how buyers prefer to acquire their products. In this connection, it is necessary to research not only what customers need but also why they buy, when they buy, and how they buy. Different distribution channels are likely to be needed for food products in Japan. This is because people are more likely to buy small quantities on a daily basis due to space being at a premium in their small apartments and refrigerators being small as a result. This contrasts with the scene in the United States where accommodation is larger, shopping more infrequent and refrigerators larger.

Other factors deriving from the nature of the market that impact on distribution strategies include the potential for the product in the international market. The larger the potential, the greater the likelihood that it will be worth investing resources to ensure control over the distribution channel. Another factor is the way the market operates – cartels or trade associations will influence whether direct involvement is a possibility and, if not, the nature of the intermediary arrangement.

Nature of product/service

Product attributes, such as degree of standardisation, extent of perishability, bulk, servicing requirements and unit price, influence both channel design and the distribution strategy. Products with a high price per unit are more likely to be sold direct to the end-user/customer, whereas bulky products often only justify direct marketing. Products that are complex, such as computers, require intermediaries to provide installation and aftersales service. Sophisticated products may justify a more direct form of distribution than fast moving consumer goods, while other products such as cosmetics need large margins to 'incentivise' the salesforce and, as a result, may be sold door-to-door. Perishable products need direct channels of distribution because of their limited life span, and bulk commodities usually require channels which minimise the number of intermediaries because of buyer resistance to high prices.

Viewed from another perspective, transportation and warehousing are critical factors for basic industrial goods; direct selling and servicing are critical factors for more sophisticated industrial products such as computers, machinery and transportation equipment, and durability, ease of servicing, and type of servicing required are factors influencing the distribution of durable consumer goods. Figure 12.3, adapted from Czinkota and Ronkainen (1998), illustrates different channel configurations according to whether the exported product is a consumer good, an industrial product or a service.

As Figure 12.3 shows, there are more intermediaries in the channel for consumer goods than in the channel for industrial products. This is possibly because of the higher price and/or larger volume orders placed by the final customer. Also, there are fewer intermediaries for services than for the other two categories and this may be due to the direct involvement of the provider of the service in the delivery of the service.

Channel alternatives

Figure 12.3

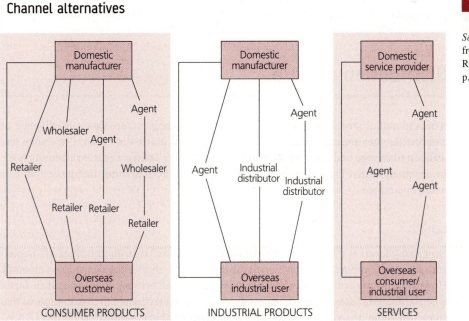

Source: Adapted from Czinkota and Ronkainen (1998), p. 385.

| Figure 12.4 | Comparing strategies | | | | | |

STRATEGY	Contractual relationship	Profit potential	Credit risk exposure	Control	Market information	Risk/ commitment
Direct sales	No	Excellent	High	Yes	Low	Low
Agent/rep.	Yes	5%–15% of price to agent/rep.	Med. high	No	Moderate	Low
Distributor	Yes	Good after discount	Low	No	Fair	Low/mod.
Licensing	Yes	You get 3%–15%	Very low	No	Fair	Low
Joint venture/ subsidiary	Yes	Very good	N/A	Maybe/yes	Very good	High

Source: Adapted from *World Trade* (1999), p. 46.

Objectives of the firm

The design of the international distribution channel will be influenced by and will also be a vehicle for implementing the objectives of the firm. Any channel of distribution must meet company objectives for overall profitability and market share. However, international channels may change as the firm's operations in the international market expand. For example, initially a firm may distribute in the international market through an agent, then it might establish its own salesforce, and finally, once significant market share is in prospect, it might establish its own retail network as happened with Country Road in the United States.

Figure 12.4 compares alternative international distribution strategies in terms of profit potential, credit exposure, control, information and risk/commitment.

Distribution criteria

It is important that the structure of distribution channels is considered in advance of entering the international market because, once put in place, distribution structures are difficult to change and a wrong decision may have long-lasting negative consequences. In designing a distribution channel decisions about the following features should be made in advance.

Length

How many levels is it necessary to have in an international distribution channel? In general, the more economically developed the country, the shorter the distribution channel. However, this may not always be the case and other factors may intervene, as in Japan where shortage of storage space necessitates an extended channel of distribution so that stock can be held at various points along the channel. This is shown in Figure 12.5.

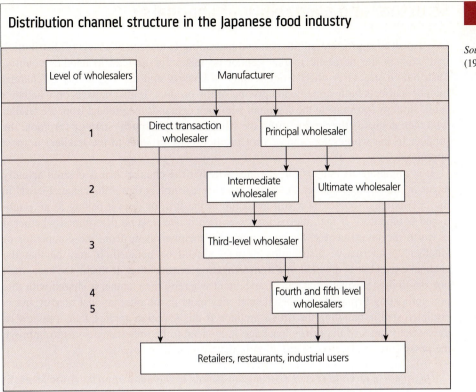

Distribution channel structure in the Japanese food industry

Source: Krause (1992), p. 140.

Width

This is determined by the number of each type of intermediary in the channel. The larger the number of similar intermediaries, the greater the width of the channel and the higher the level of competition. However, the wider the channel, the easier it is to locate effective distributors.

Density

This is the exposure or coverage desired for the product to achieve a profitable penetration of the international market (e.g. the number of sales outlets necessary to cover the whole market).

Alignment

This refers to the extent of coordination between members of the channel so as to achieve a uniform and integrated approach in getting the product to the final consumer.

Logistics

This is the physical transfer of the product from the plant in the domestic to the customer in the international market.

Structure and availability of channels

One aspect to appreciate in international marketing is that the channels of distribution that exist in the domestic market cannot be taken for granted in another country. Distribution structures differ from country to country and the availability of channel members affects both strategy and pricing of the product. It also impacts on whether a 'pull' strategy (promote to the customer who then demands the product from the retailer who then demands the product from the wholesaler) or a 'push' strategy (promote the product to the wholesaler who in turn promotes the product to the retailer) is most appropriate.

It is important to establish in advance whether the channel that is desired actually exists in the selected market. A second issue to research is that if the channel exists in the international market, is it still available to the firm or does it belong to an established competitor? If the latter is the case, then it needs to be determined whether it is worth the investment seducing the channel member away from the competitor or whether an alternative distribution channel should be pursued. It may be that the channel exists but is devoted to a non-competing organisation. If this is the case, then one possibility is to negotiate an arrangement whereby the channel is shared with this non-competing firm. Finally, the channel may exist in the international market, but is not interested in handling the firm's product. If this situation applies, then a review of the attractiveness of the firm's 'package' may need to be undertaken so as to improve the possibility of effective distribution in the target market.

One feature of channels of distribution in less developed countries is the large number of people engaged in selling very small quantities of merchandise. Although such a situation often attracts criticism from those in developed countries, given the low cost of labour and limited availability of capital, the distribution system is a rational one given the constraints under which less developed countries operate.

Cultural issues

Distribution channels are designed to bridge the gap between domestic sellers and international buyers. There are two dimensions to this gap (see Chapter 3) – one is the physical distance between buyer and seller and the other is the attitudinal and perceptual distance between buyer and seller. This latter dimension, often referred to as the psychic distance, is largely culturally influenced due to the role played in distribution channels by the formation of interpersonal relationships. Researchers such as Gatignon and Anderson (1986) have found that the greater the degree of psychic distance of the domestic from the foreign market, the less will be the firm's commitment of resources to the international market and the greater the likelihood that involvement will be via an agent rather than on a direct basis. As psychic distance is usually based on perceived risk and lack of knowledge, where this is great, use of intermediaries is a preferred option.

Japan provides a good illustration of the impact of culture on the distribution system. Because the Japanese are extremely fastidious about detail and quality of service, retailers provide home delivery, stay open 12 or 13 hours a day, are open most days, readily accept return of goods and are liberal in offering credit to regular customers. This cultural expectation of service and loyalty is passed back through the distribution channel to wholesalers and producers.

Government and legal constraints

Government regulation of distribution can impact on the design of the channel, especially when it is necessary to structure the channel to circumvent the government-regulated elements of the distribution system. In some countries, government regulation has been designed to protect small businesses (e.g. the 'large scale retail law' in Japan). Protective regulation can relate to store location, store opening hours, and the establishment of government-controlled monopolies.

Channel activities in international markets are also subject to varying legal regulations, such as retail price maintenance, turnover taxes, liability legislation, legislation covering middlemen and dealer rights, laws governing termination of agents, restrictions on territory to be covered and reciprocal selling arrangements. Legal factors such as the above will make some distribution arrangements in the international market more attractive to the firm than others.

Commercial and environmental constraints

Differences in the nature of the distribution channels between countries are due to a number of commercially related factors: in some countries, the intermediary function may rest with a particular group; in many South-East Asian countries, this function is controlled by the Chinese minority; in other countries, such as in Africa, the intermediary function is undertaken by more recently arrived immigrants (often Indians). This can engender specific attitudes in that country towards middlemen.

Customer orientation also plays a role because in some countries, intermediaries only perform a distribution function (e.g. Saudi Arabia) whereas in other countries (e.g. India), intermediaries provide full customer service.

Another variable is the breadth of the line carried by the intermediary. This can involve a wide variety of products as is the case with the indigenised successors of the trading companies from the pre-Second World War era (e.g. Dieltem or the East Asiatic Company in Thailand); whereas other intermediaries may specialise in a narrow product line. Costs and margins levied by intermediaries will also vary substantially between countries because of the degree of local competition, the differing expectation as to service to be provided, and local salespeople's wages.

Another competitive issue alluded to earlier is whether the best agents and distributors in the international market are already committed to competitors. If this is the case, then different channels of distribution may need to be used to access target customers. Veering away from the established pattern of distribution in a country may be a way of gaining a competitive advantage.

Finally, the general characteristics of the overall environment in a country are a major consideration in designing the distribution channel. The purchasing power of the customers, the demographic characteristics of the population, the lifestyle preferences of the target group, percentage of females in the workforce, the nature and size of homes and the nature/adequacy of infrastructure (power, water, transport by road, rail or sea) are just some of the factors in the wider environment which can impact on distribution. They impact on the number of stages in the channel, the size of the wholesalers and retailers and the breadth of the line carried.

Managing international distribution

Managing international distribution is critical to success in international markets because it often involves the firm accepting a lack of control in the international market in exchange for a low-risk form of market entry. This applies to most firms when they commence exporting as they usually begin exporting through agents rather than direct to the final customer in the international market. In the international market, the agent is the physical presence of the firm and can enhance or damage the image of the firm, especially if the agent pursues its own interests rather than those of its principal.

Selection

Experts estimate that more than half of all world trade is handled through agents and distributors (Classen, 1991). Given this estimate, the selection of the right agent and/or distributor for the firm in the international market is critically important. Because the agent is the face of the firm in the international market, before selecting an agent or distributor, extensive screening of as many potential intermediaries as possible is essential, according to research undertaken by Karunaratna and Johnson (1997).

The first line of inquiry is to ascertain how similar products are already being distributed in the international market, which intermediaries are used by local producers and which firms distribute imported products in the same category.

When selecting an agent or distributor, it is important to select a firm whose size is commensurate with that of the firm. If the firm in the foreign market is much larger, it is likely to merely list rather than to aggressively promote the product. If, on the other hand, the international agent is much smaller, it is unlikely that that firm can secure adequate coverage, finance sufficient inventory, and promote the products in all segments that the firm desires in order to make the export of the product to the foreign market worthwhile.

Distribution channels are heavily dependent on and influenced by relationships. Those that apply to imported products are often different from those that apply to domestic products in many countries. For this reason, it is desirable to look for an intermediary firm that is experienced in handling imported products and which understands the differences involved in dealing with foreigners.

Motivating an agent to aggressively promote a product without an established brand image in the foreign country can be a challenge. One way around this is to seek an agent already in the same area of business, that does not have a similar product. The agent is then able to flesh out the range his distributors can offer to their established clients. Therefore it is important to search out agents handling complementary products.

The seeds of a satisfactory relationship must be sown before the agency relationship commences. This requires that the firm work out in advance what it wants from the relationship and communicates this to those it approaches regarding representation. This forward planning will help avoid one common problem that arises – that of 'cherry picking'. This occurs when the intermediary decides to handle some but not all items in the range that the firm wishes to introduce to the international market. When the agency arrangement is not specific this 'cherry picking' can occur after an exclusive agency arrangement has been concluded, preventing the firm from appointing another agent to handle the lines not being promoted.

A final issue that needs to be taken into account and resolved in the process of selecting an agent is that of marketing approach and responsibility for promotion. It is important to ensure that the selected agent has a similar marketing approach to that of the firm. Otherwise there could be discordant images in overlapping markets that are served by different agents. A cause of considerable conflict between the international agent and principal is, who should pay for promotion in the international market? Firms often consider that the agent should fund promotion out of the agent's profit margin, whereas the agent feels that promotion is the responsibility of the firm. If resolution of this issue is left until after the agent is appointed, the result is that no promotion takes place. Not only should this issue be resolved before the agent is appointed but willingness to spend some portion of profit margin on promotion could be a factor in selecting the right agent.

To obtain lists of potential agents in a foreign market, there are several sources. In the first place chambers of commerce or chambers of manufactures in both the targeted country and in the exporting country could be sources of initial leads. Sometimes potential agents advertise in industry journals that circulate internationally. Another source of agents and distributors is to visit trade displays in the target market which focus on the industry of which the firm is a member. At such displays, many of those exhibiting products complementary to the firm's product could be interested potential agents. The most frequently used source of information on this subject is the trade commissioner in the target market. Not only is the trade commissioner in a position to provide a list but they can also provide background information and often a credit-check on potential intermediaries. Once a shortlist has been developed based on the factors previously discussed, then those firms remaining on the list should be compared on the basis of a grid similar to that in Table 12.1.

This grid will enable the firm to rate those intermediaries that appear most promising. The next step should be to visit the country to interview those remaining firms. Unfortunately, many firms only view the agent's office, not the agent's activity. An important part of the appraisal is to go with the agent's salespeople on calls to see how they conduct their representation of other imported products and how they are received by the trade.

Appointment

Once it has been decided which agent is to be appointed, then an agreement should be drawn up which clearly spells out the details of the arrangement. The agreement should specify which products will be represented and the boundaries of the area within which the agent will represent the firm. While the agent may wish to represent the total range,

Table 12.1 International agent selection criteria

Criteria	Weight	Distributor 1 Rating Score	Distributor 2 Rating Score	Distributor 3 Rating Score
1. Financial soundness				
2. Marketing management expertise				
3. Satisfactory trade, customer relations, and contacts				
4. Capability to provide adequate sales coverage				
5. Overall positive reputation and image				
6. Product compatibility (synergy or conflct?)				
7. Pertinent technical know-how at staff level				
8. Adequate technical facilities and service support				
9. Adequate sales infrastructure				
10. Proven performance record with client companies				
11. Positive attitude towards the company's products				
12. Trading area or region covered				
13. Excellent government relations				
14. Warehousing and storage facilities				
15. Experience in representing foreign frms				
16. Willingness to promote product/service				

Scales

Rating

5 Outstanding
4 Above average
3 Average
2 Below average
1 Unsatisfactory

Weighting

5 Critical success factor
4 Prerequisite success factor
3 Important success factor
2 Of some importance
1 Standard value

Source: Adapted from *Business International* (1983), p. 92.

care needs to be taken to ensure that the agent has the capability and distribution network in all the product areas for effective representation. If not, then it is best to restrict the range to areas where the agent is competent and appoint other agents for other areas.

Often agents will seek representation rights for a whole country or even a geographical region. It is important to check in which areas within the country or region the agent has an effective distribution network. To give an agent rights to a whole country (e.g. USA) when the agent only operates in part of it (e.g. California) is to exclude the firm's range from a major market area. If there is uncertainty as to the area of effective representation, it may be best to initially confine representation to the agent's current area of effectiveness and review the issue in two years subject to the agent's results.

Usually agents seek an exclusive arrangement that prevents the firm from appointing another agent in the country. If this is the case, it is important that the agreement be for a specified time period so that another agent can be appointed if the appointed agent does not perform or should the firm wish to establish its own sales office or manufacturing arrangement in the market. It is also useful to check that the agent does not handle any competing lines, and a clause preventing the agent from doing so should be included in the agreement. There have been cases where firms with a number of similar products have taken on the firm's line and done nothing to promote it – their motive being to keep it out of the market. Generally speaking, both parties should have an exclusive arrangement with each other, or neither party should have an exclusive arrangement with the other.

Communication and control

This phase of activity should be driven by the notion of creating a positive operating climate so as to improve chances of a long-term satisfactory relationship. To achieve this, it is desirable to promptly answer correspondence in a sympathetic and friendly manner, and to provide the agent with copies of all company material – even if this material is not directly related to the agent's duties for the principal. Such material should include company bulletins, company newsletters, staff bulletins, new product information, public relations releases and fact sheets on new products. This assists in making the agent feel part of the firm's corporate family. In addition, mention of the agent's activities should be included in the above information where possible.

Once appointed, the agent should be visited regularly. The visit should be by the executive responsible for the agency (e.g. not by the managing director or other employee on a junket!), be planned well in advance and have specific objectives that have been agreed upon with the agent in advance.

It is also important to bring the agent to the firm's domestic base shortly after appointment – the visit could be timed to coincide with a national sales conference. This visit is desirable not only to enable the agent to meet the firm's managers and view the production process, but also to enhance the agent's credibility in the other country as the firm's representative. When the agent's customers ask details about where the product is made and the agent admits that he has never seen the manufacturing process, his credibility as the firm's representative suffers.

Motivation and termination

Any relationship should be operated on the basis that it is a 'win–win' exercise for both parties rather than an arrangement where each party tries to be opportunistic and take advantage of the other. This is especially the case with agency arrangements. It is essential to create strong loyalty throughout the international distribution network. This leads to a good image in the international market and is good public relations. The philosophy underlying the relationship is that both parties have a long-term horizon for their relationship and each is willing to invest in it.

Remuneration of agents is another issue on which many international agency arrangements founder. It should conform to or preferably exceed general rates of commission in the international market. If it exceeds the prevailing rate, then the agent might be more likely to put extra effort into promoting the firm's product. If training and development is provided at the expense of the principal, this also provides an incentive, not only for the agent but also for salespersons and distributors. In most cases, the agent handles a number of lines of which the new product is only one. However, because the firm's product is unknown, it requires extra effort during the first year of its introduction to the market. The remuneration package should reflect this.

In order to ensure that the agent devotes extra effort to a new international product during the initial year when it is being introduced into the new international market, some firms pay the salary of one of the sales personnel of the agent or distributor. In return, that person sells only the firm's product. The agent wins because he still receives commission on all products sold and the firm wins because of the effort being devoted its product. Also, at varying times, some of this outlay may be claimable by the exporting firm against the government's export incentive programmes.

Transfer of knowledge and identification with the principal is important. This may be facilitated by the firm training the agent's staff – either in the foreign country or in the domestic markets. Training should be frequent and involve knowledge of the company and its products in general, in-depth knowledge of the products included in the agency arrangement, servicing of the products if applicable, how the product should be sold (taking into account cultural and commercial differences in the foreign market), and communications activities (e.g. the form and style of reporting and effective presentation of the product).

It is necessary from the outset to reach a clear understanding with the agent as to how performance of the product in the international market will be measured. This could be on the basis of market share, sales volume, number of times inventory turns over per annum, annual growth rates or extent of floor/shelf space secured for the product. Such standards should be included in the agreement if at all possible. Some of the above measures require access to industry-based market research that may not be available or reliable in many developing countries. If this is the case, objectives should be set in terms of sales volumes. Performance should be evaluated not only in relation to agreed objectives but also in terms of performance by the industry in that country and in relation to customary business practices. Furthermore, in evaluating performance it is necessary not to accept excuses for non-performance for which the agent is responsible while also being understanding about non-performance due to situations over

A motivational model for agents and distributors

Figure 12.6

Source: Noonan (1999), p. 100.

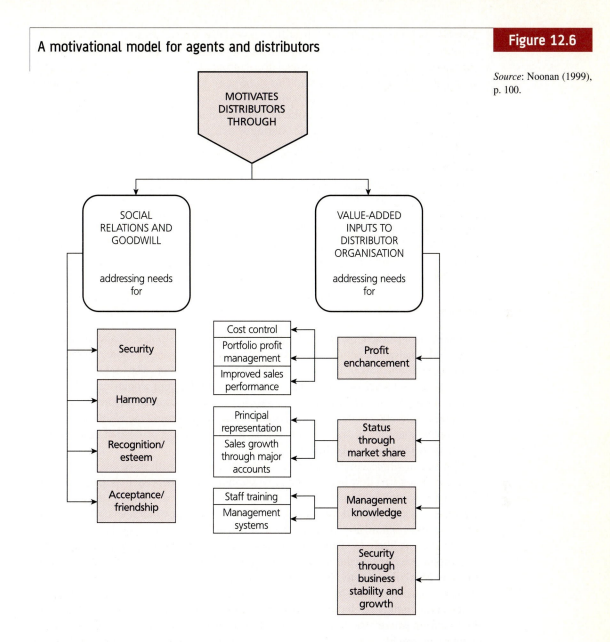

which the agent has no control (e.g. the financial crisis in Asia in late 1997). Figure 12.6 encapsulates many of the above factors.

If it is decided to terminate the arrangement, this must be handled with tact and in accordance with both the contract and accepted practice in the international country. Perceived unfair termination can provoke hostility in the trade which could impact on efforts to attract an alternative agent or to the reception of the firm's product if the firm decides to establish its own sales office or manufacturing facility in that country. Such termination can cause insecurity among others in the established distribution channel and can provoke government hostility, especially if the agent is well connected politically. Sometimes termination of agency arrangements can give rise to claims for substantial legal compensation especially if grounds for termination are not clearly spelt out in the agency agreement. This is because local courts tend to be favourably disposed towards local firms. In some countries, termination might not be possible (e.g. Saudi Arabia). In others (e.g. Latin America) it is time-consuming, expensive and requires considerable advance notice during which period little promotion or selling of the firm's product is likely to occur.

Wholesaling and retailing

The next stages in the distribution channel for most consumer goods have traditionally been wholesaling and retailing. However, patterns of distribution in many countries are changing and various intermediaries in the distribution channel between manufacturer and retailer or between manufacturer and customer are disappearing.

Wholesaling

Wholesalers undertake purchasing, selling, transportation, storage, financing and to an extent information gathering. In some countries, however, one or more of these functions may be undertaken by the manufacturer or the retailer. The status and role of the wholesaler varies from country to country. In developing countries, wholesalers play an important role in financing the flow of goods between manufacturer and retailer. Because wholesalers trade rather than manufacture and because the wholesale trade in developing countries is often dominated by minority groups of distinct ethnic origin, wholesalers often tend to be held in low esteem.

The size of wholesaling operations varies substantially, with some countries such as Finland having very few but very large wholesalers and others such as Japan having a multitude of small wholesalers. The quality of service often relates to the size of the wholesaler, especially in developing countries, with smaller wholesalers having limited capital and less know-how. In markets with fragmented wholesaling, incomplete market coverage is likely to result, with the consequence that the firm may need to undertake promotion direct to the consumer. Table 12.2 illustrates the size of wholesalers and the ratio of wholesalers to retailers in a selection of countries.

The services provided by wholesalers also depend on the nature of the competition because this influences the margins that prevail and the variety of services provided. In countries where wholesalers are numerous, margins low and competition fierce, wholesalers are likely to provide a variety of services from financing to maintenance of inventory. This is especially the case where the retail sector is small and under-financed as in Pakistan. In industrialised countries, wholesalers are facing pressure both from manufacturers who are increasingly dealing direct with retailers and from retailers who are increasingly dealing direct with manufacturers. In this situation, to justify their continued existence, wholesalers are having to provide services tailored to the needs of both manufacturer and retailer. Whereas smaller wholesalers in many countries handle only a particular category of goods, they can coexist with larger wholesalers who deal in a wide variety of unrelated products. As mentioned earlier, in developing countries, some of these larger wholesalers are the successors of the pre-Second World War

Table 12.2 Indicative wholesaling patterns in selected countries

Country	Number of wholesalers (thousand)	Employees per wholesaler	Retailers per wholesaler	Population per wholesaler
Industrialised countries				
United States	416	13	5	564
Japan	429	10	4	274
Italy	120	5	8	473
United Kingdom	80	14	3	698
Belgium	57	3	2	174
Sweden	28	7	3	145
Austria	13	12	3	582
Israel (1980)	5	8	8	782
Newly industrialised countries				
Brazil	46	10	61	2,820
South Korea	46	4	21	878
Ireland	3	14	11	1,139
Chile	1	28	42	20,856
Developing countries				
India	116	–	32	5,612
Turkey	25	4	20	1,923
Egypt	2	24	1	25,596
Kenya	2	13	1	8,257
Centrally planned economies				
Soviet Union	1	120	481	174,922
Yugoslavia	1	124	70	20,000

Note: The above fgures are only indicative, as more recent UN statistics do not differentiate between fgures for wholesalers and retailers.

Source: Adapted from Toyne and Walters (1993), and fgures based on United Nations *Statistical Yearbook*, 1983–1984, pp. 866–89, and 1979–1980, pp. 404–19; and *Statistical Abstract of the United States* (1986), p. 774.

trading companies that used to dominate international business throughout Asia. Many of these firms have integrated backwards into manufacturing and forward into retailing.

A recent development has been wholesalers integrating further forward and selling direct to the more affluent consumer.

In many Asian countries most retailing continues to involve small shops and roadside stalls selling products in small units (e.g. one cigarette stick), despite the advent of supermarkets, department stores and shopping malls. The Dutch wholesaler Macro decided in Thailand in the late 1980s to bypass the established

Table 12.3 Size of retailers in selected countries

Country	Average employment per retailer	Country	Average employment per retailer
Pakistan	1.2	Japan	4.4
Belgium	1.2	Brazil	4.5
Spain	2.1	France	4.5
Mexico	2.2	Sweden	5.3
Israel	2.3	Venezuela	7.2
China	2.4	Canada	8.6
Argentina	3.8	Ghana	10.7
United Kingdom	3.9	United States	13.3
New Zealand	4.3	Germany	13.4

Source: © Euromonitor PLC.

distribution channel for these small retailers and erect large warehouses with cash and carry facilities for wholesalers, enabling them to buy several units at a time as opposed to cases. At the same time, they emulated the US concept of forming a buyers' club allowing more affluent consumers to buy, thus bypassing the supermarket. The Macro approach has caught on and there are now similar approaches in operation in most Asian countries.

Retailing

Retailing operations vary considerably between countries – not only in terms of size of outlet but also in terms of population served and the role of retailing in the social life of the country. Table 12.3 illustrates the relative average size of retail operations between countries.

However, with developing countries, these figures do not reflect the total picture because unlicensed shops, street stalls and street vendors that play an important role in retailing in such countries are not included in the statistics. Table 12.4 provides data on different patterns of retailing between countries.

Although the number of retailers is not strongly influenced by stage of economic development attained, retailing practices are. Even within developing countries, retail patterns in major cities with large numbers of affluent people differ from patterns in smaller towns and rural communities. Size can impact on the level of service that retailers provide. Large retailers usually carry inventory, whereas smaller retailers hold little inventory, creating a need for wholesalers in the channel. Often larger retailers undertake promotion of products either on their own account or in conjunction with manufacturers (cooperative advertising). Smaller retailers expect all promotion to be provided by the manufacturer or wholesaler. It is worth keeping in mind that the concept as to what is meant by a supermarket, a pharmacy and a department store differs from other developed countries (e.g. the US) and other developing countries (e.g.

Table 12.4 Indicative retailing patterns in selected countries

Country	Population (millions)	GNP per capita (US$)	Number of retailers (thousands)	Population per retailer
Industrialised countries				
United States	235	14,080	1,923	126
Japan	119	10,100	1,721	69
Italy	57	6,390	927	61
United Kingdom	56	9,180	232	243
Belgium	10	9,130	132	75
Sweden	8	12,440	76	110
Austria	8	9,230	38	200
Israel (1980)	4	5,270	40	103
Newly industrialised countries				
Brazil	130	1,870	2,817	46
South Korea	40	2,010	946	42
Ireland	4	4,990	32	108
Chile	12	1,890	24	492
Developing countries				
India (1980)	651	260	3,760	173
Turkey (1980)	44	1,250	492	96
Egypt	45	690	2	21,161
Kenya	19	340	3	5,667
Centrally planned economies				
Soviet Union (1980)	263	–	696	379
Yugoslavia	23	2,490	80	286

Note: The above fgures are only indicative, as more recent UN statistics do not differentiate between fgures for wholesalers and retailers.
Source: Adapted from Toyne and Walters (1993), and fgures based on United Nations *Statistical Yearbook*, 1983–1984, pp. 866–90, and 1979–1980, pp. 404–19; and *Statistical Abstract of the United States* (1984), p. 799.

Indonesia). Recent affluence in developing countries has resulted in retail operations that rebut the above generalisation. See International Highlight 12.1.

Differing environments within countries cause the nature of retailing to vary. The level of a country's development and its infrastructure is likely to impact on the pattern of retailing. As an example, supermarkets and larger retail outlets tend to be more prevalent in countries where GNPs per capita are higher. Also the concentration of population within the country and concentrations of pockets of affluence are other environmental determinants of retail patterns. As a consequence, western patterns of retailing are not often appropriate for serving the needs of consumers in third world countries where traditional labour-intensive retailing is more suitable for the marketing

12.1 International highlight

Retailing in transformation

The three examples that follow show different stages of retailing in Asia – all operating in parallel for at least part of the region's population.

In early 1998 Hewlett-Packard relocated its Beijing office into a large, new, high-rise complex. Within six weeks of its relocation a myriad of new clothing shops, restaurants, cafes and bars surrounded its office building – appealing specifically to HP staff and tenants in the new building. Daily specials of merchandise, food and entertainment were offered by these retailers, targeted directly at HP and its neighbours. This rapid transformation of the retail landscape is an almost daily occurrence in the major cities of China.

Source: Corbis.

On 21 August 1998, the largest shopping mall in Asia threw open its glass and chrome doors to Bangkok's eager shoppers. Set alongside a dusty suburban highway, Seacon Square incorporates all the latest tricks of the mega-mall trade: a vast fountain-filled atrium, a 14-screen cinema complex, an amusement park complete with roller coasters – and miles and miles of shops. The arrival of Seacon Square is the largest symptom of Asia's retailing revolution. The mall craze is driven by demographics. Residents of Bangkok now earn on average around US$4,000 a year. The number of households is growing by a steady 2%–3% a year. The expanding middle class has more than enough disposable income to make a trip to the mall a feasible alternative to a visit to a pollution-choked park. As Thais find new ways to spend their money, the landscape of Bangkok is rapidly changing. The dowdy shophouses that have lined the city's commercial districts for a century are giving way to mega-malls, out-of-town hypermarkets and 24-hour convenience stores.

In May 1998 the Internet travel shop, travel.com.au, set up an online corporate site to enable business customers to manage their travel accounts over the net. One advantage is that a businesswoman in, say, Manila who needs to change flight, hotel booking and car rental can do so over the web. In mid-1998 travel.com.au was generating A$1 million per month in Internet revenue.

Sources: Adapted from Davidson (1998), and from *The Economist*, 27 August 1994, p. 59.

of staples which account for the bulk of retail spending. In such countries, to replace labour-intensive retailing on a widespread basis with supermarkets and department stores would add to the growing unemployment and possibly destroy the social fabric of shopping as a daily event involving social intercourse.

Retailing itself has gone international. For the most part this has been motivated by saturation of the domestic market and the desire to export a particular retail offering which might occupy an unfilled niche in the foreign market. Stores have opened branches in other countries and international alliances between stores have evolved to enhance their buying power. Manufacturers, having established a retail chain to sell their products in the home country, then establish retail outlets in other countries when they decide to export to that market (e.g. Country Road of Australia). The internationalisation of retailing is often stimulated by regional trade groupings, which accounts for the expansion of UK department stores such as Marks and Spencer into continental Europe and Japanese department stores such as Isetan, Daimaru and Sogo into South-East Asia. The internationalisation of retailing has been littered with failures illustrating that retailing is basically an operation that has evolved within national boundaries. It is inherently traditional and any innovation is culturally sensitive.

Legislation also has had an impact on the degree to which retailing has gone international. In France, Belgium, Japan and Italy, legislation regulates the establishment of retail operations and controls foreign ownership to preserve the role of local firms in this sector. The way these laws operate in Japan is illustrated in International Highlight 18.1 at the beginning of Chapter 18.

Global distribution issues

There are two issues that often arise when distribution is considered on a global as opposed to a national basis. These are the practicality of achieving standardisation and the frequently occurring problem of grey markets.

Standardisation

Of the marketing mix variables that are usually discussed in connection with the debate on standardisation versus differentiation, distribution receives the least attention. Most academics and practitioners believe that distribution cannot be standardised. This is true if a dichotomised approach is adopted that the firm either standardises or adapts. The reality of international marketing is that there is a continuum between standardisation and adaptation and that feasible standardisation exists somewhere along this continuum. Moreover, there are two aspects to standardisation. One aspect is *process standardisation* – this refers to the development of uniform management practices. Experience indicates that it is easier to standardise global planning and decision making than it is to standardise the global marketing mix. The other aspect is *programme standardisation* – this refers to the development of a uniform marketing mix for all international markets. As far as distribution is concerned, while it may be possible to standardise aspects of process such as types and numbers of intermediaries, difficulties are more likely to arise with programme standardisation due to the influence of both culture and tradition on international distribution channels. To achieve the greatest practical degree of standardisation for distribution channels, the factors relating to the firm, its objectives and the distinctive features of the international market should be consciously taken into account.

Grey markets and unofficial distribution channels

A grey market involves unauthorised distributors that circumvent authorised channel arrangements by buying a firm's products in low-price countries (usually from authorised distributors in that country) and selling them in high-price countries at prices lower than those offered by authorised members of the distribution channel. The goods involved are genuine branded merchandise and not counterfeit goods. They are only different in that they are sold in the market by unauthorised distributors. This reduces sales for legitimate distributors and disrupts both pricing and distribution strategies.

Grey markets have become more of a problem during recent years first due to the growth in the number of global products and second to increased international product standardisation. Being opportunistic, grey-market operators are able to respond more quickly to rapidly changing differences between markets than can global firms. In addition, fluctuations in exchange rates have been more pronounced since the major currencies in which international trade is denominated have been allowed to float. Prices are usually set by the supplier with a foreign exchange rate in mind and the price is unlikely to vary unless there is a major movement in the exchange rate. This provides the opportunity for grey market operators to take advantage of day-to-day exchange rate fluctuations.

Another reason relates to price discrimination. This occurs when the manufacturer sets different prices for different markets as part of marketing strategy, competitive reaction or discount for bulk purchase. Finally, due to fluctuations in demand, a distributor in one country may be left with large inventory that needs to be liquidated for cash flow reasons by severe discounting. The grey market operator buys the stock and resells it in a higher-price market.

When faced with a grey-market situation, many manufacturers do nothing because the cost of litigation is likely to be very expensive and judgements difficult to obtain, especially if suit is brought in a country where the action is not viewed as intrinsically illegal. In addition, legal challenges involving grey marketing have mostly failed in the courts. An alternative to seeking legal redress is to change marketing mix strategies. Changing the product strategy can involve localising the product for the specific international market. This only works if the volume in that market is sufficiently large to amortise the costs of the modification without a major increase in local prices. The manufacturer can change pricing to authorised distributors in different countries to minimise price differences between markets and/or change discount strategies to reduce overstocking. Changing the distribution strategy may involve refusal to supply dealers that stock the grey-market product, or refusal to honour warranties on products distributed via grey-market channels.

Companies in the snowboard market in Japan are now facing unfair competition from grey-market operators. These firms which have exclusivity agreements have invested heavily in advertising and sponsorship. Snowboard distributors obtain and distribute products which are supposed to be sold exclusively by contracted companies. One wholesaler viewed the problem as caused by Japanese companies. Some Japanese companies set up shops in the foreign manufacturer's country and buy directly from the snowboard manufacturer. Products are then resold in Japan. Often these shops are deliberately set up to avoid exclusivity contracts. A common technique involves a retailer in the US (often owned by Japanese interests) placing an order for say

*100 snowboards from a US manufacturer when they only need 50 boards. The
remaining 50 are shipped to Japanese retailers, thus bypassing the authorised
distributor in Japan. It was also alleged that some companies hire college
students studying abroad to pose as consumers and ship goods for sale in
Japan. Other Japanese distributors emphasised that the grey market in
Japan is being used by foreign manufacturers to try to achieve quick profits.*

Discussion so far has implied that all drivers in the economic environment of a
nation are official and legal. In many economies, particularly in the developing world,
this is not the case and a significant proportion of economic activity does not appear in
official records or statistics.

*In Myanmar (formerly Burma), prior to the advent of the SLORC government,
anecdotal comment suggested that 85% of the country's international trade did not
appear in official statistics. One reason for this was that the central government
only controlled 40% of the land area because the remainder was controlled by
various revolutionary groups, such as the Karens. In addition, the central
government had no power in that part of Myanmar which was part of the 'golden
triangle' where opium was the major source of income. The extensive common
border between Myanmar and Thailand meant that much of the country's imports
entered free of duty by being physically carried across the border. In the supply of
products to Myanmar, a significant distribution channel was via agents in Thailand.*

How to tap such a market is a challenge for the international marketer. Both markets
and activities are not all the same shade of black and different shades apply to varying
forms of illegal activity. They can range from criminal behaviour to unofficial business
practices that are widely condoned. Some of the advantages of the black economy can
be higher levels of employment due to the economic activity undertaken, increased
availability of products in the marketplace due to greater currency liquidity and
increased availability of goods and services. Apart from its illegality, disadvantages of
a black economy include negative impact on the growth of the official economy, diver-
sion of resources from public infrastructure projects into private consumption and lack
of control over a significant sector of the economy. These can operate to the country's
overall detriment.

Black markets are especially prevalent where the rule of law is deficient or applied
in an erratic or subjective fashion. For those desiring to tap this segment, it may be
necessary to trace the foreign source of the black market goods and promote to that
party, e.g. a Singapore agent for goods smuggled into eastern Indonesia. There are
of course risks involved because the practice is illegal in that it avoids payment of
duty and often contravenes intellectual property or safety laws. Black marketing is
particularly prevalent in markets such as Russia, India, China and Brazil – countries
characterised by government-owned enterprises, volumes of government regulation,
corruption and a history of the involvement of organised crime in business activities.

The growth of the Internet will further add to the use of unofficial channels because
manufacturers and users can contact and transact directly on the Internet.

In summary, it is important for the international marketer to take into account
the nature of the trading environment in the international country when preparing a
strategic plan for activity in that country. The trading environment will also impact on
the price that can be charged as well as on the most appropriate form of entry.

Internet infusion

The most promising products for trading internationally via the Internet are those where existing middlemen do not perform the traditional wholesaler functions due to the high cost of servicing small diverse and geographically dispersed players. In international marketing this results in an opportunity for SMEs to engage in international trade from which they were formerly excluded. If the Internet can perform a useful set of functions undertaken in marketplace distribution, then potentially it can absorb or render unnecessary the jobs of existing providers of those services. When this happens, the Internet reduces transaction costs because it cuts out the need for middlemen. This withering away of intermediaries because firms contact their customers direct is termed 'disintermediation'. While you can eliminate the middleman, you cannot always eliminate the function performed. Either you do it or your customers do it – if they don't want to, then despite the Internet, channel functions are unlikely to entirely disappear. There is evidence that marketplace channels may be replaced with marketspace channels, which are sometimes called cybermediaries. The functions that a channel performs are largely fixed (providing information and distributing goods and services) but the institutions that perform these functions are not. For this reason, the Internet should be regarded as a component of a firm's international marketing plans, rather than as a new phenomenon that replaces conventional methods of doing business.

Disintermediation is less likely to be the case in international marketing than in domestic marketing as one of the reasons for intermediaries in international marketing is to replace the absent principal in the foreign country. This function will still need to be performed in many cases and, as a result, the eradication of channel intermediaries and the forging of closer producer-to-consumer relationships has not occurred in the international market to the extent anticipated. Re-intermediation has, however, taken place in a number of instances – this happens when traditional middlemen find new niches for themselves in the electronic marketplace by gathering customers and information, extending online credit and providing services to complete transactions.

Physical distribution

Physical distribution is the means by which products are made available to customers where and when they want them. It includes customer service, packaging and protection, transportation, warehousing and storage, and documentation.

Customer service

The level of customer service provided to customers in international markets tends to be lower than the level in the domestic market. This is because of geographic distance, the greater possibility of mistakes, inadequate packaging, transportation delays and customs clearance problems. If the firm establishes its own distribution facilities in the international market, some of these problems can be overcome. It is not usually desirable for the international firm to maintain the same level of customer service in all markets. This is because customer service is subjective and expectations as to level vary substantially from country to country and from market to market within countries, especially as between urban and rural areas. If the level of service being provided is lower than that available from domestic suppliers in the international market, then this needs compensation if the resulting competitive disadvantage is to be removed.

Packaging and protection

Because of the extended transit times and the distances travelled by imported products in getting to market, the usual problems in physical distribution of goods are compounded. Scope for pilfering is greater and the possibility of damage in transit increases the greater the distance involved and the more stages there are involved in transit. Because imported goods often have to travel through different climatic zones there is an increased possibility of damage due to heat, rain or cold. Furthermore, as transport infrastructure in many countries in the developing world is poor, damage to consignments due to poor handling becomes more likely. Although containerisation reduces the above problems to an extent, when goods arrive in a country and containers are unloaded, pilferage and damage in transit become real problems. Thus goods destined for other countries will usually need better packaging and protection which adds to cost. The size of outer containers used in the domestic market may not be suitable either for the transportation infrastructure of the international market or for the local requirements of wholesalers or retailers. It is worth investigating in advance of shipment, what handling and transport conditions the product is likely to be subjected to, so that goods can be packaged in ways appropriate to the international market.

> *In the late 1980s Haiphong, the main port in northern Vietnam, was chaotic due to the flood of goods entering the country following the 'doi moi' liberalisation of the economy. As a result, goods were mostly stored in the open, were handled manually or moved by untrained fork-lift drivers and remained for long periods at the dock before being cleared. Many arriving consignments had been packed assuming containerised transport 'door to door', but there was no containerisation at Haiphong. Damage and pilfering were rife.*

Transportation

Choice of mode of transportation is an issue that often does not receive sufficient attention. This can be broken up into its different stages.

- *Transport of goods from factory to port of shipment.* Other shipment stages and modes might dictate the type of outer packaging and whether containers are used, even if not required for transport to the docks.

- *Transport from domestic port to international port.* Careful analysis needs to be undertaken as to the relative cost of air versus sea. Although air freight rates are usually more expensive, they may have a lower overall impact on costs. This is because the period for insurance coverage is less and the opportunity cost of funds tied up in goods in transit is lower. In addition, there is greater value due to increased customer satisfaction because transit time is shorter and goods can be delivered nearer to inland customers by air than by sea, thus reducing inland transport costs.

- *Transportation of goods from point of arrival in the international country to the customer.* Transportation infrastructure within a country varies considerably from truck and rail (e.g. in the US) to barge (in parts of Thailand) to handcart and bullock dray (in the Indian subcontinent).

Another factor impacting on selection of transport mode is the nature of the product. If the product is a spare part then the cost of machine or plant lying idle is far greater than the difference between air and sea freight rates. If the article is perishable, as with vegetables, then air may be the only feasible transport mode. In some cases, if the shipment is small, air will be cheaper because of the larger minimum quantities required for sea shipment. Freight rates are influenced by the nature of the demand for cargo. If the demand is seasonal or irregular, then rates will be higher, and if the flow of goods is mostly one way (as is the case with most countries in the Middle East), then rates are likely to be higher because there is no 'backloading' cargo available.

Warehousing and storage

Warehousing and storage facilities can be set up by the firm in the international market or provided by others in the distribution channel. If the latter is the case, the nature of warehousing in the other country needs to be investigated in advance because it can impact on the strength and design of packaging. Size requirements and storage practices for products in warehouses vary as do location and transportation distances from port or airport.

Documentation

Physical distribution of products in global markets is complicated by the need for considerable documentation. The most important documents that should accompany a shipment are:

- *export declaration* – used for statistical purposes by governments to keep track of the value and volume of goods being exported from the country;
- *bill of lading* – acknowledges receipt of goods by the carrier and serves as proof of ownership;
- *commercial invoice* – describes in detail the goods sold and the conditions accompanying the sale; and
- *certificate of origin* – specifies the exact origin of the goods and is used by the customs authority at the point of importation for specifying the applicable tariff.

Because of the complex nature of physical distribution in the international marketplace two groups of specialist firms have arisen to facilitate international transactions.

- *Customs brokers*: they act on behalf of importers and exporters to facilitate movement of goods through customs and handle documentation accompanying international shipments.

- *Freight forwarders*: they coordinate the shipping of goods from the plant in the domestic market to the international market. Their functions can include booking of cargo space, preparation of bills of lading, preparation of consular documents in the language of the international country, arranging warehouse storage and insurance, and preparation of shipping documents and forwarding them to banks, shippers or consignees as required.

Internet infusion

A substantial level of traditional trade will be influenced by the Internet and made more efficient through speedier delivery using Internet-based transport, logistics and border crossing procedures. DFAT (1999) estimates that Internet trade across borders could amount to 20% to 30% for many products because the Internet reduces the traditional barriers to international trade of distance, time and language. Whereas for bricks-and-mortar businesses, the value chain involves inbound logistics (shipping product from manufacturer/wholesaler to distribution centres) and outbound logistics (shipping product from distribution centres to retail stores), with e-business, the distribution value chain can differ widely, depending on the configuration of the value chain and the level of sourcing. Specific areas of difference are that e-business companies may ship small shipments to individual customers, so that warehousing and consolidation operations may not be required.

Although paperless trade is a reality in international business, it is still not all-encompassing and does not address the problems of customs clearance, especially in the developing world. Costs most likely to be affected by differences in the configuration of the value chain for bricks-and-mortar businesses and e-business companies are:

- *Inventory costs*: whereas with bricks-and-mortar firms some inventory needs to be located at a physical store location, e-business companies can hold inventory at a more centralised location or even not take possession of the inventory until the order arrives.

- *Order handling costs*: although bricks-and-mortar firms offer a greater variety to choose from, order costs will be greater for e-business firms, because the handling of individual customer orders is labour intensive. As a result, e-business firms may shift their distribution centres to low labour cost countries.

- *Transportation costs*: e-business firms are involved in delivering product from the manufacturing facility to the customer. As the distance from distribution centre to customer is greater and the volume of product smaller with e-business companies, transportation costs are likely to be higher.

The Internet involves a de-linking of value creation from location and this affects the motivation to locate value-adding activities in different parts of the world. There are two elements of the impact of the Internet on choice of international location:

- digitisation of value-adding content and delivery;
- the ability of the Internet to form at low cost an electronic network that connects various corners of the world.

Summary

International distribution is a critical aspect of successful international marketing. If the product cannot be delivered to the customer in the international market, sales will not occur regardless of how good the product or service is, the attractiveness of the price at which it is offered or the volume and impact of the promotion. Whether the channel is direct or indirect, the international marketer faces a major challenge in matching the international distribution system to both the objectives of the firm and the competition it faces in the international marketplace.

It is important that the channel selected by the international marketing manager will both reach the international customer and take their characteristics into account. It is also important that in the process, care is exercised in not only establishing the channel and selecting its members, but also in managing and motivating members of the channel. Differences need to be appreciated between countries as far as wholesaling and retailing are concerned as these differences can have a backwards effect on other stages in the channel.

The international manager needs to be conscious of how the channels set up in one country compare with channels set up in others. Such consciousness enables the manager to be on the lookout for economies resulting from standardising aspects of distribution on the one hand and problems which can result from differences on the other, such as 'grey markets'.

Finally, the characteristics of the physical distribution channel need to be explored as these affect the product, its pricing and its promotion. Measures must be taken to ensure that the problems of physical distribution, especially those manifested in an inability to maintain competitive levels of customer service with domestic or closer suppliers, are either overcome or compensated for in other ways.

Ethics issue

In Italy, UK Pumps Pty Ltd has had a long established agent whose performance has been disappointing. This is because the local price at which its electric motors sell makes them only just competitive due to the high margin added by the agent, which is normal for this category of product in Italy. Recently, the volume of the firm's pump products entering Italy has trebled. Investigation reveals that this increase is due to product being imported directly by Italian end users from the UK firm's Cypriot agent who operates on a commission rate half that which prevails in Italy. As a result the landed product from this source is 20% cheaper. The Italian agent is demanding UK Pumps stop the Cypriot agent selling into its territory and insists that it ceases supplying the Cypriot agent if he does not desist. Although there is nothing in the agency agreement with the Italian firm to prevent supplying this grey market operator, to continue to do so is contrary to the spirit of the agency arrangement.

If you were the export manager for UK Pumps Pty Ltd would you comply with the Italian agent's request or allow the situation to continue?

 ## Web workout

Question 1 What do you believe is the best way of using the Internet to sell a company's product in the international market? Visit ten consumer and business websites to help in your answer. You may also use any search engine to help you find websites.

Question 2 Select a local company that you are familiar with.

Your selected company is aiming to sell (or sell more of) its product in a number of international markets. Local competitors and other international companies are finding out that currently there are new possibilities of selling their product online (via the Internet).

There are big intermediaries and agent groups emerging online offering companies a variety of choices. You are required to research possible agents, exchanges, and online auctions that would be suitable to sell your product.

 ## Discussion questions

1 Why is global distribution more difficult than domestic distribution?

2 What are the advantages and disadvantages of the firm establishing its own distribution in the international market and what forms might this take?

3 How do the characteristics of the final consumer impact on a decision as to the most appropriate distribution option in international marketing?

4 What steps should be taken when selecting an international agent?

5 What criteria should be applied when managing an international agent or distributor so that the relationship might be long-lived?

6 What differences are likely to be encountered when setting up an international distribution channel for industrial products as opposed to consumer goods?

7 What are the possible risks in engaging in a partnership with an international intermediary who already handles a competitor's product?

8 How does international physical distribution differ from international channel distribution?

9 Discuss the advantages and disadvantages of the firm undertaking warehousing and storage in the international market.

 ## References

Business International (1983) 'Finding and Managing Distributors in Asia', New York, p. 92.

Classen, T.F. (1991) 'An Exporter's Guide to Selecting Foreign Sales Agents and Distribution', *Journal of European Business*, Vol. 3, No. 2, pp. 28–32.

Czinkota, M.R. and Ronkainen, I.A. (1998) *International Marketing*, 5th edn, Dryden Press, Fort Worth, Texas, p. 385.

Davidson, J. (1998) 'Retailing in Transformation', *Australian Financial Review*, 16–17 May, p. 17.

Gatignon, H. and Anderson, E. (1986) 'The Multinational Corporation's Degree of Control Over Foreign Subsidiaries: an Empirical Test of a Transaction Cost Expansion', Working Paper No. 86-041R, The Wharton School, University of Pennsylvania.

Hollensen, S. (2001) *Global Marketing – A Market-Responsive Approach*, Prentice Hall, Harlow, UK.

Karunaratna, A.R. and Johnson, L.W. (1997) 'Initiating and Maintaining Export Channel Intermediary Relationships', *Journal of International Marketing*, Vol. 5, No. 2, pp. 11–32.

Keegan, W. (1995) *Global Marketing Management*, 5th edn, Prentice Hall International, Sydney, pp. 542, 545.

Kim, K. and Frazier, G.L. (1997) in Doole, I. and Lowe, R. (eds) *International Marketing Strategy, Contemporary Readings*, International Thomson Business Press, London, pp. 297–315.

Krause, A. (1992) *Marken und Markenbildung in Japan*, GBI-Verlag, Munich.

Noonan, C. (1999) *Export Marketing: A Practical Guide to Opening and Expanding Markets Overseas*, 2nd edn, Butterworth-Heinemann, Oxford.

The Economist (1994), 27 August, p. 59.

Toyne, B. and Walters, P.G.P. (1993) *Global Marketing Management: A Strategic Perspective*, 2nd edn, Allyn and Bacon, Boston.

World Trade (1999), May, p. 46.

Case study 7

Accenture: renamed, redefined, reborn

John Brennan, Richard Burke, Declan Cahill and Chris Mulhall, Waterford Institute of Technology, Ireland

Introduction

The phenomenon of branding has gathered significant momentum in recent years, as it has come to be seen by companies as a unique differentiating characteristic and a means of building a sustainable competitive advantage. All companies desire a strong brand, and for those companies whose brands may have become staid, re-branding offers an effective means of 're-engineering' the future. In 2000, for example, 2,976 US companies were re-branded. In a global marketplace that is becoming increasingly populated with new brands, many companies are choosing to undertake a process of re-branding – and repositioning – as a way to invigorate their organisations.

That branding has received so much attention is a testament to the value companies place on it as one of the most important elements – if not the most important element – in their marketing and communications strategies. Companies may choose to re-brand for many reasons: management may want to breathe new life into a brand through a name change and repositioning effort; a merger may prompt a company to re-brand in order to avoid identification problems; or a crisis may drive a company to re-brand.

A brand is perhaps even more important in the services industry, as it comes to be associated with a level of service. In product markets, the tangible benefits of the products themselves may outweigh the influence of the brand. This case study covers two main areas: the first is the execution of an extensive international re-branding campaign in a short time frame; the second is the different attributes – financial commitment, an integrated marketing and communications programme, internal and external communications – required to make such a re-branding campaign effective.

Company background

Accenture is the world's leading management consulting and technology services company. It has an extensive global reach, employing more than 75,000 people in 47 countries. Accenture operates throughout Europe, the Americas, Asia-Pacific, the Middle East and Africa. The company recorded revenue of US$11.57 billion for the fiscal year ended 31 August 2002.

From Andersen Consulting to Accenture

Andersen Consulting was established in 1989 and operated as a separate and independent entity from the Arthur Andersen accounting firm, a distinction recognised by the United States Securities and Exchange Commission in 1990. Andersen Consulting and Arthur Andersen initiated a cross-financing agreement, which, in effect, meant that either company would compensate the other dependent upon their relative success. Andersen Consulting performed above expectations, and its superior performance resulted in it consistently redistributing its profits to Arthur Andersen in accordance with the agreement.

Arthur Andersen also changed as an organisation. In 1990, it established a non-computer consulting practice for businesses, with annual revenue of less that US$175 million, providing complementary but separate services to Andersen Consulting. However, over time, Arthur Andersen continued to expand its business capabilities to include consulting services similar to those of Andersen Consulting. This meant that Arthur Andersen's consultancy service was competing directly with Andersen Consulting for similar customers, creating confusion in the marketplace, and leading to an inevitable split between the two companies.

In 1997, Andersen Consulting sought arbitration against Arthur Andersen through the International Chamber of Commerce, citing breaches of contract by and irreconcilable differences with the accounting firm. Arthur Andersen insisted that Andersen Consulting pay US$14 billion dollars to exit Andersen Worldwide, an administrative entity, as compensation for use of the Andersen name as well as for use of technology developed by Arthur Andersen. An arbitrator's decision in August 2000 ended the protracted dispute between the two companies. The ruling released Andersen Consulting from any further obligations – financial, professional or otherwise – to Arthur Andersen or Andersen Worldwide. However, the arbitrator also ruled that the licence to use the Andersen Consulting name would expire on 31 December 2000. As a result, on 1 January 2001 – only 147 days after the arbitrator's ruling – Andersen Consulting formally launched its new name – Accenture – heralding the largest ever business-to-business services re-branding and repositioning campaign.

Some industry observers have suggested that the name change mandated by the arbitrator's decision was, in hindsight, a stroke of good fortune for Accenture because of Arthur Andersen's recent problems. It is important to remember when examining this re-branding case that while many such initiatives are proactive, this one was not. It was mandated by the arbitrator, and the change to the Accenture name occurred before the Arthur Andersen–Enron crisis. Indeed, the fact that the new Accenture identity has gained significant separation from the Andersen name reflects the success of the company's re-branding effort.

To condition the marketplace, Andersen Consulting began repositioning itself in advance of the name change to Accenture. The primary strategic motive behind re-branding and repositioning Andersen Consulting to Accenture was to enable the company to demonstrate its broad range of capabilities across consulting, technology and outsourcing. By promoting each of its core capabilities, the company hoped to illustrate that it had more to offer than IT consulting. Thus, not only did the re-branding of the company involve a name change – indeed, this was only one element of its strategy – but it also involved a new focus for the company. The positioning later evolved to include the concept of 'innovation delivered', which demonstrated the company's ability to collaborate with its clients and act as a catalyst to accelerate innovation into tangible business results.

Re-branding – the challenges faced

There were many challenges faced by the company in terms of re-branding and, subsequently, repositioning. As the title of this case suggests, a re-branding effort of this magnitude is far more than a name change. First, a new identity must be launched in order to gain brand awareness. Second, a company redefines itself and strives to make the re-branding initiative analogous to the repositioning. Third, the brand and the company

▶

are 'reborn', transferring equity from the old brand and positioning to the newly re-branded and repositioned company.

To build Accenture into an international brand that reflected the global reach of the company required a cross-departmental and international effort in the different areas of brand-building, such as print, television and air-port advertising, sponsorship and events, online marketing, thought leadership communications, and public relations. Beyond marketing strategies, this effort also involved dramatic changes across infrastructure and other areas such as legal, technology, client teams, building signage and company stationery. From the outset, the need for an integrated campaign across every facet of the organisation was necessary to make the strategy effective. The different aims of the company, such as brand awareness, brand association and transferred brand equity, all stemmed from an initial, focused strategy with clear objectives.

This strategy focused on two goals: brand name recognition (i.e. reach) and association (i.e. strategic positioning). The importance of building a strong brand to match or exceed Andersen Consulting's brand recognition was of equal – if not greater – importance to getting the brand name into the public domain. With brand awareness a prerequisite for building effective brand association, the careful selection of media was crucial to achieving the strategic goals of the campaign.

The objectives of re-branding

Accenture engaged in a major re-branding and repositioning effort to support its new business strategy and vision. This new positioning was aimed at demonstrating the company's broad range of capabilities across consulting, technology and outsourcing. That brands are so difficult to build means that to 're-build' a brand and move in a new direction is even more challenging, especially if strong associations have been built

with the old brand name, as was the case with Andersen Consulting.

The Accenture re-branding required an extensive and meticulous effort on behalf of the company to transfer its internationally renowned brand equity to its new name. The process was initiated almost immediately upon the outcome of the arbitration decision with a bold advertising campaign that featured a graphic of a partially torn Andersen Consulting logo, revealing the phrase 'Renamed. Redefined. Reborn. 01.01.01'. This initiative was designed to act as a 'teaser' campaign to heighten awareness and increase interest in the re-branding and repositioning that was to follow. In an effort to generate momentum and create a 'buzz' in the news media and the marketplace, a formal name announcement was made in late October 2000. This was followed by the global launch of the brand and word mark on 1 January 2001. The effort was one of the most highly publicised re-branding campaigns ever conducted.

From the outset, Accenture recognised that the process involved more than simply adopting a new name. Accenture viewed its brand as 'the promise it makes to its most important audiences, along with declaring its intentions for what we want to accomplish for them'. The importance placed on the new brand was further highlighted by the company's US$175 million expenditure for the global re-branding campaign. Accenture invested this significant amount into the brand to differentiate the company from competitors, create a common sense of purpose and identity, attract the best talent, and help the company enter new markets.

To ensure that the re-branding process was carried out effectively on a global scale, the company had to coordinate activities across many disciplines (marketing and communications, CIO/technical infrastructure, client teams, legal, and building and facilities, among others) across 47 countries to establish a new name, visual identity and positioning that would resonate with employees, senior executives and potential recruits worldwide. This required updating myriad branded items, including 1,500 office signs; countless pages of office stationery; 1,200 software applications; and 20,000 databases. It also meant printing 6.5 million business cards worldwide to ensure that each employee had 100 business cards at his or her disposal on the first business day of 2001.

Re-branding – an internal and external approach

The many elements of the re-branding initiative continue to be enhanced to reinforce the new name. From a basic level such as company stationery to a more advanced level such as company strategy, a clear and consistent message had to be delivered. To establish the Accenture brand in the marketplace, the Accenture name and positioning had to be at the forefront and all ties with the past eliminated.

Accenture's commitment to the re-branding is illustrated by its approach to internal and external communications. The company set ambitious targets in its re-branding programme, and this goal-driven approach focused all areas of the company – a prerequisite for a successful re-branding initiative, especially in such a short time frame. Getting the company's employees on board in the process ensured successful implementation and complemented the significant external spending the company committed to the re-branding effort.

People as part of the brand

Accenture recognised the importance of its employees throughout the re-branding process. Initially, the company launched an initiative called 'brandstorming', encouraging employees to submit brand name ideas with supporting strategic rationale. The result of brandstorming was the creation of the name Accenture. Kim Petersen, a senior manager in Accenture's office in Oslo, Norway, coined the name Accenture. He viewed the company's strategic thinking as putting an 'accent' on the 'future'. Accenture was chosen from a multitude of names created by Landor & Associates, an agency renowned for its expertise in brand building and naming, as well as from thousands of entries submitted as part of the internal brandstorming initiative. It also was screened for trademark and URL availability, as well as native speaker review and linguistic analysis for cultural sensitivities across 47 countries and 200 languages. In addition, Accenture implemented the 'Creating our future together' database, which allowed employees around the globe to contribute their ideas, thoughts and opinions throughout the entire re-branding process.

Accenture has valued the insights and input of its employees throughout the re-branding and repositioning. The company considers its employees to be the 'most important manifestation of its brand', another indication that re-branding is not simply a name change, but a means of getting the entire company on board. For a services company, this human manifestation of the brand is crucial, as employees are the main interface with customers.

The re-branding campaign – the marketing drive

The most effective way to build a brand in terms of awareness and image is through the implementation of an integrated marketing communications strategy. To make re-branding successful, it is necessary to have a coherent, consistent and forceful strategy. The international scope of Accenture's re-branding heightened the need for a message that was loud and clear.

The many elements of Accenture's campaign demonstrate the comprehensive nature of the strategy and the effectiveness of a fully integrated campaign. Individual elements such as advertising, sponsorship and public relations work most effectively when they complement and supplement each other.

▶

Integrated marketing and advertising activities

The Accenture re-branding effort had to be extremely focused in order to appeal to key target markets. This was accomplished through traditional media such as print and broadcast advertising, as well as through 'below-the-line' media such as sponsorship. It also involved activities across public relations, media and analyst relations, as well as activities linked to the company's website, accenture.com. The company has continued to 'work' the brand since the launch through public relations, advertising, thought leadership and sponsorship spending.

Advertising

Advertising has played a key role in the success of the company's re-branding. Indeed, the advertising scope and spending were significant.

The international scope of the advertising campaigns, as well as their careful placement in many different print media such as *The Economist*, have allowed the brand name to be reinforced on an international level with key audiences. National newspapers, business magazines, airport advertising and business television programming were specifically targeted in order to maximise the efficiency of the advertising spending and to target the company's key audiences.

The advertising campaign sought to build two key parts of the strategy – awareness and association – and used a variety of media to achieve its goals. The 30-second television spots during the Super Bowl offered a unique and powerful opportunity to reach Accenture's senior executive target audience. Super Bowl commercials are the prize slots in the US advertising market because of the huge audience of the event.

Accenture engaged in an aggressive advertising campaign to promote its new brand name. Between January and March 2001, 6,000 television commercials were broadcast in markets globally, including four spots that aired during the Super Bowl in the US. The ads during the Super Bowl and the company's sponsorship of major sporting events reflect the power of sports promotion in such a campaign.

Sponsorship

Sponsorship has long been considered outside the purview of traditional marketing tools, but there are several reasons that sponsorship – and sports sponsorship, in particular – was considered to be a vital element of the Accenture re-branding strategy.

The brand association that is built through the sponsorship of events is vital, and Accenture used sponsorship for this purpose. Accenture's choice of sponsorship events relates closely to its brand association strategy – the strength of a brand is dependent on its being 'carried' by an event. Sports sponsorship has the ability to achieve several goals vital to the brand, including awareness and image building, and is a complement and supplement to traditional media.

The company's choice of certain sponsorship events such as the Accenture Match Play Championship was based on a desire to be associated with a high quality event, as well as its ability to provide broad yet targeted brand reach for the company. Accenture was also involved in a number of other major sponsorship deals, including the World Soccer Dream Match in Japan and the BMW Williams F1 motor racing team. Other prominent global companies such as NEC, EMC and American Express joined with Accenture as umbrella sponsors of the World Golf Championship.

These events fulfilled the company's aims of building brand awareness and brand association. Reaching a huge global audience through these events ensured wide brand awareness, and the links with the Accenture Match Play Championship and the Formula One racing circuit fulfilled Accenture's aims of associating with 'premium' events. The experience provided solid proof that sponsorship is eminently suited to a major international re-branding campaign.

Conclusion

It is clear that by re-branding and repositioning itself as a company that delivers innovation and tangible business results to its clients, Accenture has been extremely successful. Accenture has carefully developed its brand name and initiated a concerted marketing drive in order to develop and support brand recognition. It is worth remembering that this change was not voluntary or proactive – it was mandated as part of arbitration proceedings involving the company. The fact that the change was implemented in just 147 days, and the new identity has continued to flourish throughout the much-publicised troubles at Arthur Andersen, reflects the effectiveness of Accenture's strategy and implementation.

It is little wonder that the re-branding of Andersen Consulting to Accenture is often cited as a textbook example of how to effect such a seismic change in a short period of time. If the success of Accenture's re-branding strategy can be attributed to a single element, it is the cross-organisational integrated marketing and communications campaign involved in building the brand both internally and externally. The heavy investment the company made in the Accenture brand has paid off many times over, and the company has shaped a powerful new identity for the future.

Discussion questions

1 How could Accenture further develop its image and awareness? What do you think would be the next stage of the company's marketing programme?

2 Evaluate the effectiveness of the marketing techniques used by Accenture throughout the process of re-branding itself.

3 Discuss the brand equity of Accenture. Describe the personality of the brand.

Case study 8

Kylemore Abbey: branding an international tourism product

Ann M. Torres, National University of Ireland, Galway

Introduction

Kylemore Abbey is the only Irish Abbey for the Nuns of the Order of St Benedict. Regarded as one of Ireland's most romantic buildings, Kylemore Abbey is nestled at the base of Duchruach Mountain (1,736 ft) on the northern shore of Lough Pollacappul, in the heart of the Connemara mountains. Today, the Abbey is the home of the Irish Benedictine Nuns who devote themselves to the monastic life of prayer and work. The nuns have graciously opened the estate to the education and enjoyment of all who visit, developing excellent facilities as well as conserving the many historical features. They regard it as their pride and duty to preserve and cultivate the heritage entrusted to them.

Branding an abbey

Bridgette Brew is the Marketing and Development Manager at Kylemore Abbey. Over the last four years, Bridgette has contributed to the evolution of Kylemore Abbey's brand strategy and image. However, branding an abbey, and its associated enterprises, is not an easy task and it needs to be managed with great care and consideration. Bridgette is mindful the branding strategy must promote trade, but also reflect the non-trading, or spiritual aspects, of the nuns' communal life.

Bridgette's main objective is to find a way to manage successfully the brand for a diverse product portfolio, which includes an abbey tour, restaurants, craft shops, a pottery, a fishery, walled Victorian gardens and, in the future, a 19th-century model farm. Each product within the portfolio has its own particular character, yet they all belong to the Kylemore Abbey estate. Hence, how can these distinct identities be coordinated so that customers, who are tourists from a number of countries, understand Kylemore Abbey's brand values, while still maintaining the unique character of each product? Achieving the 'right' balance between brand integration and variety in product character is a particular challenge for Bridgette in developing a lucid brand identity. The qualities the nuns wish to convey to their international customers are quality, excellence, timelessness, integrity, continuity, and handcrafted. Moreover, the nuns are concerned that the brand does not become 'too corporate', but reflects the small, private organisation they manage.

Strategic vision

The strategic vision for Kylemore Abbey must be considered in the context of the Benedictine nuns' mission. 'The Benedictine nuns are guided by the Rule of St Benedict whose wise and balanced counsel allows for the breadth of vision and an openness of spirit that adapts itself with astonishing ease and graciousness to the demands of the present moment' (Kylemore Abbey brochure, 1996/7). The Benedictine nuns, as guardians of the estate, believe their commitment to the local environs is also an important aim. Hence, they strive to ensure Kylemore Abbey is a resource that benefits not only their monastic community, but also the local community. Kylemore Abbey is a major employer in a remote, rural region, and employs 130 people during the high tourist season (i.e. April to August) and 60 during the low season. Its interdependence with the local community has afforded Kylemore Abbey the opportunity to offer a high-quality international tourism product.

Kylemore Abbey has benefited from the spectacular natural amenities in which it is located. Indeed, Connemara and the Kylemore region have a long history of tourism, which was prompted by the natural beauty of the area. This tradition of tourism was a sound foundation on which the Benedictine nuns could build a successful enterprise.

Kylemore Abbey has evolved with the growth in tourism in Ireland. In this respect, timing was excellent for ensuring growth for the estate. That is, as tourism increased in Ireland and in Connemara, it exploded in Kylemore Abbey. The Benedictine nuns, and in particular Mother Abbess Magdalena, had a strong vision for investing and reinvesting in the estate to facilitate the education and enjoyment of guests. In the achievement of this vision, their objectives were clear: to provide a high quality of service, produce and presentation. Quality was identified as a priority in all aspects of the estate's activities, and levels of quality were incrementally improved.

The long-term objectives for Kylemore Abbey's future growth are to:

- expand market share of the existing product markets (e.g. abbey tour, restaurants, retail craft shops; Victorian gardens, etc.);

- explore innovations for specialised market niches (e.g. corporate incentive market, educational and demonstration holidays, retreats/renewal programmes, etc.);

- develop new markets for new products (e.g. fully functioning 19th-century farm; book publications, cards, calendars, etc.);

- capitalise further on a strong brand presence via a number of value-added products under the Kylemore Abbey brand (e.g. home-made salad dressings, sauces, breads, sweets etc.);

- broaden the customer base by developing the mail order and Internet business as a means to exploit potential markets in Europe and North America.

Key achievements of Kylemore Abbey

Kylemore Abbey has become the biggest tourist attraction in the west of Ireland. The growth achieved over the last 10 years was supported by the Benedictine nuns' persistence in researching their market, investing in exceptional visitor facilities and culminating in quality attractions through the restoration of the abbey reception rooms, the magnificent Gothic church and the walled Victorian gardens. Indeed, efforts towards investment and conservation were recognised when Kylemore Abbey was awarded the 1995 Allied Irish Bank National Heritage Award for helping to make a better Ireland, the 1996 Western Region Architectural Award by the Royal Institute of Architects of Ireland, and more recently in 2001, the Europa Nostra Award for the walled Victorian gardens.

Since November of 1996, the abbey has remained open to visitors throughout the year. Kylemore Abbey receives over 190,000 visitors annually, and as 85% of its visitors come from abroad, it is recognised internationally (Marketing Plan, *Kylemore Abbey's Walled Victorian Gardens*, 2000). Currently, Kylemore Abbey is ranked as no. 14 among visitor attractions and no. 12 among fee-charging visitor attractions in Ireland. Visitors and tour operators consistently report very high levels of satisfaction with their visit to Kylemore Abbey estate. The Benedictine community and management team have successfully positioned Kylemore Abbey as an attraction of international quality and distinction.

Technology has played an important part in ensuring Kylemore Abbey's continued growth and favourable positioning within a competitive industry. In 1999, the management team at Kylemore Abbey commissioned an information system to track and record all visitor statistics. The addition of e-mail has made it feasible to receive electronic bookings from tour operators and to address general visitor enquiries. The website, Kylemore Abbey Online (www.kylemoreabbey.com), promotes the estate to a wider international audience.

The website not only offers information on Kylemore Abbey's history, natural environs and attractions, but also supports an online shop and sponsorship programmes. These sponsorship programmes allow people to contribute to the reforestation of Kylemore Abbey's woodlands and restoration of the Victorian walled gardens. By contributing £20 (€25.39) towards an ash tree, £25 (€31.74) towards an oak tree, or £5 (€6.35) towards flowers, Kylemore Abbey will plant a tree or flowers in the donor's name or dedicated to a named individual.

Heritage and culture tourism sector

Kylemore Abbey receives over 190,000 visitors per annum, ranking among the top visitor attractions nationally and the no. 1 tourism attraction in the west of Ireland (Bord Fáilte, *Facts 2000: Historical/Cultural Tourism Products*, 2000). Kylemore Abbey is considered to be a 'heritage' or a 'historical and cultural' tourism attraction. The Irish heritage tourism sector embraces a broad spectrum of tourism products, such as houses, castles archaeological sites, museums, galleries and interpretive centres. In addition to the environment and scenic appeal of Ireland, Irish heritage and culture are important factors that encourage people to visit. Ireland's heritage is a primary differentiating factor and an integral part of the country's overall appeal as a holiday destination (ibid.). Heritage and culture are at the core of Irish tourism and have contributed significantly to its international success as a tourist destination.

The heritage segment is among the oldest and most mature segments within the tourism market. However, the tourism industry is increasingly competitive, as 'there has been a significant investment in adding to the number of heritage sites and improving facilities at existing sites' (ibid.). Furthermore, there are new segments that are opening up with in the tourism industry, such as 'health' 'aqua tourism', and 'gardens'. Kylemore Abbey competes not only with heritage and gardens attractions but also with all other activities that visitors could pursue in their leisure time.

Kylemore Abbey's customers

With respect to customers, it is believed that visitors to Kylemore Abbey will plateau around 250,000 to 275,000 visitors per annum. The nuns view this expected stabilisation in visitors as an opportunity for the consolidation of efforts and to ensure that the high calibre of products and services is maintained. In this respect, the management team within Kylemore Abbey aims to invest further in staff training, customer service, quality and cultivating the 'right' customer by offering them the 'right' product.

Currently, 85% of Kylemore Abbey's visitors come from abroad. About half of these foreign visitors are from coaches touring the Connemara area and the other half are fly-drive customers from Shannon and Dublin airports who are driving around the west and Connemara. Typically, these are mature customers who seek a quality product and who appreciate Kylemore Abbey's beautiful natural environment, superb catering and shopping facilities. Essentially, these are customers who are seeking a 'unique experience'. Moreover, Bord Fáilte's *Visitor Attitudes Survey 2000* identified that 29% of all overseas holiday tourists (excluding Irish-born) stated that culture and history were extremely important factors when considering Ireland for holidays. Generally, this tangibility takes the form of places to visit, such as Kylemore Abbey.

Product development to meet the needs of these discerning customers is seen as an essential objective. New products and services are always considered in the context of the Benedictine nuns' overall mission and the values established in the Kylemore Abbey brand, which are: quality, heritage, uniqueness, home-made/hand-made, Irish, traditional and thoughtful.

Kylemore Abbey's branding and corporate identity

Bridgette Brew is aware that for many consumers a brand is a landmark, facilitating trade. It encapsulates identity, origin and distinction. In general, she finds consumers are increasingly sophisticated and want to know more about a product before they make a purchase or visit a tourism destination. Bridgette believes that the main undertaking for Kylemore Abbey is to manage the brand and corporate image for a diverse product portfolio for an international tourism market. The qualities the Kylemore Abbey brand aims to communicate are upmarket, homemade, unique, high quality (i.e. ingredients and materials), Irish, traditional, reliable and thoughtful. An issue remains as to how to develop this concept and communicate it to customers successfully, thereby enhancing the brand further and without diluting its value as an asset.

Bridgette reviewed the evolution of the Kylemore Abbey brand over the last few decades. In the late 1970s the brand logo was essentially the castle and a medieval letter 'K' in a dark navy colour on a cream-coloured background (see Figure 1). In the early 1980s, the brand logo retained its simplicity, although the castle and 'medieval K' were updated slightly and the main colours were changed to dark green and cream (see Figure 1).

In the early 1990s, Kylemore Abbey's brand altered dramatically. As a result of developing the storyboards for the exhibition in the recently restored abbey reception rooms and the main hall, the architect developed a stunning logo for use in signage. The logo availed of the castle's silhouette in shades of green and grey. This logo became the destination logo and was used in all the road signs leading visitors to Kylemore Abbey (see Figure 2) and in signage throughout the estate. Eventually it was incorporated in all of Kylemore Abbey's other literature and products (see Figure 3). In time, it became apparent that there were problems in reducing the logo for

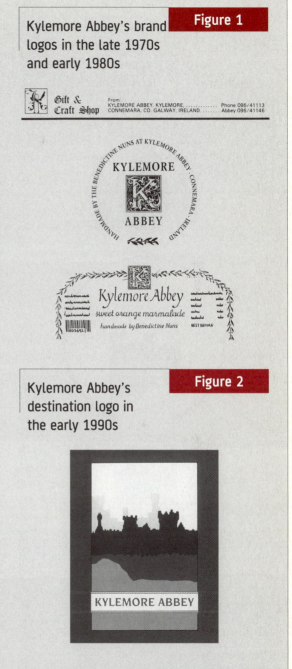

Figure 1

Kylemore Abbey's brand logos in the late 1970s and early 1980s

Figure 2

Kylemore Abbey's destination logo in the early 1990s

its use in product labels. Reproduction of the logo on a small scale was of a lesser quality than the nuns would have desired. It was also felt the integrity of the logo was diminished.

| Figure 3 | Kylemore Abbey's destination logo as applied to letterhead and product labels |

By the late 1990s, Bridgette was employed to manage Kylemore Abbey's marketing strategy and to advance its branding policy. She understood that developing a brand logo was a long-term investment. Furthermore, she recognised that an effective logo was strategic in developing a differentiated position within the tourism market. Bridgette believed that the castle silhouette developed in the early 1990s had been quite successful. Indeed, it was still effective for signage – its intended purpose – but not viable for product labelling. However, she was reluctant to abandon the castle silhouette completely as the logo still held significant brand equity with tour operators and visitors. Hence, it was decided to retain its use in signage and in communicating with tour operators and to develop a new logo for branding Kylemore Abbey's handmade products and gifts.

In developing the product logo, careful consideration was given to the use of signs and symbols and their associated meanings. Many of the nuns believed that although the castle was an important feature of the Kylemore Abbey estate, it did not reflect the monastic aspect of the abbey. Furthermore, many were uncomfortable with the castle as being the only symbol of identification for Kylemore Abbey. A number of possible logos were developed and tested. Criteria for assessment were that the new logo had to reflect Kylemore Abbey's heritage, the Benedictine nuns' monastic life, and the natural beauty of the location.

The new product logo is shown in Figure 4. Through its shape, the logo depicts the towers, turrets and gothic windows of the castle. The dove embodies the nuns' monastic life, and is perceived as being neither 'too religious' nor 'too masculine'. Furthermore, the dove has the advantage of being the international symbol of peace, which is also the motto (i.e. Pax) of the Benedictine order. The logo 'sat' on a faint image of the castle, nestled in between the mountains and the lake. The new logo's link with the castle is vital as, up until this point, it has been the main symbol of identification for Kylemore Abbey. Eventually, it should be possible for the logo to stand on its own – without the faint image of the castle (see Figure 5). Finally, the logo has been tested on a number of media (e.g. letterhead, labels, stickers, bags, pins, and fleeces), and in a number of sizes to ensure that the logo would maintain its reproduction quality. With the new product logo, it is possible to differentiate among product lines through the use of colour. The mid-range handmade products were displayed with green labels, whereas the more exclusive handmade products were displayed with gold and black labels (see Figure 6).

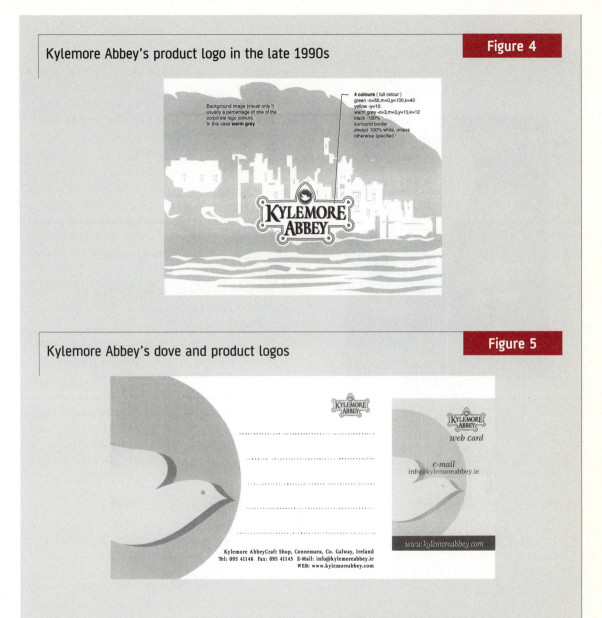

Figure 4

Kylemore Abbey's product logo in the late 1990s

Figure 5

Kylemore Abbey's dove and product logos

Future evolution

The new product logo has been received with enthusiasm and since its inception sales have increased in every product category. Furthermore, the new logo has succeeded in embedding the dove as an emblem of Kylemore Abbey. To reinforce this symbolism, Bridgette Brew developed a 'Millennium Peace Pin' in the shape of a dove, which was to be given to others as a token of friendship and peace. A faint image of the dove is also used as the background for the Kylemore Abbey website. The dove is taking greater prominence in Kylemore Abbey's literature (see Figure 5). In fact, there is some discussion as to whether, in the future, the dove

Figure 6	Kylemore Abbey's product logo as applied to labels

should become the principal symbol of Kylemore Abbey. Addressing this issue elicits other questions, such as whether the destination logo (i.e. castle silhouette) should be maintained or abandoned. Bridgette is aware that brands and their associated logos need to be revised and updated and that it is a process of constant, albeit sometimes minor, evolution.

Discussion questions

1 How realistic is the long-term vision for Kylemore Abbey?

2 How did Kylemore Abbey manage its growth?

3 How did Kylemore Abbey enhance the credibility and presence of the brand in the tourism/retail industry?

4 How will Kylemore Abbey develop its brand to an expanding product range and market segments without diluting its value?

Case study 9

2003 Special Olympics World Summer Games: the contribution of commercial sponsors[1]

Peter McNamara, Garrett Murray, Carolin Grampp, UCD Business Schools

Paul Brown, 2003 Special Olympics World Summer Games Limited

This case is intended as a basis for class discussion rather than to illustrate either effective or ineffective handling of management situations.

We wish to gratefully acknowledge the support of 2003 Special Olympics World Summer Games Limited and the 20 interviewees without whom this case could not have been undertaken. Thanks also to Kate Breslin for administrative assistance.

> *'Let me win. But if I cannot win, let me be brave in the attempt'*
> **Special Olympics Oath**

Introduction

It's June 2002 – just one year before the largest sporting event of 2003 will be held in Ireland's capital city, Dublin. The 11th Special Olympics World Summer Games[2] will bring together over 7,000 athletes with a learning disability from 166 international delegations. The sporting competition will take place over nine days, across more than 22 venues in Dublin, with the wider Games embracing the whole island of Ireland. The organisational task is immense and rests upon the shoulders of Mary Davis, CEO, the Board of Directors and her team at 2003 Special Olympics World Summer Games Limited. From their offices in central Dublin, a core team of 112 full-time employees will over the coming year manage a network of stakeholders including 30,000 volunteers, corporate sponsors, several

arms of the government and civil service, and a disparate group of suppliers, media, accommodation and sporting venues.

The 2003 Games are one of firsts. It is the first time that the Special Olympics World Summer Games (SOWSG) will take place outside of the United States. The games will be 'the largest sporting event in the world that year'.[3] It is the largest sporting event to ever occur on the island of Ireland. Through the Law Enforcement Torch Run and the Host Town Programme the Special Olympics World Summer Games will touch all parts of the island, as the athletes will spend the four days preceding the games acclimatising, training and partaking in cultural activities in over 177 towns across the island. It is intended that the Games will leave a lasting positive legacy in Ireland, raising awareness of learning disabilities through an educational programme targeted at schools and third-level institutions. It is also intended that that the World Games can positively impact upon governmental policy on learning disabilities in Ireland. Most of all it will, as always, be a Games that focuses on the athletes. Over the coming year Mary Davis needs to maintain, grow, motivate and organise her network of stakeholders if she is to make the mission of these games a reality:

> *To provide in Ireland a unique and unparalleled sporting and cultural experience for the athletes taking part, from 160 international delegations all over the world, as well as for their coaches, families,*

volunteers and sponsors, combining the excitement of sport with the opportunity for personal distinction, achievement and pride.[4]

The challenge for Mary Davis is to achieve this mission with a cash budget of €34 million and a further €23 million through in-kind product and service donations.[5]

Context: the Special Olympics movement

Eunice Kennedy-Shriver, sister of the late President J.F. Kennedy, founded the Special Olympics movement for people with learning disabilities in the United States in 1968 'in her backyard'.[6] From these humble beginnings the Special Olympics is now an international movement involving 160 nations from across the globe. Special Olympics is a year-round sports training and competition programme for children and adults with a learning or intellectual disability.[7] The organisation is founded on the belief that the people with learning disabilities can benefit, learn and enjoy, with proper instruction and encouragement, from participation in sport. It also believes:

that the community at large is united, both through participation and observation in understanding people with a learning disability in an environment of equality, respect and acceptance.[8]

The pinnacle event of the Special Olympics Calendar is the Special Olympics World Summer Games, which is held every four years. Traditionally this event has always taken place in the United States. The management challenge in running the event is comparable to any of the great events on the sporting calendar. It is expected that 7,000 athletes from over 160 international delegations will participate in the games. Additionally 3,000 coaches and

delegates, 28,000 families and friends will also attend the games; 30,000 volunteers are required to staff the organisation and operation of the games. The games will feature competition in 21 sports, in addition to a non-competitive motor activity programme.

Bertie Ahern, An Taoiseach (Prime Minister) of the Republic of Ireland, sums up the commitment of the people of Ireland to make this World Games a reality, pointing out that this is a national effort, not just a matter of money.

If you were to price this as a commercial event you couldn't run this in a small country. It is just that people have done things for nothing. A huge amount of effort by corporate leaders, by commercial companies, by stock market companies, by community organisations, by the general public just giving it their nights and their afternoons . . . It is a huge, huge commitment of people giving up their time.[9]

The state is one of the largest supporters of the World Games in terms of financial, moral and in-kind contributions. Government and international bodies have committed over €17.5 million of the total budget for hosting the games. The government of the Republic of Ireland donated over €9 million, in addition to benefit-in-kind donations. Key to the success of fundraising by the games has been the strong support of national political leaders in attracting additional funds from commercial organisations. The government of Northern Ireland has pledged €1.6 million, additionally the Fund for Ireland has pledged US$500,000 to the games. The European Union has committed €6.35 million to the games.

Notwithstanding the substantial contribution of government bodies and an expected 30,000 volunteers from the general public, the remainder of this abridged case will focus on the objectives and contributions of the commercial sponsors of the games.

Commercial sponsorship

The Premier Sponsor and the Games Partners combined are contributing over €11.5 million to the Games (see Table 1). Given the sums involved, sponsorship of the games is an investment decision. As Lisa Browne of Bank of Ireland observes:

we view sponsorship as a business decision. It is an investment and as such we expect a

Table 1 Premier Sponsor and Games Partners

Sponsor and its main business	Event sponsored	Contribution
Bank of Ireland, (Largest retail bank in Ireland) Premier Sponsor http://www.bankofreland.com	Host Town Programme	€4 million in direct fnancial contributions, plus over €1 million raised through customer coin collections and beneft-in-kind (promotion of games and banking services)
Aer Lingus (Airline) Games Partner http://www.aerlingus.com	Offcial air transport carrier	€1.27 million in fnancial contribution and beneft-in-kind (transport services)
An Post (National Post Offce company) Games Partner http://www.anpost.ie	School Enrichment Programme	€1.27 million in fnancial contribution and beneft-in-kind (communications and mail promotion)
Eircom (Largest telecommunications company in Ireland) Games Partner http://www.eircom.ie	Law Enforcement Torch Run	€1.27 million in fnancial contribution and beneft-in-kind (telecommunications)
O'Brien's Irish Sandwich Bars (Franchise company) Games Partner http://www.obriens.ie	Volunteer Programme	€1.27 million through fund raising activities, provision of food and beverages for athletes (through own resources and supplier network)
RTÉ (National TV company) Games Partner http://www.rte.ie	Support an Athlete Programme	€1.27 million in fnancial contribution and beneft-in-kind (broadcasting and media support)
Toyota (International auto manufacturer) Games Partner http://www.toyota.ie	Host Families Programme	€1.27 million in fnancial contribution and beneft-in-kind (vehicular transport)

Source: Data obtained from interviews with sponsors, except for Aer Lingus, RTÉ and Toyota, where data was obtained from secondary sources.

▶

return on our investment. The way we measure it is in terms of our marketing and business objectives.[10]

In the eyes of the sponsors the key attribute that sponsorship of the 2003 Special Olympics World Summer Games bestows upon them is association with a highly visible good cause. As Gary Finnerty of An Post put it, one of the key benefits of being a Games Partner is: 'association with a good cause and generally to be perceived as a good corporate citizen'.[11]

The commercial sponsorship of the 2003 Special Olympics World Summer Games is a pyramid structure. At the top is the Premier Sponsor, Bank of Ireland, which at the outset provided €3 million and will provide a further €1 million to promote the games. Bank of Ireland saw this as an opportunity for its customers to support the 2003 Special Olympics World Summer Games directly when the euro became Ireland's official currency in January 2002. Customers donated their old Irish coins to the games through collection bins located in each branch of the bank, raising over €1 million.[12] This contribution was in addition to the bank's own contribution of €4 million.

The next layer of sponsorship consists of Games Partners. These are six leading Irish companies, which have committed themselves to provide €1.27 million each in either cash or in kind (details of which are provided in Table 1). The third layer of sponsorship is that of suppliers who provide services including public relations, photography, design and production facilities. These companies 'provide either payment in kind or cash of £250,000 [€317,435]'.[13] The Premier Sponsor and all of the Games Partners have each a designated sporting venue during the World Games in June 2003 and also act as lead sponsor for specific programmes prior to the games. For example, Bank of Ireland's designated sporting venue during the games is Morton Stadium and is the sponsor of the Host Town Programme, which has been running since 2002 and will continue during the Games itself.

The 2003 Special Olympics World Summer Games also has the Friends 2003 Programme. This programme has a special logo that differs from the main 2003 Special Olympics World Summer Games logo.

Again it is monetary based so anyone who becomes a Friend can become a Friend for up to €10,000 and any Friend that donates over €50,000 can use the logo to address their customers and suppliers as a Friend of 2003.[14]

Branding: control is the key

Sponsors are of the opinion that the key to gaining a return on their investment is that 2003 Special Olympics World Summer Games Limited maintains tight control over the application of the brand. The games sponsorship manager, Rory Smyth, first vets all application of the brand by the individual sponsors for approval. This ensures that the image of the brand is not tarnished by inappropriate application.

The sponsors also expect the organisers to rigorously protect the brand from use by organisations other than official sponsors. According to Lorraine Keegan, the 2003 Special Olympics World Summer Games brand can only be used by the designated sponsors and by the 2003 Special Olympics World Summer Games Limited itself. Anything the sponsors want in relation to the logo has to be approved by 2003 Special Olympics World Summer Games Limited or their advertising company. 'Special Olympics are very protective of their logo, as they need to be'.[15] According to Gary Finnerty, of An Post, initially one had to contact the 2003 Special Olympics World Summer Games every time you wanted to use the logo. 'They have to work with us to use the logo correctly'.[16] With the sponsors having the use of the brand they are able to leverage it on their entire product packaging and vehicles, thus increasing awareness, as An Post has done. O'Brien's Operations Director stated, 'we have literally integrated it anywhere we can'.[17]

The regulations regarding the branding of the sponsor company are also very strict and are laid out in the sponsorship contract. For each company's designated campaign and venue their brand will be prominently placed with the brands of the all other Games Partners in view, though with a smaller logo. Bank of Ireland, as Premier Sponsor, must have its brand on everything that features the branding of the 2003 Special Olympics World Summer Games.

The Premier Sponsor

Bank of Ireland, as Premier Sponsor, has spent €4 million on its sponsorship. 'This is the biggest sponsorship in the history of the Special Olympics worldwide'.[18] Bank of Ireland regards all its sponsorship as investments that are measured against both its marketing and business objectives. The company's strategy is to make sure that 'Bank of Ireland's contribution results in a better experience for everybody that is involved'.[19] Within its sponsorship they have three marketing objectives. Firstly, to strengthen awareness of the bank's Premier Sponsorship. Secondly, to motivate target audiences to take required action and thirdly to ensure all communications demonstrate empathy with the 2003 Special Olympics World Summer Games.

Bank of Ireland is the sponsor of the Host Town Programme, which will welcome and accommodate the athletes and coaches for the four days before the World Games in June 2003. Every Host Town application form had to have the signature of the local bank manager and a staff member on its Host Town Committee, thus sponsorship of this programme has enabled the branches at a local level to take ownership of the sponsorship. The Bank of Ireland's designated sponsorship venue during the World Games is the Morton Stadium in Santry, Dublin.

Bank of Ireland has supported its sponsorship of the event with both a regionally and nationally based public relations campaign. The bank utilises the brand of the 2003 Special Olympics World Summer Games on both internal and external communication, including ATM slips. The bank also utilises its branch network to inform the public of other initiatives in which the 2003 Special Olympics World Summer Games are involved. It is also providing two days' additional leave for every two days of holidays taken by an employee to participate as a volunteer. By June 2002, one and a half thousand employees had agreed to be volunteers.[20]

Bank of Ireland's definition of a successful 2003 Special Olympics World Summer Games sponsorship is 'that people look back and say that their experience of Special Olympics was better because Bank of Ireland was a sponsor'.[21]

The Games Partners

Below we outline the activities of three of the six Games partners.

Eircom

Eircom's sponsorship of the Special Olympics is a continuation of a standing sponsorship arrangement going back 17 years. The initial sponsorship took the form of sponsoring the national Special Olympics programme called Special Olympics Ireland.

> It was a natural progression to become one of the Games Partners for the World Games . . . in a sense the sponsorship was inherited. . . . It was one of a portfolio of sponsorships that Eircom had that it saw as altruistic.[22]

Eircom is the telecommunications provider for the Games as 'that is our skills, our knowledge, and we are giving that to them'.[23] Eircom's donation is part benefit-in-kind and includes the cost of line rental and calls and other hard cash costs.

Eircom chose the Law Enforcement Torch Run as its designated sponsorship programme because it had experience of the event in its sponsorship of Special Olympics Ireland. It sees

▶

benefits in Law Enforcement Torch Run in that it has a high visibility throughout Ireland. As part of the sponsorship, Eircom is involved in the Law Enforcement Torch Run Committee on which both the Police Service of Northern Ireland (PSNI) and An Garda Siochana also serve.

Eircom liaises with the Sponsorship Manager in the 2003 Special Olympics World Summer Games and its designated venue during the Games is University College Dublin where the football and basketball tournaments will be played. The company sees this as a natural fit 'because we are involved with football'[24] (as sponsor of Ireland's Premier Football league). One way in which Eircom is supporting the Special Olympics World Summer Games is with its telephone directories that will be going to every home in the country which feature Special Olympics athletes. The 2003 Special Olympics World Summer Games branding will also be used on all billing and Eircom television commercials.

Eircom's definition of successful games includes consumer brand awareness and also the utilisation of the sponsorship within Eircom, 'as it is a very good vehicle for internal communications among staff'.[25] This is especially important for the company, as it has undergone two changes in its corporate governance structures in recent years. Eircom's brand values are described as professional, progressive and friendly so the World Games are seen as a perfect fit. Eircom intends tracking and assessing its sponsorship of games. 'The GOC seem to have very strict programmes in place[26] for the sponsors and the suppliers but Eircom also monitors the coverage the official suppliers are getting to ensure they do not lose out, as brand crowding is one of its concerns in relation to this sponsorship'.

An Post

An Post sees itself as bringing several important contributions to the games. Firstly, it sees its financial contribution as being vital to the success of the Games. Secondly, An Post sees itself as being unique in that they 'are the only sponsor with the ability to visit every home and commercial premises in Ireland on a daily basis'.[27] They also have 1,800 retail outlets throughout the Republic of Ireland. It believes this unique leveraging to promote the games to the public will help ensure the Games are a success. The company intends to mail every house in the country twice to promote the Games while also using its retail network. Thirdly, An Post believes it brings great experience to its designated sponsorship programme, the School Enrichment Programme, as it has been running a schools' programme in primary and secondary schools for the last 15 years.

An Post is also able to provide postal and logistical expertise, some of which is on a benefit-in-kind basis. An Post also contacts 2003 Special Olympics World Summer Games when running joint promotions with co-sponsors and on a regular basis to ensure it is complying with sponsorship guidelines and branding regulations as 2003 Special Olympics World Summer Games are licensed for different phases and have a strict code of vocabulary.

An Post believes there are several benefits in sponsoring an event like the 2003 Special Olympics World Summer Games. Firstly, it builds on its image as being a good corporate citizen. The organisation also sees the sponsorship as being a reflection of its staff's values. It also believes that involving the staff in 'the Games in a number of ways will result in a significant staff morale dividend'.[28] An Post in conjunction with the GOC is also planning to introduce a commemorative stamp: the designs are awaiting approval.

O'Brien's Irish Sandwich Bar

O'Brien's is somewhat different from the other Games Partners in that its contribution of €1.27 million comes in the form of direct contributions from its own funds, benefit-in-kind

contributions and voluntary financial contributions from fundraising activities organised by O'Brien's. It should be noted that O'Brien's is a small organisation, when compared with the other Games Partners. What O'Brien's may lack in direct financial resources, it more than makes up for as a passionate advocate for the Games in both the communities in which its sandwich bars operate and its wider network of commercial suppliers.

O'Brien's sponsors the Volunteer Programme and has the RDS as its designated venue. O'Brien's has the same commitment of €1.27 million as the rest of the Games Partners but much of this is in kind. It will provide 20,000 sandwiches a day for the ten days of the games. What makes it unique in comparison with the other Games Partners is that the remainder is made up of money that the organisation will fundraise: O'Brien's contract with 2003 SOWSG Limited requires it to raise specific amounts of money each month.[29] The company is in constant contact with the 2003 Special Olympics World Summer Games to inform them of its fundraising activities and in relation to the 'logos and representations of images and words they [2003 Special Olympics World Summer Games] are very thorough on it'.[30]

O'Brien's see several commercial benefits from their sponsorship of the Games. The volunteer programme is receiving national exposure through TV, newsprint and mailshot advertisements. On every campaign O'Brien's is acknowledged as the sponsor of this programme. The logic for selecting this programme is reinforced by Alyne Healy when she noted, 'we thought we would probably get the biggest coverage on that end of it [the volunteer programme]. All the 30,000 volunteers will wear a t-shirt with our logo on it.'[31]

This raises the profile of the brand. Association with a non-profit organisation further strengthens the O'Brien's brand. Again as Alyne Healy observed, 'I think everyone sees the benefit of being involved with a non-profit organisation in terms of sponsorship and brand awareness and goodwill.' For O'Brien's the definition of a successful sponsorship in this case is greater exposure of their own brand and products and that it carries out its commitment to deliver €1.27 million through fundraising and benefit-in-kind to the Games. It wants to be seen to be a company that has the capacity to deliver on its promises.

Onward to 2003

2003 Special Olympics World Summer Games Limited has achieved much since its inception. Leading a national effort, it has brought one of the world's largest sporting events to Ireland. It has raised millions of euros from the general public, commercial sponsors and the state. It has won the support of key stakeholders from the state and the commercial world to assist the promotion and funding of the games, but much remains to be done. Mary Davis and her team will have to maintain and expand its network of stakeholders if the Games is to meet its mission. By August 2002 only 18,000 of the needed 30,000 volunteers had been recruited.[32] More money needs to be raised. Some venues have yet to be built. Accommodation providers will need to cater for a vast influx of family, supporters and media. Health services will need to cope with the influx of athletes and supporters, many with special heath care needs. The local infrastructure will need to cope with the challenge of venue integration. Recall that the mission of the 2003 Special Olympics World Summer Games is:

To provide in Ireland a unique and unparalleled sporting and cultural experience for the athletes taking part, from 160 international delegations all over the world, as well as for their coaches, families, volunteers and sponsors, combining the excitement of sport with the opportunity for personal distinction, achievement and pride.[33]

Discussion questions

1 How will Mary Davis continue to manage this network over the next twelve months and in so doing create a Games to remember and bring this mission to life?

2 Discuss the role of sponsorship in the 2003 Special Olympics World Summer Games.

Notes

1 Please note that this is an abridged case study. The full case may be obtained from the European Case Clearing House. This case offers additional insights into the management of the nodal firm, 2003 Special Olympics World Summer Games Limited; the contribution of 30,000 expected public volunteers; the contribution of the state to the games and the mechanisms by which a legacy of increased awareness of learning disabilities will be left in Ireland post games. The full case is entitled: *2003 Special Olympics World Summer Games: Managing a Network of Stakeholders.*

2 The Special Olympics and the Para-Olympics are separate organisations. The Special Olympics caters for athletes with a learning disability and is independent of the Olympic movement, while the Para-Olympics caters primarily for athletes with a physical disability and takes place directly after the Olympic Summer Games.

3 Interview Mary Davis on the 'Marian Finucane Show', 1 March 2002.

4 http://www.2003specialolympics.com

5 Budget details as per fundraising section of http://www.2003specialolympics.com. This level of staffing and budget contrasts with the organisers of the 2006 Commonwealth Games, who have a full-time staff of 400. The state of Victoria has provided $84 million for sports development, much of this focusing on infrastructure development for the Commonwealth Games; 4,500 athletes will participate in these Games, versus 7,000 in the Special Olympics World Summer Games. Sources: http://www.dtscg.vic.gov.au; http://www.melbourne2006.com.au/.

6 Interview Maria Kennedy-Shriver on the 'Marian Finucane Show', 25 June 2002.

7 http://www.specialolympics.ie

8 Special Olympics Documentation.

9 Interview with An Taoiseach, 12 June 2002.

10 Interview Lisa Brown of Bank of Ireland – Sponsorship Manager 8 July 2002.

11 Interview Gary Finnerty of An Post 9 July 2002.

12 'Over €1 million raised by Bank of Ireland coin collection', Press Release, 10 September 2002, http://www.2003specialolympics.com.

13 Interview Lorraine Keegan – Sponsorship 27 March 2002.

14 Interview Lorraine Keegan – Sponsorship 27 March 2002.

15 Interview Gary Finnerty – An Post 9 July 2002.

16 Interview Lorraine Keegan – Sponsorship 27 March 2002.

17 Interview Maurice Knightly of O'Brien's – Operations Director 5 July 2002.

18 Interview Lisa Browne of Bank of Ireland – Sponsorship Manager 8 July 2002.

19 Interview Lisa Browne of Bank of Ireland – Sponsorship Manager 8 July 2002.

20 Interview Lisa Browne of Bank of Ireland – Sponsorship Manager 8 July 2002.

21 Interview Lisa Browne of Bank of Ireland – Sponsorship Manager 8 July 2002.

22 Interview Carol McMahon of Eircom 11 July 2002.

23 Interview Carol McMahon of Eircom 11 July 2002.

24 Interview Carol McMahon of Eircom 11 July 2002.

25 Interview Carol McMahon of Eircom 11 July 2002.

26 Interview Carol McMahon of Eircom 11 July 2002.

27 Interview Gary Finnerty of An Post 9 July 2002.

28 Interview Gary Finnerty of An Post 11 July 2002.

29 Interview Alyne Healy of O'Brien's – Special Olympics Co-ordinator 2003 5 July 2002.

30 Interview Alyne Healy of O'Brien's – Special Olympics Co-ordinator 2003 5 July 2002.

31 Interview with Alyne Healy of O'Brien's – Special Olympics Co-ordinator 2003 5 July 2002.

32 Mary Davis private communication 12 September 2002.

33 http://www.2003specialolympics.com

Case study 10

From exporters to global producers: the big four Australian wine companies

Catherine Welch, **University of New South Wales**

Introduction

Within the space of 15 years, the Australian wine industry has become a major player on the international stage. Total international sales of the industry as a whole increased from 8.7 million litres in 1984–85, to 38 million litres in 1989–90 and 285 million litres in 1999–2000 (reaching a value of A$1.3 billion). Australian wine companies have been able to capture market share offshore on the basis of the consistent quality of their product offering, depth of product range, reasonable pricing and technological innovation.

In this time, Australia's wine companies have gone through three phases: export growth in the 1980s, market development in the 1990s and, this decade, a transformation into fully-fledged global operators. While many small and medium-sized companies have become committed exporters, Australian wine exports are dominated by four companies whose international sales are now equivalent to, or even surpass, their domestic sales: Southcorp, Beringer Blass (formerly Mildara Blass), BRL Hardy and Orlando-Wyndham. At the same time, the export success of Australian wine has been underpinned by industry collaboration, with the industry funding an export organisation, the Australian Wine and Export Council.

The Australian wine industry's major export market remains the UK, which was its first and so far its most resounding offshore success. In 2000, Australia was expected to overtake France as the leading exporter of wine to the UK, and has an approximate market share of 20%. The UK has been an attractive market for Australian exporters in many ways. There is no significant domestic competition, there has been an increase in consumption as consumers shift away from beer, consumers respond favourably to the full flavour of Australian wine, generic images of Australia are positive, and psychic distance between the two countries is low.

The Australian industry as a whole now faces the challenge of reducing its dependence on the UK market by diversifying its exports. Key markets it has targeted this decade include Germany, the US and Japan. However, the industry faces a range of challenges in these markets: awareness among German consumers of Australian wines remains low, overall consumption in Japan remains modest, and distribution channels are very complex in the US.

The Australian wine industry faces very different conditions in its major export markets – as is the case with the food and beverage category generally, wine consumption is heavily influenced by culturally specific factors that vary from one market to the next. An industry plan, *The Marketing Decade*, argues that Australia's main markets can be divided into five categories, depending on their level of development (see Table 1). The UK is the only export market to have reached the most mature stage of development, that of category segmentation.

Meanwhile, Australia's 'Big Four' wine producers face the challenge of making a successful transition from exporters to global producers.

Beringer Blass

Mildara Blass was the product of a merger between Wolf Blass and Mildara in 1991. Mildara Blass was then acquired by Foster's Brewing Group in 1995. At that time Foster's was facing a maturation of the Australian beer

▶

Table 1 Development stage of Australia's main export markets

Market development stage	Market features	Country examples
Embryonic	Minimal consumer awareness, few brands available	Thailand, Taiwan, Korea, China
Niche presence	Limited range of brands available through mainly specialist outlets	Germany, Japan, Netherlands, Denmark, Norway, Finland, Malaysia
Volume penetration	Good range and exposure of Australian wines	USA, Canada, Switzerland, Sweden, Hong Kong, Singapore
Category status	Widespread awareness by consumers, strong representation in all distribution channels, regular exposure by media	New Zealand, Ireland
Category segmentation	Consumer knowledge high, ready availability, comprehensive range of brands, regions and price points; significant market share	United Kingdom

Source: Winemakers' Federation of Australia/Australian Wine and Brandy Corporation 2000.

market so diversification into wine was seen as an important 'growth engine' for the company by its chief executive, Ted Kunkel. The company had considered but rejected the option of acquiring foreign beer assets, believing that potential foreign markets either lacked growth or lacked stability. As Kunkel summarised, 'In countries that had the right growth profile for beer, either the country risk or the currency risk wasn't stable enough for us.'

In seeking to expand its international wine operations, Foster's has developed a 'three-channel strategy': as well as relying on its traditional channels in the wine trade, the company has acquired specialist wine packaging operations and wine clubs. The company has also explored the possibility of producing in offshore locations. In 1997 it announced a joint venture with a Chilean wine producer, Vina Sanata Carolina.

In August 2000 Foster's raised its international involvement to a new level by acquiring the Californian company Beringer Wine Estates. The company argues that the acquisition will strengthen the operations of both Beringer and Mildara Blass. Beringer currently exports a negligible proportion of its production, so will benefit from Mildara Blass's extensive international distribution network. At the same time, the Beringer acquisition is expected to assist the distribution of Mildara Blass brands in the US market. Despite these potential synergies, there was some concern expressed over the price Foster's paid for Beringer. Kunkel argues that the price paid is simply a reflection of Beringer's quality. The company is a premium wine producer, has a well-regarded management team and has been successful in building sales in the US market. As a result of the acquisition, Foster's has become the second largest wine producer in the world.

Southcorp

Southcorp's wine division was formed by bringing together the Lindemans and Penfolds brands. By 2000, the company's annual wine sales in international markets had reached $400 million and its brands were distributed in over 80 countries. Like the rest of the Australian wine industry, Southcorp is attempting to diversify its markets to reduce its dependence on the UK.

Southcorp signed a number of joint ventures in the 1990s. Together with a local partner, it launched a brand of Californian wine, and it attempted to establish production in the Languedoc region of France. Its first partnership in the region foundered, so it sought a new partner in James Herrick, an Australian who had a track record in producing his own brand of Languedoc wine. A commentator noted that Southcorp is not the only foreign producer to experience problems in the Languedoc, due to a 'clash in business cultures' and the region's tradition of winegrowing cooperatives.

Another strategy Southcorp has pursued has been to buy land for the development of vineyards. In 1997 it bought land in California which it has planted with vines. The company sees advantages in sourcing grapes offshore for its major brands, as the general manager at the time explained: 'when we have a poor vintage, as inevitably we will as an agricultural business, then we don't want to be as dependent on just Australia and Australian climatic conditions.' The Californian site was chosen because of its similarities to the Barossa Valley, thus allowing Southcorp to transfer its existing technical expertise to the new location.

Southcorp is now aiming to transform itself into the world's leading global branded wine company. Its global strategy has four main elements: building international brands, building international distribution, building volume and scale, and focusing on the premium sector. Turning to the first element, Southcorp is focusing on two global brands: Lindemans and Penfolds. Its international distribution network is already well established, this having been the focus of its earlier international marketing efforts, although distribution remains a challenge in countries such as Japan. In regard to the third element, the company has recently invested substantially in increased volume, expanding its production capacity in Australia. The last element of its global strategy, premium focus, represents a shift for the company, which in the past relied on the production of private label brands for retailers such as the British supermarkets Tesco and Sainsburys. Southcorp's acquisition of fellow Australian producer Rosemount in 2001 was an important step in this reorientation, since Rosemount has an impressive stable of high-value brands that are well recognised in international markets.

In its quest to become a global player, Southcorp has so far not taken up the option of acquiring a major US winemaker. In 2000, then general manager, Tim Park, explained that 'Southcorp was not in the business of collecting global brands, but rather in building global brands.' The following year the company did, however, announce a 50/50 joint venture with Californian producer Robert Mondavi. While the scale of collaboration between the two companies is modest, both partners in the joint venture suggested that it might be the foundation for even closer ties in the future.

BRL Hardy

BRL Hardy was formed in 1992 as a result of the merger of two wine companies, Berri Renmano and Thomas Hardy. Both companies had commenced exporting in the 1980s, and BRL Hardy was able to build upon these efforts. The company expanded its distribution network, in some cases acquiring a stake in the companies that acted as its distributors. While its distribution channels in New Zealand, the UK and US are well established, BRL Hardy is still developing its channels in Continental Europe, particularly Germany.

As well as forging partnerships for its distribution activities, BRL Hardy also sought alliances for production. It negotiated a 50/50 joint venture with a Sicilian company, Casa Vinicola Calatrasi, to market a range of wines labelled D'istinto. Under the terms of the joint venture, Casa Vinicola Calatrasi provides the grapes and the production facilities, while BRL Hardy contributes its international marketing resources. The goal of the joint venture, according to BRL Hardy Europe's marketing manager, is to 'launch the first global branded Italian wine'. BRL Hardy has also formed a 50/50 joint venture with the Chilean winemaker, Jose Canepa, to produce a new brand of wine. Jose Canapa produces the wine, with BRL Hardy providing technical and marketing resources. While its Italian joint venture gives BRL Hardy a foothold in a traditional winemaking country, its collaboration with Jose Canepa is designed to give it a share of another 'New World' success story.

BRL Hardy owns a winery in the Languedoc-Roussillon region of France, Domaine de la Baume – an acquisition made by Thomas Hardy in 1990. However, this was the company's only international acquisition in the 1990s. In the late 1990s the company signalled that it was on the lookout for a major acquisition. In 2001 it made a bid for the major US winemaker Kendall-Jackson. For Stephen Millar, BRL Hardy's chief executive, the logic behind this move was clear: 'In the wine industry there are two major opportunities – Australian wine for world markets and US wines for the US market, which is the most profitable in the world.' The acquisition fell through, but the following month BRL Hardy announced a joint venture with US company Constellation Brands. The 50/50 joint venture, Pacific Wine Partners, will allow BRL Hardy to intensify the distribution of its wines in the US. In addition, the joint venture company will operate a winery and promote a local brand, Farallon.

Orlando Wyndham

The French multinational Pernod Ricard acquired the two Australian companies Orlando and Wyndham in 1989–1990. While Pernod Ricard had been a major European player in the wine and liquor market, this acquisition represented the company's first 'New World' investment. As in the case of the other 'Big Four', the merged company began a major export push in the 1980s. Orlando Wyndham has focused on the development of a single brand, Jacob's Creek. In 1993 Jacob's Creek became the leading wine brand sold in the UK. In this early expansionary period Jacob's Creek was less successful in other markets, although sales in the US and Japan have recently been growing rapidly. While initially Jacob's Creek was synonymous with chardonnay, the company has extended the brand, most recently adding a Reserve and Limited Release range.

Since the Orlando Wyndham acquisition, Pernod Ricard has added to its 'New World' brand portfolio. It now produces wine in Argentina, Chile, South Africa and even China.

Source: Photodisc.

It has intensified its distribution efforts in Asia, so the company now markets a range of its European and New World wines in countries that are relatively new to wine-drinking. Jacob's Creek in particular is currently heavily promoted in Japan.

Conclusion

While the recent track record of the Australian wine industry's internationalisation has been nothing short of spectacular, it has not silenced all critics. Some commentators warn of looming problems that the industry will need to address:

- more than two-thirds of Australia's wine exports go to just two markets (UK and US), leaving the industry vulnerable to developments in those two countries;

- the unprecedented increase in new vineyard plantings around the world (including in Australia) may lead to a global wine glut this decade;

- Australian wine companies have been criticised for being production- not marketing-focused;

- while Southcorp, BRL Hardy and Foster's have been making foreign acquisitions, they themselves are often rumoured to be takeover targets;

- Australia faces stiff competition not just from the established European wine producing countries, but also from low-cost New World producers such as Chile.

Discussion questions

1 Compare and contrast the international expansion of the 'Big Four': Orlando-Wyndham, Mildara Blass, Southcorp and BRL Hardy. How can you account for the similarities and differences in their internationalisation strategies?

2 Do you think learning approaches to internationalisation (see Chapter 7) explain the international expansion of the 'Big Four'? Explain your answer.

3 The 'Big Four' have been very successful in the UK, but some argue that replicating this success in other key export markets may be more difficult. Why might this be the case?

4 Why have the 'Big Four' moved from being just exporters to using a range of entry modes, such as joint ventures and acquisitions?

5 What challenges are the 'Big Four' likely to face as a result of their decision to adopt entry modes other than exporting?

References

Annual reports and media releases from BRL Hardy, Foster's, Pernod Ricard and Southcorp.

Australian Bureau of Statistics, *Australian Wine and Grape Industry*, 1329.0, various years.

Evans, S. (2000) 'Wine flagships divide to conquer the US', *The Australian Financial Review*, 21–22 October, p. 11.

Gluyas, R. (2001) 'Magnum force', *Weekend Australian*, 17–18 February, pp. 29–30.

McCallum, J. and Hannen, M. (2000) 'Foster's global wine push', *BRW*, 10 November, pp. 72–78.

Rachman, G. (1999) 'The globe in a glass', *The Economist*, 18 December, pp. 95–109.

Ries, I. (2000) 'Southcorp stumbles', *The Australian Financial Review*, 16–17 September, p. 25.

Winemakers' Federation of Australia/Australian Wine and Brandy Corporation (2000) *The Marketing Decade: Setting the Australian Wine Marketing Agenda 2000–2010*.

Case study 11

Abrakebabra: capturing market share through food franchising

Rosalind Beere and Peter McNamara, UCD Business Schools

Hungry for success

Abrakebabra is Ireland's largest owned fast food franchise. The company was founded by two brothers, Graeme and Wyn Beere, in 1982. The company began from humble beginnings in the location of Rathmines, an area close to Dublin's city centre largely populated at that time by students and young workers. Graeme Beere was 22 years old, a young entrepreneur waiting for one of his many ventures to become a success. Wyn Beere was 10 years his senior, and worked in a prestigious property firm. He was a qualified chartered surveyor and had also formed a few entrepreneurial ventures. Both brothers were hungry for success and Abrakebabra was about to help them realise their dreams.

Designing a food franchise operation

The Abrakebabra concept began when Graeme realised there was a serious gap in the market for late night eating. In Dublin in the early 1980s pubs closed at 11pm and there was nowhere for the drinking masses to go. At the time, kebabs were a popular late night food item selling in London in small take-away food outlets. Graeme looked to developing something similar in Dublin. To capitalise on the kebab concept Graeme knew he had to devise a brand. The Steve Miller song 'Abracadabra' was a huge hit in 1982: with the insertion of the word kebab, a new brand name was created. With the help of a designer & friend, Donal McDonald, they came up with the logo design for Abra**kebab**ra. The logo was eye-catching and exotic, the name Abrakebabra was flanked by two palm trees all in green, with the original slogan 'Magic Food, Fast Service' in red and the surround in white (see Figure 1).

The core product was to be the doner kebab, with the help of a talented chef; the herbs and spices in the meat and the sauces were adapted to suit the Irish palate. Alongside the kebab were the usual burgers and French fries, popular with all

---

| **Figure 1** | The brand |

Source: http://www.abrakebabra.net

Sample Abrakebabra products

Figure 2

Source: http://www.abrakebabra.net

Although originally specialising in kebab-style pitta sandwiches, the menu also now encompasses burritos, hot filled baguettes and burgers. Kebabs are still the top seller, accounting for about 27% of sales. The chicken baguette has also proved to be a popular addition and has exhibited rapid sales growth. The menu features lamb, chicken, beef, pork, fish and an increasingly popular range of vegetarian options, and is constantly updated to keep apace of changing customer tastes.

The Irish palate is very particular – people are extremely finicky and fussy, not willing to experiment. To capture this market Abrakebabra needed to localise and adapt their flavours and products.

clientele. The menu was deliberately kept simple and uncomplicated. It was not until the early 1990s that Abrakebabra expanded its menu from 5 products to 35, to keep abreast of the changing Irish tastes. However, even today the kebab remains one of the top sellers, totalling 27% of overall product sales (see Figure 2 for sample of products).

Location and restaurant design were of paramount importance to the Abrakebabra branding and marketing concept. Abrakebabra's target market was young drinkers and clubbers, thus restaurants were located in areas with a high concentration of pubs and clubs.

The design of the Abrakebabra restaurant was another important key to its success. Each restaurant had seating, an important differentiating feature to the usual local 'Irish Chipper'. The interior of the restaurants was in keeping with the tri-coloured logo of red, white and green. In addition, the main counter was the focal point of the restaurant and it had the logo running lengthways along it. The menu was displayed above the service area so that the pictures of the various products would entice customers. The kebab itself was cooked on a large skewer and was displayed in the shop window so as to

Figure 3   Store frontage and interior layout

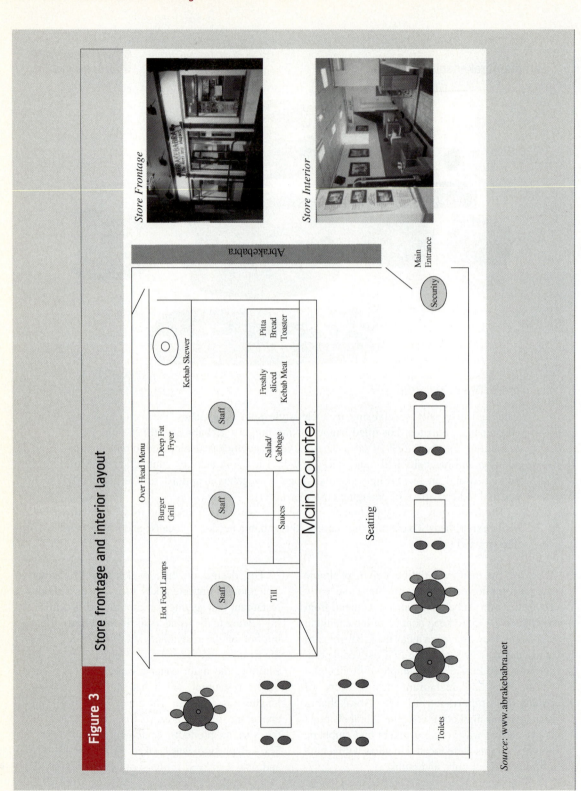

Source: www.abrakebabra.net

encourage potential walk-in customers. The rest of the restaurant was bright and tiled from floor to ceiling, both for cleanliness and visual appeal. There was modern artwork placed around the restaurants and loud music was also a recognisable feature. The design of the Abrakebabra restaurant deliberately created an atmosphere of a trendy, youth-orientated hot spot with its late opening of 4am. This was something that had never been attempted in Dublin before (see Figure 3 for samples of store frontage and interior).

Franchising: the rollout

Abrakebabra began in 1982 with the Rathmines location and within a three-year period the brothers had reached their fourth restaurant. All were highly successful; as one of the brothers put it, Abrakebabra was 'a licence to print money'. However, this success was not problem free; the two brothers were finding it increasingly difficult to maintain managerial control of all four restaurants. They wanted to expand even further, but how?

At this time McDonald's had already entered the Irish market and Wyn suggested that Abrakebabra adopted McDonald's international model of business format franchising as a solution to their growth problems. With business format the franchisees buy the entire business package and concept. Franchisees are owner operators using the franchisor's brand, products and services for a fee. The advantage of franchising from the franchisor's perspective includes low capital investment on their behalf for substantial growth and the alignment of their goals with the franchisees' – around profit maximisation. In turn, franchisees are working for themselves and, unlike a shop manager, their livelihood rests on their maximisation of profits.

Abrakebabra's franchisees make their profit from efficient management of their operations and their attraction of customers into their restaurant in preference to rival operations. Abrakebabra's franchisees were being sold a guaranteed, tried and tested formula: offering a well-known brand, quality products, bulk-buying benefits, group advertising, and a network of head office support services. Each new franchisee was set up and their location fitted to the Abrakebabra restaurant specifications. In addition, each franchisee was fully trained and given intensive support in the initial opening stages. All of these benefits make the franchisee more cost efficient than if they acted as a sole trader.

In return for these benefits the franchisee must adhere to their side of the agreement. For all of the support the Abrakebabra franchisor offers, the franchisee pays an initial set-up sum and a continuous franchise royalty fee. This covers use of the brand and operational support services. The fee is 7% of revenue (6% standard fee and 1% for group advertising). In addition, the franchisee must maintain the high standards laid out in the Abrakebabra operating guidelines. To protect the brand and group quality standards each franchisee must run their operation in accordance with the company's guiding principles.

The challenges of growth

During the early to mid 1990s this type of expansion was rapid and successful. The company opened restaurants the length and breadth of Ireland; no large town or city was left untouched. The larger the chain became the greater the brand recognition. This increased awareness of the brand in turn stimulated potential franchisees.

The company reached its peak of 60 restaurants in 1997, far exceeding the brothers' original expectations of growth. However, this rapid growth was not without problems: there were a number of factors which caused Abrakebabra to pull back and reduce their restaurant number to 56 outlets, a number that still maintains the company as the largest of its kind in Ireland.

The problems which caused this company consolidation included a serious labour shortage and a franchisee revolt. In addition, Abrakebabra still ran about 12 company-owned restaurants. A decision needed to be made about the identity of

▶

the firm. A huge majority of the company's time was being taken up running their company-owned outlets, and the franchisees were unhappy with the lack of management focus. It was at this point (1997) that the decision was made to sell off the company-owned stores. Furthermore, any franchisee that was uncommitted to the new Abrakebabra ethos was released from their contract.

Control systems to manage franchisee networks

The challenge that is faced by Abrakebabra is the high cost of monitoring franchisee standards, all of which must be absorbed from the revenues that they derive from the 6% levy on franchisee's revenues (excluding the 1% advertising levy). In relation to franchising, the quality of service at individual outlets needs to be consistent and must meet a pre-ordained minimum standard. The franchisee's quality of effort and meeting of contractual requirements needs to be continuously scrutinised. Following the franchisee revolt it was decided that Abrakebabra's core competence was not management of its own stores, but the delivery of value to franchisees.

New control systems were put in place to monitor operational standards of franchisees. Day-to-day operations were controlled through a contractually binding operations manual, which include hours of operation, prices, product quality, accounting systems, layout, décor and Abrakebabra's right to inspect the premises and make changes unilaterally. These contractual clauses allow the company to control their franchisees' daily operations and ensure that the franchisees follow the 'ideal' business format uniformly. Strategic controls were also put in place, including sales targets and objectives, expansion triggers, contract duration and a contract renewal and termination option.

Practical steps were taken to monitor performance of franchisees against these operational and strategic objectives. A network of area supervisors was created to monitor operational standards nationwide. Supervisory teams are now there to ensure that each franchisee is visited on a regular basis. This is both for support reasons but also to check standards. If one or two franchisees fail to maintain standards, this could jeopardise the overall group quality.

As well as the nationwide area supervisors, Abrakebabra uses other sources of monitoring. Customer monitoring is a well-respected tool. In every Abrakebabra restaurant there are customer comment cards, which are collected and sent to head office. Additionally, mystery shoppers are used to spot-check the quality levels of food and service in all restaurants. If a problem is identified head office will inform the relevant franchisee of the problem, ensuring immediate action is taken to resolve the issue.

With a constant focus on innovation in product, design and services, Abrakebabra is currently in the process of harnessing new technology to aid its franchising business. The introduction of a modem into each restaurant is currently under way. These modems will relay all franchisees' sales figures back to head office on a weekly basis. This system allows head office to monitor all franchises' weekly and yearly progress. In addition this information will be valuable in assessing product performance and in particular whether customers are accepting new product introductions. The information could also be of use in targeting products that are underselling and trigger a focused advertising campaign.

Abrakebabra's use of the franchising growth model has enabled them to move from an organic growth model to a centrally franchised control system. Abrakebabra is a dynamic and innovative company, with a strong ambition for future growth and expansion. These qualities combined with this new business model should enable the company to realise its ambitious growth strategy.

Discussion question

1   Critically evaluate Abrakebabra's strategy.

Case study 12

MCC − SMART Car

Seán de Búrca and Evelyn Roche, UCD Business Schools

Introduction

At the beginning of October 1998, a new car made its appearance on the European car market. The variety in colours and the remarkable design of the two-seater car attracted a great deal of attention. The message was clear: SMART had come to town and it was here to revolutionise the concepts of cars. The company behind this new venture was MCC as a joint venture between Mercedes-Benz AG and the SMH group.

Mercedes-Benz AG is wholly owned by the Daimler-Benz group and is the automotive division of the group, covering all vehicle segments. It has established a strong reputation for its high quality and superior engineering products. Indeed Mercedes prides itself on making the 'best engineered cars in the world'.

The SMH group on the other hand is a famous watch manufacturer in Switzerland. It was founded in 1983 as a merger between Switzerland's two largest companies, ASU AG and SSIH. The Swiss watch industry faced a period of crisis when the Japanese entered the market but responded to the Japanese challenge by launching a technological and marketing innovation known as the Swatch watch. This was a tremendous success. Over time SMH captured other brand names, such as Omega, Longines and Tissot.

The birth of the SMART car concept

The SMART concept was triggered firstly by environmental concerns. Consumers and manufacturers have become increasingly sensitive to the societal costs of individual transportation. For example, issues of air pollution, as well as energy and material consumption are important consumer trends. Companies are paying more and more attention to environmental issues. In particular, car companies fear that large cities might restrict conventional cars because of pollution concerns. Smaller cars that produced less pollution therefore needed to be designed and developed. Furthermore, individual car use was on the increase and the total number of registered cars as well as the average number of kilometres per capita had risen to alarming levels. These high levels resulted in a negative effect on the quality of life, such as daily traffic jams, air pollution, living space taken by highways, shortage of parking space and noise. Consumers were paying more and more attention to these environmental aspect of vehicles.

Secondly, consumers expected more from a car. Customers not only expected their car to reflect their own personality, but they expected a car to be easy and fun to drive. They were looking forward to the appearance of an environmentally friendly car with the additional advantages of requiring less parking space, lower fuel consumption, made from non-toxic and easy-to-recycle materials.

Besides the environmental aspects, consumers were also demanding high requirements on the comfort and safety aspects of small cars. Being environmentally friendly would not satisfy consumers alone. The quality and safety aspects of a car is also very important to the success of a new car.

The MCC joint venture

MCC is joint venture between Mercedes-Benz AG and the SMH group. The unlikely strategic alliance between these companies raised eyebrows

▶

in the marketplace. Industry analysts questioned why these two companies from different industries joined forces.

Mercedes-Benz (MB) was motivated into strategic alliances by its desire to enter a new market because of strong competition from Japanese manufacturers in the luxury segment of the car market. At the start of the 1990s Japanese products were competing strongly with European cars, not only in their performance, but also in their comfort and styling. Despite productivity improvements in the 1980s, European car manufacturers needed to go further to compete on both aspects of price and quality. They were also much slower to introduce new products; Japanese companies introduced new products every three years, while Europeans companies took between five and seven years.

European companies had limited product range and the profits of European manufacturers in general were low and shareholders were demanding change. Mercedes was one of the companies most affected. There were mixed reviews of the S-class car. The introduction of the S-class car was not as expected. Although the car was admired for its high level of luxury there was also criticism due to its high fuel consumption. In addition Mercedes wanted to widen its market segment. In the early 1990s the average age of MB drivers was 53; this meant that MB was only attracting a narrow segment of the market, the mature driver. To increase its customer base and widen its market segment MB needed to develop new car models to that would appeal the younger segment of the car market.

The SMH group was eager to find something else to put its brand name on. The CEO of Swatch Group (formerly SMH) wanted to change the auto industry as he had done with the watch industry. With its success in reinventing the watch industry, Swatch wanted to move into other markets. It contacted many automobile manufacturers, with no success. However, on talking with MB the concept of the SMART car was born when several dozen young jeans-and-

sweatshirt-clad engineers conceived a two-seater car combining the safety features of a Mercedes with the funkiness of a Swatch watch.

Existing small car market in Europe

Small cars have had a long tradition in Europe. The early models like the Fiat 126 offered basic transportation to lower-income groups. Mini-cars were inexpensive and easy to repair, and were mostly sold in southern Europe. Starting in the early 1990s, a new customer segment evolved. Customers were demanding stylish mini-cars with a performance similar to large cars in terms of safety and quality.

Customer trends

Ever since the 1980s European consumers have become increasingly sensitive to the societal costs of individual transportation, i.e. air pollution, energy and materials consumption. This has resulted in customers' requirements for cars changing from luxury details to aspects of less air pollution and lower fuel consumption. As environmental issues caught more and more people's attention, customers focused more on the environmental effects of cars. The need for the emergence of a 'green car' increased rapidly. Furthermore there were other concerns that also determined the customers' choice of car. Firstly, there was the space issue: there was a need for cars that were easy to park and manoeuvre in confined city centres. Secondly, price is an important issue for new entrants. A relatively low price is needed to capture customers in the new small car market. Thirdly, the local tax system has to be considered. The fact that many European countries have tax systems which rise according to the size of the vehicle implies that owning a small car is substantially cheaper than owning a large car. A mini-car can easily meet these requirements. However, there is one more factor that concerns customers of small cars and that is safety. The challenge for SMART was how to combine minimum size, driving comfort, safety and customer choice into one.

Although many auto manufacturers did not initially believe that tiny cars with almost no luggage space would make it into the highly competitive automobile market, before long they began to enter the mini-car market. Renault introduced a model mini-car in 1993. Ford, believing that smaller cars would eventually account for about one-third of the market, produced 200,000 Ka models per year. Volkswagen, GM and Rover all introduced micro-car models

and by 1997 there were dozens of mini-cars competing in the European market. The actions of competitors showed MB that it was a good time to introduce a mini-car onto the market.

Discussion questions

1 Critically evaluate the strategic alliance between Mercedes-Benz AG and the SMH group.

2 Outline and discuss the marketing strategy of MCC for the SMART car.

Part C

International
Marketing Strategy

13

Planning and strategy for international marketing

Learning objectives

After reading this chapter, you should be able to:

- describe the strategic marketing planning process and the role of scenario planning;

- explain the steps involved in the international marketing planning process;

- develop an international marketing plan;

- illustrate the challenges to effective international marketing planning; and

- discuss the requirements for practical international marketing planning.

Strategic moves of IBM and Sun Microsystems all depend on Linux

Now that the merger of Hewlett-Packard and Compaq has finally bedded down, the strategic shuffle between arch-rivals IBM and Sun Microsystems has intensified. Each is trying to move in on the other's territory.

Sun is the leading manufacturer of the powerful server computers that run the Unix operating systems based on their Solaris software. These account for approximately 60% of the server market. Sun has decided to move upmarket and compete directly with the mainframe computers, which are common in big companies' data centres.

This upscale strategy is for a number of reasons. Big customers are more reliable and more likely to buy additional services. Sun is coming under increasing competition at the low end of the market from servers running Microsoft's Windows NT software or Linux. Another reason for the move into the mainframe markets is that customers are looking for one large computer instead of many mid-sized ones. The advantages to customers are that these large computers are faster, cheaper and easier to maintain, and more flexible.

IBM is not lying down under this attack. It in turn has launched a mid-range Unix server that incorporates technology from its mainframes. In short, both companies are attacking each other's backyard. However, the real threat facing Sun and Microsoft is Linux, an operating system flexible enough to run everything from an IBM supercomputer to a Motorola cell phone. Because it is open source, Linux can be downloaded from the Internet for free, although it is typically bought by companies for free. Backed by technology giants such as Intel, IBM, HP-Compaq and Dell, Linux is causing a real stir.

Introduction

The competitive and rapidly changing environment of 2003 and beyond has prompted most firms pursuing international opportunities to use strategic market planning to identify, tap and profit from international markets. Successful companies periodically evaluate their market environments in order to assess changes in their opportunities and threats. External and internal environmental changes frequently require them to modify their objectives and sometimes change direction. As discussed in earlier chapters, changes in government regulations, emergence of new competitors, the introduction of new technology and the opening of new markets can change the way in which a firm does international business. As they gain experience, develop new competences and add more resources, firms change their objectives and sometimes their mission.

Strategic market planning in international markets is essentially a way of thinking and a mode of acting. In terms of thinking, it challenges international marketers to be constantly sensitive to changes and assess the implications for marketing. In terms of acting, marketers need to be flexible and responsive in the way they plan for and manage the firm's resources and capabilities.

Toyne and Walters (1993, p. 51) provide a useful definition of strategic market planning as follows:

> *Strategic market planning is the systematic and periodic process used by managers to examine the environments in which their company competes, the opportunities and threats they face, the goals and objectives to be achieved, and the products and services offered in order to maintain a viable fit between their company's capabilities and resources and the threats and opportunities that arise from a changing environment. Its purpose is to identify and develop a corporate purpose, objectives and goals, and plans of action that effectively relate the company, its businesses, and functional areas to their relevant environments and that enables the company to profitably exploit future marketplace opportunities in which it is likely to enjoy a competitive advantage.*

In this chapter the foundation for effective strategic market planning is laid using an adaptation of a successful firm's international marketing plan and by exploring the challenges and practical requirements for effective international marketing planning. The context and process of international marketing planning are discussed first.

The context of international strategic market planning

During the 1990s companies sought strategic market planning processes reflecting flexibility, a greater external focus and market focus with more integration of strategies and plans, rather than the rigid, internally focused and historically based systems. However, the early years of the new century are reflecting industry convergences, such as banking and insurance and computers and communications, which are transforming industries and changing their global competitive structures. The focus of strategic market planning in the future will be on balancing and matching internal and external drivers, building core competences, competing as part of 'virtual' networks involving alliance structures and building business value through customer value creation. These changes are depicted in Figure 13.1. Nowhere is this being felt more than in international marketing.

The steps proposed by many authors in the international marketing literature are embodied in the outline in Figure 13.2. It includes terms such as *mission*, *vision* and *strategy* which are now widely used, frequently with different meanings. The notes at the end of this chapter give a definition of strategic terms as a reference point.

However, the need for flexibility, quick response and agility with resources and competences has led to a resurgence in the process of scenario planning as a means of painting pictures of plausible futures that the firm may have to face.

Many leading international organisations, such as Shell, Ericsson and Fujitsu-ICL, as well as international government institutions like the IMF undertake scenario planning because of the uncertainty of future operating environments. No single outcome can be accurately forecast in times of turbulence, rapid change and convergence. Scenario planning is therefore becoming an essential capability for managing in this present environment (van der Heijden, 1996). The essential steps in scenario planning are outlined below.

● *Familiarisation* – understanding the organisation, key stakeholders, their needs and expectations.

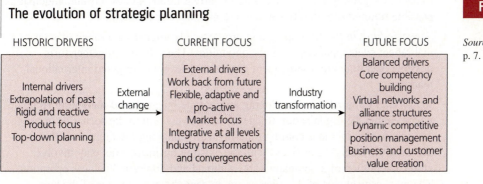

Figure 13.1

The evolution of strategic planning

HISTORIC DRIVERS   CURRENT FOCUS   FUTURE FOCUS   *Source*: Brown (1997), p. 7.

Internal drivers
Extrapolation of past
Rigid and reactive
Product focus
Top-down planning

→ External change →

External drivers
Work back from future
Flexible, adaptive and pro-active
Market focus
Integrative at all levels
Industry transformation and convergences

→ Industry transformation →

Balanced drivers
Core competency building
Virtual networks and alliance structures
Dynamic competitive position management
Business and customer value creation

EVOLUTION OVER TIME

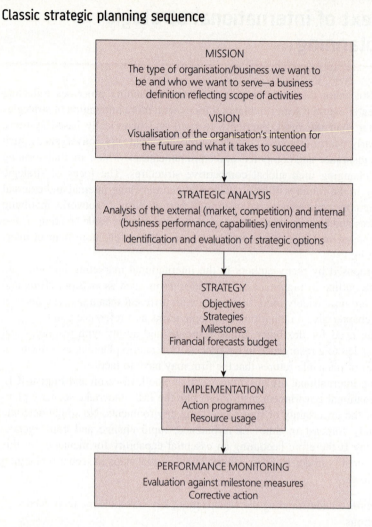

Source: Brown (1997), p. 17.

Figure 13.2 Classic strategic planning sequence

- *Discovery* – gaining an understanding of current trends and events and anticipating possible future discontinuities in the international environment.

- *Scenario building* – developing and progressively upgrading a range of scenarios that reflect events, patterns and discontinuities. These factors together form possible operating environments of the future relevant to targeted international markets.

- *Action and integration* – developing appropriate business and marketing strategies which enable the organisation to operate effectively within the scenarios generated. This phase also includes coming to terms with managing the migration; that is, blending the emerging business with the existing business. This may involve closer integration of a company's international and domestic business operations. The most critical part of this phase is to manage the expectations of the key internal and external stakeholders of the organisation.

The significance of scenarios is that each has different implications for marketing strategies in terms of what customers value and where the business value is in the changing value chain. In turn, they imply quite different investments, strategies, alliance partners and people capabilities for success and ongoing growth.

The international marketer's task is to be on the leading edge of the industry in target markets as they develop. This will involve a number of components:

- progressive scenario development which portrays realistic operating environments of the future globally and in target markets;
- integrated business and marketing strategies which exploit the opportunities and identify the threats in the emerging scenarios;
- ensuring the process of change is driven by customer considerations rather than technology and internal processes; and
- ensuring that cultural and organisation changes are planned and managed effectively to provide international capability.

Many companies use a popular form of scenario planning known as the 'Shell Method'. It relies on imagining the future rather than extrapolating from the past. The approach adopted by Ericsson is depicted in Figure 13.3.

Ericsson has developed scenarios to the year 2005 to portray possible futures for its business, its structure and its people. The company then worked back to a 'wanted' position in 2000. In 1998, it developed strategies for the business, structure and people to take it forward to its wanted position.

Focus scenario and integrated strategy

Figure 13.3

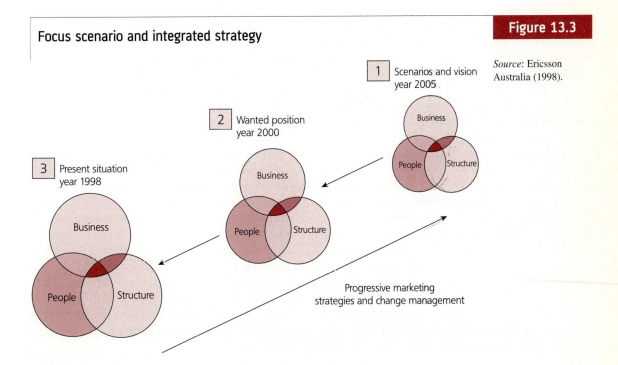

Source: Ericsson Australia (1998).

1 Scenarios and vision year 2005

Business
People   Structure

2 Wanted position year 2000

Business
People   Structure

3 Present situation year 1998

Business
People   Structure

Progressive marketing strategies and change management

13.1 International Highlight

Looking to the future

A business model can be defined as a choice of customer segments to compete in, coupled with a choice of business process or processes to apply in these segments. The more successful and lasting it is the more rigid the business process will become and be defended by managers. However, many companies have to engage continuously in scenario planning to avoid some of the rigidities that have come to mark any successful business model. For example, can Dell's extremely successful business model maintain the growth rates of the past decade? From a scenario perspective, Dell's future growth can take three directions. Firstly, it can stick to its current strategy but attempt to develop new market segments and products that fit its core direct model. Secondly, it can endeavour to break into new sophisticated products such as servers and storage devices. Finally, it can attempt to penetrate further into international markets.

Marks & Spencer's successful business model is coming under attack from focused competitors like Zara. Marks & Spencer are credited with the introduction of a true industrial approach in an industry formerly characterised by craft production. Competitors like Zara are therefore not readily identified as a threat by the management of Marks & Spencer. In the past many other companies thought the same. IBM's domination of the mainframe industry was severely disrupted by competitors DEC with their mini-computer products and later Sun and Apple with workstations and desktops. As a result, Zara's disruptive approach to fashion is causing many companies serious concern. Their 'lean' (low cost) approach to fashion is aimed at the 16–24-year-old customer segment. Their stores are located in trendy locations and kept open late, precisely in response to the targeted segment's behaviour. Key to the process innovation is the revolutionary treatment of the design step. Their scanning of fashion shows, selection of major trends, development of a library of models and postponement of final designs until after the purchase of raw materials are the key components of their process. These activities are performed continuously during the season. This continuous postponement of designs at Zara giving them an 'always in fashion' feel constitutes Zara's major innovation. Their 'freshness' in garments approach is the major challenge posed to the Marks & Spencer supply chain. On the other hand, Marks & Spencer consists of many units and sections, such as men's suits, female underwear and food. Their approach is well geared to the stable customer base among UK shoppers. Their response cannot be simple, as it is clear that the threat posed by a process-based competitor like Zara is real. As an integrated manufacturer and retailer, importing 'fresh good' (as Kenzo and Ralph Lauren do) into the textile section would only cannibalise their manufacturing unit. Given that Zara's strategy is based on a single market segment (16–24-year-olds) and uses a single business process entirely focused on that segment, makes it difficult for companies like Marks & Spencer to respond to this competitive threat, as it represents only one small but important segment of their business. Major changes will be difficult given their existing loyal customers in other segments and Zara's model has no guarantee of longevity.

Many industry analysts believe that the success of Munich-based Bayerische Motoren Werke AG (BMW) in the past was due to its ability to nurture new ideas through its integrated innovation process. Their future scenario planning is focused on unique selling propositions for each car to be launched, breakthrough innovations, concept cars to convey the brand image at automobile shows, and integrating the innovation process into BMW's core business strategy plan so that specific customer areas can be better dealt with.

The challenge is to understand future operating scenarios so that international business and marketing strategies can be progressively developed and implemented. International marketers need to manage the existing international business while progressively integrating new market opportunities presented by change. The core requirement in this challenge is to develop an effective international marketing capability so that the firm develops products and services which satisfy changing needs of target international markets in such a way as to meet financial objectives and shareholder value expectations.

Steps in the international marketing planning process

There are clearly defined steps in the international marketing planning process and the development of a marketing plan. In this section a real marketing plan of a firm (modified for confidentiality) is used to illustrate the planning elements, a similar process to that outlined in Figure 13.2. It comprises situation analysis, including SWOT, an evaluation of alternative marketing strategies, objectives and marketing strategy including the marketing mix and economic evaluation. This type of planning may focus on one country or a region such as two or three countries in an economic zone. In the example that follows the plan is for export to one country.

Case example 13.1

Background

Bathrooms Limited is a manufacturer and distributor of ceramic bathroom accessories. The company is also a leading distributor of tiling tools and accessories. The broad industry within which Bathrooms Ltd operates is the ceramic tile industry. Bathrooms Ltd's main customers are tile merchants who retail tiles and other bathroom and kitchen products. The narrower industry in which Bathrooms Ltd operates is the ceramic bathroom accessories industry.

Bathrooms Ltd is looking to expand its domestic operation by exporting. Vietnam, Japan, Singapore, Korea and Taiwan were evaluated as potential export markets. However, Japan was chosen as the market with the greatest potential.

Situation analysis

The starting point for any international marketing plan is to engage in a detailed situation analysis covering the overall business environment, market analysis, competitive analysis, the organisation's resources and capabilities and a SWOT analysis. The following is a summary for Bathrooms Ltd.

Business environment

The following is a summary of the key aspects of the business environment that will have an impact on Bathrooms Ltd's operations in Japan.

Social and cultural factors

Business is conducted in different ways in Japan: the Japanese tend to approach business with an emphasis on group spirit and harmony; seniority is also important in Japanese business dealings; the Japanese place great significance on the first meeting with a potential business partner; and business is also often approached with much

persistence and dedication, typical of the Japanese religious commitment.

Technological factors

Advances in process technology appear to be unlikely to influence products manufactured by Bathrooms Ltd as the manufacturing process remains very labour intensive to maintain quality. Major international manufacturers of ceramic bathroom products continue to use similar methods of production throughout the world.

Political and legal factors

The Japanese government is currently rectifying low business and consumer confidence by lowering interest rates on housing loans and stabilising material prices. This is expected to lead to an increase in private residential investment. Also deregulation and a reduction in barriers to imports are currently occurring in Japan.

Demographic trends

Eighty per cent of Japanese people consider themselves to be middle class. Traditional lifestyles are said to be diffusing, being replaced by a more modern and sophisticated society. The population was around 127 million in 2000 and is expected to be 128 million in 2005 with a 0.23% growth rate per year. (http://jin.jcic.or.jp/stat/stats/01CEN25.html)

Seasonal and climatic factors

Japan experiences plentiful rainfalls, with a five week rainy season in early summer, followed by a hot and humid summer. These humid and wet conditions are not conducive to the drying of the clays needed in ceramic manufacturing, which allows Bathrooms Ltd an opportunity for market entry.

Economic factors

Japan has experienced recessionary conditions over the last few years and the economy is still fairly static.

Market analysis

The product market

Bathrooms Ltd's products will be placed in the bathroom accessories market. Bathroom accessories include such products as soap holders, shelves, paper holders, towel rails and rings and robe hooks. Research into the Japanese market shows that the following types of bathroom accessories already exist: metal (both stainless steel and powder coated enamel), plastic, ceramic and porcelain.

Market characteristics and forecasts

Many freestanding homes and apartments are being built in Japan every year and there has been a move towards more upmarket home facilities. Traditionally in terms of appearance the place for bathing was not given much consideration. However, recent trends show that the Japanese want to make their bathrooms more attractive, with a demand for more western-style bathroom fittings. This would indicate a good market for bathroom accessories as a feature of these new homes.

Distribution and pricing trends

The basic distribution route for importers is from manufacturer to agent/distributor, to retail store to builder/end-user. However, some companies now deliver products direct to retailers and builders to speed up distribution. Japanese manufacturers of bathroom accessories sell their product to agents at a price of 45–55% of retail price. The pricing structure is similar for imported products with the exception of shipping, customs and tariffs.

Import positioning

Imports of bathroom accessories to Japan can be divided into two broad categories – Asian countries and the US and European countries. The Asian products are generally cheaper in price and are of lesser quality, while the US and European products are more expensive and are considered upmarket.

Market segments and target market behaviour

The two main segments for the product are home-owners and builders. Home-owners can select their bathroom accessories through a retail bathroom outlet and have them installed, or alternatively developers and builders will specify a certain type of accessory into their projects. The market can also be further segmented based on demographics, such as income and household structure.

Different marketing mixes are required for both the home-owner and the industrial user. The home-owner selects the bathroom accessories based on quality, attractiveness, functionality, colour match and overall coordination with their bathroom. Developers and builders select accessories based on functionality, quality, price and general colour match.

The agent's or distributor's decision to handle new bathroom accessories is based on complementing its existing range or serving a new niche market. Agents and distributors are interested in quality, price and delivery capability. Japanese agents are only interested in a product if it is either substantially different from, cheaper, of higher quality or more readily available than existing products.

Competitor analysis

Bathrooms Ltd's products would be competing against both domestic and imported goods of similar nature. These include products made from porcelain, ceramic, plastic, cast iron and steel. In

▶

the Japanese market porcelain and ceramic bathroom accessories are the most popular, but plastic products are now showing growth potential.

Competitors are considered to be both domestic manufacturers in Japan and also international exporters. Exporters come from Asian, European and American countries. In relation to ceramic ware, Thailand and Indonesia are the biggest exporters. TOTO and Inax are the two largest manufacturers of porcelain and ceramic ware products in Japan. Both these companies will be approached by Bathrooms Ltd in relation to distribution.

Organisational resources and capabilities

Financial capabilities

Bathrooms Ltd is a small to medium-sized, family-owned business with financial limitations. But its profit growth in recent years has given it a strong financial foundation. To assist in the financial aspects of export development Bathrooms Ltd has sought and was granted assistance from the Irish Development Authority (IDA) which provides €20,000 worth of consultancy time and subsidised international travel.

Bathrooms Ltd's domestic market share for ceramic bathroom accessories is 50–60%. This is expected to decline as both domestic and foreign competitors saturate the domestic market. In the previous three financial years Bathrooms Ltd has achieved gross profit margins of approximately 60% of sales.

Research capabilities

Much of the research required for developing its export programme will come from external assistance. Bathrooms Ltd has made contact with Japan External Trade Organisation (JETRO) and will be taking advantage of its available databases and experience. In addition, the IDA has a development office in Japan and its executives are happy to assist in relevant research.

Production capabilities

Bathrooms Ltd currently operates with excess capacity. Due to the labour intensive production process, production output can be increased by 50% with the addition of labour before further capital investment needs to be made. Development of new products is relatively inexpensive and prompt, taking approximately 6–12 weeks.

Management skills

One of Bathrooms Ltd's limitations is the lack of exporting experience of its senior managers. It plans to use the government assistance programmes to make up skill deficiencies.

Domestic distribution and suppliers

The company currently has one distributor in Dublin. This distribution network is well established and provides sufficient coverage for the domestic market. Bathrooms Ltd has two established suppliers for all its key materials.

Promotional materials

Bathrooms Ltd already maintains point-of-sale materials and other promotional materials in the domestic market. It believes that domestic material can be used/and or modified for use in export markets.

SWOT analysis

Analysis of the situation supported by detailed information (usually contained in appendices to the plan) enables executives to develop an assessment of company strengths, weakness, opportunities and threats. To be useful, these should be a short list of key factors which need to be used to advantage or addressed in the plan. The SWOT summary for Bathrooms Ltd is noted in Table 13.1.

Table 13.1 Bathrooms Ltd SWOT summary

Strengths	*Weaknesses*
• Established for 35 years, secure fnancial position, with 10% growth per annum in the past 7 years.	• Narrow product range (bathroom accessories only) may reduce competitiveness against wide range of suppliers.
• Manufactures high-quality ceramic bathroom fttings, cappings, borders, scrolls and cove tiles as well as other decorative tiles, in a large range of colours.	• Some substitute bathroom accessories are cheaper, placing ceramic products at the middle to upper end of the market.
• Ceramic bathroom accessories are considered attractive and easy to clean as opposed to metal and plastic fnishes which tarnish and scratch.	• Management has limited experience in exporting to non-English speaking countries.
• High margins allow for price competitiveness domestically and internationally.	• Higher operating costs than Asian competitors due to labour-intensive production processes and use of kilns that use large amounts of electricity.

Opportunities	*Threats*
• There are substantial numbers of apartments and freestanding houses being built in Japan every year – 150,000 freestanding homes and 300,000 apartments are scheduled for building in the coming year.	• Competition from other importers of ceramic products into Japan, together with existing competition from plastic and metal products in bathroom accessories.
• Japan is deregulating and abolishing or reducing import barriers, therefore making access to the country easier.	• Japan's economy has been on the decline for three years and looks to continue downwards for some time.
• Forming a long-standing relationship with a Japanese company may lead to other contacts or opportunities.	• The major distributors and manufacturers of bathroom accessories in Japan are operating in a cartel. The only feasible way to penetrate this market is through one of these distributors.
• Although the economy in Japan is on a downturn, sources show that the public and housing sectors continue to grow.	• Builders in Japan are slower than western builders. Also, builders in Japan have to be trained to use Bathrooms Ltd accessories effectively. High costs will be involved in this initial process.

Conclusion

The Japanese market is attractive. Bathrooms Limited has a reputation for high quality products and its access to fnancial support and export advice places it in a feasible position to succeed. However, a well-focused plan will be essential to success.

Evaluation of alternative marketing strategies

Formulation and evaluation of marketing strategies requires a clear and detailed under-standing of the international market's segmentation structure and the opportunities for valued differentiation and unique positioning. Segmentation should be founded first on need differences between customer groups which then may be reflected in particular positioning strategies. Sometimes need differences are mirrored by different demographics, geographic locations and distribution channels.

Segmenting international markets

Few companies have the resources to operate in all, or even most, of the countries around the world. Although some large companies, such as Coca-Cola, Nestlé and Ericsson, sell products in more than 150 countries, most firms focus on a much smaller set. Operating in several countries presents new challenges. The different countries of the world, even those that are close together, can vary dramatically in their economic, cultural and political make-up. Thus, just as they do within their domestic markets, international firms need to group their world markets into segments with distinct buying needs and behaviours.

Companies can segment international markets using one or a combination of several variables. They can segment by geographic location, grouping countries by regions such as South-East Asia, western Europe, North America, the Middle East or Africa. In fact, countries in many regions already have organised themselves geographically into market groups or 'Foreign Trade Zones', discussed in Chapter 18. These associations reduce trade barriers between member countries, creating larger and more homogeneous markets.

Geographic segmentation assumes that nations close to one another will have many common traits and behaviours. Although this is often the case, there are many exceptions. For example, although the United States and Canada have much in common, both differ culturally and economically from neighbouring Mexico. Even within a region, consumers can differ widely. For example, until recently, many international marketers thought that all Asian countries were the same. However, Indonesia is no more like the Philippines than Italy is like Sweden.

World markets can be segmented on the basis of economic factors. For example, countries might be grouped by population income levels or by their overall level of economic development. Some countries, such as the so-called Group of Eight – the United States, Britain, France, Germany, Japan, Canada, Russia and Italy – have established, highly industrialised economies. Other countries have newly industrialised or developing economies (Singapore, Taiwan, Korea, Brazil, Mexico). Still others are less developed (China, India). A country's economic structure shapes its population's product and service needs and, therefore, the marketing opportunities it offers.

Countries can be segmented by political and legal factors such as the type and stability of government, receptivity to foreign firms, monetary regulations, and the amount of bureaucracy. Such factors can play a crucial role in a company's choice of which countries to enter and how. Cultural factors also can be used, grouping markets according to common languages, religions, values and attitudes, customs, and behavioural patterns.

Segmenting international markets on the basis of geographic, economic, political, cultural and other factors assumes that segments should consist of clusters of countries. However, many companies use a different approach, called intermarket segmentation. Using this approach, they form segments of consumers who have similar needs and buying behaviour even though they are located in different countries. For example, brand icons like Louis Vuitton target the world's affluent, regardless of their country. And Coca-Cola uses ads filled with teenagers, sports and rock music to target the world's youth.

Emerging bases of global segmentation

Global market segmentation can be defined as country groups or individual consumer groups across countries of potential customers with homogenous attributes and similar buying behaviour.

Countries can be segmented by diffusion patterns. Some countries are fast adopters of a product, while others require a long period to adopt a product. In response to this a business could launch its products in countries that are innovators and later in those countries that are imitators or lag countries. So instead of using macro-variables to classify countries, a firm could segment on the basis of new product diffusion patterns. Usually diffusion patterns in countries differ by product, as shown in Figure 13.4 which illustrates the order and grouping of countries according to adoption-diffusion (Kumar and Echambadi, 1998).

Consumers in lag countries may learn from the product experience of lead countries resulting in a faster diffusion rate in lag markets. So lag countries that show strong learning ties with lead countries would indicate a sequential entry strategy that speeds up the diffusion in lag countries.

The maxim of 'think globally, act locally' also applies to market segmentation. Having identified and grouped countries according to adoption and diffusion patterns, it is important to look at local differences. Here a multidimensional segmentation approach is useful and more feasible for planning strategy and executing tactics. A segmentation scheme that accounts for the three dimensions – *needs, means* and *desires*

Segments based on diffusion patterns

Figure 13.4

Product categories

Segment	DVD player	Video cameras	Mobile phones	Personal computers
1	Germany, UK, France	Belgium, Denmark, Spain	Sweden, Norway	Germany, UK, France
2	Spain, Austria, Finland	Russia, Hungary, Austria	Finland, France	Norway, Austria, Germany
3	Poland, Greece, Swizerland	Germany, UK, France	Germany, UK, Italy, Hungary	Poland, Austria, Italy Hungary

Source: Adapted from Kumar and Echambadi (1998).

– is particularly useful in international marketing. For example, a potential buyer in Japan may *need* a reliable vehicle to carry two adults and one child, may have the *means* to afford a vehicle in the €20,000–25,000 range, and *desire* unique styling. Another buyer may have the *need* for a vehicle to carry small loads, the *means* to spend €10,000–15,000 and the *desire* for a working vehicle image (Neal and Wurst, 2001). These emerging forms of segmentation provide further options for the international marketer to better understand market potential and plan marketing strategy.

Market positioning for international markets

Once a company has decided which segments of the market it will enter, it must decide which 'positions' it wants to occupy in those segments.

What is market positioning?
Product position is the way the product's important attributes are defined by consumers – the place the product occupies in consumers' minds relative to competing products. Thus, Porsche is positioned as an elite performance sports car, BMW is positioned on prestige and 'sheer driving pleasure', Mercedes and Lexus are positioned on luxury, Nissan is positioned on reliability, and Subaru is positioned on value-for-money.

Consumers are overloaded with information about products and services. They cannot re-evaluate products every time they make a buying decision. To simplify buying decision making, they organise products into categories – they 'position' products, services and companies in their minds. A product's position is the complex set of perceptions, impressions and feelings that consumers hold for the product compared with competing products. The international marketer should plan positions that will give his/her firm's products the greatest advantage in selected target markets, and then design marketing mixes to create the planned positions.

Positioning strategies
Marketers can follow several positioning strategies (Rangan et al., 1992). These can be best illustrated with reference to well-known world brands. They can position their products on specific product attributes – Daihatsu advertises its low price; Saab and Peugeot promote on the basis of performance. Products can be positioned on the needs they fill or on the benefits they offer – Colgate Fluorigard reduces cavities; Aim tastes good. Or products can be positioned according to usage occasions – in the summer, Gatorade can be positioned as a beverage for replacing athletes' body fluids; in the winter, it can be positioned as the drink to use when the doctor recommends plenty of liquids. Another approach is to position the product for certain classes of users – Johnson & Johnson improved the market share for its baby shampoo by repositioning the product as one for adults who wash their hair frequently and need a gentle shampoo – they even added a variant with conditioner to reinforce this point.

A product can also be positioned directly against a competitor. For example, in advertisements for its printers, Lexmark has at times directly compared its products with Hewlett-Packard. It even supplies printer consumables like toner cartridges specifically for HP printers thus aligning itself very closely with the market leader. In its famous 'We're number two, so we try harder' campaign, Avis successfully positioned itself against the larger Hertz.

Finally, the product can be positioned for different product classes. For example, some margarines are positioned against butter, others against cooking oils. Camay hand soap is positioned with bath oils rather than with soap. Marketers often use a combination of these positioning strategies. Thus, Johnson & Johnson's Affinity shampoo is positioned as a hair conditioner for women over 40 (product class and user). It is important to understand that these positionings can differ in different cultures due to history, indigenous competitive entries and cultural context.

Choosing and implementing a positioning strategy   Some firms find it easy to choose their positioning strategy. For example, a firm that is well known for quality in certain segments will usually go for this position in an international market segment if it sees enough buyers seeking quality. But, in many cases, two or more firms will go after the same position. Then, each will have to find other ways to set itself apart, such as promising 'high quality for a lower cost' or 'high quality with more technical service'. That is, each firm must differentiate its offer by building a unique bundle of competitive advantages that appeal to a substantial group within the segment.

A simplified summary of the issues relating to segmentation and positioning, as well as marketing mix strategy alternatives for Bathrooms Limited, is provided next. In this example the firm is focusing on just one country market – Japan.

Case example 13.2

Alternative market entry strategies

While the dominance of established Japanese producers can present difficulties for importers, opportunities do exist for foreign producers with competitive products who are willing to put in the necessary effort. The foreign producer needs to fully research relevant import and distribution channels. There are three basic types of successful distribution pattern for imported products into Japan:

- using an import agent, such as a trading company, and distributing through channels already developed by the importer;
- using a company with appropriate distribution channels including companies from different industries; and
- setting up a subsidiary to develop distribution through that company.

The last option is not available to Bathrooms Ltd simply because of insufficient financial resources. Using a distributor is Bathrooms Ltd's preference because this matches the approach taken in its domestic markets. ABC Trading Co., Nikko Corp. and TOTO are three possible Japanese distributors with which a long-term relationship could be established. Japanese consumers have a high expectation of service and delivery, quality, reliability, courtesy and after-sales service. Choice of the right distributor is a critical decision.

Alternative target market and segmentation strategy

Bathrooms Ltd may market direct to retailers rather than to the distributor/wholesaler. In this option it would target retailers of bathroom, tile, hardware, building and home improvements. Alternatively, it could target just one of these retailers and then widen its market once business was established.

Beyond the segmentation approach already discussed in relation to home-owners and builders/developers, Bathrooms Ltd may segment the market based on traditional versus modern styles of bathroom accessories, or by defining geographic segments where the greatest new housing developments are taking place. The most appropriate segmentation form will be determined by current market structure and changing consumer needs.

Alternative positioning strategy

The positioning strategy would be consistent across all target markets. Middle to upper markets would apply, as Bathrooms Ltd wants to position itself as having a high-quality product with differential value.

Alternative marketing mix strategies

Distribution – If a number of distributors were to handle these products, rather than one large distributor, Bathrooms Ltd could select distributors based on geographic coverage. If two distributors were found to service similar geographic regions it may elect to supply only the more successful of the two.

Price – As retailers may not handle the same volume as distributors, Bathrooms Ltd would need to consider what price arrangements would be made when dealing with distributors versus retailers because volume discounts may become an issue.

Product – In terms of the retail target market, research may show that certain colours in the product range are preferred over others in the Japanese market. It may be more cost and time effective to export only a portion of the colour range rather than the entire range.

Promotion – The company will need to reassess its display boards and catalogues in order to project an effective sense of product quality to the Japanese, whose expectations are high. Expert advice is needed because many firms entering the Japanese market have found that high quality materials and expensive promotion are needed for this market. In addition, a video capturing the Bathrooms Ltd manufacturing plant and family owned orientation, and incorporating some of Ireland's tourist highlights, may assist the Japanese to understand the context in which the firm operates.

Corporate objectives

A firm's corporate objectives usually include a mission statement and objectives reflecting financial growth, new business and new markets. As far as possible these should be measurable so that progress can be assessed over time. Bathrooms Limited's mission statement and objectives can be found in Case Example 13.3.

Case example 13.3

Mission statement

Bathrooms Ltd will provide high quality ceramic products, at competitive prices, to both domestic and international customers' satisfaction, while providing our staff with a safe and healthy working environment by following all relevant regulatory requirements.

Corporate objectives

The major objectives to be achieved by Bathrooms Ltd in the next three years include:

- successful development of export markets, beginning with Japan by the end of 2004 and then further expansion into Vietnam in 2006;
- sales increase of 10% per annum, through the regaining of market share in the domestic market and development of new markets in Japan and South-East Asia;
- net profit to increase from 9% to 10% of sales in 2004 and maintained at this level. Gross profit to be maintained at around 60% of sales; and
- capital assets growth to be stabilised for a period of three years until the expansion into international markets requires increased manufacturing capacity.

Corporate strategy

The broad corporate strategies suggest how the corporate objectives will be achieved.

Development of export markets – management and marketing resources will be added to support focused market strategies through major distributors first in Japan, then in other targeted Asian markets.

Steady sales growth – an improved aggressive marketing strategy for domestic and export markets will include the development and implementation of translated promotional materials for foreign markets, improved and more direct salesforce efforts, use of quality assurance accreditation as a marketing tool, and ongoing investigation and further development of international markets.

Net profit increase – the combined strategies of sales growth, capacity utilisation, productivity improvements and gross margin maintenance will result in profit increases to achieve objectives.

Stabilise capital asset growth – due to substantial capital asset spending in the last 2–3 years, capital asset growth will be stabilised to allow development of efficiencies using current production capacity. This capital spending has been to improve and upgrade equipment, allowing greater capacity and more efficient production to provide the firm with an advantage when entering international markets.

Marketing objectives and strategy

Marketing objectives and strategy may address all the firm's markets or focus on individual priority markets. In Case Example 13.4 the objectives and strategy focus on Bathrooms Ltd's Japanese market. This includes marketing objectives, target markets, positioning and the marketing mix.

Case example 13.4

Marketing objectives

The fragmented nature of the Japanese market and the large number of competitive suppliers suggest realistic marketing objectives as follows:

- achieve brand awareness in target markets of 3% at end of year 1, 6% at end of year 2 and 10% at the end of year 3;

- achieve market share of relevant product markets of 0.5% at end of year 1, 1% at end of year 2 and 2% at the end of year 3.

Target markets

Bathrooms Ltd has chosen to market its products through a wholesaler/distributor to the retail markets, such as bathroom products retailers, tile retailers, hardware and building retailers and home improvement retailers. The end-user target markets include home buyers, home renovators, commercial builders and developers. Three main markets in Japan have been identified as potential areas.

Housing starts – There has been an increasing number of new housing starts occurring in the Japanese market and current information supports continued growth in this area. This is a high priority target market.

Housing reforms – The current trend is to make the amenities comfortable, clean and fun instead of merely functional. Bathrooms are now viewed as a place to relax. Research shows that out of every 1,000 established households, 710 bathrooms have been renovated. This is a high priority.

Improvement to public toilets – Public toilets have been disliked because they were dirty, dark and smelly. However, public toilets are also being renovated in order to improve the facilities and help them be perceived by the public as a place to relax and conduct grooming activities. This is a low priority target.

Market positioning

In the domestic market the lower market is satisfied by cheaper, mainly plastic, accessories. The middle market is covered by ceramic, metal, brass and other accessories. The upper market contains mostly expensive silver and gold plated or powder-coated metal screw-on accessories. Research suggests that similar lower, middle and upper market products are available in Japan.

To supply to both domestic and commercial applications in Japan, Bathrooms Ltd plans to position its products in the middle to upper end of the market. Also the company's promotional material suggests a middle to upper market position.

Marketing mix

The marketing mix strategy for exporting to Japan is consistent with Bathrooms Ltd's current operations and capabilities and fits well with existing channels of distribution in Japan.

Product – Bathrooms Ltd plans to market all its existing range of products and colours to Japan. Research conducted on the Japanese market indicates Bathrooms Ltd will have to modify and develop a number of new products to suit the market. One of the planned developments is to offer a range of screw-on accessories, to allow for quick and easy installation.

Distribution – The company has chosen to appoint one or more Japanese distributors who already have access to the entire market both demographically and geographically and can transact sales of Bathrooms Ltd products to retail outlets of tiles, building and bathroom products. The majority of freight will be shipped, the exception to this being urgent orders, which will require air freight.

Pricing – Feedback from TOTO has indicated that at the current price Bathrooms Ltd products are relatively cheap. This indicates there may be substantial opportunity for higher prices in line with positioning its products as high quality, and in the middle to upper market. The company will start with relatively high prices offering high margins to distributors with enough scope to reduce prices as required.

Promotion – Promotion consists of colour catalogues and display boards of Bathrooms Ltd products. These are designed for permanent display in retail stores. The export promotional strategy includes:

– visiting potential distributors with samples, catalogues and display boards;

– participating in relevant trade shows such as the Building Exhibition Trade Show which is run annually in Tokyo;

– advertise in relevant trade magazines and have English ads translated into Japanese with the help of JETRO and IDA; and

– create a promotion video showing Bathrooms Ltd's manufacturing facilities.

The promotional strategy needs to be dynamic and flexible responding to the changing level of experience in the Japanese market.

Economic evaluation

Economic evaluation of an international marketing strategy includes planning assumptions underpinning the logic of the plan, sales and costs forecasts, breakeven and sensitivity analyses to establish financial benchmarks and consequences of alternative possible outcomes. A summary of these is provided in Case Example 13.5 for illustrative purposes for Bathrooms Ltd. Detailed financial analysis would normally be contained in an appendix to the marketing plan.

Case example 13.5

Planning assumptions

- Growth in the bathroom market will continue in Japan at the same rate as in the previous two years.
- There will be no new revolutionary technologies or products in the next three years.
- Manufacturing cost ratios are assumed to remain constant for any additional volumes up to 150% of current output.
- Sales forecasts for pessimistic, realistic and optimistic volumes are relevant to the current economic conditions and competitive structure.
- Profit and loss forecasts are based on costs and margins ratios for the current financial year ending 2001/02, and include all relevant costs for entry into the Japanese market.
- Staff can be added and trained within two months of initial demand increase.

Forecast sales and costs

Research has revealed the following:

- The Japanese market is substantially larger than the Irish and is beyond the resources of Bathrooms Ltd to satisfy completely.
- Bathrooms Ltd's current and planned capacity will only allow sales of up to €10 million in the first three years.
- It is unlikely Bathrooms Ltd will generate substantial sales from its entry into the market in the first year, as the product and promotional materials will need to be diffused throughout retail networks to generate sales.
- Market share is likely to be low (less than 5%) for some time until the market becomes aware of the Bathrooms Ltd brand and products and adopts them.
- Japanese market sales are subjective estimates based on business and market research.

Below are the profit forecasts for the first three years of operation in the Japanese market. Forecast sales represent a small portion of the Japanese market with the 'likely' forecasts reflecting market share objectives for years 1, 2 and 3.

Profit (Loss)	Pessimistic	Likely	Optimistic
First year	(€78,000)	(€23,000)	€54,000
Second year	(€16,000)	€110,000	€254,000
Third year	€4,000	€256,000	€544,000

Breakeven analysis

It is expected a minimum of €50,000 will be spent initially in entering the Japanese market. This cost includes travel, promotional materials, wages, translations, consultancy and other costs. Calculations result in at least €1,000,000 in sales needed to break even in the first year. This falls between the likely and optimistic sales positions. Many of the costs will be incurred in initially entering the market, and the second year of trading will have lower costs and increased sales. Analysis confirms that entry into the Japanese market requires a long-term financial commitment.

Sensitivity analysis

Sensitivity analysis provides 'what if' scenarios based on possible change in variables affecting revenues and costs. Some of the volatile variables to be tested include currency fluctuations, interest rate variations, product prices, sales variations and competitor impacts on market share.

Other factors affecting sales and profit sensitivity are supply delays, loss of a distributor and changes in economic conditions affecting housing. Contingency plans will need to be developed to deal with any of these situations.

Implementation and control

Action plans for implementation

Action programme Marketing strategies should be turned into specific action programmes that answer the following questions: What will be done? When will it be done? Who is responsible for doing it? How much will it cost? For example, the international marketer may regard sales promotion as a key strategy for winning market share. A sales promotion action plan should be drawn up to outline special offers and their dates, trade shows entered, new point-of-purchase displays and other promotions. The action plan shows when activities will be started, reviewed and completed.

Budgets Action plans allow the manager to make a supporting marketing budget that is essentially a projected profit and loss statement. For revenues, it shows the forecast number of units that would be sold and the average net price. On the expense side, it shows the cost of production, distribution and marketing. The difference is the projected profit. Senior management will review the budget and either approve or modify it. Once approved, the budget is the basis for materials buying, production scheduling, personnel planning and marketing operations.

Marketing implementation Planning good strategies is only a start towards successful marketing. A brilliant marketing strategy counts for little if the company fails to implement it properly. Marketing implementation is the process that turns marketing strategies and plans into marketing actions in order to accomplish strategic marketing objectives. Implementation involves day-to-day, month-to-month activities that effectively put the marketing plan to work. Whereas marketing planning addresses the what and why of marketing activities, implementation addresses the who, where, when and how.

Successful implementation depends on several key elements. First, it requires an action programme that pulls all the people and activities together. Second, the company's formal organisational structure plays an important role in implementing international marketing strategy.

The company's decision and reward systems – operating procedures that guide planning, budgeting, compensation and other activities – also affect implementation. For example, if a company compensates managers for short-run results, they will have little incentive to work towards long-run objectives. Effective implementation also requires careful human resources planning. At all levels, the company must fill its structure and systems with people who have the needed skills, motivation and personal characteristics. In recent years, more and more companies have recognised that long-run human resources planning can give the company a strong competitive advantage. An international marketing plan will need to be supported by a commitment to training and development of required international experience.

Finally, to be successfully implemented, the firm's marketing strategies must fit with its company culture. Company culture is a system of values and beliefs shared by people in an organisation – the company's collective identity and meaning. International marketing strategies that do not fit in with the company's culture will be difficult to implement. Because company culture is so hard to change, companies usually design

Case example 13.6

Control mechanisms

Bathrooms Ltd has developed detailed action plans supporting all elements of the marketing mix including the timing of market entry activities, distributor appointments and shipping schedules to penetrate the Japanese market. An initial export marketing organisation structure has been established with sufficient people and resources to action its international marketing plan.

Performance measures and monitoring systems have been specifically designed to assist the export division to manage the new export business and control activities and expenses. These details are contained in appendices to the plan with a one- to two-page summary of important milestones included in the main planning document.

strategies that fit their current cultures, rather than trying to change their styles and cultures to fit new strategies. However, the speed of change today may force companies to be more market focused, leading many more to tackle the big challenge of culture change.

Monitoring of action plan

Marketing control   Many surprises occur during the implementation of marketing plans requiring the international marketer to practise ongoing marketing control. This involves evaluating the results of marketing strategies and plans and taking corrective action to ensure that objectives are attained. Performance in the marketplace is measured against objectives and the causes of any differences between expected and actual performance are evaluated. Corrective action to close the gaps between objectives and results may require changing the marketing action programmes or even changing the objectives.

The purpose of control is to ensure that the company achieves the sales, profits and other objectives set out in its international marketing plan (see Case Example 13.6).

Challenges to international marketing planning

Several weaknesses in international marketing planning are common among companies attempting international market expansion.

Many international marketing plans lack market reality. International marketing managers and product managers are frequently too removed from the international marketplace to maintain a handle on what is really happening in fast-changing environments. This can be rectified with a commitment to extracting timely and relevant market information and use of appropriate interpretive tools. However, often this is hard to get in Asian countries and it is necessary to maintain an ongoing on-the-spot presence. Nothing beats face-to-face contact with intermediate and end-customers.

International marketing plans are often not integrated in the business and corporate hierarchy. This is because of lack of clear vision or understanding at various levels of the strategic priorities about how various product initiatives and functional strategies fit. Where there is a lot of planning done at each level there can be misunderstanding to the point where each level prepares a full plan with either different or conflicting plans, where one level's vision is translated to another level's objectives and then to a lower level's tasks or operations. This can be resolved with a clear strategic planning framework providing a logical fit for the initiatives at various levels. The framework provided earlier in this chapter is a useful starting point.

There is often a lack of financial integration with international marketing at the business strategy level. This is because the disciplines of financial analysis and marketing analysis have not been effectively brought together to develop business strategies. Financial analysts too frequently do not understand market realities and uncertainties, while marketing analysts have limited experience in evaluating the financial impacts of proposed international marketing strategies.

Too much emphasis is given to 'the plan' document, rather than the international marketing planning process. Stories abound of plans evaluated on the basis of size or weight ('It must weigh at least 5 kilos to pass the test!'); coloured pictures; or politically correct contents ('That's what I want to hear!'). An international marketing plan should be concise, clear and directional weighing 5 grams, not 5 kilos.

Team involvement in the international marketing planning process is often lacking. Again, too much emphasis on 'the plan' document occurs without attention to the process. In the end, a plan developed but not implemented due to lack of support or understanding is a waste of resources. Those who need to support the plan, in terms of resource allocation or through implementation roles, need to be 'involved' and 'own' it in a commitment sense. This problem is endemic in organisations where objectives and priorities are unclear or conflicting divisional objectives are allowed to continue unresolved.

Traditional strategic planning does not take sufficient account of the role of key external relationships in improving competitive position. Strong relationships with key suppliers, distributors and alliance partners may lead to higher quality products and services and superior distribution/delivery systems.

A series of systematic interrelated steps is crucial in effectively formulating and implementing international marketing strategies. This reduces the risk of leaving out key issues and people, and highlights the assumptions upon which strategies are based and resources committed. The example of Bathrooms Ltd provides a detailed illustration.

In reality, organisations adopt a hybrid of management systems depending upon their size, diversity, position in the market, rate and type of external change. However, a generic series of steps in formulating and implementing international marketing strategies applies to all. The five steps discussed early in this chapter (see Figure 13.2), suggest a sequential process. In practice, the sequence will depend upon the organisation's current position in the market. For instance, business mission and vision may be

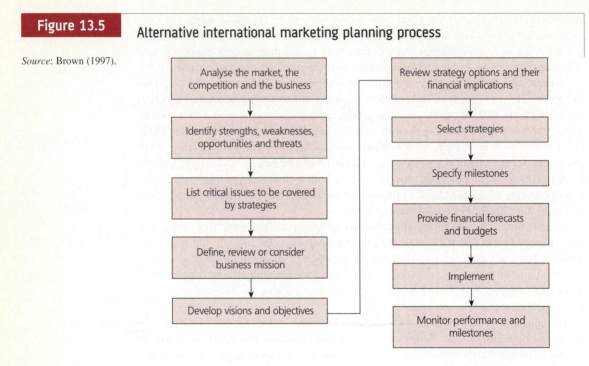

Figure 13.5   Alternative international marketing planning process

Source: Brown (1997).

well established and may require little development or review. If this is the case, they will act as the foundation from which other steps emanate. Alternatively, a company may become lost in a sea of change and need to establish its mission. It would do this through strategic analysis and a review of its broad objectives against reality. Figure 13.5 shows a different sequence of more detailed steps that would be relevant in this situation.

The challenge is to develop proactive strategies in the light of expected changes and adaptive strategies to confront unexpected changes.

All these challenges were faced by Barbeques Galore when it tackled the American market, described in International Highlight 13.2. As success was achieved in the US, the overall vision and strategy changed.

Practical international marketing planning

Developing international marketing strategies and plans often involves trade-offs in practice. The history of the firm, the relative importance of international markets, its competitive position and market trends in its home market all play a part and influence the approach taken. Three areas need to be considered: namely the starting point for international marketing planning, the inclusion of creative insight, and the influence of management aspirations.

13.2 International highlight

The hidden elements of experience and persistence

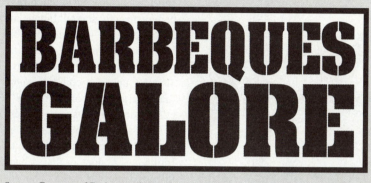

Source: Courtesy of Barbeques Galore Aust. Pty Ltd.

Whether we call it 'cooking out' in America or having a 'barbie' in Australia, this national outdoor preoccupation has enabled an Australian-based business to expand into the American market.

Barbeques Galore was formed in 1977 at Silverwater, a suburb of Sydney. The company was initially known as The Galore Group. Its NSW factory builds barbeques under the names of 'Turbo', 'Capt'n Cook', 'Bar-B-Chef' and 'Cook On'.

Market penetration in Australia or market development in US

With a large share (30%) of the Australian market and an increasingly price-competitive domestic market, the Barbeques Galore Group adopted a more aggressive international marketing strategy to achieve its objectives of sales and profit growth. Since its 1997 US listing, funds were available to expand the business in the American market. Within a period of three years it has almost been able to match its Australian sales in the US market. In 2000, Australian sales were €139 million and US sales €122 million. In 2001, Barbeques Galore was a €260 million business.

Expansion into the US created a healthy niche for the company since it seemed to be the only speciality BBQ chain in that country. The competition comes only indirectly in the form of hardware and department stores. The US barbeque and accessories market is worth €2 billion per year, so having a small piece of this market gives it far greater potential than its dominant position in the Australian market.

In 2001 Barbeques Galore had 84 stores in Australia and 68 stores in the US. (The US numbers mainly consist of franchise stores.) However, over the previous two years the company had changed its focus to operate only with company-owned stores and progressively terminated its franchises. The reason for this strategic change was because of the value-adding possibilities and learning more about the market in the event of having new competitors entering its profitable niche. The grand plan of deputy chairman, Robert Gavshon, is eventually to have 400 stores in the US.

E-commerce: threat or opportunity?

In the current economic and technological environment competitors can come from anywhere. The Internet was viewed by the company as both an opportunity and a threat. An opportunity in that it enabled Barbeques Galore to virtually become a national seller in the US, and a threat

▶

Source: Courtesy of Barbeques Galore Aust. Pty Ltd.

is to have the right mix of bricks-and-mortar and e-commerce. In 2000, Barbeques Galore opened 12 new stores and planned to open a further 10–15 stores per year over the next three years. But the US market is much bigger than what is being currently served. Financial resources, brand awareness and purchasing habits of Americans have created new possibilities to expand its American presence. Barbeques Galore has now also set up an e-commerce site and estimated that average customer online sales are worth €250 – double the average sales in US stores.

To date it seems that the mix of an international and e-commerce focus is working for Barbeques Galore in that it has doubled its size in just over four years. The growth has placed the company as an international player with the knowledge and capabilities to grow its business internationally rather than waiting for someone else to come into the Australian market.

The next challenge is where to next: Brazil, Europe, the world, or diversify into new products?

Where would you go next?

Source: Michelle Hannen, *Business Review Weekly*, 16 June 2000, p. 40.

since its expansion could be dwarfed by other multinational and pure e-commerce businesses who could establish their presence rapidly.

However, Barbeques Galore is sticking to its strategy, believing that the only way to succeed

Market-based and product-based planning

These are two approaches to practical marketing planning. The *market-based* approach proposed in this chapter is one which starts with an analysis of consumer needs. The service or product is then designed or adapted to those needs, and the strategies and marketing mix plans are developed accordingly.

This approach is most appropriate when a new product is being developed, or the intention is to modify or adapt an existing product in line with international market needs. Positioning is a key consideration in the development of the marketing strategy and plans for the new product or service.

The *product/service-based* approach is the one which is most frequently encountered in practice. It is also the one reflected in the Bathrooms Ltd example. In this case the product or service is fixed or cannot be readily changed within the available/feasible time span or resources. For example, it is not at all unusual to be facing the situation of 'a product searching for an international customer'. This situation also applies when the organisation's skills are limited (e.g. in the case of a personal services organisation such as a consultancy).

The international marketing planning approach in this case is to identify the target market segments as clearly as possible and to find these segments. The planning task is to develop appropriate programmes (distribution, pricing, communications) to reach these segments and supply them as effectively and profitably as possible (market penetration). There will be an emphasis on tactical planning. Alternatively (or additionally) it may be necessary to identify segments which are currently not catered for (market development). However, in this case, other organisations in the industry may be offering a similar service or product and all may be aiming at the same segment(s). Therefore, competition may be extreme, and it may not be possible to supply to those segment(s) profitably.

The product/service-based approach should therefore be considered as a possible short-term planning and international marketing management approach, with a market-based approach being required in the longer term.

Incorporating creative insight

One common reason or excuse given for not planning is that *the formality of carrying out the tasks and/or following a prescribed structure stifles creativity*. The challenge for the planner is to incorporate the creative insight and to identify a new or better way of doing international business.

There are ways of encouraging creativity. One approach is to question all key assertions and recommendations. Another is to discuss these areas with people with a different perspective, such as management staff or a consultant. It also helps to allow enough time in writing the plan to be able to reflect on and mull over the findings and conclusions. Leaving the writing of a report to the last minute and producing it in a rush is not conducive to creative thought.

Although lateral thinking is valuable, it is not enough to base the plan on one idea which at first sight might appear to be brilliant. The idea or insight must be relevant and capable of being put into practice. It must enhance and strengthen other marketing mix elements and help to achieve the chosen objectives. It is therefore necessary to have a sound marketing analysis and clear objectives to provide the basis for evaluating the creative insight.

The importance of management aspirations

The role of a chief executive is important in all organisations and is vital in small ones. Their personal aspirations, attitudes and expectations greatly influence the objectives, directions and activities of the organisation. Similarly, senior executives may have great influence in these important areas in the international marketing plan.

It is important for the marketing planner to understand these personal attitudes and aspirations, and to identify what drives the key influencers in the organisation. An international marketing plan which ignores this aspect may well be rejected as not 'fitting in' with the organisation. For example, the key executive(s) may have aspirations and expectations regarding the positioning and image of the organisation's product or service which are not matched by the view held by the consumer or customer in the firm's foreign markets.

The planner's task is firstly to take the time and effort to identify the key decision-makers in the organisation, and to understand their personal and management aspirations. The planner must then either make the executives understand the realities of the marketplace which may be unpalatable to them, or help the executives do the things they want to do as well as possible – if the marketplace allows this. Note that this situation is similar to the product-based approach to planning described above.

In the same vein, it is important for the international marketer to be familiar with the 'political' attitudes and factors within the organisation. These may result in some activities being accepted and others rejected. The achievability of a plan will therefore depend on these internal political influences and on minimising, avoiding or successfully countering conflict in this area.

Internet infusion

MSN – Europe's top portal While MSN lags behind AOL Time Warner in the US subscribers and behind Yahoo! Inc. in web traffic, its performance in Europe is much better. MSN is Europe's top portal. Management of MSN Europe have succeeded with a two-pronged strategy, according to Judy Gibbons, the vice-president. 'Firstly, we have taken advantage of MSN's globally recognised brand, centralised computer systems and consistent user interface, but we still think local. In France and Germany content comes from local sources. This strategy has cost us €430 million on marketing to media buyers. Secondly, to diversify our revenues we have contracted with cellular operators linking Hotmail and Messenger with mobile text messaging services. The next stage of the strategy is to turn MSN Europe into both an Internet service provider and a portal and to turn European users into paying subscribers.'

However, MSN does not have it all its own way in all parts of Europe. Yahoo! is more popular in France and Germany and offers many of the same features and will provide strong competition, but for now MSN leads the way.

Source: www.msn.com

Summary

Planning and strategy for international marketing follows a series of steps and processes which are practised by most successful international marketing firms. These include a systematic and detailed analysis of the external market environment and the internal capabilities of the firm, a clear understanding of alternatives, concise, measurable and well-communicated objectives and well thought-out marketing strategies supported by time-phased action plans and resource allocation. Financial evaluation leading to forecasts and budgets form the basis for monitoring performance and taking action to keep the business on target.

Tools such as scenario planning are now being used to build flexibility into both company response and planning processes and provide a context for international marketing planning.

The centrepiece of all international marketing planning should be detailed market analysis incorporating actionable market segmentation targets. Different approaches to segmentation should be evaluated before a segmentation scheme is settled upon. This leads to alternative choices for market positioning in the targeted international markets.

The many practical issues to be considered in international marketing planning include the management aspirations of the company, the extent to which the plan can be market-based as distinct from product-based, and the integration of the plan with the rest of the business and its competences.

Notes – definitions of strategic terms (Davies, 1995)

Action plan – A division of the overall plan into implementable pieces of work along with all the other information (how, what, when, where, why, who) that a person being given accountability for the task will need in order to do the task and get the desired result.

Milestone – An interim objective, say a quarterly measurable point, that should be reached in an annual objective.

Mission – The organisation's purpose statement.

Objective – A statement of what is going to be achieved, stated in a measurable (numeric) and time-specific way.

Strategic management – Strategic management is overall leadership of a process by which an organisation invents and reinvents positive futures for itself and organises itself to create those evolving futures in a sustainable way.

Strategic planning – A systematic methodology for charting the 'big issue' future of an organisation.

Strategy – A statement of how an objective is going to be achieved. One objective may have several strategies associated with its achievement. Strategies can cascade in hierarchies from a grand strategy, the overall 'means by which', down through successive layers to very specific 'means by which' statements. This is the hardest part, the least understood and potentially the most fruitful area.

Vision – A word picture of a desirable future state for an organisation in sufficient detail that readers can unambiguously understand and picture that future themselves.

Ethics issue

The international division of your company of which you are the manager has had several unsuccessful attempts in penetrating several Asian markets. Your board has asked you to submit a new international marketing plan. You know that this must show breakeven results in year 1 and profit from year 2 onwards for it to be acceptable to the board or otherwise they will close your division resulting in loss of your position and the jobs of your staff. Your investigations of the Asian markets clearly shows that China is by far the best prospect for your company's products but the experience of almost all companies entering the Chinese market shows that breakeven is usually not possible until three or four years of operations in that market. You are firmly convinced that your company will achieve very large profits and sales in the Chinese market in the long term. As you are the only executive with international experience and your reputation is excellent with all the board members, they will accept your recommendation.

Would you fudge the figures to show profitability in the short term to save your division and your job from extinction? Or would you present a realistic plan showing losses in the short term and profits in the long term?

Web workout

Question 1 Using the Internet find two golf-buggy sellers that compete in the same countries/markets. Compare the offers provided by each competitor and suggest ways in which they could grow their current international business.

Question 2 Are airlines considered to be truly global/international businesses? Visit the websites of British Airways, Lufthansa and Singapore Airlines. Analyse their websites taking the perspective of an international (non-English-speaking) traveller and analyse which one of these websites is mostly geared to service such needs. Select one of these companies and suggest a strategy to adopt to grow its international business.

Websites

Shell www.shell.com/au-en

Ericsson www.ericsson.com.au

Fujitsu www.fujitsu.com.au

International Monetary Fund (IMF)
   www.imf.org

Motorola www.motorola.com/

Philips www.philips.com

Panasonic www.panasonic.com.au

Nokia www.nokia.com.au

Samsung www.samsung.com.au

Matsushita
   www.panasonic.co.jp/global/index.html

Census of Japan
   www.jin.jcic.or.jp/stat

Japan External Trade Organisation
(JETRO) www.jetro.go.jp

Colgate-Palmolive www.colgate.com

Lexmark www.lexmark.com

Johnson and Johnson www.jnj.com

Avis www.avis.com

Hertz www.hertz.com.au

James Hardie Industries
www.jameshardie.com

Hewlett-Packard www.hp.com

Transgrid www.tg.nsw.gov.au

Barbeques Galore
www.barbequesgalore.com.au

World Bank www.worldbank.org

Discussion questions

1 Explain the alternative strategic planning sequences that may be used in international marketing planning.

2 What is scenario planning? Under what conditions is it useful? How important do you think scenario planning is as a context for international marketing planning?

3 Which part of the international marketing plan do you believe is most important? Why?

4 What are the most important factors in segmenting international markets?

5 Discuss the concept of market positioning. Pick a firm of your choice and outline how it positions its products in international markets.

6 Evaluate the strengths and weaknesses of Bathrooms Ltd's international marketing plan in terms of situation analysis coverage, usefulness of SWOT summary, coverage of alternatives, clarity of marketing objectives and strategies and scope of economic evaluation.

7 What are the major challenges faced by marketers in developing and implementing international marketing plans?

8 What are the practical internal issues to be addressed by marketers when developing an international marketing plan?

References

Brown, L. (1997) *Competitive Marketing Strategy*, 2nd edn, Nelson ITP, Melbourne.

Davies, M. (1995) 'Learning at Work', unpublished paper, Robertson, Queensland.

Hannen, M. (2000) 'Ambitions Galore for Barbeque Chain', *BRW*, p. 40.

Kotler, P., Armstrong, G., Brown, L. and Adam, S. (1998) *Marketing*, Prentice Hall, Melbourne.

Kumar, V. and Echambadi, R. (1998) 'Cross-National Diffusion Research: What Do We Know and How Certain Are We?', *Journal of Product Innovation Management*, Vol. 15.

Kumar, V. and Nagpal, A. (2001) 'Segmenting Global Markets', *Marketing Research*, Vol. 13, pp. 8–13.

Neal, W.D. and Wurst, J. (2001) Advances in Market Segmentation, *Marketing Research*, Vol. 13, pp. 14–19.

Rangan, V.K., Moriaty, R. and Swartz, G. (1992) *Journal of Marketing*, October pp. 72–82.

Toyne, B. and Walters, P. (1993) *Global Marketing Management: A Strategic Perspective*, Allyn and Bacon, Division of Simon & Schuster Inc, Boston.

van der Heyden, K. (1996) *Scenarios: The Art of Strategic Conversation*, John Wiley and Sons Ltd, Chichester, England.

14

Gaining international competitive advantage

Learning objectives

After studying this chapter, you should be able to:

- identify the key elements and drivers of national advantage that contribute to competitive advantage of an industry;

- determine the relevant bases of competitive advantage at the firm level and how they relate to generic competitive strategies in international markets;

- evaluate the significance of an industry value chain and how customer value can be created through restructuring it;

- conduct a systematic step process of competitive analysis in order to determine a firm's international competitiveness and most relevant positioning; and

- follow a process of competitive intelligence gathering with particular reference to the Internet as an information channel.

Technology makes the difference: Extended ERP

Computers have been used in business for fifty years. Vast changes have occurred during that time. Early systems were physically enormous and had less power than many modern wristwatches. Manipulating these systems was slow, resulting in limited information being available. As computers became more powerful and technical skills increased, businesses began to rely on the information they provided.

In the late 1990s the Internet allowed organisations to share data in a relatively straightforward manner. Software firms were quick to take advantage of this new opportunity and new enterprise applications emerged. These included online stores, eProcurement and customer relationship management, all of which could be integrated with the organisation's enterprise resource planning (ERP) system. Further advances in these technologies have allowed seamless integration between enterprises.

ERP systems dominated the enterprise software market in the mid to late 1990s. Organisations adopted ERP systems to improve business processes, reduce costs, and prepare for future growth and also to resolve Y2K and euro issues. While the rate of adoption of ERP was very high there was also much criticism for expensive overrun implementations, restricted functionality and inflexible, complicated configuration and set-up.

In parallel with the rise of ERP the Internet was moving from a messaging facility used by academics and the military to a powerful communications tool, which could be used by consumers and businesses alike.

As organisations began to improve internal processes through ERP they also began to examine how ERP and the Internet could help them improve processes which extended beyond the enterprise to their customers and suppliers.

Applications managing the supply chain, business-to-business procurement and web stores were integrated with ERP to increase the competitiveness of the enterprise and the entire supply chain. This process of integrating ERP with such applications and others such as CRM has been called Extended ERP.

Introduction

This chapter discusses the elements underlying competitive advantage and explores generic strategies relevant to firms conducting business internationally. The value chain concept is examined as a tool to help companies identify opportunities for competitive advantage in international markets. This leads into discussion of a process for analysing steps in competitor analysis ending with a brief overview of the Internet as an intelligence gathering tool.

Competitive advantage is defined as an advantage gained over competitors by offering customers greater perceived value, either through lower prices or by delivering more benefits that justify higher prices. If a company can position itself as providing superior perceived value to its selected international markets – and deliver it to customer expectations – it gains competitive advantage.

Competitive advantage is closely related to the idea of international competitiveness. This is relevant at both country and firm levels. International competitiveness at a national level is based on superior productivity performance. It is associated with rising living standards and the country's ability to stay ahead technologically and commercially in those product markets that contribute to a bigger share of world consumption and added value.

Competitiveness for the firm is closely related to its ability to increase sales, margins and profits in the international markets in which it chooses to compete – and its capability to defend its market position as new waves of competitive offers emerge (Bradley, 1999). Several frameworks have been developed to analyse both national and firm competitive advantage.

National competitive advantage

Analysis of competitive advantage by international marketing managers primarily focuses on the firm's competitive advantage. However, this is usually conditioned, in part, by a nation's competitive advantage. Michael Porter, in *Competitive Advantage of Nations* (1990, p. 71), suggests that the determinants of national advantage for an industry are fourfold.

1 *Factor conditions* – the nation's position in factors of production, such as skilled labour or infrastructure, necessary to compete in a given industry.

2 *Demand conditions* – the nature of home demand for the industry's product or service.

3 *Related and supporting industries* – the presence or absence in the nation of supplier industries and related industries that are internationally competitive.

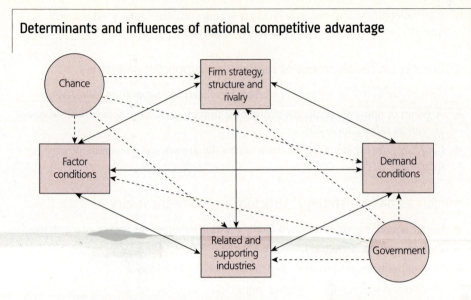

Determinants and influences of national competitive advantage

Source: Porter (1990), p. 127.

Figure 14.1

4 *Firm strategy, structure, and rivalry* – the conditions in the nation governing how companies are created, organised and managed, and the nature of domestic rivalry.

Porter's model, shown as Figure 14.1, also includes government influences and chance events. These latter elements are regarded as important influences rather than determinants.

Strong relationships between the four determinants and the two influences over time foster national competitive advantage in various industries. For each of the determinants, Porter identifies some of the influencing factors that strengthen their contribution to national advantage for an industry.

Influences on factor creation

- A cluster of domestic rivals stimulates factor creation.
- Perceived national challenges stimulate factor creation.
- Home demand influences priorities for factor-creating investments.
- Related and supporting industries create or stimulate the creation of transferable factors.

Influences on home demand conditions

- Intense rivalry increases home demand and makes it more sophisticated.
- A group of rivals builds a national image and recognition as an important competitor.
- Sophisticated factor-creating mechanisms attract foreign experts and participation by foreign firms that pull through the nation's products.
- The image of world-class related and supporting industries spills over to benefit an industry.

- Internationally successful industries producing complementary products pull through foreign demand for the industry's product.

Influences on development of related and supporting industries

- Specialised factor pools are transferable to related and supporting industries.
- A group of domestic rivals encourages the formation of more specialised suppliers as well as related industries.
- Large or growing home demand stimulates the growth and deepening of supplier industries.

Influences on firm strategy, structure and domestic rivalry

- Factor abundance or specialised factor-creating mechanisms spawn new entrants.
- Early product penetration feeds entry.
- New entrants emerge from related and supporting industries.
- World-class users enter supplying industries.

Governments

Governments can significantly influence the determinants of national advantage mainly through the creation and implementation of policies. Government policies often provide incentives for exporting in both marketing and research and development activities by firms. Examples of such policies may include:

- education and training;
- infrastructure industry regulation (e.g. telecommunications, media, transport, utilities, financial services);
- industry-specific regulation;
- purchasing and procurement;
- industry investment and assistance;
- foreign investment guidelines; and
- foreign affairs and military policies.

However, Porter (1990) believes that government cannot create competitive advantage in itself and therefore is not a determinant of competitive advantage, but it can reinforce present underlying determinants of competitive advantage.

Chance events

Chance events are occurrences that have little to do with circumstances in a nation and are often largely outside the power of firms and national governments to influence. Chance events are important because they create discontinuities that allow shifts in competitive position. Examples of such chance events include:

- acts of pure invention;
- major technological discontinuities;
- discontinuities in input costs such as the oil supply/price shocks;
- significant shifts in world financial markets or exchange rates such as the 1998 Asian crisis;
- surges of world or regional demand;
- political decisions by foreign governments; and
- wars.

By conducting analysis of this type in the firm's home country and the countries of its major competitors, a context is established for evaluating the company's competitive advantage.

Moon et al. (1998) criticise Porter's approach to the competitive advantage of nations on the grounds that it ignores the fact that in economies that are open to world trade, national competitive advantage derives from international as well as domestic activities. Each of the elements of Porter's diamond will be influenced to a greater or lesser extent by international involvement and therefore, they argue, national competitive advantage is a combination of the domestic and the international diamond as illustrated in Figure 14.2.

The generalised Double Diamond

Figure 14.2

Source: Moon et al. (1998).

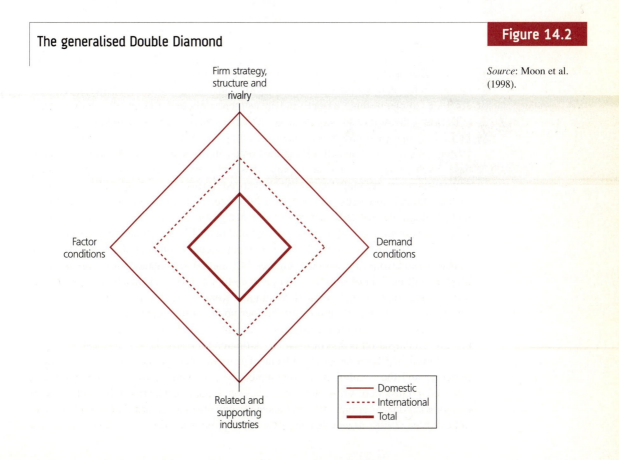

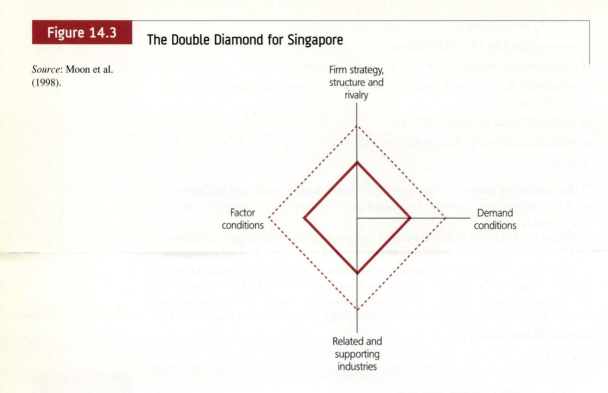

Figure 14.3

The Double Diamond for Singapore

Source: Moon et al. (1998).

The 'Double Diamond' approach overcomes the shortcoming that Porter does not include in his analysis on national competitive advantage foreign activities such as the ability to attract foreign capital and investment (inbound foreign direct investment (FDI)) and the ability to access cheap labour resources in other countries (outbound FDI). By contrast, Porter views national competitive advantage in the context of a strategy of concentrating activities in the home country and serving the world from this base. Such an approach has an export focus and does not take into account national competitiveness deriving from more advanced forms of international involvement such as strategic alliances. Moon et al. (1998) argue that this oversight has led Porter to underestimate the national competitive advantage of countries like Singapore whose success has been due both to inbound and outbound FDI. Multinational activities are also important in explaining Korea's competitiveness. Double diamonds for both Singapore and Korea are shown in Figures 14.3 and 14.4. Singapore's success has been magnified through international activities in all four points of the diamond with a strong driver being international demand conditions. Korea's success has been enhanced by foreign activities supporting three of the four points of the diamond.

An element of national competitive advantage that operates despite the move towards globalisation is that of location. Although logically the role of location should have diminished because of the advent of a more open global market, faster transportation and the revolution in communications, in many industries, localisation as reflected in clusters of firms in a specific region, remain. Clusters can be considered as geographic concentrations of interconnected companies and institutions in a particular field. Porter (1998) argues that clusters were previously based on input costs, now

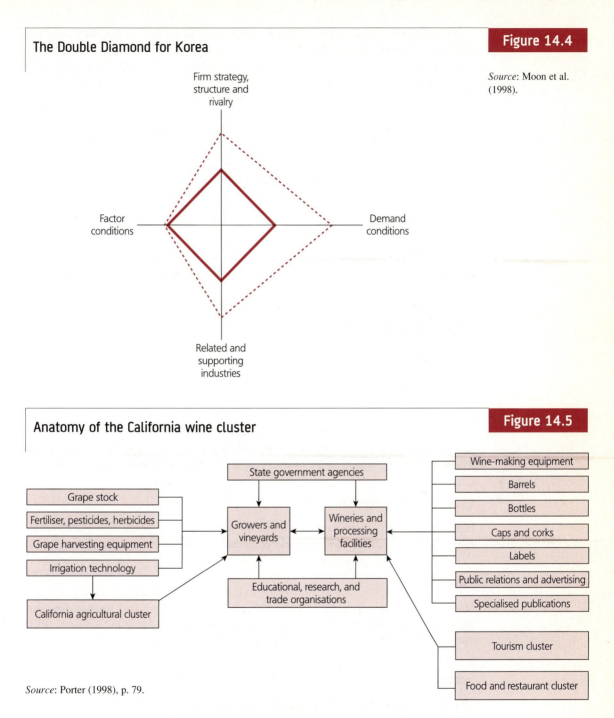

The Double Diamond for Korea

Figure 14.4

Source: Moon et al. (1998).

Firm strategy, structure and rivalry

Factor conditions

Demand conditions

Related and supporting industries

Anatomy of the California wine cluster

Figure 14.5

State government agencies

Grape stock

Fertiliser, pesticides, herbicides

Grape harvesting equipment

Irrigation technology

California agricultural cluster

Growers and vineyards

Wineries and processing facilities

Educational, research, and trade organisations

Wine-making equipment

Barrels

Bottles

Caps and corks

Labels

Public relations and advertising

Specialised publications

Tourism cluster

Food and restaurant cluster

Source: Porter (1998), p. 79.

they are based on knowledge, relationships and motivation. They can also extend downstream to customers and laterally to manufacturers of complementary products, as well as involving other stakeholders, such as universities and government. Figure 14.5 illustrates the California wine cluster.

Clusters are critical to international competitive advantage in that they result in better access to employees and suppliers, result in lower transaction costs, provide access to specialised information, create complementarities that enhance a customer's overall experience, and facilitate access to institutions and public goods. They also drive the direction and pace of innovation because members of a cluster have a better feel for the market than isolated competitors, are able to be flexible and respond to changed circumstances rapidly, and operate in an environment conducive to innovation and transmission of new ideas. Furthermore, there is a within-cluster stimulus of constant comparison with competitors, suppliers and peers. Finally clusters stimulate the formation of new businesses due to synergies leading to innovation, the ability to spot gaps and opportunities and lower barriers to entry (Porter, 1998).

Competitive advantage and generic strategies

The concepts of competitive advantage and competitive strategy at the firm level are closely related. Competitive advantage refers to the basis upon which a firm competes in its target international markets. Competitive strategy refers to how it competes.

Basic competitive strategies

More than two decades ago, Michael Porter (1980) suggested four basic competitive positioning strategies that companies can follow – three winning strategies and one losing one. The losing strategy that Porter identified is termed middle-of-the-roaders. The three winning strategies are overall cost leadership, differentiation and focus.

Overall cost leadership

Here the company works hard to achieve the lowest costs of production and distribution so that it can price lower than its competitors and win a large market share.

Differentiation

Here the company concentrates on creating a highly differentiated product line and marketing programme so that it comes across as the class leader in the industry. Most customers would prefer to own this brand if its price is not too high.

Focus

Here the company focuses its effort on serving a few market segments well rather than going after the whole market.

Companies that pursue a clear strategy – one of the above – are likely to perform well. The firm that carries out that strategy best will make the most profits. But firms that do not pursue a clear strategy – middle-of-the-roaders – do the worst. Middle-of-the-roaders try to be good on all strategic counts, but end up being not very good at anything.

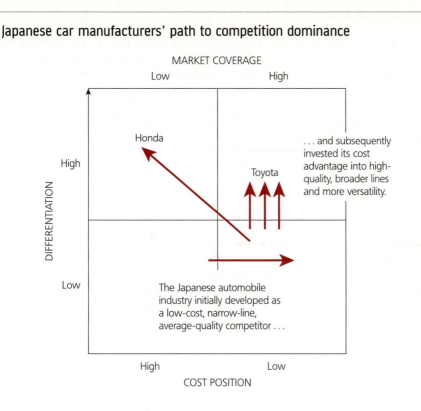

Figure 14.6

Japanese car manufacturers' path to competition dominance

Source: Brown (1997), p. 60.

These generic strategies may change over time for an individual company. For example, Figure 14.6 shows the competitive path taken internationally by Japanese car manufacturers such as Toyota and Honda. Extending from their domestic market they produced low-cost/low-price products with little differentiation. As volume grew and market coverage widened in their various Asian and American markets they improved quality and brand image and widened their ranges. While Toyota has remained in the mass market, it appears that Honda has moved to a focus strategy with high differentiation in many of its markets.

More recently, two marketing consultants, Michael Treacy and Fred Wiersema (1995), offered a new classification of competitive marketing strategies. They suggested that companies gain leadership positions by delivering superior value to their customers. Companies can develop any of three competitive advantages – called *value disciplines* – for delivering superior customer value.

Operational excellence

The company provides superior value by leading its industry in price and convenience. It works to reduce costs and to create a lean and efficient value delivery system. It serves customers who want reliable, good quality products or services, but who want them cheaply and easily. Examples include furniture company IKEA and computer company Dell.

Customer intimacy

The company provides superior value by precisely segmenting its markets and then tailoring its products or services to match exactly the needs of targeted customers. It builds detailed customer databases for segmenting and targeting, and empowers its marketing people to respond quickly to customer needs. It serves customers who are willing to pay a premium to get precisely what they want, and it will do almost anything to build long-term customer loyalty and to capture the customer's 'lifetime' value. Different but outstanding examples of this are the campaigns developed and implemented by the major consulting firms to win large government and corporate consultancy contracts.

Product leadership

The company provides superior value by offering a continuous stream of leading-edge products or services that make their own and competing products obsolete. It is open to new ideas, relentlessly pursues new solutions, and works to reduce cycle times so that it can get new products to market quickly. It serves customers who want state-of-the-art products and services, regardless of the costs in terms of price or inconvenience. Examples include Intel, Motorola and Ericsson.

Some companies successfully pursue more than one value discipline at the same time. For example, Federal Express excels at both operational excellence and customer intimacy. However, such companies are rare – few firms can be the best at more than one of these disciplines. By trying to be good at all of the value disciplines, a company usually ends up being best at none.

Treacy and Wiersema (1995) have found that leading companies operating internationally focus on and excel at a single value discipline, while meeting industry standards on the other two. They design their entire value delivery system to single-mindedly support the chosen discipline. For example, Lexmark knows that customer intimacy and product leadership are important in international markets. Compared with other low-cost suppliers of printers, it offers very good customer service and an excellent product assortment. Still, it offers less customer service and less depth in its product assortment than Canon or Hewlett-Packard that pursue customer intimacy or product leadership strategies. Instead, it focuses obsessively on operational excellence – on reducing costs and streamlining its order-to-delivery process in order to make it convenient for customers in various countries to buy just the right products at the lowest prices.

Companies targeting Asian markets need to closely consider the cultural differences between countries when positioning their value proposition. While in most Asian markets customer intimacy is highly valued because of the importance of family, friends and connections in doing business, foreign businesses need to focus on different aspects of the other value disciplines. For example, in China and South Korea negotiation is firmly focused on price, meaning that low costs and operational efficiency become important elements for doing business profitably. However, for many products and services sold to buyers in Japan and Singapore product quality is important.

Classifying competitive advantage in terms of value disciplines is appealing. It defines competitive advantage and marketing strategy in terms of the single-minded pursuit of delivering value to customers. It recognises that management must align every aspect of the company with the chosen value discipline – from its culture, to its organisation structure, to its operating and management systems and processes. The next step is to work out how value is transferred along an interconnected chain of channel players to end customers.

Value chain analysis

Firms create value for their customers by the activities they perform. The *value chain* is a tool to disaggregate a business into strategically relevant activities which create value. The value chain concept identifying the functions within the firm that create value was described in Chapter 9. This enables identification of the source of competitive advantage on both costs and differentiation. A business gains competitive advantage by performing these activities more cheaply or better than its competitors. Its value chain is part of a larger stream of strategic activities carried out by other members of the channel – suppliers, distributors and customers. It is necessary to understand the links in the chain which provide customer value to be able to restructure the offer or the industry to the firm's advantage. Figure 14.7 indicates that value chains exist at each level of a distribution channel and value is created by the linkages between players in an industry as value is transferred towards the end-buyer. The concept is summarised below.

- The value chain examines all activities a business performs by disaggregating functions into discrete but interrelated activities from which value stems.
- Examination of the value chain allows understanding of the behaviour of costs within a business and existing and potential sources of differentiation.
- Value activities are the physically and technologically distinct activities a business performs, the discrete building blocks of competitive advantage. There are primary value activities and support activities.
- Often the keys to competitive advantage are the links or relationships between activities in the value chain. For instance, vertical linkages between buyers, suppliers and ensuing channel activities can lower costs or enhance differentiation.
- A firm's competitive scope is a source of competitive advantage because it affects the value chain. This may be in terms of segment scope, the range of products and buyers, geographic scope, the range of regions; vertical scope, the extent of integration; or industry scope, the range of related industries (Brown, 1997).

The value system

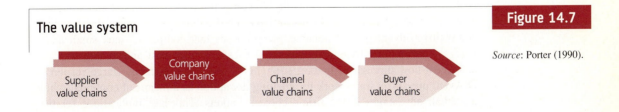

Figure 14.7

Source: Porter (1990).

Figure 14.8	The crumble effect in brokerage services

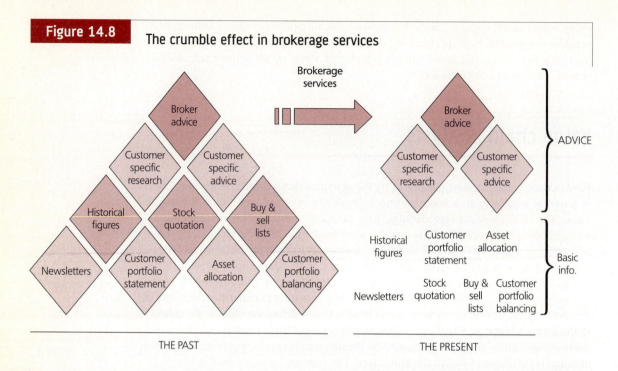

THE PAST

THE PRESENT

Changes in and convergence of information and communication technologies are restructuring traditional value chains in particular industries. An example is the unbundling of broker services in the financial sector shown in Figure 14.8. The emerging value chain in this and other industries promises to restructure those industries and redistribute value among different components and players in the value chain. For example, the international traveller can now access cash via an ATM in Beijing or London rather than take traveller's cheques and incur the cost, time and inconvenience associated with set-up and encashment. The impacts of these changes are very significant in terms of how value is delivered and which companies and networks of businesses deliver it. There will be irrevocable shifts in retailing and distribution and elimination of intermediaries, rapid shifts in market share and significant leaps forward in mass customisation. International Highlight 14.1 illustrates how time and place location of buyers is becoming less relevant. International buyers are accessing a company's products and services in an increasingly similar way to domestic customers.

The issue of sustainability of competitive advantage is questioned by some researchers. D'Aveni (1994) identifies a form of competitive intensity referred to as hyper-competition, in which competitors continually match each other's advantages in a continually unstable environment. No competitor is able to sustain an advantage. D'Aveni claims that many industries reflect this situation and the quest for sustainable competitive advantage is untenable. He proposes that companies seek small advantages on an ongoing basis as competition escalates from cost and quality to timing and know-how through to market strongholds and 'deep pockets' (large resources). D'Aveni presents a framework for creating disruption as a means of continually holding small advantages in the firm's chosen markets. This has implications for firms

14.1 International highlight

Value chains in disarray

Financial services

In the banking industry, developments in credit cards, automatic teller machines and home banking services enhance the accessibility of services to customers and have implications for the branch banking networks. The firms that lead these innovations are able to restructure the industry to their advantage.

Not only are value chains restructuring in this sector but cross-border competition in the banking industry is increasing as the functionality of virtual networks like the Internet is creating new fields of competition. Many banks are re-allocating capital to develop new positions in the financial services value chain so as to meet the challenge of new competitors that have much lower overhead structures and operating costs. This is being done to protect their domestic markets and to tap new opportunities in international markets.

Computers and software value chains

One of the largest Internet markets is for software. Downloading all kinds of software to a home or business computer is disintermediating the software retail shop. Dell Computers recognised the importance in the PC value chain of tailored products and aftersales service to PC buyers. It geared its business to direct marketing, direct delivery and direct service bypassing dealers and retailers. As a result it has built a large international business directed at market segments which value this package. Now, an increasing number of buyers are using Dell's Internet site to design and pay for their own computer packages.

Convergence of communications, media and computer value chains

The rapid trend towards the merging of telecommunications, media and computerisation creates options for the location of computer power in the communications terminal or in the telephone (communications) exchange. Understanding the value chain of the user and the benefits desired is vital. But if computer manufacturers, software firms and telecommunications equipment suppliers are able to provide better solutions to customers through their equipment they will become dominant players. We are seeing moves by Nokia and others to create wireless web devices that go well beyond the current capabilities of mobile phones.

The travel and tourism value chain

It has long been recognised that tourists buy destinations not transport. Accordingly, the airlines and travel operators market the benefits of the destination. Travel agents have traditionally been the key point of sale and service. Now an increasing number of travellers are bypassing both airlines and travel agents to organise their international travel – using the Internet as the purchasing channel for airline, hotel and tours (e.g. Ryanair.com and EasyJet.com).

operating in international markets as local and international competitors continually match strategies.

The value chain concept when applied to many corporations tends to focus on linear relationships within the chain. There is considerable emphasis on improving service and relationships that are next in line in the chain. The notion that the next person in the value chain is your customer is strongly emphasised. There can be problems if the whole chain is not improved within the context of supplying demonstrable customer value to the ultimate customer.

There is some evidence to suggest that as organisations become more involved in alliance structures and participate in the new electronic infrastructure, value creation is likely to be a multidimensional activity. Tapscott et al. (2000) paint a scene of value webs, where customer value may be created, collected and delivered within a multi-dimensional environment of interconnected businesses. This concept is explored in more detail in Chapters 17 and 19.

Competitor analysis

To plan effective competitive marketing strategies, the company needs to find out all it can about its competitors. It must constantly compare its products, prices, channels and promotion with those of close competitors. In this way the company can find areas of potential competitive advantage and disadvantage. And it can launch more effective marketing campaigns against its competitors and prepare stronger defences against competitors' actions.

But what do companies need to know about their competitors? They need to know: Who are our competitors? What are their objectives? What are their strategies? What are their strengths and weaknesses? What are their reaction patterns? Figure 14.9 shows the major steps in analysing competitors.

Identifying the company's competitors

Normally it would seem an easy task for a company to identify its competitors. Adidas knows that it competes with Nike. At the narrowest level, a company can define its competitors as other companies offering a similar product or service to the same customers at similar prices.

But companies actually face a much wider range of competitors. The company might define competitors as all firms making the same product or class of products.

Figure 14.9

Source: Kotler (2001), p. 690.

Steps in analysing competitors

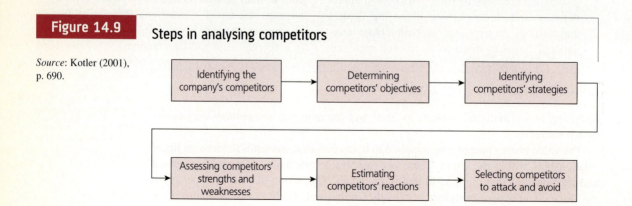

Even more broadly, competitors might include all companies making products that supply the same service. Here a car manufacturer would see itself competing against not only other car makers, but also against companies that make trucks, motorcycles or even bicycles. This is particularly true in some of the Asian developing countries, like China. Finally, and still more broadly, competitors might include all companies that compete for the same consumer dollars. Here a company would see itself competing with companies that sell major consumer durables, new homes, international holidays. Again, in countries like the Philippines, Thailand and Malaysia, for many the choice may be between an apartment and a car.

Companies must avoid 'competitor myopia'. A company is more likely to be 'buried' by its latent competitors than its current ones. For example, Kodak, in its film business, has been worrying about the growing competition from Fuji, the Japanese filmmaker. But Kodak faces a much greater threat from the recent advances in 'filmless camera' technology. Digital cameras sold by Canon and Sony take video still pictures that can be shown on a TV set, turned into hard copy, and later erased. What greater threat is there to a film business than a filmless camera?

Companies can identify their competitors from the industry point of view. They might see themselves as being in the food industry, the travel industry, or the biotechnology industry. A company must understand the competitive patterns in its industry if it hopes to be an effective 'player' in that industry. Michael Porter (1980) suggests that five major forces drive industry competition. These are shown in Figure 14.10. He proposes that the structure of the industry itself, its suppliers and its buyers have a major influence on the evolution of the industry and its profit potential. The threat of substitutes and new entrants also influences the appropriate strategies to be adopted. These parties exert differing levels of power and act as forces which shape the evolution of the industry, control the competitive balance and influence the profit potential.

Industry structure and competitive forces

Figure 14.10

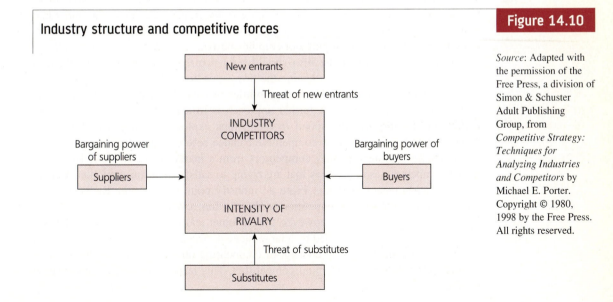

Source: Adapted with the permission of the Free Press, a division of Simon & Schuster Adult Publishing Group, from *Competitive Strategy: Techniques for Analyzing Industries and Competitors* by Michael E. Porter. Copyright © 1980, 1998 by the Free Press. All rights reserved.

Industry structure and competitive forces

Industry structure is not static. Major or minor changes may be occurring at any point in time. Some industries may be undergoing structural change or convergence with other industries. Hence, definition of the relevant 'industry' is important for structural analysis purposes. From an airline's perspective, is the relevant industry 'leisure air travel' or is it 'tourist holidays'? The latter implies that the industry includes accommodation as well as travel. Since much of the competition revolves around holiday packages in this market, through alliances or networks of airlines, hotels, coaches and resorts, the 'tourist holidays' definition may be more appropriate.

Porter (2001) has reinterpreted this model in the light of the Internet's influences on industry structure. The following observations are made in relation to each competitive force which can have both positive and negative impacts on a competitor's position.

- *New entrants*: there are reduced barriers to entry because the Internet reduces the need for a salesforce, access to distribution channels and physical assets.
- *Substitutes*: there are additional new substitution threats and potential market expansion from e-tailers offering a wide range of products and services.
- *Suppliers*: the Internet provides a channel for suppliers to end-users as well as enabling procurement processes that can standardise products and reduce differentiation.
- *Buyers*: the Internet improves bargaining power, through wider choice, and reduces switching costs.
- *Rivalry of competitors*: the Internet migrates competition to price by reducing differences among competitors, as well as widening the geographic market increasing the number of competitors.

In any industry, a small number of factors will be relevant. Analysis of industry structure using this model provides an assessment of the strength of competitive position of industry competitors as a group, and this in turn reflects on the individual industry competitor. It is useful also to assess the sustainability of a firm's competitive advantage including those of pure dot-com businesses.

The implication is that the firm should influence the balance of forces through strategic moves, thereby strengthening the firm's position. Alternatively, the strategist might reposition the firm so that its capabilities provide the best defence against the array of competitive forces. A further approach is to anticipate shifts in the factors underlying the forces and respond to them, thus exploiting change by choosing a strategy appropriate to the new competitive balance before competitors recognise it.

Companies can also identify competitors from a market point of view. Here they define competitors as companies that are trying to satisfy the same customer need or serve the same customer group. From an industry point of view, the Radisson hotel chain in Asia might see its competition as Holiday Inn, and other four-star hotel chains. From a market point of view, however, the customer really wants 'shelter and nourishment'. This need can be satisfied by a large range of accommodation houses and eating places. In general, the market concept of competition opens the company's eyes to a broader set of actual and potential competitors. This leads to better long-run market planning.

The key to identifying competitors is to link industry and market analysis by mapping out product/market segments. This will reveal that in many country markets the most important competitors to international firms are the local companies. In Japan, the interlinked ownerships of the conglomerates create barriers to entry to many markets. The local support by consumers of home-grown companies in South Korea and Thailand, particularly in tough economic times, squeezes out foreign competitors.

Determining competitors' objectives

Having identified the main competitors, the international marketer now asks: What does each competitor seek in this marketplace? What drives each competitor's behaviour?

The marketer might at first assume that all competitors will want to maximise their profits and will choose their actions accordingly. But companies differ in the emphasis they put on short-term versus long-term profits. And some competitors might be oriented towards '*satisficing*' rather than '*maximising*' profits. They have target profit goals and are satisfied in achieving them, even if more profits could have been produced by other strategies. Many competitors, like Daewoo based in Korea, adopt price penetration strategies to build market share, with profit as a secondary consideration.

Thus, marketers must look beyond competitors' profit goals. Each competitor has a mix of objectives, each with differing importance. The company wants to know the relative importance that a competitor places on current profitability, market share growth, cash flow, technological leadership, service leadership and other goals. Knowing a competitor's mix of objectives reveals whether the competitor is satisfied with its current situation and how it might react to different competitive actions. For example, a company that pursues low-cost leadership will react much more strongly to a competitor's cost-reducing manufacturing breakthrough than to the same competitor's advertising increase.

A company also must monitor its competitors' objectives for various product/market segments. If the company finds that a competitor has discovered a new segment, this might be an opportunity. If it finds that competitors plan new moves into segments now served by the company, it will be forewarned and, hopefully, forearmed.

Identifying competitors' strategies

The more that one firm's strategy resembles another firm's strategy, the more the two firms compete. In most industries, the competitors can be sorted into groups that pursue different strategies. A strategic group is a group of firms in an industry following the same or a similar strategy in a given target market. For example, in the car market in Japan, Toyota and Mazda belong to the same strategic group. Each produces a full line of medium-priced cars supported by good service. Mercedes and BMW, on the other hand, belong to a different strategic group. They produce a narrow line of very high-quality cars, offer a high level of service, and charge a premium price.

Some important insights emerge from strategic group identification. For example, if a company enters one of the groups, the members of that group become its key competitors. Thus, if a company like Ford enters the first group against Toyota and Mazda in Japan, it can succeed only if it develops some strategic advantages over these large local competitors.

Although competition is most intense within a strategic group, there is also rivalry between groups. First, some of the strategic groups may appeal to overlapping customer segments. For example, no matter what their strategy, all major car manufacturers will go after the semi-sports car segment. Second, the customers may not see much difference in the offers of different groups – they may see little difference in quality between Honda and BMW. Finally, members of one strategic group might expand into new strategy segments. Thus, Toyota's premium-quality, premium-priced line, Lexus, is designed to compete with BMW and Mercedes.

The company needs to look at all of the dimensions that identify strategic groups within the industry. It needs to know each competitor's product quality, features and mix; customer services; pricing policy; distribution coverage; salesforce strategy; and advertising and sales promotion programmes. It must also study the details of each competitor's R&D, manufacturing, purchasing, financial and other strategies.

Assessing competitors' strengths and weaknesses

Marketers need to carefully assess each competitor's strengths and weaknesses in order to answer the critical question: What can our competitors do? As a first step, companies can gather data on each competitor's goals, strategies and performance over the last few years. Admittedly, some of this information will be hard to obtain. For example, business products companies find it hard to estimate competitors' market shares because they do not have the same syndicated data services that are available to consumer packaged-goods companies. This is so, particularly in emerging markets like China, India and Indonesia.

Companies normally learn about their competitors' strengths and weaknesses through secondary data, personal experience and hearsay. They also can conduct primary marketing research with customers, suppliers and dealers. Recently, a growing number of companies have turned to benchmarking, comparing the company's products and processes to those of competitors or leading firms in other industries to find ways to improve quality and performance. Benchmarking has become a powerful tool for increasing a company's competitiveness (Larreche, 1998).

Estimating competitors' reactions

Next, the company wants to know: What will our competitors do? A competitor's objectives, strategies, and strengths and weaknesses go a long way towards explaining its likely actions, as well as its likely reactions to company moves, such as price cuts, promotion increases, or new product introductions. In addition, each competitor has a certain philosophy of doing business, a certain internal culture and guiding beliefs. International marketers need a deep understanding of a given competitor's mentality if they want to anticipate how the competitor will act or react.

Each competitor reacts differently. Some do not react quickly or strongly to a competitor's move. They may feel their customers are loyal; they may be slow in noticing the move; they may lack the funds to react. Some competitors react only to certain types of moves and not to others. They might always respond strongly to price cuts in order to signal that these will never succeed. But they might not respond at all to advertising

14.2 International highlight

Competitors' reactions to Motorola in China

In January 2003, Motorola launched a new global product line in China. The selection of China is a critical part of Motorola's strategy to show commitment to the Chinese economy. The choice is no surprise as China is the marketing fixation of every company in the industry. Motorola has invested over US$3 billion in manufacturing and research in China since 1986, more than any other western company. The commitment has paid off as Motorola sells more cell phones than anyone else in China.

Motorola does not have this market to itself. Nokia and Samsung have made serious investments and inroads in the market over the past few years. Moreover the new competition from local Chinese handset makers is more of a threat for Motorola and the other multinationals. Many of these local companies compete directly with Motorola on the low-end phones which represent the majority of sales for Motorola and other multinationals. As a result, Motorola is now focusing on models that can better handle Chinese-language

text messages and can double as karaoke machines or e-books because local companies have great difficulty in matching these. Motorola is now stressing the fun element to phones, adding value with features – sending and receiving photos. Motorola believes that such a strategy will thwart local companies in the long run as they do not have any control over the technology and own only a very small piece of the value chain.

Local manufacturers are not lying down under the challenge. Many of these companies like Ningbo Bird who have developed technology partnerships are looking to international markets for expansion. This can only lead to pressure on Motorola's worldwide sales. Motorola is fighting back by increasing its commitment to the Chinese economy. They claim with over 10,000 employees in the country they are as Chinese as anyone. Given that many local firms are government-owned and have good *quanxi* or connections with local officials, the road ahead will continue to be challenging.

increases, believing these to be less threatening. Other competitors react swiftly and strongly to any action. Many firms avoid direct competition with the local brand and look for easier prey, knowing that the local brand will react fiercely if challenged. Finally, some competitors show no predictable reaction pattern. They might or might not react on a given occasion, and there is no way to foresee what they will do based on their economics, history, or anything else.

In some industries, competitors live in relative harmony; in others, they fight constantly. Knowing how major competitors react gives the company clues on how best to attack competitors or how best to defend the company's current position in its international markets.

Selecting competitors to attack and avoid

A company has already largely selected its major competitors through prior decisions on customer targets, distribution channels and marketing-mix strategy in its international market. These decisions define the strategic group to which the company belongs. Management must now decide which competitors to compete against most vigorously. The company can focus on one of several classes of competitors.

Strong or weak competitors

Most companies prefer to aim their shots at their weak competitors. This requires fewer resources and less time. But in the process the firm may gain little. The argument could be made that the firm also should compete with strong competitors in order to sharpen its abilities. Furthermore, even strong competitors have some weaknesses, and succeeding against them often provides greater returns.

A useful tool for assessing competitor strengths and weaknesses is customer value analysis. The aim of customer value analysis is to determine the benefits that target customers value and how customers rate the relative value of various competitors' offers. In conducting a customer value analysis, the company first identifies the major attributes that customers value and the importance customers place on these attributes. Next, it assesses the company's and competitors' performance on the valued attributes. The key to gaining competitive advantage is to take each customer segment and examine how the company's offer compares with that of its major competitor. If the company's offer exceeds the competitor's offer on all important attributes, the company can charge a higher price and earn higher profits, or it can charge the same price and gain more market share. But if the company is seen as performing at a lower level than its major competitor on some important attributes, it must invest in strengthening those attributes or finding other important attributes where it can build a lead on the competitor. A detailed process for conducting customer value analysis and developing value maps is found in Best (1999).

Close or distant competitors

Most companies will compete with competitors who resemble them most. Thus, Toyota competes more against Ford than against Jaguar. At the same time, the company may want to avoid trying to 'destroy' a close competitor.

'Well-behaved' or 'disruptive' competitors

A company really needs and benefits from competitors. The existence of competitors results in several strategic benefits. Competitors may help increase total demand. They may share the costs of market and product development and help to legitimise new technologies. They may serve less attractive segments or lead to more product differentiation.

However, a company may not view all its competitors as beneficial. An industry often contains 'well-behaved' competitors and 'disruptive' competitors. Well-behaved competitors play by the rules of the industry. They favour a stable and healthy industry, set reasonable prices in relation to costs, motivate others to lower costs or improve differentiation, and accept reasonable levels of market share and profits. Disruptive competitors break the rules. They try to buy share rather than earn it, take large risks, and in general shake up the industry.

The implication is that 'well-behaved' companies would like to shape an industry that consists of only well-behaved competitors. Through careful licensing, selective retaliation and coalitions, they can shape the industry so that the competitors behave rationally and harmoniously, follow the rules, try to earn share rather than buy it, and differentiate to compete less directly. These western notions of behaviour need to be seen within the context of the varying cultures.

Obtaining competitive intelligence

The main types of information that companies need about their competitors have been described. This information must be collected, interpreted, distributed and used. The cost in money and time of gathering competitive intelligence is high, and the company must design its competitive intelligence system in a cost-effective way.

The competitive intelligence system first identifies the vital types of competitive information and the best sources of this information. Then, the system continuously collects information from the field (salesforce, channels, suppliers, market research firms and trade associations) and from published data (government publications, speeches, articles). Next the system checks the information for validity and reliability, interprets it, and organises it in an appropriate way. Finally, it sends key information to relevant decision-makers and responds to inquiries from managers about competitors. Hewlett-Packard has developed this kind of system and advertises central access points through its intranet to managers all over the world.

With this system, company managers will receive timely information about competitors in the form of phone calls, bulletins, newsletters and reports. In addition, managers can connect with the system when they need an interpretation of a competitor's sudden move, or when they want to know a competitor's weaknesses and strengths, or when they need to know how a competitor will respond to a planned company move.

Smaller companies that cannot afford to set up formal competitive intelligence offices can assign specific executives to watch specific competitors. Thus, a manager who used to work for a competitor might follow that competitor closely – he or she would be the 'in-house expert' on that competitor. Any manager needing to know the thinking of a given competitor contacts the assigned in-house expert.

The Internet represents a useful channel for the international marketer to obtain up-to-date competitive information quickly. Using a search engine like Yahoo! or Google, the starting point would be the competitor's website. This will provide information on products, services, positioning, availability and often pricing. By 'digging' through the website, recent press releases, announcements of new products, financial results and company objectives can often be found. The next step may be to visit the industry association website which may include proceedings of industry conferences, press releases about the major players' strategies and intentions, and articles on companies and the industry. This may be followed by visiting the websites of leading business magazines which record interviews and write stories about specific companies. This may include *The Economist, Business Week, Time, Financial Times Review, Far Eastern Economic Review, International Business Week* and *Fortune* magazine. ABI INFORM is a database accessible immediately within the university system. It provides a source of articles, case studies and books that may be relevant to particular companies and industries for providing competitive intelligence.

Information of this kind is continually expanding worldwide and is a source of competitive information accessible via the Internet.

Leveraging capabilities

Having identified and evaluated its major competitors, the company must now design competitive marketing strategies that will best position its offer against competitors' offers and give the company the strongest possible competitive advantage. But what marketing strategies might the company use? Which ones are best for a particular company, or for the company's different divisions and products?

No one strategy is best for all companies. Each company must determine what makes the most sense given its position in its international market and its objectives, opportunities and resources. Even within a company, different strategies may be required for different businesses or products. (Chapters 15 and 16 discuss the array of strategies available and under what conditions they are relevant.)

International marketers also need to determine how the firm's capabilities can be leveraged in international markets. One approach is to build networks to extend the value chain using alliance partners. (Alliance strategies and their implications are discussed in Chapter 17.) Another strategy for leveraging capabilities is the use of electronic commerce and electronic marketing as a means of reducing costs, increasing customer access and extending market reach.

Internet infusion

The major effects of electronic business on international competitiveness are outlined below.

Shifts in important strategic dimensions: with e-commerce, price and quality are no longer the only determinants of a firm's competitiveness. Fast delivery and customisation are also important factors – factors for which customers are willing to pay a premium. E-business, combined with flexible production systems such as computer integrated manufacturing, flexible manufacturing systems and just-in-time, makes mass customisation possible by compressing the time it takes firms to deliver products/services to customers.

Compressed value chain: not only do some of the traditional elements in the chain disappear with e-business, but also sharing demand information throughout the value chain helps plan and control upstream activities based on future demand that has already occurred downstream. In the process, excessive inventory and back orders are reduced. Online ordering and the real-time transfer of ordering information to the manufacturer significantly shorten lead times to meet customer demands.

Globalisation of markets: no longer is producing the best product or service in a country a guarantee of success, as the market is also accessible by foreign competitors.

To be competitive it is necessary to create a product or service that is attractive to global customers and at the same time is customised to specific needs in a country. No longer is it feasible for country-specific units of multinational firms to act independently from each other. To do so means that they are unable to coordinate operations between different countries, carry separate stocks for different countries and, as a consequence, they end up with a poor matching between customer demand and warehouse inventory.

Outsourcing as a strategic weapon: e-commerce makes it convenient and efficient to share information among different firms in the value chain, through the use of electronic data interchange (EDI) and the Internet. This facilitates firms outsourcing activities. Outsourcing can take the form of activities that provide little added value if done internally (e.g. bookkeeping, maintenance); activities that cannot be done due to lack of resources (e.g. R&D, logistics); activities that can be done better by other firms (e.g. advertising).

Globalisation of the supply network: international business traditionally has been inefficient and time-consuming because of the wide areas to cover and long lead times. E-business has compressed time and distance and therefore it becomes feasible for firms to overcome national boundaries and multinational activities can be executed with the efficiencies of domestic operations. As an example, Dell Computers has taken the opportunity to build a worldwide network of suppliers and customers into a virtual corporation, providing what customers want in a fast and efficient manner. Furthermore, with e-commerce, firms no longer have to confine sources of supply to domestic suppliers. A supply network on a global scale is one of the most important sources of a firm's competitiveness. This is shown in Figure 14.11.

Figure 14.11

The traditional model compared with Dell's direct business model in the personal computer industry

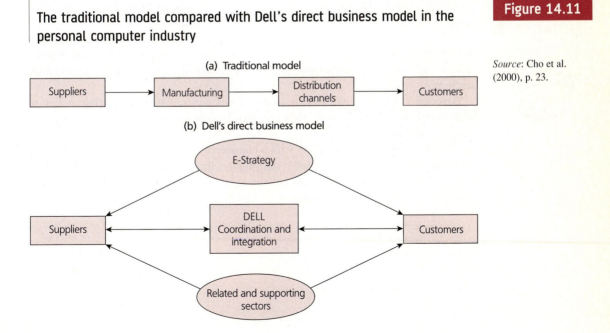

Source: Cho et al. (2000), p. 23.

Competitiveness and e-business

Theories of competitive advantage need to be modified to take account of the impact of the Internet. As an example, Porter modelled the factors causing nations to gain competitive advantage in certain industries and drew conclusions as to the implications for company strategies and national economies. His model had four determinants – factor conditions, demand conditions, related and supporting industries, and firm strategy, structure and rivalry. In addition, he included two variables external to the firm, those of government and chance.

He emphasised domestic rivalry and geographic concentration. With e-business, firms cannot restrict rivalry to the domestic scene and geographic concentration in the home country is less important. For factor conditions and demand conditions there are a number of upstream and downstream activities in the value chain to be taken into account as well as the existence of intermediaries. The possibilities in e-business of deconstruction of the value chain and of disintermediation of agents will change the businesses in the chain that are related to factor conditions and demand conditions.

In addition, the elements of domestic rivalry and the geographic concentration of related and supporting industries are both less important in e-business where geographic restriction to a certain area in a country is not very important in an increasingly digital environment. Porter largely ignored the role of human factors. These are very important in e-business because the competitiveness of an organisation can be a function of the computerised capabilities of its members. As far as factors in Porter's original diamond are concerned, according to Cho et al. (2000), e-business requires their modification as explained below.

Factor conditions: Porter's focus on domestic resources is not applicable in the Internet age. This is because the Internet, combined with an international logistics infrastructure and trade-related deregulation, enables companies to produce goods in foreign countries, i.e. countries where it is most cost-efficient to produce, and then distribute goods to the global market, or to source low-cost high-quality parts from foreign countries for incorporation into domestic production.

Related and supporting conditions: firms no longer have to rely on domestic related and supporting industries because globalisation offers the opportunity to use foreign related and supporting industries such as international logistics or communication services.

Demand conditions: with e-commerce, firms can sell their products/services to customers in the global market. They can also customise goods/services to every customer's needs to a greater extent.

Structure, strategy and rivalry: with e-commerce, through the integration of online ordering, real-time transfer of order information throughout the value chain and an efficient logistics system, a firm can get closer to both suppliers and customers so as to maximise its value to both parties.

Summary

Success as an international marketer is determined in large part by the design and implementation of an effective marketing strategy. The foundation for strategy is built on a careful assessment of a firm's competitive advantage in its targeted international markets, its relevant generic strategies, and an understanding of the value chain leading into international markets and how they are changing.

A useful starting point is to assess the competitive advantage of an industry from a national standpoint. This requires a detailed assessment of the home country national advantage using a framework similar to that developed by Michael Porter. A similar assessment could be done for the home country national advantages of major competitors and also that of the target international country market. The next level of assessment is a consideration of relevant competitive advantage options and generic strategies at the firm level. This decision is particularly important because it involves investment commitments to the relevant value model underlying the desired competitive advantage. Related to this analysis is an understanding of the industry value chain and how it is changing in relation to the creation and delivery of customer value.

In order to conduct this analysis realistically it is necessary to follow a process of competitive analysis that attempts to factor in the strategic intent and current strategies of the firm's most important competitors in its international market. A systematic analysis of competitors – both current and likely future competitors – forms the basis for the firm's positioning in its targeted international markets. In order to carry out these evaluations the firm needs to collect wide-ranging information about competitors. This process is becoming facilitated by a much greater level of electronic interconnection and use of such information channels as the Internet.

Ethics issue

Save the company or do the 'right thing'?
Your firm is losing market share at a rapid rate in an important international market as a result of the entry of a new international competitor. In a matter of months it will be necessary to pull out of the country if the trend continues. A loyal customer has illegally obtained a copy of your competitor's detailed marketing strategy and action programmes for the next year. The customer offers you the stolen document to help you out.

What would you do?

Web workout

Question 1 Select a product or service you are familiar with. Using your favourite Internet search engine (e.g. Netscape, Google or Yahoo!) select a country in the EU region and then assess whether your selected product/service is readily available or

whether there are no competitors in this area. Based on your research what conclusions can you draw?

Question 2 Select a product or service you are most familiar with (it could be the same product or service as selected in Question 1. Using the search engines type in the keywords that are associated with this product or service followed by location. (e.g. 'coffee retailers and Italy' or 'Pharmaceutical products and Ireland'). Now from the search results list yielded by the search engine select four companies that you believe may be the closest competitors to your product/service (if not sure, choose among the top 15 listings). Research the company's website. What can you tell about this company and its future outlook and customers it serves?

Websites

www.honda.com

www.toyota.com

www.dell.com.au

www.gateway.com

www.ericsson.com

www.fedex.com

www.lexmark.com

Discussion questions

1 Map out in broad terms any industry you are familiar with using Porter's model of national competitive advantage.

2 Clarify the distinction between product leadership, operational excellence and customer intimacy as a basis for competitive advantage.

3 Describe three companies operating in international markets that appear to conform with each of these three distinctive advantages outlined in question 2.

4 Michael Porter (1985) and Treacy and Wiersema (1995) suggested three winning strategies that firms can pursue. Outline these strategies.

5 Explain the concept of the value chain and indicate how it applies in an international market.

6 Describe how the value chain is designed for an international hotel company like the Sheraton.

7 What are the steps involved in systematically conducting competitive analysis?

References

Best, R. (1999) *Market Based Management*, 3rd edn, Prentice Hall, Englewood Cliffs, NJ, Chapter 4.

Bradley, F. (1999) *International Marketing Strategy*, Prentice Hall, Englewood Cliffs, NJ.

Brown, L.R. (1997) *Competitive Marketing Strategy*, 3rd edn, ITP Nelson, Melbourne.

Cho, D.S., Moon, H.C. and Park, J. (2000) 'Competitiveness Impacts of Electronic Commerce: Supply Chain Management Perspective', in *e-Commerce and Global Business Forum*, Andersen Institute for Strategic Change, Santa Cruz, CA.

D'Aveni, R.A. (1994) *Hyper-competition: Managing the Dynamics of Strategic Manouvering*, Free Press, New York.

Day, G. (1999) *The Market Driven Organisation: Understanding, Attracting and Keeping Valuable Customers*, Free Press, New York.

Kotler, P., Brown, L., Adam, S. and Armstrong, G. (2001) *Marketing*, 5th edn, Prentice Hall, Sydney.

Larreche, J-C. (1998) *Report on Competitive Fitness of Global Firms*, Pitman Publishing, London.

Moon, H.C., Rugman, A.M. and Verbeke, A. (1998) 'A Generalised Double Diamond Approach to the Global Competitiveness of Korea and Singapore', *International Business Review*, 7, pp. 135–150.

Porter, M.E. (1980) *Competitive Strategy: Techniques for Analysing Industries and Competitors*, The Free Press, New York.

Porter, M.E. (1985) *The Competitive Advantage: Creating and Sustaining Superior Performance*, The Free Press, New York.

Porter, M.E. (1990) *The Competitive Advantage of Nations*, Macmillan, London.

Porter, M.E. (1998) 'Clusters and the New Economics of Competition', *Harvard Business Review*, November–December, pp. 77–90.

Porter, M.E. (2001) 'Strategy and the Internet', *Harvard Business Review*, March, pp. 63–78.

Skotnicki, T. (2001) 'Defence business is booming', *BRW*, 6 April, p. 26.

Tapscott, D., Ticoll, D. and Lowy, A. (2000) 'Value Chains', in *Digital Capital*, Harvard Business School Press, Boston, MA.

Treacy, M. and Wiersema, F. (1995) *The Discipline of Market Leaders*, Knowledge Exchange, Santa Monica, CA.

15

International competitive marketing strategies and competitive position

Learning objectives

After studying this chapter, you should be able to:

- assess the competitive position of a firm in the international market;

- identify the characteristics of a dominant competitive position and strategies used by international firms to consolidate dominance;

- examine alternative offensive and defensive marketing strategies adopted in international markets; and

- evaluate strategies of market leaders, challengers, followers and niche specialists in international markets.

New EU regulations on anti-competitive behaviour

International practice in serious competition-law offences, such as price fixing, is routinely measured by the levels of fines and terms of imprisonment doled out to companies and executives. The US boasts the greatest successes, and is looked to by regulators in many countries as representing the benchmark of successful competition-law enforcement. Companies pay hefty fines, for example the companies involved in the worldwide 'vitamin cartel' were fined over US$1 billion. Company officers can and regularly do go to jail for instigating or participating in competition-law violations. Companies are also open to damage claims, including claims, from customers and consumers harmed by anti-competitive behaviour. US law recognises that certain types of anti-competitive practices are almost always detrimental to competition – for example price fixing, market sharing, bid rigging and restrictions on output and quota selling. EU countries in 2002 have adopted these US measures to varying degrees. But the authorities face considerable challenges if they are to translate their muscles into tangible results. The US regime, one of the only jurisdictions worldwide in which competition-law offences have been successfully prosecuted via the courts, has been highly dependent on informants and surveillance. The challenge for the EU states is to devote the same level of resources as their US counterparts.

Introduction

The purpose of this chapter is to identify the key dimensions of competitive position and provide a framework for evaluating relevant marketing strategies to be adopted in international markets.

Would the marketing strategy for international markets relevant to one airline be relevant to another? Would the strategic options be the same? No, each firm's situation is distinct. Each marketplace is unique. Firms competing in a given target market will, at any point in time, differ in their objectives and resources. Some firms will be large, others small. Some will have many resources, others will be strapped for funds. Some will be old and established, others new and fresh. Some will strive for rapid market share growth, others for long-term profits. And the firms will occupy different competitive positions in the target market. The competitive position in the international market that a firm holds at a point in time directly dictates the ability of that firm to cater for the needs of the market and, ultimately, to achieve its corporate objectives. If a firm does not have this ability, it must develop a competitive position that offers it. A firm's current position in the international market will determine, in part, what alternative positions are available to it and relevant options for strategy.

This chapter examines a variety of competitive dimensions in which a business holds a 'position' in its industry. This is examined with reference to a firm's position in the international market. Competitive position is not a precise or fixed point. It describes the relationship a company has with a market relative to its competitors in that market. It is measured in both quantitative and qualitative terms on a number of important dimensions. The relative position on each of these dimensions, when combined together, make up a business's overall competitive position.

Competitive position model

There is considerable overlap in the international business strategy and marketing literature in the use of the term 'position' and 'positioning', mainly because there are many positions that a firm may hold on different criteria. The position the firm holds on each of these shows only part of the picture. A full view of the firm, taking account of all aspects of its competitive environment, is needed to form a sound basis for international marketing strategy development.

In broad terms, competitive position is assessed on those dimensions that impact on international market performance, namely sales revenue, market share and brand/

Competitive position model

Source: Brown (1997), p. 77.

Figure 15.1

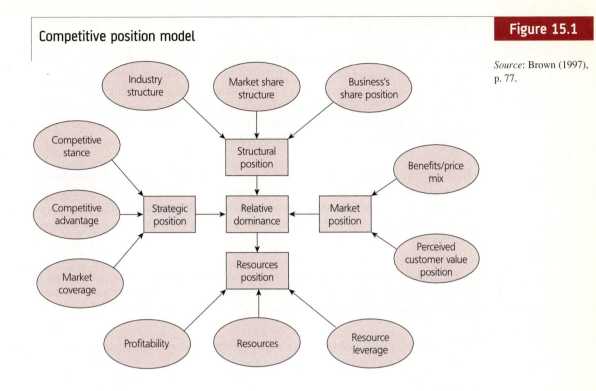

company image and on profit performance – investment levels, costs, margins, prices and productivity – which can be evaluated against important competitors. Brown (1997) proposed that competitive position is the amalgam of several key dimensions: the firm's industry and market structure, the firm's overall strategic position, its position in the marketplace, and its resource position. These dimensions are classified as structural, strategic, market and resources.

A business's relative strength or weakness in each of these dimensions provides a portrait of its international competitive position and will indicate areas of vulnerability and potential strategies for improvement. The overall competitive position model proposed by Brown is depicted in Figure 15.1.

This model provides a framework for assessing the relative dominance of a business in a defined international market or industry in terms of its competitive position from which competitive marketing strategies may be evaluated and developed.

Different international competitive positions may be strong or weak. Each position has its advantages and disadvantages – its opportunities and threats. However, some positions are more vulnerable to erosion than others. A full and objective assessment of international competitive position indicates a range of options for the future, which can be formulated as competitive marketing strategies.

Brown's model suggests that a firm should examine its position on each of the four dimensions and develop strategies to strengthen it in targeted international markets. Elements of each dimension are summarised.

Structural position

This includes an evaluation of *industry structure* as outlined in Porter's five forces model shown in Chapter 14, Figure 14.10, *market share structure* which identifies the spread of market share among the key players from monopoly structure to fragmented share holdings and the *firm's share position* – including dominance or non-dominance of the market. These three factors together provide a view of the firm's structural position and indicate both future opportunities and threats.

Industry structure level   Through innovation, technological change, alliance formation, acquisitions and direct competitive strategies the firm may act to change the balance of forces in the industry or restructure it to its advantage. The strategic alliance between Hewlett-Packard and Compaq has changed the balance of forces in the computer industry.

Market share structure   Competitor acquisitions and exit, innovation and decline of traditional leaders may result in market share restructure. This may be part of a direct strategy to strengthen the firm's position.

Firm's share position   Competitive marketing strategies targeting specific competitors may be adopted to improve competitive position moving from non-dominance to a dominant share level. Vodafone has been acquiring new firms opening up new markets in the telecommunications arena to both establish and improve its competitive position in developed and emerging markets.

Strategic position

A firm's *strategic position* is reflected in the way in which it has addressed its markets to counter competitive forces and create competitive advantage. Strategic position is composed of three elements, each of which has arisen as a result of the way the firm has operated in the past. These are competitive stance, competitive advantage and market coverage.

Analysis of a firm's strategic position may reveal opportunities to strengthen it and in turn its competitive position. Sometimes this may occur as a result of external changes in market dynamics or competitors' strategies. Usually it will be necessary for the firm to adopt innovative competitive strategies. It can impact its strategic position at three levels.

Competitive stance   This reflects the roles firms play in the international target market – that of leading, challenging, following or niching. Moves from follower to challenger to market leader will strengthen position. Similarly a niche specialist may adopt strategies to move to challenger or leader.

The competitive stance of innovator or follower is determined by the extent and timing of the introduction of new products. Competitors frequently take a deliberate decision on whether to be innovator or follower and structure their research and development functions and marketing departments accordingly. The advantages of being first into a market are well known, but the risks can be high and the costs of failure great.

Google could never be defined as an example of a first-time mover. By the time it entered the market, searching was considered a commodity. But Google is now considered one of the most popular sites on the web. Google's success stems from its use of the link structure of the web to determine what is important and what is not. Unlike its competitors it eschews banner ads; instead it offers advertisers the option of buying discrete text ads which are only shown when users search for certain words.

Long-term competitive position is strengthened by a record of successful innovations. For the business-class passenger travelling between Asia and Europe, Singapore Airlines has created an image of innovation with its lead moves of newest aircraft fleet, on-board telephone and entertainment services and its personalised cabin service.

The market leader has the position of being first in the customer's mind. This, in the long term, is supported by the highest market share. In some markets there are two or even three leaders. This characterises joint leadership. Other positions in the market are the high-share challenger, who poses a serious threat to the market leader. The *market follower* position is a stance in which the firm attempts to follow the innovative moves being made by the market leader. The remaining positions belong to specialists who focus on market niches.

Competitive advantage   Several moves are possible depending on starting position:

- from undifferentiated to low cost or differentiated;
- from low cost to differentiated as product leader or in terms of customer intimacy; or
- from differentiated to low cost and high differentiation in product or customer relationship terms.

The basis of competitive advantage, being product leadership, operational excellence and customer intimacy, was examined in Chapter 14, as was the concept of market coverage and focus. Both of these elements are relevant to assessing a firm's strategic position in its international market.

Market coverage   Moves from an unfocused to a focused position may be one option to strengthen strategic position. Another option is to extend market coverage. An example in the international airline industry is Richard Branson's Virgin Airlines. Its early strategy charter flights and low-cost transatlantic travel have now changed to differentiation through service. Customer intimacy is reflected in the availability of passenger massage services on long flights between Europe and Asia.

Market position

Market position refers to the relevant market's recognition and perception of a firm's position in the market – what it stands for and what its offerings provide relative to its competitors' offerings. For example, in the mainstream computer software market,

Microsoft is perceived to be industry leader (the standards setter) and provider of a wide range of good quality, reliable products supported by accessible aftersales service. Companies and their products become positioned in the market's collective mind on a variety of intangible and functional dimensions which are used by customers to distinguish them and assess *customer perceived value*. When international business travellers decide which airline to fly, frequently the differences in value come down to the perceived quality of the airport club lounge, the speed of luggage recovery and the attitude towards customer care taken by cabin staff.

Perceptions of quality, range, availability, image and other relevant dimensions can be measured for competing firms. Positioning studies can be used to focus a firm's attention on what target customers believe to be important to improve areas of perceived relative weakness and consolidate perceived advantages. This type of analysis provides direction to improve or reinforce market positioning in line with customer perceptions of value.

The strongest market position is one in which a firm offers superior perceived value in terms of the *benefits/price mix*, relative to its competitors. It is possible to have viable market positions in the international market in upmarket or downmarket positions provided the benefits/price mix is superior for the relevant market segment. The Japanese penchant for cars reveals a popularity of very broad offerings, from Mercedes-Benz through to bottom-of-the-range Toyotas.

Resources position

The *profitability* and *resources* elements of competitive position are internal to the company but should be assessed in relation to competitors' profitability and resources. They flag the company's ability or otherwise to fund and continue support for its strategy in relation to competitors. In international markets *resource leverage* through alliance and business partners extend the firm's capability to reach and service different market segments.

Elements such as cost structure, specific skills, responsiveness and other internal characteristics that affect success in the industry also form elements of competitive position. Frequently, as part of a competitive strategy, a business must act on costs, or know-how, or factors which make the company more market responsive, to enable it to improve competitive position. Vodafone's improved end-of-year results for 2002 surprised financial analysts and were mainly attributed to reduced cost structure.

The complete competitive position model shown as Figure 15.1 recognises the interrelationships between the dimensions of competitive position. Many of these relationships are revealed in strategic analysis of the PIMS database. Analysis of the database primarily of American and European firms reveals that high market share is correlated with high profitability, high customer value is correlated with high profitability, high product quality is associated with price premium positioning and high return on investment. Businesses with market shares above 40% were found to earn an average return on investment three times that of those with shares under 10%. The importance of share varies between industries and market situations. The higher sales volume allows the dominant firm economies of scale and learning curve effects which can translate into lower costs. Often the strong market position and leading brands owned by the dominant firm enable it to maintain higher price levels and control market price sensitivity

(Buzzell et al., 1975). These types of empirical interrelationship and the development of strategic thinking in the literature suggest that a few common profiles of competitive position are prevalent and stand out as fairly clear positions from the almost infinite number of variations of competitive position that exist.

The dominant leader in international markets

The distinguishing feature of the dominant firm is that it holds a significantly higher market share than its nearest competitor in its international market. In the short to medium term this competitive position can be almost unassailable. This is particularly so when there are effective barriers to entry of international markets as has been the case in Japan, the competition is fragmented and no other firm holds a position such that it could mount an effective challenge to the leadership position. No dominant firm is invulnerable in the long term, however. Strategies must be based on an understanding of the areas of vulnerability as well as the sources of strength. The central objective of the dominant firm is to maintain or even strengthen its future competitive position in both its current international market and any redefined future market.

Very few firms are dominant in all their international markets. Even Ericsson which has operated for decades in many international markets is not dominant in all its markets. For example, its dominance in the fixed telephone exchange market in China is not matched in Japan. Its dominance in the Hong Kong mobile market with more than 60% share is not carried across into the Indonesian market. Microsoft operating systems, Intel processors and Hewlett-Packard printers are among the few examples of worldwide dominance. But even here there are some markets like Japan in which these companies have a challenger or niche position. For some firms it is more realistic to think of dominance in perhaps one international country market or a region comprising two or three country markets.

The dominant firm has many advantages that place it in an enviable position. These include the ability to manage the market and the competition and, ultimately, to generate higher levels of profitability. This is, however, more limited in international markets where political considerations and community factors constrain super-profits resulting from dominance.

The dominant firm usually has the highest market credibility and acceptance. Product or service users see it as a company that can be trusted. This provides the opportunity to manage the flow and timing of new products, their penetration levels and the associated withdrawal of obsolete ones. While not absolute, it does give the dominant firm a measure of 'management' of the market, depending upon its level of dominance. Within the international markets for international beer brands, Heineken has highest market credibility.

The dominant firm also has the opportunity to significantly influence competitive evolution. As noted earlier, the current dominance of Microsoft with its Windows operating system and its application programs such as Microsoft Office enable it to direct the evolution of the market and manage its competitors. Microsoft has managed to form alliances with potentially threatening competitors such as Apple and Oracle and it uses market penetration strategies to keep other competitors, such as Lotus (owned by IBM), relatively small. It also faces ongoing court cases with the US anti-trust authorities in its competitive battles in a range of IT and Internet-related markets.

The dominant firm profile

Figure 15.2 shows the characteristic profile of the firm with a dominant competitive position.

Variations of this profile exist across each of the elements of competitive position although strength in each is essential for a dominant position.

Structural position and strategic position

The market share structure position is one of individual dominance. The dominant firm has a significantly higher market share than the nearest competitor. Share structure may be one of monopoly dominance as reflected in Microsoft's and Intel's position, or market share dominance such as Dell, IBM and Sun Microsystems. The danger for dominant firms lies with erosion of share by new entrants and substitutes, as well as existing rivals, to a level where individual dominance is lost.

The dominant firm is usually a market leader, a position that has historically been built by being first in the customer's mind. Kraft is synonymous with cheese, Colgate

Figure 15.2	Profile of the dominant firm

Source: Brown (1997).

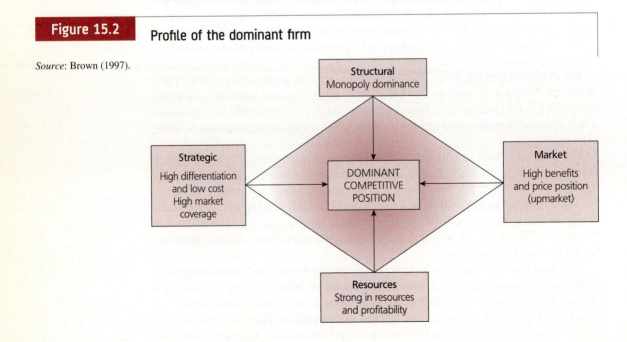

with toothpaste, Sony with consumer electronics. A dominant firm may periodically have a follower stance. This occurs when the dominant firm allows a smaller rival to offer innovative products and initiate change in a market. A stance of continuous follower mode will erode the dominant firm's competitive position and provide a platform from which the smaller firm can launch an attack.

The strongest dominant firms achieve a competitive advantage on both the cost and differentiation dimensions in mainstream markets. Dominant firms may have a differentiated position with relatively low costs.

A dominant firm must also have wide coverage of the main market segments to achieve the critical mass necessary for share leadership. A focus position may be necessary in a low segmentation market where there are similar or differentiated product offerings. The main danger to a dominant firm is to become unfocused and spread resource support too thinly. This erosion of position is usually accompanied by a declining market share. Companies like Electrolux have to work hard to prevent this by making clear their positioning to their customers in each of the segments they compete in.

Market position and resources position

Dominant firms attain their position by offering superior customer value. This may be in the form of high perceived benefits and high cost or high perceived benefits with low cost. *Yellow Pages* has an upmarket position because it offers customers superior value among their advertising alternatives.

Some dominant firms achieve a strong market position with a high-benefits/low-price position. Cadburys holds this position in the Australian and New Zealand block chocolate market. It offers superior value by combining high product quality with a low price in the face of many low-price alternatives. However, outside its dominant markets of UK, Canada and South Africa, it has niche positions in most of its international markets. The main danger to dominant firms is a drift towards inferior customer value represented by moving downmarket into a weak position.

The individual dominant firm has a relatively large resource base and usually earns higher levels of profit. Productivity levels, as reflected in cost structures and output levels, need management to maintain advantage relative to competitors. Dominant firms will usually have a strong group of alliances in international markets to create resource leverage.

Strategies for the international dominant firm

Firms seeking dominance of international markets are most likely to achieve this in either of two ways. One strategy is to focus on one international market. For example, Waterford–Wedgwood has focused on the US crystal market. A second approach is to identify a specialised market with global potential and seek to dominate it. This has been achieved by several high-technology firms in the biotech area.

15.1 International highlight

Microsoft dominance continues . . .

Microsoft's launch of launch of Windows XP is a timely reminder to its competitors that it is back from the distraction of long and messy anti-trust trial. Windows XP has been well received by consumers but Microsoft has also being focusing on developing new markets to assure its long-term growth – mainly digital entertainment, enterprise software and web services.

To understand the success of Microsoft's strategy, it is necessary to look at why it has been so successful. Microsoft, ahead of everyone else, is the provider of a 'platform'. Windows became that 'platform' – a building block that enabled developers to create applications. Microsoft sold its operating system cheaply and has done everything to make life easy for programmers. Office has beome the dominant desktop package and enjoys a market share of more than 90%.

The dominant firm must, above all else, focus on maintaining and strengthening its position of dominance in its core market. Regardless of the substantive elements of the strategy it must establish and reinforce a market leadership position while managing the competitive balance and taking heed of its obligations to the market.

Reinforce market perceptions   The dominant leader should reinforce its positioning as the standard – Coca-Cola's themes from 'the real thing' to 'always Coca-Cola' and Xerox's reinforcement of 'we invented the product' maintain the positioning of being the original. The leader may need to adopt strategies to improve the product, its service or its distribution, but the focus should be on reinforcing the leader positioning in the international market's collective mind (Ries and Trout, 1986a).

Manage the market   A dominant firm has the greatest ability to manage the market and the competition by investment in new initiatives. These enable it to maintain its market influence and its profit and cash to contain the activities of its competitors. Just as the size of a dominant leader's share should be considered and managed in relation to profit and risk, so should it manage the share levels of individual competitors. This may require strategies to limit the share growth of some competitors while enhancing the share growth of others. Market leaders have the opportunity of shaping the competition in the market by targeting the strategies they adopt. Costs, risks and protection should be considered when formulating competitor-targeted strategies.

Market and competitive obligations   The dominant firm must be aware of the social, economic and political obligations that accompany its advantageous position – a company that acquires a very high market share exposes itself to risks that its smaller competitors do not encounter. With the dominant position comes an obligation to guard against misuse of its position and to avoid behaviour that reduces the level of competition to the extent it allows it to make 'unfair' profits. Competitors, consumers and governmental authorities are more likely to take certain actions against high-share companies than against small-share ones. Microsoft is a case in point.

Offensive and defensive strategies

The character of dominant firms' strategies may be either offensive or defensive. Offensive moves are those strategic changes the market leader initiates. They are threatening to competitors when the objective is to take market share and undermine their positions through a frontal attack on selected competitors' markets. Alternatively, they are nonthreatening when they are designed to improve volume and profitability in the market as a whole.

Offensive strategies include:

● product, packaging and service innovations;
● development of new market segments;
● redefinition of the market to broaden its scope and position products more closely against broad substitutes;
● market development through product variety and distribution strategies to increase usage and widen availability; and
● international expansion to reduce the impact of global competitors.

Defensive strategies include:

● blocking competitors by brand-for-brand matching, distribution coverage and price strategies to reduce their market share and profit potential;
● pre-emption of a competitor's action by being first with a new product or distribution system; and
● use of government regulations, tariffs, import quotas or court actions to increase a competitor's cost or deny a market base.

In practice, dominant firms adopt both offensive and defensive strategies to strengthen and protect their leadership position. The strategies for competing should be related to the current experience that many firms have had with their competitors. This is discussed in more detail in Chapter 16.

Built to last

Drawing from a research project of 18 exceptional and long-lasting international companies, Collins and Porras (1994) tried to identify what made them different and able to sustain long-term dominance in their markets. These included General Electric, 3M, Walt Disney, Hewlett-Packard, Procter & Gamble, Motorola, Sony, Merck and

Boeing. They identify two key principles as internal drivers of those firms that are built to last. First, it is of critical importance to preserve and protect its core ideology. Core ideology goes beyond making money. For 3M it is respect for individual initiative, and for Boeing it is being on the leading edge of innovation – being pioneers. Second, there is a relentless drive for progress. This means urging continual change, pushing continual movement towards goals and improvement, expanding the number and variety of possibilities and being prepared to implement radical change consistent with the firm's core ideology (Collins and Porras, 1994).

We now look at specific marketing strategies that are available to market leaders, challengers, followers and nichers. These classifications often do not apply to a whole company, but only to its position in a specific industry or in a specific international market. In fact, it is likely that firms may be market leader in their domestic markets, but be a challenger, follower and nicher in other international countries.

Strategies for international market leadership

Most international markets contain an acknowledged market leader. It usually leads the other firms in price changes, new product introductions, distribution coverage and promotion spending. The market leader may or may not be admired or respected, but other firms concede its leadership position. The leader is a focal point for competitors, a company to challenge, imitate or avoid. Some of the best-known international market leaders are Toyota (cars), Kodak (photography), Dell (microcomputers), Microsoft (software), Cadbury Schweppes (chocolate confectionery), Caterpillar (earth-moving equipment), Coca-Cola (soft drinks), McDonald's (fast food) and Gillette (razor blades).

The profile of a market leader position is similar to that of the dominant competitor profile, shown again as Figure 15.3. In this section the relevant strategies for a market leader in an international market are described. They include both offensive and defensive strategies noted in the previous section.

Market leader strategies require action on three fronts: (a) the firm must find ways to expand total demand; (b) it must protect its current market share through good defensive and offensive actions; and (c) the firm may try to expand its market share further, even if market size remains constant.

Expanding the total market

The leading firm normally gains the most when the total market expands. If we make more mobile phone calls, Nokia stands to gain the most in international markets because it sells more mobile phones than its competitors. If Nokia can convince us to make calls, or make calls on more occasions, it will benefit greatly. In general, the market leader should look for new users, new uses and more usage of its products.

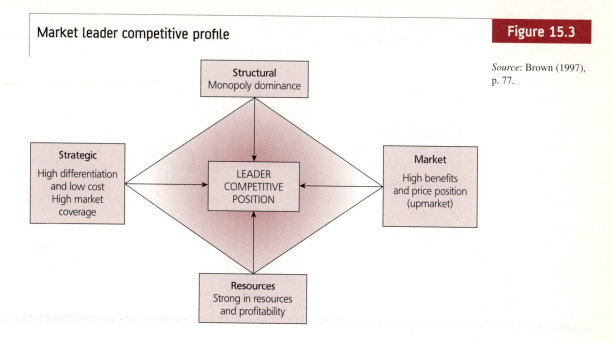

Market leader competitive profile

Figure 15.3

Source: Brown (1997), p. 77.

Protecting market share

While trying to expand total market size, the market leader should also constantly protect its current business in its international market against competitor attacks. Coca-Cola must constantly guard against Pepsi; Gillette against Bic; Kodak against Fuji; McDonald's against Burger King and KFC.

What can the market leader do to protect its position? First, it must prevent or fix weaknesses that provide opportunities for competitors. It needs to keep its costs down and its prices in line with the value the customers see in the brand. The leader should 'plug holes' so that competitors do not jump in. But the best defence is a good offence, and the best response is continuous innovation. The leader refuses to be content with the way things are and leads the industry in new products, customer services, distribution effectiveness and cost cutting. It keeps increasing its competitive effectiveness and value to customers. It takes the offensive, sets the pace and exploits competitors' weaknesses.

Increased competition in recent years has sparked management's interest in models of military warfare (Ries and Trout, 1986b; Boar, 1993; Thompson and Strickland, 1998). Leader companies have been advised to protect their market positions with competitive strategies patterned after successful military defence strategies. Six defence strategies that a market leader can use are shown in Figure 15.4.

Position defence The most basic defence is a position defence in which a company builds fortifications around its current position. But simply defending one's current position or products rarely works. Even such lasting brands as Coca-Cola and Panadol cannot be relied upon to supply all future growth and profitability for their companies.

| **Figure 15.4** | **Defence strategies** |

Source: Kotler et al. (1998), p. 728.

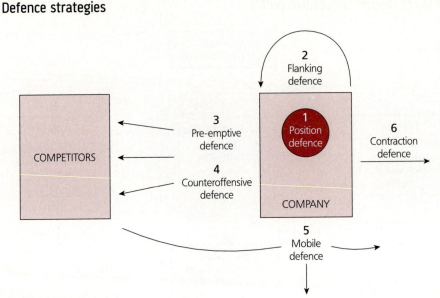

These brands must be improved and adapted to changing conditions, and new brands must be developed. Today, Coca-Cola, in spite of producing more than one-third of America's soft drinks, is aggressively extending its beverage lines and penetrating developing markets, and has diversified into desalinisation equipment and plastics.

Flanking defence   When guarding its overall position, the market leader should closely watch its weaker flanks. Smart competitors will normally attack the company's weaknesses. Thus, the Japanese successfully entered the small car market because car makers left a gaping hole in that submarket. Using a flanking defence, the company carefully checks its flanks and protects the more vulnerable areas.

Pre-emptive defence   The leader can launch a more aggressive pre-emptive defence, striking competitors before they can move against the company. A pre-emptive defence assumes that prevention is better than cure.

Counteroffensive defence   When a market leader is attacked, despite its flanking or pre-emptive efforts, it can launch a counteroffensive defence. When Fuji attacked Kodak in the film markets, Kodak counterattacked by dramatically increasing its promotion and introducing several innovative new film products. Sometimes companies hold off for a while before countering. This may seem a dangerous game of 'wait and see', but there are often good reasons for not rushing in. By waiting, the company can more fully understand the competitor's offence and perhaps find a gap through which a successful counteroffensive can be launched.

Mobile defence   A mobile defence involves more than aggressively defending a current market position. The leader stretches to new markets that can serve as future bases for defence and offence. Through market broadening, the company shifts its focus from the current product to the broader underlying consumer need.

Contraction defence   Companies may find that they cannot easily defend positions in a large number of international markets. Their resources are spread too thinly and competitors are nibbling away on several fronts. The best action then appears to be a contraction defence (or strategic withdrawal). The company gives up weaker positions and concentrates its resources on stronger ones.

Expanding market share

Market leaders can also grow by increasing their market shares further. In many markets, small market-share increases result in very large sales increases. For example, in large markets, such as financial services and telecommunications, a 1% increase in market share translates into millions of dollars profit. This also applies to smaller markets in which premium price segments exist.

For example, Mercedes holds only a small share of the total car market, but it earns high profit because it is a high-share company in its luxury car segment. And it has achieved this high share in its served market because it does other things right, such as producing high quality vehicles, giving good service and holding down its costs as well as reinforcing an image of prestige. Mercedes vehicles are widely used in many countries to transport senior government officials, visiting dignitaries and high profile entertainers.

Companies must not think, however, that gaining increased market share automatically improves profitability. Much depends on their strategies for gaining increased share. Many high-share companies endure low profitability, and many low-share companies enjoy high profitability. The cost of buying higher market share may far exceed the returns. Higher shares tend to produce higher profits only when unit costs fall with increased market share or when the company offers a superior quality product and charges a premium price that more than covers the cost of offering higher quality.

The financial risks associated with firms attempting to become market leaders in international markets must be weighed against the potential for market share gains.

Strategies for the international challenger

Firms that are second, third or lower in the international market are sometimes quite large, for example in the financial services market. These challengers can adopt one of two competitive strategies. They can attack the leader and other competitors in an aggressive bid for more market share (market challengers). Or they can play along with competitors and not rock the boat (market followers). Figure 15.5 shows the competitive position profile of market challengers.

| Figure 15.5 | Challenger competitive position profile |

Source: Brown (1997), p. 181.

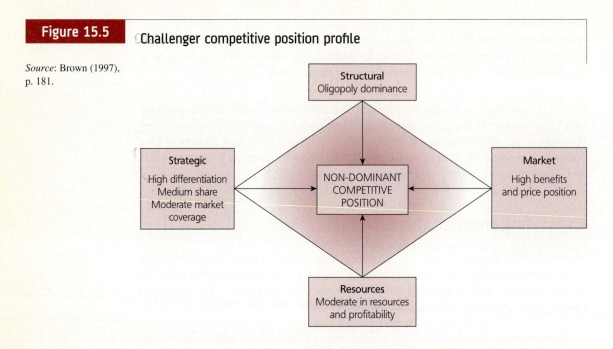

Defining the strategic objective and competitor

A market challenger must first define its strategic objective. Most market challengers seek to increase their profitability by increasing their market shares. But the strategic objective chosen depends on the competitor. In most cases the company can choose which competitors to challenge.

The challenger can attack the market leader, a high-risk but potentially high-gain strategy that makes good sense if the leader is not serving the market well. This can be a dangerous strategy for most companies targeting international markets, where political factors, interlinked loyalty for the indigenous country supplier or brand are important constraining factors. Many international beer brands have found it difficult to beat indigenous beer brands in Japan, the Philippines and China. To succeed with such an attack, a company must have some sustainable competitive advantage over the leader – a cost advantage leading to lower prices or the ability to provide better value at a premium price. In the construction equipment industry, Komatsu successfully challenged Caterpillar by offering the same quality at much lower prices. When attacking the leader a challenger must also find a way to minimise the leader's response. Otherwise its gains may be short-lived (Porter, 1985).

The challenger can avoid the leader and instead attack firms its own size, or smaller local and regional firms. Many of these firms are underfinanced and will not be serving their customers well. Several of the major international beer companies grew to their present size not by attacking large competitors, but by absorbing small local or regional competitors.

Thus, the challenger's strategic objective depends on which competitor it chooses to attack. If the company goes after the market leader, its objective may be to wrest a

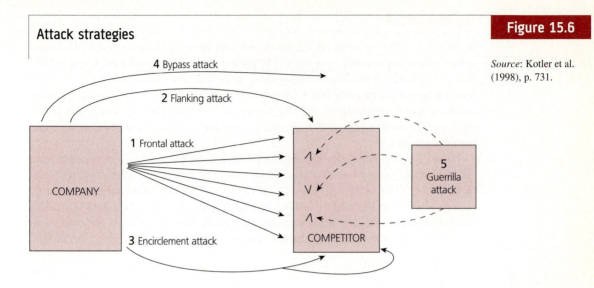

Attack strategies

Figure 15.6

Source: Kotler et al. (1998), p. 731.

certain market share. Bic knows that it can't topple Gillette in the razor market – it simply wants a larger share. Or the challenger's goal might be to take over market leadership. Dell entered the personal computer market late, as a challenger, but quickly became an important challenger to Compaq in international markets with its direct marketing and distribution strategy. If the company goes after a small local company, its objective may be to put that company out of business or buy it to gain a base in the international market. The important point remains: the company must choose its opponents carefully and have a clearly defined and attainable objective.

Choosing an attack strategy

How can the market challenger best attack the chosen competitor and achieve its strategic objectives? Five possible attack strategies are shown in Figure 15.6. When considering these strategies the firm must continually keep in mind the political and regulatory conditions of the international country and the established distributor and end-customer loyalties entrenched in many markets.

Frontal attack

In a full frontal attack, the challenger matches the competitor's product, advertising, price and distribution efforts. It attacks the competitor's strengths rather than its weaknesses. The outcome depends on who has the greater strength and endurance. Even substantial resources may not be enough to successfully challenge a firmly entrenched and resourceful competitor. If the market challenger has fewer resources or less resource leverage than the competitor, a frontal attack makes little sense. For example the world's three big couriers, Federal Express (FedEx), United Parcel Service (UPS) and DHL all follow similar frontal attack strategies in the US and Europe but compete fiercely everywhere else.

Flanking attack

Rather than attacking head on, the challenger can launch a flanking attack. The competitor often concentrates its resources to protect its strongest positions, but it usually has some weaker flanks. By attacking these weak spots the challenger can concentrate its strength against the competitor's weakness. Flank attacks make good sense when the company has fewer resources than the competitor. Another flanking strategy is to find gaps that are not being filled by the industry's products, fill them and develop them into strong segments.

Italian e-tailer Yoox.com has developed such a segment. Most Net retailers have failed to make money but Yoox.com is on course to break even after only two years in business. They offer discounts of up to 50% off retail prices on end-of-season merchandise from 300 leading fashion houses. Yoox's strategy is based on low prices and convenience. Fashion houses are happy because the alternative is the markdown rack. Yoox sells last year's merchandise and thus prevents cannibalising sales at their existing stores.

Encirclement attack

An encirclement attack involves attacking from all directions, so that the competitor must protect its front, sides and rear at the same time. The encirclement strategy makes sense when the challenger has superior resources and believes that it can quickly break the competitor's hold on the market. An example is Seiko's attack on the watch market. For several years Seiko has been gaining distribution in every major watch outlet and overwhelming competitors with its variety of constantly changing models. In most of its markets it offers over 500 models, but its marketing clout is backed by the 2,300 models it makes and sells worldwide.

Bypass attack

A bypass attack is an indirect strategy. The challenger bypasses the competitor and targets easier markets. The bypass can involve diversifying into unrelated products, moving into new geographical markets or leapfrogging into new technologies to replace existing products. Technological leapfrogging is a bypass strategy used often in high-technology industries. Instead of copying the competitor's product and mounting a costly frontal attack, the challenger patiently develops the next technology. When satisfied with its superiority, it launches an attack where it has an advantage. Thus, Minolta toppled Canon from the lead in the 35-millimetre SLR camera market when it introduced its technologically advanced auto-focusing Maxxum camera. Canon's market share dropped towards 20% while Minolta's zoomed past 30%. It took Canon three years to introduce a matching technology. A multitude of entries into the digital camera market is enabling new players in this market like Hewlett-Packard to bypass traditional leaders.

Guerrilla attack

A guerrilla attack is another option available to market challengers, especially the smaller or poorly financed challenger. The challenger makes small, periodic attacks

15.2 International highlight

Airlines jockey for competitive position in Asia-Pacific

Source: Courtesy of Singapore Airlines. Campaign created by Batey Ads, artwork courtesy of Batey Kazoo Communications Pty Ltd.

What differentiates Singapore Airlines, Qantas and Air New Zealand in the Asia-Pacific air transportation market? Each is markedly different from the other. Qantas is experienced in longer haul and has a larger, more diverse fleet of aircraft and a well-established route network. Singapore Airlines excels in service for the higher yield business traveller on Asian routes and through to Europe with a large new aircraft fleet and the 'Singapore Girl'. Air New Zealand has a reputation as a leisure airline and holds a lower overall cost structure, but restricted route access has made it difficult for it to compete with other airline frequent flyer schemes.

Several other Asian airlines – Thai, Malaysia, Garuda and Philippine Airlines – have developed competitive positions in the Asia-Pacific markets. Each carrier is attempting to dominate a segment or carve out a niche in the highly competitive international airline industry. Each uses its domestic market as a basis for loyalty building and aligns with other carriers to extend fuller international services to its customers.

While Qantas can draw on its profitable domestic market and maintain profit from its dominant positions on the London and Los Angeles market sectors, Philippine Airlines, Malaysia Airlines and Indonesia's Garuda focus on niche markets.

But the big mover in Asia-Pacific is Singapore Airlines. It owns 49% of Virgin Atlantic, it has a significant stake in the Australasian airline industry and is looking to have a bigger impact through Air New Zealand and move in on Qantas's leadership in the Pacific route to the US. These moves are designed to make Singapore Airlines the leading carrier based in the Asia-Pacific region.

The relative strength of competitive positions of these airlines will determine whether they survive the current round of industry restructuring or are forced to merge or exit the market.

Source: Thomas (1998); www.singaporeair.com/saa (accessed 28 June 2001); http://www.virgin-atlantic.com/main.asp?page=2.4 (accessed 26 June 2001); http://www.philippineair.com (accessed 29 June 2001).

to harass and demoralise the competitor, hoping eventually to establish permanent footholds. It might use selective price cuts, executive raids, intense promotional outbursts or assorted legal actions. Normally, smaller firms against larger ones take guerrilla actions but not always. Continuous guerrilla campaigns can be expensive and they must eventually be followed by a stronger attack if the challenger wishes to 'beat' the competitor. Electrolux, the world's largest white-goods producer, has continuously attacked its competitors' segments. It has spread its efforts across the entire consumer goods market. It has taken on its competitors on price in the discount markets while also competing in the middle-segment and premium segments. However, such a strategy could damage its brand appeal to some consumers. But it is hard not to be impressed by the latest product innovation – the Trilobite, named after a long extinct creature, is a robotic vacuum cleaner that uses sensors to navigate around the house.

Strategies for the international follower

Not all runner-up companies will challenge the market leader. The effort to draw away the leader's customers is never taken lightly by the leader. If the challenger's lure is lower prices, improved service or additional product features, the leader can quickly match these to defuse the attack. The leader probably has more staying power in an all-out battle. A hard fight might leave both firms weakened. Thus, the challenger must think twice before attacking. Therefore, many firms prefer to follow rather than attack the leader. Figure 15.7 shows the competitive position profile of a challenger.

A follower can gain many advantages. The market leader often bears the huge expenses involved with developing new products and markets, expanding distribution channels, and informing and educating the market. The reward for all this work and risk is normally market leadership. The market follower, on the other hand, can learn from the leader's experience and copy or improve on the leader's products and marketing programmes, usually at a much lower investment. Although the follower probably will not overtake the leader, it can often be as profitable (Haines et al., 1989).

The follower is a major target of attack by challengers. Therefore the market follower must keep its manufacturing costs low and its product quality and services high. It must also enter new markets as they open up. Following is not the same as being passive or existing as a carbon copy of the leader. The follower must define a growth path, but one that does not provoke competitive retaliation.

The market-follower firms fall into one of three broad types: the *cloner*, the *imitator* and the *adapter*. The *cloner* closely copies the leader's products, distribution, advertising and other marketing moves. The cloner attempts to live off the market leader's investments. The *imitator* copies some things from the leader but maintains some differentiation in terms of packaging, advertising, pricing and other factors. The leader doesn't mind the imitator as long as the imitator does not attack aggressively. The imitator may even help the leader avoid the charges of monopoly. Finally,

Follower competitive position profile

Source: Brown (1997), p. 241.

Figure 15.7

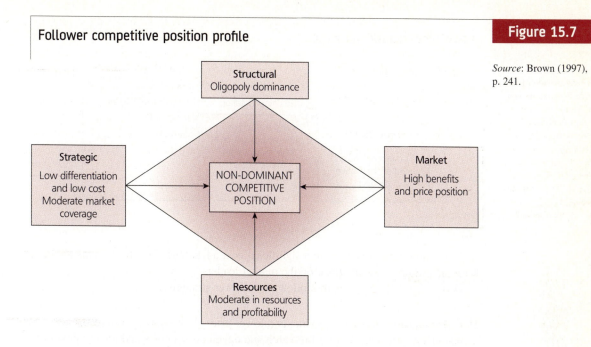

the *adapter* builds on the leader's products and marketing programmes, often improving them. The adapter may choose to sell to different markets to avoid direct confrontation with the leader. But often the adapter grows into a future challenger, as many Japanese firms have done after adapting and improving products developed elsewhere.

The firm adopting a follower strategy is quite content to remain a number two or three company. The objective is to position the firm and its products as viable alternatives to the market leader, leaving the market leader with the responsibility for market development and expansion.

The risks associated with innovation and the development of new products can be reduced by being a close follower. D'Aveni (1994) refers to one study that reports that 60% of successful patented innovations were imitated within an average of four years, and the imitating firm's development costs were at least 35% less than the innovator's.

Of course, the true follower firm is not interested in challenging the dominant firm, often out of fear of disrupting the competitive balance and causing the dominant firm to take a more offensive stance. Dominant firms are often happy to allow a follower firm to operate as a means of maintaining the existing market share structure.

Some firms take a market-follower position as a first step in challenging the market leader. This is a strategy adopted by Japanese companies in most industries in which they compete. Follower companies are able to learn from the product and marketing mistakes of the leaders and develop a product and overall market offer that is better suited to the needs of the market. Development costs are reduced by reverse engineering, the follower firm then focuses on improving process technology to reduce the costs

| Figure 15.8 | A two-step imitation process |

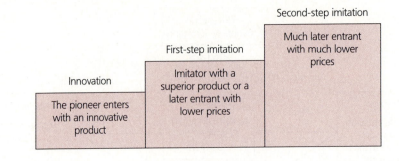

of production, often resulting in a significant cost advantage. This then forms the base for a more direct, frontal attack on the market leader.

D'Aveni (1994) suggests the following follower strategies.

1 *Imitation*: offer the same product at a lower price. This strategy requires lower manufacturing costs, reduced research and development costs and lower marketing expenditure.

2 *Adding features*: additional features that differentiate the product in a manner that is relevant to the market.

3 *Stripping down*: eliminating features to provide a more basic product at a lower price.

4 *Flanking*: stripping down and/or adding features to develop a product suited to smaller market segments.

Schnaars proposes a two-step imitation process shown in Figure 15.8.

Several examples of this two-stage process can be found. Pocket calculators were pioneered by a number of small assemblers of electronic components. The large integrated circuit manufacturers moved in quickly when they saw the market grow and forced out the small assemblers. As calculators began to appeal to the mass market beyond engineering and scientific usage, Asian manufacturers mobilised low-cost mass production and took the volume market at low prices. A similar pattern occurred with digital watches, although the Swiss manufacturers came back to appeal to certain 'style' segments, but leaving the volume low-price versions to Asian suppliers. Microwave ovens were pioneered by American firms who were later challenged by Japanese companies at lower prices. This was followed by Korean-dominated manufacture at lower costs and selling for much lower prices to supply the mass market.

Market leaders and other innovating firms will not remain idle while a follower firm piggybacks its development initiatives. The distinction between challenger and follower strategies is very fine. The follower that aims to outperform the market leader is in effect mounting a challenge and should be prepared for the competitive consequences!

Strategies for the international niche firm

Almost every international market includes firms that specialise in serving market niches. Instead of pursuing the whole market, or even large segments of the market, these firms target segments within segments, or niches. This is particularly true of small/medium-sized firms because of their limited resources. But smaller divisions of larger firms may also pursue niching strategies. The competitive position profile of a niche player is shown in Figure 15.9.

The main point is that firms with low shares of the total market can be highly profitable through smart niching.

Marketing strategy theory very often focuses on the means to rapidly penetrate a market using the support of high-level marketing expenditures in advertising, sales effort and promotion. The high profile of leading marketers, such as McDonald's, Toyota and Coca-Cola, and their enormous promotional budgets reinforces this view. Many companies, however, adopt quite different marketing strategies that aim to establish a presence in a market and then develop gradual but progressive growth. Most of these companies are relatively small in both financial resources and staff, although many medium-sized and even large companies in industrial markets and service industries adopt this marketing approach.

Niche player competitive position profile

Figure 15.9

Source: Brown (1997), p. 316.

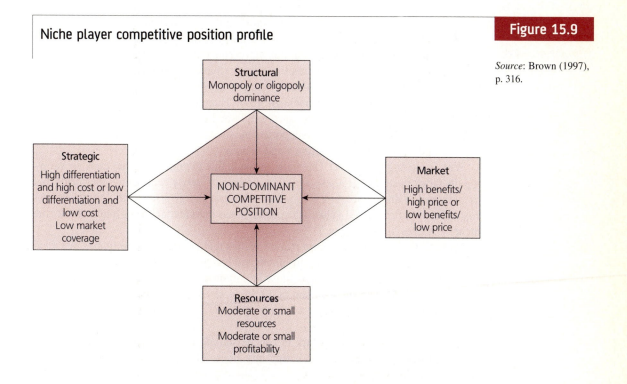

15.3 International highlight

Cadillac returns to Europe

General Motor's (GM) intends to relaunch the Cadillac into the European market at the end of 2003. It is keen to bring the Cadillac back to Europe to take on Mercedes-Benz and BMW, the German luxury brands, in their home markets. Both of these companies have been taking market share from GM in the US. GM has now decided that the best form of attack is to attack them head on in their home market. With the fall of the dollar against the euro in the past year the financial projections look good. However, GM is not looking for a big financial return; this is more a matter of psychological warfare.

Source: Adapted from James Mackintosh, *Financial Times*, 5 March 2003.

An infiltration strategy is based on a slow but increasing rate of sales and market share growth and supported by a commensurate build-up of marketing effort. Once a position is established this is consolidated and nurtured while the momentum for the development of a larger market share base builds slowly. This is contrasted with the rapid penetration strategy in which a company aims, through sheer force, to snatch market share from the existing competitors.

The essence of the infiltration strategy is that it has relatively low market impact and aims to attract minimal attention of competition in the market. The positioning of the product or the company using an infiltration strategy may range from the premium to the low end of the market. A 'market skimming' pricing strategy may appear to be similar to an infiltration strategy, but this represents only one variant.

Studies of highly successful small companies have found that in almost all cases these companies innovated and niched within a larger market rather than going after the whole market (Clifford and Cavanagh, 1988; Hamel, 2000). These studies have also found other features shared by the successful smaller companies – i.e. offering high value, charging a premium price supported by soundly based but innovative business models, and strong corporate cultures and visions.

Why is niching profitable? The main reason is that the market nicher ends up knowing the target customer group so well that it meets its needs better than other firms that casually sell to this niche. As a result, the nicher can charge a substantial mark-up over costs because of the added value; whereas the mass marketer achieves high volume, the nicher achieves high margins.

Nichers try to find one or more market niches that are safe and profitable. An ideal market niche is big enough to be profitable and has growth potential. It is one that the firm can serve effectively. Perhaps most importantly, the niche is of little interest to major competitors, and the firm can build the skills and customer goodwill to defend itself against an attacking major competitor as the niche grows and becomes more attractive.

The key idea in 'nichemanship' is specialisation. The firm must specialise along market, customer, product or marketing-mix lines. There are several specialist roles open to a market nicher.

- *End-use specialist.* The firm specialises in serving one type of end-use customer. For example, a law firm can specialise in the criminal, civil or business law markets.

- *Vertical-level specialist.* The firm specialises at some level of the production/distribution cycle. For example, a copper firm may concentrate on producing raw copper, copper components or finished copper products.

- *Customer size specialist.* The firm concentrates on selling either to small, medium or large customers. Many nichers specialise in serving small customers who are neglected by the majors. GE's concentration on the small-jet market in the early 1990s has paid off handsomely for them. While others ignored this segment GE now have a major share of this growing segment.

- *Specific customer specialist.* The firm limits its selling to one or a few major customers.

- *Geographical specialist.* The firm sells only in a certain locality, region or area of the world. For example, English retail giant Tesco has targeted eastern Europe as a high priority international market. Its hypermarkets in the western part of Poland are set to give it a strong position to develop further in the emerging volume markets of eastern Europe and Russia.

- *Product or feature specialist.* The firm specialises in producing a certain product, product line or product feature. For instance, within the laboratory equipment industry are firms that produce only microscopes or, even more narrowly, only lenses for microscopes. Food and drink is another area of product specialisation. Even Pepsi's market has splintered and big brands no longer have universal appeal. They now have developed niche products such as cherry-flavoured, caffeine-loaded Mountain Dew Code Red, Pepsi Twist and berry-flavoured Pepsi Blue.

- *Quality–price specialist.* The firm operates at the low or high end of the market. For example, Hewlett-Packard specialises in the high-quality, high-price end of the hand calculator market.

- *Service specialist.* The firm offers one or more services not available from other firms.

Niching carries a major risk in that the market niche may dry up or be attacked. That is why many companies practise multiple niching. By developing two or more niches, the company increases its chances of survival. Even some large firms prefer a multiple-niche strategy to serving the total market. One large law firm has developed a national reputation in the three areas of mergers and acquisitions, bankruptcies and prospectus development, and does little else.

Internet infusion

The pressure on travel businesses to cut costs is enormous – sandwiched on one side by airlines and hotels to cut costs and on the other by the realisation that the Internet is proving a cheap and efficient way for consumers to meet their travel requirements. Since travel agents can no longer rely on revenues from suppliers, they are being forced to charge their customers. Commissions are being replaced by fees, but charging fees is only adding to customers' incentive to use the Internet to cut agents out of the loop altogether. Ryanair and EasyJet have pioneered the direct selling of tickets via their websites. Hotels are discovering that the web can be a powerful and cheap distribution channel, and not just an online brochure. Traditional offline agents are now themselves climbing onto the Internet bandwagon to help clients manage their travel budgets.

Summary

International competitive marketing strategies are closely related to a firm's competitive position. Firms holding a dominant position usually have available a wider range of strategic alternatives than those in follower or niche positions. Also, firms starting out will be constrained by their resources, access to markets and the challenge of creating a competitive position in international markets.

The wide range of strategies relevant to the different competitive positions of dominance, market leadership, challenger, follower and niche specialist indicates the need for careful assessment and selection followed by creative implementation by the international marketer.

While some firms have been able to become market leaders or strong challengers in specific international markets, most opportunities exist for niche players. Consequently, small/medium-sized firms must master the strategies needed to succeed as specialists in an end use, specific customer, specific geographical area, product or service. When linked to electronic commerce – a subject discussed in detail in Chapter 19 – many firms have the potential to lead many of the international niche markets of the future.

Ethics issue

Your company is a major exporter of beef to Japan. Your main competition is a new large beef exporting company from Argentina. You have unconfirmed reports of contaminated beef belonging to your competitor on the Japanese wharves. Knowing the Japanese focus on hygiene you know that a rumour, whether true or unfounded, would halt your competitor's market penetration.

Would you actively spread this rumour?

Web workout

Question 1 Analyse the website of a key global beer manufacturer such as Heineken (www.heineken.com) or Budweiser (www.budweiser.com) and compare it with another European brand such as Carlsberg (http://www.carlsberg.com). What conclusions can you draw as to the information about new products and other customer retention strategies of these websites?

Question 2 Visit the website of a key European international airline and compare it with a smaller Asia-Pacific carrier such as Air India or Phillipines Airlines. What conclusions can you draw? What about Virgin Atlantic? What customer does it cater for? What position do you think Virgin Atlantic will adopt in the near future?

Websites

www.singaporeair.com

www.virgin-atlantic.com

www.philippineair.com

www.axa.com

www.singtel.com

www.british-airways.com

www.pims-europe.com

www.toyota.com.au

www.ericsson.com

www.microsoft.com

www.hp.com

www.imb.com

www.apple.com

www.sony.com

www.cadbury.com

www.fortune.com

www.boeing.com

www.3m.com

www.disney.com

www.kodak.com

www.mcdonalds.com

www.dell.com

www.gillette.com

www.nokia.com

www.pizzahut.com

www.kfc.com

www.burgerking.com

www.bicworld.com

Discussion questions

1 Evaluate the position of Coca-Cola in one of its international markets using Brown's competitive position model.

2 Identify the competitive positions of four players in the international airline passenger market. Describe their strategies and make inferences about their possible future competitive positions.

3 Hewlett-Packard dominates the printer market worldwide. Describe its offensive and defensive strategies.

4 Identify a local firm that is a market leader in one or more international markets. Summarise its strategies in those markets and compare them with typical market leader strategies.

5 Identify a local firm that is a challenger or follower in its international markets. Examine its strategies in relation to typical strategies adopted by challengers and followers.

6 What types of niche strategies are relevant to firms? Describe these strategies and give examples of firms using them.

References

Boar, B. (1993) *The Art of Strategic Planning for Information Technology*, John Wiley and Sons, New York.

Brown, A.C. (1986) Unilever Fights back in the US, *Fortune*, pp. 32–38.

Brown, L.R. (1997) *Competitive Marketing Strategy: Dynamic Manouvering for Competitive Position*, 2nd edn, ITP Nelson, Melbourne.

Brown, L.R. (2002) *Competitive Marketing Strategy: Dynamic Manouvering for Competitive Position*, 3rd edn, ITP Nelson, Melbourne.

Buzzell, R.D. and Gale, B.T. (1987) *The PIMS Principles: Linking Strategy to Performance*, The Free Press, New York, pp. 6–15, 30–35.

Buzzell, R.D., Gale, B.T. and Sultan, R.G.M. (1975) 'Market Share – A Key to profitability', *Harvard Business Review*, Jan–Feb, Vol. 53, No. 1, p. 97.

Clifford, D.K. and Cavanagh, R.E. (1988) *The Winning Performance: How America's High-growth Mid-size Companies Succeed*, Bantam Books, New York, p. 36.

Collins, J.C. and Porras, J.I. (1994) *Built to Last: Successful Habits of Visionary Companies*, Harper Books, New York.

D'Aveni, R.A. (1994) *Hyper-competition: Managing the Dynamics of Strategic Manouvering*, Free Press, New York.

Haines, D.W., Chandran, R. and Parkhe, A. (1989) 'Winning by Being First to Market . . . Or Last?', *Journal of Consumer Marketing*, Winter, Emerald Journals, MCB University Press, UK, pp. 63–69.

Hamel, G. (2000) *Leading the Revolution*, Harvard Business School Press, Boston, Ch. 3.

Kotler, P. (1998) *Marketing Management: Analysis, Planning, Implementation and Control*, Prentice Hall, Englewood Cliffs, NJ, Ch. 14.

Kotler, P., Armstrong, G., Brown, L. and Adam, S. (1998) *Marketing*, 4th edn, Prentice Hall, Melbourne.

Porter, M. (1985) 'How to Attack the Industry Leader', *Fortune*, pp. 153–166.

Ries, A. and Trout, J. (1986a) *Positioning: The Battle for your Mind*, McGraw-Hill, New York.

Ries, A. and Trout, J. (1986b) *Marketing Warfare*, McGraw-Hill, New York, pp. 55–66.

Schnaars, S.P. (1994) *Managing Imitation Strategies: How Later Entrants Seize Markets from Pioneers*, The Free Press, New York, p. 216.

Thomas, I. (1998) 'Exit Signs Light Up for Asian Airlines', *The Australian Financial Review*, 29 June, p. 3.

Thompson, A.A. and Strickland, A.J. (1998) *Strategic Management: Concepts and Cases*, 10th edn, Irwin McGraw-Hill, Boston.

16

Globalisation

Learning objectives

After studying this chapter, you should be able to:

- evaluate the forces of globalisation and the underlying philosophy of globalism;

- assess the motivations for globalisation and the six-stage internationalisation process;

- identify the elements relevant to global planning;

- use a global strategy framework;

- examine basic global competitive strategy profiles and the pitfalls of global marketing; and

- explore the rise of Asian competitors.

The global top 20	**Figure 1**

1. Ireland	11. United States
2. Switzerland	12. France
3. Sweden	13. Norway
4. Singapore	14. Portugal
5. Netherlands	15. Czech Republic
6. Denmark	16. New Zealand
7. Canada	17. Germany
8. Austria	18. Malaysia
9. United Kingdom	19. Israel
10. Finland	20. Spain

Source: Kearney (2003).

The global top 20

Ireland has again emerged as the most 'globalised' country among 62 states included in the AT Kearney/Foreign Policy magazine survey. The Republic's high level of trade and multinational investment and high telephone call volumes with the rest of the world were the key features maintaining its position at the top of the survey. By making use of several indicators – including information technology, finance, trade, personal communications, political engagement and travel – the survey reveals how a country's level of global integration spans multiple dimension.

Categories by which the index is assessed

The globalisation index aims to assess the most important components of international integration, from engagement in international relations and policy-making to trade and financial flows and the movement of people, ideas and information across borders. It tracks changes in these areas across 62 advanced economies and key emerging markets.

The index quantifies economic integration combining data on trade, foreign direct investment, portfolio capital flows and income payments and receipts.

It charts personal contact through measuring the level of international trade and tourism and international telephone traffic. Technological connectedness is counted by the total of Internet users as well as the numbers of Internet hosts and secure servers, large computers which allow Internet traffic and transactions.

The final category measured by the survey is political engagement. This is assessed by taking stock of the number of international organisations and UN Security Council missions of foreign embassies hosted.

For most variables, each year's inward and outward flows are added and the sum is divided by the country's nominal economic output or, where appropriate, its population. The political data is treated differently, with panels of data allowing comparison between countries of all sizes.

In the final calculation, foreign direct investment and portfolio capital flows are given a high weighting, due to their importance in globalisation. Internet usage and international telephone traffic are also given a high weighting reflecting their importance in the exchange of ideas.

Source: www.foreignpolicy.com; www.atkearney.com

Introduction

As we commence the new millennium, the world is becoming increasingly globally linked in terms of migration of production, technology, capital, people, information and business. Some businesses have been operating globally for many years; IBM and Nestlé are examples. However, in recent times the pace of business globalisation has increased at an exponential rate.

As markets and companies become global they face a variety of different competitive situations. One organisation may need to adopt all the strategies discussed in Chapters 15 and 19 – sometimes simultaneously across a range of different markets – and certainly over time as its competitive position changes. Strategies will include greenfields development, alliances in some markets, acquisitions in others, and a variety of offensive and defensive moves in both new and existing markets. Strategy becomes increasingly complex and multidimensional, a mosaic of different strategies in different markets – a kind of 'global chess' tied together by an overall global mentality and strategy.

This chapter looks at globalisation from a small/medium-sized firm's perspective. It presents a framework for looking at global strategy. It also identifies the benefits and costs of globalisation and the steps involved in moving to a global marketing programme. Global firms wield tremendous power and many of them are larger in terms of capitalisation than most nations, as illustrated in Table 16.1.

Table 16.1 World's 100 largest economic entities

	Feb 2001 US$ billion	Change	Rank last year		Feb 2001 US$ billion	Change	Rank last year
1 USA	14,016	–15%	1	13 Australia	373	–7%	16
2 Japan	2,955	–31%	2	14 Sweden	306	–39%	12
3 UK	2,423	–14%	3	15 Taiwan	302	–31%	15
4 France	1,380	–10%	4	16 Microsoft (US)	290	–47%	11
5 Germany	1,241	–20%	5	17 Exxon Mobil			
6 Switzerland	738	+17%	10	(US)	282	–4%	20
7 Canada	700	–19%	6	18 Pfizer (US)	237	+88%	58
8 Italy	705	–16%	7	19 Citigroup (US)	233	+25%	33
9 Hong Kong	627	–1%	9	20 South Africa	218	–6%	27
10 Holland	600	–10%	8	21 Wal-Mart (US)	212	–27%	21
11 Spain	521	+14%	14	22 Royal Dutch			
12 General Electric				(Eur)	201	+6%	32
(US)	436	–12%	13	23 Worldcom (US)	192	+32%	49

Table 16.1 (*continued*)

	Feb 2001 US$ billion	Change	Rank last year		Feb 2001 US$ billion	Change	Rank last year
24 Brazil	192*	−20%	26	55 Total/Fina/Elf			
25 BP Amoco (Eur)	185	−5%	33	(Eur)	96	+1%	NR
26 Vodafone	184	+23%	52	56 Chevron/Texaco	93	+69%	NR
27 Intel (US)	182	−40%	19	57 Morgan Chase			
28 Finland	182	−25%	17	(US)	90	+40%	83
29 South Korea	180	−30%	23	58 AT&T (US)	88	(breakup)	41
30 AIG (US)	178	+6%	39	59 Berkshire			
31 IBM (US)	173	−19%	30	Hathaway (US)	87	+21%	90
32 Merck (US)	166	+4%	43	60 Oracle (US)	86	−44%	42
33 AOL/TimeWarner				61 BankAmerica			
(US)	159	−35%	25	(US)	86	−1%	72
34 GlaxoSmithKline				62 Eli Lilly (US)	86	+18%	87
(Eur)	155	+53%	69	63 ProcterGamble			
35 Singapore	151	−12%	38	(US)	86	−38%	51
36 SBS Comm (US)	145	−11%	40	64 Tyco/Mattel (US)	85	+57%	NR
37 Belgium	137	−12%	46	65 Ireland	84	+27%	79
38 Cisco (US)	136	−72%	18	66 Astrazeneca			
39 Verizon (US)	132	+39%	81	(Eur)	83	+14%	88
40 Toyota (Jap)	132	−27%	34	67 Wells Fargo (US)	82	+30%	NR
41 Mexico	138	−12%	45	68 China Mobile			
42 Johnson &				(HK)	80	−13%	73
Johnson (US)	129	−1%	55	69 EMC (US)	76	−29%	63
43 Nokia (Eur)	125	−47%	28	70 Fannie Mae			
44 Coca-Cola (US)	120	−17%	50	(US)	76	+21%	NR
45 Malaysia	117	−34%	36	71 Nestlé (Eur)	76	+3%	87
46 Bristol-Myers				72 BellSouth (US)	76	−14%	74
(US)	114	−12%	56	73 American Home			
47 Denmark	111	+6%	68	(US)	74	+1%	NR
48 Philip Morris				74 AT&T Wireless			
(US)	105	+84%	NR	(US)	71	(breakup)	41
49 Novartis (Eur)	104	−3%	67	75 Allianz (Eur)	71	+11%	NR
50 HSBC (HK)	103	+8%	71	76 Deutsche Tel			
51 Greece	101	−46%	35	(Eur)	71	−66%	29
52 Home Depot				77 Abbott Labs			
(US)	99	−35%	47	(US)	69	+23%	NR
53 Nippon T7T				78 Pharmacia/			
(Jap)	97	−65%	22	Monsanto (US)	76	+44%	NR
54 Roche/Genen				79 Morgan Stanley			
(Eur)	97	−10%	48	(US)	67	−15%	84

Table 16.1 (*continued*)

	Feb 2001 US$ billion	Change	Rank last year		Feb 2001 US$ billion	Change	Rank last year
80 Telefonica (Eur)	67	−20%	76	91 Texas Instruments (US)	59	−16%	85
81 Amgen (US)	67	+1%	97	92 **Chile**	59	−17%	71
82 **Norway**	65	+6%	NR	93 ING (Eur)	59	−1%	NR
83 UBS (Eur)	64	+12%	NR	94 Nortel (Can)	58	−57%	57
84 Dell Computer (US)	64	−51%	54	95 Amgen (US)	57	−14%	96
85 **Israel**	63	−22%	79	96 France Telecom (Eur)	57	−57%	53
86 Sun Microsystems (US)	62	−50%	60	97 Viacom/CBS (US)	57	+54%	NR
87 Pepsico (US)	62	+17%	NR	98 Qwest Comm (US)	57	+90%	NR
88 Sony (Jap)	61	−49%	61	99 Aventis (Eur)	56	+24%	NR
89 **Portugal**	61	−23%	80	100 Hewlett-Packard (US)	56	−50%	62
90 Vivendi/Univ (Eur)	61	+22%	NR				

Source: The Sydney Morning Herald, 31 March 2001, p. 32.

Globalisation

What is globalisation?

Globalisation is the process by which firms operate on a global basis, organising their structure, capabilities, resources and people in such a way as to address the world as one market. The objective in its purest sense is to serve the global market by maximising the capabilities and advantages that individual countries have to offer – manufacturing productivity, R&D capability, market access, attractive interest rates, marketing experience. Strategic decisions are not taken from any particular country's perspective, there is no nationality bias in senior management, and it involves ongoing global searches for technology, people and alliance partners from which global competitive advantage can be achieved. In practice, this is not absolute but a matter of degree. For instance, Nestlé operations around the world are influenced by the founding culture emanating from Switzerland, as are those of Hewlett-Packard flowing from Silicon Valley, and Nokia originating from Finland.

Globalism trends

A myriad of forces are coming together in the early 2000s which are triggering the globalisation of industries, companies and individuals. Trade blocs are forming which are consolidating market regions such as the triad of Europe, North America and Japan and the regions of Asia-Pacific, southern Africa and Latin America. Global communications and media are bringing information, services, cultures and brands to all corners of the world. Industries, such as finance, computers, telecommunications and media, have become global. The demise of the England-based Barings Bank in 1995 (through transactions to the Japanese stock exchange controlled in Singapore) illustrates the interconnectedness of the finance industry. This was first demonstrated with such force in the October 1987 stock market crash. The speed and impact of financial markets' 'tornado' effect on Indonesia, Malaysia, Thailand and Korea in 1998 demonstrate this again. The impact of the devaluation of currencies in the Asian region including Japan, South American countries such as Argentina and Brazil against the US dollar is affecting many economies as well as having potential impact on the US and Europe. The slowdown of the US economy and the demise of many of the fledgling dot-coms in 2000 and in 2001/02 has reverberated around the world.

A growing number of companies around the world are looking at their business in a global context. For some this means considering the company's markets and operations together within an integrated framework. For others it means standardising products and marketing programmes and rationalising research and development and production to create global economies of scale with tactical product/service marketing done on a country-by-country basis. For a growing number of firms it means transformation from domestic or multinational players to a single global entity operating seamlessly anywhere in the world.

Nokia has already become a global company. Its mobile products division operates as a world business. New products are rolled out worldwide in months rather than years. Manufacturing has been consolidated into fewer plants, operations have been standardised so production can be moved from place to place rapidly. Human resource policies are standardised to facilitate personnel transfers.

Global advertising is consolidated through fewer agencies that design world campaigns and adaptation to local markets (Moss Kanter, 1994). The massive global advertising, promotion and publicity campaign by Microsoft to launch Windows 95 (and then Windows 98 and 2000) simultaneously around the world illustrates the speed of market penetration that can be achieved in multiple markets.

A global strategy means that a company competes on the basis of its entire combination of competences, infrastructure and products in all its markets, rather than on a country-by-country basis. To do this effectively requires integration of activities and communication between managers in different countries. Implementing the company's global strategy requires less bureaucracy, flatter organisational structures, effective and quick communication and a clear understanding in each market area of the corporate vision.

Globalism as a philosophy

Globalism is a philosophy based on an integrated, standardised world where people buy, sell and share common products, services and ideas.

McLuhan's observation in 1967 that electronic media would recreate the world into a global village was a significant articulation of the premise that media in the form of television and radio would stimulate cultural convergence around the world.

Gradually this premise was applied to marketing strategy. More than 30 years ago, Robert Buzzell questioned which elements of multinational marketing strategy could be standardised. He pointed out that various benefits could arise from standardisation, including significant cost savings, consistency with customers, improved planning and control and the exploitation of more good ideas (Buzzell, 1968).

In 1983, Theodore Levitt presented a world with globalised markets where 'global companies will systematically shape the vectors of technology and globalisation into its great strategic fecundity' (cited in Montgomery and Porter, 1991, p. 204). He concluded that the world is being driven by technology towards a converging commonality making communication, transport and travel available to all. Most people are interested in the things they have discovered or seen via the new technologies. Globalism had entered the mindset of the international marketing strategist.

> *Kenichi Ohmae suggests that on a political map boundaries between countries may be clear, but a competitive map showing flows of financial and trading activity have transcended those boundaries. This is occurring through an ever speedier flow of information.*
>
> Source: **Kenichi Ohmae (1989a), in Montgomery and Porter (1991), p. 206.**

Kenichi Ohmae defined a global economy based on the 'Triad' groups of North America, Europe and Japan (now extended to include the newly industrialised countries of Asia) (Ohmae, 1985). He also advocated strategic alliances as a key business strategy for globalisation, both for the firm itself and for marketing products and services into the global 'Triad' markets (Ohmae, 1989b).

Hamel and Prahalad's *Competing for the Future* is a culmination of global business strategy grounded on strategic intent that typically searches for global dominance through the development and leverage of global core competences.

> *Organisations should view strategic intent as being the underling component of their strategic foundation. Hamel and Prahalad refer to this as a strategic architecture capstone. This strategic architecture aims at pointing organisations to a desired future position, however the strategic intent provides the fuel for the journey. The fuel is needed for both emotional and intellectual areas within the organisation. Thus strategic architecture is seen as the brain and strategic intent is the heart of the organisation.*
>
> Source: **Hamel and Prahalad (1994), p. 129.**

Hamel and Prahalad (1994) contend that core competences for a firm must pass three tests.

1 *Customer value.* A core competence must make a disproportionate contribution to customer-perceived value.
2 *Competitor differentiation.* To qualify as a core competence, a capability must be competitively unique.
3 *Extendability.* Core competences must be the gateways to tomorrow's markets.

Hamel and Prahalad reinforce the global strategy framework of strategic intent supported by core competences, with a model for global multistage competition.

Throughout the 1990s globalism has been embraced by a growing group of business strategists and developed to the point where there is a distinct sphere of global business strategy thought and application.

Often globalisation is regarded as synonymous with Americanisation because most of the world's global firms originated there. However, A.T. Kearney have developed a Globalisation Index which uses as measures of globalisation, foreign trade, Internet use, international telephone traffic and number of international visitors. Notably it excludes a nation's cultural impact on the rest of the world. The top 15 globalised countries according to the A.T. Kearney Index were Singapore, Netherlands, Sweden, Switzerland, Finland, Ireland, Austria, United Kingdom, Norway, Canada, Denmark, United States, Italy, Germany and Portugal.

Source: *USA Today*, 8 January 2001, p. 6a.

Motivations for globalisation

Companies that operate in global industries, where their strategic positions in specific markets are strongly affected by their overall global positions, must think and act globally. Thus, car firms must organise globally if they are to gain purchasing, manufacturing, financial and marketing advantages. Firms in a global industry must compete on a worldwide basis if they are to succeed.

Any of several factors might draw a company into the global arena. Global competitors might attack the company's domestic market by offering better products or lower prices. The company might want to counterattack these competitors in their home markets to tie up their resources. Or the company might discover foreign markets that present higher profit opportunities than the domestic market. The company's domestic market might be shrinking or the company might need an enlarged customer base in order to achieve economies of scale. Or it might want to reduce its dependence on any one market so as to reduce its risk. Finally, the company's customers might be expanding and require international servicing.

Before going into foreign markets, the company must weigh several risks and answer many questions about its ability to operate globally. Can the company learn to understand the preferences and buyer behaviour of consumers in other countries? Can it offer competitively attractive products? Will it be able to adapt to another country's business cultures and be able to deal effectively with foreign nationals? Do the company's managers have the necessary international experience? Has management considered the impact of foreign regulations and political environments? These questions have been discussed in detail in earlier chapters.

There are many reasons motivating firms to go global. Three reasons apply to most firms. First, competition and customers – in many industries, competitors can access customers almost anywhere. In contrast, many customers that are going global want their key suppliers to be there to service them. Second, technology evolves at different speeds in different countries. As a major driver of change and competitive advantage, it is no longer sufficient to source technologies from one country only. If a business is located close to leading-edge technology development, it is likely to be closer to the early adopters phase of new markets (as discussed in relation to lead users in Chapter 5). Third, economies of doing business are changing in terms of cost of funds, cost of labour, availability of specialised skills and opportunities for standardisation. As an example, manufacturing advantages for textiles moved from Hong Kong to Taiwan, Korea and Mauritius, then to China. A global approach enables the firm to plan for and respond to these changes in relation to both the costs and quality of its inputs.

Yip (1992) classifies the drivers of globalisation under four headings.

- *Market drivers.* These include rising expectations, converging per capita incomes, convergence of lifestyles and tastes, increasing travel, establishment of more world brands, emergence of global market segments (e.g. teenagers), the push to have global advertising campaigns and the Internet.
- *Cost drivers.* These include the push for economies of scale, accelerating technological innovation, advances in transportation, transferring operations to newly industrialising countries in search of lower labour costs and the increasing cost of product development relative to the market life of the product.
- *Government drivers.* These include the reduction in trade barriers, the formation of more regional trade groupings, privatisation of government businesses and the reduction in the number of state-dominated economies.
- *Competitive drivers.* These include the continuing expansion in world trade, increasing levels of foreign ownership, more companies seeking to operate on a global as opposed to a national basis and the formation of global strategic alliances.

Characteristics of the global firm

Daniels and Frost, in a paper entitled 'On Becoming a Global Corporation' (*Stage by Stage*, 1988) developed a typology for the global firm, the highlights of which are as follows:

- has a business concept rather than a geographic concept with a focus on how you do business rather than where you do business;
- is decentralised rather than centralised and is willing to do business in any location and does not worry about centralising activities in a particular location;
- adopts a holistic view of its operation and believes that any part of the business should reflect the whole of the business (i.e. its genetic code). The firm has shared values, attitudes and beliefs that are evident wherever it chooses to do business, and are apparent to its stakeholders;
- consciously eliminates the isolation that precludes the sharing of information and deliberately lowers the boundaries between members of its value chain;
- builds trust between members of the organisation and the networks in which the elements of the organisation are embedded so as to speed up communication and decision making and overcome the 'not invented here' syndrome;
- goes out of its way to be a good corporate citizen in the countries in which it operates, and caters to local tastes without sacrificing economies of scale;

- operates as a coordinator among members of its network of companies rather than as a controller. This enables the amplification and interpretation of communications and facilitates the sharing of experiences;

- actively works to remove duplication of facilities and achieve economies of scale by leveraging knowledge. This is reflected in its pursuing outsourcing;

- encourages horizontal communication within the group from one level to another, rather than vertical communication from operating level up to CEO, across to CEO in a different country, then down to operating level in the other country;

- understands the worldwide economics of the businesses in which it is involved and engages in cross-subsidisation between areas of activity as required with a focus on long-term financial rewards rather than short-term gains.

Global or multinational?

One of the most vigorous debates in international marketing is the preference for multi-national or global marketing. For the strategist, this debate raises many key questions including:

- Which approach provides a better picture for developing future competitive position – an aggregation of several national and industry competitive position models or a model that starts with an overall global competitive position?

- Which elements of the marketing mix or aspects of the value chain can be effectively standardised or modified to service global customer sets?

- Which external or environmental variables (such as economical, political, legal and cultural variables) require analysis that goes below a global perspective to a regional or national level?

- What is the impact of global telecommunications, media and computing on the development of effective international competitive marketing strategy?

- How does a multinational firm convert to a global company?

- Is true globalisation really ever possible – or even desirable?

The issues relevant to the standardisation versus adaptation debate were discussed in Chapter 8. Although the issue has been vigorously debated, there is increasing recognition that a global strategy can possess sufficient flexibility to have a standardised business strategy and yet still market and deliver products adapted for many different markets. Quelch and Hoff (1986) (in Barnevik and Moss Kanter, 1994) developed a Global Marketing Planning Matrix accommodating both standardisation and adaptation. This matrix is presented in Figure 16.1.

Now companies do not just need to debate over whether they are going to standardise their products or customise their products for the potential global market. There is a new manufacturing technique that with the help of the Internet and advanced machinery technology will allow individual customers to design their own products. It's called mass customisation and is now a serious competitive issue in the global marketplace. The companies that are involved in mass customisation are instantly global because they use interactive websites to reach global customers. See International Highlight 16.1.

Figure 16.1   Global planning matrix

		ADAPTATION		STANDARDISATION	
		FULL	PARTIAL	FULL	PARTIAL
Business functions	Research and development				
	Finance and accounting				
	Manufacturing				
	Procurement				
	Marketing				
Products	Low cultural grounding High economies or efficiencies				
	High cultural grounding High economies or efficiencies				
	High cultural grounding Low economies or efficiencies				
Marketing mix elements	Product design				
	Brand name				
	Product positioning				
	Packaging				
	Advertising theme				
	Pricing				
	Advertising copy				
	Distribution				
	Sales promotion				
	Customer service				
Countries Region 1	Country A				
	Country B				
	Country C				
Region 2	Country D				
	Country E				

16.1 **International highlight**

Global market of one

At the forefront of the mass customisation revolution are companies like Dell Computer (www.dell.com). Since 1996 a significant portion of Dell's business has come from people who visit its website to customise their made-to-order PCs. Despite the technology companies' down-turn in 2001, Dell still maintained relatively strong profitability. Dell's initial focus was to cater for the business market or those purchasing their second computer. The thinking was that online customisation required the customer to know at least some basic requirements for their

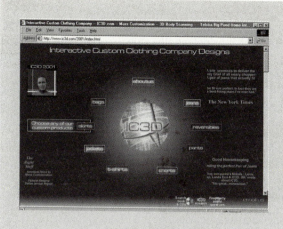

'to be configured' PC. Also, typical business users in most cases have their own IT departments who fine-tune their company's hardware to organisational needs. Therefore, if a problem arose with their company's PC, in most cases they would solve the problem on their own before consulting Dell. As a result the servicing costs of Dell were kept to a minimum.

Following this trend Gateway 2000 in the US (www.gateway.com) established a similar business model. However, to avoid competing head-on with Dell, its focus was two-fold – the individual customer and small to medium-sized business. As a result these two companies have different cost structures and different customer segments. A late entrant to online customisation was Compaq (www.compaq.com). Its bricks-and-mortar business and global alliances hindered its initial push to online customisation. However, Compaq succeeded in convincing both its distribution partners and customers about the benefits of online customisation. Even Apple has entered the game, lifting sagging fortunes with its build-to-order store. The advent of the mass customisation model also enabled small players/resellers to become customisation players by adopting the Dell model and configuring budget computers for their customers.

As customers become more empowered in the computer industry they can also apply the same principle to cars. Car manufacturers, such as Daimler Chrysler (Mercedes-Benz), Ford and BMW use their websites to stimulate demand for their products. These companies allow customers to configure their own car, make the order online, select the nearest dealer for pick up and then trace their car being built and trace its current transit location.

Another example of mass customisation has developed in the clothing industry. Interactive Custom Clothes (www.ic3d.com) launched two years ago offers a dizzying array of made-to-measure men's and women's jeans that give customers a plethora of choices – including style, fit and fabrics. Customers even choose the colour of rivets and pocket labels for a perfect individualised fit. The costs of the jeans vary from $65 for denim up to $250 for silk velvet. The measurements and specifications sent by the customer are placed into a computer intelligence system, which generates a pattern to the customer's size. The information is then downloaded and entered into an industrial cutter, which takes 42 seconds to cut the pieces of cloth needed to make the pair of jeans. They are then sent on to a sewing shop and shipped to the customer in about a week. Levi Strauss (www.levis.com) has also been offering its Personal Pair customised women's jeans. Meanwhile another company, Squash-Blossom (www.squash-blossom.com), has found success online by allowing customers to design their own children's clothes, make purchases and place orders online.

As consumers become more aware of the products and services offered in the global marketplace, companies will need to be able to give each individual exactly what they want. Because if they can't, other more advanced companies will. Most of us are probably using customisation tools every day   My Yahoo!, My Netscape, MySchwab. Does your favourite website customise the content to your needs and liking?

Source: Mathieson (1998); James (1999); Brady et al. (2001).

Global strategy framework

Every industry has aspects that are global or potentially global – global meaning that there are intercountry connections. A strategy is global to the extent that it is integrated across countries. This does not equate with any one element, such as global manufacturing or standardised global products. A global strategy is a flexible combination of many elements. George Yip (1992) suggests that a total global strategy usually has three separate steps or components:

● *Step one* is the development of a core strategy, which is the basis of the firm's competitive advantage.

● *Step two* involves the internationalisation of the strategy through expansion of activities and adaptation of the core strategy to several country markets.

● *Step three* integrates the strategy across countries. At this stage globalisation is achieved. This involves managing for worldwide business leverage and competitive advantage.

Yip's (1992) framework for global strategy is shown as Figure 16.2.

Industry globalisation drivers that reflect underlying market, cost, government and competitive conditions create the potential for a business to achieve the benefits of a global strategy. This occurs if it can set global strategy levers such as market coverage, standardised products and global marketing appropriately relative to the industry drivers and relative to the position and resources of the business and the parent company. The company's ability to implement a global strategy determines how substantial are the benefits to be achieved. The global strategy will also determine how the organisation should be structured and managed.

Globalisation strategy is multidimensional, requiring choices along at least five strategic dimensions.

1 *Market participation* relates to the choice of country markets and the level of activity in these countries.

Figure 16.2	A framework for global strategy

Source: Adapted from Yip (1992), p. 8.

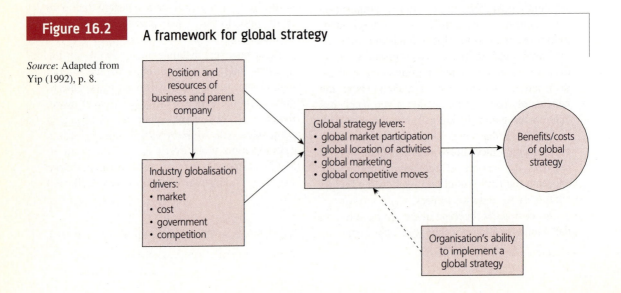

2 *Product/service standardisation* involves the extent to which standardisation or differentiation exists in each country.

3 *Location of value-adding activities* requires choices of location of each of those activities in the business's value chain from R&D to service back-up.

4 *Marketing* involves choices about worldwide use of brand names, advertising, sales strategies and service.

5 *Competitive moves* relate to the extent to which moves in specific countries form part of a global competitive strategy.

The benefits and drawbacks of global strategy need to be evaluated by firms in this situation. International Highlight 16.2 reflects the difficulties experienced by firms in developing and implementing a global strategy.

In summary, the benefits of global strategy fall into the four areas of cost reduction, improved quality of products and programmes, enhanced customer preference and increased competitive leverage.

Drawbacks generally lie in standardisation of products, services and processes, which may not meet the needs of a specific country's customers well. Also competitive positions may substantially differ between countries, making some strategies much less effective in specific countries than in other countries. Management and coordination costs may also be significant through the creation of additional overheads and reporting requirements.

16.2 International highlight

Trials and tribulations of globalisation

Opponents of globalisation claim that poor countries are losers from global integration. A new report from the World Bank challenges that proposition. The report suggests that if you divide poor countries into those that are 'more globalised' and those that are 'less globalised', with globalisation measured simply as a rise in the ratio of trade to national income, you find that more globalised countries have seen income per person fall.

Between 1945 and 1980, the World Bank reckons, economic integration was concentrated among rich countries. Since 1980 that has changed. Manufactured goods rose from 25% of poor country exports in 1980 to more than 80% in 1998. This integration was concentrated in two dozen countries – including China, India and Mexico – that are home to 3 billion people. Over the past two decades, these countries have doubled their ratio of trade to national income. In the 1990s their GDP per head grew by an annual average of 5%. Life expectancy and schooling levels increased.

Another 2 billion people live in the rest of the developing world, where the story is rather different. In these 'less globalised' countries, including much of Africa, the ratio of trade to national output has fallen. In the past decade, income per head has shrunk, and the number of people in poverty has risen. In short, the poor countries that are in the biggest trouble are those that have globalised the least. The challenge for development – and the World Bank – is to reverse this marginalisation.

Source: 'Globalization, Growth and Poverty', World Bank policy research report, December 2001.

The globalisation of an industry can be used to advantage as we see in the trans-formation of Foster's Brewing Group.

A different global brew from Foster's

The purchase of Beringer Wine Estates of California has transformed the Foster's Brewing Group from an Australian brewer into an international beverage company. Foster's acquired Beringer at a time when there were moves towards rationalisation of the Australian wine industry so that there would be fewer, bigger producers with the scale to handle a big export business and supply multinational retailers. Faced with the prospect of growth levels in the beer business of somewhere between inflation and 5% in the financial year 2000/01, Foster's set out to find another growth engine for the company. Growth through acquisition of a foreign brewer was considered but, according to CEO Kukkel [sic], the countries Foster's would be comfortable entering had mature beer markets and with those having the right growth profile for beer, either the country risk or the currency risk was unacceptable to the firm. Any new acquisition was to be in the international market. With 90% of company earnings and assets in Australia, Foster's wanted to spread its geographic risk. The transformation of Foster's into a global beverage business is even more remarkable considering that it only entered the wine business in 1996 with the purchase of Mildara-Blass.

Source: BRW, 10 November 2000, pp. 72–78.

Basic competitive strategy profiles

Most of the basic competitive strategy profiles described in Chapter 15 apply in a global context. Also the *built-to-last* characteristics proposed by Collins and Porras (1994) should be considered and the research findings of Treacy and Wiersema (1995) on market leaders apply.

Global leader strategy

Innovator in technologies, products and markets with high global share and wide country market coverage.

Microsoft, Cisco, Coca-Cola, Intel and Nokia are clear global leaders in their respective markets. Each adopts aggressive global strategies designed to be ahead of competitors in new expanding markets. Intel and Boeing lead in their respective technologies. Microsoft, through a range of alliances with computer makers, dominates the operating systems and application software for PCs. Coca-Cola's focus on brand management, worldwide coverage and intensive distribution and advertising makes it the leading and most profitable soft drink company in the world. Nokia's brand positioning segmentation and product line strategy has made it a global leader in mobile phone handsets. Cisco dominates the supply of routers and equipment associated with the Internet.

Global challenger strategy 1

Frontal or encirclement attack on the leader in all markets with increasing country market coverage and high global share but less than the leader.

Komatsu is a major threat to Caterpillar's leadership as is Pepsi's challenge to Coca-Cola in many of its major markets. News Corporation is a challenger in many of its media markets around the world – film, television, newspapers, and cable and satellite networks.

Global challenger strategy 2

Flanking or bypassing world leader with increasing country market coverage and high global share but less than the leader.

Burger King's challenge to McDonald's and Mobil Oil's to Shell involve strategies to map out new geographic markets in which the leaders are weak.

Global follower strategy

Rapid imitation of leader or challenger with moderate country market coverage and emphasis on price sensitive markets. The result is overall moderate share with high shares in selected country markets.

Examples include Hyundai, Daewoo and Sanyo.

Global niche strategy 1

Rapid penetration of narrow market segments by selective targeting of country markets and a small share of the overall market.

Examples include BMW, Toshiba (laptops), Vodafone and IKEA (furniture).

Global niche strategy 2

Infiltration, slow penetration of selected narrow markets with focus on selected country markets and a low share of the overall market.

Many food products fall into this category – wine, cheese, beer and dairy products.

Global collaborator strategy

Innovator in research and development of technologies, products and markets, sets standards and shares them with other firms. This shows small or moderate country market shares, but high shares when all strategic 'standards users' are included.

For example, Hewlett-Packard sells many of its competitors' products to provide its customers with tailored solutions in its 'network systems' division. Sony provides Trinitron screens to PC vendors as well as for sale in its own products. Other companies generating sales and share growth through collaboration are Philips and Canon.

The pitfalls of global marketing

Once the global strategy is right, the pitfalls of global marketing lie in implementation. This may involve a combination of vertical integration, joint ventures and alliances depending upon regulatory, competitive and market conditions in target countries. Global niche strategies, particularly, are likely to require alliance arrangements as a means of leveraging resources. There are several critical success factors to be considered to avoid the pitfalls in global marketing.

Key success factors are both external and internal. External factors relate to market, competitive, regulatory and industry conditions, which provide opportunities in world markets for a profitable fit to the company's competences. These external factors must be considered in the context of future conditions. For instance, major world car manufacturers competed for the contract to produce the 'Chinese People's Car' on the basis of expected growth in purchasing power and progressive deregulation of this massive market.

However, many of the success factors are internal. First, they involve attitude. People in the company must perceive it as a global operation treating the world as one market and the competitors as global. Second, the company must develop global strategic capability. This requires information processing capability including development of systems for tracking political changes, technological innovation, threatening competitive moves having global significance, and analytical sophistication of managers. Probably the greatest challenges involve the development and understanding of a shared vision and corporate culture and identity by people in different countries and divisions which can be translated into managing innovation and strategic change. Global teams working on R&D, new product roll-outs, and common service strategies, need to facilitate coordination across functions and countries. This is a major challenge for even the most experienced global companies.

A number of issues and questions need to be looked at by marketers in the context of implementation of global marketing.

Can a global marketing approach embrace both

(a) positioning the same product differently in each national market, and

(b) positioning the product the same way in each national market, but modifying the product to meet the needs of each market?

The answer to this is: think global – act local.

Global marketing implies some form of standardisation. Is the potential for standardisation (with respect to any or all of the marketing mix) greater for certain types of products than it is for others?

Global marketing implies that world wants are becoming homogenised, and proponents point to global customer segments and global brands targeting those segments. Are these products of general appeal, or are they products aimed at a relatively restricted upscale international customer segment?

Global marketing implies that customers behave the same way in different countries. Do the same market segments exist in all countries and, if so, are they of the same significance? Alternatively, are similarities in customer behaviour restricted to a relatively limited number of target segments while for the most part there are substantial differences between countries?

Global marketing implies a universal preference for low price at acceptable quality. However, what does this mean for:

(a) the drivers of brand preference?

(b) the impact of government subsidies/duties on a price positioning strategy?

(c) a standardised low price being 'overpriced' in some countries and 'underpriced' in others?

Global marketing implies economies of scale. How far is this moderated by technological developments and demand differences, which require more tailored marketing mix approaches?

Global marketing may not take into account external constraints such as:

(a) government and trade restrictions;

(b) the nature of marketing infrastructure in each country;

(c) interdependencies with resource markets, like availability of raw materials or low cost and skilled labour;

(d) the competitive situation in each market.

Globalisation from a macro perspective

The previous discussion has focused solely on globalisation from the perspective of the firm, i.e. a micro perspective. Such a perspective implies that globalisation is inevitable, it is the way of the future, and that it will dictate a nation's future economic policies. US texts on international marketing, usually written from the perspective of transnational firms, put a positive spin on it. They argue it is inevitable for reasons as varied as rising fixed costs, the rapid dissemination of information, the need to increase expenditure on R&D to bring new products to market, the rapid dispersion of technology, shortening product life cycles, converging consumer tastes and the increased value being placed by the share market on brand equity.

In such an environment, globalisation is essential from a profit perspective because it facilitates serving customers on a global basis, in bringing products to market more quickly, being able to introduce products into several countries simultaneously, and reducing promotion costs by having a single brand. Such a micro perspective on globalisation leads to it being viewed in terms of profitability considerations only. Firms, however, have many stakeholders other than their shareholders and it is relevant to view globalisation in the context of other stakeholders as well, in view of the pervasive effect it is alleged to have on the lives we all lead. From a macro perspective, the spin on globalisation does not appear to be as positive. Figure 16.3 illustrates this.

In Figure 16.3 the top line represents the rapid growth since 1980 in financial assets as measured by stock market capitalisation. The second line shows the rise in GDP, being the market value of output of goods and services that bring about growth in

Source:
D. Korten (1999)
dkorten@bainbridge.net.
Reproduced with
permission of David
Korten.

Figure 16.3	Globalisation – a macro view

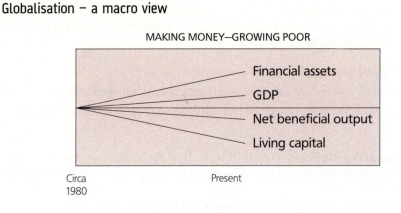

Circa 1980   Present

corporate profits and thence in share prices. As can be seen, GDP growth has not been as rapid as that in financial assets. The third line shows 'net beneficial output' when GDP is discounted to allow for expenditures on products harmful to society, defence expenditures and depreciation. The net beneficial output since 1980 has in fact declined.

Globalisation has also had a number of social costs, e.g. when rationalisation by transnational firms results in unemployment in a location. Therefore when these social costs which include resource depletion, social fragmentation and environmental degradation are taken into account, what Korten refers to as living capital has substantially declined during the two decades when globalisation has rapidly risen. His analysis indicates that a macro perspective on globalisation is different from the micro perspective. This issue can be explored at the social/cultural level, the economic/financial level, the political/legal level and the technological level.

Social/Cultural

The UK, Germany, France and Holland are considered multicultural nations from a European perspective. However, globalisation promotes homogeneity of culture, not the celebration of diverse individuality as with multiculturalism. Each country has its national icons, many of which take the form of brands or companies. Globalisation causes a loss of such icons as when successful local firms are acquired by transnational companies (TNCs). The loss of such icons impacts on cultural identity. Also, globalisation often results in importing the cultural baggage of other nations. This is exacerbated when the content of the local media is dominated by international interests. In these circumstances, globalisation can be synonymous with Americanisation, with consequent reduction of other nations' cultural identity.

Economic/Financial

Research shows that, overall, TNCs do not create employment in other countries, nor shift production away from developed to developing countries (Martin and Schumann,

1997). Although the top 500 firms in the world account for 25% of global production, they only account for 0.1% of the global workforce. Globalisation is accentuating wealth divisions in many societies throughout the world. This is evidenced in higher salaries paid to chief executive officers (a trend led by TNCs), by an expanding gap between salaries paid in commercial/technical sectors and those paid in the social service/education sectors, and by urban areas becoming richer and rural areas poorer. TNCs are able to exert influence on governments by shifting or threatening to shift capital from one country to another.

Political/Legal

Globalisation calls into question the democratic process as it exposes countries to influences by 'non-elected' bodies such as the World Trade Organisation and the International Monetary Fund. These bodies, however, are subject to influence by countries from whom the majority of TNCs come. Furthermore, there is opportunity for 'non-elected' TNCs to influence local governments via lobbying and contributions to party funds. This could result in an eventual change in the focus of local governments from looking after the citizens that elect it to protecting the interests of the TNCs that fund it. Globalisation can also become an excuse to impose 'western' norms on other countries, such as those relating to employment, worker safety and human rights. TNCs are able to evade national laws as they relate to various elements of the marketing mix, on local subsidiaries' contribution to the balance of payments by exporting, on controls over imports and exports to protect local firms. Finally, do global firms make a contribution to host countries sufficient to compensate for the costs of social dislocation caused when the dictates of their global activities bring about rationalisation or elimination of a local operation in another country?

Technology

TNCs often supply outmoded plant and equipment when they invest in international markets. The development of the motor vehicle industries in India and Iran were retarded for years when UK firm Leyland shipped plant to India to build the Morris Isis, and Hillman shipped plant to build the Hillman Hunter in Iran. TNCs often ship to developing countries products banned for sale on health or safety grounds in the home country. Finally TNCs can use their power to challenge intellectual property protection at the national level if it suits their commercial convenience.

When the impact of globalisation on the marketing mix is considered, further macro issues come to light. For countries with few global firms, it is appropriate to consider how relevant it is to such countries. Certainly, as has been pointed out, SMEs in these countries have to compete with global firms in international markets and in their own markets; and they have to compete with the subsidiaries of global firms. Yet is globalisation as relevant to firms in these countries as it is to firms in countries that have spawned most of the world's transnational companies? We consider this proposition in relation to each element of the marketing mix below.

Product. There is a problem regarding standards. Whose standards for a product should apply? Should they be the standards drawn up in host country or global standards reflecting the interests of TNCs that are lobbied by their governments via international trade forums such as the World Trade Organisation? Globalisation can retard innovation within a country. With rationalisation of activities between countries in which the TNC operates, it might be decided to have all R&D for the firm undertaken outside the host country. Another product-related problem with globalisation is that the country of origin and national identity of products becomes masked. Products previously actually made in the host country may no longer be manufactured there with globalisation, yet the illusion of local manufacture is created by phrases such as 'designed in', 'assembled in', 'fabricated in', etc.

Promotion. With globalisation, messages are increasingly received from sources outside the country. Such promotional messages may not be sensitive to either the culture or social circumstances of the country and may arouse the ire of the elected government of that country because that government has less control over the messages its citizens receive. This is particularly the case when the offending messages beamed from outside the country breach local government regulations on promotion and advertising. China has expressed concern over this and the fact that the messages received may have a destabilising effect on its regime especially in making its citizens discontented because they cannot have what people have in other countries. Global firms are increasingly promoting themselves via sponsoring global events such as World Cup Football, which can have the effect of diverting sponsorship from local to global events to the detriment of local sporting and cultural groups and possibly of local firms.

Pricing. Corporate citizens of any country should pay a reasonable economic rent for operating in that country. Globalisation has resulted in some TNCs evading their responsibilities in this connection, with the result that the taxation burden falls more heavily on local firms. Financial engineering and operation of the global money market facilitates such evasion. Some global firms avoid their taxation obligations via transfer pricing as discussed in Chapter 11. Global firms are able to set the prices to be charged in the host country by reference to their global strategy and not by reference to the local market. In implementation of this global pricing approach they may evade local government-imposed price controls and regulations by dumping, price fixing and price discrimination. As a consequence of their operation in the local market, foreign government laws regarding competitive pricing are imposed on subsidiaries of TNCs – e.g. the US Anti Trust Act.

Distribution. In general, because of the power they wield, when TNCs enter a country they may take over control of established channels or reduce the number of stages in such channels, thus creating intermediary unemployment. When they set up their own intermediary operations these are often less amenable to local government control. The same applies to physical distribution, and global firms now account for an increasing percentage of transport and the charges that are set for it. In cases where TNCs control distribution channels in a country, the government of that country is likely to encounter greater difficulty in tracking and taxing the distribution of goods.

An understanding of the macro aspects of globalisation is essential when implementing a firm's global strategy in international markets. It sensitises managers to how such globalisation efforts might be perceived at the local level. It enables an assessment of the likelihood that the local government might engage in defensive intervention and impose regulations on the operation of the global firm's subsidiary, or offensive intervention and nationalise the operation of the global firm's local subsidiary.

The growth of Asian competitors

Few Asian corporations (other than Japanese) are global. Samsung from Korea is one. This chaebol (conglomerate) has a world-leading 17% share of the computer chip market. But like many small firms exposed to global markets it is being radically restructured to maintain profitability (Ihlwan and Bremmer, 1998). However, there are many companies within the region that are becoming more global.

Many businesses venturing into Asian markets are finding that their toughest competitors are not other western multinationals or Japanese companies, but lesser-known Asian companies based in other Asian countries. These Asian competitors are using quite different strategies. Although the strategies differ by industry, home country and company culture, Williamson (1997) reports there are eight strategies that have been identified as general rules to be studied by any company intending on competing successfully within Asian markets. These are summarised.

1. It's always best to be a first mover

Emerging multinationals believe that it is better to be the first in a market and enjoy the first pick of partners, sites and resources, as well as being able to establish products and brands cheaply, before the marketing channels become cluttered with competing offers. They believe that although some mistakes will be made in the first instance, the first mover advantages will allow the company to fix these mistakes with time to recover before other competitors can take the dominant position.

To justify the early entry into markets, many Asian companies imagine the worst case scenarios of entering a new market or industry. If they believe they can weather the worst case scenario then the worst will pass and the upside will develop as time goes on. This first mover approach has seen many Asian companies entering frontier Asian markets, such as Cambodia, Myanmar and Vietnam, well before western companies do. For example in 2001 Taiwanese companies' cumulative investment in Vietnam was higher than all the European Union countries combined and more than double the total investment of either Japan or the US.

2. Control the bottlenecks

Bottlenecks occur when propriety technologies, specialised skills, distributions networks and resources are limited. Many Asian companies have been investing in these areas to take control of the bottlenecks and also influence their competitors' volume growth and cost structures. This leverage has been especially great in the emerging markets that grow rapidly.

Taiwan's Acer company is using this approach in the personal computer business. There has been a mass of entrants into this market, with new competitors moving into the assembling of new computers. This has caused a severe bottleneck in other links in the industries value chain, in sourcing key component technologies, manufacturing key components at high volumes, brand building, logistics and channel management. Acer's strategy is to invest in these bottlenecks through global brand building, advanced logistic and distribution systems and highly efficient design and manufacture of key components.

3. Build walled cities

At the core of most of the large emerging multinationals are walled cities – one or more industries in which the company holds a dominant position. Some examples are the Indonesian company Salim Group which dominates Indonesia's cement industry, controls more than 60% of the flour milling and has approximately 85% of the noodle market. Charoen Pokphand of Thailand controls more than 50% of large-scale production of animal feed in Thailand.

These walled cities provide protection against competitive attack, often with the aid of governments with exclusive licences or concessions granted for these companies. Walled cities also provide a reliable source of free cash flow that can be used for investment in international expansion.

Traditionally, walled cities were found in the company's home country, as with the examples mentioned above; however, now some emerging Asian multinationals intend to build walled cities in pan-Asian product segments. For example, the Salim Group plans to build a pan-Asian and ultimately global position in the oleochemicals. This move involves having plants in the Philippines, Batam Island off Singapore, China and Malaysia, as well as the acquisition of 50% of an Australian producer of oleochemicals and interest in a producer in Germany. These actions are motivated by more than just market share motives, it comes from the desire *'to be the head of a chicken*, [rather] *than the tail of a cow'*. Dominance in large segments is preferable; however, growth through dominance in multiple smaller segments (the head of the chicken) is always considered better than being a follower in a large business driven by others (the tail of the cow).

4. Bring market transactions in-house

Asian nations have poorly developed markets for inputs (e.g. raw materials and energy) and services (e.g. distribution, logistics and financing) which reflect Asian companies' preference for controlling the sources of supply, distribution and ancillary services. This has been a powerful force behind vertical integration in Asia and the formation of conglomerates.

One example is Formosa Plastics in Taiwan. It is vertically integrated in the polyvinyl chloride (PVC) plastics industry, from basic feedstocks right through to finished goods. As for conglomerates, the empire of Robert Kuok, a Chinese Malaysian entrepreneur is a good example. The empire extends into areas as diverse as sugar plantations, tin mining, TV broadcasting and newspaper publishing.

In 2001, Jiang Miankeng was the most influential person shaping technology in China. He organised private funding to launch China Netcom in 1999 to compete with a new broadband network against former monopoly China Telecom. He also partnered with Taiwanese billionaire Winston Wong to build semi-conductor plants in Shanghai (Lee-Young, 2001).

Emerging Asian multinationals actively seek involvement in upstream and downstream industries, while western corporations are outsourcing non-core activities. Asian companies in contrast take comfort in knowing they control their sources of supply. This also helps them to build strong trusting relationships, which are often bolstered by cross-shareholdings and family or ethnic ties. This is also reflected in more cross-border Asian alliances.

5. Leverage your host government's goals

Asian governments will give monopoly rights, concessions and protection to companies whose goals are aligned with theirs. Asian governments believe that regulations to steer their country's goals and growth in the right direction are needed.

One of Asia's goals is to reduce the migration from the rural areas into the city by increasing employment opportunities in the country regions. Chareon Pokphand's successful entry into the poultry business was due to the improved income opportunities from this business to country areas. This is also the reason for Chareon Pokphand's welcomed expansion into 80 other regions in China. The message is clear: making the government your silent partner is an important part of the new Asian game.

6. Encourage company networks and information sharing

In Asian companies the extended family is the core of the cooperative business network. This means that many companies are run like family dynasties, often under a powerful patriarch. From this system has sprung the extended networked organisations that rely on continual information sharing among all their business units. The flow of information is two-way which serves as a strong competitive advantage for those companies in the family as they have access to technology and market intelligence, which is relatively hard to come by in Asian countries. Acer is one company that takes a networked approach.

7. Commercialise on others' inventions

Western companies' lead in technological advancement was out of reach of Asian companies a decade ago. Today the gap between leading technological companies in the US or Japan and Asia has closed. Many Asian companies are now developing direct links, via partnerships, investment or alliances, with companies on the technological cutting-edge.

The emerging Asian competitors excel at bringing technologies, pioneered by cutting-edge technology companies, into development and production at very low costs. Samsung in Korea and Creative Technology in Singapore are examples of this.

8. Asian companies rewrite the rules

The most common way western companies have entered Asian markets in the past is by joint ventures with Asian companies, where the western company usually held more power and gained much more from the partnership through connections with local distribution and political networks. Asian companies have now grown and they have also begun to rewrite the ways in which joint ventures are formed and managed, which presents western companies with yet another challenge when entering the Asian markets of today.

The emerging Asian multinationals have built up strong finances, resources, systems and technical skills. This means they want much more from their partnerships with western companies. They are looking for companies that provide them with more resources and partners that provide them access to other profitable markets. They want equal partnerships or partnerships that see them as the lead player.

These strategies, while relevant, are being reviewed in the light of the Asian financial crisis in terms of establishing which are most critical for competitive success.

Internet infusion

The Internet has stimulated globalisation because it advantages countries with leading technology such as the US from which a majority of global firms emanate. The drivers of Internet demand are communications (e-mail and information) and commerce. The enablers of such demand are access, security and bandwidth and these require significant investment – investment which global firms may be best able to provide.

Jupiter Communications (see Plumley, 2000, p. 19), depict the evolution of e-commerce from domestic to global as shown in Figure 16.4.

Globalisation is likely to be influenced by a number of factors in the e-business environment.

Global integration. This is driven by supply-based pressures. There is no evidence that e-business has removed the underlying pressures impacting upon business in the global environment – environmental, technological, economic and cultural. These are still there but they impact in a different way due to e-business, e.g. there is a cultural preference for cash over credit in India and China; and there is weak protection of intellectual property rights for information given over the Internet.

Local responsiveness. This is driven by demand-based pressures. These can be expected to evolve as consumer access widens, and if the promise that technology changes the nature of the relationship between customer and producer proves true. Extraneous factors may operate – the reason why online shopping in Europe is more successful than in the US is because retail opening hours are much shorter.

Transaction completeness. This is driven by contracting pressures to outsource as many non-core activities as possible. The Internet facilitates this. Given the fewer complications with international commodity trade, this has proved amenable to Internet trading and is reflected in Internet auctions replacing global commodity exchanges.

Figure 16.4

From domestic to global e-business

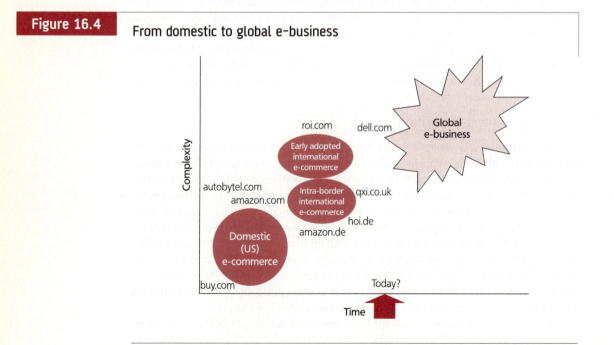

Summary

Products, markets, companies and lifestyles are becoming more global as people travel and communication links provide 'real time' reporting of events. This is particularly common in sport and is exemplified by the Soccer World Cup Final played between Germany and Brazil in Japan in July 2002. Hundreds of millions watched on television, global sponsors advertised, players became household names in all corners of the globe and the soccer culture with all its associated products took another step towards full globalisation.

For companies to take advantage of these trends they need to develop a global philosophy and think of the world as one marketplace. However, for almost all businesses the steps to globalism are progressive, the risks and capability limitations act as constraints, and the economic shocks such as those experienced in Asia and Japan in the late 1990s provide setbacks.

The issue of standardised versus adapted product offerings continues to be assessed by most companies but the move towards mass customisation is changing the economics of adaptation.

A global strategy framework assists firms in assessing the external factors, internal capabilities and the benefits and costs of global strategies. This is reviewed in the light of different competitive strategies – global leaders, challengers, followers, nichers and global collaborators.

Despite the downturn in Asian economic growth, there are many successful Asian companies becoming more global.

Ethics issue

You are the international marketing manager of an import/export company based in Hong Kong. You trade globally in top brand merchandise sourcing products from global manufacturers and sell to retail chains in the US, Europe, Japan, South-East Asia and Australia. You are aware of a ruling by the European Court of Justice in Luxembourg in July 1998 outlawing the distribution of upmarket brands to discount chains in Europe without the prior agreement of manufacturers. You are also aware that your main competitor disregards this ruling and sells at a discount in the so-called 'grey' market from its Asian base.

Large British and European discount chains have approached you, being outside the EU, to supply top brand products to them at a discount without the agreement of manufacturers.

These potential deals would launch your business into the big league and also ensure lucrative business in the US. Despite the deals' illegality, their size is tempting. What would you do?

Web workout

Question 1 Visit three car manufacturers of your choice. Compare their offerings in terms of customisation of their products to individual needs. Which one do you think has products more suited to the global market?

Question 2 Visit your favourite sports shoe manufacturer. Why is it your favourite shoe manufacturer? Would you expect it to custom-design shoes for you?

Websites

www.foreignpolicy.com

www.atkearney.com

www.fosters.com.au

www.ibm.com

www.microsoft.com

www.nortel.com

www.bt.co.uk

www.telstra.com

www.dell.com

www.gateway.com

www.compaq.com

www.ic3d.com

www.squash-blossom.com

www.mhhe.com/primis

www.businessweek.com

www.brw.com.au

www.visa.com

www.nokia.com

www.mcdonalds.com

www.exxon.com

www.vodafone.co.uk

Discussion questions

1 List the main factors driving businesses towards globalisation.
2 What are the main inhibitors to operating a global business?
3 How does the philosophy of globalism differ from multinational marketing?
4 What are the main management motivations for going global?
5 How valid is the step-by-step internationalisation process in a world in which some new businesses gain immediate global access through the Internet?
6 Using a specific industry like pharmaceuticals or the car industry, select a leading company to focus upon. Describe their global strategy framework with reference to Yip's model in Figure 16.2.
7 What macro issues are emerging in the debate on globalisation?

References

Brady, D., Kerwin, K., Welch, D. and Lee, L. (2001) 'Customising For The Masses', *Business Week*, 20 March; www.businessweek.com, accessed 30 June 2001.

Business Review Weekly (2000), 10 November, pp. 72–78.

Buzzell, R.D. (1968) 'Can You Standardise Multinational Marketing?', *Harvard Business Review*, pp. 103–107.

Collins, J.C. and Porras, J.I. (1994) *Built To Last: Successful Habits of Visionary Companies*, Harper Business, New York, 1994.

Daniels, J.L. and Frost, N.C. (1988) 'On Becoming a Global Corporation', *Stage by Stage*, Nolan, Norton & Co, One Cranberry Hill, MA.

Fletcher, R. (2000) 'The Impact of Globalisation on National Sovereignty', *Journal of Current Research in Global Business*, Vol. 2 No. 2, Fall, pp. 95–103. John A. Walker College of Business, Appalachian States University, North Carolina.

Hamel, G. and Prahalad, C.K. (1994) *Competing for the Future*, Harvard Business School Press, Boston, 1994.

Ihlwan, M. and Bremmer, B. (1998) 'Samsung: A King Without Money', *The Australian Financial Review*, 20 March, p. 31.

James, D. (1999) 'New Ease of Production Makes the Pursuit of Mass Rather Critical', *BRW*, 15 March; http://www.brw.com.au/newsadmin/stories/brw/19990315/1552.htm (accessed 20 June 2001).

Kearney, A.T. (2003) 'The Global Top 20', *Foreign Policy Magazine*, January-February.

Korten, D.C. (1999) 'The Dark Side of Globalisation: Financial and Corporate Rule', *Proceedings of the Annual Meeting of the Academy of International Business*, Charleston, SC, 22–24 November.

Lee-Young, J. (2001) 'The Digital Prince of China', *The Industry Standard*, pp. 38–39.

Levitt, T. (1983) 'The Globalization of Markets', *Harvard Business Review*, May–June, in Montgomery, C.A. and Porter, M.E. (1991) *Strategy – Seeking and Securing Competitive Advantage*, Harvard Business School Publishing, Boston, MA, p. 204.

McLuhan, M., Fiore, Q. and Agel, J. (2001) *The Medium is the Message*, Gingko Press, Inc., Corte Madera, California.

Martin, H.P. and Schumann, H. (1997) *The Global Trap*, Zed Books, London.

Mathieson, R. (1998) 'Market of One: Mass Customization Meets the Net', *E Business*, June; http://www.hp.com/Ebusiness/m_customization.html.

Moss Kanter, R. (1994) 'Afterword: What Thinking Global Really Means', *Global Strategies: Insights from the World's Leading Thinkers*, Harvard Business Review Book Series.

Ohmae, K. (1985) *Triad Power*, Free Press, New York, 1985.

Ohmae, K. (1989a) 'Managing in a Borderless World', *Harvard Business Review*, May–June, in Montgomery, C.A. and Porter, M.E. (1991) *Strategy – Seeking and Securing Competitive Advantage*, Harvard Business School Publishing, Boston, MA, p. 206.

Ohmae, K. (1989b) 'The Global Logic of Strategic Alliances', *Harvard Business Review*, March–April, in Barnevik, P. and Moss Kanter, R. (1994) *Global Strategies – Insights from the World's Leading Thinkers*, Harvard Business Review Book Series, Boston, MA, p. 109.

Ohmae, K. (1995) *The End of The Nation State*, Harper Collins, London, p. 80.

Plumley, D.J. (2000) Global eCommerce: The Market, Challenges and Opportunities, Browne Global Solutions, January.

Quelch, J.A. and Hoff, E.J. (1986) 'Customizing Global Marketing', *Harvard Business Review*, May–June, in Barnevik, P. and Moss Kanter, R., *Global Strategies – Insights from the World's Leading Thinkers*, Harvard Business School Publishing, Boston, MA, p. 181.

Treacy, M. and Wiersema, F. (1995) *The Discipline of Market Leaders*, Addison Wesley, Reading, MA, pp. 31–41.

USA Today (2001), 8 January, p. 6a.

Williamson, P.J. (1997) 'Asia's New Competitive Game', *Harvard Business Review*, September–October, pp. 55–67.

World Bank (2001) 'Globalization, Growth and Poverty', World Bank policy research report, December 2001.

Yip, G. (1992) *Total Global Strategies: Managing your Worldwide Competitive Advantage*, Prentice Hall, Ch. 1, pp. 1–29.

17

Relationships, networks and strategic alliances

Learning objectives

After reading this chapter, you should be able to:

- explain the network paradigm and the central role of relationships;

- describe different types of strategic alliances in international business;

- describe the new type of organisation known as the virtual organisation;

- outline the elements used to model how industries transform and develop;

- illustrate alliances that have been formed by market leaders, challengers, followers and specialists; and

- discuss the factors relevant to the success and failure of alliance relationships.

Revolution of the supply side

Business to business – B2B – Internet applications have revolutionised the way in which companies interact with their suppliers. By integrating systems and networks, companies within a supply chain have developed faster and more efficient transactions than ever before. Nowhere is this more evident than in procurement and many dot-com companies have sprung up purely to service this sector of the market.

One of the best known of these is BuildOnline, the first e-commerce site for Europe's $750 billion construction industry. Working on the premise that materials and services typically account for 65% of total construction cost, BuildOnline enables buyers and sellers to come together via an Internet marketplace. The site also allows all parties involved in a construction project to link up with one another enabling them to seamlessly manage every stage of the construction process from design and tender to building and maintenance, all online.

More recently, B2B e-commerce company CrossBrowse launched CateringBuyer.com. This e-marketplace is an independent trading site linking buyers and sellers in the catering industry. IBM assisted the company in developing a business model and provided management consulting along with support in applications development.

Another successful B2B venture is IngredientsNet.com. It has positioned itself as the world's first and most comprehensive B2B marketplace dedicated to the food industry. The Boston Consulting Group estimates that the global online B2B market will be worth $5 trillion in 2003. IngredientsNet.com predicts that at least 20% of this value will be traded online. Ingredients include raw materials for the food processing indurate, skimmed milk powder, butter, vegetable oils and flour.

The global marketplace treats these products as commodities, with often the only difference being price. The IngredientsNet.com B2B model took many of the non-price variables and brought together buyers and sellers whose only remaining 'haggle' related to price. One third of the participant companies are US firms with the remainder being European and include clients such as Nestlé, Kraft and Unilever.

Introduction

Successful international marketers have realised the vital role of strategic alliances, marketing relationships and competitive networks in their ability to expand their international businesses. For example, to develop and sustain profitable business in the Indian Ocean island of Mauritius it is essential for a firm to develop alliances and close relationships with at least one of three dominant companies – Rogers & Co. Ltd, Island Blyth and Harel Mallac & Co. Ltd. This will ensure access to hotels, supermarkets, sugar plantations, textile manufacturers, travel services, consulting and almost the entire import/export industry. Cross-directorships occur on the boards of all three companies as well as the Mauritius Commercial Bank – the dominant financial institution. A close personal relationship with just one senior director is enough to get access to this market. Close connections exist between all important government agencies and the political hierarchy. These three companies have close connections with South Africa and other African markets and can provide a gateway for the firm into African markets. This example provides a microcosm of the important elements in alliance strategies, which are discussed in this chapter.

It is important for the firm to see itself as part of a competitive network of inter-related firms bound together by relationships of mutual benefit. It is also important to see the emerging opportunities of information technology linkages creating 'virtual' organisations. This new form of organisation is made up of alliances held together by relationships between players and linked together by electronic communication and information networks. When viewed holistically it is possible to see how industries are becoming transformed. Alliance strategies incorporating these elements can create competitive advantage – whether for leaders, challengers, followers or niche market specialists. This chapter begins with an overview of networks, relationships and strategic alliances.

Relationships and networks

There is a marketing genre that emphasises the role of relationships and networks in international marketing as opposed to the more traditional marketing management approach. This new genre which had its origins in Europe (especially Scandinavia) is especially relevant when doing business in Asia where business has been conducted for centuries based on relationships as epitomised in concepts such as 'guanxi' (inside connections and personal ties). Although there is an element of opportunistic advantage in relationship marketing, there is usually an underpinning of personal liking, trust and loyalty.

Healey et al. (2001) explored the linkage between relationship marketing and networks. They arrived at the following classification.

Relationship marketing involves a dyadic buyer–seller relationship that tends to ignore the role of other elements in the distribution channel and the role of other stakeholders – it is only concerned with the focal relationship.

17.1 International highlight

The new relationship marketing perspective

Once upon a time . . .

. . . in a village in ancient China there was a young rice merchant, Ming Hua. He was one of six rice merchants in that village. He was sitting in his store waiting for customers, but business was not good. One day Ming Hua realised that he had to think more about the villagers and their desires, and not just distribute rice to those that came into his store. He understood that he had to provide villagers with more value and something different from what the other merchants offered them. He decided to develop a record of his customers' eating habits and ordering periods and to start to deliver rice to them.

To begin with, Ming Hua walked around the village and knocked on his customers' doors asking:

- how many members were there in the household;

- how many bowls of rice did they cook on any given day; and

- how big was the rice jar of the household.

Then he offered every customer:

- free home delivery; and

- a service to replenish the rice jar of the household at regular intervals.

By establishing these records and developing these new services, Ming Hua managed to create more extensive and deeper relationships with the villagers, first with his old customers, then with other villagers. Eventually the size of his business increased and he had to employ more people. Ming Hua spent his time visiting villagers and handling the contacts with his suppliers, a limited number of rice farmers whom he knew well.

The above story illustrates how Ming Hua, the simple rice merchant, through using what today would be called a relationship marketing strategy, changed his role from a transaction-oriented channel member to a value-enhancing relationship manager, thus creating a competitive advantage over rivals who continued to employ a traditional strategy. He included three typical tactical elements of a relationship strategy.

Source: Corbis.

1 The seeking of direct contacts with customers and other stakeholders such as rice farmers.

2 The building up of a database covering necessary information about customers and others.

3 The development of a customer-oriented service system.

It is possible also to distinguish three strategic elements of a typical relationship marketing approach:

1 Redefinition of the business as a service business and the key competitive element as service competition – i.e. competing with a total service, not just the sale of rice.

2 Looking at the organisation from a process management perspective and not from a functional perspective – i.e. managing the process of creating value for the villagers.

3 Establishing partnerships and a network to handle the whole service process – i.e. close contacts with well-known rice farmers.

Source: Grönroos, C. (1996) 'Relationship Marketing Logic', *Australasian Marketing Journal*, Vol. 4, No. 1, p. 8.

Neo-relationship marketing, although still dyadic, goes beyond the relationship between buyer and seller and includes all marketing relationships aimed at ensuring success. It includes both focal and connected relationships.

Network theories are more complex structures involving all elements that directly or indirectly influence a transaction and cater for the situation that international marketing can occur by the linking of a network in one country with a network in another.

The common element in the above is that of interdependent relationships rather than of one-off transactions.

Relationships have substance in that they must be recognised; they need to be managed; they can be a solution to a problem; they may involve a technical content in that they can result in the linking of production processes of two different firms; and they have a social content in that they involve trust, commitment and power. Relationships are assets in that they optimise the time spent and activities undertaken by both parties (e.g. if one party trusts the other, they do not need to spend time checking on credentials or pre-qualification); they provide access to the resources and skills of the other party; and they allow division of tasks between the parties. On the other hand, relationships have disadvantages in that they restrict the firm's autonomy, they require resources to manage, and the future of the firm can become dependent on others over whom the firm has no control.

Commitment to continue and develop a relationship is affected by many factors. Morgan and Hunt (1994) suggest these include trust, relationship benefits, shared values and relationship termination costs. An investigation of 136 international business relationships by Holm et al. (1996) shows that relationship profitability is directly affected by relationship commitment and indirectly through commitment by business network connections. They found that the relationship development process needs to be coordinated with ongoing processes in other connected relationships of the partners. Cooperative relationships such as formal alliances are more likely to be successful if the partners can bring their business networks into the alliance.

Relationships are connected to each other and form part of the firm's wider network. The consequent network is likely to have the following characteristics:

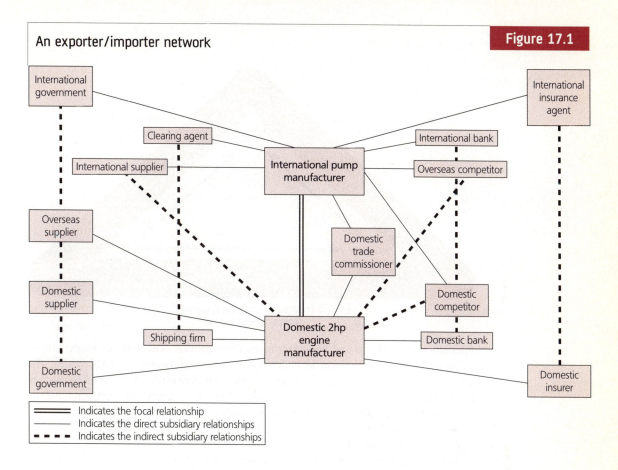

An exporter/importer network

Figure 17.1

- *reciprocity* – contributions of each party are not expected to be in balance for each specific transaction, but rather over the total relationship;
- *interdependence* – the parties are knowledgeable about each other and draw on this information when solving problems;
- *loose coupling* – while the network does not involve formal legal obligations, it does provide a reasonably stable framework for interaction and communication;
- *power* – this is used to exploit the interdependencies that exist in the network; and
- *boundedness* – because the network in which a firm is embedded in its own country becomes linked to the network of the importer or partner in the other country and that network in turn is linked to other networks, it is difficult to place a boundary around networks.

A simple illustration of the operation of networks in international marketing is provided in Figure 17.1 which illustrates a hypothetical transaction between an exporter of 2hp engines and an international manufacturer of pumps.

At the centre of the network approach is the concept of relationships, which implies interdependence, a medium- to longer-term time horizon, and the need for exporters and importers or alliance partners to develop knowledge about each other. This enables the firm both to export its products and to gain access to resources such as the

Figure 17.2 The network model

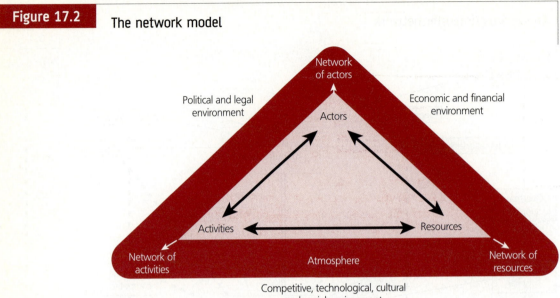

Political and legal environment

Economic and financial environment

Network of actors

Actors

Activities

Resources

Network of activities

Atmosphere

Network of resources

Competitive, technological, cultural and social environment

international salesforce and important market information. The network model shown in Figure 17.2 depicts the interdependence between actors, resources and activities. The network concept of actors carrying out activities that transform resources takes place in an atmosphere that encompasses the attitudes of the players towards each other and the relationship. Atmosphere includes elements such as trust, power and dependency. This all occurs in the wider environment which places pressure on the network and relationships as well as providing opportunities.

In an international marketing context competition usually occurs between networks. This is evident in the export market for cars when comparing Ford UK and Toyota Japan targeting the Thai market. Figure 17.3 reflects a network view of competition in which raw material and parts suppliers, advertising agencies, car manufacturers and dealers are closely tied to a network seeking to obtain customers. Even customers become part of that network after purchase when they return for car servicing, parts and exercise of warranties. Globalisation of this industry is at a stage where different elements of the value chain, from R&D to manufacture to distribution and sales, are centred around locations and skills bases that exhibit world's best practice and competence in these functions. These form part of the multiple networks that take the product range to its end-user markets. It is the total network and its interlinkages that enable a car manufacturer to compete at the point of sale in its various international markets.

Hence, an international network can be thought of as a process of building relations with other firms to create the necessary infrastructure for effective competition in international markets. These networks change over time with changes in the environment and the atmosphere between actors. Fletcher (1996) explored changes in the international networks within the context of countertrade in the Vietnamese coal and Vietnamese seafood industries. These and other studies indicate the relevance of network competition in an international marketing environment. When firms decide to develop alliance agreements networks become more formalised, usually with the intention of cementing longer-term relationships.

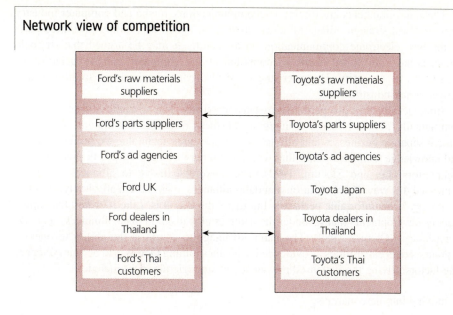

Network view of competition

Figure 17.3

Strategic alliances

Companies are combining resources, knowledge and technology to create new markets and restructure old ones. The alliance between the powerful Microsoft and telecommunications players in the Asian region to create new electronic networks is having a major impact on existing network services. The alliances occurring in imaging applications involving Kodak, Motorola, AT&T, Philips, Silicon Graphics and Apple illustrate the new types of alliances. Similarly, the emerging interactive TV market opportunity has brought together Time Warner, Sega, Toshiba, Matsushita and others. In a broader global media context, the union of AOL and Time Warner has combined 'old' economy and 'new' economy business (Hale, 2000).

AOL Time Warner Inc. is an integrated, Internet-powered media and communications company. The company was formed in connection with the merger of America Online Inc. and Time Warner Inc. on 11 January 2001. As a result of the merger, America Online and Time Warner each became wholly owned subsidiaries of AOL Time Warner. The company's fundamental business areas comprise America Online, consisting principally of interactive services, web brands, Internet technologies and e-commerce; cable, consisting principally of interests in cable television systems; filmed entertainment, consisting principally of interests in filmed entertainment and television production; networks, consisting principally of interests in cable and broadcast television networks; music, consisting principally of interests in recorded music and music publishing; and publishing, consisting principally of interests in magazine publishing, book publishing and direct marketing.

This indicates how companies need to combine competences to enable them to have a strong global position in future markets.

These developments are forcing telecommunications, media and computer industry firms to form strategic alliances across industries, aimed at building profitable parts of the new electronic communication infrastructure. It may be argued that strategic alliances have developed in the telecommunications, computer and media industries simply out of necessity. However, the trend also exists in the more traditional and conventional industries.

Strategic alliances are partnerships between firms. The strategic alliance partners contractually pool, exchange or integrate business resources for mutual gain. They remain separate businesses and aim to learn and acquire technologies, products, skills and knowledge from each other that would not otherwise be available to them or their competitors (Lei and Slocum, 1992). The inexorable move to alliances has been expressed this way: 'Globalisation mandates alliances, makes them absolutely essential to strategy. Uncomfortable perhaps – but that's the way it is. Like it or not, the simultaneous developments that go under the name of globalisation make alliances – entente – necessary' (Ohmae, 1989). The main advantage to a firm is the ability to operate beyond its own capabilities as evidenced in airlines joining One World or Star Alliance. The factors driving the increased prevalence of strategic alliances include:

- moving into new markets;
- filling knowledge gaps;
- pooling to gain operational economies;
- building complementary resource capabilities; and
- speeding up new product introduction (time-based competition).

Strategic alliances are now viewed as a more effective diversification strategy than the traditional conglomerate approach. Human relationships between alliance members are a major influence on the development and maintenance of strategic alliances, especially for senior management. The drivers of international strategic alliances can be internal or external.

Internal drivers

Internal drivers are reflected in the value chain as shown in Chapter 8, Figure 8.1. With internal drivers, the strategic linkages in the value chain can be either vertical or horizontal.

Vertical – these are alliances across different levels and are designed to improve the product offering. They can include distribution or outsourcing arrangements and customer supplier relationships.

Horizontal – these can be within individual elements of the value chains so as to reduce investment or to access markets. By contrast with vertical alliances, horizontal alliances are usually driven by the desire to achieve economies. The linkages can be either in support activities (e.g. human resource management as with Boeing and Lockheed sharing staff; technology development as with Airbus Industries; procurement as with cooperative buying arrangements between retail chains); or in primary activities (e.g. logistics as with code sharing by airlines; manufacturing as with model sharing between Ford and Mazda; and in marketing/sales).

External drivers

External drivers of strategic alliances are related to competitive threat or advantage. They may be motivated by a desire to tie up sources of inputs, to obtain insider status in international markets, improve chances of securing government business, to be more acceptable to government in the international market or to access low-cost product for marketing back in the domestic market.

Classification of strategic alliances

Strategic alliances have been identified in different ways. Table 17.1 provides a classification of alliances based on different kinds of strategies and relationships (Stafford, 1994).

Table 17.1 Cooperative strategies relationships

Corporate strategies	Contract	Creative joint venture	Acquisitive joint venture
Hand-over	A	B	C
Trade	D	E	F
Pool	G	H	I

Strategy defnitions

Hand-over: one-way transfer of a resource or chain activity where one partner literally hands over to the other.

Trade: two-way exchange between partners trading complementary outputs or value chain activities with one another.

Pool: partners share the same value chain activity or common resource.

Relationships defnitions

Contracts: non-equity agreements specifying the cooperative contributions and powers of each partner.

Creative joint ventures: partners contribute resources to the formation of a new separate subsidiary, jointly owned by the partners.

Acquisitive joint venture: one partner acquires partial interest of the other, and the partners work together with joint management teams and joint-owned assets.

Source: Adapted from Stafford (1994), pp. 65–67.

Table 17.2 Radisson Hotel Australasia's strategic alliances

Cooperative strategies relationships	Contract	Creative JV	Acquisitive JV
Hand-over [one way]	• RHW • Global Distribution Systems (Southern Cross, Fantasia) • Suppliers		
Trade [two-way exchange]	• RHW (Reservation System) • Hotel Property Owners • Qantas • Ansett Airlines • Telstra		
Pool [share value chain]	• RHW (Development)	• Malaysian partner	• Indonesian partner

Source: Adapted from Stafford (1994), pp. 65–67.

The letters A to I in Table 17.1 indicate the different combinations of strategies and relationships. An illustration of this model can be seen with reference to the international hospitality industry. Radisson Hotels of Australasia (RHA) holds the franchise for Radisson hotels in the South-East Asia region including Australia from the American franchisor, Radisson Hospitality Worldwide (RHW). RHA is a hotel management services company linked to the RHW system and to hotels in Australia, Indonesia and Malaysia.

Using Stafford's Cooperative Strategies typology of alliance types, RHA's main strategic alliances are shown in Table 17.2. Most are contract relationships involving 'hand-over' and 'trade' strategies. Three alliances are 'pool' strategies with joint venture relationships.

RHA's strategic alliance relationships are shown in more detail in Figure 17.4. Its most important alliance is with RHW, which is a contract as an exclusive licensee to develop the Radisson Hotel franchise in Australia and the South West Pacific.

Three types of cooperative strategy operate between RHW and RHA. RHW's provision of its centralised Pierre reservation system provides the trading network for RHA to receive reservations for its hotels and give reservations to other regions of the RHW group. RHW also provides a 'hand-over' of its brand name, hotel systems, Radisson product types, training and advertising/sales support. RHW's resource support of RHA's Asian developments represents a 'pool' cooperative strategy. Both RHW and RHA have a 'hand-over' contract with TIAS which links the Pierre reservation system with the Sabre and Galileo distribution systems. RHW and RHA pay a fee for usage of these systems when bookings are made in Radisson hotels.

RHA's contractual relationship with individual property owners represents a trade strategy. RHA has individual contracts with each property owner who provides the hotel building and working capital. RHA provides the Radisson brand name, network, hotel systems and management services.

Details of RHA's strategic alliances

Figure 17.4

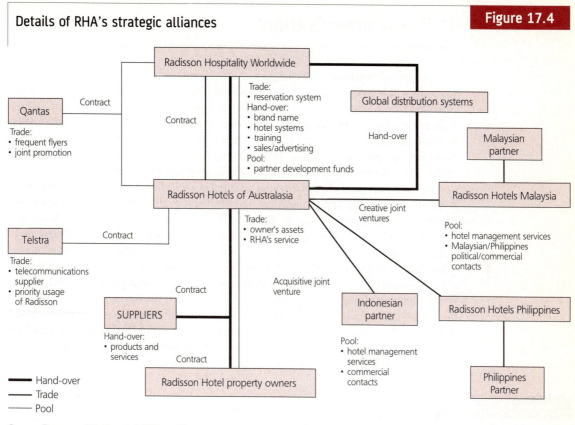

Source: Brown and Pattinson (1995), p. 47.

The Qantas contract with RHW includes RHA hotels. Qantas has provided Radisson with cooperative advertising and joint promotion of Radisson properties to enable its frequent flyers to obtain points towards free tickets from their accommodation. Radisson enhances the relationship between Qantas and its frequent flyers while gaining accommodation revenue from the relationship.

RHA also has a trade relationship with Qantas and other airlines and other package holiday sections of major airlines to the leisure market in the form of short-term joint promotions of package holidays incorporating Radisson resort hotels.

The Telstra/RHA trade is an alliance which makes Telstra the main supplier of telecommunications products and services to Radisson in return for preferred usage by Telstra staff of Radisson Hotels.

RHA has three joint ventures involving 'pooling' strategies. Joint venture companies set up in Malaysia and the Philippines involve powerful local groups. RHA provides hotel management services pooled with political and commercial networks provided by partners in Malaysia and the Philippines.

An acquisitive joint venture with an Indonesian partner where the partner has acquired a minority equity in RHA is a similar pooling 'strategy' using the Indonesian partner's commercial contacts in its home country.

The new organisation

The process of organisational change and developments in technology are converging to produce new types of business organisations. The new information infrastructure has provided a foundation for a new form of organisation – the 'virtual corporation', which does not exist in the bricks-and-mortar sense. Its purpose is to link, using information technology, people, assets and ideas to enable an opportunistic network of organisations to join quickly to exploit fast-changing opportunities (Davidow and Malone, 1992). The characteristics of the virtual organisation are shown in Figure 17.5.

The most important characteristic of a virtual organisation is that it is created to meet a specific opportunity in a defined time period (Priess et al., 1996). Communication and the pursuit of common objectives form the basis for relationships between firms and individuals who will increasingly be electronically connected through the new electronic information infrastructure whose public channel is represented by the Internet (Davidow and Malone, 1992). For example, the Virtual Vineyards website represents a large number of vineyards in California as well as related food products. Expert commentary on vintages and quality is included to assist the buyer in making purchase decisions – all of which can be done online. Some of these aspects were discussed in Chapter 5, while e-commerce is described in more detail in Chapter 19. Here the combination of alliance formation and electronic networks is discussed with reference to their potential for industry transformation.

Figure 17.5   Characteristics of the virtual organisation

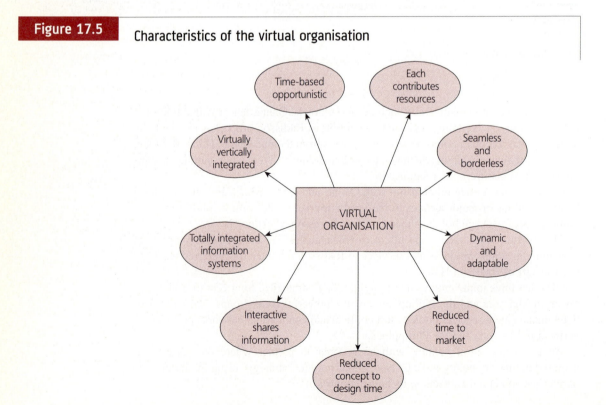

Industry transformation

Alliance formation and electronic information infrastructure

The cross-border nature of the new infrastructure means that vast pools of commercial knowledge are rapidly moving around the world through the infrastructure, challenging businesses in all industries to view the accumulation of knowledge and the conversion of it to commercially profitable outcomes as a cornerstone of strategy formulation. The new electronic information infrastructure is transforming individuals, businesses and industries as it impacts on industry structures, alliance structures and marketing strategies. The interactions of the electronic infrastructure with industry structure, alliance structure and marketing strategy constitutes the basis for an industry transformation model (Brown et al., 1995).

This model, shown in Figure 17.6, is based on the premise that the electronic information infrastructure acting as a global facilitator can transform industry structure, alliance structure and marketing strategy by working with one or more of these elements.

Electronic infrastructure and industry structure

Three key effects of the interaction of the electronic information infrastructure on industry structure include: rapid globalisation of industries, the multidimensionality of value-addition, and the levels of barriers to entry.

Entry into the information infrastructure through avenues such as the World Wide Web and other access points opens the door to a global marketplace. Development of appropriate intra- and inter-corporate infrastructure linking to these services

---

Industry transformation model

Figure 17.6

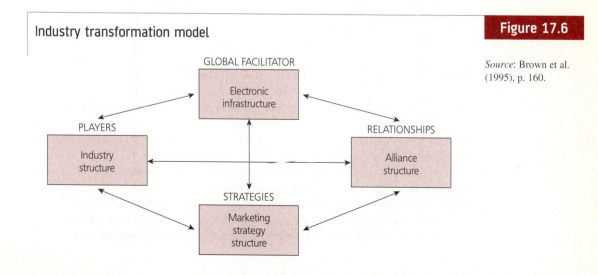

Source: Brown et al. (1995), p. 160.

enables businesses to perform 'co-R&D and co-marketing' in different time zones and geographic areas. The era of continuous 24-hour global R&D and marketing through a complex web of strategic alliances is now a reality.

The World Wide Web and other networks that connect to it can be viewed not only as an infrastructure but also as a marketplace. The new 'marketspace' as defined by Rayport and Sviokla moves the marketplace transaction from an interaction between a physical seller and a physical buyer to an electronic or 'marketspace' transaction (Rayport and Sviokla, 1994).

Value is created in marketspace through the management of content, context and infrastructure. These elements cover (Rayport and Sviokla, 1994):

- *content* – which is either physical product extended by information services or the information itself;
- *context* – the electronic channel or access mode, such as TV, computer or mobile phone; and
- *infrastructure* – the electronic infrastructure operators which together create the channel, such as digital TV, the Internet and the mobile communication networks.

Information networks such as the World Wide Web allow connection to a network by an individual from any dimension of space. This means that value adding through using the networks can be multidimensional. The Porter notion of value chains and exchange discussed in Chapter 14 has been challenged by the notion of value constellations and utility. The new infrastructure greatly facilitates the development of effective value-constellations (Ramirez and Normann, 1994).

The information infrastructure has significant implications for barriers to entry. There will be instances where entry into the new infrastructure will offer global business opportunities previously unimagined by the entrants. However, in some well-established, information-based service industries, the prevailing industry-specific information infrastructure may constitute a significant barrier to entry. For example, the well-established Global Distribution Systems (GDS) in the airline and travel industry represents powerful prevailing information infrastructures to which existing and prospective players must gain access to be able to participate in that industry (Brown et al., 1995).

Electronic infrastructure and alliance structure

Which organisational structures are appropriate to maximise utility from the electronic infrastructure? Strategic alliances are an effective means of gaining knowledge which is becoming more important today in creating value than the traditional elements of capital, land and labour (Badaracco, 1991).

The combination of strategic alliances and the electronic infrastructure leads to the theme of the virtual organisation discussed earlier in this chapter. Goldman, Nagel and Preiss from the Agile Manufacturing Enterprise Forum (AMEF) at the Lehigh University's Iacocca Institute have proposed a model of a virtual organisation made of many strategic alliances linked through a powerful information infrastructure.

The key feature of the virtual organisation structure is agility:

For a company to be agile is to be capable of operating profitably in a competitive environment of continually, and unpredictably, changing customer opportunities. For an individual to be agile is to be capable of contributing to the bottom line of a company that is constantly reorganising its human and technological resources in response to unpredictably changing customer opportunities.

Source: Goldman et al., 1995, pp. 3–4.

Individuals, teams, businesses (in strategic alliances) and even industries (especially within converged industry structures) are all reconfigurable in this model. Goldman et al. (1995) have renamed the virtual corporation, the agile corporation in their model.

Electronic infrastructure and marketing strategy

Defining the information infrastructure as a 'marketspace' implies that there will be marketing strategies that will lead to value addition and competitive advantage available within this dimension. Marketspace strategy proposes that value is created through the manipulation of content, context and infrastructure defined earlier. Focus on any one (or a mix or all) of these strategies may lead to new marketing strategies that redefine high value-added activities. For example, educational material available any time any place with video support, a chat room for student discussion, convenient access to instructors via e-mail with self-paced immediately graded tutorials. All this together with relevant feedback provides substantial added value in all components – content, context via computer access, and infrastructure which enables electronic discussion forums to occur between people widely separated in space.

A concerted strategic focus on particular infrastructure may lead to a transformation or significant redefinition of the industries that a business may be in. Examples of industries undergoing transformation are entertainment, education, banking and financial services, and medical services. At the same time new alliances are being created as new players enter these industries. These transformational changes will redirect businesses targeting international markets from being product-driven organisations to companies driven by information-based services.

Alliance strategies for creating competitive advantage

While a particular market may be the focus of attention, if the context is global the firm will need to consider alliances with firms in the same or related industries to put together an appropriate alliance network strategy. If the strategy does not involve alliances then a change in perspective is needed. In an alliance network, the firm must consider the overall strategy of the group of which it is a part. The basis of competitive advantage and market coverage needs to be looked at from the alliance network's viewpoint as noted earlier when discussing network-based competition.

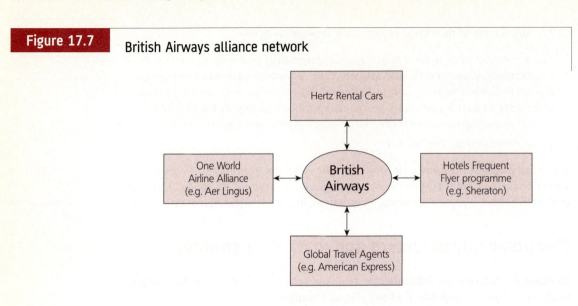

Figure 17.7   British Airways alliance network

Market leader alliance strategies

If the intent is to rapidly achieve leadership in the new market and to have a major impact, the firm needs to develop a network of alliances that can quickly deliver innovative products and services with appropriate support and resource leverage. The alliance network must be planned with foresight to include additional or different alliance players as the market evolves and as competition responds to the new entrant. All of the principles associated with market leadership strategies discussed in earlier chapters apply. The strategy should contain the following elements:

- focus on mainstream markets;
- resource leverage for rapid penetration entry;
- market positioning to take the high and middle end of the market; and
- integration of alliance partners into a seamless organisation to deliver the offer.

In the travel industry many companies have formed a range of alliance relationships, for example the One World membership or Star is designed to deliver worldwide passenger travel. A simplified picture of the One World alliance network is shown in Figure 17.7.

Alliance strategies for challengers and followers

To be a major threat, it is necessary to design a challenger alliance network with sufficient resource leverage to have a major impact on the market. Market entry may be narrowly focused on key market segments or focused on broader market coverage. The specific strategy will be determined in part by the strength of incumbent competitors. The principles discussed in Chapter 15 on challenger and follower strategies apply.

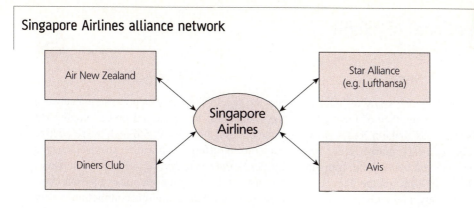

Singapore Airlines alliance network

Figure 17.8

Followers usually rely for their success on speed of implementation and lower costs. Here the alliance network requires the following elements:

- an alliance configuration of small units;
- communication lines and relationships enabling rapid decision making and implementation;
- low cost structures;
- a well-organised competitive intelligence system providing early information on competition developments and initiatives; and
- competences in imitating and improving products, services, delivery processes and customer communications.

The alliance network of Singapore Airlines is shown in part in Figure 17.8.

The Star Alliance, which is the catalyst for Singapore Airlines' multi-airline alliance network, was formed in May 1997 by six regional airlines. Singapore Airlines formalised its participation in April 1999 and became part of the IT infrastructure which enables customers to use an agent from any Alliance member to help them plan a series of flights across all Alliance airlines. The Alliance has a separate, permanent IT organisation, called Star IT, which is made up of IT team members from the Alliance airlines and works to ensure that the Alliance's strategy is compatible with each individual company's objectives. It has a variety of ongoing global IT projects all involving Star Alliance airlines covering reservations departure control and frequent flyer programmes. In the Asia-Pacific region the airline alliances are becoming even closer as Singapore Airlines seeks to acquire a larger equity share of Air New Zealand, which in turn has absorbed some regional airlines (Chung, 2000).

Alliance strategies for niche specialists

Chapter 15 discussed appropriate strategies for niche specialists. The alliance network for new market entry should be composed of partners that specialise in various parts of the value chain relevant to the target market – product or service supply, specialised distribution, specialised customer communication and specialised support services.

17.2 International highlight

Renault's alliance with Nissan

The Nissan recovery story is a study of how to manage an alliance in the the face of great cultural diversity. Nissan was making losses year after year and losing domestic market share for over a decade. Management blamed the strength of the yen and the poor state of the Japanese economy for the company's situation, ignoring the fact that competitors like Honda and Toyota were doing well.

After the alliance, cross-functional teams were organised to break down the barriers between departments. One of the main cost-saving actions was the development of platform sharing between the companies. Work started on developing the same building blocks, even though the respective cars looked different. This alliance was managed by developing synergy between the companies but also by keeping the identities of each company separate. Managing this contraction is very important: identity matters because it is the basis of motivation. Renault people therefore identify with their company brand and Nissan people with theirs, with Renault as the European core and Nissan focusing on Asia and America.

Implementation and management of strategic alliances

Ultimately successful international alliances depend upon the relational exchanges that occur in international marketing. Returning to the central focus of network competition based around relationships it is clear to see the complexity that exists. The marketing relationships include supplier partnerships, lateral partnerships involving competitors and frequently governments, buyer partnerships which encompass intermediate and ultimate customers and internal partnerships involving employees, business units and functional departments. The effectiveness of all these partnerships and relationships will determine the overall effectiveness and longevity of the network and the alliance strategy.

Research into international business relationships by Holm et al. (1996) points to some of the causes of implementation problems. They suggest that the strategic fit between alliance partners is brought about by the relationship development process. For the most part, the process leading up to formal agreement is conducted by top management, whereas the process of implementation is dealt with by middle management. The relative understandings and commitments of the different management levels can be quite different. Relationship commitment is affected by positive factors such as trust, acquiescence and relationship benefits, as well as negative influences like propensity to leave and uncertainty. It is no wonder that this myriad of interrelationships causes difficulties in alliances in practice.

The implementation of strategic alliances can be difficult and time-consuming, particularly cross-cultural alliances. The failure rate is high. Most strategic alliances do not seem to have lived up to initial management expectations over time. One study suggests that 7 out of 10 joint ventures fail to meet either partner's management expectations (Stafford, 1994). The challenges and obstacles to strategic alliances may be summarised as:

- autonomy of alliance members;
- forward momentum;
- focus on the external environment;
- politicking – internal agendas that may go against alliance development;
- commitment to change and innovation;
- learning – desire and commitment to learning about each other;
- people – having the best people committed to the alliance;
- 'black box' – fear of giving away something; and
- culture.

Studies on the matching of partners has led to the following observations about the success of strategic alliances (Lorange et al., 1992):

- ventures tend to be more successful where partners are homogeneous;
- ventures are less successful where neither partner has products, services, assets or experience related to its venture; and
- ventures last longer between partners of similar cultures, asset sizes and venturing experience levels.

The high levels of management energy required to initiate, develop and maintain alliances with a substantial number of members is a major challenge. This is a special problem for management of the alliance founder or alliance deal driver. It is particularly pertinent with the alliances developed by Rupert Murdoch of News Corporation with John Malone of TCI, America's largest cable operator. Their surfeit of alliances in the last few years has shaped media programming and entertainment content not only in the US, but worldwide. The big joint ventures include Fox Liberty Networks LLC, Fox Family Worldwide Inc. and United Video Satellite Group (Chenoweth, 1998).

In relation to the management of people in a virtual organisation, Handy (1995) suggests seven elements of trust are critical success factors. These include:

- don't place blind trust in everyone;
- trust needs boundaries;
- trust demands learning;
- trust requires toughness especially when wrong matches are made;
- trust includes component parts which must bond to goals of the whole virtual organisation;
- trust still requires 'touch' or physical face-to-face contact throughout the virtual organisation, although this may not be in the conventional workplace environment; and
- trust requires a multiplicity of strong leaders in the virtual organisation.

A final issue is that of terminating strategic alliances because successful strategic alliance management involves knowing when to end it. Often this can be planned for from the inception stage, especially when the alliance is to be terminated by development into a merger or an acquisition by one party of the other. Not so easy to plan for is termination by 'walking away'. This, however, may be easy if the alliance was formed for the purpose of undertaking a specific project, and at the conclusion of the project there are no further benefits to be gained from continuing the alliance.

The issues outlined above point towards a complex set of human behaviours that may make or break the formation and development of strategic alliances.

Internet infusion

Underlying relationships, networks and alliances in the international electronic environment is the concept of the rational as opposed to the biological man. Because the biological man acts on his feelings, it is the biological man that underlies relationships and networks (Ambler and Styles, 2000). On the other hand, the Internet is based on rationality. This raises the question as to whether there is a future for relationships in the Internet age. Although the Internet is based on rationality, does it entirely do away with both memory and affect? While there may appear to be an apparent inconsistency between e-business and relationships, it will be argued that relationships, networks and alliances have a definite role in international e-business.

Relationships in marketspace

Information technology (IT) has altered social exchange in the interaction process. This has led to relationships becoming more impersonal and more formalised as the relationship atmosphere has changed. However, businesses still need to interact, albeit in different ways, as interactions remain at the heart of successful relationships and successful relationships are fundamental to successful business. Figure 17.9 shows typical applications of IT and how they have replaced situations where face-to-face activities were formerly involved.

Figure 17.9   Physical versus virtual value chain

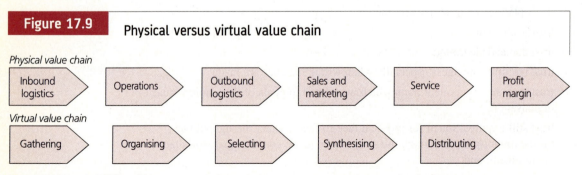

Physical value chain

Inbound logistics → Operations → Outbound logistics → Sales and marketing → Service → Profit margin

Virtual value chain

Gathering → Organising → Selecting → Synthesising → Distributing

Source: Speier et al. (1998), p. 266.

The virtual organisation is a collection of business units in which people and work processes from the business units interact intensively in order to perform work which benefits all. They enable organisational and/or personal competences to be brought together when needed and disbanded when no longer needed. They mirror the fluidity of the global marketplace. The virtual corporation assesses all marketing activities across the entire global value chain in order to 'virtually vertically integrate' across a 'web of companies'.

These marketing relationships can be characterised as virtual when a significant amount of activity between relationship partners occurs outside their organisational domains and therefore in a non-'face-to-face' context. The management orientation will need to go beyond the command and control model and focus on cooperation as a basis for the interaction. These virtual relationships/organisations will develop a culture and identity of their own. This will be apart and distinct from that of the two parent organisations.

The importance of trust in e-business is high. The physical separation of buyer and seller, the physical separation of the buyers and the merchandise, and the perceived insecurity of the Internet, all challenge marketers to find new ways to initiate and develop relationships with their customers. When there is no personal face-to-face contact between seller and customer, building and maintaining trust is more difficult to achieve. This is particularly relevant when doing business in Asia where trust is an important element of a relationship.

Indicators of trust are twofold – experience-based and cue-based. Experience-based indicators are the result of an exchange that has taken place, whereas cue-based indicators occur prior to the exchange and create trust by the customer in advance of the purchase. E-business marketers therefore should focus on providing cues to potential customers or business partners so that they trust the company sufficiently to engage in the initial transaction.

In cue-based trust, the cues, which may serve as indicators of trustworthiness, may consist of return policies, name recognition, the professional look of the website, a privacy and security policy, availability of company address and phone number for alternative ordering procedures, and references and testimonials from existing customers.

Networks in marketspace

According to Poon and Jevons (1997), the Internet provides small businesses with the opportunity to share information and experiences. This can lead to collaboration such as the sharing of customer orders or a number of small firms jointly bidding on a large project. Because the Internet is a virtual borderless platform on which suppliers, customers, competitors and network partners can interact, it enables the formation and maintenance of business network links that would otherwise be prohibited by barriers such as distance, time and limited resources. Networks involve establishing linkages both upstream and downstream with networks in other countries to facilitate efficiencies in the transnational value chain. This requires efficient and continually evolving communication between the various members of the network. The Internet can facilitate this because of the instantaneous way it communicates over both geographical and psychic distances. However, although the Internet does allow freer and easier flow of communication, it does not replace the need for personal relationship building, especially in cultures that are high context in character such as Thailand or Japan.

Strategic alliances in marketspace

Inkpen and Currall (2000) argue that alliances driven by the Internet will operate under different assumptions and create substantially different management challenges from traditional global alliances. Traditional alliances, because of their coordination and competitive costs, tend to be transitional. Many smaller firms shy away from alliances because of the complexities associated with both forming and terminating them.

By comparison, the Internet will dissolve many of the constraints of time and geography and make it possible for organisations to connect and collaborate across borders. In the Internet economy, alliances will become easier both to create and terminate, and location and size will become less critical as variables. The classic market entry form of a bricks-and-mortar joint venture will decline in relevance as firms discover that relationships can be easily and efficiently established electronically. Personal interactions which are expensive and time consuming offer the prospect of being largely replaced by electronic interchanges. However, during the alliance formation stage, face-to-face interaction is still likely to be critical. As the alliance develops and matures, electronic interactions between the partners may be sufficient to maintain the alliance. Although foreign market entry alliances will still be formed, the Internet is likely to shift the focus of the objective in alliance formation away from market entry towards the achievement of strategic efficiency. In addition, firms will be able to access international markets that were previously beyond their reach.

Summary

Companies today are unable to dominate any technology, business or market region alone. They need to develop networks of strategic alliances that provide access to technologies, new products and new markets. These alliance arrangements encompass both a variety of strategies and relationships.

The convergence of telecommunications, computers, software and media industries has resulted in a new information infrastructure – the most public embodiment being the Internet. In response, new organisations are being created to take advantage of those opportunities – 'virtual' organisations, which involve linkages and alliances by companies in pursuit of common objectives and markets.

Many industries are undergoing transformation due to the impact of electronic communication structures and the formation of alliance networks. An industry transformation model incorporating electronic information infrastructure, industry structure and alliance structure helps us describe the key elements relevant to the development of marketing strategies. Alliance strategies for market leaders, challengers, followers and niche specialists are considered in terms of creating competitive advantage.

Finally, the organisation must consider the requirements of common objectives, cultures and trust required to implement and maintain successful alliance strategies.

Ethics issue

Your company has just signed a very important alliance with a distributor in a foreign country. The distributor dominates the market area relevant to your company's products and has all of the right government and industry connections to introduce your products very successfully.

You have been told by the senior marketing executive of your alliance partner firm that it is essential to provide 'monetary benefits' to a number of government officials and industry facilitators; these include, wharf personnel, customs, and transport companies. This is to ensure minimal 'red tape' and disruption to the flow of your products through to customers.

You believe these to be bribes and know that your firm will turn a 'blind eye' to this issue even though bribes are illegal in the foreign country.

How would you handle this?

Web workout

Question 1 Using the search engine of your choice (if you do not have one use www.google.com) find websites that allow you to send free SMS (Short Message Service) to mobile phone users. Try to determine who are their partners and whether there are any restrictions as to where the SMS can be sent.

Question 2 Pretend you want to plan your around-the-world holiday using the Internet. Using your favourite travel website or an airline, select a few destinations, car hire and accommodation you wish to consider. See what packages are on offer and whether you can create your own booking with your preferred hotel, car hire company and airline. Show the travel deals and best prices that can also be arranged in line with your preferences.

Websites

www.airnz.co.nz	www.hertz.com
www.aoltimewarner.com	www.kodak.com
www.att.com	www.mercedesbenz.com
www.avis.com	www.newscorp.com
www.bosch.com	www.philips.com
www.csr.com.au	www.qantas.com.au
www.ford.com	www.radisson.com
www.fox.com	www.sabre.com
www.caterbuyer.com	www.sega.com
www.buildonline.com	www.star-alliance.com
www.ingredientsnet.com	www.toshiba.co.uk
www.galileo.com	www.toyota.com
www.harelmallac.com	www.virtualvineyards.com

Discussion questions

1 Given the experience of limited success of many alliance partnerships, why do so many companies develop alliance networks?

2 Describe the network concept and its key elements. Outline an example of network-based competition in a specific industry or between two competitors.

3 Why is it that information is creating new business? Give examples of some new products or businesses which are purely information based and are selling internationally.

4 Traditional industry structure analysis (discussed in Chapter 13) is being augmented by analysis of alliance structure and electronic infrastructures. How do these additional elements (i.e. alliances and electronic infrastructure) create added value in international markets? Use an example to illustrate.

5 Identify a company adopting a niche strategy with its international business. Outline its alliance partners and relationship network.

6 What do you consider are the main factors needed to ensure longevity of alliances in international markets?

7 By accessing the Internet go to the home page of BA, Air France, Delta Airlines, Qantas and Singapore Airlines and study their services and linkages with other websites. From this study, see if you can identify their main alliance partners.

8 Identify a European company that is part of an alliance network which is challenging the leaders in the international market. Draw up the alliance network to illustrate.

References

Ambler, T. and Styles, C. (2000) 'The Silk Road to International Marketing: Profit and Passion', in *Global Business*, Pearson Education Ltd, London.

AOL Time Warner website – www.aol.com/marketguide (accessed 1 July 2001).

Badaracco, J.L. Jr (1991) *The Knowledge Link: How Firms Compete Through Strategic Alliances*, Harvard Business School Press, Boston, p. 1.

Brown, L. and Pattinson, H. (1995) 'Information Technology and Telecommunications: Impacts on Strategic Alliance Formation and Management', *Management Decision*, Vol. 33, No. 4, p. 48.

Brown, L., Pattinson, H. and Perrott, B. (1995) 'Marketing Strategy Implications of the New Electronic Information Infrastructure for the International Hospitality and Travel Industry', Paper submission to the 1995 Marketing Science Conference, 2–5 July, Sydney.

Brown, L.R. (1997) *Competitive Marketing Strategy: Dynamic Manoeuvring for Competitive Position*, 2nd edn, Nelson, Melbourne, Ch. 16.

Chenoweth, N. (1998) 'The Big Dealers', *The Australian Financial Review*, 27–28 June, pp. 22–23.

Chung, Daphne (2000) 'Reaching for the Stars', *MIS Australia*, May 2000, pp. 43–47.

Davidow, W.H. and Malone, M.S. (1992) *The Virtual Corporation*, HarperCollins, New York.

Fletcher, R. (1996) 'Network Theory and Countertrade Transactions', *International Business Review*, Vol. 5, No. 2, p. 169.

Goldman, S.L., Nagel, R.N. and Preiss, K. (1995) *Agile Competitors and Virtual Organisations: Strategies for Enriching the Customer*, Van Nostrand Reinhold, New York, pp. 3–4.

Grönroos, C. (1996) 'Relationship Marketing Logic', *Asia–Australia Marketing Journal*, Vol. 4, No. 1, pp. 7–18.

Hale, B. (2000) 'AOL–Time Warner deal shifts the media landscape', *BRW*, 21 January, pp. 26–27.

Handy, C. (1995) 'Trust and the Virtual Organisation', *Harvard Business Review*, May–June, pp. 44–48.

Healey, M., Hastings, K., Brown, L. and Gardiner, M. (2001) 'The Old, the New and the Complicated: A Trilogy of Marketing Relationships', *European Journal of Marketing*, Vol. 35, No. 1/2, pp. 182–93.

Holm, D., Eriksson, K. and Johanson, J. (1996) 'Business Networks and Cooperation in International Business Relationships', *Journal of International Business Studies*, Special Issue, pp. 1033–53.

Inkpen, A. and Currall, S.C. (2000) 'Joint venture trust: Interpersonal, intergroup and interfirm levels', in De Rond, M. and Faulkner, D. (eds), *Cooperative Strategies: Economic, Business and Organizational Issues*, Oxford: Oxford University Press, pp. 324–340.

Lei, D. and Slocum, J.W. (1992) 'Global Strategy, Competence-Building and Strategic Alliances', *California Management Review*, Fall, pp. 81–82.

Lorange, P., Roos, J. and Bronn, P.S. (1992) 'Building Successful Strategic Alliances', *Long Range Planning*, December, p. 15.

Morgan, R. and Hunt, S. (1994) 'The Commitment–Trust Theory of Relationship Marketing', *Journal of Marketing*, July, Vol. 58 No. 3.

Ohmae, K. (1989) 'The Global Logic of Strategic Alliances', *Harvard Business Review*, March–April, in Barnevik, P. and Moss Kanter, R. (eds) (1994) *Global Strategies: Insights from the World's Leading Thinkers*, Harvard Business School Press, Boston, p. 109.

Poon, S. and Jevons, C. (1997) 'Internet-enabled International Marketing: A Small Business Network Perspective.' *Journal of Marketing Management*, Vol. 13, pp. 29–41.

Priess, K., Goldman, S.L. and Nagel, R.N. (1996) *Cooperate to Compete: Building Agile Business Relationships*, Van Nostrand Reinhold, New York, pp. 158–161.

Ramirez R. and Normann R. (1994) 'From Value Chain to Value Constellation', Paper presented at the *14th Annual Strategic Management Society Conference*, pp. 2–3. Also 'From Value Chain to Value Constellation: Designing Interactive Strategy', *Harvard Business Review*, July–August 1993, pp. 65–66.

Rayport, J.F. and Sviokla, J.J. (1994) 'Managing in the Marketspace', *Harvard Business Review*, November–December, p. 142.

Speier, C., Harvey, M.G. and Palmer, J. (1998) 'Virtual Management of Global Marketing Relationships', *Journal of World Business*, Vol. 33, No. 3, pp. 263–76.

Stafford, E.R. (1994) 'Using Co-operative Strategies to Make Alliances Work', *Long Range Planning*, June, Figure 1 and pp. 65–67.

Case study 13

Megazyme

Angela Kennedy, UCD Business Schools
Megazyme International Ireland Ltd, Bray Business Park, Bray, Co. Wicklow, Ireland

Late in September 2002, Angela Kennedy, Business Director, and Dr Barry McCleary, Technical Director, sat in the 'conference room' to again review the final figures and data for their five-year business plan and competitive strategy for the next several years. McCleary was excited as he had just received his first GMO enzyme which had resulted from a partnership agreement involving the sponsorship of a PhD student placement in a university in the UK. Potentially, this recombinant enzyme technology was the key to Megazyme's future and thus held great significance for the company. The directors wanted to build on Megazyme's existing strengths to stimulate more impressive performance in the years ahead.

Evolution of the company – background

Megazyme International is a knowledge-based, privately owned biotechnology company, and was founded in Australia in 1989 by Dr Barry McCleary and Angela Kennedy. McCleary obtained his PhD and DScAgr degrees from University of Sydney and had the opportunity to research in the Howard Hughes Medical Foundation, University of Miami (Fulbright Foundation Scholarship), Unilever Research, Bedford, England (Nuffield Foundation Scholarship), ETH Zurich and Biocon Bio-chemicals, Cork. He is the author of over 100 scientific papers in his area of expertise and has been awarded the Guthrie Medal by the Royal Australian Chemical Institute for 'contributions to cereal chemistry in Australia in the broadest sense', and more recently (2002) the Harvey W. Wiley Medal by the Association of Official

Analytical Chemists (USA) for 'career achievements in analytical chemistry'.

Kennedy started her career as a science technologist and obtained her MBA degree (Hons I) from UCD, in 2002. She has brought to the company her scientific base and her extensive knowledge in the marketing and sales of medical products and clinical diagnostic reagents. She is ideally suited to promote and develop overseas markets for the products that Megazyme develops and is responsible for both the export marketing strategy and overall corporate strategy. With this pool of knowledge and experience, Dr McCleary and Ms Kennedy make a formidable team.

It was while in his position of Senior Research Scientist with the New South Wales Department of Agriculture, Sydney, Australia, that the embryonic seeds for the formulation of Megazyme were sown. Dr McCleary says the company was born of his frustration with the existing analytical methods, which were either archaic or non-existent. Consequently, the company was set up with the aim of developing and supplying new and innovative diagnostic test kits and reagents for the cereals, food, feed and fermentation industries. Having developed the business successfully over the past ten years Megazyme's vision for the future is to become a specialised, world-class manufacturer and supplier of high-quality and innovative test technology for the cereals, food, feed and fermentation industries.

Products: diagnostic test kits and reagents

The company's product range presently numbers over 225, as listed in the Megazyme 2002/2003

►

catalogue, and includes the following product groups:

- *diagnostic test kits* for measurement of key components in food, feed and agricultural products;
- specialised *reagents* used in laboratory analyses;
- high-purity, analytical grade *enzymes* for research and analytical purposes;
- pure *polysaccharides* for use as analytical reagents;
- *tablet tests* for measurement of enzyme activity;
- *oligosaccharides* used as chromatographic standards.

The test kits and test tablets that are produced by Megazyme are used to measure components that allow quality control in numerous processes involving the use of agricultural plant products. Such components include sugar compounds and enzymes. The specificity and simplicity of the Megazyme enzymatic methods make them ideal for measuring key quality parameters and consequently many of the test methods have been validated by scientific and industry associations. Additional advantages of using test kits of this nature is that they contain ready-to-use reagents which yield time savings and laboratory safety hazards are minimised.

More specifically the test kits find widespread application in the malting, brewing, baking, animal feed, silage, detergents, textiles, milling and food industries. The products are also widely used in research and analytical laboratories within government, industrial and university facilities. All of the world's major enzyme manufacturers are customers including Genencor, Danisco, Quest (Division of ICI, Ireland), DSM (Holland and France) and Novozymes (Denmark, USA and China). Most of the major food and brewing companies also are customers, including Unilever, H.J. Heinz, Kellogg's,

Weetabix, Nestlé, Guinness, Anheuser-Busch, Coors and Procter & Gamble. Presently the Company's customer database is a valuable resource, containing details of 2,000 customers worldwide.

Technological innovation (R&D)

Megazyme is a very active and progressive biotechnology company. The company's approach is to identify products for development that are responsive to the needs of its customers. The company is committed to the development of new and innovative test technology. More than 90% of the products listed in the Megazyme catalogue were developed by the company, and Megazyme is the sole world supplier of these products. Where the company has decided to manufacture products that are already supplied by other companies, the philosophy has been to supply a superior product at a lower price.

Megazyme's investment in R&D has led to a wealth of innovation. Expenditure on in-house R&D has been >12% per annum of total turnover. From the outset, the company knew that simply developing improved test procedures was not sufficient. Consequently, many of the test kits have been validated as Official Standard Methods by international scientific associations such as American Association of Cereal Chemists (AACC), Association of Official Analytical Chemists (AOAC), European Brewing Congress (EBC), American Society for Brewing Chemists (ASBC), Royal Australian Chemical Institute (RACI), and International Association for Cereal Science and Technology (ICC). This stamp of approval from international bodies has formed the foundation of the company's global marketing strategy.

- seven of the Megazyme procedures are AACC standard methods;
- five of the methods have been adopted as AOAC (most prestigious official scientific/industry analytical association in the world) standard methods;

- four of the Megazyme methods have been accepted by the ICC;
- nine of the Megazyme methods are RACI standard procedures.

Product, quality, cost

The company has achieved and sustained superior performance in the marketplace by the continual exploitation of its assets: product purity, international test methods and outstanding customer value. While the competitors may meet Megazyme's prices in the marketplace, they cannot match the 'purity' and innovative nature of the products supplied. In many cases, the Megazyme enzymes are orders of magnitude purer than competitors' products.

Megazyme test methods could potentially be copied by competitors, but for the last ten years the company has positioned itself in the marketplace and secured a large database of buyers from bluechip companies, such as H.J. Heinz, Kellogg's, USA; Anheuser Busch, USA; Coors, USA; and other major food and starch companies. The barriers to entry are high for competitors, given that the Megazyme test procedures are validated as world standard methods. This process of international, interlaboratory evaluation and acceptance of each test procedure by scientific technical committees, such as those within AOAC International, is extremely tedious and costly and can take anything from one to three years before final approval is achieved.

However, the company has achieved an international reputation based on pioneering new test methodologies aimed at *sensing, serving and satisfying* customer needs, which in turn, has kept Megazyme ahead of the competition. Since 1989, Megazyme has become a globally recognised leader in the development of high purity enzymes and innovative test kits and reagents. Megazyme's unique positioning is best described in both Tables 1 and 2 below, outlining the purity of the enzymes employed in the test kits; internationally accepted test methods; and value for money for the customer.

The market – market development, size and structure

One of the fastest growing sectors, both in food as well as in feed additives, is enzymes. In food, enzymes are used as processing aids, while in feed they are used to aid feed conversion. Parallel to the growth of the enzyme market worldwide, is the requirement for measurement of enzyme activity. The enzyme sector is now the fastest growing sector for Megazyme, representing 21% of total sales in 2002.

At present, Megazyme exports 98% of products from Ireland to over 50 countries, worldwide. The total turnover is derived from sales in Europe of 55%, USA 25%, Far East 15% and the rest from the Middle East. No figures are available for market share (%) of the 'Food Analysis

---

Table 1 Purity, value, innovation

Purity	• The highest purity enzymes available
Methods	• Internationally accepted test methods
	• Industry leader in pioneering new methods for enzyme and carbohydrate measurement
Value	• Provision of highest purity products at less than 50% of the cost of competitors.

▶

Table 2 Value creation

Customer needs	Megazyme value	Competitive advantage
Simple and reliable tests to measure enzyme activity	Product quality, consistency and reliability	Products are highly purified. Very low levels of contamination
Methods that their customers can use, i.e. which are standardised	Customers can save considerable time in the labs because tests are quick to do. 70 minutes versus 24 hrs	Internationally accepted methods from AOAC, AACC Reinventing new standards
Screening for new activities	Technical support and back-up, response within 48 hours. In-house leading-edge research	Industry leader in pioneering new methods for measurement
Quality control for their products	Manufacturer and methods developer	Reputation for high value products, i.e. lower prices but superior products

Figure 1 Megazyme (turnover as % of cumulative historical sales)

Source: Megazyme (2002).

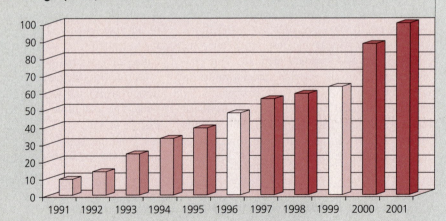

Reagents and Test Kit' market. Exhaustive searches have been conducted with MCI, Euromonitor and other marketing agencies both in Europe and the USA which have failed to come up with any statistics for the Food Test Kit market. This also confirms the fact that Megazyme is operating within its own market-space and is considered to have an almost monopolistic position where competitors are few and market entry costs are high.

The future growth forecasts for Megazyme are based on the company's historical sales over the past five years (refer to Figure 1). Market trends and statistics for the growing enzyme

Table 3 US diagnostic enzyme demand ($ million)

Item	1992	1996	2001	2006	2011
Diagnostic product shipments	7,475	9,056	11,660	15,750	21,500
$enzyme/$000diagnostic shpts	5.2	7.1	8.1	8.8	9.4
Diagnostic enzyme demand	<u>39</u>	<u>64</u>	<u>95</u>	<u>139</u>	<u>203</u>
Polymerases	8	15	24	33	45
Nucleases	6	9	14	21	29
Other	25	40	57	85	129
% Diagnostic	6.4	7.2	8.0	8.4	9.0
Total enzyme demand	610	885	1,190	1,645	2,250

Source: The Freedonia Group, Inc.

market in the US are also included as a predictor of potential growth areas for Megazyme. The aim of Megazyme is to continue to predict and follow the trends in enzyme development, and to develop test kits to match the perceived needs of the industrial enzyme producers. This will be achieved both by continual adaptation of the Megazyme range of products to suit customer needs and by development of new products (i.e. substrates) for measurement of enzyme activity.

Enzyme demand: Demand for diagnostic enzymes is projected to increase by 7.9% per annum to total sales of $139 million by 2006. Growth will be fuelled by increased emphasis on preventative medicine, self-treatment, and surgical and diagnostic procedures, all of which promote the use of diagnostic tests. The growth in demand for diagnostic enzymes in the US is shown in Table 3.

The US diagnostics market is served by numerous enzyme companies, most of which are biochemical companies which also manufacture research enzymes. With a few exceptions, large industrial enzyme suppliers are not involved with the diagnostics market, due to the considerable downstream processing needed to produce the requisite chemical purity.

In Table 4 a breakdown of sales by individual company, together with principal product line for the top enzyme manufacturers is shown. This sector accounted for 21% of Megazyme's turnover for 2002 and Megazyme supplies assay methods for the enzyme formulations for 60% of these US companies. Genentech and Genzyme are involved in therapeutics, and consequently are not potential customers for Megazyme.

US industry market share: The US enzyme market is characterised by large producers, who dominate most commodity-type end use applications, and suppliers of high-value enzyme-based therapeuticals. The market is dominated by six producers: Novozymes, Genencor, Genentech, Genzyme, DSM and Chr. Hansen who together account for more than half of total enzyme sales in 2001. Four of these companies, Novozymes, Genencor, DSM and Chr. Hansen, are leaders due to their dominance of key large-volume sectors, including detergents and food and beverage processing. For the year 2002, these four major enzyme producers accounted for 15% of Megazyme turnover. Other market leaders, Genentech and Genzyme, have attained their strong position by securing market exclusivity for enzyme-based therapeutics, either by patent or by other means (e.g. orphan drug status),

Table 4 US enzyme sales by company, 2001* ($ million)

Company (division)	Total company revenues	Estimated US enzyme revenue	Principal product line	Megazyme customer
Archer-Daniels-Midland	12,877	30	Corn refining	No
Chr. Hansen	558	45	Dairy	✓
Danisco	2,127	35	Bakery	✓
DSM	7,129	55	Industrial, pharmaceutical	✓
Genencor	326	155	Industrial, speciality	✓
Genentech	2,212	115	Therapeutic	No
Genzyme	1,224	60	Therapeutic	No
Johnson & Johnson	33,004	30	Therapeutic	✓
Maxygen	31	6	Industrial, speciality	✓
New England Biolabs	30	15	Research, speciality	No
Novozymes	633	190	Industrial, speciality	✓
Promega	>120	20	Research, speciality	No
Roche	17,277	35	Research, speciality	✓
Valley Research	10	8	Industrial, pharmaceutical	✓

*Fiscal years may vary; may include non-US sales.
Source: The Freedonia Group, Inc.

which assure a period of minimal competition and relatively high profit margins.

Global enzyme demand: In 2001, the world market for enzymes (including industrial and speciality) was estimated to be worth more than $2 billion. While US enzyme demand generally follows broad world consumption trends, there are a couple of distinct differences. For example, the US accounts for the majority of high-value enzymes used in the therapeutic segment and is also the largest user of corn-refining enzymes due to the country's agricultural dominance. Regulations and growing consumer activism in the European Community have mitigated penetration of enzymes (particularly genetically engineered types) in agricultural and food processing markets.

Despite the anti-GMO sentiment that has swept across Europe, this continent remains the leading market for enzymes worldwide. In large part, this is due to the presence of the headquarters of several of the leading producers, Novozymes, DSM, Danisco and others, in western Europe. These companies are major contributors to the Scandinavian economy and have not engendered the ill-will among Europeans that certain US-based purveyors of GMOs have.

The brand

Megazyme has developed a strong international brand among bluechip companies, such as Nestlé, Kellogg's, Anheuser-Busch, Novozymes, DSM, Coors, and many more. As part of its trademark policy the company has invested in protecting both the name and mark, 'MEGAZYME' and the logo worldwide, and is now synonymous with high purity enzymes, quality and innovation. On occasion, the company has successfully appealed possible infringements. Megazyme has invested in its trademark policy as it believes that it is an intangible asset of the company which therefore represents a value, and when considering an exit strategy the value of this trademark protection and/or intellectual property will be of extreme significance.

Sales and distribution

The key to success in any business, not just the food test kit and reagents market, is in getting the right product to the customer on time, every time. From inception, Megazyme adopted a 'born-global' strategy. The company has representation via a network of seven agents worldwide, in the following countries: Japan, Korea, Taiwan, Australia, Holland, Spain and Finland. Products are shipped via FedEx from Ireland and sold by the agent at a profit. Agents now account for 21% of Megazyme turnover.

E-business (*www.megazyme.com*)

In 1994, Megazyme established and launched its website. Internet trading allowed the company to expand its global markets and to lead rather than follow. The products and services offered by Megazyme matched the Net audience; companies in the supply chain already used the Net, and potential customers were scientists, who were among the early adopters of the Internet as a resource facility. The company continued to focus and expand on its website offerings adding the following features over the years: *New Products, International Agents, Products, Purchase Payment Details, Company Profile, Standard Methods, Scientific Publications, Media News, Customer Feedback, Industries We Serve, Technical Support and FAQs.* One of the prime objectives of the site was to give customers more and better information about the company's products and services.

By 2001, Megazyme had become an e-business success story:

- 35–40% of all worldwide sales were conducted via the website/e-mail.
- 50% of all new customers were attracted via the web (average 6 per week).
- The site attracted an average of 160,000 hits per month.
- The effective use of Internet technologies transformed the company's efficiency and profitability.

E-business has been of immense value in developing Megazyme's global reputation and is evidenced by the company receiving several awards, namely:

- DHL Export Award 1998 (Finalist);
- Eircom/Irish independent 'Business of the Year 2000' for best use of Internet technology;
- Spider Awards – Best Use of IT in International Markets (shortlisted to 5 out of 100 companies), 2001.

Competition

In 2003, there were four major global contenders in the food test kit and reagents market. However, the company's present range of products overlaps with less than 10% of competitor products since Megazyme is the sole world supplier of 90% of the products in the 2002/2003 catalogue. The majors are as follows:

- *Sigma Diagnostics*, USA (> 85,000 products/global leader in life/science products);
- *R-Biopharm GmbH*, Germany (previously Boehringer Mannheim – clinical diagnostics + food and feed analysis kits);
- *Scil Diagnostics*, Germany (founded 1999, management team formerly with

▶

Roche/Boehringer Mannheim – veterinary diagnostics/proteins and food and human diagnostics);

- *Seikagaku*, Japan (enzymes, carbohydrates, and oligosaccharides).

Management was intent on both expanding the present range of test kits and enzymes and diversifying into new markets. By building on the existing range the company could potentially tap into the database of 2,000 customers and penetrate deeper into the food test kit market and ultimately become a one-stop resource for the carbohydrate-active enzyme market.

Historic strategy

Until recently Megazyme purified enzymes from commercially available industrial preparations using conventional chromatographic procedures, such as ion exchange, hydrophobic and gel permeation chromatography. This type of technology allowed the directors to concentrate on building market share and expanding the range of enzymes and test kits to the present, i.e. 225 products in Megazyme's 2002/2003 catalogue. Throughout the development of the business, the directors of Megazyme maintained a hands-on role in the manufacturing process and technological advances within the industry in order to maintain the company's position as a leading supplier of test kits and reagents for the cereals and allied industries.

Future strategy

Recombinant DNA technology: Recombinant DNA technology is vital to the consideration of the modern enzyme industry, as the majority of enzymes are produced via recombinant methods. Recombinant DNA techniques enable the researcher to alter substances in order to transform them into targeted products with specific performance attributes. By introducing recombinant DNA technology to Megazyme this new capability will enable the company to rapidly respond to increasing demand for stable, high purity enzymes with exacting substrate specificities. In order to exploit strong market growth and new market opportunities, Megazyme is now setting up a new Molecular Biology Division. This will necessitate the expansion of the plant by 1,200 sq m at an estimated cost of €1.5 million, including fit-out of new laboratories.

Kennedy closed the management meeting with a list of priorities arising from the meeting, including recruitment of two new staff to head up the new Molecular Biology Division; initiation of architects' drawings for new extension to plant; cost analysis on new plant and equipment; funding and R&D grants and other considerations. McCleary was already preoccupied with the protocols for the first new Megazyme recombinant enzyme diagnostic test kit, namely the Lactose Assay Kit, and a list of immediate targets for other test methods to follow.

There was a palpable excitement in the room as both directors stood up from the meeting, both equally convinced about the feasibility of a molecular biology-driven expansion for the company.

Discussion questions

1 What are the key critical success factors for a biotechnology company?

2 What is biotechnology?

3 Discuss the potential of biotechnology and life sciences.

4 Does Megazyme have a sustainable competitive advantage? Why?

5 Outline the Megazyme marketing strategy.

6 What are the challenges and opportunities facing Megazyme?

Case study 14

Waterford Crystal – the Japan challenge

Thomas O'Toole and Eugene Crehan, **Waterford Institute of Technology**

Introduction

The Waterford Crystal story began in the port city of Waterford in 1783 when the Penrose brothers, George and William, started their crystal manufacturing business. Today, Waterford is recognised throughout the world for its high quality crystal, sold in over 90 countries. Waterford is part of the Waterford-Wedgwood Group (group turnover in excess of €1 billion). Recent acquisitions by the Group have given it a better global economic balance taking market growth and currency movements into account. Today the Group's brands include Waterford, Wedgwood, Rosenthal, Hutschenreuther, All-Clad and Aisling Linens. Many of these main brands have subsidiary brands for different price points, such as Marquis by Waterford Crystal. The Marquis product is a lead-crystal (ensures a quality crystal) but at a lower price point than the main brand. Each of the Waterford-Wedgwood brands has a greater degree of exposure to a specific currency than another, for example, Waterford in US dollars, Wedgwood in yen and sterling, and Rosenthal in euros. This has reduced the currency exposure of the group, headquartered in Kilbarry in Waterford City.

The lead market for the Waterford Crystal brand is the United States, where the brand has been actively promoted for over half a century. Waterford gains significant exposure, in several international markets, from its association with premier sporting events. By creating magnificent trophies for the winners of such events, Waterford is placed in the hands of some of the greatest sportswomen and men of our time. The fans of these sports stars see Waterford as a reward for success, achievement and excellence.

This message of success is reinforced in the corporate arena where Waterford is frequently chosen to reward outstanding achievement. One promotional event that illustrated the international presence of the Waterford Crystal brand was the Waterford New Year's Eve crystal ball, an impressive crystal structure, almost 2 metres in diameter, lowered in Times Square, New York, on 31 December 1999, to ring in the new millennium. This event was watched by almost one billion TV viewers across the globe. This is now an annual event that further increases Waterford's brand awareness in non-US markets and provides additional momentum to the brand in those markets.

Waterford's objectives for entering new markets, in recent decades, were not unlike those of other companies. They included the following:

- Reduce dependency on the lead markets of USA and Ireland via access to new consumers, in Europe, Japan, Australia and Asia.

- Enhance long-term sales growth and profits for Waterford and the Waterford-Wedgwood group.

- Access to lower-cost European crystal suppliers allowed Waterford to achieve lower price points and compete in new markets.

- Continued product innovation particularly through supplier and customer networks.

Waterford has had a small foothold in the Japanese market and is considering ways of developing this presence, on a budget modest in comparison with some other higher-priced luxury goods brands.

Gifting and brand choice

Today over 80% of Waterford Crystal purchased by consumers is intended as gifts. The psychology of gifting is very similar throughout the world. Basically, the giver wishes to alter the relationship between him or her and the receiver and in doing so influence the receiver's perception of him or her. Research commissioned by Waterford Crystal has increased its understanding on the type and value of gifts given by people, depending on the relationship of the giver and receiver and the particular gift occasion. This information in turn has guided Waterford in determining its product offering for individual markets.

Gift giving is an art form in Japan and is especially pronounced during the bonus seasons. Although the Japanese economy has slowed over the last 10 years, it is still one of the top economies in the world (population 126 million). Japanese consumers are recognised as being very brand literate and conscious. They seek brands that are recognisable and have a 'pedigree', especially if craftsmanship is involved in the manufacture of the product. Their perspective of a brand is influenced by the product, its packaging, in-store displays, the knowledge of the staff in the store and brand visibility including above-the-line marketing communications. Entry to the Japanese market presented Waterford with a great opportunity and many challenges. Unlike many other brand categories, there is a low awareness of the crystal product category and therefore consumers buy according to aesthetic and other factors. The growth in wine consumption has benefited crystal manufacturers and the Japanese consumer is slowly shifting to more quality products for wine consumption. However, handmade drink ware items are expected to have exactly the same dimensions as the consumer expects high quality finishes in all cases – the understanding of quality is one-dimensional and exact. Classic heavy-cut designs are not suitable to many Japanese tastes and such designs

give a masculine image in a market dominated by the female decision-maker.

Waterford Crystal's Japanese owner profile is of a female, who is married, aged over 35 with a high disposable income and influenced by western lifestyle. Waterford also appeals to the corporate market for gifts and to the single, 25 years of age and over, male interested in high quality drink ware. The Waterford Crystal brand is sold in its classic styles alongside Marquis that has a more contemporary design with lighter cuts. Waterford is positioned at the premium end of the market and Marquis at the more accessible gifting price points.

Waterford's product and promotional strategy

Waterford Crystal has a very successful track record of new product development. Waterford's most successful giftware collection was 'the Millennium range'. This was a range of champagne flutes and giftware items themed around the universal 'toasts' of Love, Happiness, Health, Prosperity and Peace. The concept of this offering was clearly understood by consumers in most developed countries. Items from the collection were ideal gifts for individuals and couples at various gift-giving occasions. At the end of the 1990s the Millennium collection from Waterford was very much in vogue, in several international markets, as a gift or as an heirloom to mark the passing of the millennium. It had relevance to cross-cultural consumer segments in several markets. The marketing communication was simple and consistent and the price was accessible to many consumers. This resulted in the recruitment of new Waterford consumers across many cultures.

Waterford decided to tailor the product offering for new markets by selecting the most appropriate items, from its extensive range, which would address consumer needs in the chosen new market. For example, the Japanese prefer less weight, greater functionality and free flowing designs. In addition, consumer pricing has to be aligned to the established price points regarded as 'appropriate' for gifting items. In Japan, these price points are fixed based on the relationship and status of the giver and receiver. As costs increase and prices are adjusted upwards, new products are required to back-fill the gaps created by vacating the key price points. As these key price points do not change, Waterford's sub-brand Marquis back-fills the lower price points.

In order to access new consumers in new markets, Waterford adapted elements of the marketing mix. This varied from the physical adaptations of product sizes for Asian markets to more symbolic adaptation vis-à-vis packaging configuration, for example, a two-piece gift box and the use of different colour packaging for certain markets. For example, the brand livery carried elements of green in Japan to reinforce Irish craftsmanship to Japanese consumers. Waterford sent artisans from its factories to Japan and other countries to conduct 'crystal cutting and engraving' events in retail outlets in order to reinforce the craftsmanship behind the brand. As the marketing infrastructure varied across cultures, Waterford has had to decide which marketing and promotional decisions to decentralise for greater effectiveness. With direction from central marketing, the market-based brand managers developed local campaigns that were implemented with local support from Waterford's sister company, Wedgwood. The coordination of many individual marketing programmes into one effective multinational marketing plan allows Waterford to monitor brand progress across geographical and cultural boundaries.

To develop the Waterford Crystal brand in Japan, one option was to spend significant funds, over a period of time, on creating widespread awareness of a consumer brand. Another was to leverage the brand's success in other markets, for example, through world tour golf or tennis events being staged in Japan. Another was to leverage the success of its sister brand, Wedgwood, in the Japanese market, by accessing its chain of retail shops. These shops have been re-branded as Waterford-Wedgwood.

Waterford has completed physical and symbolic customisation of product offerings for specific markets. For example, specific ranges were developed for Canada, the Northern Lights collection, and for Australia, the Australian Heritage collection; in addition, some size and weight adjustments were made for certain Asian markets. Symbolic changes such as modifying packaging and quantity per pack were made for other markets. When Italian consumers purchase stemware sets, they select 12 settings of each stem glass instead of the European norm of 6 place settings. In some markets the inclusion of coloured items is more important for merchandising reasons, to attract the consumer's eye, than for commercial reasons. Waterford Crystal was one of the first crystal companies to use a fashion designer, John Rocha, to design new crystal products. This initiative helped to make the brand more appealing to younger consumers. The ranges designed by John Rocha were visually different from existing Waterford designs, which increased Waterford Crystal's appeal in new markets.

Distribution and sales

Waterford Crystal is aware of the complexity of the international marketplace and the challenges of coordinating marketing strategies and activities across countries and cultures. To increase understanding of cultural differences and their potential impact on the variables in the marketing mix, Waterford positioned market brand managers in key international markets. These brand managers provided a conduit to Waterford central marketing and contributed to the tailoring of products and marketing activities for host countries. Waterford leverages the strengths of retailer relationships of its sister company, Wedgwood, to access distribution in new markets. Waterford analysed the opportunities and costs of various options for distribution in international markets. Decisions had to be taken regarding which markets to enter and the market segments in which to participate. Utilising the Wedgwood distribution infrastructure, which had already been established in Japan, Asia, Australia and Canada, allowed Waterford to quickly gain access to new consumers. By working in a mutually beneficial partnership with Wedgwood, Waterford entered new department stores and speciality stores in the above-mentioned markets. Waterford provided brand direction while Wedgwood's local experience accelerated Waterford's penetration of the new markets.

There is limited shelf space for both Wedgwood and Waterford in the traditional distribution channels in Japan. Wedgwood has 60 concession shops in department stores. The Wedgwood brand awareness is over 60% in Japan while Waterford's is still in low single figures. The Waterford-Wedgwood Group is developing a range of crystal to test market under the Wedgwood brand name. Distribution in Japan is multilayered and complex and can impose a considerable multiple on the final price. Waterford-Wedgwood products can be found in boutiques, concessions in stores, department stores, owned stores, third-party outlets, and in other speciality retailers. Retailers favour established (luxury) brands and brands with highly visible presence in stores via advertising, public relations and location. The brand owners are expected to invest in above- and below-the-line advertising as the retailers do not take this risk. Due to the current economic climate in Japan, some department stores are struggling and therefore are reducing shelf space given to tabletop items. In addition, Japanese consumers are exploring new distribution channels including direct mail and the Internet. Given the sophistication of the Japanese buyer, there has been a growth in speciality stores representing smaller manufacturers, thus meeting the characteristic Japanese consumer's need for something different.

Discussion question

Discuss options available to Waterford to grow its business in the Japanese market, including investing in the development of a consumer brand, distribution via sister company Wedgwood and the opportunity for Waterford to re-brand its crystal and market as Wedgwood in Japan.

Case study 15

Bulmers: a case in strategic learning

Paul Ryan, National University of Ireland, Galway
Mike Moroney, National University of Ireland, Galway
Will Geoghegan, National University of Ireland, Galway
Max Hayes, UCD Business Schools

It was autumn 2002, and the apples were maturing in the orchards that supplied the raw material for Bulmers, the brand that had become synonymous with cider in Ireland. For Brendan McGuinness, Managing Director of Bulmers for more than a quarter of a century, harvest time always prompted reflection on past developments and future challenges. Looking back, he could derive considerable satisfaction from the repositioning, since the late 1980s, of the company's Original Vintage Cider from a cheap, downmarket drink with a poor image, to being one of Ireland's premium and most popular alcoholic beverages. The transformation in the company itself had been no less impressive.

However, Brendan McGuinness was not one to dwell long on past successes. The drinks industry in Ireland, as elsewhere, was dynamic and the nature and scale of change presented many challenges to Bulmers, externally in its markets and internally within the company. In 2002, there were two issues that particularly occupied the thoughts of Brendan McGuinness and his management team. Firstly, the successful repositioning of the company's core product brought its own challenge, that of continued domestic market growth for Original Vintage Cider. Furthermore, for the first time, the company confronted the issue of significant expansion into overseas markets. Secondly, changing market tastes had indicated the need for a new version of the Original Vintage Cider, with lower calories and a lighter taste.

It was clear to Brendan McGuinness that the implications of these challenges were potentially as significant as the previous repositioning of the company's core product. It was important to embrace the changes that would result from these challenges. However, from experience, Brendan McGuinness also knew that the appropriate lessons of the past needed to be carried into new areas of business.

Company background and history

Bulmers Co. is Ireland's leading manufacturer of cider. Its activities began in 1935, when a Clonmel native, William Magner, decided to produce the drink commercially in Dowds Lane, Clonmel. In 1937 he joined forces with the established English cider maker H.P. Bulmer and Co. In 1949 Magner retired from the firm and the name Bulmers came to the fore. In 1964 it changed its name to Showerings (Ireland) Ltd and moved its operations to Annerville, which is located about three miles from the centre of Clonmel town. It is currently one of the main employers of the regional town of Clonmel with 470 people in its ranks. In 1999 it further showed its commitment to future growth with a €24.4 million extension including a €12.7 million bottling line, a new 75-unit tank farm with a storage capacity of 16.5 million litres, fully automated processing facilities and a new 75,000 sq ft warehouse. It announced further plans in 2001 for another plant increase in the magnitude of €25.4 million.

In 2001 the company changed its name back to Bulmers to reflect the importance of the brand to the company and to further heighten its profile among the general public and licensed trade. However, Bulmers cider is not the only brand

▶

produced in the Clonmel plant. It also manufactures Strongbow Cider, Linden Village Cider, Samsons Cider, Ritz Crisp Dry Perry, Cidona, Britvic Orange Juices (Orange, Pineapple, Grapefruit, Tomato, Tomato Cocktail) and Britvic Orange 55.

The group context (C&C)

The Cantrell and Cochrane (C&C) group currently controls the Bulmers company. Allied Domecq and Guinness UDV previously owned C&C. However, in 1998 Guinness sold their 49% stake to Allied Domecq and in 1999 Allied Domecq sold the entire C&C group to a consortium of private equity funds lead by BC Partners, a leading European venture capital company, with the support of the management of the group. The company still remains a private entity and was due to float an initial public offering in July 2002, but postponed it due to the turbulence of international equity markets during the summer of 2002.

Bulmers is just one entity within the C&C portfolio, which also has several other operating companies such as C&C Ireland (producer and distributor of soft drinks such as Club, Mi-Wadi, 7-Up, Pepsi), C&C International (producer and distributor of alcoholic products such as Carolans, Tullamore Dew, Irish Mist, Frangelico), C&C Wholesale (company-owned wholesaler to service on-trade nationally), Grants of Ireland (wine and spirit merchants), Findlaters (wine merchants) and Tayto (snack food producer). However, the importance of the Bulmers product cannot be overemphasised in relation to the C&C portfolio. In June 2003 C&C decided to move its financial year end from August to February to avoid it ending at the group's peak selling season for its largest brand, Bulmers cider.

Repositioning Bulmers

The image of cider in the late 1980s was appallingly bad. It was thought of as cheap, strong in alcohol and was associated with binge drinking and unruly behaviour. It served as a convenient scapegoat for the alcohol abuse problems of the time. This poor image also existed amongst the licensed trade and many publicans refused to stock the drink because of this perceived image problem. Added to this it had low margins and showed little promise of future growth.

Bulmers decided to start off their marketing campaign in 1988 with a strategy of drawing parallels with the beer Industry. They initially tried to position the product as a beer, using rather tacky advertising such as ZZ Top-type advertisements, reinforced with rather coarse posters saying 'everything close tastes like pils'. This approach did not do anything for the brand or the correction of the image problems that it was suffering from. As Managing Director Brendan McGuinness recalled:

Clearly the first attempt to reposition cider as beer failed and it was out of that we said let's get back to basics and the basics were telling us that it was all about tradition, naturalness and heritage. Those are our properties.

From this early failure Brendan McGuinness and his management team learned a very valuable lesson: cider was not beer, and trying to fool the consumer through a smokescreen of advertising portraying it as such was not going to work. Through an extensive marketing research effort they were able to identify several key attributes of the product. These would serve as the creative platform that they built upon. Cider has several qualities that beer does not possess. It is natural, made from apples. As Colin Gordon (Marketing Director from 1989 to 1994) stated:

Apples growing and then being crushed, wow, brilliant! It is not as if it's a funny thing that takes place with chemistry in the background. Apples grow, apples get crushed, and it gets bottled. . . . There you go more or less. Well yes, that is it essentially. Leave aside all the consumers and all the research that we did, even just watching the whole process gave you that kind of confidence that, you know, this is something that you could get a lot of movement out of.

It is also seen as being a very traditional product that has been around for a long time (having been introduced to Britain by the Druids and further perfected by the Romans and the Norman invaders). This also led Bulmers to believe in a sense of heritage that beer did not have. Beer could be seen as relatively modern and artificial compared with wine and cider. However, none of these points of differentiation had been inculcated in the mindset of the consumers. Brendan McGuinness noted this fact:

We did a lot of research at the time that showed that cider in general had enough properties that beer did not have. It was seen as natural and was made with apples. It was seen as being a very traditional product that had been around for a long time, traditional in the terms you know wine is traditional whereas beer is new. It was seen as having heritage as a category and it was out of that that we said, well, what are our points of difference to beer so let's focus on tradition, natural and heritage as our creative platform.

Key research carried out by Bulmers' marketing department showed that people were put off by the product's negative image and its adverse effects. Bulmers at this time had colloquial labels such as 'lunatic juice' or 'rocket fuel' and this was in part due to the high alcohol content of the drink. Nevertheless they discovered that the public would not like to see the drink removed from the marketplace. Essentially people had a certain regard for the product but abhorred the image and baggage that came with it. This research also allowed Bulmers' management to identify the faults in their previous strategy of positioning the product head to head with beer and highlighted the fact that it was too big a challenge to try to convert all lager drinkers to cider drinkers. The fact was acknowledged that this would never happen, so they now looked at their own drinkers. They established three varieties of Bulmers' drinker: the first being the regular core drinker, the second being the regular repertoire drinker and the third being the occasional repertoire drinker. The regular core drinker drank cider the majority of the time due to its taste and alcohol strength. The regular repertoire drinker was identified as the kind of consumer who went out to play a football match on a Wednesday night and started off on Bulmers before moving on to Guinness after two or three pints, simply using Bulmers for the refreshment value. The final category that they identified was that of the occasional repertoire drinker who only drank Bulmers when he was in the countryside or when the sun shone on a Sunday afternoon.

Colum Carey (Managing Director of The Research Centre, a research company engaged by Bulmers) summarised the classification thus:

Instead of saying all or nothing you started to say just let me hang out with you sometimes. Rather than have a gang that insists that you either hang around with them all the time or you are not part of the gang, this was, no, you can hang around with us on Tuesday or whenever, you can play football with this group, your old college mates are that group, the friends you grew up with on the street are that group, your wife's friends are that group. You don't need to bring them all together into the party and you don't have to choose between them.

Now that Bulmers had identified their drinkers and separated them into categories, the problem faced was how were they going to expand ▶

this circle and bring in more consumers? Bulmers management decided that rather than trying to make everyone a regular core drinker, they would first attempt to move people from the occasional repertoire bracket to regular repertoire, then from regular repertoire to regular core drinker. The idea was as Colin Gordon (Marketing Director) said, 'to move the centre out all the time, try to make the centre the bigger part all the time'.

Bulmers could also look to learn from Guinness's success with their product positioning using such attributes as tradition and culture. Bulmers then identified this gap at the start of the 1990s when Guinness went off in a new direction, forsaking its image of tradition, naturalness and culture. At this time Guinness pursued a variety of strategies aimed at positioning their product as 'cool and hip' rather than emphasising the ingredients and heritage of the product. Brendan McGuinness cited the fact that, 'We almost moved into all of that ground that Guinness used to occupy and, let's be honest, that was helpful'.

Image makeover

Simultaneously, the poor image of cider was a critical issue that Bulmers' management needed to address. Colum Carey recalls that, 'The image was the tail on the kite that was pulling the kite down, so you had to cut that free so that it could soar'. The first element addressed was the image of cider as having very high strength. This was compounded by the sort of adverse coverage that cider was receiving in the media in this regard. Newspaper headlines such as 'Cider crazed youths', 'Residents at war on cider parties and vandals', 'Cider thugs started library blaze', 'Cider party turned nasty, court told' were commonplace. Needless to say this did little for the Bulmers image in the mindset of the general public.

Brendan McGuinness identified the problem thus:

I think a lot of the poor image had probably come from the history of cider being very cheap. Historically it was always very high strength. We were getting very bad headlines in the media. Clearly when we investigated a lot of those cases it was apparent that not just alcohol was involved. It was under-age drinking. Today it would be Alco-pops getting the brunt of it, but cider was the convenient scapegoat of the day. Where was it all coming from? It really started life as a very marginal category. It started life at very high alcohol and it was very cheap. It was sold primarily in flagons and it was for thirst-quenching purposes. Also I suppose the history of the company is that the strength was never really controlled in the early days. You could get cider at 4% alcohol one day and another day you could be getting it at 8.5% and that is how it sort of got its reputation of 'Johnny Jump up' and 'Drives you crazy' and stuff like that. So there is a whole history of it being a cottage industry, which wasn't very well controlled, therefore it got its poor reputation. The only way to resolve that was to go through what we call a total repositioning exercise and that involved a whole range of initiatives. Obviously we had problems with consumer attitudes to cider, we had huge problems with perceived trade attitudes to cider as well in those days with Bulmers – they wouldn't stock it or were reluctant to stock it because of the type of consumers it attracted. We also had a problem with the media in that any form of alcohol abuse by the young was attributed to cider so we addressed these three areas. To do that, clearly advertising was an issue, public relations was an issue, we had to look at the product, we had to look at the pricing and packaging. So I would summarise it by saying that every single element of the marketing mix needed a remake. It is difficult to capture in a short period the extent of the remake the brand went through and the consistency with which we followed all that. In terms of the product itself, it was a 5.5% or 6% alcohol product, high alcohol, so on a phased basis we reduced the alcohol level down to the current 4.5% to bring it in line with beer.

In 1988 the Cider Industry Council (CIC) was set up with a substantial initial fund of IRL£100,000. Its aims (as stated on the website) were:

● to encourage an appreciation of cider amongst responsible and mature drinkers;

● to encourage the use of cider in cooking as an accompaniment to food;

● to help combat under-age drinking.

It played a very important role for all of the industry members in changing the media and consumer attitudes to the product. Colin Gordon reflected on the motives for the creation of the Cider Industry Council:

We were always scared that a misreported accident attributed to cider would have a seriously detrimental impact on the whole business. Trade could have delisted us and whatever . . . So everything we did was fundamentally around how to continually improve the image, where we could bring truth into the public domain, truth around under-age drinking, truth in terms of what the causes of under-age drinking were, as well as what the products were that were actually involved in the under-age drinking scene at the time. Truth also in terms of how any so-called park parties and so on were reported, because regularly they were cited as cider parties.

Figure 1 illustrates how effective the establishment of the Council proved over time.

Further marketing initiatives

Other efforts to reposition Bulmers in the mind of the consumer were used. The first of these measures was to repackage the product to bring

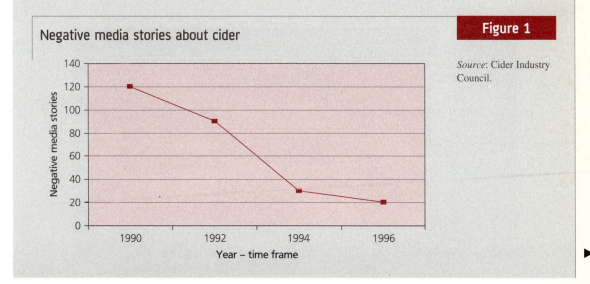

Negative media stories about cider

Figure 1

Source: Cider Industry Council.

it more clearly in line with premium product industry norms. This involved first of all introducing the product in draught, long-neck bottle and can forms. Another major step in this strategy was to discontinue with the two-litre plastic flagon, which had become renowned for underage drinking and its relative inexpensiveness. The major success of this repackaging was the introduction of the glass pint bottle traditionally served with a glass of ice, which has become synonymous with Bulmers in Ireland (as shown in the sample advertisement that follows*). Brendan McGuinness highlighted the emergence of this strategy:

I think we recognised how some people were beginning to use it and developed that as opposed to starting out from the very outset saying we want to create this concept, no. We noticed that people were beginning to use the pint bottle over ice as a refreshment proposition. Sunday morning, usage pattern, we recognised that and started building on it. We upgraded the packaging and put nice foil packaging on it, took it out of the Sunday morning hangover cure area and into the occasional refreshment area and it is now supported separately with advertising. To me that is a good example of recognising a trend that was beginning to emerge and grabbing it and taking ownership of it and developing it and bringing it to a position where the pint bottle is about one third of our business.

Bulmers also decided to stop the in-pub promotion policy, which was deemed by management to show Bulmers in a bad light. The assumption was made that by giving free Bulmers in pubs and bars, Bulmers were increasing the negative image through encouraging drunkenness. This was stopped completely and the money was utilised elsewhere in the marketing budget. One of the measures taken in attempting to upgrade their image was the sponsorship of golf events. Colin Gordon recalled:

I was very conscious that you went into trade and regularly the bar owner would tell you that 'I'm not going to have that in here because I've heard a bad story' or 'I've had a bad experience'. A lot of it was driven by the promotions that were run. The promotions on cider tended to be a

PINT BOTTLE & ICE

volume-driven activity rather than an image-building activity and therefore for a lot of publicans as indeed consumers, their only real experience of cider were people drinking it and getting too much of it and becoming slightly negative, image-wise, because of it. We withdrew all promotions to the trade, every single thing and we put all the money into image correction.

Another issue addressed was the relatively low price of Bulmers in relation to the other major beers. The price was increased to reflect its new premium product positioning. This was not done overnight, however. The late 1980s and early 1990s was a time of very high inflation in Ireland. This allowed Bulmers to employ a phased increase in the price of their product over an eight-year period. Initially it was brought up to the level of stout prices. Next it was increased to the price of ale and then to the same level as lager. In 1994 and 1996 the Irish government introduced two selective duty increases, which meant that cider prices went up but beer was not subject to this. This allowed Bulmers to pass on these duties to the consumer and again increase the price of the brand. This resulted in a position where from 1996 Bulmers sold at a premium to lager.

Advertising consistency

One aspect of the Bulmers strategy that has proved unflagging during the years has been their commitment to consistency of message. This has been achieved through several media all portraying the same messages, those of naturalness, tradition and heritage. They have kept the theme of time in all of their advertisements. It initially began as 'Nothing added but time' ('Scrumpy Jack', the English cider company, humorously responded to this with their own campaign slogan of 'nothing added but apples'). This proved to be very successful for Bulmers. The next campaign focused on 'All in its own good time'. This in turn was superseded by 'Time dedicated to you' (as shown in the advertisement below*).

Colin Gordon reflected on the inception of the idea and the snowballing consequences:

Once you had the copy line, it actually became unstoppable what you could put in against it. So, 'nothing added but time' allowed you to be natural. What is natural? Well, standing in the middle of a river fishing on your own is as natural as you can think of. You have time; you have all day to fish. You can pick on the tradition, the craft, heritage, all to do with time. You

TIME DEDICATED TO YOU   BULMERS

could pick on the absence of things because of the nothing added part of the by-line. It really became a way of having one central ad and then having loads of different themes to address different consumers in different ways to try and tweak people's emotional response to the image, giving it absolutely something unique within the long alcohol business.

John Keogh (Bulmers Marketing Director 1994–2001), however, noted how the exercise in stability could be a struggle over time:

The people who worked on the brand changed over time, the creatives changed, the marketing people changed, the account handlers changed in the agency, the administrators in the Cider Industry Council, everyone. I remember worrying every time there was change, particularly on the creative side, that the new team would want to do something new. You know, 'Ah for Christ's sake you've been doing that for the last . . . you can't keep doing that, you've got to do something new, you got to go challenge the customers'.

John Keogh thus commented on the process of educating the new management team on the consistent nature of the Bulmers' marketing plan:

You do need to get somebody into the mindset of the brand, not the mindset of 'I'm the new broom, I'm going to do something distinctly different to what was done before and I'm gonna take this brand on to the next level'. Like you'd know a Bulmers concept, you knew it was right or wrong instantly.

The dedication (as in 'Time dedicated to you') aspect highlighted that single-minded devotion to success is needed to be first in a particular field. Bulmers used many symbols and legends in different areas to draw a parallel between themselves and the person that puts in everything to succeed. For example, 'Jules Leotard', the world's first flying trapeze artist, is depicted in one of their advertisements. Another advertisement focused on the 'ski jump', featuring Sondre Nordheim, the first person to 'fly' through the air.

The second creative platform added was that of 'craft'. The advertising reflected the brand's mood and style but successfully added another aspect to the brand's character (as shown in the example below which focuses on the time and craft necessary to produce the product*). The aim of this constant brand building and learning was to allow the Bulmers brand to evolve while at the same time retaining the initial focus and qualities that were identified at the outset of the campaign.

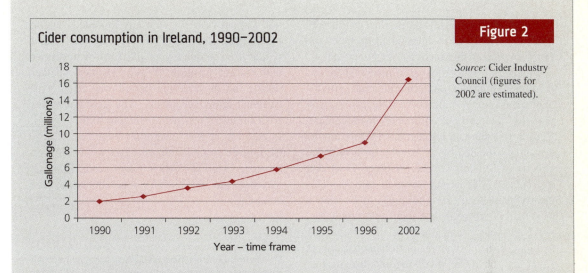

Cider consumption in Ireland, 1990–2002

Figure 2

Source: Cider Industry Council (figures for 2002 are estimated).

The set of initiatives involved in the repositioning strategy proved to be immensely successful in the enhancement of the image attached to Bulmers cider. They significantly changed the image of a product that looked to be in decline. The result was a huge increase in the sales of cider (see Figure 2), of which Bulmers as the dominant market leader was the chief beneficiary.

Future challenges

By 2002, the repositioning of Bulmers in the domestic market was largely complete. The fruits of the company's success were clearly evident. Bulmers' share of the Irish beer market stood at over 10% from a meagre 2% in 1988. Moreover, consumption of cider in 2002 was an impressive 55 million litres (equivalent to 15 litres per head p.a.) and was worth more than €200 million annually. Of this total, Bulmers accounted for the vast proportion. It commanded 89% of the 'on-trade' market, which in turn accounted for some 75% of total cider sales.

Such success brought its own issues. It was evident to Bulmers' management that continuing to grow in Ireland at the pace of the recent past

would pose challenges. With a market share of over 10% for a product with a minority taste, further gains in the domestic beer market would be hard won but nonetheless achievable. The hegemony of Guinness was again an issue, in terms both of long-established consumer preferences and the marketing and distribution muscle of the St James Gate giant. Nationally, at 5.63 million hectolitres in 2001, beer consumption in Ireland was down by 1.3% on 1999 levels (Irish Brewers Association data). At the same time, sparked by media reports focusing on late-night street violence involving young people, elements of public opinion were pushing for greater regulation of alcohol advertising and pub opening hours. Finally, the prospective banning of smoking in pubs and restaurants from 1 January 2004 was causing concern to many in the licensed and tourism industries.

Against this background, Brendan McGuinness and his team had begun to pursue the expansion of Bulmers Original Vintage Cider into overseas markets. A limited product roll-out had already taken place in the US and the UK. Test marketing was carried out in London and Glasgow, involving expenditure believed to be in the region of €3 million in total. Early results from similar test marketing in New York and Boston

▶

were encouraging, with the product being well received among the Irish emigrant diaspora and in established Irish-American neighbourhoods.

Apart from general issues of market share and continued domestic and international growth, shifts in consumer preferences were also exercising the thoughts of Bulmers' management. Market research had highlighted a desire among certain consumers, many female, for a different version of Bulmers Original Vintage Cider that was lighter in taste and lower in calories. This clearly pointed to an opportunity to develop a new market segment, one that traditionally had not been heavy consumers of the product. A tentative decision was made to launch Bulmers Light in mid-2003, involving the use of pub endorsements as a marketing tool.

While this opportunity was potentially an exciting one, the company was aware that it was not without risk. As with any modified version of an established core product, Bulmers Light would need to quickly establish its own identity and market position. Warm summer weather during the introduction period was critical for early consumer acceptance. The record of recent Irish summers was not auspicious in this regard. In addition, it was uncertain what effect, if any, the introduction of Bulmers Light would have on the core Original Vintage Cider product, which had been so successfully repositioned by the company.

---

* All advertising concepts developed by Young Euro RSCG Dublin, Ireland. Young Euro RSCG have been involved with repositioning the Bulmers brand in the Republic of Ireland and have worked very closely with the Bulmers marketing teams on the implementation of this strategy as well as lauching Bulmers Light and Magners International.

Case study 16

Know thy competitor

Katherine Rodionoff and Richard Fletcher, University of Technology, Sydney

Background

The Australian-owned manufacturer Cereol Farm is a provider of nutritious and tasty health food. Beginning in 1898, the company was the first to introduce peanut butter to the Australian market. Since this time, they have continued to be innovation driven and to date provide an extensive range of over 135 individual products with exports going to over 30 countries worldwide. Food categories manufactured by Cereol Farm include cereals, soy beverages, spreads, snacks, occasion foods and vegetarian convenience foods.

Among Cereol Farm's product portfolio is Bix-o-weet, a flake cereal biscuit, which has been the number one selling breakfast cereal in Australia for over 32 years. Bix-o-weet did not, however, originate in Australia, the formula was purchased by Cereol Farm in 1937 from the Whitworth brothers who had started the UK company Weetabix in 1932. Ironically, over 50 years later, Cereol Farm wished to enter the UK market with a competitive product to rival Weetabix.

The UK cereal market

The UK enjoys the highest global per capita consumption of cereal at 7.62 kg per annum, with approximately 95% of the population eating cereal. The UK cereal market grew by 13% in the period 1993–1996 with a market value of £1034.7m in 1996. Much of this growth was attributed to the growing market share of 'private label' product, which at this time accounted for 12% market share by value. Growth also came from new product development (NPD).

The UK breakfast cereal market is extremely concentrated with the top three manufacturers, Kelloggs, Cereal Partners and Weetabix holding over 70% of total value sales (see Figure 1). Consumers generally switch between brands in the same categories rather than across categories, making it easier for manufacturers to segment the market based on behaviour.

The UK retail food trade consists of predominantly major multiple supermarkets and discount supermarkets. The major multiple supermarkets dominate the retail industry, with

Corporate share of the UK cereal market, 1996

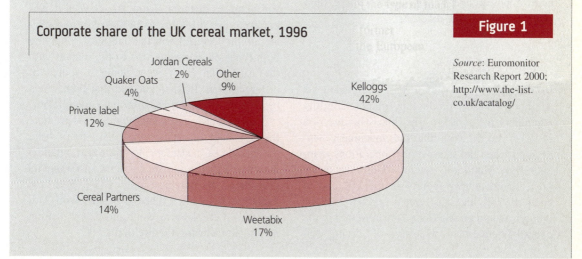

Figure 1

Source: Euromonitor Research Report 2000; http://www.the-list.co.uk/acatalog/

Jordan Cereals 2%
Quaker Oats 4%
Private label 12%
Cereal Partners 14%
Weetabix 17%
Other 9%
Kelloggs 42%

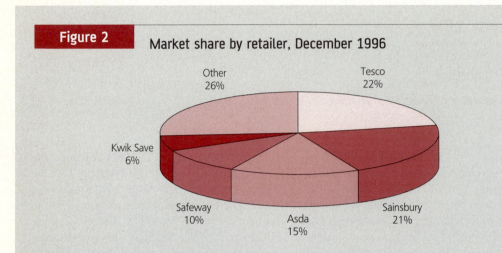

Figure 2   Market share by retailer, December 1996

Other
26%

Tesco
22%

Kwik Save
6%

Safeway
10%

Asda
15%

Sainsbury
21%

independent food stores, convenience and discount stores contributing the remainder. The main retailers and select discounters served over 70% of the consumer market in 1996 (see Figure 2). Retailers, when dealing with small manufacturers are often the price makers, with the manufacturers being the price takers. This is a result of the fierce competition between retailers, which use frequent price discounting, making profit margins on products including breakfast cereals very thin. Larger manufacturers such as Weetabix and Kelloggs who have maintained a long-term market presence and built up brand equity with consumers, have greater price control power due to consumers pulling their products through the retailers.

The idea is conceived

In the mid-1990s Cereol Farm upgraded its Melbourne-based production plant including machinery for its Bix-o-weet line. The question of what to do with the old machinery was decided when the international operations manager Tony Matthews, saw an opportunity to set up a manufacturing facility in the UK and to enter the UK breakfast cereal market. He saw that this would enable Cereol Farm to satisfy the overall international objectives of serving cul-

turally similar markets while increasing revenue. In this they would benefit from the low cost of manufacturing in the UK. The opportunity took the form of manufacturing a 'private label' brand for the UK discount supermarkets as the current supplier of the flake cereal biscuit refused to serve this market segment due to low margins. The 'private label' market was rising rapidly and Cereol Farm saw this as a golden opportunity to serve a niche that was being neglected.

Entering the market

Although the UK flake cereal biscuit, Weetabix was slightly different from Bix-o-weet it was believed that Weetabix would be easy to replicate, giving Cereol Farm the option of supplying both types of wheat biscuits to the market with the Australian Bix-o-weet being a source of differentiation. It was expected that both wheat biscuits would be sold to discount supermarkets.

Cereol Farm used distributors to promote their product to retailers, as they didn't have the resources necessary to approach retailers directly. A distributor by the name of Granovita guaranteed to purchase both Bix-o-weet and Weetabix lines after successful talks with Aldi and Lidl. Cereol Farm went ahead with setting up a manufacturing facility in the UK.

Problems

While the facility was being set up in the UK, it was reported that people employed by the competitor Weetabix had been to the plant, and that aerial photographs of the production plant had also been taken. This proved to be the start of a long line of attacking moves initiated by Weetabix to retain their dominance and ultimately become the only player in the category for wheat flake biscuits.

Faced with the opening of the Cereol Farm plant in 1999 and the potential threat to its complete dominance of the marketplace, Weetabix changed their strategic direction and started aggressively pursuing Cereol Farm's business. Weetabix, renowned for supplying only the major multiples, initiated talks with the discounters, namely Aldi and Lidl (Cereol Farm's accounts). They cut margins to below the cost of production and offered an 'under the table' incentive of over £200,000. In December 1999 and again in January 2000, Granovita informed Cereol Farm that they had lost the two respective discounter accounts. Discussions held with most other discounter retailers ended in the same fashion, with Weetabix undercutting the competition. Another attacking move was found to be Weetabix's registering of the *Fruiti-bix* trademark a day before Cereol Farm was scheduled to.

Upon further research into its rival, Cereol Farm was able to discover why Weetabix was so dominant in its market and had the ability to fend off the competition so completely.

- Weetabix was a six product company (see Table 1) with Weetabix being its lifeline. It was poor at product innovation and survived primarily through category domination. It was in three market sectors and possessed the brand leaders, Alpen in cereals, Ready Brek in the hot sector, and Weetabix in the whole wheat biscuit category.

- Weetabix charged a premium for its product. Its ability to command high margins was partly due to its long history in the

Table 1 Weetabix's product range
Weetabix + Fruiti-bix variant
Alpen
Crunchy Bran
Weetos
Advantage
Ready Brek

marketplace. Children had grown up on the cereal and when they had grown into adults and produced families of their own, they fed Weetabix to their own children. This produced high loyalty and penetration levels in the UK market. The resulting high margins made it possible for Weetabix to undercut their competitors by realising a loss on the Weetabix brand and offsetting this against high margin gains from other product offerings. If this did not work, Weetabix simply acquired small rivals (this had happened to the last two companies that had offered the whole wheat biscuit).

- Weetabix had developed personal relationships with its wholesale distributors over the years. It delivered promptly and had a high reputation for quality and reliability, winning a gold medal for services to wholesalers from the 'Federation of Wholesale Distributors'. This meant that competitors could not gain an advantage over Weetabix through trade marketing as Weetabix offered reasonable margins and delivered on promises.

- Weetabix had a low employee turnover with employees committed to the company for the long term. This resulted in experienced management teams having a deep understanding of the brand and a long-term survival strategy for the company.

- Weetabix was a highly secretive company which did not like speaking to the press,

▶

public or competitors alike. Information was limited to what could be found in the annual report. Most voting shares were privately owned; however, the non-voting shares were listed on the small UK 'Of ex' exchange due to the lax disclosure requirements. This meant that institutional investors could not build up powerful shareholdings in order to influence the running of the company.

With the insights gained from market research, Cereol Farm realised that Weetabix's major weakness was in its limited range of products offered. Cereol Farm, being a long time innovator, entered into a joint venture with another long established cereal manufacturer and together they are developing new breakfast cereals to launch onto the UK market. Time can only tell how successful they will be.

Discussion questions

1 What should Cereol Farm have done more extensively before entering the UK market?

2 What enabled Weetabix to keep Cereol Farm out of the UK market?

3 Explain Weetabix's main motivation in keeping Cereol Farm out of the UK market.

4 Was Weetabix an ethical competitor?

5 You are now managing director of Cereol Farm, what alternatives other than a joint venture are open to you if you wish to remain in the UK cereal market?

6 Consider Porter's Five Forces Model as discussed in Chapter 14 and discuss the extent to which it can and cannot be applied in this case.

Case study 17

AIB Credit Card Centre (CCC): supplier management and relationship development

Seán de Búrca and Thomas Downes, UCD Business Schools

Introduction

It was ten past five on Friday evening and the Operations Manager of AIB's Credit Card Centre, was staring blindly out his office window. Yet deep in the back of his mind he was thinking deeply about how this changing purchasing function was going to integrate effectively and successfully into the future strategic plans of the unit. He had arranged a meeting with the Purchasing Officer for 10am the next morning and therefore he was making some notes. His main concern was to organise the next Vendor Day and he knew that before this could be done, the management team had to decide on how they were going to raise the significance of vendor management to a strategic level in the unit so as to meet the challenges and demands of the future.

Background

In the past the purchasing function at CCC had been given very little attention and it was considered a simple routine task that required minor effort. To associate it with management would be unheard of, and thus there was no real focus. There was a wide range of suppliers and the attitude was very much adversarial, based on a win–lose situation. There was very little contact between the parties and the communication flows were quite limited. The purchasing function as it stood was very much into stationery. The person doing the job looked after the buying of paper, pens, paper clips and that sort of stuff. All the other areas were outsourced. CCC used agencies for all other market-to-market items like print, continuous stationery, services, terminals, machines etc. This proved extremely expensive as the agency costing structure allowed them to add on 17% to what they spent and obviously there was no real incentive for the agencies to be cutting costs. And since CCC was not fully aware of the nature of these activities, they just accepted the fact and learned nothing in the process. As the years went on, the costs that they were incurring got higher and higher, and the marketing department was reporting a huge amount of spend on the prime print area. The marketing manager and the management team realised that these expenses could be avoided, so they set about taking on the task of purchasing themselves. They felt that if savings could be made then they should make them. It sounded so simple but as they quickly learned it wasn't the simplicity that was the issue, it was the efficiency.

Types of suppliers

To clarify, CCC has two types of suppliers:

1 *Issuing*: which consists mainly of stationery – continuous stationery i.e. statements, card mailers, pin mailer, and envelopes; also plastics (on the product side).

2 *Acquiring*: Technology – terminal providers and maintenance service providers, machines, IT providers and IT third party contractors.

CCC started to take the print purchasing away from the agencies and the role was taken on internally without a formal purchasing department set up. As a result, there was a serious lack of procedures and that point was becoming increasingly evident.

It was at this stage that the management started looking down the ISO route. From a cost control point of view, management need to make some major changes in the internal structure and current methods of operations. One of the major bond rules of the ISO system was purchasing and therefore this option seemed suitable for the unit at the time.

In addition there was also an element of competitive advantage as no other credit card company in the world had ISO. The head of CCC at the time was a major champion in initiating this change. He had a reputation for being good at visualising and projecting out, and his backing was quite important. To begin the process they had an internal audit in the acquiring side (terminals, machines, maintenance, software, etc.) of operations. When the auditor asked to see the procedures and there was none, it only highlighted further the need for some sort of structure that would ensure consistency. Hence the auditor was retained for about six months, during which time he wrote procedures for them. Clearly the ISO offered a framework that could tighten up procedures as well as get an international accreditation that was seen to be something of real value.

It was decided to take the ISO route and nine months later it was achieved. Emerging out of ISO, CCC started to think about their relationships with suppliers. Procedures continued to be developed and information collected for entry onto their database. They started recording what and how many orders were sent out, if they got back on time, and whether or not there were any problems. Good vendors were kept on the Approved Vendors List. CCC started informing the supplies that they were being graded, and that if problems arose on a regular basis that they would be struck off this list. At the beginning it was really difficult to understand what the ISO manuals were calling for. Building the procedures was a critical part of this change and it was important to be precise and inclusive as well as leaving some flexibility for change.

Initially CCC was very much control focused and quality assurance was a major issue. They were checking everything that was coming in and stickers were flying everywhere. Basically it was a controllable approach where the suppliers were told exactly what was expected of them. Product specifications were placed on all their main products. A goods inwards piece was designed as well as building a goods inward quality area downstairs. Quality questionnaires were designed. A PC-based system was put up for maintaining what vendors were on, what grades they had, and how many corrective actions they had received. This tracking of information had not been done in the past and so it constituted a major change in the handling of these relationships. Thus it was taken as given that problems would arise, but with procedures in place as well as people downstairs receiving and checking, that these problems could be reduced. The supplier base slowly began to narrow but really it had not yet reduced to a desired level. All this was built up during a six-month period leading up to the first ISO audit.

Still the focus seemed to be on developing internal structures, and the communication between AIB and the suppliers had changed only incrementally. The suppliers would have noticed the formalisation of orders and corrective action procedures and would have known that CCC was going for ISO, but they had not yet been brought into this change.

Vendor Day

CCC decided to bring their suppliers together to have a frank and open discussion about their relationships; it was called Vendor Day. The vendor representatives were generally from a high level in their organisation, predominantly sales reps and CEOs, and there was a high level of response. AIB (CCC) took the value chain model as a framework and realised they didn't control it. So in order to manage it more effectively they needed their suppliers to buy into their ethos and quality concept.

During the course of the discussions with their suppliers, CCC management accepted that this was a two-way street and that they didn't intend to 'beat the other guy up'. In addition, they openly highlighted the areas that had been deficient such as quality control, quality assurance, internal procedures, and structure. They outlined that they intended to operate with a consistent approach that would be value led rather than price led. Furthermore they emphasised the fact that they would be quality focused as well as partnership driven. This consistent approach applied to all suppliers with regards to ordering, lead times, and delivery requirements. Value led meant getting the right quality, to the right place, at the right time as well as at the right price. The quality focus emphasised quality assurance rather than quality control. Most importantly they wanted future relationships to be partnership driven. This meant joint objectives, openness and trust, coupled with a more win–win type relationship that was mutually supportive.

CCC acknowledged that they needed to work together and that it was in their best interests to offer whatever help they could to buy the vendors into the concept of adding value to both their businesses. Small group discussions were organised and a number of interesting issues emerged.

- *Customer usage*: suppliers don't know what the finished product is used for.
- *Communication*: people don't know who they will be dealing with as personnel are always changing.
- *Delivery*: needs to be more flexible.
- *Audit*: should companies that already have ISO be audited?
- *Corrective action requests*: larger suppliers are more vulnerable to the 4 CARs threat (more supplies, more errors).
- *Certificate of analysis*: is it needed with each order?
- *Ideal vendor*: zero defects is impossible!

- *Communication*: there is a need for defined points of contact, and a need for a hierarchy of contact points.
- *CARs*: what type of defect gives rise to a CAR particularly in software?
- *CcAIB*: sometimes do not deliver resources/specifications on time.
- *Incoming inspection*: will the quarantine area eventually disappear? And if so, then the first ones to see the problems will be the customers.
- *Pricing*: should not be uppermost in choosing vendors.
- *Customer-held stock*: there should be procedures for stock levels being looked at on a more regular basis.
- *Visits*: were encouraged.
- *ISO manual*: can CCC send a copy to all vendors outlining ISO and their procedures?
- Vendors should be offered greater *opportunities* within the IB group if they are approved vendors with CCC.

After discussing the feedback with the suppliers CCC introduced the concept of quality audits. Since most of the suppliers may not have been familiar with quality audits, it was important to communicate to them the surrounding issues encompassing such a procedure so they could change and adapt accordingly. The main purpose of the quality audit was to evaluate to what extent the vendor's quality system complies with the CCC requirements. Its primary aim was to help the vendor improve and build a closer partnership with CCC and outlined how CCC would approach the vendor pre-audit, during and post audit.

How can the CCC help you

The discussion closed with the issue of assistance. CCC offered a helpline for vendors to call if they had any questions on how or what

▶

changes needed to be made to get up to speed. Training programmes were also mentioned and suppliers were invited to take part in these activities so as to aid in their development. CCC announced that they would be making more visits as well as encouraging the vendors to do the same. The Certificate of Vendor Relationship and the Best Vendor Award were also ways in which CCC could help: i.e. if you worked with us, we would reward you with something of value that will assist your future business.

At the end of the day CCC management had much to consider. They were convinced that the strategic role of purchasing and supplier relationship had an important part to play in the future of CCC. Were they really doing the right thing? Could they get more from working closer with their suppliers than mere quality improvement? Do they have the right balance? Where should the future focus lie? And how can they communicate this both internally and externally? How well do they really know their suppliers?

Part D

Contemporary Challenges in International Marketing

18

Incorporating international trade relations into international marketing

After studying this chapter,
you should be able to:

- appreciate the role of
  international trade
  relations in marketing
  international products
  and services;

- recognise how the role of
  government impacts on
  international marketing;

- learn how multilateral
  trade relations have
  evolved and their likely
  directions in the years
  ahead;

- appreciate how bilateral
  trade relations operate
  and how they can be
  used by businesspersons
  to address problems of
  access or impediment
  in the international
  market; and

- discuss the advantages
  and disadvantages of
  entering into commodity
  agreements and the
  impact of managed
  trade.

Working for manufacturers without factories

A growing number of large firms in manufacturing are separating the physical production of goods from the research and development and marketing stages of the production process, relying for the former on a dense network of independent (but often closely monitored) suppliers and for the latter on their own efforts. As the tasks directly performed by these firms have shifted to higher-value added activities, the number of jobs within subcontractors located in both developed and developing countries has increased rapidly. Such subcontracting is popular in the garment and footwear industries but is also spreading to other manufacturing activities as well as services. A prominent example is Nike (United States).

Nike subcontracts 100% of its goods production. Nike itself currently employs 9,000 people, while nearly 75,000 people are employed by its independent subcontractors located in different countries. These figures reflect the division of labour in value added: Nike's own team of highly skilled workers focuses on the services part of the production process, including design, product development, marketing, distribution, data processing, sales and administrative tasks. Labour-intensive manufacturing tasks are performed by the workforce at the subcontractors' facilities in developing countries. Apart from a powerful media-driven image, a key source of the company's profitability is its performance-oriented inventory-control system, Futures. Nike manages to get orders from retailers in advance in return for guaranteed delivery times and discounts, making it possible for it to organise timely production from its different producers located abroad.

The location of Nike's subcontractors and the associated employment has shifted over time. From its inception, the company sourced almost all its shoes from independent producers. But the original suppliers in Japan, the United States and the United Kingdom have in part been replaced by producers in developing countries, including China (which now supplies about 25% of Nike's shoes) and the Republic of Korea, Malaysia, Taiwan Province of China and Thailand. In an attempt to achieve both flexibility and stability, Nike has created a set of clearly differentiated supply relationships that have implications for the quality of employment provided by subcontractors.

There are three groups of suppliers in Nike's network:

1 Developed partners (Taiwan and South Korea)
2 Developing sources (Thailand, China, Indonesia)
3 Volume producers (South Korea)

The most important are what the company calls the *developed partners* mainly located in the Republic of Korea and Taiwan Province of China, who participate in joint product development and concentrate on the production of newest product designs. Given the rising labour costs in these locations, labour-intensive activities previously performed by suppliers in these countries were relocated to other countries.

Introduction

 International trade relations are part of a country's total relationship with other countries. They are interrelated with political relationships which are increasingly influenced by trade considerations; cultural relationships which frequently operate as a vehicle to expand services exports such as stage productions, films, music and art works; defence relationships which are influenced by the potential to sell military hardware; civil aviation relationships which involve landing rights and bilateral agreements to access other markets; immigration relationships including issues such as business migration; and finally, development assistance relationships where the tying of aid to trade is a common practice. Figure 18.1 illustrates how political relationships are perceived to facilitate commercial relationships in various countries in Asia.

A series of recent global changes have served to further shift the focus of international relations towards trade. The redrawing of the global atlas following the collapse of communism has caused a shift in eastern Europe and the former USSR from politics to trade, especially obtaining benefits from the World Trade Organisation and membership of regional trade groupings such as the European Union. In addition, with the absence of a cold war threat, global defence expenditures have fallen and political competition between countries is more by trade than by war. The increase of tribalism, rather than the nation state, is a source of conflict. In places such as Africa and the former Yugoslavia, a dilemma for international governments is whether they should also target their trade relations activity towards the tribal group or the alternative government as opposed to just the federal government in power.

Globally there has been an overall reduction in aid from the richer to the poorer nations. This reduction has been in grants as well as in low-interest, long-term loans. The political motivation for aid has diminished as the cold war recedes and debt levels in the wealthy nations increase. Reduction in aid increases the pressure to trade and developing countries are increasingly exploring trade expansion as an alternative to aid.

Marketing context

Both international trade relations and marketing are about access – to world markets, to regional markets or to single country markets. The bottom line is that a firm cannot market its goods abroad if the goods are not allowed entry. Issues of access can be short-term, as with temporary quarantine bans, or long-term. Impediments to access are driven by:

- firms in another country that want to keep out imports;
- governments that want to raise revenue by using tariffs; and
- firms or governments that wish to favour specific countries.

Love thy neighbour

Source: International Business Asia, 17 November 1997. Reproduced with the permission of the Charlton Group.

Figure 18.1

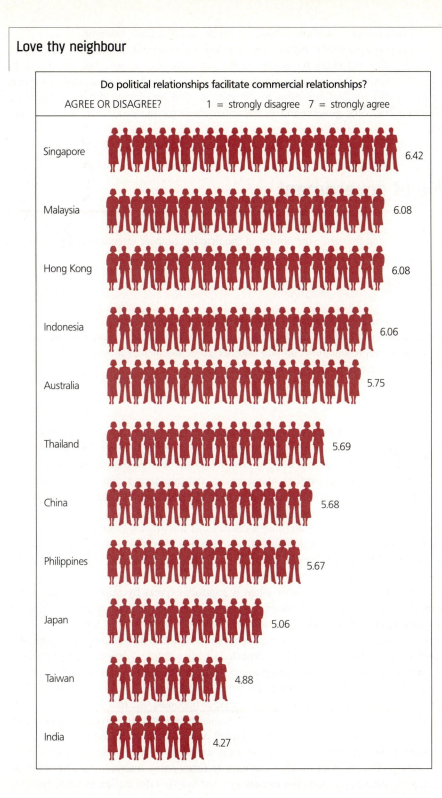

Do political relationships facilitate commercial relationships?

AGREE OR DISAGREE?   1 = strongly disagree   7 = strongly agree

Singapore — 6.42

Malaysia — 6.08

Hong Kong — 6.08

Indonesia — 6.06

Australia — 5.75

Thailand — 5.69

China — 5.68

Philippines — 5.67

Japan — 5.06

Taiwan — 4.88

India — 4.27

The principal vehicles for impediments are tariff and non-tariff barriers.

Marketing is also about maximising international competitiveness. Trade relations and trade policy activities by governments can adversely impact on the ability to compete. It can do this by reducing the value offered to the international customer, by creating different relationships in the market, and by placing different emphasis on the importance of government in the value chain for the product or service being offered.

Role of government

Governments can influence the ability of the firm to compete internationally.

Domestic

Government operates as a partner in the firm's network as a regulator, as a facilitator, and as a customer. Each of these roles by the government can become the subject of trade relations representations should another government feel they adversely impact on its firms entering the international market.

Regulator

The government can impose bans on its firms exporting to specific international countries as happens when it supports UN embargoes on trade with countries such as Iraq. Its actions in the domestic market can raise the costs of exporting. Examples of such actions are export inspection fees, stamp duties and transaction charges and either not allowing or making difficult the claiming back of import duties paid on the imported content of products subsequently exported.

Another area where the government operates as a regulator is in the imposition of standards. Standards may be deliberately set different from those of other countries so as to make it difficult for foreign products to enter the market, or (allegedly) may be imposed for quarantine or health reasons.

Government acts as a regulator when it controls exports by imposing bans on the export of certain products for security reasons. Examples include actions by the US under its foreign military sales programme.

There are many ways by which a government can act as a facilitator of exports if it chooses to do so. When a product is exported, it can refund any taxes or import duties paid. Many governments have a programme of export incentives. Often other countries argue that these incentives amount to dumping or in other ways result in injury to their domestic suppliers. When this occurs, the matter becomes one that is settled via trade relations representations and discussion. In some cases, domestic governments deliberately create a favourable financial environment for exported products.

Domestic governments' international representatives such as trade commissioners and embassy officials can provide assistance to firms going international. Not only do these representatives provide direct assistance and market information to firms, but they also lobby international government departments and ministers on behalf of the interests of these firms.

Other ways in which a government facilitates firms is via the provision of investment incentives. These encourage firms from abroad to invest in the domestic market, especially in joint ventures.

Customer

The government is also a customer for many firms. In the process, they add credibility to firms' claims of expertise, especially in countries where government endorsement is respected. Governments also give preference to local products and legislation such as 'Buy Local' Acts allows governments to buy from local sources even if those sources are more expensive than international sources.

Often the domestic government gives aid to other countries and this aid is usually given to advance the donor's commercial interests. There may be a requirement for the aid to be tied to procurement of certain products, or the aid is given as part of a joint government/private sector assistance package to the other country that resulted from bilateral trade discussions.

Foreign

Foreign governments can also operate as regulator, facilitator and as customer.

Regulator

Foreign governments can impose duties on products entering their domain. They can also impose a variety of non-tariff barriers, such as quotas, licences, quarantine regulations and health requirements. They may impose standards not only on the product but also on the way it is promoted, the way it is distributed, and the way it is priced.

Facilitator

Foreign governments can act as a facilitator, not so much with exports unless a countertrade arrangement is involved, but more when investment in their country is concerned. Governments often offer incentives to foreign firms to invest in either priority regions in the country or in priority industries or for the transfer of unique technology or in all three areas. The incentives can relate to free or concessional duties on the importation of capital equipment, components or raw materials; tax holidays; absence of restrictions on the repatriation of profits, capital or dividends; or concessions on local taxes and imposts.

Customer

Because of the large volume of purchasing in the government sector, international governments can be major customers for imported products, services and projects. Often their trade relations activities reflect their using the leverage of their purchasing to facilitate other commercial objectives. This often happens with offsets programmes (see section on Countertrade).

Influence and government

If the firm is able to involve its government as a partner in its international network, this is likely to improve its international competitiveness. The government using its 'trade relations clout' can assist firms' entry into international markets. Government involvement improves the attractiveness of the firm's offer because in many countries buyers want the security of dealing with international firms that have the active support of their government.

18.1 International highlight

Johannesburg Earth Summit failure

The United Nations World Summit for Sustainable Development held in Johannesburg in 2003 confirmed for many the lack of commitment to the eradication of poverty. The summit was to build on the historic Rio conference held 10 years ago. The main objective was to drive efforts to tackle the crisis of world poverty and environmental degradation. The overall assessment is that little has so far been delivered for the poor or for the environment. When it comes to tackling these issues the summit's implementation plan is high on rhetoric with little real commitment. For example, as regards tackling the main problem areas Paul Brown in the *Irish Times* outlines the successes and failures:

Water and sanitation – the summit agreed to halving the number without basic sanitation by 2015 alongside plans to provide clean water for half those without it.

Poverty – recognition that poverty and environmental degradation are linked and the cycle needs to broken. The aim is to halve the 1.2 billion who live on less than $1 a day.

Energy and climate change – no targets, greatest single failure of the summit.

Health – commitment to restore fish stocks urgently and focus on marine pollution and illegal fishing.

Sustainable consumption – agreement to develop an action programme in 20 years and to give shoppers informative eco-labels.

Biodiversity, natural resources – aim to reduce loss of biodiversity significantly by 2010 and attempt to strengthen forest law and reduce illegal logging.

Africa – agreement on land tenure, women's right to inherit land, and food security plans as well as recognition that Africa need special attention.

Trade and globalisation – agreed to give environment treaties equal standing with the WHO.

Human rights – relationship between human rights and the environment was recognised with some resistance from the G7 group.

There seems to be no political will on the part of world's leaders – some, like US President Bush, did not even turn up and many of the leaders who did attend gave grand speeches but little was reflected in their negotiating positions. This fortress mentality means that there is little hope that the World Trade Organisation's new development round will genuinely face up to the changes needed to make international trade a force for poverty reduction.

Another issue is how the firm can enlist the support of its government to help it win international business. The firm can directly approach the relevant government department for assistance. It can also initiate an approach through indirect means, such as via the industry association to which it belongs; by lobbying ministers and officials through third parties such as professional lobbyists; by approaching local political representatives such as a member of parliament or responsible minister; or it can work through local or regional government bodies. Some of these may have a pre-existing relationship with the international market such as a 'sister city' relationship.

There are five major ways for government to influence the trade activities of other countries. These are: participation in multilateral forums, membership of regional trade groupings, bilateral trade relations with countries on an individual basis, entering into commodity agreements, and insisting on managing the trade in certain product categories. The firm can influence each of the above in order to improve business prospects. A trade relations approach by the firm need not be confined to one of the above but may include several as they interact and overlap, as the following illustrates.

International trade issues can be addressed on a multilateral basis, on a regional basis, or on a bilateral basis.

Multilateral trade relations

Purpose

The purpose of multilateral trading systems such as the General Agreement on Tariffs and Trade (GATT) is to remove restrictions on trade worldwide. In pursuit of this objective, it supports structural change and economic growth in the overall world economy. It does this in two ways. The first is by promoting trade liberalisation. Bodies such as the GATT (now the World Trade Organisation) believe that overall economic growth will be enhanced if all countries remove their barriers to trade and liberalise their existing measures for protecting local producers and using imports to raise revenue. The second is by establishing a framework of rules for the conduct of trade policy by nations.

History

Following the depression of the 1930s, in the years leading up to the Second World War, there was chaos in international trade. Following the Second World War, it was felt by the victorious nations that in order to facilitate world recovery, a new trading order should be introduced which allowed each member nation to pursue its comparative advantage and stimulate the flow of trade which the Second World War had interfered with. It was presumed that the main barriers to trade were tariff barriers and the reduction of these should be targeted. It was also considered that the main reason for the introduction of tariffs by a nation was to protect its infant industries. Therefore the focus of this new world trade order was on manufactures.

The above resulted in the formation of the GATT in 1947. This body aimed to provide a secure and predictable international trading environment in which the progressive liberalisation of trade could continue. Since its formation, there have been a number of major forums where GATT members come together to debate major issues of concern. Known as GATT rounds, these go on for several years at a time. The last GATT round was the Uruguay Round. This was arguably the most significant of all and resulted in the GATT renaming itself the World Trade Organisation (WTO). As of 26 July 2001, there were 142 signatories to the WTO accounting for over 90% of world trade.

Operation

The GATT operated on the basis of a set of rules agreed on a multilateral basis governing the behaviour of governments. It provided a forum for trade negotiations designed to liberalise the international trading environment. It also provided an international court in which governments could resolve disputes on trade issues with other governments.

The objectives of GATT were to reduce tariffs on goods, prohibit restrictions on the quantities of goods that could be traded and eliminate other non-tariff barriers to trade in goods. It also aimed to eliminate all forms of trade discrimination through the operation of the Most Favoured principle Nation (MFN). All GATT members agreed to the MFN principle by which they undertook to accord to any GATT member the same treatment as they accorded to their most favoured trading partner.

The GATT objectives were to be achieved by a range of measures:

- *Non-discrimination.* This involved ensuring that nations did not discriminate in their trade and treated all other nations equally. Both the MFN and an agreement by GATT members not to introduce any new preferences were to be the means for eliminating discrimination.

- *Open markets.* Signatories agreed that any forms of protection they implemented would be transparent to all and not hidden; that they would work towards reducing tariffs and that, once reduced, these tariffs would not be subsequently increased; and that restrictions on the quantities of a product allowed to be imported (QRs) would only be imposed if a country was experiencing serious balance of payments problems.

- *Fair trade.* All the world's exporters were to have the chance to compete with each other on fair and equal terms. To this end, export subsidies on manufactures were prohibited and limits were imposed on subsidisation of primary products.

- *Settlement of trading disputes.* If both parties to the dispute were GATT members, then they were required to consult with each other. If they could not settle the dispute by consultation, then the GATT would arbitrate the issue.

- *Stability and predictability.* All members were to facilitate stable trading conditions and governments should not subject importers to constant changes in regulations or other aspects of gaining access to their markets.

Current focus

Although earlier GATT rounds had endeavoured to update GATT rules and provisions to take into account the changing international trading scene, in reality little had changed in the two decades prior to the conclusion of the Uruguay Round in 1994. There was considerable dissatisfaction with the operation of the GATT. The less developed nations, although members, claimed that they were disadvantaged compared with the developed nations. The GATT appeared to be unable to address issues of agricultural protectionism that resulted in inefficient agricultural producers in developed countries receiving subsidies to produce agricultural products surplus to domestic requirements. These surpluses were then dumped on world markets to the detriment of efficient producers who were mostly from the developing countries. Protection of intellectual property was another area which GATT did not cover and this was of concern to developed countries whose products were being copied by operators in the developing countries. The growth in international trade in services was expanding faster than that of goods and was not adequately catered for by existing GATT rules. Increasingly, investment in manufacturing in a foreign country was the alternative to supply of goods and this facet of international activity also was not covered in GATT. Finally, there was increasing dissatisfaction with the effectiveness of GATT in resolving disputes.

These shortcomings led to the Uruguay Round. This was the toughest of the eight GATT rounds and lasted seven and a half years. The results represented a major achievement in addressing the shortcomings mentioned above. However, there is always a gap between the rhetoric and the implementation. The most important outcomes are listed below:

- *Agriculture.* Because an average cut of 36% in tariffs was agreed to, access for agricultural products to other markets was likely to significantly improve. In addition, the extent of subsidisation of agricultural products for export was curtailed both by agreement to reduce measures to support agricultural production by 20% and by the cutting of export subsidies by 36%.

- *Industry.* Tariffs on most industrial products were reduced by one-third which was considerably in excess of tariff cuts negotiated at previous GATT Rounds.

- *Services.* For the first time, international trade in services was to be governed by the rules of fair trade. This trade was valued at US$960 billion as at 1994. Seventy nations entered into binding commitments as far as their trade in services was concerned.

- *Intellectual property.* A new agreement covering intellectual property (TRIPS) was drawn up providing both specific rules and rules for dispute resolution. Because individual countries had different laws and varying degrees of enforcement where breach of intellectual property rights was concerned, transition periods were provided to enable countries to bring their practices into line with the provisions of the TRIPS agreement. The transition periods were one year for developed countries, five years for developing countries and eleven years for the least developed of the developing countries.

- *Investment.* A new agreement covering investment (TRIMS) was arrived at. This limited the scope for foreign governments to attach onerous conditions to investment approvals or link such approvals to receipt of other advantages, which might be viewed as discriminatory.

The Uruguay Round resulted in the formation of the World Trade Organisation (WTO) which commenced with 120 members. This number has now risen to 142 and there are other countries, including China, seeking membership. The WTO has inherited a substantial agenda for implementation from the Uruguay Round. Some of the major issues confronting the WTO are its focus on single-sector negotiations such as telecommunications, and providing less opportunity for trade-offs and mutual concessions. It will also have to grapple with the growing friction between the US and the EU over issues of extraterritoriality, such as trade with Cuba and Libya, and the feeling of many developing countries that they got relatively little out of the Uruguay Round.

In order to implement the above agreed outcomes, a new round of multilateral trade talks was held in Seattle in 1999 known as the 'Millennium Round'. This was a disaster and this can be attributed to a number of factors including disenchantment with globalisation and suspicion by the developing countries that the WTO would continue the GATT tradition of being a 'rich man's club'. Despite the rhetoric, little had been done by the developed countries to address agricultural subsidies that prevented efficient agricultural producing nations (many in the developing world) from selling into developed country markets. Subsidies paid to farmers in the European Union, the US and Japan are now valued at US$29.4 billion, a figure not seen since the mid-1980s. The US continues to hide behind the requirement that agreements made by the President had to be referred to Congress so as to delay implementation – the Clinton administration allowed the 'Fast Track Legislation' that would overcome this anomaly to lapse in 1994.

The consequence is a lack of enthusiasm by a number of Asian countries for the WTO, illustrated in the following:

The push for further trade liberalisation is making many Asian governments uneasy. These governments argue that, given the troubled state of Asia's economies, this is hardly the time to start tinkering with the world trading system. These countries are reluctant to further open their domestic markets to foreign competition and they have already encountered difficulties translating the WTO's current liberalisation pledges into domestic legislation.

Source: *Far Eastern Economic Review*, 21 May 1998.

Items under current discussion at the WTO include anti-bribery measures, trade and competition policy, and trade and the environment. Items already scheduled for further action include agriculture, services and intellectual property rights. New issues likely to be raised in the next WTO round include electronic commerce, liberalisation of investment flows, elimination of textile quotas, anti-dumping policy, labour standards and further reduction of industrial tariffs.

One area where developing countries have been disappointed at the lack of progress has been in implementing the TRIPS (Trade Related Aspects of Intellectual Property Rights). In theory, TRIPS should benefit both rich and poor nations alike. However, it was pushed onto the trade agenda by the US, Europe and Japan which hold the lion's share of world patents and whose companies wanted more protection abroad. It required the developing countries to bring their legal protection and enforcement systems up to western levels but to date has given them nothing in return. In fact, the recent disputes over 'copy cat' life-saving drugs to treat AIDS has highlighted the gulf between developed and developing countries over patent protection and related TRIPS issues.

Regional trade groupings

Regional trade groupings (RTGs) are being pursued to a greater extent than at any time during the last 50 years. This increased focus on regional trade groupings is a sign of loss of faith in the multilateral trade system. The move towards RTGs gained additional stimulus during the early years of the Uruguay Round when few thought that it would be successful. One of the ironies is that the United States, which has been a major champion of non-discrimination, has itself entered into a major regional trade grouping – the North American Free Trade Area.

As mentioned in Chapter 2, RTGs can take different forms (from simple to complex):

- they can be *preferential tariff arrangements* whereby the members extend lower tariff rates to other members, but apply normal tariffs to non-members;
- next they can be a grouping committed to the *free trade area*, where tariffs between member countries are dropped completely;
- then follows the *customs union* in which members have standard external barriers to imports;
- after that they can form a *common market* where labour and capital flow freely across members' borders; and
- finally they can be an *economic union* where there is coordination of fiscal and monetary policies.

Purpose

A regional trade grouping is a preferential economic arrangement between a group of countries. This arrangement is intended to reduce intraregional barriers to trade in goods, services or investment, or all three. It stimulates trade between members of the group. Successful regional trade groupings usually contain members with similar per capita GNP, geographic proximity, compatible trading regimes or a political commitment to membership of a regional organisation.

There are a number of factors which have stimulated the formation of regional trade groupings:

- *Political.* A joining of forces in trade activities may be viewed as a prelude to some form of political unity. This was an important reason underlying the moves towards European economic unity and is believed to be the motivation behind the accession of the former centrally planned economies in Europe to the European Union.
- *Trade, economics and investment.* This results from a desire to eliminate unnecessary customs and transport procedures, to reduce technological and regulatory barriers to production, and to rationalise and concentrate production to achieve economies of scale. Economic factors also come into play, particularly when an RTG moves from a free trade area to an economic union. For example,

underlying the transition from the European Economic Community to an economic union were issues such as control over interest rates, inflation and employment. RTGs are also motivated by a desire to achieve gains from intensified competition within the wider economic grouping and attract foreign investment to the wider region because of its enhanced attractiveness as a market.

- *Globalisation.* The increasing movement towards globalisation is resulting in greater mobility in factors of production. Firms wish to operate in wider markets than in single countries and regional trade groupings provide insider status in a much larger market.

- *Marketing.* Reasons in this category include the need for multinationals to access consumers in new countries. As domestic markets become saturated, smaller nations and their companies are defending themselves against global competition by securing the protection of being a member of a regional trade grouping and firms are rationalising their production within a region by having separate plants in each country produce separate components of the final product. In addition, other factors include the willingness of nations to cede partial sovereignty to supra-national organisations so as to obtain benefits in international trade and increased consumer mobility and convergence of their needs.

History

Since the Second World War, the formation of a regional grouping in Europe has been the most prominent example of the move towards RTGs and has created a situation which others sought to emulate. There are now 32 such groupings in operation. They can take a number of different forms. These forms involve varying degrees of commitment and the surrendering of differing degrees of national sovereignty. In terms of commitment and lessening of national sovereignty, forms include preferential trade agreements, such as the Carribbean Basin Initiative; free trade areas, such as the North American Free Trade Area; customs unions, such as the South African Customs Union; common markets, such as the Central American Common Market; and economic unions, such as the European Union.

Regional trade groupings are here to stay. They discriminate explicitly and implicitly against outsiders by only granting preferences to member countries. They are not a violation of the WTO as long as barriers are not raised against third countries – however, most RTGs do involve such barriers. Despite this apparent breach, the formation of RTGs has not been strongly contested. This is because very few members of the WTO are not members of an RTG and some RTGs also have a political agenda, such as the promotion of democracy in their region.

Operation

RTGs can vary between two extremes. At one extreme, they aim to free up trade, they are open to new members and they have common agreements covering all members. As such they complement rather than inhibit free trade. This type of grouping usually takes place between countries that are natural partners in that they are contiguous and undertake a substantial percentage of their overall international trade with each other. These types of RTGs are known as GATT+ types on the presumption that the reduction of barriers is negotiated by like-minded participants and extended on an MFN basis to all other WTO members.

At the other extreme are RTGs that are limited in product coverage, have different rules for different countries, are antagonistic to outsiders and only admit new members on discriminatory conditions. The European Union is an example of this type. Those RTGs that limit free trade are often referred to as 'hub and spoke' agreements as they are usually between a large country and several smaller countries, as is the case with the North American Free Trade Area. These RTGs are more likely to resist rather than pursue multilateral trade liberalisation. Figure 18.2 shows regional trade groupings as at 1995. Since that time, while the number of RTGs has not increased, the number of nations seeking access to RTGs has.

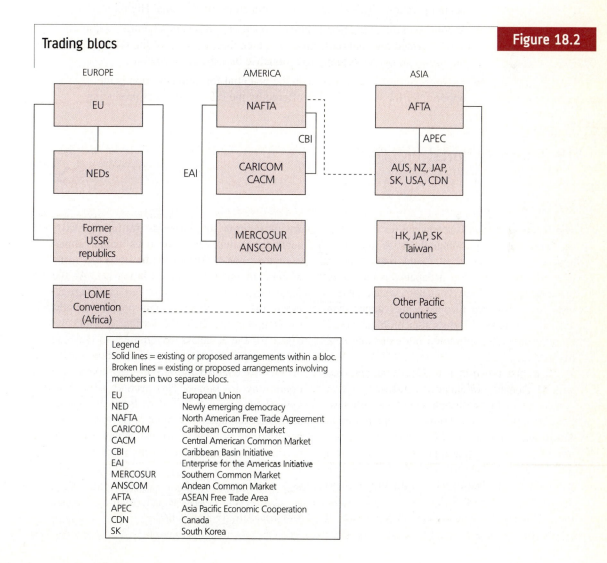

Trading blocs

Figure 18.2

RTGs can be viewed from both an insider and an outsider perspective. The perspective of a firm already operating within the RTG or wishing to operate in the region will be different from that of a firm outside the region wishing to trade with countries in the region.

Insider perspective

The insider perspective involves considerations as to how to expand business, where to produce, the potential for rationalising operations, and opportunities for standardisation.

- *Expansion.* One attraction of RTGs to firms is the resulting access to a larger market. There is also the potential for the firm to establish itself in one country in the grouping and, once successful there, expand to other countries in the group.
- *Production.* The next decision is in which of the member countries should the firm begin operations. This situation is illustrated in International Highlight 18.2.
- *Rationalisation.* If the firm is already operating in several countries within the newly formed regional trade grouping, then the formation of the RTG provides the firm with the opportunity to rationalise its existing operations.
- *Standardisation.* Associated with the potential for rationalisation is the opportunity for standardisation offered by the RTG. Instead of producing

18.2 International highlight

Toys"Я"Us

The Japanese market is renowned for its numerous barriers to entry. When Toys"Я"Us investigated this market, they found that a major impediment to operating in Japan was the Large Scale Retail Store Law (Daitenho) which made it virtually impossible to open stores larger than 450 square metres. Unless this problem could be overcome, the firm could not enter this new market.

Their first move was to form a partnership with McDonald's of Japan which had excellent contacts with Japanese politicians and officials, especially those in the Ministry of International Trade and Industry (MITI). The key factor, however, was the joint approach (adopted with the US government) to persuade the Japanese government to liberalise the Daitenho. Due to their lobbying, Toys"Я"Us were able to make liberalising the Daitenho one of the key issues in the Structural Impediments Initiatives (SII) negotiations with Japan – talks which aimed to remove non-tariff barriers faced by US firms wishing to enter the Japanese market. At the same time, via a public relations campaign in Japan, the firm actively sought popular support for changing the Daitenho so that it would be easier for the Japanese government to concede on this issue in the trade talks. Modification of the law enabled the US firm to commence operations in Japan. The second store was opened by then US President Bush during his state visit to Japan as a symbol of how the SII negotiations had begun to tear down structural barriers to trade and investment in Japan.

Source: Lewis Cohen, Si-Well International, presentation to the Association of Japanese Business Studies Conference, Washington, DC, 13–15 June 1997.

different products for each market in the group, it may be possible to produce the same product or at least to reduce the differences because of the likelihood of increasing homogenisation of demand within the group. The potential for standardisation will vary according to the nature of the product, the racial composition of the region and differences in per capita GDP, religion, climate, stage of industrial development, languages spoken and levels of education.

Considering the marketing mix variables, with product there will be a need to adjust positioning strategy of brands because of differences in strategy between countries in the group – for example, Palmolive is positioned as a beauty soap in Italy and as a family soap in the UK. With price, reductions will be possible because of the absence of tariff and non-tariff barriers. Tax harmonisation within the group and the need for price coordination in the light of differences in affordability across member countries will also be a consideration. As far as promotion is concerned, the need for multilingual sales personnel and executives who can operate in all member countries will increase. Also media focus may need to switch from national media to regional media and from national facilitators such as advertising agencies and market research agencies to firms competent to operate across the region. Finally, with distribution, the RTG will eliminate border controls on transportation and reduce grey markets within the region.

Outsider perspective

If it is possible, the ideal situation is to lobby government to exclude from the arrangement products currently exported to countries in the new regional trade grouping. Where this is not possible, the greatest worry to the outsider is loss of a traditional market because competitors within the new group no longer face the same barriers as the outsider. This problem caused considerable concern when the UK entered the European Common Market and Australian products were no longer accorded preferential entry to the UK market under the British Commonwealth Preference Scheme. In this circumstance the challenge is to acquire insider status. Possible ways of achieving this are as follows:

- the government becomes a member of the RTG;
- the government applies for associate membership. A number of former colonies and small countries obtained associate membership of the European Community;
- the government secures a continuation of privileged access or negotiates phased-down arrangements, as New Zealand was able to do when the European Common Market was formed;
- components are assembled in one of the member countries. The Japanese automobile manufacturers achieved this with their automotive transplant factories in the European Community;
- the firm forms a strategic alliance with a firm already operating inside the RTG. This could take the form of a manufacturing under licence arrangement (MUL); or
- manufacture in a country that is a member of the RTG. This could involve acquiring a firm already there or entering into a joint venture.

Current focus

Because of the momentum with the formation of regional trade groupings and fear of the isolation of not being a member of one of them, countries in increasing numbers are seeking membership. Figure 18.3 shows how the original 'Triad' of the EU, North America and Japan has expanded to the North American Free Trade Area (NAFTA), western Europe and Japan, Australia and 'tiger' economies. The figure also shows South and Central America seeking to join NAFTA, central and eastern Europe seeking to join western Europe, and developing countries in Asia seeking to join Japan, Australia and the tigers.

The potential for expansion of RTGs is illustrated by the Third Summit of the Americas in Quebec City, April 2001. The agenda included discussions on expanding NAFTA to include all countries (34) from the Bering Strait to Cape Horn – 800 million people and a combined GDP of US$11 trillion, making it the largest free trade zone on the planet.

Expansion of RTGs can bring with it a host of problems as illustrated by the proposed enlargement of the EU as shown in Figure 18.4.

The EU plans to admit 12 new members (possibly 13 if Turkey can allay human rights concerns) in two waves. The first would involve Cyprus, Czech Republic, Estonia, Hungary, Poland and Slovenia. The second wave would include Bulgaria, Latvia, Lithuania, Malta, Romania and Slovakia. Many people within the current EU view the enlargement as a vehicle for the creation of a homogenous superstate that will be marked by loss of national identities, national cultures and national languages.

Figure 18.3   'Triad' and the world economy

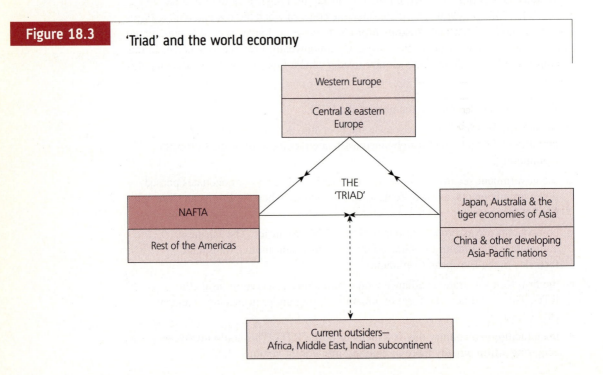

Knocking on the door

Figure 18.4

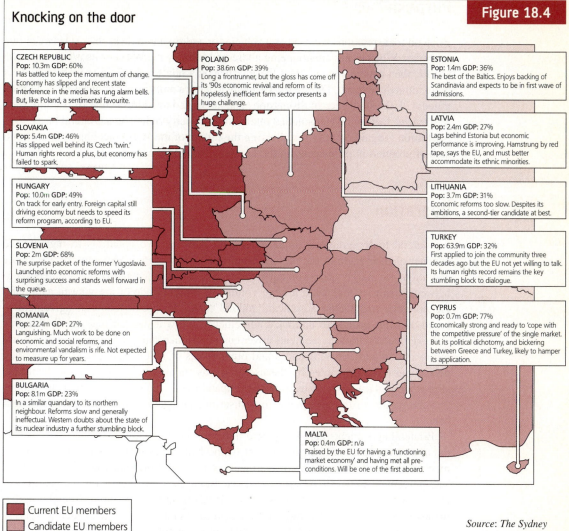

CZECH REPUBLIC
Pop: 10.3m **GDP:** 60%
Has battled to keep the momentum of change.
Economy has slipped and recent state
interference in the media has rung alarm bells.
But, like Poland, a sentimental favourite.

SLOVAKIA
Pop: 5.4m **GDP:** 46%
Has slipped well behind its Czech 'twin.'
Human rights record a plus, but economy has
failed to spark.

HUNGARY
Pop: 10.0m **GDP:** 49%
On track for early entry. Foreign capital still
driving economy but needs to speed its
reform program, according to EU.

SLOVENIA
Pop: 2m **GDP:** 68%
The surprise packet of the former Yugoslavia.
Launched into economic reforms with
surprising success and stands well forward in
the queue.

ROMANIA
Pop: 22.4m **GDP:** 27%
Languishing. Much work to be done on
economic and social reforms, and
environmental vandalism is rife. Not expected
to measure up for years.

BULGARIA
Pop: 8.1m **GDP:** 23%
In a similar quandary to its northern
neighbour. Reforms slow and generally
ineffectual. Western doubts about the state of
its nuclear industry a further stumbling block.

POLAND
Pop: 38.6m **GDP:** 39%
Long a frontrunner, but the gloss has come off
its '90s economic revival and reform of its
hopelessly inefficient farm sector presents a
huge challenge.

ESTONIA
Pop: 1.4m **GDP:** 36%
The best of the Baltics. Enjoys backing of
Scandinavia and expects to be in first wave of
admissions.

LATVIA
Pop: 2.4m **GDP:** 27%
Lags behind Estonia but economic
performance is improving. Hamstrung by red
tape, says the EU, and must better
accommodate its ethnic minorities.

LITHUANIA
Pop: 3.7m **GDP:** 31%
Economic reforms too slow. Despites its
ambitions, a second-tier candidate at best.

TURKEY
Pop: 63.9m **GDP:** 32%
First applied to join the community three
decades ago but the EU not yet willing to talk.
Its human rights record remains the key
stumbling block to dialogue.

CYPRUS
Pop: 0.7m **GDP:** 77%
Economically strong and ready to 'cope with
the competitive pressure' of the single market.
But its political dichotomy, and bickering
between Greece and Turkey, likely to hamper
its application.

MALTA
Pop: 0.4m **GDP:** n/a
Praised by the EU for having a 'functioning
market economy' and having met all preconditions. Will be one of the first aboard.

Current EU members
Candidate EU members
Non EU members

* GDP per head as a % of EU average 1999

Source: *The Sydney
Morning Herald*, 16–17
June 2001, p. 35.

Bilateral trade relations

This is the oldest and most common form of international trade relations. Issues of 'fair'
trade and market access are often dealt with bilaterally, outside the scrutiny of the WTO
and in ways that may be at variance with WTO rules. One of these rules is that of non-
discrimination, and, by their very nature, bilateral agreements tend to discriminate in
favour of both parties. Because some of the bilateral undertakings entered into are not
always a matter of public record, the WTO principle of transparency is sometimes
breached in bilateral trade relations.

Purpose

Bilateral trade relations are used as a vehicle for addressing trade problems between two countries. When issues are not being addressed fully by the WTO or its predecessor the GATT, then nations may address these issues on a bilateral basis in order to achieve a more immediate result. During the Uruguay Round, a number of countries became frustrated with the slow pace of discussions and attempted to address areas of friction, such as services, foreign investment and intellectual property rights, on a bilateral basis. This frustration is again on the rise following the failure of the WTO meeting in Seattle and lack of progress in implementing the Uruguay Round outcomes.

Operation

A bilateral trade agreement is an agreement between two countries to regulate the conduct of their trade to the mutual benefit of both parties. It seeks to provide stable conditions for market access on equal terms. These agreements are usually entered into between countries that share a large volume of mutual trade or are viewed as having the potential to develop significant mutual trade. The basic bilateral agreement is based on MFN principles and most agreements follow a standard pattern. Within this context, bilateral trade agreements cover customs duties and internal taxes, issues relating to import and export licences and other issues of mutual interest. However, they go beyond these principles by the use of words such as 'take measures to facilitate, strengthen and diversify so as to further expand trade'. This type of statement implies that the parties to the agreement may discriminate against outsiders to their mutual benefit.

Bilateral agreements may be entered into for specific commercial purposes, such as the agreement between the government of the Kingdom of Thailand and the government of the Federal Republic of Germany concerning Financial Cooperation (1983). The agreement between Australia and the Republic of Hungary on the Reciprocal Promotion and Protection of Investments (1992) is another example. Bilateral agreements because of their 'umbrella' nature tend to remain in force a considerable period of time. They may be updated by the addition of a supplementary document.

The implementation of bilateral trade agreements is usually via regular rounds of trade discussions held alternately in each country. Basically, the trade agreement serves as an umbrella under which discussions between the two countries on trade matters can take place. It is at these discussions that specific problems can be raised. The firm needs to ensure that it has input into the matters on the agenda for the discussion. Often this can be achieved through membership of groups involved in advising the official delegation. Members may be drawn from the relevant panel of the trade development board or the appropriate business cooperation committee or chamber of commerce between each country.

Bilateral trade relations can be advanced by regular meetings of officials from both countries. Often these are called joint trade committees. Increasingly, the 'official' talks take place at the same time as talks between business groups from both countries. At the conclusion of both sets of talks, officials and businesspeople come together for a joint meeting.

Bilateral trade relations can also be advanced by regular meetings of ministers from both countries. Known as joint ministerial meetings, these meetings provide opportunity for private sector involvement. There may be opportunity for businesspeople to accompany the ministerial party as advisers.

Finally, bilateral trade relations can be advanced by visits of appropriate ministers to the other country.

Current focus

The current focus of bilateral agreements and associated rounds of trade talks and the issues raised for firms are as follows:

- *Exchange of information* – as far as areas of joint interest are concerned. From the firm's perspective, would this exchange of information benefit its international activities?

- *Exchange of representatives* – these could be commercial, industrial or technical representatives. The firm might consider providing a person who would be placed in a key decision-making or advisory area in another country. Alternatively, there is the opportunity to favourably predispose officials from the other country towards the firm's technology by providing a short-term placement within their company in the domestic market.

- *Holding of trade fairs/exchange of trade missions* – in each country. The issue for the firm is whether it should participate in the activity directed towards the other country because of the blessing of both governments.

- *Lists of product* – which each side wishes to trade with the other. Are the products or services of the firm included in the list? If not, can the firm lobby the Department of Foreign Trade to have them included at the next round of bilateral trade talks?

- *Investment clauses* – these detail areas in which new investment is sought. Is the firm's industry covered?

- *General problems in the bilateral trade* – these could include a wide variety of issues, such as shipping services, cost of insurance or need for concessional credit. If the firm faces a general problem which impedes its trade with the country, can it arrange for it to be discussed under the umbrella of the trade agreement?

- *Specific problems in the bilateral trade* – these may also take the form of barriers to future trade development. If the firm has a specific problem, can it arrange for it to be included in trade talks between the two countries?

- *Establishment of new groups to facilitate trade objectives* – an example would be the establishment of a country-to-country institute to promote people-to-people contacts. Groups of this nature provide opportunities for the firm to network and it may consider membership because of this.

Bilateral trade agreements do not usually cover:

- goods supplied under aid, whether grant or loan;
- advantages of access with bordering countries to facilitate frontier traffic;
- tariff preferences currently in force which result from multilateral activities;
- existing obligations or measures resulting from international commodity agreements; or
- measures necessary for balance of payments or health, safety or quarantine reasons.

Basically, enforcing the provisions of bilateral trade agreements depends on the goodwill of both parties. Often, the rhetoric of cooperation is pushed far ahead of reality due to a lack of genuine interest. It often boils down to how important the parties are to each other. Goodwill in the associated trade discussions largely depends on reciprocal advantage. If a country wants a concession from the other country, it has to offer something in return. However, success in this connection is likely to depend on whether one country is willing to reduce existing barriers against the other country for products which they produce more efficiently.

Sometimes in bilateral trade relations problems are created so as to provide negotiating coin for future discussions. For example, a perceived health or quarantine problem may result in a blanket prohibition of a product. Individual nations then lobby to prove that the prohibition should not apply to them as the problem does not exist in their country. In return for accepting this representation, the first country requests as a trade-off, solution to a pre-existing problem in their trade with the second country. In negotiating reciprocal reductions to barriers to trade, it is preferable to focus on areas of growth in the other economy. This is because growth areas are better placed to weather any additional competition as a result of the reduction in protection, whereas barriers are more entrenched in declining industries and more difficult to dislodge because of greater employment effects.

It is also easier to negotiate away revenue-motivated as opposed to protectionist-motivated barriers because the latter have social implications and are more sensitive in terms of domestic politics. Barriers to trade are driven by different reasons in each country. It is useful to research these differing motivations as this will assist in formulating the optimal negotiation strategy.

Lobbying

The firm may lobby its government to raise an issue under the bilateral trade agreement. This is particularly the case where the problem relates to gaining access to the market in that country, to restrictions on operating in that country, to being able to market its products and services in that country, or to a regulatory practice in that country which discriminates against its product. In order to improve its lobbying effectiveness, a firm with a strong interest in a particular country should consider joining the bilateral business group, participating in government-sponsored trade missions to that country, asking to brief ministers and officials prior to trade talks, and supporting government advertising or public relations activities in the international market.

18.3 International highlight

Bilateral arrangements on the increase

The failure by the WTO to achieve collective agreement on a number of pressing issues during the last few years has caused countries to look to bilateral arrangements to address their major trade problems. Of interest is that the new arrangements go beyond bilateral trade agreements and are being proposed as free trade agreements. Singapore and Japan signed such a free trade agreement in October 2000. It represents Japan's desire to develop a stronger presence in the region via economic and financial ties and will cover trade in goods, services, regulatory procedures, investment and competi-

tion policy. Japan is also exploring the possibility of a similar trade agreement with South Korea, while Singapore recently penned an agreement with New Zealand. These developments are causing some international concern with EU officials who worry that such bilateral agreements could undermine moves to relaunch a new round of global trade talks under the WTO.

Source: Adapted from *World Trade*, January 2001; the *Bulletin*, 5 December 2000 and 15 May 2001 and *The Sydney Morning Herald*, 2–3 June 2001 and 14–15 July 2001.

Subsidies

An issue increasingly raised in bilateral trade relations discussions is that of governments subsidising exports. Frequently, the subsidy issue is raised when there is a downturn in the domestic industry as periodically happens when there is a recession. Many subsidies are disguised, and often they are embedded in the structure of the economy or industry in such a way that they are inseparable from its operation. This is illustrated in the case of the timber industry in Canada.

> *For almost 20 years Canada and the United States have been at loggerheads over softwood lumber, with the US claiming Canadian producers are subsidised and imposing countervailing duties to compensate, and the Canadians claiming they have a different system and the Americans are engaging in protectionism by another means. Despite undertaking three investigations, the US has not been able to prove its claim and the claim was thrown out by the disputes panel of the United States–Canada Free Trade Agreement in 1992. The Canadians are now proposing to seek resolution under NAFTA and if necessary will take the issue to the WTO.*
>
> *Source*: adapted from *The Economist*, 24 March 2001, p. 24.

Hitherto discussion has centred on trade relations applying to products and services in general. There are trade relations activities that are confined to specific product groups. These are known as commodity agreements.

Commodity agreements

Commodity agreements were introduced to create predictability and security in the international trade for specific commodities. They evolved when the percentage of world trade that was resources- or agriculture-based was much greater than it is today. They usually involve both the buyer and the seller, and sometimes include a price support or buffer stock mechanism. The intention is to increase stability for both buyer and seller by ironing out sharp price fluctuations. In this way it was hoped to increase overall consumption of the product. Furthermore, the security of agreed remunerative prices permits the gradual expansion of production of the commodity. Membership of these arrangements could involve both public and private sectors.

The position today is that commodity agreements have diminished in significance. Their role has changed from a market-stabilising role to more of an information exchange function. This is because some of the previous economic type commodity agreements which regulated production collapsed, e.g. the International Tin Agreement. The focus of current commodity agreements is on the threat of substitute products and the gathering and supply of worldwide data and statistics on production and trade in the commodity covered.

Commodity agreements can benefit a firm involved with the commodity covered as synergies arise from exporting as a group and the exchange of information enables early warning of threats which might arise from producers outside the arrangement or from substitute products. Cooperating with customers to the mutual advantage of both parties has a stabilising effect on the trade in what might otherwise be a volatile commodity.

A final aspect of international trade relations concerns the practice of managed trade.

Managed trade

Managed trade is not free trade as envisioned by the World Trade Organisation because it restricts the operation of the market by government decision or decree.

In addition, it is not appropriate to call it protectionist as government involvement may be motivated by other reasons, such as to assist reduction of national debt, achieve investment goals or acquire new technology. Managed trade can be defined as direct intervention by government in trade and investment so as to better manage its own economy and its interaction with the international economy. There are two main forms of managed trade. These are government intervention and voluntary restraints.

Government intervention

The EU and the US have reached agreement to resolve outstanding disputes over the operation of the 1996 D'Amato Act penalising firms investing more than US$40 million in Iran or Libyan energy sectors and the Helms Burton Law banning trade with Cuba. Triggered by US sanctions against a consortium led *by Total being involved in Iranian gas development, the agreement will apply to Gazprom of Russia and Petronas of Malaysia as well. It heralds a weakening in the US propensity to impose sanctions on firms outside its jurisdiction who trade with its perceived enemies.*

With this type of managed trade, governments are exercising their sovereign rights. Intervention can include the following forms:

- *Embargoes.* Often embargoes are imposed for political reasons. As long as the resulting restraint of trade is predictable and non-discriminatory, then embargoes are defensible.

- *Import quotas.* These are generally protectionist in motivation and are subject to more criticism than tariffs. The excuse that they are imposed for balance of payments reasons has been used so frequently that this form of managed trade is viewed with suspicion.

- *Other non-tariff barriers.* These include health and safety regulations, standards for products, certification and recognition requirements for professional services, giving preference to domestic providers when government purchases are involved, and import inspection procedures and costs.

- *Countertrade.* An increasing number of governments mandate countertrade as a condition of contract when government purchases are involved, or when the availability of foreign exchange is scarce. While all forms of countertrade can be mandated, offsets is the most usual form of mandated countertrade.

- *Export assistance.* This takes a variety of forms including tax incentives, low interest loans, assistance with promotion, provision of information on the potential and restraints in international markets, trade representation and formation of export groups or consortia to bid on projects. A number of these are alleged to interfere with free market activities and, when they do so, they can be regarded as managed trade. The trend with export assistance is to help firms further back along the supply chain. One example is the provision of investment incentives for export-generating industries.

If the firm feels that it is disadvantaged by any of the above forms of intervention by the international government, it can lobby its government to provide advice and possibly compensatory assistance or apply pressure to the other government to reduce the disadvantages faced by the firm.

Voluntary restraints

Despite the high-sounding diplomatic phrases which surround them, voluntary restraints are akin to blackmail because there is nothing genuinely voluntary about them. Governments are often subject to intense lobbying by sectoral interests to restrict imports because of their impact on higher-priced domestic products. Approaches to the WTO can be time consuming and may not succeed. As the competitive threat may come from a variety of countries, neither an appeal to relevant RTGs nor bilateral negotiation is likely to yield a speedy resolution.

As an alternative, the country threatens to impose highly restrictive import quotas on the product, but offers to negotiate much more liberal quotas if interests in the major supplying countries agree to accept the restriction on imports. All parties often agree to this negotiated arrangement. This is because the importing country can avoid seeking approval from the WTO for the quota system it proposes, and because the exporting country receives guaranteed access for a fixed quantity for an agreed period.

Voluntary restraint arrangements (VRAs) tend to apply to 'smokestack industries', such as steel and automobiles and examples exist in both these areas where the US has used VRAs as a form of protectionism. Prior to the conclusion of the Uruguay Round, VRAs increased in incidence and it was estimated in 1993 that one-third of imports of manufactures into the US were covered by VRAs. The conclusion of the Uruguay Round raised hopes that VRAs would disappear as it was recognised that it was a trade-distorting practice. However, as many of the WTO's measures have not yet been implemented and global economic circumstances are likely to stimulate protectionism, it would be premature to say that VRAs will shortly disappear.

Internet infusion

E-business is an issue that affects the ability of countries to compete with each other and one that has the potential to confer monopoly power on some countries at the expense of others due to its interactive, borderless and timely nature. As such, it is a subject that is increasingly likely to appear on the agendas of countries' multilateral, regional and bilateral trade relationships. However, historically nation states have only had limited success at creating global treaties that succeed in practice. Furthermore, such treaties take ages to negotiate (e.g. the GATT Uruguay Round) and, given the pace of Internet technology, they run the risk of limping behind economic reality. In the multilateral arena, the World Trade Organisation is focusing on e-commerce issues, such as privacy, customs duties, modes of delivery, international procurement, intellectual property, standards and the use of telecommunications networks. WTO agreements applicable in this context are the General Agreement on Trade in Services (GATS); the Agreement on Basic Telecommunications of 1997 and the Information Technology Agreement of 1996. The World Intellectual Property Organisation (WIPO) has established benchmarks for treating various forms of intellectual property in cyberspace and has set up an Arbitration and Mediation Centre. The Organisation for Economic Cooperation and Development (OECD) hosted an international conference on e-commerce in 1998 and operates a number of working parties on e-commerce issues.

At the regional level, various bodies are addressing e-commerce issues. For example, the Asia Pacific Economic Cooperation Group (APEC) has created an inter-connecting framework that aims to foster competitive network development and an authentication task group that aims to foster user confidence in e-commerce.

As the importance of e-commerce grows in international trade, this new form of commerce is likely to be included in bilateral negotiations between countries. It may be included in general trade agreements between countries or be the subject of specific agreements.

Summary

Although there is much in the media about international trade relations in its various forms – multilateral, regional and bilateral – there is a tendency on the part of business executives to regard it as a political exercise undertaken by bureaucrats and ministers. There is considerable advantage to the firm to become actively involved in international trade relations activities concerning international markets in which the firm is involved or interested, or in issues which impact on the future profitability of the firm.

In the first place it is necessary for the firm to strengthen its relations with the government. This will mean that its interests are more likely to be taken into account when issues of interest to the firm are being negotiated in a multilateral context. It will also improve chances that impediments faced by the firm in specific international markets are raised by government in either regional trade forums or in bilateral discussions. To facilitate this improvement in relations with the home government, the firm should become actively involved in business groups focusing on trade development with an area or with a region. Such involvement is likely to result in collective strength when lobbying government, being called upon to offer advice to government on trade with the country/region involved, and possible invitation to become a member of an official trade delegation to the country.

The second step is for the firm to strengthen its relationship with the foreign government. While this may be achieved via the firm's agent or joint venture partner in the other country, it should also be undertaken directly by the firm. Membership of bodies involved in advancing trade between countries adds credibility to the firm's approach to officials, as does involvement in official talks as an adviser or by accompanying government ministers on their visits to the other country.

Such relationships with government will improve the competitiveness of the networks involved in international operations and serve both to minimise impediments and maximise facilitation by government.

Ethics issue

You are a major exporter of fresh fruit and an industry spokesperson from the Canary Islands. The Minister for Trade has asked that you attend the next meeting of the Spanish/Finnish Ministerial Commission where Finnish restrictions on the import of Spanish fresh fruit on quarantine grounds will be debated. It is felt that the restriction is motivated more by protectionist than quarantine reasons. The Minister will be arguing that the ban on Spanish apples should not apply to product from the Canary Islands as being an island state it does not have the disease problems that plague the mainland. The day before you were scheduled to leave for Finland, you are advised of an isolated instance of mainland fruit fly in the north-east part of the island. This was immediately treated.

If you were the industry spokesperson would you inform the Minister and would you advise the Minister to inform the Finns of the recent occurrence of fruit fly?

Web workout

Question 1 Visit the EU website and research under procurement. What have you found out? Are there any opportunities for international marketers outside the EU?

Question 2 Visit websites for the Singapore Government Electronic Business Partner (http://www.gebiz.gov.sg/) and US Agency for International Development (http://www.usaid.gov/). Find out how these agencies can be used to market products and services in the international market.

Websites

European Union www.europa.eu.int

NAFTA www.nafta-sec-alena.org/

World Trade Organisation www.wto.org

Governments on the Web www.gksoft.com/govt/en/

Discussion questions

1 Why has the prime emphasis in international relations shifted from the political to the commercial?

2 How do international trade relations impact on marketing?

3 Discuss the role of government as both a regulator and a facilitator in international trade.

4 Comment on ways in which the government can be an ally in overcoming impediments and facilitating access to international markets.

5 In what ways has the World Trade Organisation gone beyond the GATT in its approach to international marketing issues?

6 Why is the World Trade Organisation sometimes referred to as 'the rich man's club'?

7 How do bilateral trade relations differ from multilateral trade relations? Under what circumstances can the latter be more effective than the former?

8 Do you consider that managed trade will disappear when the WTO implements the outcomes of the Uruguay Round?

References

Brown, P. (2002) 'Assessment of the Successes and Failures of the Summit', *The Irish Times*, 4 September.

Cohen, L. (1997) Presentation to the Association of Japanese Business Studies Conference, Washington DC, 13–15 June.

Kakarti, J.G. (1996) 'Opportunities and Challenges of Doing Business in Asean', *Journal of Global Marketing*, Vol. 9, No. 3, pp. 47–65.

Quelch, J.A., Buzzell, R.D. and Salame, E.R. (1992) *The Marketing Challenge of Europe 1992*, Addison Wesley, Reading, UK.

19

Electronic commerce in international marketing

Learning objectives

After reading this chapter, you should be able to:

- describe the elements of e-commerce and their relevance to international marketing;

- outline different international marketing business models of e-commerce;

- explain the Internet as a new marketplace and its potential business benefits;

- outline the challenges to established international marketers in migrating their businesses from 'place' to 'space' marketing; and

- describe the different forms of 'B-web'.

To B or not to B: that is the question

B-webs – appealing models for the international marketer The industrial revolution of the past century revolved around creating value within the individual corporation. Its primary role was to lower transaction costs and thus prices. So, for instance, the Ford Motor Company bought power plants and shipping companies to reduce its overall production costs.

In the 21st century we are entering the era of B-webs. This new form of competing revolves around a closely linked system of business actors such as suppliers, service providers, distributors and infrastructure providers as well as customers. All these players use the Internet as a common platform for business communication and transactions. The new digital economy creates value by redefining existing business models and by exploiting the power of business webs (B-webs). Industry by industry B-webs are replacing old, competitive models of the firm. International marketers have heard of many other names that at first sight may resemble a B-web cluster: virtual corporation, kieretsu (the interconnected companies with cross-ownership which are typically found in Japan), bamboo network, outsourcing partnerships or econets. Here, traditionally one company usually holds a major share of the web profits. The B-web concept rewrites the competitive engagement rules. Although members must cooperate in order for the web to succeed, they also compete vigorously with one another. Furthermore, one B-web competes with other webs. It is not unusual to find a B-web ally to be also a member of other competitive B-webs.

Classifying B-webs With the Internet being a publicly available platform an unprecedented inter-corporation integration of processes is taking place through B-webs. Any company wanting to succeed and survive in this competitive environment must decide which webs to join and what specific roles it wishes to play in them. This places a great challenge on international marketers since there is a large spectrum of emerging B-web models. It is important to first understand which of the basic types of B-webs are relevant – an agora, aggregation, value chain, alliance or distributive network or a hybrid model of these (Table 19.1).

Tapscott et al. (2000) have classified B-webs according to their level of control and degree of value integration.

1 *Agora* – works as a facilitator between the seller and the buyer. Prices are determined via a real time on-the-spot negotiation. The price negotiation can take the form of haggling, auction or exchange. The examples of companies trading in the agora space are eBay and Priceline which operate in a number of international markets.

2 *Aggregation* – here one company leads the web by positioning itself as a value-adding intermediary between suppliers (producers) and customers. The leading aggregator company will take charge in selecting value, pricing, segment targeting and augmentation of the product/service. Companies competing in the aggregator B-web include E*Trade which aggregates services of many companies from stock-quoting services, news services, research companies and software developers to deliver a virtual stockbroking service.

Table 19.1 The key dimensions of the B-web options

	Agora	Aggregation	Value chain	Alliance	Distributive network
Main feature	Dynamic pricing	Selection and convenience	Process integration	Creativity	Allocation/distribution
Value Proposition	Liquidity – converting goods into a desirable price	Optimisation of selection, organisation, price, convenience, matching and fulflment	Design and delivery of an integrated product or service that meets a specifc set of customer needs	Creative collaboration in aid of a goal shared across a community of contributors	Facilitate the exchange and delivery of information, goods and services
Role of customer	Market participant	Buyer	Value driver	Contributor	Sender/recipient Network optimisation
competences (KSF)	Timing Market intelligence	Market segmentation Supplier offerings Fulflment	Innovation Supply chain management	Community Creativity Standards and roles	Visibility and transparency
Essential processes	Price discovery	Needs matching	Product design Supply chain management	Innovation	Distribution
Examples of B-web actors	Yahoo! classifeds eBay Priceline NASDAQ Free-Markets	Amazon.com Chemdex HomeAdvisor E*Trade Travelocity WSJI	Cisco Systems Dell Computer General Motors Celestica Bidcom	America Online NetNoir Linux MP3 Wintel	Enron UPS AT&T Wells Fargo

Source: Tapscott et al. (2000) Table adapted from http://www.agilebrain.com/tapscott.html

---

3 *Value chain* – the 'key' company sits at the top of the B-web to manage customer relationships and marketing while other B-web members provide specific support activities. Examples of companies competing in the value chain B-web are Cisco, Dell and General Motors. The key company designs core technologies, coordinates processes across the B-web, markets and manages relationships while its B-web partners handle most of the manufacturing, fulfilment, and customer service.

4 *Alliance* – the fourth B-web in Tapscott et al.'s classification, high in value integration but low in hierarchical control. This web enables a large number of companies and/or individuals to work towards a common goal. End-customers or users are often active contributors. Their operations are more casual and there is no single individual or company controlling the web. The Open Source programming (www.opensource.org) movement and Linux, where programmers from around the world collaborate and offer their product for free, are examples of an alliance.

5 *Distributive network* – the fifth type of B-web identified by Tapscott et al., in which a distribution network facilitates exchange and the delivery of goods, services and information. Companies like Federal Express network with a number of players in their distribution systems to facilitate a total logistics solution for their larger clients.

The rise of B-webs forces organisations to rethink their current and sometimes obsolete competitive strategies. To become leading companies or to maintain current leadership positions international marketers need to guide their organisations to an appropriate B-web strategy.

Which B-web strategy, or strategies, will be most appropriate for your business and its marketing effort?

Options for membership of different types of B-webs provide opportunities for the international marketer to participate in international markets which, prior to Internet connectivity, would have been prohibitively expensive or too risky.

Introduction

Only five years ago the term 'electronic commerce' or 'e-commerce' was the buzzword for many businesses. Today it is set to have a major impact on international marketing. Internet stocks such as Yahoo!, Amazon.com, AOL Time Warner and Sony Music are strengthening their market positions at the New York stock exchange in relation to the 2000–2001 'Tech Wreck' that resulted in many online companies failing, due to their inability to deliver customer value and ultimately profitability. While there are some outstanding examples of success in electronic commerce, such as Cisco and Dell, Office Depot or Ryanair in Ireland, most companies have not yet worked out how to benefit fully from the electronic business interface.

A 2001 survey of CIOs (corporate information officers) and CEOs indicated that there are new drivers in the inter-networked enterprises and industries. The word e-business or e-commerce is no longer prominent. The new thinking includes better management of customer relationships and on top of the agenda now is investment in relevant CRM (customer relationship management) systems. Of the 224 executives surveyed, 18% indicated CRM was the most important technology decision the company has/or will face in 2001. Further, 20% indicated that the electronic (or e-business) infrastructure is now coming to prominence, while a further 16% perceived ERP (enterprise resource planning) as their most important decision. This survey also indicated that there is still not enough money or CEO-level support for new technologies. Sixty per cent of companies see no active involvement of their CEOs in making technology decisions.

For the 224 executives surveyed, new technology is forming a basis of their corporate strategy. Fifty-eight per cent indicated that the main reason is to improve efficiency, 55% said it is to improve customer service and only 8% said that the decision was not tied to a specific business goal. Forty-seven of those surveyed also indicated that their technology strategy was designed to move ahead of their competitors and 37% acquired new technology to catch up to competitors.

A further study conducted by Insead Business School, France, indicated that the level of e-business readiness and organisational fitness to implement such initiatives varied across industries and the players in these industries.

The 'e-readiness' figures shown in Figure 19.1 indicate that consumer goods as well as the process industries are considered laggards while financial and computer electronics have greater capabilities in implementing e-business initiatives.

A further analysis indicated that companies should no longer focus primarily on building up necessary hardware but should also begin to integrate their business strategy thinking and to integrate inter- and intra-organisational processes in order to fine-tune their corporate position.

Dimensions such as mission and vision, corporate culture, customer orientation, organisation and systems, planning and intelligence, human resources, technical resources, innovation, market strategy, performance, financial, marketing operations should now form an integral part of electronic business strategy. On these dimensions Nokia is considered to be a global leader, as shown in Figure 19.2.

Organisations can use these benchmarks to assess their current position against world's best practices and begin to improve their positions in the global context.

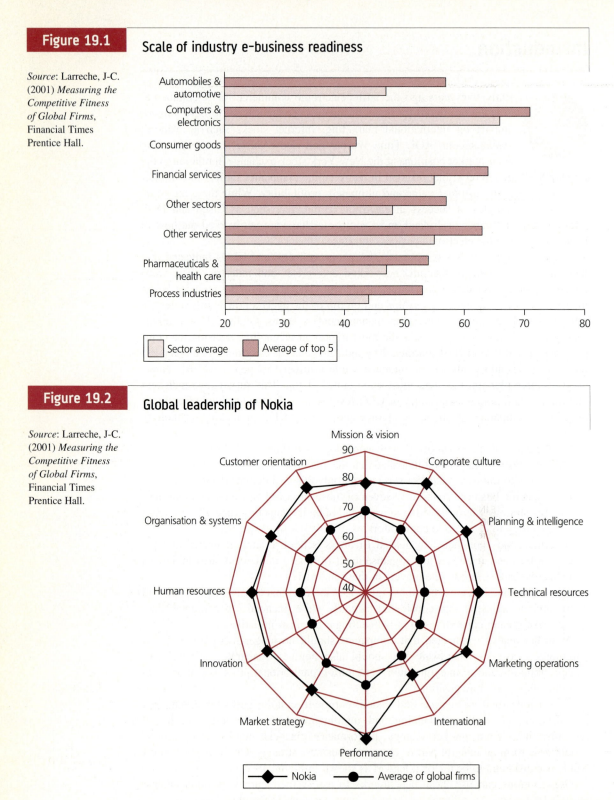

Figure 19.1

Scale of industry e-business readiness

Source: Larreche, J-C.
(2001) *Measuring the
Competitive Fitness
of Global Firms*,
Financial Times
Prentice Hall.

Figure 19.2

Global leadership of Nokia

Source: Larreche, J-C.
(2001) *Measuring the
Competitive Fitness
of Global Firms*,
Financial Times
Prentice Hall.

This chapter builds on discussions in Chapters 5 and 16 and explores the scope of e-commerce in international marketing and the Internet as a commercial marketplace. Several e-commerce business models are outlined with reference to successful cyberspace businesses. Finally, some of the challenges to international marketing in an e-commerce environment are canvassed.

Overview of electronic commerce

Definitions and scope

Electronic commerce is the exchange of business information and transactions using electronic methods. These include internal and external computer-connected networks such as the Internet, the sending of purchase orders to suppliers via electronic data interchange (EDI), the use of telephone and fax to conduct transactions, the use of ATMs, EFTPOS, wireless networks and smart cards to facilitate payment and obtain digital cash. E-commerce includes all the means by which activities and transactions are conducted in a 'space' environment as compared with a physical 'place' environment. Several of these elements are summarised in Figure 19.3.

The figure highlights the types of digital products and services that will be large contributors to e-commerce revenues in the future – information, books, CDs, software, video, education and medical services. It also points to the central role of financial transactions

E-commerce – what does it include?

Figure 19.3

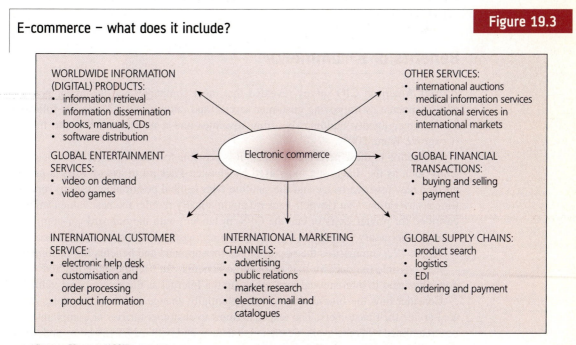

Source: Konana (1997).

Figure 19.4

The role of different networks in e-commerce

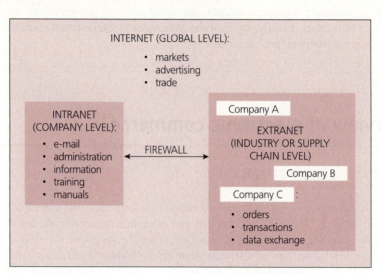

and payment systems – from a marketing viewpoint, the emergence of new electronic marketing channels for advertising, PR, market research and 'shop'-front business as well as the transformational effect on customer service and supply chain costs and benefits.

The central role of computer-to-computer exchange is most visibly described in terms of intranets (within the corporation), extranets (between the corporation and its suppliers or customers) and the Internet – the public communication network. These are depicted in Figure 19.4.

Benefits of e-commerce

A 2001 American CIO survey revealed that most companies see the major benefits of e-commerce as improving customer service and cutting costs. These are followed by customer loyalty building, boosting revenues and a new channel to the market (Cosgrove Ware, 2001).

In addition to these perceived benefits it is possible to create new services electronically such as the diagnostic tools used by Hewlett-Packard to assess when a printer needs a new toner cartridge and the satellite GPS (global positioning system) services for car navigation. Can Hewlett-Packard automatically reorder the best value available cartridge for printer users or can the GPS, in tandem with the onboard-car-computer, arrange a necessary service for the car? These services can add value to the offer.

Figure 19.5 summarises the opportunities for suppliers and benefits for customers.

It is possible to conceive that all of these benefits can become more marked when doing business in international markets using the Internet as the e-commerce vehicle.

Consider how the Internet has or can potentially change the way companies interact/service their customers. The response times to customer queries or complaints can be streamlined by being available on a global basis and with a 24/7 (24 hours and seven days a week) framework. The story below (International Highlight 19.1) outlines how electronic commerce and electronic networks can provide such service.

Supplier opportunities and customer benefits

Figure 19.5

SUPPLIER OPPORTUNITY	CUSTOMER BENEFIT
Global presence	Global choice
Improved competitiveness	Quality of service
Mass customisation and consumerism	Personalised products and service
Shorten or eradicate supply chains	Rapid response to needs
Substantial cost savings	Substantial price reductions
Novel business opportunities	New products and services

19.1 International highlight

'Hello, this is Belinda from Bangalore. How may I help you?'

Belinda Jones is a typical graduate student from UCLA University. She wears bell-bottom jeans and is a loyal fan of *Buffy the Vampire Slayer* and never misses her dose of *Boston Public*. Or so says Belinda, if asked while taking calls from Americans. However, her real name would be difficult to pronounce: Aathimantharai Dalelsinghji. After they listen more closely, they will detect a Midwestern dialect with a touch of Asian: Aathimantharai is Indian. She is part of a growing business trend in the southern Indian region of Bangalore that is saving western companies millions of dollars while earning young Indian university graduates their first real rupees. When Americans are calling a toll-free number in the US to report a broken fridge, kettle or any other appliance or complain about wrong delivery of an item ordered from the catalogue or over the Internet, the call is most probably routed through fast fibre-optic cables to a centre in India. Belinda is polite and eager to assist, and most importantly sounds just like the girl next door and not someone 10,000 km away. But wait, in order to get into the role, Aathimantharai Dalelsinghji (Belinda Jones) even created an American family history. Her brother is 15 and her parents have migrated from Ireland and she got her degree from UCLA.

'A personal relationship with the customers is most important,' says Aathimantharai who is working in one of a dozen of Bangalore's global call centres. She further says, 'It doesn't matter if I am really Belinda, Bronwyn, Bettina or Aathimantharai. What matters is that I've helped the customer.'

Thousands of Indian college graduates are lining up for such jobs. Upon successful job application they will receive months of speech training for American and British accents based on the customers' companies they will represent. They will watch and learn sporting activities, get a good dose of the client's country sitcoms to bridge the cultural canyon between Bangalore, Boston, Birmingham, Berlin, Brussels or Brisbane. According to Customerasset.com and NASSCOM, international call centres located in India will generate $15 billion in revenue by 2008.

Global companies are following customer demand for 24-hour and 7-days-a-week access to company products and customer representatives. The advent of the Internet and hence global markets are forcing companies to use the Internet technology to aid their backroom operations to please their customers.

Companies who use such services are Altavista, Shutterfly and major PC companies.

Who are you speaking to the next time you are calling an 0800 number?

Source: Based on information from www.customerasset.com; www.247customers.com

E-commerce leaders

In May 2001, the US-based Economist Intelligence Unit (EIU) published its 'E-business Readiness Rankings' for over 60 countries. The top 13 countries identified as 'e-business leaders' are as follows:

1	US	**8**	Finland
2	Australia	**9**	Denmark
3	UK	**10**	Netherlands
4	Canada	**11**	Switzerland
5	Norway	**12**	Germany
6	Sweden	**13**	Hong Kong
7	Singapore		

19.2 International highlight

Power of the web – some companies will have to face the music or become small players

The Internet revolution has created a new type of customer – the Netizen:

- the one who wants to sample the product before he or she buys it;
- the one who wants only breaking news about their favourite topic;
- the one who wants relevant information provided to them instantly;
- the one who wants to create/bundle their own product;
- the one who will switch between companies to get what they want.

Vivendi Universal with its portfolio of top artists dominates the music business. But being the market leader sometimes means that the leader takes its customers for granted. In the past the costs for new companies establishing themselves as record producers required large investments in cash and assets and then hopefully a very large slice of luck to sign up 'chart busting' artists. However, the establishment of the web has created new possibilities for new and lesser-known companies to communicate effectively with their customers at a fraction of the cost. Companies began setting up their own websites and signing up new artists at low cost. The power of the web meant that music lovers were able to listen to new or existing artists' recordings or their 'work in progress' and then vote whether they liked what they heard. This works as instant market research. Furthermore customers were then able to order their music CDs based on what they had heard.

Using this model there is virtually no inventory and hence the costs of establishing new artists are much lower while the revenues and profits are channelled into promoting the artists. But the online creativity did not stop there. The new online players have begun emerging and challenging the old market leaders in the way the music is played, recorded and exchanged. Real time video and music streaming, peer-to-peer exchange of Napster or legally downloading and storing music using MP3 technologies are winning over even the most traditional customers.

In early 2000 and 2001 with e-commerce still in its early stage of development and with many companies (start-ups) going 'belly up' due to poor online business models, Vivendi Universal with a portfolio of artists, such as Eminem, Blink 182, Sting and Sisquo, was a laggard in transforming its business to an online model. Vivendi Universal did not initially see the need for investing in or competing with lesser online brands since it had the copyright on the key artists. The emergence of new players such as Napster and Gnutella has turned the entire concept of exchanging and buying music over the Internet on its head. Furthermore, the customers have become more Net savvy. Put simply, they have become Netizens.

The statistics for the global market in general and the US market in particular indicate that the Internet is becoming the most preferred channel for buying music. Until 2001 the company saw no reason to pursue online sales like its smaller competitors and it had no clear strategy or clear distribution points on the Net. In 2001 many online companies were applying for bankruptcy. However, everything changed after the merger of AOL and Time Warner, making it the largest offline and online entertainment organisation in the world. AOL Time Warner began attracting smaller record labels and establishing its role of intermediary between music labels, the artists and the consumer. Armed with its own record label 'Warner Music' it has been able to eat into the revenues of Vivendi Universal.

Vivendi Universal realised that out of every dollar spent in the US on music the online purchases account for 25% of total sales. With profitability and growth heading in favour of online services, future revenues are threatened. As well, new players such as MP3 were making inroads and becoming the standard technology platform for exchanging music over the Net.

Vivendi Universal has had no time to wait. It had to launch an aggressive online strategy or become a minor online player in the global music market.

It began the process of creating a superportal for the music industry in 2001 and it began its international acquisitions of key and emerging players in the online music business. Its portfolio in 2001 consisted of:

1 *MP3* – an online music store that allows its 14 million users to legally store, purchase and play songs including those they already own – enabling users to listen to their music online from a central storage point.

2 *Duet* – launched in the second-quarter of 2001, it is streaming music from Sony Records and Vivendi Universal musicians. The music downloads will also be part of the service.

3 *E-music* – operates such sites as rollingstone.com and downbeat.com which have over two million loyal readers.

4 *Farmclub* – a promotional site where unsigned artists can post music is drawing over a million users. This service lets Universal discover and promote potential new starts at a fraction of the usual cost.

5 *GetMusic* – has an over two million fan site that is selling clothing and videos. It also has chat rooms and interviews with the stars.

Vivendi is now strongly positioned to appeal to the new customer, the Netizen, and is using the power of the web to reduce costs and achieve even greater global reach in attracting new and retaining existing customers. Since it now has a well-established network of services that its customers seek, it can now embark on the next stage – to enlist smaller labels to be alliance partners in its global Internet empire. It seems that the smaller labels will have no choice but to sign up if they wish to reach global customers or they will have to resort to niche marketing.

Electronic commerce business models for international marketing

A significant number of e-commerce models are being used by companies operating in international markets. Lawrence et al. (1998, pp. 20–22) describe seven specific business models ranging from a low-cost poster/billboard approach to a virtual store model. Timmers (1997) provides a framework for categorising business models based on two dimensions: single function/multiple functions and traditional/new activities. He describes nine different models. In this section four broad categories are noted and two detailed examples of successful models are portrayed to provide international marketers with an indication of how e-commerce can be implemented.

As shown in Figure 19.6, e-commerce can be subdivided into four distinct categories:

- business-to-business;
- business-to-consumer;
- business-to-government; and
- consumer-to-government.

Business-to-business

An example of the business-to-business category would be a company that uses a network for ordering its supplies, receiving invoices and making payments. This category

---

Figure 19.6   Categories of electronic commerce

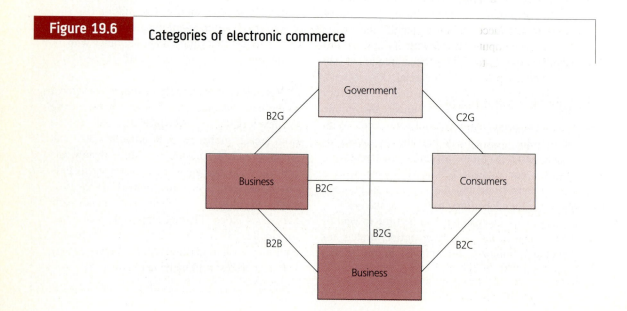

of electronic commerce has been well established for several years, particularly using EDI over private or value-added networks.

Business-to-consumer

The business-to-consumer category relates largely to electronic retailing. This category has expanded greatly with the advent of the World Wide Web. There are now virtual shopping malls offering all manner of consumer goods from cakes and wine to computers and motor cars.

Business-to-government

This category covers all transactions between companies and government organisations. For example, in the US the details of forthcoming government procurements are published over the Internet and companies can respond electronically. Currently this category is in its infancy, but could expand quite rapidly as governments use their own operations to promote awareness and growth of electronic commerce. In addition to public procurement, administrations may also offer the option of electronic commerce interchange for such transactions as VAT returns and the payment of corporate taxes.

Consumer-to-government

The consumer-to-government category has not yet emerged; however, in the wake of the growth of both the business-to-consumer and the business-to-government categories, governments may extend electronic interaction to such areas as welfare payments and self-assessed tax returns.

One of the most successful business-to-business models is used by Cisco – a provider of routers and computer networking equipment. Figure 19.7 depicts the type of model used in the business-to-business (B2B) environment.

B2B online – what happens

- The customer (top left) accesses the website and orders equipment. As part of this process, the customer actually accesses applications on the site as well as internal data from the company. These processes ensure that the customer is ordering a viable configuration of equipment, and that the necessary parts are available.
- The transaction flows directly into the company's own system. Payment information is sent to the appropriate bank, and the transaction processing system (middle of figure) exchanges the necessary information with the company's customer database, product database and financial/billing databases.
- If the customer has questions, they too can be directed to the website. This then transmits them to the customer service centre, which also has access to customer, product and billing data and can respond appropriately.

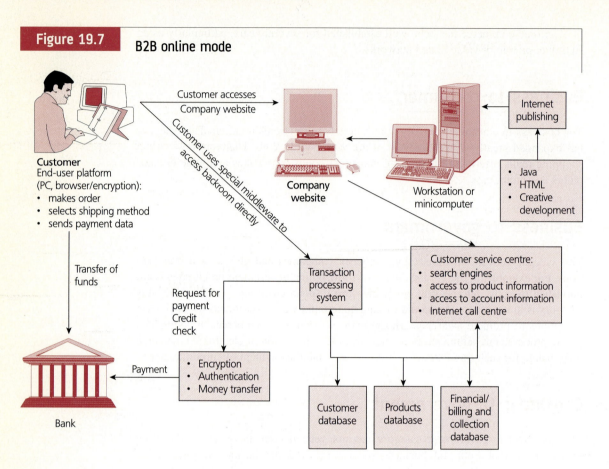

| Figure 19.7 | B2B online mode |

Customer accesses Company website

Customer uses special middleware to access backroom directly

Customer
End-user platform
(PC, browser/encryption):
• makes order
• selects shipping method
• sends payment data

Company website

Workstation or minicomputer

Internet publishing

• Java
• HTML
• Creative development

Transfer of funds

Request for payment
Credit check

Transaction processing system

Customer service centre:
• search engines
• access to product information
• access to account information
• Internet call centre

Payment

• Encryption
• Authentication
• Money transfer

Bank

Customer database

Products database

Financial/ billing and collection database

Another frequently quoted consumer-to-consumer model is Amazon.com. Starting out as an electronic bookstore it has now moved into music and other product. Its model, and that of Barnes&Noble Online, is shown in Figure 19.8.

Bookshop online – what happens

The customer at his computer initiates a purchase by ordering a book and issuing payment data. The customer then does nothing more. Once the order has been received the website puts a series of activities into play:

● the order goes to the transaction processing system, which accesses and updates product, customer and warehouse/shipping data;

● the order is fulfilled by sending information to the warehouse, which has its own databases;

● information also goes to the customer service centre.

This model highlights the added value provided by the virtual consumer community to customers in evaluating books for purchase.

Online bookshop mode

Figure 19.8

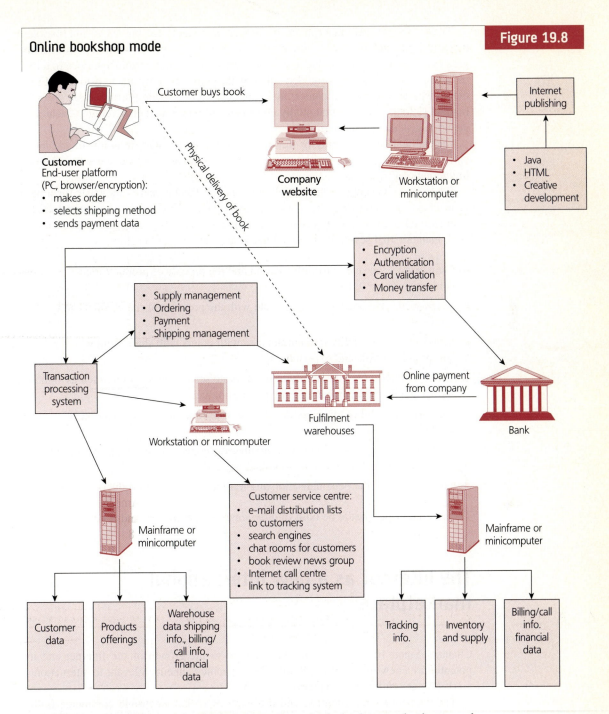

Customer buys book

Customer
End-user platform
(PC, browser/encryption):
- makes order
- selects shipping method
- sends payment data

Physical delivery of book

Company website

Workstation or minicomputer

Internet publishing

- Java
- HTML
- Creative development

- Encryption
- Authentication
- Card validation
- Money transfer

- Supply management
- Ordering
- Payment
- Shipping management

Transaction processing system

Workstation or minicomputer

Fulfilment warehouses

Online payment from company

Bank

Mainframe or minicomputer

Customer service centre:
- e-mail distribution lists to customers
- search engines
- chat rooms for customers
- book review news group
- Internet call centre
- link to tracking system

Mainframe or minicomputer

Customer data

Products offerings

Warehouse data shipping info., billing/ call info., financial data

Tracking info.

Inventory and supply

Billing/call info. financial data

Another successful model which encompasses both business-to-business and business-to-consumer is Dell Computers. It enables customers to configure their own PC with peripherals and software from basic configurations targeted for different types of buyers. Customers can price their desired configurations then trade off performance/ price combinations before finalising a purchase decision.

These three models incorporate a number of benefits for buyers in international markets. They include lower costs in terms of search time and transmission processing, greater buying convenience due to 24-hour access and higher customer service in terms of information availability provided either by the company or by other customers. From the viewpoint of these companies, there are cost savings made in transaction processing and selling, loyalty is potentially enhanced and wider market coverage is achieved generating share and sales growth.

Careful and detailed study of these models is a useful starting point for the international marketer to determine how customer value and business value can be achieved in international markets.

Research by Champy et al. (1996) suggests that the Internet is the basis for a new value chain they refer to as the 'consumption process'. This needs to be understood by international marketers in terms of how their customers buy electronically. Champy et al. maintain that seven fundamental needs are shared by all customers:

- *knowledge* – the search for information and the process of product/price comparisons;
- *interaction* – the need to communicate with the provider of the products and services;
- *networking* – the ability to communicate with others who share similar consumption needs and experiences;
- *sensory experience* – the ability to incorporate sensory perceptions such as sight, sound, smell and feel when making purchasing decisions;
- *ubiquity* – the ability to access the service or product when and where it is needed;
- *aggregation* – the assimilation of a number of related products and services that fulfil every step of the consumption process; and
- *customisation* – the personalisation and individualisation of products and services.

These components should be built into the international marketer's strategy.

The Internet as a new international marketplace

Chapters 5 and 16 have provided background to the growth of the Internet and its potential as a new marketplace. Some of the specific elements relevant to international marketing are outlined in this section.

The focal point for adoption and diffusion of global electronic commerce is the Internet. There is little agreement as to the actual size or overall potential of the Internet, except that it is big – and growing. Whether accessed by personal computer, mobile phone, web-based TV or Internet appliance, it is expected that high-speed Internet (broadband) access will become commonplace in the home and workplace. By 2004, it is projected that over 709 million will have access to the Internet (cyberatlas.com).

Revenue on the Internet typically comes from three sources – advertising, content (products, services and information) and electronic transactions. However, as noted earlier, few companies have been able to capitalise yet. Nevertheless, the Internet is spawning the growth of electronic communities which have the power to reshape the structure of industries, alliances between companies, the marketing strategies companies use to compete and reach customers, and the ways in which customers consume products and services (Hagel and Armstrong, 1997).

Research by Quelch and Klien (1996) also concludes that the Internet will revolutionise the dynamics of international commerce and, in particular, lead to the more rapid internationalisation of small to medium-sized enterprises (SMEs). They maintain that the competitive advantages of economies of scale will be reduced, global advertising costs will be less and small companies offering specialised niche products will be able to find the volume of customers globally to succeed through the worldwide reach of the Internet. Hamill (1997) also concludes that the Internet can provide SMEs with a low-cost gateway to global markets by helping to overcome many of the barriers to internationalisation commonly experienced by small companies.

For international marketers, the Internet offers a number of steps in building e-commerce in their international markets. Ghosh (1998) points to four levels.

1   Customer service

It is possible to provide almost the same level of service to customers as a salesperson at lower cost through a website. For example, Federal Express makes it easy for customers to order courier services online, pay electronically and track delivery status.

Through data warehousing and data mining using new Internet technologies it is possible to personalise interactions with customers and build customer loyalty. In addition new services can be provided at low cost such as Amazon.com's book review service provided by customers and book critics.

Investments in the Internet channel to enhance customer service displace the traditional sales, marketing and service costs. Increasingly higher levels of service can be offered at low incremental cost. These possibilities are quite feasible for the SME doing international business.

2   Pirating the value chain

It is possible for a participant in the value chain to take on the role of other participants. For instance, a publisher of books like Pearson Education could deliver content electronically to libraries, doing away with physical delivery, sales agents and distributors in various countries. It could go further and take on the role of retailer of academic books if it developed alliances and supply channels including books published by others. However, to succeed, the 'pirating' the company needs to build new skills to be able to provide the required customer value.

3   Digital value creation

Companies can decide to innovate and introduce new products and services. This can be done by supplying digitally what is supplied physically by someone else. For example, universities might provide an online research service at lower cost than is currently provided physically by commercial research firms. Similarly, small specialist consulting firms may find online markets and erode the high price/high margin general services of firms that have a physical presence in those markets.

4 Creating a customer magnet

'Stores' that establish a strong position or dominant brand on the Internet can grow rapidly, benefiting from the fact that customers feel comfortable returning to the places they know. In order for companies to achieve this it is likely that there will need to be alliances and various forms of product and customer specialisation in order to create a leading brand presence.

For a firm or alliance group to exploit these opportunities in international markets it will be necessary for them to explore in detail and answer a number of key questions proposed by Ghosh (1998). These questions, noted in Table 19.2, represent a useful starting point.

In a comprehensive overview of e-commerce on the Internet from an American perspective the conclusion of multiple analysts is that businesses are ahead of consumers in embracing the Internet. Even slow-growing business markets are larger than fast-growing consumer sectors (Hof and McWilliams, 1998). Table 19.3 shows predictions by Forrester Research Inc. of early and later adoption categories of products and services in business and consumer markets.

It is challenging to provide a stocktake of the business adoption of electronic commerce in international markets because of the rapid changes that are occurring almost on a daily basis. Significant transformation has occurred and there are already success stories in the financial services and retail sectors of many economies, particularly in business-to-business transactions. International Highlight 19.3 describes a case in the airline industry.

The front runners

Early adopters of electronic commerce have been those involved in well-defined supply chains – such as the automotive industry. Car manufacturers were faced with pressures to reduce inventories and improve their ordering processes.

Financial institutions were an early user of electronic settlements both domestically and internationally. Banks have rapidly extended the use of ATM transactions and there is now an inexorable move to Internet banking. This is an illustration of an industry in which business-to-business e-commerce has been extended to business-to-consumer as the technology becomes available and as consumers become more sophisticated in its use and are able to secure its advantages.

The travel industry is in a similar position. Airlines were early adopters in transactions between one another and their agents and suppliers. They are now moving to online transactions with their customers to maximise loadings on planes and reduce costs (see International Highlight 19.3).

Industries that deal in information are now rapidly moving to electronic commerce by digitising their product and providing it online. This can be seen in entertainment and publishing. The transition to digital TV will provide a further avenue and incentive for electronic commerce.

Table 19.2 Internet marketplace checklist

Increase service levels and cut costs

1 How much does it cost me to provide services that customers could get for themselves over the Internet?

2 How can I use the information I have about individual customers to make it easier for them to do business with me?

3 What help can I give customers by using the experience of other customers or the expertise of my employees?

4 Will I be at a significant disadvantage if my competitors provide these capabilities to customers before I do?

Consolidating the distribution channel

1 Can I realise significant margins by consolidating parts of the value chain to my customers?

2 Can I create significant value for customers by reducing the number of entities they have to deal with in the value chain?

3 What additional skills would I need to develop or acquire to take over the function of others in my value chain?

4 Will I be at a competitive disadvantage if someone else moves first to consolidate the value chain?

Leveraging digital assets

1 Can I offer additional information or transaction services to my existing customer base?

2 Can I address the needs of new customer segments by repackaging my current information assets or by creating new business propositions using the Internet?

3 Can I use my ability to attract customers to generate new sources of revenue, such as advertising or sales of complementary products?

4 Will my current business be significantly harmed by other companies providing some of the value I currently offer on an à la carte basis?

Creating a customer magnet

1 Can my industry be divided into logical product, customer or business-model segments that could evolve into customer magnets?

2 What services could an industry magnet offer my customers that would make it efficient for them to select and purchase products and services?

3 What partnerships or alliances could I create to establish the critical mass needed to become an industry magnet?

4 Will the emergence of a competing industry magnet hurt my relationships with customers or my margins?

Table 19.3 Predicted early and later adoption of product and service categories

	Early adoption	Later adoption
Business purchases	**Durable goods** – led by makers of computers and other high tech hardware, more than 75% of manufacturers will conduct business-to-business commerce over the Internet by 2004 with sales reaching $208 billion. **Procurement** – businesses will buy most of their supplies, such as office goods, equipment. Projected sales by 2004 are $2.8 trillion.	**Services** – doctors, lawyers and accountants generally provide their services in person, one reason why the sector is slower to adopt e-commerce. Projected sales by 2004 are $21 billion. **Transportation** – the majority of transport companies are already committed to EDI. Sales may reach $450 million by 2004. **E-learning** – organisations are now finding new ways for educating their employees. The organisational curricula first have to be transferred electronically. Projected sales $27 billion by 2005.
Consumer purchases	**Travel** – flyers are bedevilling agents by browsing the net for bargain fares. Estimated sales in 2004: $212 billion. **Computer hardware & software** – it is an ideal sector for e-commerce. Buyers tend to be Net savvy, and you do not need to squeeze or try on the merchandise. $11 billion by 2004. **Books and music** – this is a sector where online purchases may raise total spending, not just cannibalise sales from brick-and-mortar merchants. The 2004 forecast is $9 billion.	**Housing** – the Internet is a great place to research houses, apartments and mortgage loans but transactions are still being conducted via the traditional methods. **Food and beverages** – supermarkets will not be shutting doors and moving purely online anytime soon. Sales may reach $1.1 billion by 2003. **Services** – Telemedicine notwithstanding, health care is still face-to-face business. The same applies for other services, except for computer updates and fixes which are native to online.

Source: Mandel and Hof (2001), pp. 43–53; Forrester Research (www.forrester.com – press releases, accessed 25 and 28 August 2001); Gartner Group Research (www.gartner.com – press releases, accessed 20 August 2001); pay News (http://www.epaynews.com/statistics/index.html, accessed 29 August 2001).

19.3 International highlight

Ryanair at Internet takeoff speed

Although it is another miserable day in Dublin, Ryanair is far from being miserable. With airfares such as London to Venice at $89 and not $915 or London to Oslo at $48 and not $800, Ryanair is putting a smile on all the faces of international budget-conscious travellers.

Ryanair, an Irish-based company which was established less than three decades ago is now in the phase of European/international expansion. Historically, the European market was serviced by a host of national carriers with high operating costs and often-monopolistic behaviours.

European skies deregulation in the 1990s gave way to the Ryanair business model. The Ryanair business model and strategy was to appeal to budget-conscious customers who will trade off some perks for cheap and yet reliable air travel and are willing to use computer-mediated customer interfaces. It is not targeting the business traveller whose demands are different, such as last minute rescheduling, frequent services, or handy locations. Ryanair customers are not worried when their plane lands on an airport that is 80 km away from the city centre or that there are no high-end airport facilities or that the plane is 40 minutes late. All they are after is cheap and safe air transportation. This Ryanair does best. Ryanair fares are as low as one-tenth of the price of national carriers. At first it seems that such pricing resembled the dot-com mania of 1999–2000 where the customer was serviced well below cost. But Ryanair has managed to undercut its rivals and still return profits. Ryanair's philosophy for success is a constant quest for cutting costs. Ryanair market value has risen tenfold to $4 billion since its 1997 public offer. It is now bigger than Sweden's SAS, the same size as AirFrance,

or a touch smaller than British Airways valued at around $5.5 billion. The stock trades on the same NASDAQ exchange as some of the ill-fated or emergency crash-landed dot-coms, but Ryanair's fortune is steeply taking off.

In order to deliver such cheap or competitively priced services, Ryanair is on a constant lookout for cost savings. It has already changed its airports to cheaper locations – hence reducing the per customer charge from $12 to $1.50. It does not offer free refreshments on the flight. The next phase of cost savings involves the Internet.

In 2000, a Ryanair.com website was launched with an aim of bypassing expensive intermediaries such as travel agents. This switch to Internet-based services has instantly saved Ryanair $6 million in commission fees. Furthermore the availability of booking online or via a call centre has increased the frequency of purchases per customer. By doing away with most of the travel agents it has put the customer in charge of their ordering.

In March 2001, Ryanair sold over 400,000 bookings per week and 65% of those were made online. Today travel agents only constitute 8% of its business. With such success not a week goes by without a new pitch from a European politician to persuade Ryanair to begin to service their constituency. Are you unhappy with the price of air travel, are you in the government election period? Ask your politician.

Typically any company's international expansion would require a well positioned network of travel agents to generate sales, but Ryanair already has a well established and hassle-free network – the Internet network. Austria, Spain, Hungary or Slovakia, are you ready for Ryanair landing? Log on to the Ryanair.com website and click 'yes'.

The extent to which Internet opportunities can be exploited in international markets will be determined in part by the external drivers of customers, competitors and technology and internal drivers represented by company capability and its ability to utilise an Internet strategy.

Figure 19.9	Strategic positioning for Internet applications

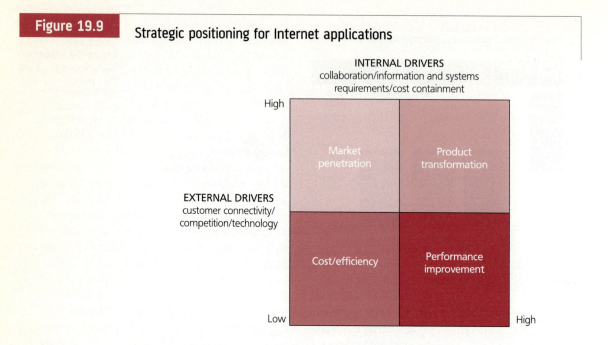

Cronin (1996) presents a strategic positioning matrix for identifying the forces that influence and shape the type of Internet application most likely to add value and lead to competitive advantage at different stages of a company's development. The matrix is shown in Figure 19.9. According to Cronin, the Internet's competitive value for a particular organisation will reflect the interaction of customer connectivity and external competitive forces with internal network access and core applications. Four main competitive advantages are available for Internet connectivity which are outlined in the four quadrants.

Cost/efficiency savings are achieved through substituting the Internet for other communications channels with vendors, information providers and business partners. Performance improvements come from the widespread internal use of the Internet to integrate information resources, support virtual teams and facilitate distributed decision making and organisational flexibility. Market penetration can be achieved through high external connectivity with customers, including public websites and online customer support. Where high internal and external drivers exist, product transformations generated from the development of Internet-based products and services can redefine the company's strategic position.

The challenge of moving from 'place' to 'space'

A business start-up 'born' as an e-commerce-based business does not have any tradition or technological and cultural legacies to consider in targeting international markets. However, established exporters and international marketers find themselves with

Planning the migration

Figure 19.10

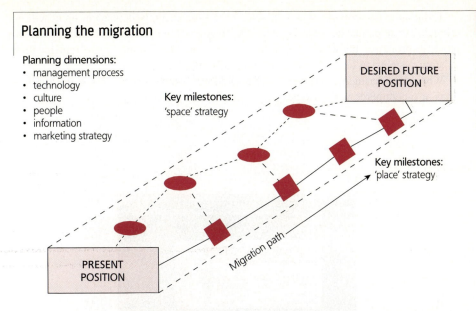

Planning dimensions:
* management process
* technology
* culture
* people
* information
* marketing strategy

Key milestones:
'space' strategy

DESIRED FUTURE
POSITION

Key milestones:
'place' strategy

Migration path

PRESENT
POSITION

Source: Bruce Perrott
PhD and Linden Brown
PhD, presentation to
the MSI INFORMS
Conference, Insead,
Fontainbleau,
11 July 1998.

systems, processes, investments, channel relationships and people in place in the traditional environment of physical marketplace transactions and relationships. The challenge then lies in managing the migration from a full marketplace environment towards a marketspace business. Figure 19.10 depicts a company over time managing a place and space environment as part of an integrated business strategy. The challenges in implementing an effective migration strategy are both internal and external.

Internal planning requirements go beyond the role of international marketing to include the process of change management. Usually the hardest things to change are people and the traditional culture of the organisation. New technologies, skills and marketing tools of information capture and customer interactivity need to be developed. Many firms are well placed to make this transition in international markets if attitudes to change are flexible. The question of global positioning versus local adaptation of product, service, advertising and availability needs to be addressed by the international marketer when conducting e-commerce online in targeted international markets.

The external international marketing challenges of e-commerce should not be underestimated. Markets, cultures and individual customers need to be closely assessed in terms of their readiness and capability for online business. Trust and relationships remain central to international marketing and the final assessment must be based on the firm's ability to deliver superior perceived customer value. The potential will vary by market and by type of product or service. Issues such as actual and perceived security of payment, legality of contracts agreed online and government intervention to collect taxes and impose controls are factors still in transition. Information privacy is a concern to consumers worried about 'identity theft'.

The challenge of differential pricing to different markets and customer segments takes on a new dimension when customers can shop globally for specific items either from the same corporation or from its competitors.

The problem of different software standards between Oracle, SAP and Peoplesoft means that data cannot easily be exchanged. Congestion on the Internet is a problem today – it is likely to be much worse by 2004.

The quality of networks which businesses are increasingly dependent upon will be critical if system crashes are to be avoided. Businesses must streamline their order and payment processes before moving into e-commerce. Most simply try to transfer their existing systems on to the Net (Gross and Sager, 1998).

When considering many of the issues raised in the chapters of this book, the implications of e-commerce will raise new questions for consideration.

Internet infusion

Here come the Cyberbanks First Direct (www.firstdirect.com), set up in 1989 by Britain's Midland Bank, now a division of HSBC in the UK (HSBC Bank plc), operates entirely by telephone, fax and Internet – no branches and no physical presence.

With 925,000 customers and adding 11,000 new ones each month this represents the future model and force of financial services.

Bank 24, a three-year-old Deutsche Bank offshoot that offers banking and brokerage services online, has 1.4 million online customer accounts. Banco Directo of Spain has 110,000 clients. The arrival of the euro in 2002, Europe's common currency, has made direct banking across borders easier and will drive the restructure of retail banking. It is estimated that 30% of 300 million Europeans will be banking this way in 2003. No bank has yet launched a Europe-wide operation, but the payoff will come when Europe is treated as a single market of 300 million account holders.

New competitors, such as US online brokerage firm – E*Trade – charging low flat brokerage fees are entering Europe with joint ventures and licensing arrangements in the major markets of Britain, Sweden, France and Germany.

The strength of the online mortgage brokers is that they provide a single listing point for the range of loan products. This allows customers to compare rate prices, conditions and fees before making any decision and without having to move between sites.

Source: Woodruff (1998); Wang (1998); http://www.ecommercetimes.com/perl/story/1340.html (accessed 24 August 2001); http://www.deutsche-bank-24.de (accessed 21 August 2001); http://www.firstdirect.com/homepage_prospect.shtml (accessed 19 November 2003).

Summary

The opportunities and challenges of e-commerce in international marketing are profound. While there are a relatively small number of companies, mainly in the IT industry, profiting, the potential benefits of e-commerce are large for firms operating in international markets.

There are several well-documented successful business models in both business-to-business and business-to-consumer markets. There are also several useful international marketing frameworks which point to the strategies relevant to customer service enhancement, product and market extension, business building in the value chain, and creation of customer magnets.

Electronic commerce is finding its largest markets in the business-to-business sector. Consumer markets are expected to follow. The international marketer needs to assess the readiness and capability of its target customer markets to operate online as well as the firm's own culture and capability to deliver. However, by developing the capability the firm also has the opportunity to look for new customers who value online purchasing and relationships.

For established international marketing firms a major challenge exists regarding how to progressively migrate from a 'place' business towards a 'space' business. This is accompanied by many external issues in transition–payment–security–legality of contracts, government involvement and privacy of information.

Ethics issue

Your company has developed a very sophisticated customer database from your new-generation real-time interactive website. You have developed the trust of customers who have provided personal information ranging from credit details through to family members' personal habits and lifestyles. Your database is so rich in information it is a virtual storybook of 'The Days Of Our Lives' of your customers. As such, it represents a marketing 'goldmine'. Until now you have been using this data-mine to personalise your company's own offerings to its customers. However, contact with several global companies has convinced you that your database and interactive utilisation of it is worth much more than your current international business of products and services. One global company known as a 'Mover and Shaker', but also known to flaunt privacy of information laws and ethics, wants to buy your system including the database for a huge sum of money. You know that it will on-sell the system to any companies that will pay the price as well as using it for its own global business.

How would you handle this?

Web workout

Question 1 Visit two websites in each the following industries: financial services, entertainment, travel and retailing. Which of these industries will be significantly affected by the Internet, and which ones will have their business models changed on a more incremental basis? On what basis did you form your opinion?

Question 2 Companies operating on the Internet are under constant pressure to come up with a business model where users will have to pay for things they used to get for free. Which of the following areas do you think the customers will be paying for and which areas will remain free?

The services to consider are as follows: Internet access, search engines, analysed information, entertainment, specialised services, commodity data, shopping information, online purchase capabilities.

You may want to browse the Internet to visit a range of websites relating to the above services to help you with your analysis.

Discussion questions

1 How would you define e-commerce? Look for alternative definitions and identify the common elements.

2 What are the relevance and benefits of e-commerce for international marketing? Illustrate using examples.

3 Describe one of the successful e-commerce business models used in practice with reference to a company.

4 Based on Ghosh's four levels of Internet commerce explain how companies could adopt strategies in their international markets to:
   (a) enhance customer service;
   (b) 'pirate' the value chain;
   (c) create digital value; and
   (d) create a customer magnet.

5 With reference to EU markets, which product and service sectors are most likely to grow first using e-commerce?

6 What must firms manage in order to move their business into the 'space' environment in their international markets? Give examples of firms that appear to be doing this effectively.

7 Champy et al. (1996) maintain that seven fundamental needs are shared by all customers. Search for two or three websites that reflect these needs best.

8 Search the Internet for business-to-business and business-to-consumer websites for both products and services businesses. Compare sites in terms of their e-commerce capability and appeal.

References

Business Week, European Edition (1998) 'The Click Here Economy', 22 June, pp. 64–65.

Business Week, European Edition (1998) 'E-Commerce: More Buzz than Byte?', 27 July, p. 17.

Champy, J., Buday, R. and Nohria, N. (1996) 'Creating the Electronic Community', *Information Week*, Vol. 583, 10 June, pp. 57–64.

Cosgrove Ware, L. (2001) CIO, http://www2.cio.com/research/surveyreport.cfm?id=18 (accessed 12 August 2001).

Cronin, M. (1996) *The Internet Strategy Handbook: Lessons from the New Frontiers of Business*, Harvard Business School, Boston, cited in Hamill, J. (1997) p. 304.

Ghosh, S. (1998) 'Making Business Sense of the Internet', *Harvard Business Review*, March–April, pp. 126–135.

Gross, N. and Sager, I. (1998) 'Caution Signs Along the Road', *Business Week*, 22 June, pp. 86–87.

Hagel, J. and Armstrong, A.G. (1997) *Net.Gain: Expanding Markets through Virtual Communities*, Harvard Business School Press, Boston.

Hamill, J. (1997) 'The Internet and International Marketing', *International Marketing Review*, Vol. 14, No. 5, pp. 300–323.

Hof, R.D. and McWilliams, G. (1998) 'How the Internet Changes Almost Everything', *Business Week*, 22 June, p. 68.

Konana, P. (1997) 'An Introduction to Electronic Commerce', Class Presentation, University of Texas, September.

Larreche, J-C. (2001) *Measuring the Competitive Fitness of Global Firms*, Financial Times, Prentice Hall.

Larreche, J-C. and Heineken, A.H. (2001) 'Competitive Fitness of Global Firms Report', Insead, France; http://www.insead.fr/projects/compfit/2001Menu.htm.

Lawrence, E., Corbitt, B., Tidwell, A., Fisher, J. and Lawrence, J. (1998) *Internet Commerce: Digital Models for Business*, John Wiley and Sons, Brisbane.

Mandel, M. and Hof, R. (2001) 'Rethinking the Internet', *Business Week*, 26 March, pp. 43–53.

Perrott, B. and Brown, L. (1998) Presentation to the MSI INFORMS Conference, Insead, France, 11 July.

Quelch, J.A. and Klein, L.R. (1996) 'The Internet and International Marketing', *Sloan Management Review*, Spring, pp. 60–75.

Tapscott, D., Ticoll, D. and Lowy, A. (2000) *Digital Capital*, Harvard Business School Press, Boston.

Tapscott, D., Ticoll, D. and Lowy, A. (2001) 'Internet Nirvana, Business 2.0'; http://www.business2.com/webfile/0,1638,8850,00.html (accessed 20 August 2001).

Timmers, P. (1997) 'Internet Electronic Commerce Business Models', *European Commission*, 10 September; http://www.ispo.cec.be/ecommerce/introduc.htm.

Woodruff, D. (1998) 'Twilight of the Teller?', *Business Week, European Edition*, 20 July, pp. 16–17.

Case study 18

www.coffeelife.net.cn

James Duan, **Business Director, Ogilvy Interactive Worldwide**

Introduction

The International Coffee Organisation (ICO) was founded in London in 1963. It is an inter-governmental body whose members are coffee exporting and importing countries. One of the ICO's objectives is to develop demand for coffee in emerging markets, particularly in China. The ICO holds an International Coffee Festival every year in China to promote coffee culture in the country. In the year 2000, the theme of the festival was to 'meet on the coffee net'. The ICO launched a website during the festival as part of its ongoing public relations campaign.

Background

China has a population exceeding 1.2 billion. As a result of its 'open door' policy, China's economic growth has been among the strongest in the world in the past two decades, and it has become one of the world's largest markets for consumer goods.

Multinationals such as Maxwell House and Nestlé entered the Chinese coffee market more than a decade ago. There is no shortage of coffee types. About 85% of consumer demand is for soluble coffee, especially in the form of coffee mixes. However, the coffee market in China is still at the embryonic stage. Total coffee consumption has been stagnant in relation to other drinks, lagging well behind the world average by a large gap.

In China, coffee is considered a typical western drink. The scene of highly visible westerners drinking coffee at Starbucks and at other coffee bars throughout China has reinforced this impression. But although there is a high level of awareness of coffee drinking in big cities, most people in China have limited knowledge about the beverage. Few have ever tasted it, and far fewer could be classified as heavy drinkers.

Several reasons exist for this resistance to coffee. Foremost is China's thousand-year-old tea culture, presenting a major barrier to coffee acceptance. Another is the high cost of coffee. For instance, a cup of coffee usually costs between 22 and 27 Chinese yuan (€3–4). A third reason lies in the coffee itself. It is understood to have an unpleasant 'bitter' taste, is bad for digestion and causes sleeping problems.

Despite these negative perceptions, research shows there is a growing interest in all forms of coffee consumption. Coffee bars and coffee shops are flourishing in major cities. Coffee is becoming emblematic of modern lifestyle, which deeply influences young and fashion-conscious Chinese consumers. Many people believe coffee is able to refresh the mind. To some, drinking coffee is also a signifier of a happy and active life.

The annual coffee festival has become an established event in China, and the idea of the coffee culture has captured the imagination of the new generation of Chinese. An increasing number of companies, coffee shops, bars and restaurants have been involved in this event. The ICO launched a website during the 2000 festival, with the aim of building a platform for the ongoing promotion of coffee culture in China.

Why Internet?

This is the first time that the ICO has used the Internet to promote the festival. This has resulted from several factors. First, the Internet has taken

Table 1 Internet users by age

<18	18–24	25–30	31–35	36–40	41–50	51–60	>60
1.65%	46.77%	29.18%	10.03%	5.59%	5.07%	1.30%	0.41%

Source: China Internet Network Information Center (June 2000).

Table 2 Internet users by education

Under High School	High School	2–3 Years Diploma	Bachelor's Degree	Master's Degree	Doctoral Degree
2.54%	12.79%	32.81%	45.93%	4.94%	0.99%

Source: China Internet Network Information Center (June 2000).

Table 3 Time spend on the Internet each week (hours)

<1	1–5	6–10	11–20	>20
0.02%	20.70%	26.01%	30.72%	22.55%

Source: China Internet Network Information Center (June 2000).

off at a rapid pace in China, becoming a hot phenomenon in people's lives. The total number of Internet users increased from 12 million in 1998 to 16 million in April 2000, and a majority of these users dwelt in 20 or so primary cities. Secondly, the image of the Internet itself is modern and western, which coincides with the perceptions of coffee in China. Thirdly, the demographics of the Internet users match that of the target audience, i.e. young, active, well-educated and with high disposable incomes (see Tables 1 and 2). Fourthly, the Internet is an ideal tool to spread detailed information about coffee. An average Net user spends over 16 hours online each week (Table 3), much longer than conventional mass media. Fifthly, surfing the Internet is a kind of virtual experience, so it is possible to connect coffee culture with this interesting phenomenon. Finally, the website could serve as a permanent platform for future promotions.

The campaign plan

The objective of Festival 2000 was to influence the consumer to think of coffee as the preferred drink. During the festival, the ICO aimed to spread knowledge about coffee, help consumers understand the benefits of coffee and encourage them to try coffee products. The ICO hoped that the campaign would help to build a positive image about coffee culture as being intelligent, modern and even a little mysterious. As a secondary objective, the campaign would help the related businesses to connect with their targets.

As mentioned earlier, the theme of the campaign was to 'meet on the coffee net'. This was not simply understood as meeting people online. It was also about meeting the 'surfer' him or herself by venturing onto the Internet. Through the combination of the Internet, coffee and adventure, people could gain information and experience, and express their own understanding of what coffee is all about. Therefore, lifestyle and coffee culture were the focus of the campaign.

The profile of the target audience was as follows.

Demographics

- 20 to 35 years;
- higher education (bachelor degree or above);
- professionals with medium to high monthly income.

Psychographics

- fashion-conscious;
- advocate western lifestyle;
- drinking coffee is associated with their lifestyle values;

- their knowledge about coffee is limited;
- Internet is a part of their life – surfing the web is a regular activity.

The website

The website was launched during the festival in April 2000. The website introduced coffee knowledge, including coffee history, plantation, production, product etc. Business information, such as listing coffee product multinationals, was included. Comprehensive information news about coffee consumption in China was also included, particularly the activities and news releases during the festival.

To help viewers 'taste coffee life' online, every coffee type was assigned to a different lifestyle. For instance, black coffee was associated with 'a businessman who is fighting for his career path'. Table 4 gives the examples of such associations for other coffee types. The concept of 'meeting on the Net' was executed through various creative strategies. Through the use of colour, portraits, scenes, music, animation, etc., viewers were able to view different lifestyle models. They could also feel the romantic atmosphere surrounding the magic of coffee, and share their feelings with others.

A BBS (bulletin board system) was developed to encourage interactivity. The BBS allowed users to share opinions and information with the community. Viewers could post messages whenever they liked on the BBS. They

---

Table 4 Image associations for different coffee types

Black coffee	A businessman, fighting for his career path
Instant coffee	A young man, active and busy
Espresso	A middle-aged man, successful in life
Ice coffee latte	A 16-year-old student, life is joyful and easy
Mocha coffee	A young woman, just beginning her new family
Cappuccino	A charming girl, attractive

could also make free links to their home page and post news of their interests. Coffee business organisations used the BBS to send invitations to consumers to attend their events during the festival. Many viewers were able to fill out offer forms to receive free samples from sponsors. It is worth pointing out that building a customised interface such as a BBS on the web was very expensive, compared with the development of information pages or online catalogues.

Drive-to-web strategy

Even the best websites need a well-designed and well-executed drive-to-web strategy to take the target viewers to the site. For the Coffeelife website, banners were used as the key strategy to attract traffic. That is, the ICO paid other websites for the banners that it placed on these websites. A popular website normally charged 166 Chinese yuan (€21) for a thousand impressions. Although banner ads risk having a low click-through rate (the average was about 3% at the time), they offered the ICO the potential to target its message by choosing the right website to identify individual Internet users. Two banners were designed for the campaign. The first banner was targeted at those who were interested in coffee, those who had a strong opinion about coffee, and those who knew coffee to some extent, but wanted to gain in-depth knowledge.

The second banner was designed to attract young people who did not yet have a fixed lifestyle or developed life values. These were searching for a lifestyle and atmosphere that suited them, and regular Net surfing was already a feature in their lives. The two banners received awards for their designers' creative thinking.

These banners were placed at popular portal sites during the festival to gain maximum exposure in Chinese cities. Coffeelife.net.cn was also linked to related websites, such as Maxwell House, Nescafé, etc. In offline support, the ICO promoted the website through newsletters, exhibitions in primary business locations and radio.

Results

During the festival, the site attracted 12,000 page views every day from about 20,000 different people. On average, each viewer read about 10 pages, and 10% of the viewers visited the site more than once. Since the web promotion stopped, the website content has not been refreshed. Soon after the festival, the site's daily page view dropped to 4,000, and active viewers dropped to under 1,000. During the festival, the BBS and community sections were very active. The site received over 1,000 postings. A large number of electronic cards were also downloaded.

Discussion questions

1 Is the Internet an appropriate promotional tool for the ICO?
2 Evaluate the drive-to-web strategy.
3 What should the ICO do to attract return visits by the viewers?
4 What should the ICO do more for its online campaign?

Case study 19

Combining ERP and Internet technologies

Seán de Búrca, Brian Fynes and Evelyn Roche, UCD Business Schools

Introduction

Computers have been used in business for fifty years. Vast changes have occurred during that time. Early systems were physically enormous and had less power than many modern wristwatches. Manipulating these systems was slow, resulting in limited information being available. As computers became more powerful and technical skills increased, businesses began to rely on the information they provided.

In the late 1990s the Internet allowed organisations to share data in a relatively straightforward manner. Software firms were quick to take advantage of this new opportunity and new enterprise applications emerged. These included online stores, e-procurement and customer relationship management (CRM), all of which could be integrated with the organisation's enterprise requirements packages (ERP) system. Further advances in these technologies have allowed seamless integration between enterprises.

Background

Enterprise requirements packages (ERPs) are designed to model and automate many of the business processes of an organisation, such as customer order fulfilment and manufacturing. The goal of ERP solutions is to integrate information across the company and eliminate complex, expensive links between computer systems that were never meant to talk to each other. It can therefore be seen as a software mirror image of the major business processes of an organisation. Despite the cost of implementing ERP systems they succeeded because the cost of developing an in-house IT system with similar functionality would have been prohibitive and have taken a

long time, possibly so long that it would be of no use as the company's business processes would have changed in the meantime.

Benefits of ERPs

Many companies were attracted by the opportunity of replacing a tangle of complex obsolete applications on different platforms with one single integrated application from a reputable vendor. Improved business processes and the resultant cost savings are generally cited as the main reasons for embarking on ERP implementations.

O'Leary (2000) details the main benefits of ERPs:

- ERPs integrate a firm's activities, forcing organisations out of traditional, functional and locational silos. Duplicate databases are replaced by a single entity and processes are generally integrated across the organisation.

- The best practices contained within ERP systems help organisations improve the way they do business.

- Processes can be standardised across the organisation. A single view of the firm can be presented.

- ERP systems use a single common database eliminating data duplication. This allows information to be viewed throughout the firm, increasing decision-making capabilities and removing opportunities for information to be used as a bargaining chip.

- Once information is entered into an ERP system it is immediately available to all relevant users throughout the system for planning and control, thus facilitating better planning and control.

- The common data structure and integrated processes facilitate inter-organisation communication and collaboration.

Davenport (2000) lists other benefits including cycle time reduction, faster information trans-actions, better financial management and laying the foundations for electronic commerce through its emphasis on shared data across functions, a prerequisite for e-commerce.

While the ERP may provide many advantages to those who have implemented it, it also poses many challenges. Laudon and Laudon (2000) identified five potential areas: implementation, cost/benefit analysis, achieving robustness, attaining interoperability and realising strategic value.

Impact of the Internet

The closing years of the twentieth century saw huge resources spent on implementing ERP systems. However, in parallel the Internet revolution was taking place. The Internet revolutionised communications for businesses as documents could be exchanged almost instantly by e-mail, websites displayed information and allowed companies to sell their products online. However, it soon became apparent that if organisations were truly to benefit from the Internet they would need to integrate their web stores with their ERP systems.

Combining ERP and Internet technologies

Having implemented an ERP system, companies must decide whether they want to take advantage of new technologies and extend their business processes over the Internet. There are three applications in particular that need to be high-lighted: supply chain integration, e-procurement and CRM.

Supply chain management

Supply chain management comprises the busi-ness processes that bring a product or service to market, including coordination, communication and collaboration among suppliers; manufactur-ing, materials, transportation and warehouse management; and procurement, distribution, wholesale, and service and sales channels. In the traditional model, the supply chain is typically designed around functions rather than process; as a complex and relatively static entity, it is more often reactive than proactive.

Internet technologies have opened enormous possibilities for organisations to share data. Pure-play dot-coms, many of which have now gone bankrupt, dominated the first wave of e-business. The prime reason for their failure was the absence of business processes behind their websites. However, we are now witnessing the second wave whereby established companies are adding an e-business dimension to their portfolio. These companies bring their business experience to e-business; however, the creation of e-supply chains is central to the success of these ventures (van Hoek, 2001).

An adoption of an integrated approach throughout the supply chain requires a trade-off between autonomy and control in which the balance is unique within each supply partner relationship (Graham and Hardaker, 1997). Partners in virtual integration need to be willing to allow each other to view their systems and processes in order for the end-to-end process to work correctly. Organisations also need to understand the implications of integration across the entire supply chain (Venkatraman and Henderson, 1998). The Internet has allowed a shift towards dynamic communication and improved integration, often ahead of the physical movement of goods. Indeed, Graham and Hardaker (1997) believe that the digital age has seen information functioning as a unique source of competitive advantage; virtual supply chain activities in marketspace can operate completely independently of the physical value chain.

▶

Michael Porter acknowledges the impact of the Internet on the supply chain (Porter, 2001). He states that IT has a pervasive influence on the value chain and that the current stage in IT evolution is enabling the integration of the value chain and the entire value system, i.e. the set of values for an entire industry. Porter asserts that the Internet is the most powerful tool available today for enhancing operational effectiveness, as it allows the exchange of real-time information thereby creating improvements throughout the value chain. He cautions that the advent of Internet technologies alone will not help firms achieve competitive advantage as traditional sources such as scale, human resources and investments in physical assets continue to play prominent roles. Indeed, the open nature of Internet technologies makes it easier for companies to use them. This minimises the opportunity for them to deliver competitive advantage.

Van Hoek (2001) describes the e-supply chain as the physical dimension of e-business which provides the base level of operational performance, i.e. order fulfilment etc., but also allows the development of more advanced e-business applications. Electronic supply chain management (e-SCM) represents a philosophy of managing technology and processes in such a way that the enterprise optimises the delivery of goods, services and information from the supplier to the customer. The result is an e-supply chain or 'supply web' that gives the organisations involved access to all the critical information they need to plan their development, manufacturing, distribution and warehousing operations whenever and wherever they need it.

E-SCM therefore requires change across the supply chain – change to management practices, performance metrics and business processes. Two major factors underpin the success of e-SCM (Norris et al., 2001). Firstly, all firms involved must view collaboration as a strategic asset and an operational priority in order to foster trust among trading partners. Secondly, e-SCM allows information visibility across the supply chain to become a replacement for inventory; it must therefore be managed with strict policies, disciplines and monitoring. Many commentators are agreed on the first point. For example Kehoe and Boughton (2001) say that total cycle time compression and inventory cost reduction will only occur when the entire supply chain is optimised rather than individual enterprises. Forrester Research (Forrester, 2000) draws the same conclusion, stating that all steps in the supply chain from design to aftersales service must become an integrated flow of information. For example, Cisco currently shares sales information with its manufacturers.

Instead of being linear and fixed, the e-supply chain is an enhanced network, a complex but well-defined web of relationships with multiple channels and an open flow of information. Modern organisations are undergoing rapid, complex and fundamental change. Businesses have to work directly with customers, suppliers, partners and sometimes even competitors, in order to respond more quickly and intelligently to change.

With the growth of e-commerce, customers are demanding faster turnaround and greater customisation than ever before. At the same time, companies are looking for innovative ways to make their businesses more consumer-centric. They need to improve their relationships with customers and create customer loyalty or stickiness. With competitive power up for grabs in most vertical markets, companies across all industries are discovering that the best and often only way to achieve tough business goals is to implement e-SCM.

E-SCM provides organisations with significantly increased strategic options for achieving long-term flexibility and adaptability – a critical competitive advantage. E-SCM also levels the playing field between large and small companies, allowing any size enterprise to access suppliers and customers around the world.

While the technology to enable e-commerce activities may be with us and many organisations are embracing the e-SCM approach, there is evidence to suggest that e-business is still largely driven by sales and marketing rather than an integral business model (van Hoek, 2001).

Organisations must move quickly to take advantage of e-SCM capabilities but they must ensure that their own ERP systems are implemented correctly first. Without properly functioning ERP systems e-SCM may do nothing more than create upstream and downstream problems at Internet speed (Norris et al., 2000).

Cisco, Dell and Sun Microsystems are among the companies that have made the greatest strides towards fully integrating their supply chains. Cisco claims to take 90% of its orders over the Internet, fewer than 50% being touched by a Cisco employee. According to Pete Rukavina, Cisco's Director of Global Supply Management, they have six virtual employees, who use Cisco processes and are measured against Cisco metrics, located around the world. Cisco's suppliers, distributors and contract manufacturers are linked through Cisco's extranet.

Cisco operates in a no-warehouse, no-inventory, no-paper-invoice environment. For example if a customer orders a network product from Cisco, the order information is routed to a contract manufacturer. When the contractor has finished the product it goes through an in-house testing phase. Cisco has online access to the product during testing; when the testing is complete Cisco sends the customer's shipping details to the contractor (Koch, 2000).

The challenges organisations face when implementing ERP are exacerbated when implementing e-SCM, as organisations do not have control of their partners' systems. Relationships with business partners are therefore of paramount importance to the success of e-SCM initiatives, all parties needing to recognise that success for one part of the supply chain means success for all (Scalet, 2001). This theme is central to the US-based National Institute for Supply Chain Integration:

Every firm in a supply chain must look after its own interests and its own shareholders first and foremost. That is the fundamental nature of free enterprise, and the source of its strength. It is also the source of much inefficiency within chains as each link works to enlarge its own portion of the consumer dollar, which must be shared by all in the chain. To turn this strong tendency in a different direction it is necessary that the new direction be more beneficial to each member than the present.

Source: Rationale for founding the National Institute for Supply Chain Integration (NISCI); www.nisci.com

Exchange of accurate and up-to-date information will help organisations share best practices. Relationships are a competitive advantage built on trust between the partners. Traditionally relationships in supply chains have centred on shaving the supplier's margin, but in a collaborative environment organisations will need to optimise the processes for their mutual benefit.

Companies like Cisco are avoiding the traditional approach and are supporting rather than pressurising suppliers, according to CEO Pete Slovik: 'If we can help the suppliers reach their goals then we can count on them to give us priority when we have problems' (Koch, 2000). Cisco has since taken its programme further, dealing not only with its own suppliers but with its suppliers' suppliers. Cisco wants to have information transparency at each level (Koch, 2000).

This partnership aspect is a trade-off between autonomy and control, of which the balance decided upon is unique to partner relationships. Allowing all partners in the supply chain to dynamically view and manage both demand and capacity data raises the opportunity for the simultaneous improvement in customer service level and the reduction in overall inventory levels and associated costs (Kehoe and Boughton, 2001).

As well as managing the physical supply chain, applications managing the financial supply chain (FSC) are emerging. The FSC is described as the transactions related to the flow of cash from receipt of the customer's order, through to billing and payment with related receipt and payment of the supplier's invoice. This process is also referred to as the 'cash-to-cash' cycle. The purpose of FSC applications is to allow organisations to manage their receivables, plan the organisation's financial future and reduce their working capital needs.

For FSC systems to operate effectively all business partners need to be involved. The technology then tracks financial documents to provide proactive intelligence and indicate problems that may arise. FSC technology will therefore provide chief financial officers (CFOs) with the ability to anticipate, identify and correct errors much earlier in the order fulfilment process. The main benefits of these systems are reduced working capital borrowing, improved cash flow and reduced processing and reconciliation costs. These improvements can have follow-on benefits in the organisation resulting in improved partner relationships and improved supply chain activity.

Convincing all business partners to become involved in an FSC project will pose a considerable challenge to organisations, much more so than recruiting partner firms for an e-SCM project. However organisations can use other technologies to optimise their FSC in advance of recruiting all business partners – for example, electronic invoice presentment and payment (EIPP) and online dispute resolution and self-service customer support.

However, organisations willing to share information with their supply chain partners may be few. Many companies believe that their own information gives them a crucial competitive advantage and have no desire to share it freely.

E-SCM allows us to get information more quickly and it reduces the period of uncertainty. It does not improve machine changeover time or cost or improve physical transport difficulties. Supply chains still need to be managed, organ-

isations will still need to manage the balance between ability to respond to customers and the desire to hold zero inventory.

Organisations wishing to integrate their supply chains will face many barriers, both internally and externally:

- Organisations are already communicating with each other but they need to move to the next phase where they are coordinating on a timely basis before they can collaborate, i.e. share information electronically.

- Collaboration implies visibility of internal activities and metrics by external parties. An organisation's ability to perform is therefore a lot more transparent, and therefore puts pressure on the organisation to execute correctly.

- To optimise supply chain processes, organisations will need to be able to make decisions more rapidly; they will have to respond within a matter of days and hours.

- Managers need to be rewarded on how they optimise the entire supply chain rather than their own specific link.

- Change management will be an issue. People throughout the organisation need to be able to manage the impact of having a faster flow of information.

- Many organisations feel that their current information is too unreliable to share with the other supply chain participants (Forrester, 2000).

- Forrester also points out that many organisations feel that they do not have the technical resources to support integrated supply chain management.

E-procurement

Business-to-business e-procurement is defined as intercompany trade where the final order is placed online. It can take place in an e-marketplace or directly between two organisations. E-procurement software automates the purchasing process using Internet technologies. Requisitioners can access the system via a standard browser where they are routed to company-approved catalogues, either internal or external. The external catalogues can be at sellers' sites or Net-markets to which the buyer and seller have subscribed. The objective is that a seamless transaction is created between the buyer's ERP system and the seller's ERP system when the purchase order is approved by the buying origination. To allow this to happen the buyer's e-procurement application must be integrated with its ERP system and the seller's online catalogue must be integrated with its ERP system.

High-tech manufacturing, financial services and telecommunications companies have spearheaded the drive towards e-procurement. These companies have also made e-procurement available to large numbers of end-users. This is allowing end-users to work more closely with their suppliers and reduces the workload on other areas of the organisation in terms of workflow and contract compliance.

While linking to internal catalogues or the suppliers' external catalogues has helped the procurement process, software vendors, realising that an aggregated model would be far more efficient, began developing Net-market or portal software. This allowed buyers to access several sellers by accessing a single external marketplace. While online marketplaces are still very much in their infancy, their promise is virtually unlimited. These online 'bazaars' have already taken on a variety of incarnations, each suited to a different purpose. For example (Berryman and Heck, 2001):

- The *catalogue model* aggregates suppliers and buyers, particularly in industries that have a high potential for volume transactions in small-ticket items. Among the best-known exchanges in this category are Grainger, which eases high-volume

buying for factories in virtually any industry, and SciQuest, which does the same for buyers and suppliers of health care products.

- The *auction model* matches buyers and sellers of unique products with differing perceptions of value, e.g. Imark.com which sells used capital equipment. Meanwhile, the exchange model has a real-time, bid–ask matching process and works best when prices are volatile. Among the best-known examples of this model are eSteel and PaperExchange.

- The *consortium model* bands large organisations together with their trading partners and suppliers. Best known is 'Covisint', the GM/Ford/DaimlerChrysler joint venture. The objective of these exchanges is to reduce bid/offer spreads and reduce transaction costs by matching buyers and sellers.

Net-markets can therefore be vertical, aligned with an industry, or horizontal, focused on many. They can also have many titles such as independent trading exchanges, private trading exchanges, digital exchange, trading hub, virtual trading network etc. (White, 2001).

Customer relationship management

CRM stands for customer relationship management. It is a strategy used to learn more about customers' needs and behaviours in order to develop stronger relationships with them. CRM is as a process that will help bring together lots of pieces of information about customers, sales, marketing effectiveness, responsiveness and market trends.

The idea of CRM is that it helps businesses use technology and human resources to gain insight into the behaviour of customers and the value of those customers. If CRM works as intended, a business can (Deck, 2001);

▶

- provide better customer service;
- make call centres more efficient;
- cross-sell products more effectively;
- help sales staff close deals faster;
- simplify marketing and sales processes;
- discover new customers;
- increase customer revenues.

CRM systems organise companies in such a way that they can handle their business through whichever channel they choose. This has the double benefit of getting closer to offering customers the service levels they require and giving the organisation a holistic view of the customer so that it can understand customer behaviour and profitability across channels (*CIO*, 2000).

For CRM to be truly effective, an organisation must first decide what kind of customer information it is looking for and it must decide what it intends to do with that information. For example, many financial institutions keep track of customers' life stages in order to market appropriate banking products like mortgages or life assurance to them at the right time to fit their needs. The more channels a customer can use to access a company the greater need there is for the type of single centralised customer view a CRM system can provide. For example, an organisation may contact its customers via mail campaigns, websites, brick-and-mortar stores, call centres, mobile salesforce staff and marketing and advertising efforts. Solid CRM systems link up each of these points. This collected data flows between operational systems (like sales and inventory systems) and analytical systems that can help sort through these records for patterns. Company analysts can then comb through the data to obtain a holistic view of each customer and pinpoint areas where better services are needed.

CRM systems, therefore, gathering information about all the customer contact points, are increasingly vital to people who are in contact with customers. Access to CRM data from mobile devices such as PDAs, laptops and mobile phones is becoming increasingly important.

ERP CRM integration

As ERP systems contain vast amounts of data about and relevant to customers, integration between these two applications is vital. Proper integration can provide the ability to access any customer information, including service issues to avoid being blind-sided by complaints when making a sales call.

Companies face a number of integration, interoperability and performance challenges when they link their e-CRM solutions to back-office systems. According to a recent AMR report (AMR, 2001) a successful CRM strategy must include access to back-office information. Such useful customer data might include what marketing or telemarketing efforts have been directed at a particular customer, whether past goods arrived on time at the customer's door, or whether the customer is also a supplier of the company and, if so, what the relationship is between the two companies. RCM's ability to cross-sell and up-sell can be hampered because much of the data it needs to do this is contained in ERP systems (Earls, 2001). The ERP data must be merged with the functionality of CRM.

In a recent white paper, Hewlett-Packard described how it identified three essential points of integration when implementing the Sales Force Automation (SFA) element of Oracle's CRM solution Firstly, it had to be integrated to all points and types of customer sales contacts from whatever channel – the Web, phone, e-mail, fax, chat room, and so on. Secondly, it had to be integrated with other HP business functions, including marketing, call centre, telesales and service, and finally to HP's SAP system. HP believed that this level of integration was essential if it was to enable its customers to believe that they were dealing with someone who fully understands their issues (HP, 2001).

The importance of ERP data to CRM projects is stressed by Nelle Schantz, CRM Program Director at SAS: 'Bridging the gap between front office and back office systems is crucial to the success of CRM in order to have a fully automated, complete picture of a customer. This allows businesses to focus on growth and increasing revenue rather than simply reducing costs as they did with enterprise resource planning implementations. It is vital to take data stored in ERP systems and turn it into usable knowledge' (*CIO*, 2000a).

Best of breed?

When deciding to replace legacy systems, organisations are confronted with the decision as to whether to choose best-of-breed systems or an ERP system. A best-of-breed system provides the best product available for each system function (Windsor, 2001); for example the firm would choose a separate finance package, a separate sales package, a separate production package. The advantage is that the firm should get the system and functionality it wants (O'Leary, 2000). O'Leary goes on to list some of the disadvantages of the best-of-breed approach; higher search costs, different look and feel per application, integration costs, diversified skill sets required to support them, and synchronisation issues due to different upgrade timetables. Windsor counters these points saying that best-of-breed vendors are investing hugely in integration and the ERP vendors are promoting their application partnerships, i.e. they are making it easy for best-of-breed solutions to integrate with them.

The best of breed versus single vendor quandary remains for organisations extending their ERP systems. There are best-of-breed vendors of SCM, CRM, B2B software and many vendors of associated specialist or niche products such as strategic sourcing and settlement. These vendors have been building their products and markets while the ERP vendors were concentrating on their core products. The ERP vendors have now responded and have developed or acquired their own 'extended' product suite. Organisations now have to determine whether to stick with one vendor or choose the best-of-breed route for extended ERP. The situation is complicated by the arrival of enterprise application integration (EAI) software which reduce the integration problems associated with best-of-breed solutions. According to the ARC Advisory Group, sales of EAI packages have been growing at more than 100% annually, and they expect that trend to continue (Fulcher, 2000). AMR concludes that the choice comes down to factors such as requirements for length of deployment time and depth of functionality. Deloitte's 1999 B2B survey found that organisations were fairly split between B2B and best-of-breed approaches (Deloitte, 1999).

In summary this case study has reviewed the literature relating to how organisations can derive value from their ERP implementations. Organisations can achieve this through a programme of continuous business improvement both within the enterprise and by extending processes to partners. They can build upon their ERP backbone with a range of e-SCM, B2B, CRM and business intelligence products. However, organisations wishing to extend their processes will have to develop more trusting and collaborative relationships with their business partners. To achieve competitive advantage thorough combining ERP and Internet technologies, organisations will have to embrace complex changes and confront the challenges head on.

References

AMR (2001) Report on Enterprise Application, 2001.

Berryman, K. and Heck, S. (2001) 'Is the Third Time the Charm for B2B?', *The McKinsey Quarterly*, No. 2.

CIO (2000) 'Staying Ahead of the CRM Curve' November 15; www.cio.com.

▶

CIO (2000a) 'Closing the CRM Loop', *CIO Magazine*, Nov; www.cio.com.

Cisco (1999) 'Networking the Supply Chain for Competitive Advantage. An Overview of the Cisco Networked Supply Chain Management Solution', www.cisco.com.

CTP (1999) 'The Transformation of ERP: From Money Pit to Money Pot'.

Davenport, T. (2000) *Mission Critical: Realising The Promise of Enterprise Systems*, Harvard Business School Press.

Deck, B. (2001) 'What is CRM?', www.darwinmag.com.

Deloitte Consulting (1999) 'Leveraging the e-Business Marketplace – Business-to-Business e-Procurement Trends, Opportunities, and Challenges'.

Deloitte Consulting (1999a) 'ERP's Second Wave, Maximising the Value of ERP-Enabled Processes'.

Earls, A. (2001) 'Integrating ERP and CRM, www.ebizq.net.

Forrester Research (2000) www.forrester.com – website press release statistics.

Fulcher, J. (2000) 'Extended Enterprise Systems', *Manufacturing Systems*, Vol. 18, No. 12, pp. 38–40.

Graham, G. and Hardaker, G. (2000) 'Supply Chain Management across the Internet', *International Journal of Physical Distribution and Logistics Management*, Vol. 30, No. 3/4, pp. 286–295.

HP (2001) 'Implementing a CRM Solution', HP Consulting White Paper.

Kehoe, D. and Boughton, N. (2001) 'Internet Based Supply Chain Management – A Classification of Approaches to Manufacturing, Planning and Control', *International Journal of Operations and Production Management*, Vol. 21, No. 4, pp. 516–524.

Koch, C. (2000) 'The Big Payoff – Supply Chain Management' *CIO Magazine*, October; www.cio.com.

Laudon, P. and Laudon, M. (2000) '*Management Information Systems, Organisation and Technology in the Networked Enterprise*', 6th edn, Prentice Hall.

Norris, G., Hurley, J.R., Hartley, K.M., Dunleavy, J.R. and Balls, J.D. (2000) *E-Business and ERP, Transforming the Enterprise*, John Wiley.

O'Leary, S. (2000) *Enterprise Resource Planning Systems, Life Cycle, Electronic Commerce and Risk*, Cambridge University Press.

Porter, M. (2001) 'Strategy and the Internet', *Harvard Business Review*, March, pp. 63–78.

Scalet, S.D. (2001) 'The Cost of Secrecy', *CIO Magazine*, July; www.cio.com.

Van Hoek, S. (2001) 'E-Supply Chains – Virtually Non-Existing', *Supply Chain Management: An International Journal*, Vol. 6, No. 1, pp. 21–28.

Venkatraman, N. and Henderson, J.C. (1998) 'Real Strategies for Virtual Organising', *Sloan Management Review*, Fall, pp. 33–47.

White, A. (2000) 'The Rise and Fall of the Trading Exchange', www.ascet.com.

Windsor, B. (2001) 'Best of Breed vs. ERP. A Debate Running Out of Steam?', www.hrmsoftware.com.

Discussion questions

1 What are the key issues for businesses as they prepare to extend the capabilities of their ERP systems and integrate with business partners?

2 Given the heavy cost of ERP implementations, volumes have been written in the trade press questioning whether they deliver advantages. Many would argue that these advantages were never clearly enunciated to begin with and that ERP implementation was a necessity, an essential cost of doing business rather than anything else. Discuss.

3 How can organisations build on their ERP infrastructure to achieve competitive advantage?

4 Having implemented ERP, companies must decide whether they want to take advantage of new technologies and extend their business processes over the Internet. Discuss the benefits and challenges confronting companies in their attempt to integrate e-SMC, e-procurement and customer relationship management applications.

Index